SCOPE 28

Environmental Consequences
of Nuclear War

Volume II

Ecological and Agricultural Effects

SCOPE 28

Environmental Consequences of Nuclear War

Volume II

Ecological and Agricultural Effects

Mark A. Harwell and Thomas C. Hutchinson

with

Wendell P. Cropper, Jr, Christine C. Harwell, and Herbert D. Grover

Additional Contributions by:
L. C. Bliss, J. A. Clark, J. K. Detling, A. C. Freeman, J. P. Grime,
J. D. Hanson, M. Havas, R. Herrera, A. Keast, G. J. Kelly, J. R. Kelly,
P. M. Kelly, N. K. Lukyanov, J. McKenna, S. J. McNaughton, K. Meema,
R. L. Myers, T. Ohkita, S. Pacenka, D. Pimentel, V. M. Ponomarev,
J. Porter, S. J. Risch, M. J. Salinger, Y. Shimazu, T. Sinclair,
D. Sisler, R. B. Stewart, Y. M. Svirezhev, P. B. Tinker, Z. Uchijima,
M. H. Unsworth, T. Urabe, J. Vandermeer, M. Verstraete, D. W. H. Walton,
G. F. White, R. C, Worrest, E. Zubrow

Published on behalf of the
Scientific Committee on Problems of the Environment (SCOPE)
of the
International Council of Scientific Unions (ICSU)
by
JOHN WILEY & SONS
Chichester · New York · Brisbane · Toronto · Singapore

British Library Cataloguing in Publication Data

Harwell, Mark A.
  Environmental consequences of nuclear war.—
  (SCOPE; 28)
  Vol. 2 : Ecological, agricultural and human effects
  1. Nuclear warfare—Environmental aspects
  I. Title   II. Hutchinson, Thomas C.
  III. International Council of Scientific Unions
  Scientific Committee on Problems of the Environment
  IV. International Council of Scientific Unions
  574.5   QH545.N83

  ISBN 0 471 90898 3

Library of Congress Cataloging in Publication Data

Harwell, Mark A.
  Environmental consequences of nuclear war.

  (SCOPE ; 28)
  Includes index.
  Contents: —V. 2. Ecological, agricultural,
and human effects.
    1. Nuclear warfare—Environmental aspects—
Addresses, essays, lectures. I. Hutchinson, Thomas C.
II. International Council of Scientific Unions.
Scientific Committee on Problems of the Environment.
III. Title. IV. Series: SCOPE (Series) ; 28.
  U263.H37   1985   574.5'222   85-20114

  ISBN 0 471 90898 3 (v. 2)

Printed and bound in Great Britain

Funds to meet SCOPE expenses are provided by contributions from SCOPE National Committees, an annual subvention from ICSU (and through ICSU, from UNESCO), an annual subvention from the French Ministère de l'Environment et du Cadre de Vie, contracts with UN Bodies, particularly UNEP, and grants from Foundations and industrial enterprises.

International Council of Scientific Unions (ICSU)
Scientific Committee on Problems of the Environment (SCOPE)

SCOPE is one of a number of committees established by a non-governmental group of scientific organizations, the International Council of Scientific Unions (ICSU). The membership of ICSU includes representatives from 68 National Academies of Science, 18 International Unions, and 12 other bodies called Scientific Associates. To cover multidisciplinary activities which include the interests of several unions, ICSU has established 10 scientific committees, of which SCOPE is one. Currently, representatives of 34 member countries and 15 Unions and Scientific Committees participate in the work of SCOPE, which directs particular attention to the needs of developing countries. SCOPE was established in 1969 in response to the environmental concerns emerging at that time; ICSU recognized that many of these concerns required scientific inputs spanning several disciplines and ICSU Unions. SCOPE's first task was to prepare a report on Global Environmental Monitoring (SCOPE 1, 1971) for the UN Stockholm Conference on the Human Environment.

The mandate of SCOPE is to assemble, review, and assess the information available on human-induced environmental changes and the effects of these changes on humans; to assess and evaluate the methodologies of measurement of environmental parameters; to provide an intelligence service on current research; and by the recruitment of the best available scientific information and constructive thinking to establish itself as a corpus of informed advice for the benefit of centres of fundamental research and of organizations and agencies operationally engaged in studies of the environment.

SCOPE is governed by a General Assembly, which meets every three years. Between such meetings its activities are directed by the Executive Committee.

R. E. Munn
Editor-in-Chief
SCOPE Publications

Executive Secretary: V. Plocq

Secretariat: 51 Bld de Montmorency
　　　　　　75016 PARIS

The editors wish to thank the following organizations for giving permission to reproduce copyright material:

Figure 1.3. Reproduced from C. Raunkier, *The Life Forms of Plants and Statistical Plant Geography*, 1934, by permission of Oxford University Press.

Figures 1.4, 1.5. Reproduced from J. Levitt, *Responses of Plants to Environmental Stresses*, 1972, by permission of Academic Press.

Figure 1.8. Reproduced from M. G. R. Cannell and L. J. Sheppard, *Forestry*, **55**, 137–153, 1982, by permission of Oxford University Press.

Figure 1.9. Reproduced from C. Glerum, *Can. J. Plant Science,* **53**, 881–889, 1973, by permission of the Agricultural Institute of Canada.

Figures 1.10, 1.11, Tables 1.6, 1.7. Reproduced from P. H. Li and A. Sakai, *Plant Cold Hardiness and Freezing Stress, Volume 2*, 1982, by permission of Academic Press.

Figure 1.15, Table 3.4. Reproduced from M. A. Harwell, *Nuclear Winter: The Human and Environmental Consequences of Nuclear War*, by permission of Springer-Verlag, New York.

Figure 1.18. Reproduced from D. B. Carter and J. R. Mather, *Publications in Climatology*, **19**(4), 305–395, 1966, by permission of C. W. Thornthwaite Associates.

Figure 1.19a. Reproduced from H. Leith, *Human Ecology*, **1**, 303–332, 1973, by permission of Plenum Publishing Corporation.

Figure 1.22. Reproduced from R. H. Whittaker, *Communities and Ecosystems*, 2nd edition, 1975, by permission of Macmillan Publishing Company.

Figure 3.3, 3.7, Table 3.12. Reprinted with permission from F. W. Whicker and V. Shultz, *Radioecology: Nuclear Energy and the Environment, Vol. 1*, 1982. Copyright CRC Press, Inc., Boca Raton, Fl.

Figure 3.5. Reproduced from *Health Physics* Vol. 23, p. 519–527 by permission of the Health Physics Society.

Table 1.5. Reproduced from J. Levitt, *Responses of Plants to Environmental Stresses, Vol 1*, 2nd edn., 1980, by permission of Academic Press.

Tables 1.8, 1.9. Reproduced from T. C. Hutchinson, *Journal of Ecology*, **55**, 291–299, 1967, by permission of Blackwell Scientific Publications Limited.

Table 1.13. Reproduced from E. P. Odum, *Science*, **164**, 1969, by permission of the American Association for the Advancement of Science. Copyright 1969 by the AAAS.

Table 1.16. Reproduced from V. Stoy, *Physiol. Plant. Suppl.*, **IV**, 1–25, 1965, by permission of Physiologia Plantarum.

Acknowledgements

The biological portion of the ENUWAR study has been a unique undertaking to synthesize information from a very broad range of disciplines in order to establish the state of the current understanding about the global consequences of large-scale nuclear war. We have relied on the contributions, analyses, discussions, and advice from approximately 200 scientists from over 30 countries around the world, especially through participation at a series of technical workshops. Consequently, the present volume is the product of many people, whose contributions we gratefully acknowledge.

Foremost among these are the three who are listed as primary contributors to the overall volume; this volume could not have been prepared without their contributions. Wendell Cropper, Jr., was the mainstay of the food calculations and the analyses of agricultural productivity, central elements in the Volume II analyses, and he provided considerable insight into ecological and other assessments. Christine Harwell provided invaluable coordination of the overall biological study, a monumental task for a project involving so many scientists from so many countries; she also took on the jobs of preparing Chapter 6 from widely divergent inputs and of editing the entire volume. Herb Grover helped initiate the ENUWAR study and was there at the end to help pull together the ecological analyses. We also particularly acknowledge the coordinating assistance of Ann Freeman as indispensable to the successful completion of the project.

The technical workshops that focused on the biological issues were held in Paris, France (October, 1984) concerning radiation effects; Essex, England (January, 1985) concerning Northern temperate agricultural effects; Hiroshima and Tokyo, Japan (February, 1985) concerning human effects; Toronto, Canada (March, 1985) concerning Northern temperate ecosystem effects; Melbourne, Australia (March, 1985) concerning Southern Hemisphere agricultural and ecosystem effects; Caracas, Venezuela (April, 1985) concerning tropical agricultural and ecosystem effects; and Essex, England (June, 1985) concerning research needs and in review of the draft manuscript. Other workshops were held to plan the ENUWAR project and to identify the specific issues requiring attention; these included workshops held in London, England (April, 1983); Stockholm, Sweden (November, 1983); New Delhi, India (February, 1984); and Leningrad, U.S.S.R. (May, 1984).

We are particularly indebted to the chairpersons of each of the biological technical meetings: Mike Unsworth and Bernard Tinker at the first Essex workshop; Barrie Pittock and Jim Salinger at the Melbourne workshop; Rafael Herrera at the Caracas workshop. Each contributed generously of his time to the success of the workshops by helping to identify the appropriate mix of disciplines and people to participate and by providing the logistical support needed to conduct the workshops under very tight time constraints.

We are quite grateful for the contributions of all of the participants at the various workshops, including preparation of discussion papers, participation in the workshop deliberations, and providing advice and ideas for our approach. A list of participants is included in an appendix to this volume, as there are too many to list here. We wish to make particular note of those who acted as leaders or rapporteurs in the various working groups into which each workshop divided and who prepared synopses of the working groups' consensus: Thomas Rosswall at Stockholm and New Delhi; Yuri Svirezhev and Nick Lukyanov at Leningrad; Charles Shapiro and Warren Sinclair at Paris; Mike Unsworth, Bernard Tinker, Herb Grover, and John Porter at Essex; Larry Bliss, Phil Grime, Jake Levitt, David Walton, Jack Kelly, Russ Wein, Leslie Cwynar, and Charles Shapiro at Toronto; Gilbert White and Takeshi Ohkita at Hiroshima and Tokyo; Jim Salinger and Neil Cherry at Melbourne; Rafael Herrera, Steve Risch, John Vandermeer, Ann Freeman, and Kersti Meema at Caracas.

Certain people among the the workshop participants performed additional roles that were invaluable to this project: Steve Risch contributed to several meetings and provided unique insights into the potential consequences of nuclear war on humans, along with John Vandermeer and Ezra Zubrow. Bob Stewart was responsible for the computer simulations of grain production in Canada and for many ideas concerning effects on agricultural productivity. Grahame Kelly, David Walton, Allyn Seymour, and John Teal provided substantial written inputs on potential effects on marine ecosystems. Phil Grime wrote on the importance of plant strategies in recovery processes. Jim Salinger wrote substantial inputs on potential effects on Australia and New Zealand. Ron Myers conducted an extensive literature review concerning freeze effects on sub-tropical ecosystems and crops. Bob Worrest assumed responsibility for synthesizing the literature on UV-B effects on biological systems. Zenbei Uchijima provided the detailed information on vulnerabilities of rice crops. Jim Detling was responsible for the simulations of temperate grassland effects, along with Jon Hanson. Jack Kelly coordinated the estuarine ecosystem simulations using the Narragansett Bay model, conducted by Jim McKenna. Sam McNaughton used his model of tropical grassland ecosystems for evaluating potential effects. Tom Sinclair performed analyses using his soybean productivity model. Mick Kelly provided an invaluable service in helping us understand the projections from the climatic scientists. Alan Keast, Magda Havas, and Steve Pacenka prepared substantial inputs on effects on freshwater ecosystems. Josef Svoboda and Harry Taylor provided written inputs on radiation effects. David Pimentel prepared a discussion paper on issues of human energy subsidies to agriculture. John Porter prepared maps of crop distributions around the Northern Hemisphere. Tatsuo Urabe conducted simulations of large warhead detonations over Hiroshima for comparison with the 1945 bombing. Yuri Svirezhev coordinated an extensive effort by the Soviet Academy of Sciences' Laboratory of Mathematical Ecology in evaluating global consequences. Dick Warrick provided much insight from experiences in his project on climate effects on global productivity. Dan Sisler was a valuable resource for food stores and distribution information. Michel Verstraete conducted statistical analyses of the relationships between average temperatures and growing season length.

The final workshop at Essex involved a team of scientists who simultaneously provided technical review on drafts of the manuscript, assistance in finalizing the report, and suggestions on research needs, all of which were of considerable benefit to us. We are especially grateful to Phil Grime, who chaired this group, and to Larry Bliss; these two took on the substantial task of final review of the completed draft. The other participants are also acknowledged for their participation and advice, including: John Bromley, John Edwards, Herb Grover, Alexander Kuzin, Alex Leaf, Nick Lukyanov, Takeshi Ohkita, Steve Risch, Jim Salinger, Bob Stewart, Yuri Svirezhev, Mike Unsworth, and David Walton. We also received comments on drafts of this manuscript from the Volume I authors, including Barrie Pittock, Tom Ackerman, Paul Crutzen, Mike MacCracken, Charles Shapiro, and Rich Turco. Other reviewers of at least parts of the manuscript drafts included: Jack Kelly, Karin Limburg, Tom Malone, Simon Levin, Steve Schneider, Dick Warrick, David Weinstein, Gilbert White, and Ezra Zubrow.

In addition to the workshop process, we benefited greatly from discussions with many scientists who could not attend the technical workshops. These included: Vladimir Alexandrov, Wilfred Bach, John Bardach, Barbara Bedford, Pall Bergthorsson, Helmgeir Björnsson, Elaine Birk, Sandra Brown, Edith Brown-Weiss, Dick Carpenter, Len Chambers, Curt Covey, Paul Dayton, Don DeAngelis, Olafur Dyrmundson, Barry Edmonston, John Edsall, Tom Eisner, John Farrington, Bob Friedman, John Haaga, Doug Haith, Robert Heaney, Craig Heller, Howard Hjort, Bob Kates, Peter Kauppi, Tom Kirchner, Jerry Kuhn, Michael Latham, Jennifer Leaning, Peter Lert, Patricia Lewis, Simon Levin, Julius London, Ariel Lugo, Jag Maini, Ramon Margalef, John Mason, Dennis Meadows, Judy Meyer, Cedric Milner, Hal Mooney, Sergey Pitovranov, Bob Platt, Larry Ragsdale, Peter Raven, David Reichle, Alan Robock, Ed Rykiel, Carl Sagan, John Schalles, Jacob Scherr, Doug Scott, Chris Shoemaker, Ralph Slatyer, Rich Small, Joe Soldat, Allan

Solomon, Dick Tracy, Peter Vitousek, Paul Waggoner, Dick Waring, David Weinstein, Elaine Wheaten, Dan Williams, Peter Wills, and George Woodwell. We especially appreciate the cooperation of Martin Parry, director of the IIASA project on global climate and productivity relationships, and the advice and assistance of Joe Rotblat.

It should be clear from the extensive listing above and in the appendix that this report represents ideas from many people. We have attempted to reflect accurately the consensus of these scientists, but we assume responsibility for any errors or omissions. The time allocated for the entire process, from project initiation through completion of the workshops, to the final writing and review, has been extremely brief for such a large and complex project. This has inevitably led to the potential for uneven treatment or omission of issues. However, we feel this report presents a comprehensive and balanced contribution to an ongoing process of scientific debate and clarification concerning issues that must remain academic and not a part of the human experience. That so many people volunteered their time and energy in this intensive effort is a testament to the nature of the peril for Earth and the commitment of the scientific community.

We were guided in this integrative undertaking by the SCOPE–ENUWAR Steering Committee, who also arranged funding for the workshops and partial support for the research at Cornell University and the University of Toronto. The work at Cornell was assisted by the technical research of Karin Limburg and the administrative support of Roberta Sardo and Kathy Wilson. We gratefully acknowledge the substantial funding contributed by Cornell University for the research conducted there. The research at the University of Toronto was made possible by the invaluable assistance of Kersti Meema, who helped prepare Chapters 1 and 3 and who organized the Toronto workshop.

Finally, we wish to recognize Sir Frederick Warner, who guided us through this project with wisdom and patience and in the process won the admiration and respect of all.

Mark A. Harwell
Center for Environmental Research
Cornell University
Ithaca, New York 14853
USA

Thomas C. Hutchinson
Institute for Environmental Studies
University of Toronto
Toronto, Ontario M5S 1A1
Canada

Contents

**3   Additional Potential Effects of Nuclear War on
      Ecological Systems**   173

Thomas C. Hutchinson, Mark A. Harwell,
Wendell P. Cropper, Jr., and Herbert D. Grover

Foreword

Beginning in the summer of 1982, approximately 300 scientists from more than 30 countries and a wide range of disciplines, under the auspices of the International Council of Scientific Unions (ICSU), joined in a deliberative effort to appraise the state of knowledge of the possible environmental consequences of nuclear war. Although it has been recognized since the first nuclear explosions over Hiroshima and Nagasaki in 1945 that multiple detonations could cause massive destruction on people and their culture, the effects of life support systems of air, water, and soil and on organisms received relatively little emphasis in public discussion.

In the mid-1970s, attention began to turn to the whole range of consequences that might be expected to follow a large-scale exchange of nuclear weapons. This reflected a growing recognition of the immense number and yield of thermonuclear devices in the arsenals of the nuclear powers. The renewed activities also reflected concern with effects beyond the direct destruction of cities and human life. While interest still centered on the well-studied issues of direct blast, thermal effects, and radioactive fallout from ground and air bursts, scientists began to consider the large-scale consequences (e.g., from possible global depletion of ozone and from perturbations to the atmosphere). This concern was manifested in studies of information that had accumulated from the detonations at Hiroshima and Nagasaki and the subsequent series of nuclear tests, and with extrapolation of these data to situations in which the current nuclear arsenal might be used. Among the analyses were those by the U.S. Senate Committee on Foreign Relations (1975), the U.S. National Academy of Sciences (1975), the Office of Technology Assessment of the U.S. Congress (1979), the United Nations Environment Programme (1980), the United Nations (1980), and A. Katz (1982).

In 1982, several organizations and individual scientists launched new examinations of anticipated global effects, including those of the American Association for the Advancement of Science, the U.S. National Academy of Sciences, and the World Health Organization. Appraisals commissioned by the Royal Swedish Academy of Sciences published in Ambio in April 1982 were particularly influential. A paper in that issue by P. Crutzen and J. Birks had been intended to deal with possible effects on the stratospheric ozone layer and regional air quality. While it did suggest that ozone changes might be of significance, the new suggestion was that smoke and soot generated by large urban and forest fires might cause reductions in light at the Earth's surface, inducing profound changes in weather. These suggestions stimulated a new round of research and appraisal around the world. Not since the 1960s, when agitation about the consequences of delayed radioactive fallout from bomb tests in the 1950s resulted in the signing in 1963 of the Treaty Banning Nuclear Weapon Tests in the Atmosphere, in Outer Space, and Under Water, had as much thoughtful attention been marshalled by scientists and citizens.

At its General Assembly in Ottawa in June 1982, the Scientific Committee on Problems of the Environment (SCOPE)—one of the ten Scientific Committees of the International Council of Scientific Unions (ICSU)—concluded that "the risk of nuclear warfare overshadows all other hazards to humanity and its habitat" and asked its Executive Committee to consider what further action might be appropriate for SCOPE. In September 1982, the General Assembly of ICSU passed the following resolution:

> *Recognizing* the need for public understanding of the possible consequences of the nuclear arms race and the scientific competence that can be mobilized by ICSU to make an assessment of the biological, medical and physical effects of the large-scale use of nuclear weapons.

> *Urges* the Executive Board to appoint a special committee to study these effects and to prepare a report for wide dissemination that would be an unemotional, nonpolitical, authoritative and readily understandable statement of the effects of nuclear war, even a limited one, on human beings and on other parts of the biosphere.

Accordingly, a Steering Committee for the SCOPE–ENUWAR (Environmental Effects of Nuclear War) study was established, with responsibility to initiate the study requested by ICSU and to oversee the selection and recruitment of participants. A SCOPE–ENUWAR coordinating office was established at the University of Essex. From the outset it was agreed that the report would not deal explicitly with questions of public policy, but would focus on scientific knowledge of physical effects and biological response. International aspects of the direct medical effects have already been dealt with explicitly by the World Health Organization, and thus are not taken up in this study.

The SCOPE–ENUWAR process involved the active collaboration of scientists, bringing together the insights and skills of numerous disciplines. Preparatory workshops were held in London and Stockholm, and major workshops were convened in New Delhi, Leningrad, Paris, Hiroshima and Tokyo, Delft, Toronto, Caracas, Melbourne, and finally at the University of Essex in an attempt to arrive at a consensus. Smaller groups gathered in a variety of other places, chiefly in connection with meetings of International Scientific Unions. Meanwhile, new findings were becoming available as noted in appropriate parts of this report, and further studies of likely effects were published (Turco et al., 1983; Ehrlich et al., 1983; Aleksandrov et al., 1983; Openshaw et al., 1983; World Health Organization, 1984; Covey et al., 1984; London and White, 1984; United Nations, 1984; Harwell, 1984; National Research Council, 1985; The Royal Society of Canada, 1985; The Royal Society of New Zealand, 1985).

Support for the project came from individual donations of time and from organizational grants. The Steering Committee is particularly grateful to those who committed the extensive time and effort to prepare the two volumes reporting these important scientific results. Barrie Pittock, Thomas Ackerman, Paul Crutzen, Michael MacCracken, Charles Shapiro, and Richard Turco have been responsible for preparation of the volume on physical and atmospheric effects. Mark Harwell, Thomas Hutchinson, Wendell Cropper, Jr., Christine Harwell, and Herbert Grover have played the major role in preparing the volume on ecological and agricultural effects. Both sets of authors were assisted by many colleagues, listed elsewhere in these volumes, who collaborated with them and generously gave of their time to participate in discussion, analysis, writing, and review. It was very much a cooperative, voluntary effort.

The collaboration among these scientists was made possible by financial contributions covering the costs of travel, assistance by post-doctoral fellows, workshop arrangements, and secretarial support. Initial grants making possible the planning of the project came from the SCOPE Executive Committee, using contributions from its 36 member academies of science, and from ICSU. The Royal Society of London hosted the preliminary and concluding workshops and funded the SCOPE–ENUWAR office. Other workshops were hosted by the Royal Swedish Academy of Sciences, the Indian National Science Academy, the Academy of Sciences of the U.S.S.R., la Maison de Chimie of France, the T.N.O. Institute of Applied Geosciences of the Netherlands, the Australian Academy of Science jointly with the Royal Society of New Zealand, the United Nations University and the Venezuelian Institute of Scientific Investigation. Major grants for travel and other expenses were provided by the Carnegie Corporation of New York, The General Service Foundation, The Andrew W. Mellon Foundation, the W. Alton Jones Foundation, and The Rockefeller Brothers Fund.

Recognizing that the issues dealt with in this report transcend science and technology and involve moral and ethical issues, SCOPE–ENUWAR co-sponsored an *ad hoc* meeting of scientists and scholars of ethics and morality at the Rockefeller Conference and Study Centre, Bellagio, Italy, in November 1984. The conference took note of the preliminary findings that a significant nuclear exchange could lead to an unprecedented climatic perturbation, killing crops and threatening countries distant from the target areas with mass starvation. A statement called for the development of more effective cooperative efforts for dealing with common interests and problems and urged collaboration between science and religion in the "... quest for a just and peaceful world" (*Bulletin of Atomic Scientists,* April 1985, pp. 49–50).

The Steering Committee has elected to publish the results of the SCOPE-ENUWAR studies in two volumes. The first volume deals with the physical aspects of the environmental impact of a nuclear war. The second volume addresses the biological impacts, principally the ecological and agricultural effects. As further background for the reader, each volume includes the Executive Summary of the companion volume, with its explanation of findings and research recommendations, as an appendix. In addition, the Committee has commissioned a less technical account intended for wide international distribution to fulfill the ICSU request for a "... readily understandable statement of the effects of nuclear war." It is anticipated that this third volume will be translated into several languages.

The two volumes present a general consensus among the scientists concerned with the study. There is not unanimity on all points, but a concentrated effort has been made to describe those remaining points at issue. These unresolved issues suggest research that should be pursued in order to reduce the present degree of uncertainty. The report should be regarded as the first attempt by an international scientific group to bring together what is known, and what must still be learned, about the possible global environmental effects of nuclear war. It should not be the last. It should be taken as a point of departure rather than as a completed investigation.

A recurring issue in the recent discussion of the long-term, global environmental consequences of a nuclear war has been the degree to which uncertainties preclude a conclusion regarding the plausibility of severe effects. These uncertainties are of two kinds: (1) those resulting from the nature of human actions (e.g., number of weapons, yields, targets, height of detonation, time of conflict, accidents resulting from technological failure, societal response to an outbreak of hostilities); and (2) those resulting from an incomplete state of knowledge concerning physical and biological processes and the limited ability to simulate them faithfully by mathematical models.

Clearly, the specific circumstances of a large-scale nuclear war cannot be predicted with confidence, and the history of past wars reminds us that even carefully planned military actions rarely develop as expected. Thus, detailed scenarios of possible nuclear exchanges must remain highly speculative. Wherever practicable, as a basis for estimating environmental effects, the report considers specific ranges of physical parameters and responses—such as a given mass of smoke injected into the atmosphere, or the occurrence of a freezing episode—that are consistent with the detailed technical analyses, yet are not peculiar to any specific war scenario. In the absence of a nuclear war, many of the specific effects will continue to be in doubt.

Although uncertainties associated with knowledge of physical and biological processes could be substantially reduced by further research, some of these uncertainties are bound to remain large for many years, as explained in the report.

The report does not attempt to provide a single estimate of the likely consequences for humans and their societies of the physical and biological changes projected to be possible after a nuclear war. One reason is that the combinations of possible environmental perturbations are so large and the varieties of environmental and human systems are so numerous and complex that it would be an impossible task to look with detail into all of the ways in which those perturbations might result in an impact. Further, the environmental disruptions and dislocations from nuclear war would be of a magnitude for which there is no precedent. Our present interdependent, highly organized world has never experienced anything approaching the annihilation of people, structures, resources, and disruption of communications that would accompany a major exchange, even if severe climatic and environmental disturbances were not to follow it. The latter could aggravate the consequences profoundly. How the environmental perturbations which would occur at unprecedented scales and intensities would affect the functioning of human society is a highly uncertain subject requiring concerted research and evaluation. Nevertheless, whatever the uncertainties, there can be no doubt that there is a considerable probability a major nuclear war could gravely disrupt the global environment and world society. All possible effects do not have the same probability of occurrence. Sharpening these probabilities is a matter for a continuing research agenda.

The bases for these statements are to be found in the report, along with references to supporting or relevant information. From them we draw the following general conclusions:

1. Multiple nuclear detonations would result in considerable direct physical effects from blast, thermal radiation, and local fallout. The latter would be particularly important if substantial numbers of surface bursts were to occur since lethal levels of radiation from local fallout would extend hundreds of kilometers downwind of detonations.

2. There is substantial reason to believe that a major nuclear war could lead to large-scale climatic perturbations involving drastic reductions in light

levels and temperatures over large regions within days and changes in precipitation patterns for periods of days, weeks, months, or longer. Episodes of short term, sharply depressed temperatures could also produce serious impacts—particularly if they occurred during critical periods within the growing season. There is no reason to assert confidently that there would be no effects of this character and, despite uncertainties in our understanding, it would be a grave error to ignore these potential environmental effects. Any consideration of a post-nuclear-war world would have to consider the consequences of the *totality* of physical effects. The biological effects then follow.

3. The systems that currently support the vast majority of humans on Earth (specifically, agricultural production and distribution systems) are exceedingly vulnerable to the types of perturbations associated with climatic effects and societal disruptions. Should those systems be disrupted on a regional or global scale, large numbers of human fatalities associated with insufficient food supplies would be inevitable. Damage to the food distribution and agricultural infrastructure alone, (i.e., without any climatic perturbations) would put a large portion of the Earth's population in jeopardy of a drastic reduction in food availability.

4. Other indirect effects from nuclear war could individually and in combination be serious. These include disruptions of communications, power distribution, and societal systems on an unprecedented scale. In addition, potential physical effects include reduction in stratospheric ózone and, after any smoke had cleared, associated enhancement of ultraviolet radiation; significant global-scale radioactive fallout; and localized areas of toxic levels of air and water pollution.

5. Therefore, the indirect effects on populations of a large-scale nuclear war, particularly the climatic effects caused by smoke, could be potentially more consequential globally than the direct effects, and *the risks of unprecedented consequences are great for noncombatant and combatant countries alike.*

A new perspective on the possible consequences of nuclear war that takes into account these findings is clearly indicated. In these circumstances, it would be prudent for the world scientific community to continue research on the entire range of possible effects, with close interaction between biologists and physical scientists. It would be appropriate for an international group of scientists to reappraise those findings periodically and to report its appraisal to governments and citizen groups. Increased attention is urgently required to develop a better understanding of potential societal responses to nuclear war in order to frame new global perspectives on the large-scale, environmental consequences. This task is a special challenge to social scientists.

In arriving at these conclusions, we have been moderate in several respects. We have tried to state and examine all challenges to theories about environmental effects of nuclear war, to minimize speculative positions and to factor valid criticisms into discussions and conclusions. Uncertainties in the projections could either reduce or enhance the estimated effects in specific cases. Nevertheless, as representatives of the world scientific community drawn together in this study, we conclude that many of the serious global environmental effects are sufficiently probable to require widespread concern. Because of the possibility of a tragedy of an unprecedented dimension, any disposition to minimize or ignore the widespread environmental effects of a nuclear war would be a fundamental disservice to the future of global civilization.

SCOPE–ENUWAR Steering Committee

Sir Frederick Warner, University of Essex, U.K., *Chairman*
J. Benard, Ecole Superieure de Chimie, Paris, France
S. K. D. Bergström, Karolinska Institutet, Stockholm, Sweden
P. J. Crutzen, Max-Planck-Institut für Chemie, Mainz, F.R.G.
T. F. Malone, (ICSU Representative) St. Joseph College, U.S.A.
M. K. G. Menon, Planning Commission, New Delhi, India
M. Nagai, United Nations University, Tokyo, Japan
G. K. Skryabin, Akademia Nauk, Moscow, U.S.S.R.
G. F. White, University of Colorado, U.S.A.

VOLUME II

Executive Summary

The potential consequences to the global environment of a nuclear war have been the focus of several studies in the four decades since the first detonations of nuclear weapons in Japan. During this time, the *potential consequences* that would ensue from a modern nuclear war have increased dramatically, and the combination of much larger yields and much greater numbers of nuclear warheads could now result in a large-scale nuclear war having little in common with the relatively limited experiences of Hiroshima and Nagasaki. Simultaneously, the projections of the magnitude of impacts from a nuclear war have also increased steadily; however, the *perception of the consequences* of a large-scale nuclear war consistently have lagged behind the reality. New global-scale phenomena continue to be identified, even up to the present, and there remains a concern that decision-makers are operating with obsolete analyses and basing their policies on a foundation of misunderstanding of the total consequences of nuclear war.

The SCOPE–ENUWAR project had as one of its objectives the development of a comprehensive understanding of the nature of a post-nuclear war world, based on the full range of available information and models. Volume I of the ENUWAR report presented the bases for estimating potential effects on the physical environment, including possible climatic disturbances as well as fallout, UV-B, air pollutants, and other effects. The present volume takes up where the first left off, by specifically considering the potential consequences of such physical and chemical stresses on biological systems and on the ultimate endpoint of concern, i.e., effects on the global human population.

The approach taken in the biological analyses was to synthesize current understanding of the responses of ecological and agricultural systems to perturbations, relying on the expertise of over 200 scientists from over 30 countries around the Earth. Much of the synthesis took place in the context of a series of workshops that addressed specific issues; other work included conducting simulation modelling and performing detailed calculations of potential effects on the human populations of representative countries. We do not present the evaluation of a single nuclear war scenario as estimated by a single methodology; rather, a suite of methodologies were drawn upon collectively to develop an image of the aftermath of a large-scale nuclear war. The range of possible nuclear war scenarios is great; the estimates from the physical scientists of potential climatic consequences are not yet certain and continue to evolve with time. Those estimates are complex in their spatial and temporal distribution over the Earth, and the global landscape is covered by extremely complex ecological, agricultural, and human systems that react to perturbations in complex manners. For these reasons, the present volume investigates the vulnerability of these systems to the types of perturbations possible after a nuclear war, offering readers the opportunity to form their own specific projections of biological and human consequences by providing calculations of vulnerabilities to benchmark assumptions.

Nevertheless, many conclusions are evident from considering these vulnerabilities to nuclear war perturbations. These include:

- Natural ecosystems are vulnerable to extreme climatic disturbances, with differential vulnerability depending on the ecosystem type, location, and season of effects. Temperature effects would be dominant for terrestrial ecosystems in the Northern Hemisphere and in the tropics and sub-tropics; light reductions would be most important for oceanic ecosystems; precipitation effects would be more important to grasslands and many Southern Hemisphere ecosystems.

- The potential for synergistic responses and propagation of effects through ecosystems implies much greater impacts than can be understood by addressing perturbations in isolation. For example, increased exposure to UV-B and to mixtures of air pollutants and radiation, while not crucially harmful for any one stress, might collectively be very detrimental or lethal to sensitive systems because of synergistic interactions.

- Fires as a direct consequence of a major nuclear exchange could consume large areas of natural ecosystems, but fire-vulnerable ecosystems are generally adapted to survive or regenerate via a post-fire succession. Other direct effects of nuclear detonations on ecological systems would be limited in extent or effect.

- The recovery of natural ecosystems from the climatic stresses postulated for an acute phase following following a major nuclear war would depend on normal adaptations to disturbance, such as through presence of spores, seed banks, seedling banks, vegetative growth, and coppicing. For some systems, the initial damage could be very great and recovery very slow, with full recovery to the pre-disturbed state being unlikely. Human-ecosystem interactions could act to retard ecological recovery.

- Because of limitations in the amounts of utilizable energy, natural ecosystems cannot replace agricultural systems in supporting the majority of humans on Earth, even if those natural ecosystems were not to suffer any impacts from nuclear war.

- Consequently, human populations are highly vulnerable to disruptions in agricultural systems.

- Agricultural systems are very sensitive to climatic and societal disturbances occurring on regional to global scales, with reductions in or even total loss of crop yields possible in response to many of the potential stresses. These conclusions consistently follow from a suite of approaches to evaluating vulnerabilities, including historical precedents, statistical analyses, physiological and mechanistic relationships, simulation modelling, and reliance on expert judgment.

- The vulnerabilities of agricultural productivity to climatic perturbations are a function of a number of different factors, any one of which could be limiting. These factors include: insufficient integrated thermal time for crops over the growing season; shortening of the growing season by reduction in a frost-free period in response to average temperature reductions; increasing of the time required for crop maturation in response to reduced temperatures; the combination of the latter two factors to result in insufficient time for crops to mature prior to onset of killing cold temperatures; insufficient integrated time of sunlight over the growing season for crop maturation; insufficient precipitation for crop yields to remain at high levels; and the occurrence of brief episodic events of chilling or freezing temperatures at critical times during the growing season.

- Potential disruptions in agricultural productivity and/or in exchange of food across national boundaries in the aftermath of a large-scale nuclear war are factors to which the human population is highly vulnerable. Vulnerability is manifested in the quantities and duration of food stores existing at any point in time, such that loss of the continued agricultural productivity or imports that maintain food levels would lead to depletion of food stores for much of the world's human population in a time period before it is likely that agricultural productivity could be resumed.

- Under such a situation, the majority of the world's population is at risk of starvation in the aftermath of a nuclear war. Risk is therefore exported from combatant countries to non-combatant countries, especially those dependent on others for food and energy subsidies and those whose food stores are small relative to the population.

- The high sensitivity of agricultural systems to even relatively small alterations in climatic conditions indicates that many of the unresolved issues among the physical scientists are less important, since even their lower estimates of many effects could be devastating to agricultural production and thereby to human populations on regional or wider scales.

- Longer-term climatic disturbances, if they were to occur, would be at least as important to human survival as the acute, early extremes of temperature and light reductions, suggesting that much greater attention should be given to those issues. Similarly, much greater attention is needed to resolve uncertainties in precipitation reduction estimates, since many of the agricultural systems are water-limited, and reduced precipitation can significantly reduce total production.

- Factors related to the possibility and rates of redevelopment of an agricultural base for the human population would have much influence on the long-term consequences to the human population. Interactions with societal factors would be very important.

- Global fallout is not likely to result in major ecological, agricultural, or human effects, as compared to effects of other global disturbances. Local fallout, on the other hand, could be highly consequential to natural and agricultural systems and to humans; however, the extent of coverage of lethal levels of local fallout and the levels of internal doses to humans from such fallout are inadequately characterized.

- Human populations are highly vulnerable to possible societal disruptions within combatant and non-combatant countries after a large-scale nuclear war, such as in the consequent problems of distribution of food and other limited resources among the immediate survivors. This is an area requiring a level of serious scientific investigation that has not yet been brought to bear on these issues.

As a part of the SCOPE–ENUWAR project, a workshop was held in Hiroshima, Japan, in order for the scientists to gain a fuller appreciation of the human consequences of nuclear detonations. The considerations listed above indicate that as devastating as the Japanese atomic bombings were, as consequential to their victims even to the present day, and as important to the development of the 20th Century, they cannot provide a sense of what the global aftermath of a modern nuclear war could be like. Hiroshima today is a thriving, dynamic city reborn from complete devastation by interactions and support from the outside world; after a large-scale nuclear war, there would be essentially no outside world, and qualitatively new global-scale effects would occur that could devastate not just an urban population but the entirety of humanity. Although issues remain to be resolved, the information in this volume demonstrates some of the great vulnerabilities of agricultural, ecological, and societal support systems to the potential direct and indirect consequences of nuclear war. This demonstration of global frailties mandates the formulation of new global perspectives on avoiding the aftermath of nuclear war.

VOLUME II

Introduction

This report presents the results of an international, cooperative effort involving scientists from extremely diverse fields of expertise. The SCOPE–ENUWAR biological analyses have sought consensus among experts, and synthesis from existing information and understanding, in order to evaluate the potential consequences to the natural environment and to human environments of the short- and long-term consequences of a large-scale nuclear war. Yet among the most common questions we are asked are: Why study these issues? Aren't the consequences of direct effects bad enough? Why worry about natural ecosystems and people in non-combatant nations when hundreds of millions of humans would die directly or shortly thereafter? Aren't there too many uncertainties in the climatic issues, making a further look at the consequences to biological systems premature?

Why, indeed? The answer is found in the endpoint of such analyses: impacts on humans and society. Our premise is that the consequences to the global human population are precisely what one should focus upon; all the rest are merely intermediary steps in making that evaluation. Projecting darkness at noon and subfreezing temperatures in July does not paint a picture which is complete enough to understand the total effects of nuclear war; humans simply would not die from a reduction in sunlight for a few weeks, and the world's human population would not likely be greatly reduced by freezing to death. The present analyses show that if substantial global climatic and other disturbances were to occur after a nuclear war, effects on the agricultural and ecological bases which support the Earth's human population would probably lead indirectly to the subsequent loss of hundreds of millions or even billions of human lives. A major conclusion of the current work on the vulnerability of human and natural systems is that the mechanism most likely to lead to the greatest consequences to humans from a nuclear war is not the blast wave, not the thermal pulse, not direct radiation, nor even fallout; rather, it is *mass starvation.*

We do not know this, however, from single analyses of the specific effects of a specified hypothetical nuclear war. Such an approach was not possible or desirable, because of the large uncertainties in the physical analyses and in nuclear war scenarios; the continuously evolving nature of the projections by the physical scientists; the complexity of interactions of possible nuclear-war induced disturbances across the global landscape and over time; and the complexities of ecological, agricultural, and societal systems and their responses to perturbations. There will always be uncertainties in the physical projections, in part because the global atmospheric systems are so complex that they can never be perfectly predicted, in part because many of the variables in climate assessments cannot be measured at their appropriate scale, and experimentation at the global scale is not possible. Further, the exact scenario of a nuclear war could only be defined as it occurred, not in some pre-war speculation. Delaying the biological assessments until the physical uncertainties are resolved, then, is never to do them. But already it is clear that nuclear war-induced climatic perturbations are a *plausible* consequence of nuclear war.

Because of this, the present analyses are focused on characterizing the *vulnerability* of biological and human systems to the types and ranges of perturbations that could follow a large-scale nuclear war. For instance, by examining the current status and potential duration of global food supplies, we can characterize the vulnerability of the human population to global-scale disruptions in food production and distribution systems. Whereas we are not predicting that a global-scale *elimination* of these systems would necessarily follow a large-scale nuclear war, it does appear that humans have the potential through nuclear war to *disrupt* global agricultural, ecological, and societal systems on a scale unprecedented in extent or intensity.

There is a great opportunity for feedback from the biological analyses into the physical studies. For instance, many of the issues in dispute for climatic consequences involve the early, acute time period, with arguments over the intensity of initial temperature decreases. Analyses of the concomitant impacts on agricultural systems, however, indicate that even for smaller temperature decreases, the effects on regional and global agricultural productivity would still be devastating. Similar responses can be expected for many natural ecosystems if affected in their vulnerable growing seasons, or should tropical and sub-tropical systems suffer freezing or chilling. Hence, much of the dispute would seem to be irrelevant to the central issue of overriding importance: human survival. We are coming to the realization that the *duration* of climatic changes of a few degrees is more important, within limits, than how extreme the initial temperature drop would be; this indicates a clear need for longer-term analyses. How quickly temperatures would drop and the nature of their temporal patchiness might be as important as how low they drop. We do emphasize, however, that extreme temperature excursions for quite limited periods can be extremely damaging if occurring in certain regions or in the active growing season. Duration of extremes are more important for ecosystems which are not adapted to or used to experiencing such extremes. The potential reduction in precipitation in the longer-term, chronic phase following a nuclear war appears to be biologically more important for many systems than the loss of incident sunlight during the acute period. The degree of spatial and temporal heterogeneity of climatic effects requires considerably more study. Different issues are key for different regions, as seen by the biological analyses thus far; e.g., Australian agricultural systems are most vulnerable to changes in precipitation; pelagic marine ecosystems are most vulnerable to prolonged decreased light inputs; many agricultural systems and tropical ecosystems are most vulnerable to low temperature excursions. Other considerations are that external radiation doses anticipated from global fallout, which have been well investigated, are not very significant with respect to inducing human and biological effects; but local fallout and internal doses, which are rarely analyzed and are poorly understood, would likely be of critical importance to millions of humans and to natural and agricultural systems after a nuclear war. These and a large number of other findings from biological considerations need to be integrated into a physical effects research program in order to make it more relevant.

Biological responses can have direct feedback to the physical processes themselves. For instance, changes in biological systems on a large scale would likely affect surface albedo. The possibility of the creation of large areas of standing dead biomass from temperature-induced impacts on tropical forests leads to the consideration of massive fires extending into the several-year time frame, potentially prolonging climatic effects; similar fires can follow from coniferous forests killed by local fallout, and by grassland, forest, and other ecosystems subject to reduced precipitation. Further, biologically mediated processes affect or control many atmospheric processes, e.g., via changes in CO_2 inputs and sinks, changes in the rates of evapotranspiration, and the global cycles of other atmospheric gases. The biological record can be instructive in evaluating previous catastrophic events, especially those which have concerned periods of weeks, months, or years of lowered temperatures with frosts occurring in the growing season. Such climatic analogs, including the Little Ice Age and volcanic events, have been inadequately investigated so far. And human-ecological interactions, such as desertification resulting from overexploitation for resources, can extend climatic effects in time and space. Clearly, the feedbacks are many, and physical analyses will be incomplete and often less relevant without their consideration.

What if it is found that there would be no nuclear war-induced climatic perturbations? There are still many global biological issues resulting from nuclear war that require careful attention. The current arsenals of strategic nuclear weapons are so large that the effects seen at Hiroshima and Nagasaki are grossly inadequate as models of a modern nuclear war. Issues such as prompt fallout, UV-B enhancement, pyrotoxins, habitat destruction, acidic fogs, elevated NO_x and HCl levels, and fire-caused high CO levels, among many others, could affect the human and biological systems on a local or global scale. The potential for synergistic effects among these stresses is very high, but almost no work has been done in this area. Linkages of agricultural and ecological effects to impacts on human societal systems are extremely important; for example, reduced agricultural productivity from loss of fossil fuel subsidies alone could tremendously decrease world food yields, and disruption of food imports to many countries in the world could lead to large consequences even for humans far removed from the theatres of nuclear war. It is apparent that should major climatic disturbances occur, human consequences would be devastating; but the converse is not true, that minor or no climatic effects would result in only limited impacts on the global human population.

Just as the studies of nuclear war climatic effects have provided incentives to the development of general circulation models and other techniques for understanding atmospheric systems, nuclear war-induced stresses on the environment provide an ideal framework to develop the general field of stress ecology, an area greatly in need of an infusion of resources and new ideas, and an area of considerable importance in the current affairs of the citizens of the world in coping with increasing anthropogenic stresses on the environment. Indeed, one of the most amazing things evident from enumerating the consequences of nuclear war is that virtually every environmental problem we are currently confronting would be a direct result of nuclear war—only on a scale and intensity of unprecedented magnitude. The development of the next generation of ecosystem models and the assembly of extensive data bases of microcosms and whole ecosystems experimentally subjected to perturbations are exactly the areas of research needed to characterize environmental responses to large-scale stresses. It has been a quarter of a century since there was a substantial experimental effort in characterizing the effects on biological systems of nuclear war. We still draw primarily from the seminal work of Platt, Woodwell, and others in evaluating the effects of radiation on ecosystems, but few of the other nuclear war-related stresses on the environment have been treated explicitly. Yet this is the most important environmental issue ever facing humans.

The question should not be, 'Why study the biological effects?' but, rather, 'Why have we waited this long?' It is even more imperative today, since the new perspective on nuclear war is that a modern nuclear war would almost certainly export its devastation far beyond the combatant countries, particularly but not exclusively if there were major climatic impacts. The agricultural, ecological, and human vulnerabilities to perturbations on a global scale suggest that the indirect effects are likely to be much more consequential than the direct effects of the detonations themselves, and these effects would define what the post-nuclear war world would be like for the 4 billion or so immediate survivors. Understanding how different a picture of consequences this is compared to the limited perspective drawn from nuclear tests and the relatively small-scale nuclear detonations on Japan can only be accomplished by understanding the vulnerability of the human support systems to the potential stresses of a modern nuclear war. It is unreasonable to expect decision-makers to develop appropriate nuclear policies when they only have an inadequate and obsolete perception of the consequences of nuclear war.

PART I

Ecological Effects

The immediate effects of nuclear detonations would have devastating consequences for human populations. But the larger-scale, longer-term, and indirect effects of a nuclear war would present unprecedented stresses on all the biological constituents of Earth. The physical nature of those perturbations is discussed in the companion volume to this study (Volume I, Pittock et al., 1985; see Appendix C for a summary). Here we examine the consequences of those stresses on the biological systems of concern, specifically ecological, agricultural, and human systems.

Part I begins with a background discussion in Chapter 1 of those principles relevant to the ecological responses to nuclear war. Chapter 2 assesses the vulnerabilities and likely responses of ecosystems to the potential acute and chronic climatic perturbations. Chapter 3 first examines the ecological effects from other nuclear war stresses (e.g., UV-B, radiation, pollutants), then summarizes the total consequences on different ecosystems.

Environmental Consequences of Nuclear War Volume II:
Ecological and Agricultural Effects
Edited by M.A. Harwell and T.C. Hutchinson
© 1985 SCOPE. Published by John Wiley & Sons Ltd

CHAPTER 1

Ecological Principles Relevant to Nuclear War

THOMAS C. HUTCHINSON, WENDELL P. CROPPER, JR., AND HERBERT D. GROVER

Contributions by: J. P. Grime, C. C. Harwell, M. A. Harwell, K. Meema, D. W. H. Walton

1.1 INTRODUCTION

Nuclear war represents the most significant environmental threat of our times. The potential combined effects of reduced temperatures, light, and precipitation, exposure to ionizing radiation and enhanced UV-B, and the release of various toxicants into the environment would result in the short-term devastation, and long-term impairment of recovery for exposed biological communities. In this chapter, some of the ecological principles we feel are necessary to understand the subsequent analyses are introduced.

The ecological principles outlined are very basic ones; we anticipate a readership trained in a broad range of disciplines, including those unfamiliar with the academic discipline of ecology. We include substantial discussion in this chapter on ecophysiology (i.e., the responses of organisms to their environment) because this is relevant to the new understanding of the potential climatic consequences of nuclear war (see Volume I). In particular, the physiological sensitivity of organisms to reduced levels of light and temperature are a key part of the analysis of the potential ecological effects (Chapters 2 and 3) and agricultural effects (Part II) of nuclear war.

Much of the ecological analysis has been organized around major biological units called biomes. In this chapter, we describe the biome concept and discuss some of the environmental–climatic factors that are believed to control biome distribution. A description is also included of the current geographical distribution and productivity of those biomes that are discussed in Chapter 2. Emphasis is given in this chapter to plants because of their controlling influence on ecosystem functions through their role as primary producers. Future reports are needed to address more fully the potential effects on animals. Much more research needs to be done on both plant and

3

animal responses to the types of perturbations possible for the aftermath of a nuclear war. (See Appendix B for a brief listing of research needs.)

Another important element for analysis of the potential ecological consequences of nuclear war concerns recovery processes. As the post-nuclear war environmental extremes ameliorate, ecological communities in devastated regions would begin to reorganize. It is not possible to predict the course of such a succession precisely, but some principles concerning post-perturbation replacement (such as seed banks and germination), relevant successional patterns, and organism strategies are discussed.

1.2. ECOPHYSIOLOGY

1.2.1. Plant Responses to Low Temperatures

The ecological significance of low temperature tolerance, or the lack of it, as a normal response to an environmental stress is well documented by Larcher and Bauer (1981). They point out that for 64% of the Earth's land mass, the mean minimum temperature is below 0°C, and for 48% it is below − 10°C. Forests occupy large areas in Siberia, Alaska, Scandinavia, and Canada, where temperature drops regularly below − 50°C. Tundra species occupy areas further north, where temperatures may not be necessarily more extreme, but where winds increase the winter desiccation problems. An absolute temperature minimum of − 68°C was recorded at Verkhoyansk in lowland Siberia, and one of − 71°C at Olimyakon in eastern Siberia. Larcher and Bauer (1981) noted that absolute minima of − 45°C to − 55°C are reported from Antarctic coastal stations, and temperatures of − 90°C have been reported from continental Antarctica.

Freezing temperatures are clearly a normal event for a majority of the Earth's surface, and adaptations of plants and animals enabling them to live through the normal seasonality of cold in temperate regions reflect this. However, the cold or freezing adaptations generally do not provide protection from temperature extremes well beyond those normally experienced by the organism.

Major patterns of vegetation distribution (i.e., of communities, ecosystems, and biomes) reflect annual and seasonal low temperatures. Each species has its particular temperature limits, but generalized responses occur. For example, the northern latitudinal and altitudinal distributional limits of broad-leaved evergreen woody plants are probably determined by low winter temperatures (Sakai and Wardle, 1978; Larcher, 1981; and Lavagne and Muotte, 1971). Similarly, the northern limits of the temperate deciduous forests of North America and Eurasia correlate well with the threshold for deep supercooling of their tissues; i.e., − 40°C to − 45°C (George et al., 1974; Quamme, 1976; and Rajashekar and Burke, 1978). Using these survival limits of distribution for groups of species against low temperature thresholds, Larcher (1981) used Hoffman's data to construct a world map for vegetation based on five temperature-stress categories. The thresholds are shown in Figure 1.1 using the following categories:

- Zone A: a frost-free zone;

- Zone B: a zone with episodic frosts having lower limits down to − 10°C;

- Zone C: a zone of cold winters, with an average annual minimum of − 10°C to − 40°C. This zone delineates the northern limits of most of the north temperate deciduous forests. Within Zone C, the − 30°C isotherm coincides with the geographic limits of many herbaceous perennial species that are unprotected in winter.

- Zone D: a zone with an average annual minimum temperature below − 40 °C; this zone includes the coniferous boreal and tundra ecosystems;

- Zone E: the polar ice caps, which are substantially devoid of vegetation.

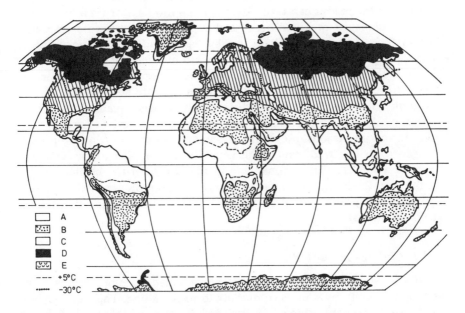

Figure 1.1   Map of low-temperature threshold limiting plant distribution on the Earth. A: frost-free zone; B: zone with episodic frosts down to − 10°C; C: zone with average annual minimum between − 10°C and − 40°C; D: zone with average annual minimum below − 40°C; E: polar ice; - - - : + 5°C lowest temperature isotherm; · · · : − 30°C average annual minimum isotherm. From Larcher and Bauer (1981)

It should follow that if generations of rather rigorous natural selection and adaptation have accommodated plant communities and taxa to their low temperature exposures, then a sudden change in this low temperature exposure might take them beyond their tolerance limits. The climatic disturbances following a nuclear war could cause temperature excursions beyond seasonal or even annual temperature limits. Relatively small ambient alterations applied over many generations can cause the shifting of the boundaries of floras, such as latitudinal shifts during the recent Ice Ages, but short-term events (i.e., applied over time periods of weeks to a few years) might cause local or regional extinctions, without causing latitudinal or altitudinal displacements. The potential for the latter category of climatic perturbations is documented in Volume I and summarized in Appendix C. A more complete description of the types of climatic stresses of biological relevance is provided at the beginnings of Chapters 2 and 4.

Biota respond not only to seasonal and annual mean temperatures, but also to episodic and periodic events. Low temperatures may follow polar air mass intrusions, which on clear nights can cause sudden severe frosts in the temperate region or summer frosts in the boreal region. At high altitudes, frost can occur at any time of the year, even in desert regions. These episodic temperature excursions can take place within a few days or even hours, and plants are damaged or killed because they have very little cold resistance when in the active growth phase if they have insufficient opportunity to enhance their cold tolerance. A major concern of effects of a nuclear war in summer is that both temperate crops and native species would suffer severe damage from sudden freezing at a time when they are most susceptible.

Periodic cold stress is experienced seasonally, allowing plants enough time to adapt gradually (Larcher and Bauer, 1981). Only severe or exceptionally long, continuous periods of extremely low temperatures in winter represent a danger to acclimatized plants. This generalization applies to the ecological effects of a nuclear war commencing in the Northern Hemisphere winter months; i.e., the ability of plants to survive and regrow when climate subsequently ameliorated would be affected by the intensity and duration of extreme temperatures.

1.2.1.1. Chilling-Sensitive Plants

Many sensitive plants can be damaged or killed at temperatures above the freezing point, by what is commonly termed chilling. This phenomenon has long been recognized (e.g., Molisch (1896) reported that in 1844, Hardy found that in tests on 56 tropical species, 25 were killed at 1°C to 5°C).

Chilling temperature is defined as any temperature sufficiently cool to produce injury, but not cold enough to freeze the plant. In most cases the plants do not suffer chilling injury until the temperature drops below +10

°C. For warm temperate, sub-tropical, or tropical plants, the possibility of temperatures being reduced to +10°C for days or weeks during a nuclear war-induced climatic event seems possible (Volume I, Pittock et al., 1985). In some cases, severe damage can occur at temperature exceeding +10°C; for example, flowering rice and sugar cane suffer damage at 15°C (Adiv, 1968; Tsunoda et al., 1968; Levitt, 1977). (See the discussion on rice in Chapter 4.)

As with frost damage, the intensity and duration of chilling are critical to the damage, as are intrinsic features of the plant species. This is illustrated in Figure 1.2 for chilling exposure of *Saintpaulia* leaves to temperatures from 7°C to 1°C for 1 to 72 hours. At 1°C, irreversible damage occurred within minutes of exposure, while 12-hour exposure caused death of all leaves. In contrast, an 8-hour exposure to 5°C was needed before damage occurred, and more than 48 hours exposure was needed to damage more than 50% of the leaves irreversibly.

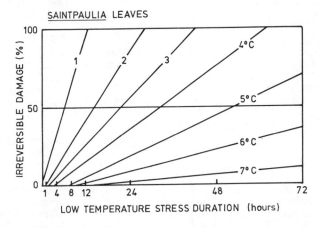

Figure 1.2   Dose dependence of chilling injury in leaves of *Saintpaulia*, Rhapsody strain. The duration of low temperature exposures required to cause various percentages of irreversible injury are shown. From Larcher and Bauer (1981)

Chilling excursions, such as the friagems in Brazil and Amazonia, are known to have devastating effects on native tropical flora and tropical or sub-tropical crops. Larcher and Bauer (1981) noted that certain tropical rainforest plants and mangroves, many cultivated and ornamental plants of tropical origin, tropical seagrasses, tropical C_4 fodder grasses, and vegetables of tropical origin suffer visible injury after exposure to chilling temperatures (Table 1.1). This table clearly shows the extreme sensitivity of many mangrove species, including *Avicennia* and *Rhizophora*, to temperatures from 1 °C to 4°C for as little as 24 hours (Larcher and Bauer, 1981).

TABLE 1.1.

SUSCEPTIBILITY TO LOW TEMPERATURE STRESS
FOR LEAVES OF CHILLING-SENSITIVE CORMOPHYTES [a]

Species	Chilling injury at °C	Duration of chilling at the indicated temperature	Reference
1. WOODY PLANTS IN THEIR NATURAL HABITAT (PUERTO RICO)			
Guarea guara	4	24 hr	Biebl (1964)
Marcgravia sintenisii	4	24 hr	Biebl (1964)
Avicennia nitida	3	24 hr	Biebl (1964)
Marcgravia rectiflora	0.5-1	24 hr	Biebl (1964)
Cecropia peltata	0.5-1	24 hr	Biebl (1964)
Rhizophora mangle	0 - 1	24 hr	Biebl (1964)
Psychotria berteriana	0 - 1	24 hr	Biebl (1964)
2. HERBACEOUS PLANTS IN THEIR NATURAL HABITAT			
Pilea obtusata	< 4	24 hr	Biebl (1964)
Ruellia coccinea	< 4	24 hr	Biebl (1964)
Psychotria uliginosa	1	24 hr	Biebl (1964)
Peperomia hernandifolia	0 - 1	24 hr	Biebl (1964)
Passiflora edulis	0	5 d	Patterson et al. (1976)
Passiflora edulis	0	25 d	Patterson et al. (1976)
3. CULTIVATED PLANTS OF TROPICAL ORIGIN			
Phalaenopsis	7	< 8 hr	McConnell and Sheenan (1978)
Episcia reptans	5	1 hr	Wilson and Crawford (1974); Wilson (1978)
Eranthemum tricolor	< 4	2 d	Molisch (1897)
Impatiens sultani	< 3	1.5 d	Spranger (1941)
Peperomia arifolia	< 3	1.5 d	Spranger (1941)
Schismatoglottis pulchra	< 3	2 d	Spranger (1941)
Scindapsus pictus	4.5	< 4 d	McWilliams and Smith (1978)
Maranta leuconeura	4.5	4 d	McWilliams and Smith (1978)
Begonia stigmatosa	< 4	5 d	Molisch (1897)
Piper decurrens	< 3	5 d	Spranger (1941)
Peperomia argyrea	< 4	5-7 d	Molisch (1897)
Lycopersicon esculentum	< 5	> 6 d	Seible (1939)
Eranthemum tuberculatum	< 4	11 d	Molisch (1897)
Zebrina pendula	< 5	> 14 d	Seible (1939)
4. TROPICAL SEAGRASSES			
Syringodium filiforme	2	1 hr	McMillan (1979)
Thalassia testudinum	2	4 hr	McMillan (1979)
Halodule wrightii	2	1 d	McMillan (1979)

[a] Data from Larcher and Bauer (1981).

Despite the widespread use of maize (*Zea mays*) in temperate regions, it is very susceptible to chilling injury in various ways. For example, Crevecoeur et al. (1983) studied physiological and ultrastructural effects on the germination of kernels under sub-minimal temperatures. When exposed to chilling lasting for more than 6 to 8 days, the ability of maize embryos to resume growth declined. After a 26-day chilling period, all embryos had died. Significant ultrastructural changes also occurred, with the nucleolus becoming fibrillar and unusual ribonucleoprotein granules appearing, in addition to large decreases in chromatid transcription. By extrapolation, one month of a nuclear war-induced chilling that occurred after seeds were sown in the spring would be enough to devastate maize crops, even without the occurrence of freezing temperatures

Hodgins and Van Huystee (1985) found that maize seedlings exposed to 12°C for 6 days were unable to synthesize chlorophyll, even though fully illuminated. However, when subsequently returned to 28°C, chlorophyll synthesis was restored, though the seedlings had etiolated (i.e., become elongated, pale, and thin) by this time. Biochemical examination of seedlings at different stages of the 12°C chilling showed an accumulation of chlorophyll precursors but an absence of aminolevulinic acid, an essential factor in the synthesis of the porphyrin ring of the chlorophyll molecule. Thus, chilling at a temperature as high as 12°C causes potentially debilitating metabolic disorders in maize, even though this temperature is a good deal higher than the point of freezing-induced death.

Any low temperature excursions which caused chilling in tropical regions and which persisted for even a few days would have devastating effects. Freezing temperatures would be worse, since most low altitude tropical plants have no mechanism for avoiding ice crystal formation within cells and would be killed. Ripening fruits of both tropical and sub-tropical plants are also especially susceptible to cold.

1.2.1.2. Differences in Freezing Resistance and Killing Temperatures

The tolerance of all plants to low temperatures is increased at lower tissue water content (Kappen and Lange, 1970a; Lipman, 1936; Mazur, 1969). In an air-dry state, most microorganisms, mosses, algae, lichens, and ferns are able to survive extreme temperatures (e.g., immersion in liquid nitrogen). Bacteria and yeast are especially able to tolerate very low temperatures, though abilities vary a great deal. There is a cryophile microbial flora that is best adapted to low temperatures, just as there are other groups that can tolerate very high temperatures. Dried seeds are also able to tolerate low temperatures, with tolerances at the maximum in dried conditions.

The crucial survival factor for many organisms would be whether they were dry or wet, growing or dormant at the onset of nuclear war-induced

climatic extremes. Dry seeds are characteristic of grasslands and other temperate ecosystems, especially for weedy species. The seeds and fruit of the
tropical rainforest species, in contrast, are predominantly fleshy, enhancing
sensitivity to freezing. On the other hand, the compilation of data from
Larcher and Bauer (1981) (Table 1.2) emphasizes the remarkable cold tolerances of many groups of organisms and indicates that many plant species
would survive if in a dried condition. Even tropical mosses and ferns showed
chilling tolerance, and temperatures from between 0°C to − 7°C were necessary to kill them (Biebl, 1964, 1967). Clearly mosses and many ferns have
remarkable tolerances irrespective of geographic origin.

It should also be noted that some permanently ice-covered lakes occur
in the Canadian arctic; yet, in the waters beneath the ice, phytoplankton,
zooplankton, bacteria, and fungi exist. Also, the well-known phenomenon
of ice-algae occurs in polar marine waters, where attached to the bottom of
the ice-pack and often embedded in the ice itself at temperatures of − 4°C
and at very low light levels, an annual prolific colonization by unicellular
diatoms and chrysophytes regularly occurs. Often these ice algae peak in
productivity before spring break-up of the ice pack occurs (Aragno, 1981).
Thus, a well-adapted algal flora can exploit cold environments with low light
and short summers, and life is possible at about 0°C for a wide variety of
microorganisms and functions. Other examples include fungal pathogens
that infect alpine fir trees and grow under snow cover, and algae and fungi
that grow on or through the melting snow pack (Aragno, 1981).

Larcher and Bauer (1981) used data from many sources (Tables 1.3 and
1.4) to analyze the potential frost resistance of many species of plants. These
were also analyzed according to their ecosystem of origin. Not surprisingly,
tropical and sub-tropical plants are largely susceptible to freezing throughout their lives. Most of these species are unable to frost harden, so that their
freezing point lies between − 1°C to − 3°C. Markley et al. (1982) point out
that few species, except mangroves and seagrasses, are distributed from the
tropics into temperate coastlines. McMillan (1979) studied three of the seagrasses (*Thalassia testudinum*, *Syringodium filiforme*, and *Halodule wrightii*)
collected from the western tropical Atlantic. All three showed leaf and plant
damage to various degrees when exposed to chilling temperatures, with populations of more tropical origin showing the most chilling damage and those
from more temperate populations showing the least injury at 2°C to 4°C.
Similarly, tropical mangroves are more sensitive to low temperatures than
are sub-tropical species.

The C_4 grasses and the sugar cane relatives from Australia, New Zealand,
and the Pacific tropical and sub-tropical areas are very sensitive (Rowley
et al., 1975; Ivory and Whiteman,1978; Miller, 1976). Another group of extremely sensitive plants are those growing in warm temperate coastal regions
where frosts are very rare. The tropical lianas and epiphytes are typically

TABLE 1.2

POTENTIAL COLD RESISTANCE OF ALGAE, LICHENS,
AND MOSSES IN THE HYDRATED STATE[a]

Plant and habitat		Injury below indicated temperature (°C)	Reference
1. ALGAE			
Arctic seas		-8 to -28	Biebl (1968, 1970)
Intertidal		-2 to -4	Biebl (1968, 1970)
Sublittoral			
Temperate seas			
Intertidal	Chlorophyceae	-8 to -25	Terumoto (1964); Biebl (1958,
	Phaeophyceae	-40 to -60	Parker (1960) 1972)
	Rhodophyceae	-7 to -8 (-70)[b]	Biebl (1939, 1958);
			Terumoto (1964); Migita (1966)
Sublittoral		-2 to +4	Biebl (1958, 1970)
Tropical seas			
Intertidal		-2 to +11	Biebl (1962)
Sublittoral		+3 to +14	Biebl (1962)
Arctic and Antarctic freshwaters			
Cyanophyceae		-70 to -196	Holm-Hansen (1963)
Phycophyta		-15 to -30	Holm-Hansen (1963); Biebl (1969)
Temperate lakes			
Cyanophyceae		(-25) -70 to -196	Holm-Hansen (1963)
Phycophyta		-2 to -20	Terumoto (1964); Duthie (1964);
			Biebl (1967); Schölm (1968)
Tropical lakes		n.d.[c]	
Hot springs		[+15 to +20][d]	Soeder and Stengel (1974);
			Brock (1978)
Epiphytic and epipetric algae		-70 to -196	Kärcher (1931); Edlich (1936)
Soil algae		-25 to -196	Holm-Hansen (1963)
Snow algae		ca. -40	Göppert (1878)
2. LICHENS			
Arctic, Antarctic		-80 to -196	Kappen and Lange (1972);
			Riedmüller-Schölm (1974)
Desert, High mountains		-78	Kappen and Lange (1970b, 1972)
Temperate zone		-50 and below	Kappen and Lange (1972)
3. MOSSES			
Arctic		-50 to -80	Riedmüller-Schölm (1974)
Temperate zone			
Marchantiales		-5 to -10	Clausen (1964), Dircksen (1964)
Jungermanniales		-10 to -15	Clausen (1964), Dircksen (1964)
Musci (Hydrophytes)		-8 to -20	Irmscher (1912), Dircksen (1964)
Musci (bogs)		-7 to -15	Dircksen (1964)
Musci (forest floor)		(-10) -15 to -35 (-55)	Irmscher (1912); Dircksen (1964);
			Hudson and Brustkern (1965);
			Antropova (1974)
Musci (epiphytic, epipetric)		-15 to -30	Irmscher (1912)
Humid tropics		< 0 to -7 (-16)	Biebl (1964, 1967)

[a] Data from Larcher and Bauer (1981).   [c] n.d. No experimental data available.
[b] Exceptional values indicated by parentheses.   [d] Estimated from growth limitations indicated by brackets.

TABLE 1.3

POTENTIAL FROST RESISTANCE OF
HERBACEOUS VASCULAR PLANTS[a]

Plant group	Frost resistance			Reference
	(lowest temperature (°C) sustained without lethal injury)			
	Leaves	Shoot apex	Subterraneous organs	

1. PTERIDOPHYTES

Plant group	Leaves	Shoot apex	Subterraneous organs	Reference
Tropical ferns	0 to -2			Biebl (1964)
Temperate ferns	-13 to -25		-7 to -12	Kappen (1964)
Subarctic (Lycopodium)	-80			Riedmüller-Schölm (1974)

2. GRAMINOIDS

Plant group	Leaves	Shoot apex	Subterraneous organs	Reference
Tropical and subtropical grasses	-1 to -4	-4 to -6		Rowley et al. (1975); Ivory and Whiteman (1978)
Temperate grasses	-20 to -25	-5 to -30	-7 to -20	Till (1956); Fowler et al. (1977); Fuller and Eagles (1978); Noshiro and Sakai (1979)
Steppe grasses	n.d.[b]			
Alpine sedges	(-70)[c]	(-70)	(-70)	Kainmüller (1975)
Arctic graminoids	n.d.			

3. HERBACEOUS DICOTYLEDONS

Plant group	Leaves	Shoot apex	Subterraneous organs	Reference
Tropical herbs	-1 to -2			Biebl (1964)
Meadow plants	-15 to -25	-10 to -20	-5 to -15	Schnetter (1965); Noshiro and Sakai (1979),
Temperate forest herbs	-10 to -20	10 to -20	-7 to -11	Till (1956)
Geophytes	-5 to -12	ca. -10	-7 to -14	Till (1956); Goryshina (1972); Lundquist and Pellett (1976)
Halophytes	-10 to -2	ca. -20	-10 to -20	Kappen (1969); Maier and Kappen (1979)
Winter-annual desert plants	-6 to -10			Lona (1963)
Arctic and alpine rosette and cushion plants	-20 to -50	-30 to -50	-20 to -60	Ulmer (1937); Sakai and Otsuka (1970); Kainmüller (1975)
Tropical high mountain plants	-7 to -12			Larcher (1975)

[a] Data from Larcher and Bauer (1981).

[b] No experimental data available.   [c] Parentheses denote exceptional values.

very sensitive to frost. It seems a general phenomenon, however, that during seasonally dormant or inactive periods, such as droughts in tropical systems and winter in temperate systems, plant freezing tolerance is greater, and such ecosystems are more resistant to cold temperatures than ecosystems that are constantly moist and warm. It should also be emphasized that in ecosystems with very little seasonal temperature variation, as in many evergreen tropical areas, sudden temperature drops would likely be devastating because of lack of adaptation. The generalization that ecosystems can tolerate normally experienced extremes, but not extremes for which there is little previous experience, seems to be true for low temperature, as it is for drought, darkness, hurricanes, and other climatic extremes.

Having said this, it also needs to be recognized that substantial differences occur within and across species, even within an ecosystem at a specified location. The individual can alter its response somewhat, provided it is not killed outright by the first exposure to the new (surprise) circumstances. Further, population-level accommodations can occur if there is a diversity of tolerances among the individuals in the population. The hardening and acclimation of temperate forest trees on a seasonal basis is one clear example. Some cold adaptation has also been demonstrated in sub-tropical grasses (e.g., *Paspalum dilotatum* and *Evengrostis curvula*) (Rowely et al., 1975), as well as in citrus species growing in Florida (Yelenosky, 1975).

Sudden freezes have led to disasters to the citrus groves of Florida on numerous occasions this century, seemingly most frequent over the past decade. This is an example of a semi-tropical crop grown beyond the limits if its normal range, and provides a dramatic demonstration of the disaster which a nuclear war could bring to agricultural systems everywhere and to ecosystems in the tropics and sub-tropics should frost occur, especially if chilling temperatures were prolonged.

The acclimation or hardening of plants to tolerate low temperatures is reversible and temporary. If, for example, some sub-tropical species were to acclimate to chilling conditions, the acclimation might be of little value in the climatic conditions after a large-scale nuclear war, as the acclimation would be lost as temperatures increased, and the plants would be just as sensitive to damage from subsequent chilling as they were to the first.

Subterranean organs generally are less adapted to very low temperatures than are plant parts exposed at or above the soil surface. This is illustrated in Table 1.3. It is not normally disadvantageous, however, since the substantial insulating properties of soils ameliorates air temperatures within a few centimeters of the surface. Low growth forms and lack of trees or shrubs in exposed arctic and alpine areas, together with the development of belowground perennating (over-wintering) and storage organs, emphasize this point. The classification by Raunkiaer (1909, 1928) indicated that both latitudinal and altitudinal vegetation types change in relative abundance based

TABLE 1.4

POTENTIAL RESISTANCE OF WOODY PLANTS
TO LOW TEMPERATURES AND FROST[a]

(lowest sustained temperatures without lethal injury) (^{o}C)			
Plant group	Leaves	Buds	Flower buds
1. TROPICAL REGIONS			
Forest and fruit trees	+4 to -3	down to -5	
Tropical palms	$(-1)^{b}$ -3 to -5	[-3 to -5][c]	
Lianas	+4 to 0		
Mangroves	+4 to -4		
2. SUBTROPICAL REGIONS			
Evergreen trees and shrubs	(-2) -4 to -6 (-8)	-6 to -12	
Drought and deciduous trees		ca. -14	
Subtropical palms	-5 to -12	down to -14	
3. MARITIME-TEMPERATE REGIONS			
Conifers	-10 to -20	-10 to -25	(-10)
Arcto-tertiary flora	-10 to -15	-8 to -15	
Evergreen broad-leaved trees and shrubs	-7 to -15 (-20)	-10 to -18	down to -17
Mediterranean scherophylls	-5 to -12 (-15)	-8 to -18	-10 to -16
Warm-temperate deciduous trees		-15 to -30	-15 to -30
Ericaceous heath shrubs	-15 to -30	-20 to -30	-15 to -25
4. REGIONS WITH SEVERE WINTERS			
Conifers	-40 to -70 (-196)	-30 to -70 (-196)	
Temperate deciduous trees		-25 to -35 (-60)	-25 to -40
Boreal deciduous trees		-30 to -80 (-196)	
Arctic and alpine dwarf shrubs	-30 to -50 (-80)	-20 to -40	

[a] Data from Larcher and Bauer (1981).

[b] Parentheses denote exceptional values.

[c] Brackets denote estimations from observations of occasional frost injury

TABLE 1.4 continued

Plant group	Stem	Roots	References
1. TROPICAL REGIONS			
Forest and fruit trees		down to -5	Biebl (1964); Sakai (1972,1978b,c)
Tropical palms			Biebl (1964); Smith (1964); Larcher (1980b)
Lianas			Biebl (1964)
Mangroves			Biebl (1964); McMillan (1975)
2. SUBTROPICAL REGIONS			
Evergreen trees and shrubs		-6 to -15	Larcher (1971); Layton and Parsons (1972); Sakai (1972, 1978b); Yelenosky (1977)
Drought and deciduous trees		-15 to -20	Larcher (1971); Sakai (1978b)
Subtropical palms			Larcher (1980a); Larcher and Winter (1982)
3. MARITIME-TEMPERATE REGIONS			
Conifers	-15 to -30	-10 to -20	Parker (1960); Larcher (1954, 1970); Sakai and Okada (1971); Havis (1976); Sakai (1978b)
Arcto-tertiary flora	-8 to -18		Sakai (1971)
Evergreen broad-leaved trees and shrubs	-10 to -20	-7 to -9	Sakai (1972); Havis (1976); Sakai and Wardle (1978);Sakai and Hakoda (1979)
Mediterranean sclerophylls	-8 to -22[d]		Larcher (1954, 1970); Sakai (1978b)
Warm-temperate deciduous	-20 to -40[d]		Larcher (1970); Sakai (1971, 1972, 1978b,c); Sakai and Weiser (1973); Kaku and Iwaya (1978)
Ericaceous heath shrubs	-15 to -35	-10 to -20	Till (1956); Havis (1976); Sakai and Miwa (1979)
4. REGIONS WITH SEVERE WINTERS			
Conifers	-50 to -196	-20 to -35	Pisek and Schiessl (1947); Parker (1962); Sakai and Okada (1971);Havis (1976); Sakai (1978a,1979)
Temperate deciduous trees	-30 to -50[d]	-15 to -25	Till (1956); Pisek (1958);Parker (1962); Sakai (1972,1978c); Sakai and Weiser (1973); George et al. (1974)
Boreal deciduous trees	down to -196		Sakai (1965); Sakai and Weiser (1973); Sakai (1978c)
Arctic and alpine dwarf trees	-30 to -50	-10 to -30	Ulmer (1937); Pisek and Schiessl (1947); Sakai and Otsuka (1970);Riedmüller-Schölm (1974); Larcher (1977).

[d] Stem resistance limited by deep supercooling of xylem.

on the position of perennating buds (meristems surviving dormant periods). In tropical evergreen ecosystems, the great majority of species have buds well above the ground, whereas in seasonal forests, a mixture of woody perennials or herbaceous perennial (phanaeophytes and hemicryptophytes) occurs (Figure 1.3), with annual species surviving during the cold or drought seasons as well-protected dry seeds. In cold polar regions, the perennating buds are at or below the ground surface. This life-form sequence along climatic gradients is to a large extent based on progressive protection of vital meristems against cold and drought. It means that cold-temperate and polar ecosystems are at least partially pre-adapted (by chance) to the climatic disturbances that a nuclear war could impose.

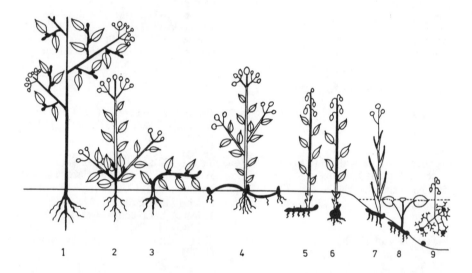

Figure 1.3   The relative positions of the perennating parts of four life forms. (1) Phanerophytes, (2–3) Chamaephytes, (4) Hemicryptophytes, and (5–9) Crypto-phytes. The persistent axes and surviving buds are shown in black. From Raunkiaer (1934)

1.2.1.3 Acclimation and Hardening

Hardening is a sequential process, as described in Tumanov (1962), Weiser (1970), Kacperska-Palacz (1978), and Tyurina et al. (1978). Initial hardening is achieved at temperatures from 0°C to 5°C, which makes it possible for moderate frosts to be survived. Subsequent, sustained frosts lead to complete hardiness, in those plant species capable of developing it, so that the plants achieve their limits of freezing tolerance. At this stage of hardening, woody boreal species (e.g., *Abies, Picea, Pinus, Salix, Betula,* and *Ribes*) are resistant to extreme temperatures, even including immersion in liquid nitrogen (– 196°C). Some herbaceous plants of the northern woods, tundra, and high mountains also exhibit unlimited freezing tolerance.

Differences between hardened and unhardened plants are striking in their temperature limits (Table 1.5). Cold periods occurring during the winter can induce additional cold-tolerance within a few days for plants already hardened. However, dehardening by warming to above-freezing, especially if temperatures suddenly rise to greater than + 10°C in winter in cold temperate regions, takes place even faster, being completed within 1–2 days of persistent warm temperatures This phenomenon leads to premature bud break and subsequent frost damage to shrubs and trees. A lack of continuous below-freezing temperatures following a nuclear war could cause this

TABLE 1.5

KILLING TEMPERATURES FOR PLANTS IN THE FROZEN STATE[a]

Species	Killing temperature (°C) when frozen		Reference
	Unhardened	Hardened	
Potato tuber	-2		Maximov (1914)
Red beet root	-2		Maximov (1914)
Wheat		-12, -15	Tumanov and Borodin (1930)
Cabbage	-2	-6, -20	Levitt (1939)
			Kohn and Levitt (1965)
Vaccinium vitis idea	-2	-22	Ulmer (1937)
Erica carnea	-4	-19	Ulmer (1937)
Sempervivum glaucum	-3	-25	Kessler (1935)
Rhododendron ferrugineum	-4	-28	Ulmer (1937)
Globularia nudicaulis	-4	-19	Ulmer (1937)
Globularia cordifolia	-4	-19	Ulmer (1937)
Saxifraga caesia	-4	-30	Ulmer (1937)
Homogyne alpina	-4	-18	Ulmer (1937)
Saxifraga aizoon	-4	-19	Ulmer (1937)
Hedra helix	-5	-18	Kessler (1935)
Rhododendron hirsutum	-5	-29	Ulmer (1937)
Saxifraga cordifolia	-5	-19	Kessler (1935)
Carex firma	-6	-30	Ulmer (1937)
Pinus mugo	-6	-41	Ulmer (1937)
Empetrum nigrum	-6	-29	Ulmer (1937)
Juniperus nana	-8	-26	Ulmer (1937)
Pinus cembra	-9	-38	Ulmer (1937)
Pinus cembra	-10	-40	Pisek (1950)

[a] Data from Levitt (1980).

phenomenon, especially in more southerly latitudes, such as 30°N–40°N. Examples of the seasonal and shorter term changes in freezing tolerances are shown in Figures 1.4–1.6 .

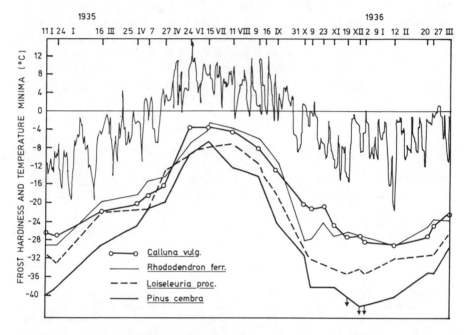

Figure 1.4   Seasonal changes in freezing tolerance of four evergreen species compared with the daily temperature minima. From Levitt (1972)

Cannell (1985) noted that frost hardening is an active metabolic process and that there is abundant evidence that complete hardening of temperate woody species occurs only if the plants receive a sequenced change in conditions from long, warm days ⇒ short, warm days ⇒ short, cool days ⇒ short, frosty days. All steps in the sequence are essential. If the short, warm day (autumn) step is omitted, then the trees do not harden fully. In autumn before the second stage of hardening is induced by decreased daylengths, the difference between ambient temperatures and the hardiness of the shoots (defined by the killing temperatures for that time of the year) can be less than during the summer, indicating an increased vulnerability to frost damage. This is illustrated by Figure 1.7 (Timmis, 1978), which shows that in the absence of the short, warm days, both in spring and autumn while active growth occurs, hardening is insufficient to prevent damage at temperatures as high as − 3°C to − 10°C. Other examples of this induction of cold hardiness are shown in Figures 1.8 and 1.9.

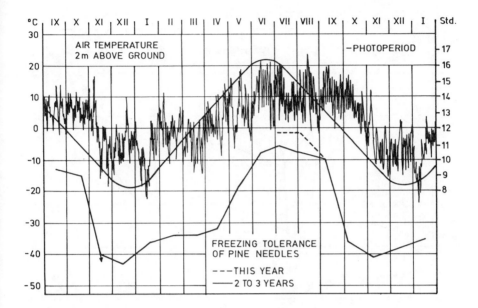

Figure 1.5 Seasonal changes in air temperature (daily extremes), photoperiod (upper curve), and freezing tolerance (lower curve) of pine needles, from September 1965 to January 1967. From Levitt (1972)

Though the hardening sequence described by Cannell (1985) needs to be met both in the correct order and for the appropriate minimum length of time, there is some evidence that acclimation can be achieved in the early autumn. Simonovitch (1982) noted that, for black locust (*Robinia pseudoacacia*) growing at about 45°N latitude, the triggering effects of cool night temperatures or shortening daylengths are completed by mid-September; these effects are instrumental in promoting cessation of growth, leaf senescence, and the migration of nutrients and metabolites needed for the final process of bark cell hardening. Over a 15-year period, these trees attained winter hardiness of bark tissues at almost the same time each year, despite the occurrence in some years of moderately warm conditions. Simonovitch et al. (1975) suggested that an endogenous clock mechanism in bark cells drives the hardening reaction to completion in the autumn, to a considerable extent irrespective of light or low temperatures. Many of the black locust bark cells that were maintained for 5 weeks in the dark at 10°C were able to survive immersion in liquid nitrogen, indicating that extreme hardiness was attained (Figure 1.10). Under normal conditions, these trees do not reach total tolerance to liquid nitrogen by mid-October.

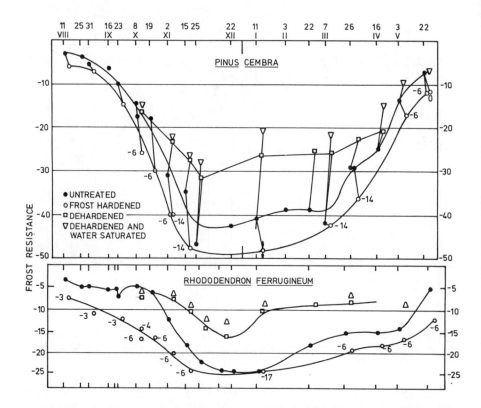

Figure 1.6   Seasonal course of the *actual* frost resistance in the habitat, the *potential* resistance after cold hardening, and the *minimal* resistance after artificial dehardening of leaves of *Pinus cembra* and *Rhododendron ferrugineum* from the alpine timber line in Europe. The difference between minimal and potential frost resistance is a measure of the degree to which the state of hardening can be influenced by weather conditions. From Larcher and Bauer (1981)

In terms of potential acute temperature drop following a nuclear war, severe damage to Northern Hemisphere temperate forest trees would be likely if this drop occurred before September; however, later in the autumn, the most northerly forested ecosystems of the boreal regions might be either already winter hardened or could continue to harden, even as smoke- and dust-induced darkness occurred. On admittedly limited data, it can be suggested that if a nuclear war-induced climatic disturbance commenced in mid-September, then forests in eastern North America and Europe north of 50°N latitude would already be winter acclimated. Likewise, if an acute, extreme temperature excursion commenced in mid-October, forests above

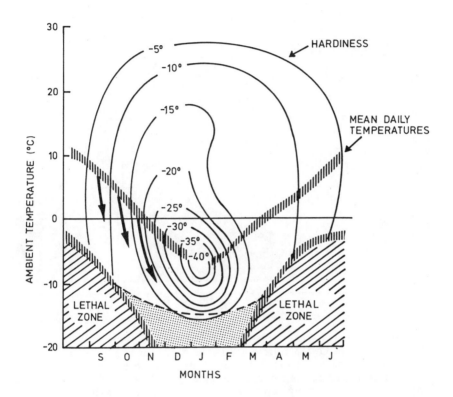

Figure 1.7 Relation between seasonal changes in ambient air temperature and development of hardiness. If premature cooling occurs in September–October, before hardening has developed fully, then exposure to −10°C to −20°C can be lethal. Adapted from Timmis (1978)

45°N would be acclimated; those north of 40°N would be well on their way to acclimation and might be able to complete it, thus avoiding frost damage, so long as temperatures did not drop immediately to lows of −20°C to −40°C.

Though northern temperate trees, such as oak, black locust, spruce, and beech, are frost hardened in a sequence which involves a daylength or photoperiod trigger, not all woody species are initiated in this way. Eucalyptes and other woody angiosperm genera of the Southern Hemisphere have evolved frost tolerance mechanisms to survive brief and occasional frost (down to about −8°C to −16°C) and resume growth within a few days of warm weather recurring (Paton, 1978, 1982, and unpublished data). The photoperiodic insensitivity of *Eucalyptus* is notable for the rapidity with which hardening or dehardening can occur, compared with Northern Hemi-

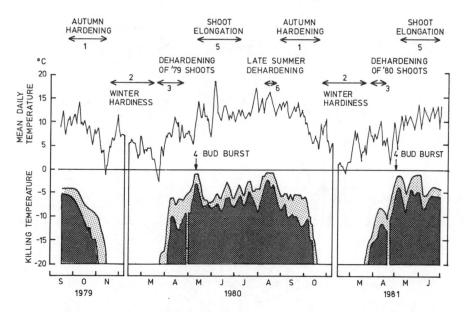

Figure 1.8   Seasonal changes in the frost hardiness of shoots on 7–10 year-old trees of *Picea sitchensis* of Queen Charlotte Islands provenvance growing in Scotland. Darkly shaded = damage score 2; stipled = damage score 1; curves were fitted through a total of 302 points. Shoots were hardy to below −20°C from December to February. Mean daily temperatures have been smoothed by taking 3-day moving means. From Cannell and Sheppard (1982)

sphere trees. They have not evolved either the deep supercooling mechanism, which would allow them to tolerate to −40°C, or the dehydration freezing tolerance mechanism, which would allow even greater cold tolerances. Since *Eucalyptus* is very widely planted in many parts of the world, frost tolerance is a factor to be considered. For example, large plantations of *E. viminalis* were killed in southern U.S.S.R. in 1950 when temperatures dropped to −13°C for several days. In the 1970s, severe frost damage occurred in Northern California and in Brazil.

   The geographic distributions of species, genera, and families are at least partially determined by minimum temperatures (Yoshie and Sakai, 1982); woody plants from different geographic locations (and climates) exhibit large and gradual (clinal) differences in freezing resistance. Oohata and Sakai (1982) reported data for winter hardiness of 48 species of pine (*Pinus*) from a wide range of latitudes and for 9 species of the subgenus *Strobus*. Several species were uninjured at −80°C while others, such as *Pinus caribaea*, were damaged at temperatures below −9°C, and *P. leiophylla* and *P. lawsonii* at

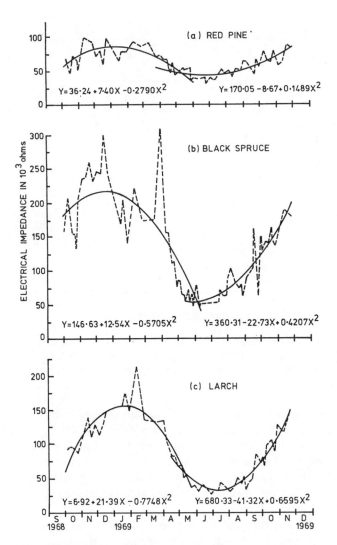

Figure 1.9 Electrical impedance trends for (a) red pine, (b) black spruce, and (c) larch. The electrical impedance increased gradually during October and November in the pines and rapidly in the other species. It remained relatively unchanged during the winter months. In April and May, the impedance decreased gradually in the pines and drastically in the other species, to a minimum. In August, the impedance started to increase again. The two second-degree curves were calculated from the October 1968–July 1969 and June–November 1969 measurements. The curves indicate the trends, and the measured data demonstrate the variations that were encountered from one week to the next. The reading at each date is based on an average of five trees, with two measurements per tree. From Glerum (1973)

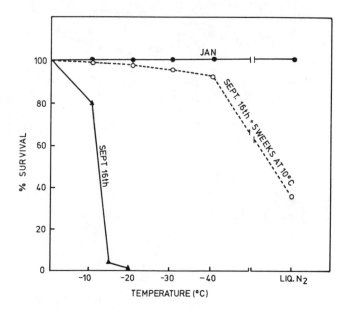

Figure 1.10   Freezing tolerance of bark of sections of the trunk of black locust tree on Sept. 16; on Oct. 17 after storage for 5 weeks at 10°C in the dark; and in January; measured in terms of survival after freezing to various temperatures. From Siminovitch (1982)

−8°C. Some boreal and sub-boreal Canadian species, such as *P. banksiana*, *P. strobus* and *P. resinosa*, could tolerate −80°C (Table 1.6). Figure 1.11 shows a highly significant correlation between the freezing resistance of each pine species and the mean air temperature in the coldest month within the natural distribution range. Freezing resistance was greatest in these species from areas with a low mean warm index and a corresponding high negative cold index.

Intraspecific and ecotypic differences in freezing resistance and in timing of cold hardening in the autumn also occur. Northern populations harden earlier than those from southern and coastal regions (Smithberg and Weiser, 1968). These facts suggest that winter minimal temperatures and frost intensity are important selective factors in species adaptations to cold climates.

Differences in life form allow for differences in freezing resistance, as demonstrated by Yoshie and Sakai (1982) (Table 1.7). They found that the hardiest winter buds are the woody shrubs and trees with the over-wintering buds located well above the ground (phanerophytes). Subterranean organs of hemicryptophytes, which have buds at the soil surface, are much hardier

TABLE 1.6

FREEZING RESISTANCES IN <u>PINUS</u> SPP.[a]

Pinus species		Mean Warmth Index (°C/month)	Mean Cold Index (°C/month)	Mean Air Temp. of Coldest Month (°C)	Freezing Resistance (°C)
1. SUBGENUS STROBUS					
SUBSECT.:					
Cembrae	P. koraiensis	43	-78	-15	-70
	P. pumila	20	-116	-18	-70[b]
	P. cembra	24	-53	-7	-70[b]
Strobi	P. strobus	62	-41	-7	-80[b]
	P. monticola	47	-21	-1	-80[b]
	P. ayacahuite	95	0	10	-15
	P. peuce	51	-35	-6	-40
	P. griffithii	71	-17	-2	-35
Cembroides	P. cembroides	113	-1	8	-12
Gerardianae	P. bungeana	81	-34	-7	-30
2. SUBGENUS PINUS					
SUBSECT.:					
Leiophyllae	P. leiophylla	105	0	10	-8
Canarienses	P. canariensis	57	-1	7	-22
Sylvestres	P. resinosa	55	-52	-9	-80[b]
	P. nigra	81	-11	1	-40
	P. mugo	44	-27	-4	-70[b]
	P. densiflora	86	-15	0	-60
	P. insularis	179	0	15	-7
	P. merkusii	211	0	20	-10
Australes	P. palstris	156	0	9	-18
	P. taeda	147	-1	8	-23
	P. elliottii	165	0	10	-22
	P. caribaea	221	0	20	-9
Ponderosae	P. ponderosa	60	-32	-4	-26
	P. engelmannii	120	0	8	-15
	P. michoacana	134	0	12	-10
	P. lawsonii	155	0	14	-8
Contortae	P. banksiana	38	-100	-20	-80[b]
	P. contorta	30	-51	-7	-75[b]
	P. clausa	195	0	14	-14
Oocarpae	P. radiata	92	0	9	-13
	P. patula	100	0	9	-15
	P. greggii	114	0	8	-15

[a] Data from Oohata and Sakai (1982).

[b] Uninjured at the lowest temperature indicated.

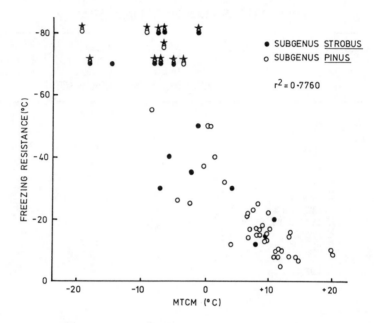

Figure 1.11   Relation between freezing resistance of each pine species and mean air temperature in the coldest month (MTCM) at the natural distribution range. Star = uninjured at the lowest temperature. From Oohata and Sakai (1982)

in those plants growing at the edge of forests than in plants well within the forest. Differences in hardiness of subterranean organs among different life forms and microhabitats were found to be much greater in Japan than in Scandinavia (Till, 1956). Yoshie and Sakai (1982) accounted for this by the much more severe winter experienced at Hokkaido than at Gottingen.

1.2.1.4 Supercooling and Dehydration—Mechanisms of Frost Hardening

Plant structures that can survive extreme low winter temperatures do so by two primary mechanisms that involve either tolerating or avoiding ice formation (Levitt, 1980). Cells that survive by tolerance dehydrate intracellularly in the winter, and extracellular water freezes without injuring the living cellular constituents. In mid-winter, such plant tissue is extremely hardy, and can withstand immersion in liquid nitrogen ($-196°C$) without injury (Sakai, 1960). In contrast, plant cells that survive by avoidance of ice formation do so by supercooling of the tissues. A supercooled solution remains liquid below its equilibrium freezing point (Becwar and Burke, 1982) and is said to be deep supercooled when it remains liquid to the low temperature limit for supercooling, the homogeneous nucleation temperature for the solution. This is about − 40°C for plant solutions and sets the lower limit on winter hardiness in supercooling plants.

Becwar and Burke (1982) noted that in terms of ecological significance, most eastern deciduous forest trees of North America have tissues that can supercool. Their northern distribution limit closely parallels the − 40°C average annual minimum temperature isotherm for North America, at which temperature tissues freeze and are injured. In contrast, boreal forest trees of more northerly latitudes, where − 40°C temperatures occur regularly, survive freezing by tolerating the ice that forms, a mechanism which is not limited by extreme low temperatures. Much of the ice damage problem is avoided by dehydration of tissues. Becwar and Burke (1982) reviewed literature on the mid-winter hardiness of timberline or treeline species of Europe, Japan, and America. Treeline minimum average temperatures were reported to be consistently between − 40°C and − 43°C.

It is apparent from this that if a nuclear war-induced climatic disturbance were to occur after winter hardening, even the worst scenarios would not likely cause death of the northerly boreal forest species, especially coniferous ones with an ice-tolerance dehydration system. However, if winter temperatures went much below − 40°C in areas where supercooling predominates (e.g., in the eastern deciduous forests of the United States, at the higher altitudes in the Rocky Mountains, and in the mountains of northern and central Europe), then those woody species could be severely harmed or fatally damaged. Even in that case, however, the cambial cells at the base of the trunk are often best protected by soil and thicker bark, so that coppicing or adventitious shoots might be produced at the base of surviving trees, allowing eventual recovery.

The possibility of a nuclear war pushing temperatures below the tolerance limits of timberline species in either winter or summer seems a real one. The timberline is at about 3400 m over a very wide and heterogeneous area. Becwar and Burke (1982) suggested that the environment on passing through the timberline changes gradually, but the plants respond discontinuously to the gradient of worsening environmental factors. That is, a small change in a single environmental factor can cause severe plant stress damage. Such responses to temperature stresses are well known. For example, Engleman spruce twigs survive prolonged winter exposure at − 35°C, but are injured after brief exposure to − 45°C (Becwar et al., 1981); wheat leaves survive prolonged exposure to − 1°C, but are killed after brief exposure to − 17°C (Gusta et al., 1975).

The differential distribution of the two major mechanisms of freezing tolerance are illustrated for North America in Figure 1.12. Rajashekar and Burke (1978) pointed out that conifers and deciduous species of the northern boreal forest cover large areas of Canada, Alaska, and Northern Eurasia,

TABLE 1.7

FREEZING RESISTANCE OF DORMANT BUDS,
LEAVES, RHIZOMES, AND ROOTS[a]

Species	Dormant Buds	Leaves	Freezing Resistance (°C) Rhizomes	Roots
1. PHANEROPHYTES				
Quercus mongolica var. grosseserrata	-20			
Juglans ailanthifolia	-30			
Carpinus cordata	-17			
Cornus controversa	-25			
Cercidiphyllum japonicum	-25			
Fraxinus sp.	-25			
Tilia maximowicziana	-30			
Magnolia kobus var. borealis	-25			
Sorbus alnifolia	-25			
Acer mono var. mayrii	-15			
Acer palmatum var. amoenum	-25			
Hydrangea petiolaris	-20			
2. CHAMAEPHYTES (Forest Floor)				
Daphne pseudo-mezereum var. jezoensis	-20	-7		-5[b]
Pachysandra terminalis	-20	-20	-7	-5[b]
Euonymus fortunei var. radicans	-20	-20		-10
Lycopodium obscurum	-20	-20		
Lycopodium serratum var. serratum	-20	-15, -20		-10
Pyrola secunda	-17	-15	-5	
Pyrola incarnata	-15	-15	-7	
Pyrola alpina	-15	-12	-5	
Pyrola renifolia	-12	-12	-5	
Oxalis acetosella	-12	-7	-5	-5
Tripterospermum japonicum	-15	-5		
3. CHAMAEPHYTES (Forest Margin)				
Lycopodium clavatum var. nipponicum	-25	-15, -25		

[a] Data from Yoshie and Sakai (1982).

[b] Injured at indicated temperature.

TABLE 1.7 continued.

Species	Dormant Buds	Leaves	Freezing Resistance (°C) Rhizomes	Roots
4. HEMICRYPTOPHYTES (Forest Floor)				
Tiarella polyphylla	-10	-7	-10	-5
Agrimonia pilosa	-10		-7	-5[b]
Maianthemum dilatatum	-10		-5	-5
Chamaele decumbens	-5[b]		-5[b]	-5[b]
Sanicula chinensis	-5		-5	-5[b]
5. HEMICRYPTOPHYTES (Forest Margin)				
Oenothera sp.	-12	-12		-7, -12
Miscanthus sinensis	-7		-7	-7
Filipendula sp.	-12		-10	-5[b]
Solidago virga-aurea	-12		-10	-10
Plantago asiatica	-10		-10	-10
Trifolium pratense	-5		-5[b]	-5[b]
Petasites japonicus var. giganteus	-5		-5[b]	-5[b]
Leibnitzia anandria	-7		-7	-5
Artemisia montana	-10		-7	-7
Artemisia japonica	-12		-12	-12
Anaphalis margaritacea	-7		-7	-7
Sanguisorba tenuifolia var. alba	-7		-7	-5
Lysimachia vulgaris var. davurica	-7		-7	-7
6. GEOPHYTES (Forest Floor)				
Phryma leptostachya var. asiatica	-5[b]		-5[b]	-5[b]
Cacalia delphiniifolia	-5[b]		-5[b]	-5[b]
Cacalia auriculata var. kamtschatica	-5[b]		-5[b]	-5[b]
Sceptridium multifidum var. robustum	-5	-17	-5[b]	-5[b]
Lilium cordatum var. glehnii	-5[b]		-5[b] (bulb)	-5[b]
Adoxa moschatellina	-5[b]		-5[b]	-5[b]

Figure 1.12   Hardiness zone map of North America. The map is divided into three hardiness regions. Region A has average annual minimums below − 40°C and extreme minimums much lower. Region B has finite probability of − 40°C minimums. Region C has very little probability of − 40°C. Deep undercooling trees only occur in the very southern parts of region A; however, they dominate the forests in regions B and C. Adapted from Rajashekar and Burke (1978)

and do not deep undercool. Most deciduous species native to the eastern deciduous forest, which covers the eastern half of the U.S.A., do deep undercool. Such deep undercooling trees dominate the forests in regions B and C, where the probability of temperatures of − 40°C occurring is low. Hence, we estimate that should a major nuclear war cause winter temperatures to plunge below − 40°C for extended periods or below − 50°C for brief periods, then the native species would simply not be able to survive. If even temperatures of − 20°C were reached in latitudes below about 34°N for the United States, the native vegetation would not be adapted to survive, except for alpine species.

1.2.2. Responses of Plants to Low Light

The acute phase of post-nuclear war climatic disturbances outlined in Volume I could be sufficiently severe that in Northern mid-latitudes, light could be reduced by 90% or more. Even as conditions subsequently ameliorated during a chronic period, light reductions by 5% to 10% could occur. This decreased light would be accompanied by lower temperatures. Since productivity of green plants, the essential primary producers for all natural and agricultural ecosystems, is achieved through light-mediated photosynthesis, significant reduction of light would cause a reduction in photosynthesis and possibly alter other related physiological processes.

The more severe temperature excursions of the acute phase following a summer nuclear war could lead to a sudden onset of temperatures well below freezing. Since it is at just such a stage in the post-war climate that accompanying light levels would be minimal, it is important to recognize for terrestrial ecosystems that it is the low temperatures which would have the predominant acute period effects. If grasslands and temperate forests were subject to subfreezing temperatures, it would matter little with regard to vegetation whether darkness or full sunlight prevailed. For many animals however, the intensity of light and number of daylight hours would be important to finding food.

In aquatic systems, light, rather than temperature, determines productivity rates and reduced light levels would cause an almost linear reduction in photosynthesis. If low light were to be prolonged, the normal trophic interactions and successional and seasonal patterns of species replacements would be severely altered. Light would become the dominant controlling factor.

1.2.2.1. Plant Responses to Prolonged Light Reductions

Much research over the past 50 years has demonstrated the great difference among and within species in their ability to grow in deep shade versus in open habitats exposed to direct solar illumination. Many plants, especially forest species, normally grow under deeply shaded conditions, with light intensities of 10% to $\leq 1\%$ of that reaching the upper canopy. Similarly, in tall grasslands, low growing species and the basal leaves of grasses typically occur at very low light intensities.

Grime (1979) suggested that shade is only important in climatic regimes conducive to the development of dense canopies. In normally functioning ecosystems, shade frequently coincides with the high temperatures and humidities of tropical and sub-tropical climates year-round, or temperate regions during summer, and with conditions of mineral nutrient depletion associated with the development of a large biomass. It is likely, therefore, that many plant characteristics described as shade adaptations are, in fact, more related to simultaneous tolerance to shade, high temperatures, and mineral nutrient stress. This being the case, a low light intensity accompanied by low temperatures imposed as a consequence of a nuclear war would probably present a novel climatic event.

Few plant species are able to survive continuous low light conditions because of limitations in photosynthesis. Beneath dense tree canopies, especially canopies composed of evergreen species, herbaceous species are sparse, and, consequently, vertical light gradients are less pronounced near the forest floor. Ability to compete for light under such circumstances is likely to be of secondary importance compared with an ability to tolerate shade.

The effects of shade upon growth rate and morphology of plants have been examined by many researchers (e.g., Burns, 1923; Blackman and Rutter, 1948; Grime and Jeffery, 1965; Loach, 1970). In general, plants in shaded conditions produce less dry matter, develop larger internodes and petioles, and produce larger, thinner leaves. However, species differ considerably in their responses. Loach (1970) and others have shown that greatest plasticity (i.e., ability to alter leaf shape and size) occurs in those species for which deep shade is an unusual or transitory occurrence, whereas those species or populations which occur in continuous deep shade do not make such leaf morphological adjustments.

Grime (1966) and Grime and Hunt (1975) found in comparative studies that shade-tolerant herbs and tree seedlings show a consistent, slow growth rate, which is genetically determined (Mahmoud and Grime, 1974). Shade-tolerant plants are better able to exploit shaded locations by having rapid photosynthetic fixation of carbon at low light intensities, coupled with lower respiratory rates; plants that require full sunlight respire more rapidly, but photosynthesize at the same or lower rate than the shade-tolerant species. If a nuclear war caused reduced light intensities for prolonged periods, the shade-tolerant plants would be at an advantage compared to those species from open habitats. However, this general statement needs qualification, since low light would be accompanied by low temperatures, which would reduce respiration rates. Nevertheless, the advantage of shade-tolerant species would probably remain, if they and shade-intolerant species are equally metabolically slowed by lowered temperatures.

An unresolved issue for botanists is how long species could tolerate low light levels and which species might prevail. Very little literature exists on plant survival in the dark. The study by Hutchinson (1967) emphasized the remarkable tolerance of some species to this unnatural condition. He examined the comparative ability of 25 native species from the U.K. to survive in complete darkness and considered the effects of soil nutrition, air temperature, and the influence of seed size on survivorship. Survivorship was also examined relative to the habitat in which the species normally occur. These included open habitats, short grasslands, tall herb and grassland sites, and woodlands. Species varied in seed weight by up to 70-fold. Data are given in Tables 1.8 and 1.9.

On nutrient-poor soil at low temperatures (5°C–7°C), longevity was greatest. The woodland grass *Deschampsia flexuosa* survived in the dark for 280 days as seedlings, after being grown in the light for 20 days, and for 252 days when initially grown for 40 days in the light. On nutrient-sufficient loam, longevity was less. In contrast, species from open and lightly shaded habitats survived about 50 to 60 days under the same circumstances at 5°C to 7 °C. This indicates that even very young seedlings might be able to survive low temperatures and low light for a number of months. However, higher temperatures (15°C–17°C) were found to result in decreased survivorship, presumably because of higher metabolic activity and concomitant higher respiratory loss.

Based on this limited data base, woodland species would appear be at a distinct advantage in temperate regions. The general response within a habitat category is that the slower the growth, the longer the survival. Plants on nutrient-poor soils survive longer than on nutrient-sufficient soils. This could have implications for agricultural crops, which would normally be planted on fertile soils. Species from tall herb and tall grassland communities are intermediate between the woodland and open community types in their longevity, and grasses are generally more persistent than dicotyledons. Particularly on infertile acidic soils, seedlings were found to be capable of remarkable persistence and resumed normal healthy growth when light conditions improved. This could be relevant to the change from acute to the chronic climatic phase after a nuclear war.

In tropical regions, the severity of any climatic change as a result of a nuclear exchange is anticipated to be much less than in the mid-latitudes of the Northern Hemisphere. Deep shade as a result of reduced sunlight is unlikely. However, since the ground flora of evergreen tropical forest are adapted to life in uniform deep shade, no effect from light reductions would

TABLE 1.8

LONGEVITY OF SEEDLINGS GROWN IN DARKNESS[a],[b]

Species	Acidic Soil			Calcareous Soil			Mean survival time
	Pre-treatment period		R.G.R.[c]	Pre-treatment period		R.G.R.[c]	
	0 days	30 days		0 days	30 days		
Anagallis arvensis	28	28[d]	0.56	18	18	0.60	23
Arabidopsis thaliana	40[d]	43	0.17	30	43	0.63	39
Hordeum murinum	44	39	0.55	44	43	0.52	42
Lotus corniculatus	45	48	0.31	35[d]	48	0.39	44
Scabiosa columbaria	45	36[d]	0.19	39[d]	31[d]	0.33	38
Thlaspi arvense	24	22	0.37	25[d]	17	0.56	22
Ulex europaeus	49[d]	47	0.22	64	38	0.12	48
Brachypodium pinnatum	54[d]	42	0.29	28	49	0.41	43
Utrica dioica	44	38	0.41	39[d]	35	0.36	39
Zema erecta	44	68	0.21	45	75	0.25	58
Brachypodium sylvaticum	104	67	0.24	97	58	0.40	82
Deschampsia caespitosa	55[d]	58	0.81	62[d]	59	0.60	57
Geum urbanum	50	70	0.50	48	57	0.63	56
Hypericum hirsutum	45	64	0.47	40	44	0.57	49

[a] Data from Hutchinson (1967).

[b] The longevity (days) of seedlings of fourteen species grown on two contrasting soils in continuous darkness after being grown in the light for 0 or 30 days at 15°C. Longevity is given as the time from commencement of dark treatment until 100% death occurred. The mean survival time of each species is also given as the mean of its longevity on both soils and after both pre-treatment periods. The relative growth rates were measured over the first 28 days from germination. The soils used were a phosphorus-deficient colluvial soil, pH 5.8, from exposed Old Red Sandstone ledges at Jedburgh, Roxburghshire; and a brown-calcareous soil, pH 7.3, from the North Downs, which was both phosphorus and nitrogen deficient.

[c] Relative growth rate.　　[d] Seedlings attacked by fungi.

be likely, even with a decrease by 50%. Unfortunately, the shade might be accompanied by low temperatures which would be very damaging to tropical ecosystems (see Chapter 2).

1.2.2.2. Effects of Shade on Photosynthesis

Many species and ecosystems have a fine balance between net primary production and the needs for food reserves to last through seasonally cold winters or dry seasons; there is a similar balance between net primary production and the high respiratory rates in tropical and sub-tropical ecosystems. Ecosystem maintenance depends directly on adequate photosynthesis which, in turn, depends upon adequate light, both in quantity and quality. Disruption of photosynthesis by attenuation of incident sunlight, as is possible during an acute climatic disturbance phase after a nuclear war, would have serious consequences that would propagate through foodchains, including those upon which humans depend. Primary production would be reduced roughly in proportion to the degree of light attenuation, assuming the plants were actively growing, and assuming, perhaps unrealistically, that the plants remained otherwise undamaged.

The relationship between increasing incident light (quantum flux density) and rate of photosynthesis is illustrated for two ecotypes of the European goldenrod (*Solidago virgaurea*) (Figure 1.13). One ecotype was collected from a sunny, open field and the other from a shaded woodland (Björkman and Holmgren, 1963). Photosynthetic response increased linearly with increasing light intensities at low levels. The shade-tolerant ecotype was able to photosynthesize more rapidly than the sun ecotype at lower flux densities. However, the sun ecotype was able to maintain the linear relationship at higher light intensities than the shade-tolerant ecotype. Thus, at fluxes above 500 $\mu E \cdot m^2 \cdot sec^{-1}$, it photosynthesized more rapidly. Full sunlight is well above photosynthetic saturation level of an isolated ecotype, largely because of restrictions in quantity of chlorophyll available for interception. For shade-tolerant ecotypes, light intensity could be decreased further before direct reductions in photosynthesis would ensue.

The photosynthetic rate responses to light intensity also differs among species (Figure 1.14) in their ability to photosynthesize at high light intensity and in their ability to adapt (Björkman, 1981). Those that cannot adapt or have a limited ability would be at a disadvantage if significant light attenuation followed a major nuclear war. Adaptation would not be immediate, perhaps requiring a few weeks. A key factor then, would be how long an acute phase light attenuation would last. Further, synergisms with accompanying reduced temperatures are largely unknown.

Berry (1985) suggested that about 3% of total incident sunlight energy is stored in the form of chemical bonds in plants under optimal conditions

TABLE 1.9

LONGEVITY OF SEEDLINGS GROWN IN DARKNESS
ON DIFFERENT SOILS[a,b]

A. At 5°C-7°C

	Acidic Soil Pre-treatment period		Loam Pre-treatment period		Mean survival time
	20 days	40 days	20 days	40 days	
Betula pubescens	50	100	56	51	64
Erophila verna	Failed	10	43	100	72[c]
Galium aparine	60	146	74	65	52
Hieracium pilosella	140	220	63	65	108
Koeleria gracilis	233	197	81	220[d]	189
Arrhenatherum elatius	170		140	209	179
Betonica officinalis	Failed	252	230	138	184[c]
Deschampsia flexuosa	281	169	133	240	227
Digitalis purpurea	146	188	75	187	144
Zerna ramosa	190		152	210	185

a Data from Hutchinson (1967).

b Longevity is given as the time (days) from initiation of the dark treatment until 100% seedling death occurred. The seedlings were grown for 20-40 days in the light prior to dark treatment. The mean survival time of each species at each temperature is also given as the mean of its longevity on both soils and after both light treatments. The relative growth rates were measured over the 42 days following germination. The soils used were a fertile loam from Newcastle University Experimental Gardens, pH 5.6, and an alluvial silt from Gosforth, Northumberland, pH 3.8, which was highly infertile and produced symptoms of heavy metal toxicity in several species.

c Mean survival time on loam only.

d Seedlings attacked by fungi.

TABLE 1.9 continued

B. At 15°C-17°C

	Acidic soil			Loam			
	Pre-treatment period		R.G.R.[e]	Pre-treatment period		R.G.R.[e]	Mean survival time
	20 days	40 days		20 days	40 days		
Betula pubescens	50[d]	68	0.43	20[d]	48[d]	0.53	47
Erophila verna	Failed	-	-	20	33[d]	1.12	27[c]
Galium aparine	43[d]	10	0.08	40[d]	40[d]	0.40	33
Hieracium pilosella	39[d]	40	0.23	18	16[d]	0.83	28
Koeleria gracilis	63[d]	68	0.24	38[d]	40[d]	0.89	52
Arrhenatherum elatius	48	46	0.08	40[d]	57[d]	0.73	48[c]
Betonica officinalis	Failed	-	-	64[d]	74[d]	0.63	69[c]
Deschampsia flexuosa	90[d]	89[d]	0.16	42[d]	64[d]	0.74	71
Digitalis purpurea	57[d]	28[d]	0.08	33[d]	65[d]	0.70	46
Zerna ramosa	50[d]	65[d]	0.14	38[d]	50[d]	0.54	52

[e] Relative growth rate.

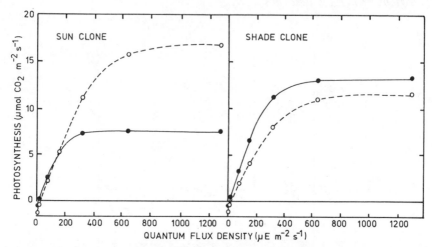

Figure 1.13 Rate of photosynthesis as a function of incident quantum flux density in clones of sun and shade ecotypes of *Salidago virgaurea*, grown at 6.6 (•) and 33.1 (o) μE m^{-2} day^{-1}. Measurements were made at 320 μbar O_2, and a leaf temperature of 22°C. From Björkman (1981)

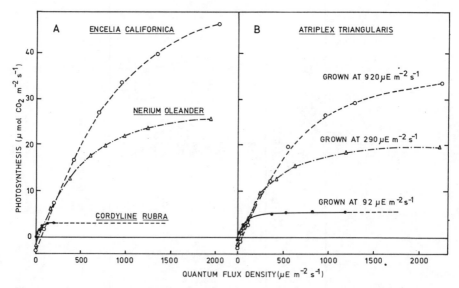

Figure 1.14 Rate of net photosynthesis as a function of incident quantum flux density (400–700 nm) for A: the sun species *Encelia californica* and *Nerium oleander rubra*, grown under natural daylight (approx. 40 μE m^{-2} day^{-1}), and the shade species *Cordyline rubra* grown in its native rain forest habitat (0.3 μE m^{-2} day^{-1}); and B: the sun species *Atriplex triangularis*, grown under three different light intensity regimes. All measurements were made in air of normal CO_2 and O_2 partial pressures and a leaf temperature of 25°C or 30°C. From Björkman (1981)

and that the photosynthetic efficiency is reduced at increasing light levels approaching saturation. Net primary production rates are always lower, however, than photosynthetic carbon fixation rates because some of the captured energy is needed to provide maintenance for the plants or to offset energy losses to grazing by animals, pathogens, and other factors.

Since the linear relationship between absorbed light and photosynthesis only holds at lower light intensities, it is important to consider how much light is needed for saturation in natural vegetation stands. Studies have been done on individual leaves and on canopies *in situ*. Light interception is a function of spatial arrangements of many overlapping leaves in a forest or a grassland. Some light is transmitted through leaves, while other is reflected or absorbed. As the light intensity decreases with depth in the canopy, the characteristics of the leaves change, such that they require less light for saturation (Figure 1.15). The light response of the whole forest canopy is

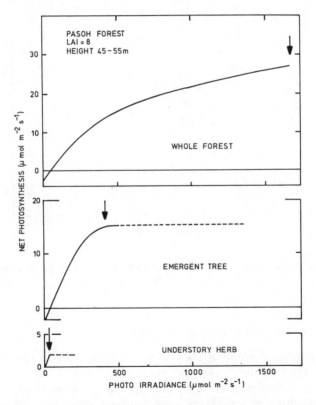

Figure 1.15 Effect of canopy depth and light saturation on photosynthesis as determined for a whole forest, for individual emergent trees, and for understory herbs. From Harwell (1984)

a sum of the responses of all the leaves to the light levels that penetrate to their micro-habitats (Berry and Downton,1982). The net result is that it takes much higher light to saturate the entire canopy than for any single component (Figure 1.15).

Leaf area index (LAI; i.e., the amount of leaf surface area present per unit area of ground) is also an important factor. LAI is a composite of all species and takes account of overlapping leaves; it is determined by the phenological (developmental-seasonal) stage and is affected by limitations of water and nutrients. In water- or nutrient-deficient ecosystems, fewer leaves are formed; thus, the leaf area index is reduced, and the maximum ecosystem interception of light for photosynthesis is reduced. In these areas, much of the incident sunlight strikes the soil and is not available for photosynthesis. In such situations, a reduction in light to the individual plant would directly reduce photosynthesis (Figure 1.16).

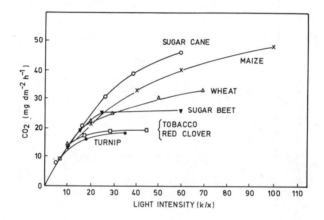

Figure 1.16   Light response curves of photosynthesis for different crop plants. Attached leaves, CO_2 concentration = 0.03 vol. %; temperature = 20°C. From Stoy (1965)

1.2.3 Animal Responses to Low Temperatures [1]

The responses of some of the major animal groups to low temperature stress and their potential for survival after a nuclear war are considered in this section. Animals are subjected to the same kinds of climatic seasonal fluctuations as are plants, and similarly many animals are adapted

[1] This section prepared by K. Meema.

to cold temperature extremes, which enable them to survive winter conditions in northern latitudes and in alpine areas. Animals exposed to freezing temperatures avoid lethal freezing of body tissues by either behavioral or physiological mechanisms. Some terrestrial insects and frogs, however, are able to allow their body tissues to freeze and thaw with no adverse effects. Animals may be divided into two groups according to their ability of regulate their body temperatures; homeotherms (birds and mammals), which maintain their internal body temperature at a relatively constant value by metabolic processes regardless of environmental temperature fluctuations, and poikilotherms (all other animals), which have body temperatures that vary according to ambient environmental temperatures. It would be expected that homeotherms that are not adapted to cold temperatures would suffer more severely in the event of reduced temperatures following a nuclear war than their poikilothermic counterparts, since they must maintain a high internal temperature. If, however, temperatures dropped below freezing in areas not usually experiencing such temperatures, both groups would be in danger of body tissue freezing.

1.2.3.1 Freezing Tolerance of Terrestrial Insects

Since terrestrial insects of temperate and polar regions must normally survive sub-freezing temperatures, a number of behavioral and physiological responses to these temperatures have developed. Apart from those insects that avoid cold temperatures by migration, two groups of insects that are not injured during their overwintering in either the dormant or diapause stage have evolved mechanisms similar to plants, specifically: 1.) insects which are freeze-sensitive but prevent ice formation in their tissues, and 2.) insects able to tolerate the freezing of their extracellular fluids (e.g., beetles, flies, wasps) (Storey and Storey, 1983). The majority of insects overwinter using the latter strategy.

Freeze-sensitive insects prevent the formation of ice through the use of cryoprotectant (anti-freeze) compounds (e.g., glycerol and sorbitol), which aid in the supercooling of body fluids and elimination of ice nucleation sites in the body (e.g., emptying of the gut contents). Glycerol both lowers the freezing point of tissues and increases supercooling (Cloudsley-Thompson, 1970) and is the most prevalent cryoprotectant. Supercooling temperatures in the larvae of the Canadian hymenopteran *Bracon cephi* were found to vary in direct proportion to the glycerol concentrations (Salt, 1959). The cues for hibernation are important, since these cryoprotectants are produced before hibernation.

The mechanism of freeze tolerance is similar to that of plants and some microorganisms and can be remarkable in its extent. For example, the gall fly larva is able to withstand temperatures of $-40°C$ during winter. The insect is able to control the amount of ice formation and protect the cells from dehydration and osmotic damage (Storey and Storey, 1983). Freeze-tolerant species decrease free cellular water, which would otherwise form lethal ice crystals, by expelling this free water to extracellular spaces or by increasing bound water through the action of cryoprotectants. These cryoprotectants also lower the freezing point of intracellular water and increase osmotic pressure to prevent cellular dehydration (Storey and Storey, 1983). Again, the most common cryoprotectant is glycerol, which is synthesized in response to cooling. Sorbitol, however, is produced in response to temperatures of 5 °C to − 8°C, the supercooling point. It is interesting to note that species that are freeze-tolerant in the winter are able to withstand low temperatures in the summer by supercooling to an extent beyond that which occurs in the winter. This implies that freeze-tolerance is a seasonal response, similar to hardening in plants.

1.2.3.2 Freezing Resistance in Freshwater Fishes

Freshwater systems could be expected to cool significantly following a nuclear war, and surface ice could result. Freshwater fish are not in great danger of freezing, as the freezing point of freshwater is nearly 0.5°C above the freezing point of their body fluids (DeVries, 1971). However, in lakes that did freeze to the bottom, fish would be in danger of freezing. Some species can normally avoid freezing by burrowing into the mud at the bottom and overwintering in an inactive state (Nikolsky, 1963). The greatest danger of lowered temperatures for freshwater fish is the decrease in dissolved oxygen content of the water brought on by the complete coverage and formation of surface ice to a considerable depth. Fish not in the inactive, semi-dormant state (i.e., with normal oxygen consumption rates) and some fish with limited oxygen requirements are in danger of suffocation from a reduced oxygen supply. This winter kill frequently occurs during severe winters in lakes that do not normally freeze over.

1.2.3.3 Response of Amphibians to Cold Temperatures

Most amphibians (with the exception of freeze-tolerant terrestrial frogs) avoid freezing temperatures by the behavioral mechanism of burrowing deep into the soil or mud, or they remain at the bottoms of lakes and ponds where the minimum temperature is usually 4°C. Brattstom (1970) suggested that cold may be the factor that restricts certain species to the tropics; this is supported by evidence that amphibian cold-tolerance increases with latitude. Thus, many amphibians in the tropics might not be able to tolerate the chilling associated with the lowered temperatures possible after a nuclear war. Those in temperate climates, which normally have to survive seasonal fluctuations, might not have the instinct, the proper environmental cues, or proper sequence of environmental cues to survive a rapid and substantial decrease in temperature.

Drought conditions would affect the ability of this group to survive, since water loss, respiration, and breeding activity depend on humidity and the availability of surface moisture.

1.2.3.4 Freezing Resistance in Frogs

Terrestrial frogs that hibernate on the land (e.g., *Hyla versicolor, H. crucifer,* and *Rana sylvatica* [Schmid, 1982], and *Pseudacris triseriata maculata* [MacArthur and Dandy, 1982]) are the only known vertebrates that can withstand the freezing of extracellular fluid. This freezing appears to occur when the ambient temperature is lowered to approximately $-2°C$, and the animals are able to survive several days at temperatures as low as $-6°C$ (Storey and Storey, 1984). Tadpoles are reported to survive in frozen shallow waters for several days. During freezing, the extracellular fluids and blood are frozen, and breathing and heartbeat cease. Though tissues rely on degradation of endogenous substrates locally for cellular energy, the anoxia tolerance of tissues, particularly those in the brain, probably determines the length of time in the freezing state (Storey and Storey, 1984). The accumulation of metabolic wastes and end products must also be tolerated.

Both glycerol and glucose have been found to act as cryoprotectants in the tissues and urine of these frogs. Interestingly, the rapid synthesis of these cryoprotectants is in direct response to exposure to subzero temperatures, in contrast to the production of cryoprotectants during an acclimation period in freeze-tolerant insects (Storey and Storey, 1983). This appears to be a mechanism of conservation; if the temperatures do not drop to below freezing, the cryoprotectant is not produced, and the animal does not have to convert excess glucose to glycogen in the spring.

Photoperiod is not a triggering mechanism for cryoprotectant production in frogs, although burrowing may be. Since these frogs live in northern latitudes, they burrow under the leaf litter and snow, which offer protection from extremely cold temperatures. Frogs are unable to survive temperatures of $-30°C$. The question remains as to whether frogs would have the instinct to burrow if the temperature dropped in the summer.

1.2.3.5 Response of Reptiles to Cold Temperatures

The number of species of reptiles, including snakes, declines markedly along a gradient from the tropics to temperate latitudes. Lizards, alligators, crocodiles, turtles, and tortoises are scarce or absent in cold temperate regions. Reptiles survive in cold temperate climates by behavioral adaptations to maintain their body heat at levels that allow them to be active during spring, summer, and autumn, and by hibernation during winter.

Most reptiles, such as land tortoises, diurnal snakes, and lizards, primarily gain heat from solar insolation, using it to attain body temperatures at which activities can be performed. The changes in body posture and contours enable maximization of insolation striking the surface of the animal. Many snakes in cold temperate regions hibernate in well-insulated locations during the cold winters. Sudden temperature decreases with accompaning decreases in solar insolation following a nuclear war would be devastating to these animals.

1.2.3.6 Responses of Birds to Cold Stress

Avifauna are particularly vulnerable to cold stress because of their high metabolic requirements. In most situations, their high mobility allows for avoidance of cold temperatures. However, some birds can effectively regulate their body temperatures, even under severe cold conditions. For example, Veghte (1964) found that body temperatures of the gray jay remained unchanged between January (temperatures as low as − 40°C) and July (average temperatures 15°C).

Behavioral responses to cold include postural changes and plumage adjustment, as well as movement into sheltered areas. The latter response is not as widely used as with mammals, since birds do not hibernate. However, willow ptarmigan do burrow in the snow, and cavities in trees are used by woodpeckers. Dawson and Hudson (1970) have reviewed the anatomical adaptations that conserve heat in birds living in northern climates, which include heavier plumages than in those birds that migrate, and countercurrent vascular flow in unfeathered areas of birds. Larger digestive capacity in some boreal finches increases the storage capacity of food.

Muscular thermogenesis (i.e., shivering) was suggested to be the major means of thermoregulation by West (1965), who studied the relationship between electrical activity of muscles and ambient temperature. Non-shivering thermogenesis, demonstrated by many mammalian species, does not appear to be used (Dawson and Hudson, 1970).

Environmental parameters can influence the basal metabolic rate of some bird species. Some northern species are able to maintain higher metabolic rates in winter than in summer. For example, evening grosbeaks and house sparrows that have been cold acclimated are able to maintain higher metabolic rates under severe cold stress than those of the same species that have not been acclimated (Hart, 1962). Basal metabolic rate of the northwest crow was about 20% higher in winter than in summer in Alaska. However, other species, such as yellow bunting (Wallgren, 1954), cardinal (Dawson, 1958), and gray jay (Veghte, 1964), have basal metabolic rates which do not vary with the seasons. Acclimation appears to be important in some species, since experiments show that birds exposed to low temperatures increase their metabolic activity, thermogenic capacity, and cold resistance within 1 to 4 weeks (Dawson and Hudson, 1970). Furthermore, Chaffee et al.(1963) found that exposure of various sparrows to 1 °C for 7 weeks caused an increased in the size of the heart, kidney, and liver, and an increase in myoglobin content. Increased thyroid activity has also been found (Miller, 1939).

1.2.3.7 Responses of Hibernating Animals

Both acclimation and hibernation may be used as mechanisms to tolerate cold temperatures in hibernating mammals. Acclimation may occur before hibernation, but this is not necessary. Typical physiological changes occurring during acclimation include: lowered oxygen consumption, increased non-shivering thermogenesis, decreased shivering, and increased quantity of unsaturated fats (which remain more fluid at lower temperatures than saturated fats).

Hibernation is the state of inactivity in mammals with accompanying physiological changes, such as lowered body temperature and decreased heart rate. It is triggered by different environmental cues or other mechanisms in different animals. The woodchuck (*Marmota monax*), for example, requires food deprivation before it will hibernate (Davis, 1967). Other animals respond to decreases in temperature, changes in photoperiod, or a combination of these factors. For example, a short photoperiod and low temperatures induce hibernation in the arctic ground squirrel (*Spermophilus undutatus*) (Drescher, 1967). There are also differences in the intensity of environmental cues needed to induce hibernation. Some species are able to enter into hibernation without external cues, but in response to an internally regulated annual circadian rhythm (Hudson, 1973). These species include many of the ground squirrels (e.g., *Citellus* and *Spermophilus*), the hedgehog (*Erinaceus europaeus*), many chipmunk species (e.g., *Tamias striatus* and *Eutamias* spp.), and the bat *Myotis lucifugus* (Hudson, 1973). In the event of an unnatural, sudden drop in temperature, those species that hibernate in response to internal cues would perish if the climatic conditions were severe and hibernation were not induced.

Hudson (1973) concluded that the cue for periodic arousal from the torpid state of mammals during hibernation relates to their excretion requirements. However, the triggers for complete arousal from hibernation are likely to be as complex as the mechanisms which induce hibernation. Squirrels wake at intervals to feed in winter months. Those animals dependent on temperature increases for complete arousal would be the most likely to survive a nuclear war-induced climatic perturbation, since this would ensure that they would not be aroused during periods of severe cold.

1.2.3.8 Responses of Non-Hibernating Mammals to Cold Temperatures

Non-hibernating mammals living at northern latitudes or in alpine areas must be able to tolerate cold temperatures either on a nightly or seasonal basis. In regions that experience severe temperatures, such as the arctic, mammals cannot rely strictly on increased metabolic heat production through increased food consumption. The obvious way in which many mammals are able to withstand cold temperatures is through insulation provided by fur; arctic animals have coats much thicker than those animals of comparable size in the tropics. Those that are not able to coat themselves sufficiently with fur because of size constraints spend much of their time in borrows beneath insulating snow.

The extremities of animals tend to be less well covered in fur to facilitate movement. The temperature gradient present within the limbs result from either vasoconstriction (Adams,1963) or a countercurrent vascular system, which prevents rapid loss of heat from the body. In this system, warm arterial blood loses heat to cool venous blood as it is returned back to the heart. A review of the literature concerning countercurrent blood flow may be found in Whittow (1971).

Other adaptations to cold temperatures include: increased heat production by shivering and increased shivering efficiency; increased peripheral vascularization; increased total blood volume; and altered neuronal and hormonal levels (Adams, 1971).

1.2.3.9 Survivability

Despite the adaptations that enable various groups of animals living in temperate regions to cope with low temperatures, these will not necessarily ensure that they would be able to survive the climatic conditions after a nuclear war. The timing of the nuclear war would be a major factor in survivability of many groups, the least damage occurring in the winter, when many animals would be in a dormant state or acclimated to lowered temperatures. The key factors in determining survivability are : 1.) the cues that control acclimation and hibernation/dormancy; and 2.) the need and availability of food sources during the period of reduced temperatures and thereafter. For example, insects that are freeze-tolerant and respond directly to decreases in temperature would be able to survive the period of cold. However, it is essential that they feed once temperatures increased (Storey, pers. comm.).

Since temperature is not often the only cue for hibernation and dormancy, it is unlikely that many species that are sensitive to freezing temperatures would be protected by going into hibernation. The length of time for acclimation would also be important, especially since the acute decrease in temperature is predicted to be sudden. Animals with migratory instincts not reliant solely on temperature decreases, and those animals living in warmer climates, would be unlikely to survive major cooling events because they would not have the behavioral or physiological adaptations characteristic of cold-hardy animals. Migratory birds and mammals might well suffer severely, as the appropriate triggers for migration would not likely be present.

Many migratory birds in the Northern Hemisphere travel from the tropics or sub-tropics to temperate regions. Even for those used to arriving in polar regions while ice is still on the sea or land, a prolonged, unmelted snowpack could cause catastrophic losses of young or of unhatched eggs. Many of these species (e.g., ducks, geese, ravens, sandpipers, and plovers) could be greatly reduced in numbers if sub-freezing temperatures prevented the normal cycle of food availability in spring or summer. A premature southward migration because of nuclear war-induced freezing could equally leave the birds with insufficient food reserves to make the return northerly migration, or could leave young to die. Catastrophe could occur if the normal stop-over areas for resting or feeding, in mid-latitudes, were under the influence of nuclear war-induced climatic alterations.

For migratory animals such as caribou or reindeer, the timing for the seasonal migrations is critical in terms of food supply and arrival in calving grounds. Predation is also a factor which is dependent on the vigor of the herds and on the availability of stragglers and of unprotected young. Native human populations harvest these herds for essential protein. It is entirely conceivable that a sudden onset of an acute climatic phase after a nuclear war could severely and perhaps fatally disrupt the balances and migratory instincts.

1.3 PLANT STRATEGIES RELEVANT TO NUCLEAR WAR [1]

1.3.1 Introduction

The task of predicting the effect upon the planet of a major nuclear war would be greatly simplified if the now rapidly evolving models of world climate and its potential disruption by nuclear war could be complemented by general models of the functional characteristics of the world's ecosystems. At present, ecologists are sharply divided in their assessment of the feasibility of devising predictive models of ecosystem and community functioning and response to perturbation. In consequence, whereas several ecosystem models are used in assessing the potential consequences of nuclear war (Chapter 2), another approach preferred by many ecologists is to concentrate upon those systems and organisms for which detailed information is available. This section explores the alternative approach using existing knowledge and theory,

---

[1] This section based on a paper prepared by J.P. Grime.

which are now sufficient to allow some general predictions of variation in sensitivity and resilience in biota. The concepts developed here rely heavily upon 'strategy' theories (Ramenski, 1938; Grime, 1978) of ecological specialization, and they are illustrated mainly by reference to terrestrial plants. However, most of the principles can be readily adapted to fungi (Pugh, 1980), algae (Dring, 1982), and animals (Greenslade, 1983). Reference will be made to three types of plant strategies: 1.) primary strategies of established (mature) plants; 2.) strategies of growth response to temperature; and 3.) regenerative strategies.

1.3.2 Primary Strategies of Established Plants

One approach that has been used to summarize the main types of ecological specialization in the established phase of plant and animal life-histories (Ramenski, 1938; Grime, 1974) is to define three primary ecological strategies, each corresponding to habitat conditions characterized by reference to the quantity and continuity of resource supply (Table 1.10).

TABLE 1.10

CONDITIONS OF RESOURCE SUPPLY ASSOCIATED
WITH THREE PRIMARY STRATEGIES[a]

STRATEGY	RESOURCE SUPPLY
Ruderal (ephemeral)	Temporarily abundant
Competitor	Continuously abundant but subject to local and/or progressive depletion as resources are exploited
Stress-tolerator	Continuously scarce

[a] After Grime (1979)

For plants, it has been recognized that the extreme conditions favoring either competitors, stress-tolerators, or ruderals (i.e., weedy species) form only part of the range of environments occurring in nature. The full spectrum of habitat conditions and their associated strategies can be described as a unilateral triangle (Grime, 1974), in which the relative importance of competition, stress, and disturbance is represented by three sets of contours. This model allows recognition of not only the three extremes of plant specialization described above, but also a range of intermediate strategies associated with less extreme equilibria among stress, disturbance, and competition. A review of the full implications of the model has been presented elsewhere (Grime, 1979). Essential features of the primary strategies are summarized in Table 1.11, which also draws attention to the features of plants most relevant to predictions of sensitivity to nuclear war-induced climatic disturbances and to the potential for recovery.

1.3.3 Strategies of Growth Response to Temperature

Since both the acute and chronic phases following a major nuclear war could involve depressions of temperature, it is desirable to examine existing knowledge of plant responses to temperature. Considerable research has been conducted on: 1.) the relative cold-hardiness of species of different geographical distribution and origins, and 2.) the efficiency of C_3 and C_4 and CAM photosynthetic systems under various temperature regimes. Although these types of studies provide information relevant to the post-nuclear war analysis, further insights are required. In order to devise adequate predictions of plant survival and recovery, it is necessary to assess the extent to which growth (i.e., the construction of plant tissue through division and expansion of cells) would be disrupted by altered climate. In particular, we need to differentiate between plants that would remain dormant and those that would continue to grow or would initiate growth during the period of low temperature and insolation following a nuclear war, although possibly with severe penalties. This growth would commence after the sub-freezing phase ended, since growth is obviously temperature limited.

Grime (1983) suggested that some predictions of how plants would respond to lowered temperatures can be obtained by reference to recent theories relating the amount of DNA in plant cell nuclei (known as the nuclear DNA content of plants) to the climatic conditions to which their growth has been attuned by natural selection.

Differences in nuclear DNA content exist on a broad geographical scale. Whereas plants of low nuclear DNA content are ubiqituous, species with high values appear to be restricted to regions in which cool temperatures are experienced during the growing season. The data are consistent with the hypothesis that climate has operated upon nuclear DNA content, especially through differential sensitivity of cell division and cell expansion to low temperatures.

At one extreme are the vernal geophytes with massive DNA contents. In these plants, growth at cold temperatures in the early spring is achieved mainly by expansion of large cells formed during warm conditions of the previous summer, rather than by cell division. The other extreme corresponds to the wide range of vascular plants in which growth is restricted to relatively warm conditions. Natural selection for rapid rates of plant development by both cell division and cell expansion appears to have resulted in

TABLE 1.11

CHARACTERISTICS OF PLANT STRATEGIES AS RELEVANT
TO RESPONSES TO NUCLEAR WAR[a,b]

		COMPETITIVE	STRESS-TOLERANT	RUDERAL
•o	Life-forms	Herbs, shrubs, and trees	Lichens, bryophytes, herbs, shrubs, and trees	Herbs, bryophytes
	Morphology	High dense canopy of leaves. Extensive lateral spread above and below ground	Extremely wide range of growth forms	Small stature, limited lateral spread
o	Life-span	Long or relatively short	Long - very long	Very short
•o	Longevity of leaves and roots	Relatively short	Long	Short
	Leaf phenology	Well-defined peaks of leaf production coinciding with periods of maximum potential productivity	Evergreens, with various patterns of leaf production	Short phase of leaf production in period of high potential productivity
o	Reproduction	Established plants usually reproduce each year	Intermittent reproduction over a long life-history	Prolific reproduction early in life-history
o	Proportion of annual production devoted to seeds	Relatively small	Small	Large
•	Perennation	Dormant buds and seeds	Stress-tolerant leaves and roots	Dormant seeds
o	Maximum potential relative growth-rate	Rapid	Slow	Rapid

[a] After Grime (1979).
[b] Code indicates the following:

o - particularly relevant to recovery
• - particularly relevant to susceptibility in the acute phase.
•o - particularly relevant to both susceptibility in acute phase and to recovery.

TABLE 1.11 continued.

	COMPETITIVE	STRESS-TOLERANT	RUDERAL
o Photosynthesis and uptake of mineral nutrients	Strongly seasonal, coinciding with long continuous period of vegetative growth	Opportunistic, often uncoupled from vegetative growth	Opportunistic, coinciding with vegetative growth
• Acclimation of photosynthesis, mineral nutrition and tissue hardiness to seasonal change in temperature, light and moisture supply	Weakly developed	Strongly developed	Weakly developed
•o Storage of photosynthate and mineral nutrients	Most photosynthate and mineral nutrients are rapidly incorporated into vegetative structure but a proportion is stored and forms the capital for expansion of growth in the following growing season	Storage systems in leaves, stems and/or roots	Confined to seeds
• Defense against herbivory	Often ineffective	Usually effective	Often ineffective
•o Litter decomposition	Rapid	Slow	Rapid
Associated regenerative strategies[c]	V, S, W, B_s	V, B_j, W	S, W, B_s
o Role in secondary successions in productive habitats	Relatively early	Late	Early

[c] Key for regenerative strategies (see Table 1.12): V - vegetative expansion, S - seasonal regeneration in vegetation gaps, W - numerous small, widely dispersed seeds or spores, B_s - persistent seed or spore bank, B_j - persistent juveniles.

reductions in cell size, cell cycle length, and nuclear DNA content. The vernal geophytes could be at an advantage if chronic decreases in temperature were to be sustained over several growing seasons. However, many arctic and alpine species are of the second type, i.e., with small cells, short cell life cycles, and low DNA content. This type is best able to exploit abrupt and brief opportunities for growth.

1.3.4 Regenerative Strategies

The regenerative strategies of plants can be considered for insights into effects of nuclear war. Five major types of regenerative strategies are distinguished in Table 1.12, which contains a brief description of the seed bank types (discussed later in this chapter) and habitat conditions with which each strategy appears to be associated. When these concepts are used in predictions of nuclear war-induced effects, it is necessary to bear in mind that

TABLE 1.12

FIVE REGENERATIVE STRATEGIES OF WIDESPREAD
OCCURRENCE IN TERRESTRIAL VEGETATION[a]

STRATEGY	HABITAT CONDITIONS TO WHICH STRATEGY APPEARS TO BE ADAPTED
Vegetative expansion (V)	Productive or unproductive habitats subject to low intensities of disturbance
Seasonal regeneration in vegetation gaps (S) (seed banks transient)	Habitats subjected to seasonally predictable distrubance by climate or biotic factors
Regeneration involving persistent seed or spore bank (B_s)	Habitats subjected to spatially predictable but temporally unpredictable disturbance
Regeneration involving numerous widely despersed seeds or spores (W) (seed banks usually transient)	Habitats relatively inaccessible (cliffs, tree trunk, etc.) or subjected to spatially unpredictable disturbance
Regeneration involving persistant juveniles (B_j) (seed banks transient or non-existent)	Unproductive habitats sunjected to low intensities of disturbance

[a] After Grime (1979).

TABLE 1.13

TRENDS IN ECOSYSTEM SUCCESSIONAL DEVELOPMENT[a]

ECOSYSTEM ATTRIBUTES	DEVELOPMENTAL STAGES	MATURE STAGES
Community Energetics		
Gross production/community respiration (P/R ratio)	greater or less than 1	approaches 1
Gross production/standing crop biomass (P/B ratio)	high	low
Biomass supported/unit energy flow (B/E ratio)	low	high
Net community production	high	low
Food chains	linear, predominantly grazing	weblike, predominately detritus
Community Structure		
Total organic matter	small	large
Inorganic nutrients	extrabiotic	intrabiotic
Species diversity - variety	low	high
Species diversity - equitability	low	high
Biochemical diversity	low	high
Stratification and spatial heterogeneity (pattern diversity)	poorly organized	well organized
Life History		
Niche specialization	broad	narrow
Size of organism	small	large
Life cycles	short, simple	long, complex
Nutrient Cycling		
Mineral cycles	open	closed
Nutrient exchange rate between organism and environment	rapid	slow
Role of detritus in nutrient regeneration	unimportant	important
Selection Pressure		
Growth form	for rapid growth	for feedback control
Production	quantity	quality
Overall Homeostasis		
Internal symbiosis	undeveloped	developed
Nutrient conservation	poor	good
Stability (resistance to external perturbations)	poor	good
Entropy	high	low
Information	low	high

[a] Based on Odum (1969).

some plant species and genotypes exhibit several of the regenerative strategies listed in Table 1.13. This fact is relevant to assessments of both sensitivity and potential for recovery. Two of the strategies (V and B_s) would likely favor resistance during an acute phase of extreme temperatures, since these categories often involve, respectively, the maintenance of dormant buds and dormant seeds at or below the soil surface.

1.3.5 Susceptibility During an Acute Phase Following a Nuclear War

The extent of the mortalities suffered by particular plant populations during extreme temperature decreases would depend upon many factors, including geographical location, season, intensity and rate of onset of low temperatures, plant physiology, and plant strategy. Assessing the effects of frost damage from an abrupt drop in temperature would rely primarily upon existing physiological data dealt with in detail elsewhere in this volume. Predictions of frost and fire damage would vary considerably according to the season at which the event occurred, with greatest mortality if the perturbation occurred during the growing season.

Several additions or refinements to physiologically based predictions are suggested by strategy concepts. The most important of these derives from major differences in the relative sensitivity of established plants and their propagules. An extensive literature (Brenchley, 1918; Brenchley and Warrington, 1933; Chippendale and Milton, 1934; Crocker, 1938; Major and Pyott, 1966; Went, 1969; Zobel, 1969; Marks, 1974; Symonides, 1978; Thompson, 1977; Grime, 1981; Grandstom, 1982; Keddy and Reznicek, 1982; Cavers, 1983; During and ter Horst, 1983; Conn et al., 1984; Nakagoshi et al., 1983) shows that plants that exploit habitats subject to spatially predictable disturbances (e.g., arable fields, pastures, marshland, heathland, savannah, chaparral, taiga, secondary tropical forest) tend to accumulate large reserves of spores or seeds (known as seed banks), which persist either in the soil or, more rarely, attached to the parent plants. The propagules form an inconspicuous but extremely resistant component of many plant populations in vegetation types where cycles of destruction and regeneration are a normal feature of the vegetation dynamics. Ungerminated seeds, especially in temperate regions and where they have not imbibed water, are relatively resistant to temperature fluctuations. Along with any surviving shoot bases and rhizomes, seeds could be expected to confer resilience on populations, even in circumstances if there were large-scale mortality of the established vegetation (Section 1.4).

Transient seed banks, which occur for many species, provide a less certain means of survival. A large number of trees, shrubs, and grasses are known to regenerate each year by producing a single crop of seeds, which after a short period on the soil surface, germinate synchronously in a particular season.

Quite clearly, timing of the climatic disturbance in relation to season would determine whether populations dependent upon this type of regeneration would suffer catastrophic mortalities.

If widespread destruction of the established vegetation occurred in response to chilling, fire, or other perturbations, the most vulnerable plants would likely be those in which regeneration relies wholly upon a bank of juveniles (seedlings, sporelings, or saplings). This type of regeneration is particularly characteristic of ferns, gymnosperms, primitive families of woody angiosperms, and in primary tropical rainforest; it is also common in a wide range of slow-growing plants of late successional vegetation. In many of these plants, seeds or spores are produced only intermittently and tend to germinate with little delay. Recovery of systems having seedling banks, rather than seed banks, would be exceedingly vulnerable to extreme perturbations, in which the adult and regenerative components would be killed simultaneously.

1.3.6 Recovery After an Acute Phase

The vegetation recovery processes after a nuclear war would be considerably affected by the severity and differential effects of the initial perturbations. If the impacts were severe, the greatest risks of total extinction would be expected in relatively stress-tolerant species, including many of the late successional dominant forest trees of temperate and tropical forests. On first inspection, this prediction may seem paradoxical, since many of the temperate forest trees normally endure considerable climatic extremes in their natural habitats. If the impacts of the acute phase were restricted to effects of low temperature and reduced insolation experienced in the winter by acclimated plants, high survival could be expected. However, this is the most optimistic of the range of possible scenarios; at the other extreme could be situations in which a summer perturbation might eliminate (at least locally) the many species in which there is no capacity for re-sprouting and in which seed banks are transient or non-existent.

If mass destruction of the established vegetation in temperate regions occurred (e.g., from an extreme climatic disturbance in summer), the early phases of recovery would likely be similar to those familiar in large areas of deforested and derelict landscape. For example, in many parts of ex-industrial sites in northern England at the present time, late successional trees, shrubs, herbs, and cryptograms are quite localized; many areas of wasteland succession remain suspended indefinitely at a low diversity stage of competitive-dominance by a relatively small number of mobile, early successional herbs and shrubs (Grime, 1979). The lack of seed banks, poor dispersal ability, slow-growth, and delayed reproduction of late-successional species (Table 1.11) could be expected to retard the process of recovery. A state of suspended recovery is often apparent in areas of severe industrial devastation, such as around major smelters and in heavily industrialized regions of Europe (Amiro and Courtin, 1981).

The species that could be expected to expand fastest after nuclear war-induced severe disturbances would almost certainly include those herbs and shrubs that possess several different types of regenerative strategies. These are plants which have shown a formidable ability to survive disturbance as underground buds or seeds, and to disperse widely over the landscape, to colonize open ground, and subsequently to monopolize extensive areas by prolific seeding or clonal expansion.

In addition to the truncation of the succession to forest, there might occur aspects of recovery peculiar to the post-nuclear war conditions. For example, during the later part of an acute phase, when temperatures and insolation might be adequate for growth but remained depressed from normal, plants that are normally capable of winter or spring growth (including many geophytes and grasses of high DNA content) might commence growth in conditions which would lead to etiolation, wasteage of storage reserves, and susceptibility to fungal attack. Although this might not cause mortalities directly, it would likely play a significant role in the competitive interactions that would determine the composition of recolonizing communities.

An additional and more unpredictable element to be accommodated in the recovery assessment would be the potential population explosion of insect herbivores in the absence of avian predators and applications of insecticides. Particularly since the ruderal and competitive early successional plants are weakly defended (Coley, 1983; see Table 1.11), this could have devastating effects on the early recovery process and might lead to the temporary emergence of some unfamiliar vegetation dominants. It is possible, therefore, that succession could follow an erratic course until populations of insect parasitoids and returning insectivorous birds became re-established and stabilized.

Many ecosystems experience considerable year-to-year variation in climate without major repercussions, and it is therefore tempting to propose that the major effects of climate on vegetation following a nuclear war would be those arising from extreme temperature excursions during an acute phase. While this might apply to many ecosystems, some possible exceptions exist. For example, vegetation types established in a Mediterranean climate might well survive an acute phase as bulbs or dormant seeds; however, the life cycles of most of the geophytes and grasses of Mediterranean climates are closely adapted to alternating wet-cool and hot-dry seasons, both of which processes are essential to plant development. Physiological studies of these processes (e.g., Hartsema, 1961) suggest a degree of developmental inflexibility that could lead to failure if the climate remained variable into a chronic phase.

1.3.7 Summary

From plant strategy concepts the following may be concluded concerning terrestrial vegetation sensitivity and recovery potential:

1.) Resistance to damage from low temperature and insolation during an acute phase would be greatest in stress-tolerant plants of unproductive habitats or late successional communities, but these same plants would face the highest risk of local extinction if there were widespread destruction of the established vegetation.

2.) Survival and recovery would be enhanced in plant populations maintaining a persistent bank of buds or seeds within the soil.

3.) Resilience would be greatest in vegetation where cycles of destruction and regeneration are already a normal feature of the vegetation dynamics.

4.) Where severe vegetation damage occurred in temperate and tropical regions, recolonization would involve the mobile, early-successional herbs and shrubs that currently dominate derelict ex-industrial or ex-agricultural landscapes, where succession could remain truncated indefinitely over extensive areas.

5.) Initial loss of predators (especially insectivorous birds) could lead to severe damage of the recovering vegetation by insect outbreaks; this could lead to erratic and unusual patterns of vegetation development.

6.) Species normally capable of winter or spring growth in cold conditions (many geophytes and grasses) could continue or commence shoot expansion during the post-nuclear war conditions; this would have deleterious effects and reduce their competitive ability in relation to plants which remained inactive.

7.) Where there is protracted disruption of seasonality, such as for the wet-cool, dry-hot seasonal pattern of Mediterranean climates, severe effects could be expected in plants with determinate life-cycles.

1.4 SEED BANKS AND REGENERATION

1.4.1 Occurrence of Seed Banks

If nuclear war were to result in large-scale mortality to plants in an ecosystem, then the long-term consequences to that ecosystem would depend to a great extent on the ability of individual species to regenerate. This would involve the attributes exemplified in post-fire successions, such as the ability to survive extreme physical conditions and to regenerate from buds or belowground perennating organs that have survived buried in the soil. Another factor in regeneration would be the ability to repopulate an area as a consequence of seeds remaining viable until conditions became suitable for germination. Species that would seem pre-adapted include those that already experience severe climatic stress and normally have seed banks which persist and accumulate in the soil following dispersal from the parent plants.

The possession of a sizeable seed bank is an adaptation for survival during unfavorable conditions, often of a seasonal nature, e.g., droughts, freezing, severe cold, or low light. Other ecosystems do not have sizeable seed banks, and most seeds germinate soon after release. In comparing transient and persistent seed banks, it seems clear that a majority of the seeds of persistent seed banks are deeply buried, which helps the viability of seeds because of lower soil temperatures, darkness, or increased CO_2 levels, each of which may inhibit germination.

Some species (e.g., willow [Salix]) have seeds that are viable for only a few days after dispersal. Others have seeds with thick seed coats and large food reserves that can persist for decades (e.g., some legumes). Selective pressures within habitats seem to have played a large role in seed persistence. The best-documented examples of species which accumulate large seed reservoirs in the soil are the ruderals (weeds) of arable fields (Brenchley and Warington, 1930; Roberts, 1970). Such ruderals appear in large numbers when the habitat is disturbed, for example by plowing.

Large seed banks are particularly characteristic of shrubs and perennial herbs occurring in habitats subjected to intermittent damage by fire (Grime, 1979). In addition, large seed banks occur in shore-line habitats, in species colonizing seasonally water-logged grasslands, and in many natural grasslands. In vegetation subjected to summer drought, persistent seed banks are accumulated by both perennial herbs and winter annuals (King, 1976; Thompson, 1977).

1.4.2 Regeneration from a Seed Bank

Those species with a substantial seed bank buried in the soil would be at an advantage in recovery following destructive freezing temperatures or extensive fires following a nuclear war. Species that lack a seed bank are especially common in wet tropical evergreen ecosystems, where seedling banks are more common (see Chapter 2 for discussion of specific ecosystem responses). Regeneration from banks of persistent seeds in shrubs and trees in those ecosystems would be restricted to species associated with frequently disturbed habitats.

The closed-cone pines (e.g., in California, the New Jersey Pine Barrens, and the Appalachians) and the jack pine stands of the North American boreal forests provide an unusual addition to the seed bank species. It has been shown that the seed-containing cones, which often persist on the trees for years, are specifically adapted to release their seeds after periodic destruction by fire (Vogl, 1973). The actual forest stands are often short-lived (30–75 years) and composed of even-aged trees. Release of seeds from the cones occurs when the cones open upon exposure to high temperatures, which destroy the resins which normally keep such cones closed. Soon after a fire, enormous numbers of pine seedlings appear. Such adaptations might be advantageous to regeneration after a nuclear war, following fires directly caused by the nuclear war, or fires in stands killed by climatic stresses, which in turn increases the fuel load available to burn.

Seed banks of tundra and boreal forests, as well as those in most subtropical and tropical ecosystems, have received very little attention. McGraw (1980) collected soil from a cottongrass (*Eriophorum vaginatum*) tussock tundra in Alaska and determined the distribution, abundance, and germination patterns of buried viable seeds. Seeds of *Carex bigelowii*, *E. vaginatum*, and *Ledum palustre* were abundant, and smaller amounts of other species were also present. Buried seeds were found to a depth of 21 cm below the soil surface. When exposed to favorable conditions, germination took place initially rapidly then more slowly. Another interesting example of a tundra plant with a persistent seed bank is that of *Lupinus articus* seed, estimated to be 10,000 years old, which was recovered from permanently frozen lemming burrows and found to be viable (Porsild et al., 1967).

1.4.3 Regeneration by Vegetative Means

Many plant species produce new shoots vegetatively, such as from stolons, rhizomes, tussocks, or suckers; spreading by runners; splitting of bulbs; or by coppicing. After fires in frequently burned ecosystems, vegetative recovery is often rapid, often involving species with perennating organs at or below the surface, with protected apical meristems (e.g., bulb- and corm-forming species in prairies, grasslands, chaparral, and Mediterranean habitats). Grasses have an intercalary meristem located at or below the soil surface, between the root and leaf blade, which enables them to re-sprout after defoliation by fire, grazing, mowing, cutting, or air pollution. Often ruderal and post-fire colonizers combine effective widespread dispersal by wind-borne seeds (e.g., fireweed [*Epilobium angustifolium*], and hawkweeds [*Hieracium* spp.]), with effective vegetative spread as soon as seedlings are established. Such pioneer colonizers can be expected to be effective in regenerating after a nuclear war.

Some woody species have a high capacity to coppice, i.e., produce new shoots from dormant buds located near the base of the plant, or to produce suckers. Trees such as aspen, other poplars, willows, fir, and maples regenerate in this way after the trunk or branches are cut or burned.

1.5 COMMUNITY SUCCESSION

Plant communities are subject to temporal changes, both in species composition and in the relative importance of constituent life-forms. Such changes may be described as successional or, in some cases, cyclical. Successions may occur over very long time periods, or they may be typically interrupted at a certain stage, such as when fire occurs in pine forests and the forest is turned back to an earlier successional stage. Primary succession involves primitive soils or bare ground exposed for the first time; pioneer plants move in, generally with dispatch. Primary succession occurs on rock surfaces, on foredunes of sand-dunes, on muds and sediments of infilling lakes, and on exposed glacial moraines and tills as glaciers retreat. Secondary succession involves recolonization after an existing plant community is destroyed and soils are exposed. Secondary successions occur on abandoned agricultural fields; after fires in forests, chaparral, and grasslands; and following clear-cutting, extensive hurricane damage, and other major disturbances.

Odum (1971) characterized the maturation and development of ecosystems as a strategy of increased control of the physical environment, which provides the biota with maximum protection from environmental perturbations. The culmination of this dynamic and largely predictable (unidirectional) process of community-controlled modification of the environment can be a stabilized ecosystem. In the course of a succession, biomass increases, species diversity increases, food chains become more complex, vertical stratification develops, detritus and organic matter increase, nutrient cycling becomes tighter as less nutrients are lost from the system, while long-lived and larger organisms enter the system and niche differentiation accelerates. This is further explained in Table 1.13.

Given all of these processes and changes leading in the common direction of enhanced stability, we need to determine as best we can the effects of nuclear war-induced perturbations which, in the short term at least, would likely cause instability. We need to examine which ecosystems have particular resistance to such stresses and what the prospects are for regeneration of the systems. This analysis is described in Chapter 2 for several biomes. Clearly, those ecosystems which are regularly subject to stresses such as fire, clearance, and grazing are likely to have species components in them that may respond better to nuclear war-induced stresses than other ecosystems, where such interventions are unknown or so rare as to be beyond the life spans or generation times of key (dominant) components.

While the particular paths of regeneration and post-nuclear war succession cannot be predicted with certainty, it seems most likely that they would follow known paths in ecosystems where disturbance is a regular phenomenon. We might anticipate greater long-term damage, other things being equal, in those systems unaccustomed and therefore probably unadapted to major disturbance (Chapter 2). For the former systems, we predict no surprises, but for the latter (e.g., for cactus deserts, evergreen rain forests, and mangrove swamps) confident predictions become more difficult.

1.6 WORLD BIOMES

1.6.1 Introduction

Biome is a general term used to identify a biotic community type, dominant over broad geographical regions. There are a number of classification systems used in categorizing and naming biomes, several of which are widely accepted. In all but a few cases, the name given to a biome reflects in some way the geographic placement and overall structure of the plant community present, and frequently gives some indication of climate. Thus we see terms such as 'north temperate deciduous forest', or 'tropical desert scrubland'.

Temperature and precipitation to a very large extent determine the distribution of terrestrial ecosystems in complex ways, yielding a broad range of identifiable communities. Because variation in climate is less pronounced near the equator, vulnerability to changes in environmental conditions increases with decreasing latitude. Thus, nuclear war in northern latitudes might cause smaller or briefer climatic disturbances in equatorial latitudes, but the biota of those regions are not adapted to even moderate changes in light, temperature, or precipitation regimes beyond the normal diurnal or seasonal fluctuations. For example, evergreen wet tropical rainforests in lowland areas experience almost no seasonal temperature change.

1.6.2 Distribution of Biomes

A simple classification of biomes can be made by comparing regional temperature and moisture regimes and relating these climatic factors to the general physiognomy of the plant community (Figure 1.17). No single climatic variable can be used to classify terrestrial biomes; for example, several biomes receive about the same amount of annual precipitation but differ greatly in mean annual temperature. The climatic effects of nuclear war could alter the atmosphere so that temperature and precipitation regimes characteristic of northerly, dry, cold biomes would extend to more temperate, mesic biomes.

Temperature and precipitation influence biological activity in a number of different ways. For plants, temperature and precipitation can be combined as indices that reflect the potential availability of moisture for primary production (Figure 1.18). Tropical forests, north temperate forests, and tundra are similar when compared on the basis of moisture availability, but potential evapotranspiration is much higher in tropical forests. This separation is

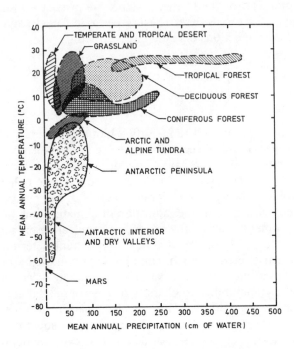

Figure 1.17   Terrestrial biomes in relation to mean annual temperature and precipitation

largely influenced by the temperature regime across the latitudinal range occupied by these biomes. In contrast, desert shrublands and grassland biomes occur in areas of low moisture availability and high potential evapotranspiration.

The importance of precipitation and evapotranspiration to net primary production (the amount of photosynthetic carbon fixed by plants minus that respired by plants or consumed by animals) can be seen in Figure 1.19. Net primary production (NPP) increases almost linearly up to about 1,000 mm·yr^{-1} of precipitation, with a plateau in response above about 1,800 mm·yr^{-1}. What is not shown in these figures is that for some ecosystems, evapotranspiration may exceed precipitation, causing water stress and limiting primary production. Thus, moderate decreases in average temperatures of 1°C to 2°C if occurring *alone* can increase potential primary productivity. But cooler average growing season temperatures could well occur with increases in freeze frequency, damaging plants before seed maturation.

There are several ways to combine climatic indices to describe the distribution of major biotic communities (see Emanuel et al., 1985). A simplified vegetation map of the world is shown in Figure 1.20. Of course, this

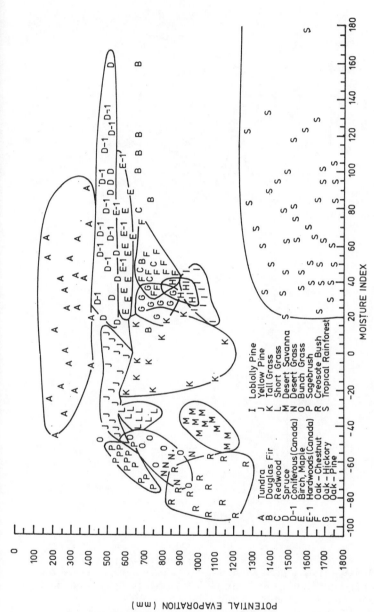

Figure 1.18   Relation between distribution of communities and climate, where climate is defined as potential evapotranspiration, and a moisture index. The moisture index is calculated as follows:

$$\text{Moisture Index} = \frac{\text{Annual Water Surplus} - \text{Annual Water Deficit}}{\text{Annual Potential Evapotranspiration}} \times 100$$

From Carter and Mather (1966)

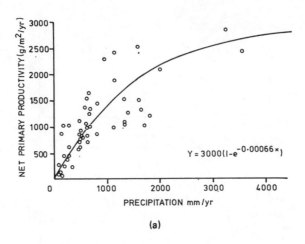

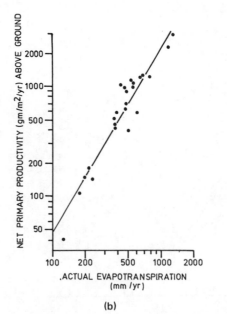

Figure 1.19 A: Net primary productivity, above and below ground, in relation to mean annual precipitation. From Lieth (1973). B: Net primary productivity in relation to actual evapotranspiration. From Whittaker (1975)

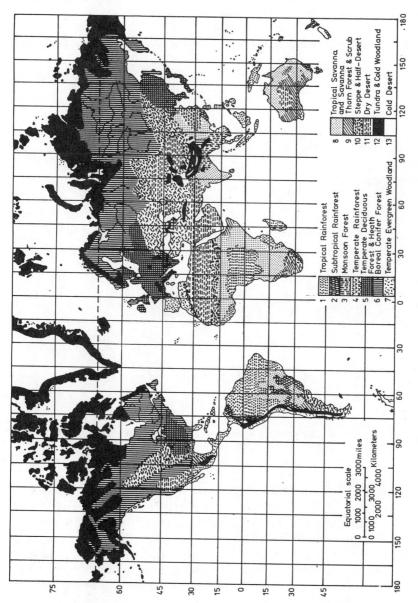

Figure 1.20   Terrestrial biomes of the Earth. From Dansereau (1957)

broad-scale depiction does not resolve elevational variation in biome type, as illustrated in Figure 1.21. Thus, an increase in latitude is similar to an increase in elevation, so that biomes characteristic of northern latitudes can be found at high elevations in equatorial latitudes.

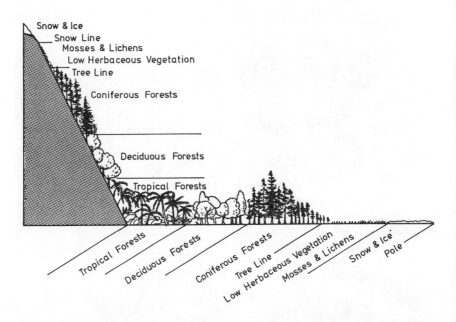

Figure 1.21   Comparison between latitudinal and altitudinal community types in North America. From Clapham (1983)

Two climatic features that are not depicted in the figures discussed thus far are seasonal variability in temperature and precipitation. Biomes characteristic of equatorial latitudes experience relatively constant temperature and precipitation conditions throughout the year. Temperate biomes are variously adapted to seasonal variability in temperature and precipitation. Fall and winter dormancy mechanisms are commonly found in biota living above approximately 30°N latitude, so that some temperate species would be susceptible to the climatic disturbances following a nuclear war only during the growing season, while subtropical and tropical species would be highly vulnerable during the entire year.

1.6.3 Production within World Biomes

Table 1.14 summarizes information on the areal extent and biological productivity of major world biomes. Extreme desert, rock, sand, and ice cover the greatest proportion of the Earth's land surface (16%), yet account for less than 1% of the biological production. Tropical rainforest covers about 11% of all land surface, but accounts for the greatest proportion of terrestrial net primary production (32%), plant biomass (42%), and animal biomass (33%) of any single biome type. Species diversity (richness) is also highest in the tropics.

Open ocean is the predominant marine biome type (Table 1.14). However, all of the other marine biomes shown contribute proportionally more to total marine net primary production, plant biomass, and animal biomass than their areal extent would predict. Thus, continental shelf, estuarine, upwellings, and reef systems are more productive per unit area than is open ocean.

Although marine systems account for 71% of the Earth's surface, only 32% of the net primary production occurs in these ecosystems, and less than 1% of the plant biomass is found there. In contrast, about 50% of the world's animal biomass is found in marine systems, reflecting the dynamic relationship that exists between consumers and primary producers. That is, a relatively small amount of plant biomass supports a large consumer component, because of rapid turnover and high net primary production by the plants that are present. As a result, changes in marine production capacity can rapidly cascade through the food chain having second- and third-order effects on consumers, such as zooplankton and pelagic fishes, and even shorebird populations (e.g., El Niño of 1982–83).

1.6.4 Soil Factors

One final factor of potential importance to the agricultural and ecological responses to the perturbations after a nuclear war is that of soil type. The behavior of radionuclides, for example, would be strongly influenced by the physical and chemical properties of soils, the presence or absence of a permafrost, the height of the water table, and the level of microbial activity in the soil. These features of soils, as well as the soil types themselves, are substantially determined by climatic conditions, as illustrated in Figure 1.22.

Rates of nutrient cycling and litter decomposition would affect radionuclide pathways and retention time. Actual rates of evapotranspiration in comparison with inputs of water from precipitation and other sources would determine whether leaching into groundwater or runoff to watersheds would predominate, or whether an upward evaporative movement prevailed, with associated long retention times.

TABLE 1.14

REPRESENTATIVE PRODUCTION AND BIOMASS SUMMARIES
FOR BIOMES OF THE EARTH[a]

Ecosystem Type	Area 10^6 km^2 (% world total[b])	NPP g·m^-2·year^-1 (%world total[c])	Mean Plant Biomass kg·m^-2 (% world total [c])	Animal Consum. 10^6 t·year^-1	Animal Product. 10^6 t·year^-1	Animal Biomass 10^6 t (% world total[c])
TERRESTRIAL						
Tropical rainforest	17.0 (11.4%)	2200 (32.5%)	45 (41.6%)	2600	260	330 (32.8%)
Tropical seasonal forest	7.5 (5.0%)	1600 (10.4%)	35 (14.1%)	720	72	90 (9.0%)
Temperate evergreen	5.0 (3.4%)	1300 (5.7%)	35 (9.5%)	260	26	50 (5.0%)
Temperate deciduous	7.0 (4.7%)	1200 (7.3%)	30 (11.4%)	420	42	110 (10.9%)
Boreal Forest	12.0 (8.1%)	800 (8.3%)	20 (13.1%)	380	38	57 (5.7%)
Woodland & shrubland	8.5 (5.7%)	700 (5.2%)	6 (2.7%)	300	30	40 (4.0%)
Savannah	15.0 (10.1%)	900 (11.7%)	4 (3.3%)	2000	300	220 (21.9%)
Temperate grassland	9.0 (6.0%)	600 (4.7%)	1.6 (0.8%)	540	80	60 (6.0%)
Tundra & alpine	8.0 (5.4%)	140 (0.96%)	0.6 (0.3%)	33	3	3.5 (0.3%)
Desert & Semi-desert scrub	18.0 (12.1%)	90 (1.4%)	0.7 (0.7%)	48	7	8 (0.8%)
Extreme desert & rock, sand and ice	24.0 (16.1%)	3 (0.06%)	0.02 (< 0.1%)	0.2	0.02	0.02 (<0.1%)
Cultivated land	14.0 (9.4%)	650 (7.9%)	1 (0.8%)	90	9	6 (0.6%)
Swamp & marsh	2.0 (1.3%)	2000 (3.5%)	15 (1.6%)	320	32	20 (2.0%)
Lake & Stream	2.0 (1.3%)	250 (0.4%)	0.02 (< 0.1%)	100	10	10 (1.0%)
Total Continental	149 (29%)	773[b] (68%[d])	12.3[b] (99.8%[d])	7810	909	1005 (50.2%[d])

[a] Data from Whittaker (1975).
[b] Averaged separately for terrestrial and marine biomes
[c] Based on world net production or biomass for terrestrial and marine biomes separately.
[d] Based on terrestrial + marine totals.

TABLE 1.14 continued

Ecosystem Type	Area 10⁶ km² (% world total[b])	NPP g·m⁻²·year⁻¹ (%world total[c])	Mean Plant Biomass kg·m⁻² (% world total[c])	Animal Consum. 10⁶ t·year⁻¹	Animal Product. 10⁶ t·year⁻¹	Animal Biomass 10⁶ t (% world total[c])
MARINE						
Open ocean	332.0 (92%)	125 (75.5%)	0.003 (25.6%)	16,600	2,500	800 (80.2%)
Upwellings	0.4 (0.1%)	500 (0.4%)	0.02 (0.2%)	70	11	4 (0.4%)
Continental shelf	26.6 (7.4%)	360 (17.5%)	0.01 (6.9%)	3,000	430	160 (16.0%)
Algal beds & reefs	0.6 (0.1%)	2,500 (2.9%)	2 (30.8%)	240	36	12 (1.2%)
Estuaries	1.4 (0.4%)	1,500 (3.8%)	1 (35.9%)	320	48	21 (2.1%)
Total Marine	361 (71%)	152[e] (32%[d])	0.01[b] (0.2%[d])	20,230	3,025	997 (49.8%[d])
WORLD TOTALS	510	333	3.6	28,040	3,934	2002

[c] Based on world net production of biomass for terrestrial and marine biomes separately.

[e] Weighted by system.

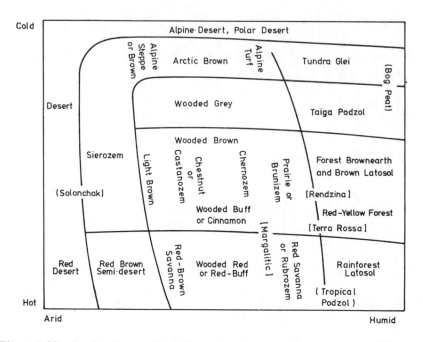

Figure 1.22   Great soil groups in relation to climate. Zonal great groups are shown by relative positions along climatic gradients of humidity on the horizontal axis, and temperature on the vertical. In intermediate climates, both grass dominated and nongrass communities are written on the vertical; soils formed by woodlands and shrublands (or, in the arctic, in tundra) are written on the horizontal for the same climates. Certain nonzonal great soil groups are also shown; those formed with impeded drainage or special conditions of water movement in parentheses. Terminologies and numbers of great soil groups vary among authors. Forest brown earths as used here include more than one group in most classifications; brown latosols occur in tropical mountain forests. From Whittaker (1975)

REFERENCES

Adams, T. (1963). Mechanisms of cold acclimation in the cat. *J. Appl. Physiol.*, **18**, 778–780.

Adams, T. (1971). Carnivores. In Whittow, G.C. (Ed.). *Comparative Physiology of Thermoregulation.* Volume 2: 152–191. Academic Press, Inc.. New York.

Adiv, C.R. (1968). Testing rice seedlings for cold water tolerance. *Crop Sci.*, **8**, 264–265.

Amiro, B. C., and Courtin, G.M. (1981). Patterns of vegetation in the vicinity of an industrial disturbed ecosystem, Sudbury, Ontario. *Can. J. Bot.*, **59**, 1623–1639.

Antropova, T.A. (1974). The seasonal changes of cold and heat resistance of cells in two moss species. *Bot. Zh.*, **59**, 117–122. (in Russian).

Aragno, M. (1981). Responses of microorganisms to temperature. In Lange, O.L., Nobel, C.B., and Ziegler, H. (Eds.). *Physiological Plant Ecology.* Vol. 1: 339–37. Springer-Verlag, New York.

Becwar, M.R., and Burke, M.J. (1982). Winter hardiness limitations and physiography of woody timberline flora. In Li, P.H., and Sakai, A. (Eds.). *Plant Cold Hardiness and Freezing Stress. Mechanisms and Crop Implications.* Vol. 2: 307–324. Academic Press, New York.

Becwar, M.R., Rajashekar, C., Hansen-Bristow, K.J., and Burke, M.J. (1981). Undercooling of tissue water and winter hardiness limitations in timberline flora. *Plant Physiol.,* **68**, 11–114.

Berry, J.A. (1985). The effects of nuclear winter on global productivity. Paper contributed to SCOPE–ENUWAR Toronto Workshop.

Berry, J.A., and Downton, W.J.S. (1982). Environmental regulation of photosynthesis. In *Photosynthesis: Development of Carbon Metabolism and Plant Productivity.* Academic Press, Inc. New York.

Biebl, R. (1939). Über die Temperaturresistenz von Meeresalgen verschiederner Klimazonenn und verschieden tiefer Standorte. *Jahrb wiss Bot.,* **88**, 389–420.

Biebl, R. (1958). Temperatur- und osmotische Resistenz von Meeresalgen der bretonischen Küste. *Protoplasma,* **50**, 218–242.

Biebl, R. (1962). Temperaturresistenz tropischer Meersalgen. (Verglichen mit jener der Algen in temperierten Meersgebieten). *Bot. Marina,* **4**, 241–254.

Biebl, R. (1964). Temperaturresistenz tropischer planzer auf Puerto Rico. *Protoplasma,* **59**, 133–156.

Biebl, R. (1967). Temperaturresistenz einiger Grünalgen warmer Bäche auf Island. *Botaniste,* **50**, 33–42.

Biebl, R. (1968). Über Wärmehaushalt und Temperaturresistenz arktischer Pflanzen in Westgrönland. *Flora Abt. B,* **157**, 327–354.

Biebl, R. (1969). Untersuchungen zur Temperaturresistenz arktischer Süsswasseralgen im Raum von Barrow, Alaska. *Mikroskopie,* **25**, 3–6.

Biebl, R. (1970). Vergleichende Untersuchungen zur Temperaturresistenz von Meeresalgen entlang der pazifischen Küste Nordamerikas. *Protoplasma,* **69**, 61–63.

Biebl, R. (1972). Studien zur Temperaturresistenz der Gezeitenalge *Ulva pertusa* Kjellmann. *Bot. Marina,* **15**, 139–143.

Björkman, O. (1981). Responses to different quantum flux densities. In Lange, O.L., Nobel, P.S., Osmond, C.B., and Ziegler, H.Z. (Eds..) *Physiological Plant Ecology.* Vol. 1: 57–108. Springer-Verlag, New York.

Björkman, O., and Holmgren, P. (1963). Adaptability of the photosynthetic apparatus to light intensity in ecotypes from exposed and shaded habitats. *Plant Physiol.,* **16**, 889–914.

Blackman, G.E., and Rutter, A.J. (1948). Physiological and ecological studies in the analysis of plant environment. XI. A further assessment of the influence of shading on the growth of different species in the vegetative phase. *Ann. Bot.* N.S., **23**, 51–63.

Brattstom, B.H. (1970). Amphibia. In Whittow, G.Ç. (Ed.). *Comparative Physiology of Thermoregulation.* Vol. 1: 135–166. Academic Press, Inc., New York.

Brenchley, W.E. (1918). Buried weed seeds. *J. Agric. Sci.,* **9**, 1–31.

Brenchley, W.E., and Warington, K. (1930). The weed seed population of arable soil. I. Numerical estimation of viable seeds and observations on their natural dormancy. *J. Ecol.,* **18**, 235–272.

Brenchley, W.E., and Warrington, K. (1933). The weed seed populations of arable soil. II. Influence of crop, soil and methods of cultivation upon the relative abundance of viable seeds. *J. Ecol.*, **21**, 103–127.

Brock, T.D. (1978). *Thermophilic Microorganisms and Life at High Temperatures.* Springer-Verlag, New York: 465 pages.

Burns, G.P. (1923). Studies in tolerance of New England forest trees. IV. Minimum light requirements referred to a definite standard. *Bull. Vermont Agr. Sta.*, **235**, 15–25.

Cannell, M.G.R. (1985). *Effects of a nuclear winter on temperate forests—some notes.* Paper presented at Toronto SCOPE–ENUWAR Workshop, March 1985.

Cannell, M.G.R., and Sheppard, L.J. (1982). Seasonal changes in the frost hardiness of provenances of *Picea sitchensis* in Scotland. *Forestry*, **55**, 137–153.

Carter, D.B., and Mather, J.R. (1983). Climatic classification for environmental biology. C.W. Thornwaite Associates, *Publications in Climatology*, **19** (4), 305–395.

Cavers, P.B. (1983). Seed demography. *Can. J. Bot.*, **61**, 3578–3590.

Chaffee, R.R., Mayhew, W.W., Drebin, M., and Cassuto, Y. (1963). Studies on thermogenesis in cold-acclimated birds. *Can. J. Biochem. Physiol.*, **41**, 2215–2220.

Chippindale, H.G., and Milton, W.E.J. (1934). On the viable seeds present in the soil beneath pastures. *J. Ecol.*, bld 22, 508–531.

Clapham Jr., W.B. (1983). *Natural Ecosystems.* 2nd Edition., Macmillan Pub. Co., Inc., New York: 282 pages.

Clausen, E. (1964). The tolerance of hepatics to desiccation and temperature. *Bryologist*, **67**, 411–417.

Cloudsley-Thompson, J.L. (1970). Terrestrial invertebrates. In Whittow, G.C. (Ed.). *Comparative Physiology of Thermoregulation*, Volume 1. Invertebrates and Non-mammalian Vertebrates. 15–18. Academic Press, Inc., New York.

Coley, P.D. (1983). Herbivory and defensive characteristics of tree secies in a lowland tropical forest. *Ecol. Monographs*, **53** (2), 209–233.

Conn, J.S., Cochrane, C.L., and de Lapp, J.A. (1984). Soil seed bank change after forest clearing and agricultural use in Alaska. *Weed Sci.*, **32**, 343–347.

Crèvecoeur, M., Deltour, R., and Bronchart, R. (1983). Effects of subminimal temperature or physiology and ultrastructure of *Zea mays* embryo during germination. *Can. J. Bot.*, **61**, 1117–1125.

Crocker, W. (1938). Life span of seeds. *Bot. Rev.*, **4**, 235–274.

Dansereau, P. (1957). *Biogeography—An Ecological Perspective.* Ronald Press Co., New York.

Davis, D.E. (1967). The role of environmental foctors in hibernation of woodchucks (*Marmota monax*). *Ecology*. **48**, 683–689.

Dawson, W.R. (1958). Relation of oxygen comsumption and evaporative water loss to temperature in the cardinal. *Physiol. Zool.*, **31**, 37–48.

Dawson, W.R.. and Hudson, J.W. (1970). Birds. In Whittow, G.C. (Ed.). *Comparative Physiology of Thermoregulation.* Volume 1. Invertebrates and Nonmammalian Vertebrates. 224–310. Academic Press, New York.

DeVries, A.L. (1971). Freezing resistance in fishes. In Hoar, W.S., and Randall, D.J. (Eds.). *Fish Physiology.* Volume VI. Environmental Relations and Behavior. 157–189. Academic Press, New York.

Dircksen, A. (1964). *Vergleichende Untersuchungen zur Frost-, Hitze- und Austrocknungsresistenz einheimischer Laub- und Lebermoose unter besonderer Berücksichtigung jahreszeitlicher Veränderungen.* Dissertation. Göttingen.

Drescher, J.W. (1967). Environmental influences on initiation and maintenance of hibernation in the Arctic ground squirrel, *Citrellus undulatus*. *Ecology*, **48**, 962–966.

Dring, M.J. (1982). *The Biology of Marine Plants*. Edward Arnold, London: 199 pages.

During, H.J., and ter Horst, B. (1983). The diaspore bank of bryophytes and ferns in chalk grassland. *Lindbergia*, **9**, 57–64.

Duthie, H.C. (1964). The survival of desmids in ice. *Brit. Phyc. Bull.*, **2**, 376–377.

Edlich, F. (1936). Einwirkung von Temperatur und Wasser auf aerophile Algen. *Arch. Mikrobiol.*, **7**, 62–109.

Emanuel, W.R., Shugart, H.H., and Stevenson, M.P. (1985). Climatic change and the broad-scale distribution of terrestrial ecosystem complexes. *Climatic Change*, **7**, 29–43.

Fowler, D.B., Dvorak, J., and Gusta, L.V. (1977). Comparative cold hardiness of several *Triticum* species and *Secale cereale* L. *Crop Sci.*, **17**, 941–943.

Fuller, M.P., and Eagles, C.F. (1978). A seedling test for cold hardiness in *Lolium perenne* L. *J. Agric. Sci. Camb.*, **91**, 217–222.

George, M.F., Burke, M.J., Pelleth, H.M., and Johnson, A.G. (1974). Low temperature exotherms and woody plants distribution. *Hort. Sci.*, **9**, 519–522.

Glerum, C. (1973). Annual trends in frost hardiness and electrical impedence of seven coniferous species. *Can. J. Plant Sci.*, **53**, 881–889.

Göppert, H.R. (1878) as cited in Kol, E. (1968). *Kryobiologie. I. Kryovegetation*. Schweizerbart, Stuttgart.

Goryshina, T.K. (1972). Recherches écophysiologiques sur les plants éphémériodes printaniéres dans les chênaies de la zone forêt-steppe de la russie centrale. *Oecol. Plant.*, **7**, 241–258.

Grandstrom, A. (1982). Seed banks in five boreal forest stands originating between 1810 and 1963. *Can. J. Bot.*, **60**, 1815–1821.

Greenslade, P.J.M. (1983). Adversity selection and the habitat templet. *Amer. Nat.*, **122**, 352–365.

Grime, J.P. (1966). Shade avoidance and tolerance in flowering plants. In Bainbridge, R., Evans, G.C., and Rackham, O. (Eds.). *Light as an Ecological Factor*. 281–301. Blackwell, Oxford.

Grime, J.P. (1974). Vegetation classification by reference to strategies. *Nature*, **250**, 2–31.

Grime, J.P. (1978). Interpretation of small-scale patterns in the distribution of plant species in space and time. In Woldendrop, J.W. (Ed.). *A Synthesis of Demographic and Experimental Approaches to the Functioning of Plants*. 101–124. Wageningen.

Grime, J.P. (1979). *Plant Strategies and Vegetation Processes*. John Wiley & Sons, Chichester: 222 pages.

Grime, J.P. (1981). The role of seed dormancy in vegetation dynamics. *Ann. Applied Biol.*, **98**, 555–558.

Grime, J.P. (1983). Prediction of weed and crop response to climate based upon measurements of nuclear DNA content. *Aspects Appl. Biol.*, **4**, 87–98.

Grime, J.P., and Hunt, R. (1975). Relative growth rate: Its range and adaptive significance in a local flora. *J. Ecol.*, **63**, 393–422.

Grime, J.P., and Jeffery, D.W. (1965). Seedling establishment in vertical gradients of sunlight. *J. Ecol.*, **53**, 621–642.

Gusta, L.V., Burke, M.J., and Kapoor, A.C. (1975). Determination of unfrozen water in einter cereals at subfreezing temperatures. *Plant Physiol.*, **56**, 707–709.

Hart, J.S. (1962). Seasonal acclimation in four species of small wild birds. *Physiol. Zool.*, **35**, 224–236.

Hartsema, A.M. (1961). The influence of temperature on flower formation and flowering of bulbous and tuberous plants. *Handbuch Pflanzphysiologie*, **18**, 123–167.

Harwell, M.A. (1984). *Nuclear Winter: The Human and Environmental Consequences of Nuclear War.* Springer-Verlag, New York: 179 pages.

Havis, J.R. (1976). Root hardiness of woody ornamentals. *Hort. Sci.*, **11**, 385–386.

Hodgins, R., and Van Huystee, R.B. (1985). Chilling-induced chlorosis in maize (*Zea mays*). *Can. J. Bot.*, **63**, 711–715.

Holm-Hansen, O. (1963). Viability of blue-green and green algae after freezing. *Plant Physiol.*, **16**, 530–540.

Hudson, J.W. (1973). Torpidity in mammals. In Whittow, G.C. (Ed.). *Comparative Physiology of Thermoregulation.* Vol.3. Special Aspects of Thermoregulation. 98–165. Academic Press, New York.

Hudson, M.A., and Brustkern, P. (1965). Resistance of young and mature leaves of *Mnium undulatum* (L.) to frost. *Planta*, **66**, 135–155.

Hutchinson, T.C. (1967). Comparative studies of the ability of species to withstand prolonged periods of darkness. *J. Ecol.*, **55**, 291–299.

Irmscher, E. (1912). Über die Resistenz der Laubmoose gegen Austrocknung und Kälte. *Jahrb wiss Bot.*, **50**, 387–449.

Ivory, D.A., and Whiteman, P.C. (1978). Effects of environmental and plant factors on foliar freezing resistance in tropical grasses. II: Comparison of frost resistance between cultivars of *Cenchrus ciliaris*, *Chloris gayana* and *Setaria anceps*. *Aust. J. Agric. Res.*, **29**, 261–266.

Kacperska-Palacz (1978). Mechanism of cold acclimation in herbaceous plants. In Li, P.H., and Sakai, A. (Eds.). *Plant Cold Hardiness and Freezing Stress, Mechanisms and Crop Implications.* 139–152. Academic Press, New York.

Kainmüller, C. (1975). Temperaturresistenz von Hochgebirgspflanzen. *Anz. math.-naturw Klasse Österr Akad Wiss*, 67–75.

Kaku, S., and Iwaya, M. (1978). Low temperature exotherms in xylems of evergreen and deciduous broadleaved trees in Japan with references to freezing resistance and distribution range. In Li, P.H., and Sakai, A. (Eds.). *Plant Cold Hardiness and Freezing Stress.* 227–239. Academic Press, New York.

Kappen, L. (1964). Untersuchungen über den Jahreslauf der Frost-, Hitze- und Austrocknungsresistenz von Sporophyten einheimischer. Polypodiaceen. *Flora*, **155**, 124–166.

Kappen, L. (1969). Frostresistenz einheimischer Halophyten in Beziehung zu ihrem Salz-, Zucker- und Wassergehalt im Sommer und Winter. *Flora*, **158**, 232–260.

Kappen, L., and Lange, O.L. (1970a). Kälteresistenz von Flechten aus verschiedenen Klimagebieten. *Dtsch. Bot. Ges. Neue. Folge.*, **4**, 61–65.

Kappen, L., and Lange, O.L. (1970b). The cold resistance of phycobionts from macrolichens of various habitats. *Lichenologist*, **4**, 289–293.

Kappen, L., and Lange, O.L. (1972). Die Kälteresistenz einiger Makrolichenen. *Flora*, **161**, 1–29.

Kärcher, H. (1931). Über Kälteresistenz einiger Pilze und Algen. *Planta*, **14**, 515–516.

Keddy, P.A., and Reznieck, A.A. (1982). The role of seed banks in the persistence of Ontario's coastal plain flora. *Amer J. Bot.*, **69**, 13–22.

Kessler, W. (1935). Über die inneren Ursachen der Kälteresistenz der Pflanzen. *Planta*, **24**, 312–352.

King, T.J. (1976). The viable seed content of ant-hill and pasture soil. *New Phytol.,* **77**, 143–147.

Kohn, H., and Levitt, J. (1965). Interrelations between photoperiod, frost hardiness and sulfhydryl groups in cabbage. *Plant Physiol.,* **41**, 792–796.

Larcher, W. (1954). Die Kälteresistenz mediterraner Immergrüner und ihre Beeinflussbarkeit. *Planta,* **44**, 607–638.

Larcher, W. (1970). Kälteresistenz und Überwinterungsvermögen mediterraner Holzpflanzen. *Oecol. Plant.,* **5**, 267–286.

Larcher, W. (1971). Die Kälteresistenz von Obstbäumen und Ziergehölzen subtropischer Herkunft. *Oecol. Plant,* **6**, 1–14.

Larcher, W. (1975). Pflanzenökologische Beobachtungen in der Páramostufe der venezolanischen Anden. *Anz. Oesterr. Akad. Wiss. Math-naturw Kl.,* 194–213.

Larcher, W. (1977). Ergebnisse des IBP-Projekts 'Zwergstrauchheide Patscherkofel'. *Sitz. Ber. Oesterr. Akad. Wiss. Math-naturw. Kl., Abt. 1,* **186**, 301–371.

Larcher, W. (1980a). Untersuchungen zur Frostresistenz von Palmen. *Anz. Oesterr. Akad. Wiss. Math-naturw. Kl., Jg. 1980,* **3**, 1–12.

Larcher, W. (1980b). Klimastress im Gebirge—Adaptationstraining und Selektionsfilter für Pflanzen. *Rheinisch-Westfäl Akad Wiss Vorträge,* N. 291: 49–88. Westdeutscher Berlag, Opladen.

Larcher, W. (1981). Low temperature effects on Mediterranean sclerophylls: An unconventional viewpoint. In Margais, N.S., and Mooney, H.A. (Eds.). *Components of Productivity of Mediterranean Regions: Basic and Applied Aspects.* June Publishers, The Hague.

Larcher, W. (1982). Typology of freezing phenomenon among vascular plants and evolutionary trends in frost acclimation. In Li, P.H., and Sakai, A. (Eds.). *Plant Cold Hardiness and Freezing Stress. Mechanisms and Crop Implications.* Vol. 2: 417–426. Academic Press, New York.

Larcher, W., and Bauer, H. (1981). Ecological significance of resistance to low temperature. In Lange, O.L., Nobel, P.S., Osmond, C.B., and Ziegler, H. (Eds.). *Physiological Plant Ecology.* Volume 1: 403–437. Springer-Verlag, New York.

Larcher, W., and Bodner, M. (1980). Dosisletalität-Nomogramm zur Charakteristik der Erkältungsempfindlicheit tropischer Pflanzen. *Agnew. Bot.,* **54**, 273–278.

Larcher, W., and Winter, A. (1982). Frost susceptibility of palms: Experimental data and their interpretation. *Principes,* 26.

Lavagne, A., and Muotte, P. (1971). Premieres observations chorologiques et phenologiques sur les ripisilves à *Nerium oleadner* (Neriaies) en Provence. *Ann. Univ. Prevence Marseille,* **15**, 135–155.

Layton, C., and Parsons, A. (1972). Frost resistance of seedlings of two ages of some southern Australian woody species. *Bull. Torrey Bot. Club,* **99**, 118–122.

Levitt, J. (1939). The relation of cabbage hardiness to bound water, unfrozen water, and cell contraction when frozen. *Plant Physiol.,* **14**, 93–112.

Levitt, J. (1980). *Responses of Plants to Environmental Stresses.* Volumes 1 and 2. Academic Press, New York: 497 and 606 pages.

Lieth, H. (1973). Primary production: Terrestrial ecosystems. *Human Ecology.,* **1**, 303–332.

Lipman, C.B. (1936). The tolerance to liquid air temperatures by dry mass protonema. *Bull. Torrey Bot. Club,* **64**, 515–518.

Loach, K. (1970). Shade tolerance in tree seedlings. II. Growth analysis of plants raised under artificial shade. *New Phytol.,* **69**, 273–286.

Lona, F. (1963). Caratteristiche termoperiodiche e di resistenza al freddo di alcune piante dei deserti circummediterranei. *Giron. Bot. Ital.,* **70**, 565–574.

Lundquist, V., and Pellett, H. (1976). Preliminary survey of cold hardiness levels of several bulbous ornamental plant species. *Hort. Sci.,* **11**. 161–162.

MacArthur, D.L., and Dandy, J.W.T. (1982). Physiological aspects of overwintering in the boreal chorus frog (*Pseudacris triseriata maculata*). *Comp. Biochem. Physiol.,* **72A**. 137–141.

Mahmoud, A., and Grime. J.P. (1974). A comparison of negative relative growth rates in shaded seedlings. *New Phytol.,* **73**, 1215–1219.

Maier, M., and Kappen, L. (1979). Cellular compartmentalization of salt ions and protective agents with respect to freezing tolerance of leaves. *Oecologia,* **38**, 303–316.

Major. J. and Pyott, W.T. (1966). Buried viable seeds in two California bunch grass sites and their bearing on the definition of a flora. *Vegetation,* **13**, 253–282.

Marks, P.L. (1974). The role of pin cherry (*Prunus pensylvannica* L.) in the maintenance of stability in northern hardwood ecosystems. *Ecol. Monogr.,* **44**, 73–88.

Markley, J.C., McMillan, C., and Thompson, G.A. (1982). Latitudinal differentiation in response to chilling temperatures among populations of 3 mangroves (*Avecennia germinans, Laguncularia racemosa* and *Rhizophora mangle*) from the western tropical Atlantic and Pacific Panama. *Can. J. Bot.,* **60**, 2704–2715.

Maximov, N.A. (1914). Experimentelle und kritische Untersuchungen ber das Gefrieren und Erfrieren der Pflanzen. *Jahrb. Wiss. Bot.,* **53**, 327–420.

Mazur, P. (1969). Freezing injury in plants. *Ann. Rev. Plant Physiol.,* **20**, 419–448.

McConnell, D.B., and Sheehan, T.J. (1978). Anatomical aspects of chilling injury to leaves of *Phalaenopsis* Bl. *Hort Sci.,* **13**, 705–706.

McGraw, J.B. (1980). Seed bank size and distribution of seeds in cottongrass tussock, Eagle Creek, Alaska. *Can. J. Bot.,* **58**, 1607–1611.

McMillan, C. (1975). Adaptive differentiation to chilling in mangrove populations. In Walsh, G.E., Snedaker, S.C., and Teas, H.J. (Eds.). *Proceedings of the International Symposium on the Biological Management of Mangroves.* 62–68. University of Florida Press, Gainesville.

McMillan. C. (1979). Differentiation in response to chilling temperatures among populations of three marine spermatophytes, *Thalassia testudinum, Syringodium filiforme,* and *Halodules wrightii. Am. J. Bot.,* **66**, 810–819.

McWilliams, E.L., and Smith, C.W. (1978). Chilling injury in *Scindapsus pictus, Aphelandra squarrosa* and *Maranta leuconeura. Hort. Sci.,* **13**, 179–180.

Migita, S. (1966). Freeze-preservation of *Porphyra* thalli in viable state. II. Effect of cooling velocity and water content of thalli on the frost resistance. *Bull. Fac. Fisheries, Nagasaki Univ.,* **21**, 131–138.

Miller, D.S. (1939). A study of the physiology of the sparrow thyroid. *J. Exptl. Zool.,* **80**, 259–281.

Miller, J.D. (1976). Cold resistance in sugar cane relatives. *Sugar y Azucar,* March 1976.

Molisch. H. (1896). Das Erfrieren von Pflanzen bei Temperaturen über dem Eispunkt. *Sitzber. Kaiserlichen Akad. Wiss. Wein. Math. Naturwiss. Kl.,* **105**, 1–14.

Molisch, H. (1897). *Untersuchungen über daas Erfrieren der Pflanzen.* Fischer, Jena.

Nakagoshi, N., Nehira, K., and Nakane, K. (1983). Regeneration of vegetation in the burned forest in S. Hiroshima. IV. Buried viable seeds in the early stages of succession. *Memoirs of the Faculty of Integrated Arts and Sciences, Hiroshima* Univ., Series IV, **8**, 87–110.

Nikolsky, G.V. (1963). *The Ecology of Fishes.* Academic Press, New York: 352 pages.

Noshiro, M., and Sakai, A. (1979). Freezing resistance of herbaceous plants. *Low Temp. Sci. Ser.* **B, 37**, 11–18.

Odum, E. (1969). The strategy of ecosystem development. *Science*, **164**, 262–270.

Odum, E. (1971). *Fundamentals of Ecology*, 3rd. Ed. Saunders, Philadelphia: 574 pages.

Oohata, S., and Sakai, A. (1982). Freezing resistance and thermal indices with reference to distribution of the genus *Pinus*. In Li, P.H., and Sakai, A. (Eds.). *Plant Cold Hardiness and Freezing Stress. Mechanisms and Crop Implications*. Vol. 2: 437–446. Academic Press, New York.

Parker, J. (1960). Survival of woody plants at extremely low temperatures. *Nature*, **187**, 1133.

Parker, J. (1962). Seasonal changes in cold resistance and free sugars of some hardwood tree barks. *For. Sci.*, **8**, 255–262.

Patterson, B.D., Murata, T., and Graham, D. (1976). Electrolyte leakage induced by chilling in *Passiflora* species tolerant to different climates. *Aust. J. Plant Physiol.*, **3**, 435–442.

Paton, D.M. (1978). *Eucalyptus* physiology. 1. Photoperiodic responses. *Australian J.Bot.*, **26**, 633–642.

Paton, D.M. (1982). A mechanism for frost resistance in *Eucalyptus*. In Li, P.H., and Sakai, A. (Eds.). *Plant Cold Hardiness and Freezing Stress. Mechanisms and Crop Implications*. Vol. 2: 77–92. Academic Press, New York.

Pisek, A. (1950). Frosthärte und Zusammensetzung des Zellsaftes bei *Rhododendron ferrungineum, Pinus cembra* und *Picea excelsa*. *Protoplasma*, **39**, 129–146.

Pisek, A. (1958). Versuche zur Frostresistenzprüfung von Rinde, Winterknospen und Blüte einiger Arten von Obsthölzern. *Gartenbauwissenschaft*, **23**, 54–74.

Pisek, A., and Schiessl, R. (1947). Die Temperaturbeeinflussberkeit der Frosthärte von Nadelhölzern und Zwergsträuchern an der alpinen Waldgrenze. *Ber. Naturwiss- med Ver Innsbruck*, **47**, 33–52.

Pittock, A.B., Ackerman, T.A., Crutzen, P., MacCracken, M., Shapiro, C., and Turco, R.P. (1985). *The Environmental Consequences of Nuclear War*. Volume I: Physical. SCOPE 28a. John Wiley & Sons, Chichester.

Porsild, A.E., Harington, C.R., and Mulligan, G.A. (1967). *Lupinus arcticus* Wats. grown from seed of Pleistocene age. *Science*, **158**, 113–114.

Pugh, G.J.F. (1980). Strategies in fungal ecology. *Trans. Brit. Mycol. Soc.*, **75**, 1–14.

Quamme, H.A. (1976). Relations of the low temperature exotherm to apple and pear production in North America. *Can. J. Plant Sci.*, **56**, 493–500.

Rajashekar, C., and Burke, M.J. (1978). The occurrence of deep undercooling in the genera *Pyrus, Prunus,* and *Rosa*: A preliminary report. In Li, P.H., and Sakai, A. (Eds.). *Plant Cold Hardiness and Freezing Stress. Mechanisms and Crop Implications*. Vol. 2: 213–225. Academic Press, New York.

Ramenski, L.G. (1938). *Introduction to the Geobotanical Study of Complex Vegetations*. Selkozgiz, Moscow.

Raunkiaer, C. (1909). Formationsundersogelse og Formatranstatisk. *Bot. Tidsskr.*, **30**, 20–132.

Raunkiaer, C. (1928). Dominansareal, Artstaethed og Formations-dominanter. *Kgl. Danske Videnskabernes Selskab. Biol. Medd. Kbh.*, **7**, 1.

Raunkiaer, C. (1934). *The Life Forms of Plants and Statistical Plant Geography*. Clarendon Press, Oxford: 632 pages.

Riedmüller-Schölm, H.E. (1974). The temperature resistance of Alaskan plants from the continental boreal zone. *Flora*, **163**, 230–250.

Roberts, H.A. (1970). Viable weed seeds in cultivated soils. *Rep. Natn. Veg. Res. Stn.*, 25–38.

Rowley, J.A., Tunnicliffe, C.G., and Taylor, A.O. (1975). Freezing sensitivity of leaf tissue of C_4 grasses. *Aust. J. Plant Physiol.*, **2**, 447–451.

Rozenweig, M.L. (1968). Net primary production of terrestrial communities: Prediction from climatological data. *American Naturalist*, **102**, 67–74.

Sakai, A. (1960). Survival of the twig of woody plants at − 196°C. *Nature*, **185**, 393–394.

Sakai, A. (1965). Survival of plant tissue at super low temperatures. III. Relation between effective prefreezing temperatures and the degree of frost hardiness. *Plant Physiol.*, **40**, 882–887.

Sakai, A. (1971). Freezing resistance of relicts form the arcto-tertiary flora. *New Phytol.*, **70**, 1199–1205.

Sakai, A. (1972). Freezing resistance of evergreen and broad-leaf trees indigenous to Japan. *J. Jap. For. Soc.*, **54**, 333–339.

Sakai, A. (1978a). Low temperature exotherm of winter buds of hardy conifers. *Plant Cell Physiol.*, **19**, 1439–1446.

Sakai, A. (1978b). Frost hardiness of flowering and ornamental trees. *J. Jap. Soc. Hortic. Sci.*, **47**, 248–260.

Sakai, A. (1978c). Freezing tolerance of evergreen and deciduous broadleaved trees in Japan with reference to tree regions. *Low Temp. Sci. Ser.* **B**, **36**, 1–19.

Sakai, A. (1979). Freezing avoidance mechanism of primordial shoots of conifer buds. *Plant Cell Physiol.*, **20**, 1381–1390.

Sakai, A., and Hakoda, N. (1979). Cold hardiness of the genus *Camellia*. *Am. Soc. Hort. Sci.* **104**, 53–57.

Sakai, A., and Miwa, S. (1979). Frost hardiness of *Ericoideae*. *Am. Soc. Hort. Sci.*, **104**, 26–28.

Sakai, A., and Okada, S. (1971). Freezing resistance of conifers. *Silvae Genetica*, **20**, 53–100.

Sakai, A., and Otsuka, K. (1970). Freezing resistance of alpine plants. *Ecology*, **51**, 665–671.

Sakai, A., and Wardle, P. (1978). Freezing resistance of New Zealand trees and shrubs. *N.Z. J. Ecol.*, **1**, 51–61.

Sakai, A., and Weiser, C.J. (1973). Freezing resistance of trees in North America with reference to tree regions. *Ecology*, **54**, 118–126.

Salt, R.W. (1959). Role of glycerol in the cold-hardening of *Bracon cephi* (Gahan). *Can. J. Zool.*, **37**, 59–69.

Schmid, W.D. (1982). Survival of frogs in low temperatures. *Science*, **215**, 697–698.

Schnetter, M.L. (1965). Frostresistenzuntersuchungen an *Bellis perennis*, *Plantago media* und *Helleborus niger* im Jahresablauf. *Biol. Cbl.*, **84**, 469–487.

Schölm, H.E. (1968). Untersuchungen zur Hitze- und Frostresistenz einheimischer Süsswasseralgen. *Protoplasma*, **65**, 97–118.

Schwarz, W. (1968). Der Einfluss der temperatur und Tageslänge auf die Frostyhärte der Zirbe. In Polster, H. (Ed.). *Klimaresistenz Photosynthese und Stoffproduktion*. Deut. Akad. Landwirtsch, Berlin.

Seible, D. (1939). Ein Beitrag zur Frage der Kältesch den an Pflanzen bei Temperaturen über dem Gefrierpunkt. *Beitr. Biol. Pflanz.*, **26**, 289–330.

Seymour, A. H. (1982). The impact on ocean ecosystems. *Ambio*, **11**, 132–137.

Simonivitch, D. (1982). Major acclimation in living bark of September 16 Black Locust tree trunk sections after 5 weeks at 10°C in the dark—evidence for endogenous rhythms in winter hardening. In Li, P.H., and Sakai, A. (Eds.). *Plant Cold Hardiness and Freezing Stress. Mechanisms and Crop Implications*. Vol. 2: 117–128. Academic Press, New York.

Simonivitch, D. , Singh, J., and de la Roche, I.A. (1975). Studies on membranes in plant cells resistant to extreme freezing. 1. Augmentation of phospholipids and membrane substance without changes in unsaturation of fatty acids during hardening of black locust bark. *Cryobiology,* 12, 144–153.

Smith, D. (1964). More about cold tolerance: Effects of a hard freezing upon cultivated palms during December 1962. *Principles,* 8, 26–39.

Smithberg, M.H., and Weiser, C.J. (1968). Patterns of variation among climatic races of red-osier dogwood. *Ecology,* 49, 495–505.

Soeder, C., and Stengel, E. (1974). Physico-chemical factors affecting metabolism and growth rate. In Stewart, W.D.P. (Ed.). *Algal Physiology and Biochemistry.* Volume 10: 714–740. Blackwell, Oxford.

Spranger, E. (1941). Das Erfrieren der Pflanzen über 0°C mit besonderer Berücksichtigung der Warmhauspflanzen. *Gartenbauwissenschaft.,* 16, 90–128.

Storey, K.B., and Storey, J.M. (1983). Biochemistry of freeze tolerance in terrestrial insects. *Trends Biochem. Sci.,* 7, 242–245.

Storey, K.B., and Storey, J.M. (1984). Biochemical adaption for freezing tolerance in the wood frog, *Rana Sylvatica, J. Comp. Physiol.* B, 155, 29–36.

Stoy. V. (1965). Photosynthesis, respiration, and carbohydrate accumulation in spring wheat in relation to yield. *Plant Physiol. Suppl.,* IV, 1–125.

Symonides, E. (1978). Diaspores in the soils of Spergulo-Corynephoretum numbers, distribution and specific composition. *Ekologia Polska,* 26, 111–122.

Terumoto, I. (1964). Frost resistance in some marine algae from the winter intertidal zone. *Low Temp. Sci.* B, 22, 19–28.

Thompson, K. (1977). *An ecological investigation of germination responses to diurnal fluctuations of temperature.* PhD. Thesis. University of Sheffield, U.K.

Till, O. (1956). Über die Frosthärte von Pflanzen sommergrünner Laubwälder. *Flora,* 143, 499–542.

Timmis, R. (1978). Frost Hardening of Containerized Conifer Seedlings under Constant and Sequenced Temperatures. *Weyerhaeuser Comp. Forestry Res. Tech. Report 042-3301/78/37.* Weyerhaeuser Co., Tacoma, Washington: 21 pages.

Tsunoda, K. Fugimura, K. Nakahari, T., and Oyamado, Z. (1968). Studies on the testing methods for cooling tolerance in rice plants. 1. An improved method by means of short term treatment with cool and deep water. *Jap. J. Breed.,* 18, 33–40.

Tumanov, I.I. (1962) *Frost resistance of fruit trees.* 16th Intern. Hort. Congress. Bruxelles, 1962, 737–743.

Tumanov, I.I., and Borodin, I.N. (1930). Untersuchungen über die Kälteresistenz von Winterkulturen durch direktes Gefrieren und indirekt Methoden. *Phytopathol. Z.,* 1, 575–604.

Tyurina, M.M., Gogoleva, G.A., Jegurasdova, A.S., and Bulatova, T.G. (1978). Interaction between development of frost resistance and dormancy in plants. *Acta. Hort.,* 81, 51–60.

Ulmer, W. (1937). Über den Jahresgangder Frosthärte einiger immergrüner Arten der alpinen Stufe, sowie der Zirbe und der Fitche. *Jahrb. Wiss. Bot.,* 84, 553–592.

van der Pijl, A. (1972). *Principles of Dispersal in Higher Plants.* Springer-Verlag, Berlin: 161 pages.

Veghte, J.H. (1964). Thermal and metabolic responses of the gray jay to cold stress. *Physiol. Zool.,* 37, 316–328.

Vogl, R.J. (1973). Ecology of knobcone pine in the Santa Anna Mountains, California. *Ecol. Monogr.,* 43, 125–143.

Wallgren, H. (1954). Energy metabolism of two species of the genus Emberiza as correlated with distribution and migration. *Acta Zool. Fennica,* 84, 1–110.

Weiser, C.J. (1970). Cold resistance and injury in woody plants. *Science*, **169**, 1269–1278.

Went, F.W. (1969). A long term test of seed longevity II. *Aliso*, **7**, 1–12.

West, G.C. (1965). Shivering and heat production in wild birds. *Physiol. Zool.* **38**, 111–120.

Whittaker, R.H. (1975). *Communities and Ecosystems*. Macmillan Pub. Co. Inc., New York: 385 pages.

Whittow, G.C. (1971). Ungulates. In Whittow, G.C. (Ed.). *Comparative Physiology of Thermoregulation*. Volume 2: 192–282. Academic Press, Inc., New York.

Wilson, J.M. (1978). Leaf respiration and ATP levels at chilling temperatures. *New Phytol.*, **80**, 325–334.

Wilson, J.M., and Crawford, R.M.M. (1974). The acclimatization of plants to chilling temperatures in relation to the fatty-acid composition of leaf polar lipids. *New Phytol.*, **73**, 805–820.

Wolcott, R.H. (1946). *Animal Biology*. 3rd. Edition. McGraw Hill, New York.

Worrest, R. (1983). Impact of ultraviolet-B radiation (290–320 nm) upon marine microalgae. *Plant Physiol.*, **58**, 428–434.

Yelenosky, G. (1975). Cold hardening of *Citrus* stems. *Plant Physiol.*, **56**, 540–543.

Yelenosky, G. (1977). The potential of *Citrus* to survive freezes. *Proc. Int. Soc. Citriculture*, **1**, 199–203.

Yoshie, F., and Sakai, A. (1982). Freezing resistance of temperate deciduous forest plants in relation to their life form and microhabitat. In Li, P.H., and Sakai, A. (Eds.). *Plant Cold Hardiness and Freezing Stress. Mechanisms and Crop Implications*. Vol. 2: 427–436. Academic Press, New York.

Zobel, D.B. (1969). Factors affecting the distribution of *Pinus pungens*, an Appalachian endemic. *Ecol. Monogr.*, **39**, 303–333.

Environmental Consequences of Nuclear War Volume II:
Ecological and Agricultural Effects
Edited by M.A. Harwell and T.C. Hutchinson
© 1985 SCOPE. Published by John Wiley & Sons Ltd

CHAPTER 2
Vulnerability of Ecological Systems to Climatic Effects of Nuclear War

MARK A. HARWELL , THOMAS C. HUTCHINSON ,
WENDELL P. CROPPER , JR., AND CHRISTINE C. HARWELL

Primary Contributions by : L. C. Bliss, J. K. Detling, H. D. Grover,
J. D. Hanson, A. Keast, G. J. Kelly, J, R. Kelly, S. J. McNaughton,
R. L. Myers, S. Pacenka, V. M. Ponomarev, M. J. Salinger, D. W. H. Walton

Additional Contributions by : Toronto Workshop participants,
Caracas Ecosystems Working Group participants,
Melbourne Biology Working Group participants

2.1 INTRODUCTION

The potential perturbations to ecological systems that could result from a large-scale nuclear war include: 1.) direct effects of nuclear detonations; 2.) climatic disturbances; 3.) other global-scale disturbances such as fallout and enhanced UV-B; and 4.) localized disturbances such as air and water pollution.

The direct effects involve initial ionizing radiation (i.e., gamma rays and fast neutrons emitted from the fireball) and thermal radiation, each of which initially is limited to a relatively small area around a nuclear explosion. As discussed in Harwell (1984), the effects of blast are insignificant to the Earth's ecosystems in areal extent. Areas affected by initial ionizing radiation are even smaller than for blast for the size of nuclear warheads in current arsenals and, thus, these effects are also unimportant to ecosystems. Thermal radiation does offer the potential for greater ecological damage insofar as targets in grasslands and forests (e.g., missile silos) could have nuclear bursts that initiate fires in those systems. This issue is discussed further in Chapter 3.

The *indirect* effects on ecosystems of nuclear war cannot be so easily dismissed, however. The remainder of this chapter addresses the vulnerabilities

TABLE 2.1

ESTIMATES OF CLIMATIC RESPONSES TO
NORTHERN HEMISPHERE SUMMER AND WINTER NUCLEAR WARS[a]

A. SUMMER WAR

REGION	PHASE		
	ACUTE (1ST FEW WEEKS)	INTERMEDIATE (1-6 MONTHS)	CHRONIC (1-FEW YEARS)
	(DEGREES C. BELOW SEASONAL AVERAGE)		
N. Hem. Mid-Latitude Cont. Interiors	-15 to -35 under dense smoke[b]	-5 to -30	0 to -10
N. Hem Sea Surface[c] (Ice Free)	0 to -1	-1 to -3 and local anomalies	0 to -4 and local anomalies
Tropical Cont. Interiors	0 to -15	0 to -15	0 to -5
Coastal Areas[c]	0 to -5 very variable unless offshore wind, when: -15 to -35	0 to -5 very variable unless offshore wind, when: -5 to -30	0 to -5 variable
N. Hem. & Tropics Small Islands[c]	0 to -5	0 to -5	0 to -5
S. Hem. Mid-Latitude Cont. Interiors	initial 0 to +5 then 0 to -10 in patches	0 to -15	0 to -5
S. Hem. Sea Surface[c] (Ice Free)	0	0 to -2	0 to -4
S. Mid-Latitude Coastal Areas	0	0 to -15 in offshore winds	0 to -5
S. Hem. Small Islands	0	0 to -5	0 to -5

[a] From Volume I, Pittock et al. (1985).

[b] Smoke clouds with an absorption optical depth of 2 or more, remaining overhead for several days.

[c] These figures are climatological average estimates. Local anomalies may exceed these limits, especially with respect to changes in oceanic behavior, such as upwelling or El Niño-type anomalies.

B. WINTER NUCLEAR WAR

REGION	ACUTE (1ST FEW WEEKS)	PHASE INTERMEDIATE (1-6 MONTHS)	CHRONIC (1-FEW YEARS)
	(DEGREES C. BELOW SEASONAL AVERAGE)		
N. Hem Mid-Latitude Cont. Interiors	0 to -20 under dense smoke[b]	0 to -15	0 to -5
N. Hem Sea Surface[c] (Ice Free)	0	0 to -2 and local anomalies	0 to -3 and local anomalies
Tropical Cont. Interiors	0 to -15	0 to -5	0 to -3
Coastal Areas[c]	0 to -5 very variable unless offshore wind, when: 0 to -20	0 to -5 very variable unless offshore wind, when: 0 to -15	0 to -3
N. Hem. & Tropics Small Islands[c]	0 to -5	0 to -5	0 to -5
S. Hem. Mid-Latitude Cont. Interiors	0	0 to -10	0 to -5
S. Hem. Sea Surface[c] (Ice Free)	0	0 to -1	0 to -1
S. Mid-Latitude Coastal Areas	0	0 to -10 in offshore winds	0 to -5
S. Hem. Small Islands	0	0 to -5	0 to -5

of ecosystems to the types of climatic disturbances that have been characterized as possible after a large-scale nuclear war. Chapter 3 is concerned with other local- and global-scale disturbances to ecosystems.

In analyzing the potential vulnerability of ecosystems to climatic disturbances, the effects were related to categories of stresses rather than to specific values for temperature, light, and precipitation reductions predicted from particular simulations by atmospheric scientists. In that regard, the estimates of the effects on the biological systems of Earth would not be strictly dependent on resolution of the uncertainties in the atmospheric projections, which continue to be updated following new analyses, and which are often scenario dependent. Designing classes of stresses, with alternatives among them to cover the range of possible climatic impacts, was considered sufficient for most of the purposes and uncertainties associated with the biological analyses.

The stresses considered follow the values provided by Volume 1 (summarized in Table 2.1); additional discussion of this approach is given at the beginning of Chapter 4. The resistance of an ecosystem type to an environmental perturbation, such as temperature decreases, was matched with assumed exposures to that parameter that the ecosystem would experience under various scenarios. It is this combination of considerations that is important to establishing the vulnerabilities of ecosystems to the perturbations that could result from a nuclear war.

The analyses were based upon a variety of considerations. For the more extreme stresses possible in the acute phase after a large-scale nuclear war, physiological-level information (discussed in Chapter 1) formed the primary basis for estimates of effects, since it was felt that the first-order effects on organisms would dominate the early responses of the systems to physical stresses. These estimates were primarily accomplished in the various technical workshops that specifically addressed the potential effects on ecosystems in the Northern temperate, tropical, and Southern temperate regions of the world, reaching as broad a consensus as possible among the workshop participants as to the probable responses of the ecosystems to perturbations. Notes from these workshops, prepared discussion papers, additional information from the literature, and discussions with specialists collectively provided much of the information base for the following discussions.

For lesser perturbations, such as those during a chronic period of climatic disturbances, or following a relatively mild acute climatic disturbance, a number of computer simulation models were additionally drawn upon. These were developed to analyze the productivity and components of particular ecosystem types as functions of the physical environment. It was felt that the lesser stresses examined do not exceed the bounds for which these models are reasonably reliable, a situation not the case for extreme, acute stresses. Many of these models provide conservative estimates of chronic-phase ecosystem response (i.e., underestimates), because potential acute-phase alterations of ecosystem structure and composition were not considered where perennial organisms dominate. These simulations are a useful guide to potential ecosystem sensitivity, and as simulations of possible effects of milder climatic disturbances. Simulations cannot provide precise predictions of ecosystem biomass, productivity, or species composition changes following a nuclear war. However, the model results are useful as a guide to the type of responses that could occur, even with relatively small climatic disturbances.

The analyses that follow, then, are based on a suite of approaches: physiological information, historical analogs, simulation and statistical analyses, and expert judgment. Because of the great complexity of ecosystems across the global landscape and the temporal and spatial complexity of potential nuclear-war induced climatic disturbances, it is not possible uniquely to characterize the effects on ecosystems. A biome approach has been chosen as an appropriate level for generalization of potential effects. In separate sections that follow, Northern Hemisphere temperate terrestrial ecosystems, aquatic ecosystems, tropical ecosystems, and Southern Hemisphere extra-tropical ecosystems are addressed.

It should be noted that the ecosystem discussions emphasize effects on the primary producers, in large part because those components are fundamental to the total ecosystem and are often especially vulnerable to the types of perturbations considered here. Estimates of effects on fauna are largely based on those mediated through changes in food supplies. Further study of effects on trophic structures and of indirect effects on species propagated through the complex interactions of ecosystems is required.

2.2 POTENTIAL EFECTS ON NORTHERN TEMPERATE TERRESTRIAL ECOSYSTEMS

2.2.1 Potential Effects on Arctic and Boreal Ecosystems [1]

2.2.1.1 Estimation of Vulnerabilities to Acute Climatic Disturbances

This discussion is concerned with landscapes north of about 65°N latitude, including the northern taiga (forests), lichen-woodland, tundra, and other more northern arctic ecosystems. This area is characterized by very small human populations, essentially no agricultural development, and

---

[1] Note: much of this section follows from the Toronto working group on ecosystems effects, chaired by L.C. Bliss, and from the discussion papers prepared for the workshop by Bliss and by J.Svoboda and H.W. Taylor

limited human impacts on ecosystems. Humans are primarily supported by natural animal populations, and therefore their diets are predominantly protein rather than fiber and carbohydrates, as found in the diets of most human populations. In this regard, maintenance of the natural ecosystems, especially the total productivity of the plant communities and the persistence of particular food- source animal populations, is essential for maintenance of the indigenous human population.

The taiga, i.e., a boreal (subarctic) ecosystem, typically forms cold-limited needle-leaved forests across climatic ranges extending around the Earth in the northern parts of North America and Eurasia. These circumpolar ecosystems occupy about 10×10^6 km^2 of the Earth's surface. Tundras do not have trees, and are characterized by the dominance on a more local scale of shrubs, grasses, herbs, mosses, and lichens. With low levels of temperature and precipitation, these semi-arid landscapes demonstrate characteristics of deserts.

If acute nuclear-war induced climatic disturbances were to occur in the *autumn or winter*, the effects would be considerably mitigated. From water relation studies of black spruce in Alberta (van Zindern Bakker, 1974) and the Northwest Territories of Canada (Black and Bliss, 1980), and studies of Jack pine in northeastern Alberta (Mayo et al., 1980), it appears that boreal conifers conduct little if any photosynthesis during this period, probably because their root systems are not active. Thus, a reduction in temperature and associated light levels in an acute response during this period would not reduce primary production directly in northern forests and arctic ecosystems since the plants would be dormant.

The separate question of freeze-induced mortalities of the plant species seems not to be a major problem for a winter-onset war, although sudden severe temperature decreases could cause frost cracks and increased disease susceptibility. In the dormant state, most arctic and boreal vegetation could withstand temperatures down to $-50°C$ to $-70°C$ or below, well under the minimal temperatures expected in a post-nuclear war environment. In addition, the landscapes are usually covered by snow and ice, which provide a protective blanket for understory plants and components of the soil subsystems.

A winter-onset war could also affect an ecosystem by delayed impacts, specifically by the extension of winter temperatures into the following spring and summer. Again in the case of tundra ecosystems, these effects would appear to be small for the plants. There are few field data from the low arctic to indicate how shrubs or other dominants would respond to a summer with little or no plant growth as a result of an unusually prolonged winter season. However, many arctic species have been maintained in cold laboratory environments for 12 to 24 months, brought out of dormancy, and subsequently resumed normal growth. By extrapolation, one can assume the same would be the case in the aftermath of post-war climatic disturbances that occurred in the winter season and under the conditions in which the environment did not warm sufficiently to release the plants from the cold-hardened state. Plants in the high arctic would be little affected if they experienced no summer at all. For instance, in 1964 there were large areas in which snowmelt did not occur until early August, yet the arctic plants survived and flowered in the following year (Savile, 1972). It is less clear what the effects would be if a very brief summer were to be experienced, followed by early initiation of the following winter.

Effects on arctic animals would be much more pronounced than effects on plants, although less than on animals in biomes at lower latitudes in the Northern Hemisphere. Extending the length of the winter period might be a major cause of animal mortality, especially for birds and for mammals that do not hibernate. Resident bird populations would probably survive increased winter cold, although population reductions of up to one-third seem possible. Large herbivores would be more susceptible to population reductions, especially if temperature reductions extended into May and June. In that instance, winter foraging for food of low nutritional value would be extended into periods of calving and lactation, and temperature effects could lead to increased mortality among newborn populations. Carnivores such as foxes and wolves would also be adversely affected, although with a greater delay period; increased food supplies would occur initially as their prey species experienced increased mortality, but eventually the reduced secondary production would propagate to reduced carnivore production. Small mammals would be less affected by maintaining themselves under a snow pack, unless they consumed all of their food within their home range before productivity could be restored. The decomposer system, by contrast, would probably not experience long-lasting effects.

Effects on boreal and arctic ecosystems from nuclear-war induced climatic disturbances occurring in the *summer* could be far more significant. The impact of reductions of temperature below freezing on actively growing tissues of trees, shrubs, graminoids, and forbs would be considerable. Little is known about the level of cold hardiness of arctic plants in the summer. Studies by Somers (1981) on *Salix arctica* at 75°N and by Sakai and Otsuka (1970) on alpine species in Japan suggest that arctic plant species may tolerate temperatures of $-5°C$ to $-10°C$ during the growing season. If temperature and light reductions occurred gradually over a two-week period or longer, an additional increase in cold hardiness might be induced, further minimizing freezing damage to plants. However, more rapid reductions in temperatures would not allow acclimatization; in that instance, it is not clear what proportion of the tundra plant community would be killed.

For lichen-woodlands and taiga, a drop in summer temperatures would kill the new growth of conifers (e.g., *Larix, Pinus, Picea,* and *Abies*) and deciduous trees and shrubs (e.g., *Populus, Betula, Alnus,* and *Salix*). Unless summer temperatures dropped below − 10°C, the older needles of the conifers and the older branches of the deciduous species would largely survive. If subfreezing temperatures were experienced, high mortality of the plant community could be expected; however, individual trees and shrubs could survive, and for many species, resprouting of new growth from the shoot base could occur for perhaps 10–20% of the populations (e.g., for shrubs, black spruce, Jack pine, poplars, and birches). Dwarf shrubs and the graminoids would survive if temperatures dropped more gradually, especially if they were covered by a protective snow blanket prior to severe temperature reductions. This snow cover would prevent rapid freezing of the soil subsystem, providing time for cold hardiness of root systems to develop. Lichens and mosses would be little affected.

In the tundra, arctic shrubs, grasses, and forbs would all be considerably affected by the combination of cold and reduced light levels if occurring in the summer, but the plant communities would largely survive, although recovery rates might be quite slow. Shrubs would be most severely affected, with extensive dying back to ground level; most graminoids, herbs, and dwarf shrubs would survive. In the high arctic (> 70°N latitude), early onset of snows in August are seen to force the plants into early dormancy, and the systems survive. Arctic species function normally in summer temperatures of only 3°C to 10°C, and they maintain at least a limited level of cold hardiness in summer (low temperature limits are about − 5°C to − 10°C) (Somers, 1981). The potential initial reduction in light and temperatures following a nuclear war could trigger an increase in cold hardiness, down to − 20°C to − 30°C within 7 to 10 days. Arctic plants are relatively long-lived (20 to 100+ years), and the loss of seed production for one or two years would have little impact on the survival of many plant species. Although in general some seed banks are present, even in the high arctic, certain dominant species (e.g., *Carex aquatilis, C. bigelowii, C. stans, Alopecurus alpinus, Luzula confusa,* and *L. nivalis*) produce little or no ripe seed each year. Should populations of these dominants be eliminated over large areas, recolonization would be very slow, and forage for large herbivores would be severely reduced. There are very few ruderal or pioneer species in the arctic to initiate succession. Thus, plant reestablishment would result from resprouting and from species in the soil seed bank.

In general, survival of arctic animals would be reduced if the plants upon which secondary production is based were damaged, killed, or buried in snow. If animals are unable to replace energy reserves over the summer season, increased mortality would ensue after a few months. Large herbivores would require a growing season of about two months prior to the onset of a nuclear war-triggered cold period in order to gain enough energy reserves to last through the subsequent period of 8 to 10 months with only limited foraging. Invertebrate populations would be reduced by direct mortality, but the species would not be eliminated, since most species require more than one year to complete their life cycles, and immature stages (e.g., eggs, larvae, pupae, and nymphs) could survive within the soil and litter until the following growing season. Large mammal populations could survive extreme climatic disturbances for a number of months, but only a few large and small herbivore populations could survive until the next summer, and then only provided that they were already located in a highly favorable winter-grazing habitat. Should surface vegetation be sealed in ice, small mammals and large mammals would be eliminated from large areas (Fuller et al., 1977; Miller et al., 1975). In these circumstances birds, both migratory and resident, could be eliminated. The soil fauna and flora would survive essentially intact.

2.2.1.2 Vulnerabilities to Chronic Climatic Disturbances

The considerations thus far have dealt with the response to an extreme acute period of climatic disturbances affecting arctic and boreal ecosystems in the winter or the summer. We next consider effects on arctic ecosystems from potential chronic reductions in temperature, light levels, and precipitation. In order to help evaluate the vulnerability of these ecosystems to chronic temperature decreases, these discussions focus on average temperature reductions of about 3°C below normal, persisting throughout the growing season. These are partially based on the estimations of effects on arctic ecosystems from the Little Ice Age (Andrews et al., 1976; Dyke, 1978, 1979) and on many years of observation of the effects of unusually cold or warm summers on the phenology and plant growth in the arctic (Svoboda, 1982).

A decrease in the average temperature by 3°C would probably result in delayed or incomplete snowmelt, resulting in a shallower or absent biologically active layer in the soil. Reduced average temperatures could be expected to result in a delay in ice break-up in river and lake systems and an earlier incidence of freezing in the following fall. There would be a decreased number of degree-days above freezing, upon which primary production is dependent. Old unmelted snow would result in firn formation, an initial phase of ice crust formation, if the chronic effects lasted longer than a single year.

The lack of snowmelt or ice break in the Arctic Ocean could also result in an increased albedo throughout the year, with subsequent increased loss of radiant energy from the arctic regions. Note, however, that this effect would be mitigated if sufficient particulates from a disturbed atmosphere were to be deposited on top of the ice cover. It is unclear from the atmospheric analyses how prevalent such a particulate cover on these regions would be. One analysis (Warren and Wiscombe, 1985) indicated that there might be sufficient smoke and soot from a perturbed atmosphere to result in significant reduction in the albedo of Greenland and arctic sea ice. Further, they suggested that upon melting each year, the deposited polluted layer would become reexposed and, therefore, repeatedly reduce the albedo. Subsequent snowfall would again increase the albedo until the next snow melt. This could affect both the nature and timing of the snowmelt process and extend the climatic responses in time.

Climatic alterations could result in the vascular plants of boreal and low arctic regions experiencing a prolonged period of winter dormancy and concomitant delayed initiation of the growing season by up to a month. Thus, most of the life cycle would develop after the summer solstice, a period of declining solar irradiation, adding a further limitation to the solar radiation already decreased by smoke. Growth of plants would probably begin, but the normal life cycles might well not be completed. In general, in highly seasonal ecosystems the life cycles of the constituent plants must coincide with cycles of the physical environment. If buds break dormancy too early, they are killed by frost; likewise, if they are delayed too long in appearance, there would be insufficient time for the life cycle to be completed and for fruits to ripen. The chronic climatic disturbances could result in sporadic occurrence of flowering, or incomplete fruit development. If the chronic phase lasted for several years, these effects would be more severe (Dahl, 1985).

Considerable enhancement of the extent and frequency of fires could occur if large-scale die-off of taiga trees occurred during an acute period, and fuel moisture conditions permitted. Low arctic animal populations would probably be severely affected because of a general shortage of food resources from reduced primary production. Predators and scavengers might temporarily have an increased food supply, but the decline in carnivore populations would eventually follow the decline in herbivores.

Within boreal forests there are herb and shrub species that rapidly recolonize sites disturbed by fire or tree harvest (e.g., fireweed, grasses, willows, and birches). These species would be present in the seed bank following disturbance and would facilitate recolonization of denuded lands.Resprouting of woody species, as discussed previously, would also enhance plant succession.

In the high arctic, the chronic reductions in temperature and light could result in snow cover for the entire summer, and vegetation would not grow. Snow cover would enhance long-term plant community survival if the plants did not break out of dormancy and cold hardiness. However, under such conditions all land-bound vertebrates could starve within a few months. The bird populations would also be severely affected by the loss of breeding grounds, as they would not be able to return to their nesting sites, nor would they be able to find adequate food.

2.2.1.3 Inferences from Previous Modelling Studies

These estimates of the potential effects of nuclear war on arctic ecosystems are reinforced by some previous analyses of tundra ecosystem models under simulated conditions of reduced temperatures (Cooper et al., 1979). Two separate tundra models were analyzed. The first was a model of the physical processes affecting photosynthesis rates for individual plant leaves and, by extrapolation, primary production (Miller and Tieszen, 1972). The model shows that plant production is almost totally temperature- and insolation-dependent, and that soil moisture is not a major limiting factor, at least for the wet soils of the Barrow, Alaska area, for which the model was calibrated. Other data show the importance of temperature in controlling photosynthesis rates (Hartgerink and Mayo, 1976; Addison and Bliss, 1984).

The model results reported by Cooper et al. (1979) approximate a 25% reduction in primary production for each 2°C drop in temperature. Field data, however, do not support this model. Over a three-year period, mean weekly temperature and total degree-days over a 50-day growing season changed 3-fold, yet plant production within two communities changed less than 10% (Bliss, 1977). This illustrates that current models can be helpful in explaining responses of individual species, but community and ecosystem responses may be quite different. A major factor is the role of food reserves (carbohydrates and fats) in perennial species. This limits the usefulness of these simulation models to plants that store limited food resources. Other, more useful ecosystem models for arctic systems were not available for evaluating potential effects of nuclear war.

2.2.2 Potential Effects on Forest Ecosystems [2]

2.2.2.1 Vulnerabilities to Acute Climatic Disturbances

The second major class of ecosystems that were considered includes the deciduous and coniferous forests that occur in the temperate regions of the Northern Hemisphere. The deciduous forests of North America, Europe, and Eastern Asia are broad-leaved, consisting of oak, maple, beech, birch, and ash, and many other species of trees, including mixtures of conifers. These ecosystems are characterized by relatively high species diversity and productivity. Temperate coniferous forests occur in a variety of regions and climates, ranging from dry, fire-maintained ecosystems to the massive forests found in the cool maritime climate of the Pacific Northwest region of North America.

One particular consideration for the temperate Northern Hemisphere forests is that they are located in the probable latitudinal bands of the nuclear war itself. Thus, these systems could experience more intense climatic

---

[2] The discussions in this section are based primarily on the conclusions of the ecosystems working group at the Toronto conference, chaired by L.C. Bliss.

disturbances than other ecosystems, and there would be a greater input of other stresses, such as radiation, pyrotoxins, particulates, and toxic gases. These are independently considered elsewhere (Chapter 3), but the potential for synergisms should always be kept in mind.

The possible effects from acute reductions in temperature and light would be considerably less if imposed in winter as compared to in the summer. For the more northern and mountainous deciduous and coniferous forests, the trees would be in a state of winter dormancy. Substantial undercooling would permit bud primordia to survive unfrozen to temperatures of about $-40°C$ (see further discussion in Chapter 1 of cold-hardiness of temperate species). Thus, trees would not suffer substantial mortality from the direct effects of cold. In these areas, snow cover might protect the understory plant species as well. In southern coniferous forests, the trees would be much less cold hardy, especially pines, and a substantial fraction of the trees, shrubs, and herbs would be killed, at least back to ground level. Subsequent snow associated with the initial stages of nuclear war-induced climatic changes might provide protection to the understory species. Reduced light levels would not affect coniferous plants much or deciduous plants at all because of the reduced rates of photosynthesis during these periods.

A variety of factors would influence the survival and recovery of mammal and bird populations following a winter-onset war. Northern animals might tolerate climatic stress better, but southern populations might encounter higher levels of food availability because of the existence of less snow cover than in northern areas. Severe climatic disturbances could reduce primary productivity, possibly to levels insufficient for maintaining animal populations. Although decomposer activity is reduced by decreasing temperatures, climatic stresses would probably not eliminate many decomposer organisms (soil invertebrates, bacteria. and fungi). Similarly, mycorrhizal infection of tree roots might decrease under reduced temperatures, but the resistance of mycorrhizal spores and inoculum to stress would prevent those species from being eliminated. In general, these forest ecosystems have a diversity of species well adapted to colonization following major disturbances.

One possible climatic response to a summer-onset nuclear war is the occurrence of subfreezing temperatures, brought on very rapidly in combatant-zone latitudes. Sudden freezing would be expected to result in widespread loss of the current season's foliage. However, that alone is not expected to cause long-term effects for the trees, as some forests can experience large foliage losses from insect consumption and continue to survive into the next season. Aboveground tree mortality from reduced temperatures could also occur. Among the deciduous species (e.g., oak, maple, beech), some might be able to resprout in the next warm growing season. If temperatures remained below freezing for two or more months, however, most species of trees could survive only in very low numbers (below 10%), if at all. If temperatures remained below freezing for weeks to months, many shrubs would be killed outright, and the tops of all herbaceous species would be killed. Significant losses of nutrients might occur in forests with high levels of tree mortality, because of reduced uptake and immobilization of nutrients. This effect could be particularly important in regions of normal or increased precipitation.

Large and small mammals could be eliminated because of insufficient food, coupled with extremes of temperature. Likewise, other than a few hardy winter residents, birds would probably be killed. The soil subsystems, however, would remain essentially intact.

In subsequent years, those forests that had experienced substantial mortality of at least the aboveground portions of the trees could be subject to great increases in insect outbreaks. Fire could also be extensive in these systems, thereby extending ecosystem stresses well into the future following the acute phase, even if there were no chronic climatic effects. The relatively high density of viable seeds in these types of forests promotes recovery of a forest community after perturbation. However, the combinations of perturbations and the probable propagation of indirect effects throughout the ecosystem indicate that it is not possible to describe precisely the extent or ultimate effects of these potential post-war perturbations.

2.2.2.2 Vulnerabilities to Chronic Climatic Disturbances

The vulnerability of forest ecosystems to potential chronic conditions, i.e., temperature reductions of a few degrees, light reductions of 5–20%, and precipitation reductions of up to 50%, are more difficult to characterize. It is clear that chronic temperature reductions could result in delayed growing season initiation and an earlier onset of winter; further, the variance in temperature could result in episodes of near- or sub-freezing temperatures being experienced well into a growing season. This would result in the increased mortality of plants and, especially, in the interruption of the normal life cycles of plants. However, if subfreezing temperatures were not experienced within a growing season and if the precipitation were not reduced substantially, reductions in temperature alone could result in *increased* primary productivity in those forests that are at least partially limited by soil moisture stress. On the other hand, photosynthesis and respiration rates would *decrease* with reduced temperatures; thus, the integrated effect of these processes would be difficult to predict. A mechanistic simulation model could be used to explore this problem. In the event of reduced precipitation, there could be a substantially increased incidence of fires, which would have a considerable effect on forests not accustomed to experiencing a high fire frequency. Reduced light levels associated with the chronic phase could be expected to reduce productivity in many forests.

2.2.2.3 Results from Previous Modelling Studies

For deciduous forests, there are simulation models that can be used to look more carefully at the effects of the chronic perturbations and the propagation of those effects throughout the ecosystem and over time. One set of such simulations was reported in Harwell (1984). The FORNUT model (Weinstein, 1983) was designed to test the effects of environmental perturbations on the primary productivity and species composition of Eastern deciduous forests of the United States (Harwell and Weinstein, 1982; Weinstein and Shugart, 1983). The version used for these simulations was calibrated to the mixed conifer-hardwood forest of the Southern Appalachian Mountains based on data from eastern Tennessee. FORNUT is based on the forest-gap replacement concept, in which simulations monitor the birth, growth, and death processes for individual trees.

The results of the FORNUT simulations should not be interpreted as predictions of species composition or ecosystem characteristics following a nuclear war. The model was not initialized with conditions appropriate for a forest severely damaged by acute-phase climatic or other disturbances. The model is more appropriately evaluated as part of an analysis of forest sensitivity to relatively mild climatic stresses, potentially occurring in an acute phase in some regions or a chronic phase elsewhere. With severe acute disruptions, FORNUT simulations would probably greatly underestimate effects and the time required for forest recovery. On the other hand, simulating chronic stresses lasting for 5 years may overestimate the consequences of shorter-term chronic perturbations.

Results from the FORNUT simulations are shown in Figure 2.1. The 0°C case is the control simulation, demonstrating the successional development of the forest over the fifty-year period, beginning with the forest as currently constituted. Chronic temperature reductions were imposed for the first five years of the simulation, with subsequent return to normal temperature conditions for the remainder of the simulation period. During that period, the total biomass of the control forest trees increased by about two-thirds. Simulations of an average 3°C drop resulted in an initial decrease in biomass by about 25%, with return to the unstressed trajectory in about three or four decades. By contrast, reductions in average air temperatures of 6°C led to an 80% reduction in the biomass of the forest, with the peak loss occurring a few years *after* the temperatures had returned to normal. Moreover, the reductions in biomass had not returned to normal conditions by the end of the simulation period; i.e., even 50 years after temperatures returned to pre-war levels, the forest biomass would be less than one-half its value had there not been the chronic stress lasting for the first five years. A similar pattern ensued after a 9°C reduction in temperature.

Another set of simulations was conducted to evaluate the effect of reduced

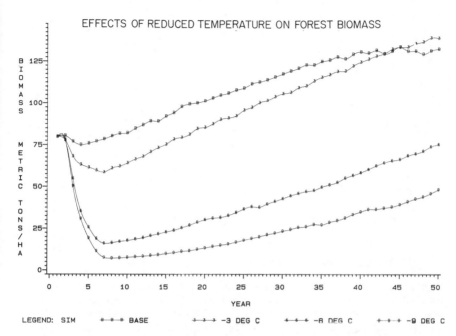

Figure 2.1   Effects of reduced air temperatures on forest biomass. Reductions in average annual air temperatures imposed for first five years at levels of 0°C (base case), 3°C, 6°C, and 9°C. Simulations performed using FORNUT model. From Harwell (1984)

precipitation on the forest structure and productivity if that co-occurred with a 6°C decrease, again having the stresses last only for the first 5 years of a 50-year simulation (Figure 2.2). As in the other simulations, no account was taken of the effects from the acute period of nuclear war stresses. Three simulations were run, with reductions in precipitation by 0%, 10%, and 25%. The results indicate that for this forest, primary productivity is far more sensitive to a 6°C reduction than to precipitation reductions. Simulations were also conducted to test the effect of reduced insolation on the forest with and without a simultaneous reduction in precipitation. Figure 2.3 indicates that a 25% reduction in precipitation alone is about equivalent in effect to a 50% reduction in insolation lasting for one year (a situation *not* expected to be an outcome of nuclear war), and these in turn are only somewhat greater in effect than the 3°C reduction if that occurred alone (Figure 2.1).

The FORNUT model was also examined for species compositional effects from the chronic stresses. The model maintains number, size, and age information for each individual tree in the simulation plots. These were used to estimate the biomass levels for the dominant tree species at the end of

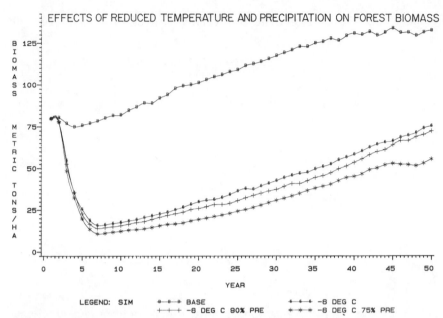

Figure 2.2 Effects of reduced precipitation on forest biomass. Air temperatures reduced by 0°C and 6°C, and precipitation reduced 0%, 10%, and 25% for first five years. Simulations performed using FORNUT model. From Harwell (1984)

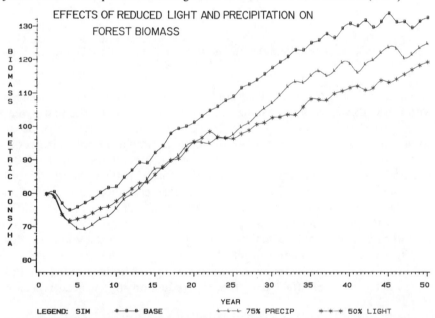

Figure 2.3 Effects of light and precipitation reductions on forest biomass. Reduction of 75% for precipitation imposed for first five years only; reduction of 50% for light imposed for first year only. Simulations performed using FORNUT model. From Harwell (1984)

the fifty-year simulation period for the control forest simulation and for simulated temperature reductions of 3°C, 6°C, 9°C (Figure 2.2), and a 25% precipitation reduction, and a 50% reduction in insolation (Figure 2.5), each acting independently. Compositional changes were limited for the 3°C case, with only sourwood (*Oxydendron arboreum*) being eliminated from the forest. However, a 6°C or a 9°C reduction resulted in a relative increase in red maple (*Acer rubrum*), ash (*Fraxinus americana*), and black cherry (*Prunus serotina*), but a loss of hickory (*Carya glabra*), tulip poplar (*Liriodendron tulipifera*), blackgum (*Nyssa sylvatica*), sourwood (*Oxydendron arboreum*), and oak (*Quercus prinus*). The responses are roughly correlated with the geographical ranges of the tree species: those species distributed over a wide latitudinal range tended to increase, while species with a more restricted southerly distribution were reduced or eliminated. In contrast, reductions in either precipitation or insolation were found to have no significant effect on the composition of the dominant trees in the forest.

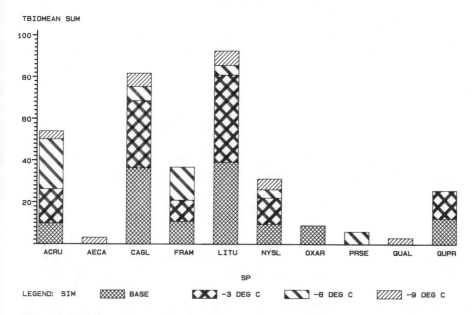

Figure 2.4   Effects of reduced air temperature on forest composition. Biomass values reported for species at fifty years, with temperature reductions occurring only for first five years. Species code: AECA, *Aesculus octandra*; ACRU, *Acer rubrum*; CAGL. *Carya glabra*; FRAM, *Fraxinus americana*; LITU, *Liriodendron tulipifera*; NYSL, *Nyssa sylvatica*; OXAR, *Oxydendron aboreum*; PRSE *Prunus serotina*; QUAL, *Quercus alba*; QUPR, *Quercus prinus*. From Harwell (1984)

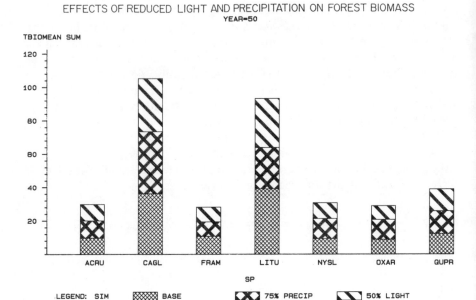

EFFECTS OF REDUCED LIGHT AND PRECIPITATION ON FOREST BIOMASS
YEAR=50

Figure 2.5 Effects of 50% light and 75% precipitation reductions on forest biomass. Reductions for first five years only. Simulations performed using FOR-NUT model. Species code as in Figure 2.4. From Harwell (1984)

These simulations (Harwell, 1984) are illustrative of the types of effects that could occur on the plant components of forested ecosystems following possible chronic stresses associated with nuclear war. First, there is the potential for long-term reductions in *primary productivity* lasting for decades after the perturbations ceased and the climate returned to normal. This expectation of slow recovery is related only to chronic stresses, and does not include the probably much more marked forest alterations in response to the acute stresses. It also does not include the likelihood of increased fires during the same period. Either case would considerably retard the projected rates of recovery, as would human exploitation. Second, changes in the species *composition* of the forest could occur under some of the stress conditions; these changes reflect the propagation of effects through the mechanism of species interactions, as trees more sensitive to temperature or other reductions became replaced by more hardy species. Third, although the model does not link the forest to the animal communities associated with it, the reductions in productivity could be expected to translate into at least as great a reduction in secondary productivity, and the shifts in species composition among plants is both an indicator of and an initiating factor in animal community alterations. Indeed, experience would suggest that the animal populations would undergo more significant impacts than indicated for the relatively stable tree community.

2.2.3 Potential Effects on Temperate Grassland Ecosystems [3]

2.2.3.1 Vulnerabilities to Acute Climatic Disturbances.

Temperate grasslands occur in large areas of the moderately dry and continental climates of North America and Eurasia. They are dominated by graminoids and herbs that die back to ground level each year, with relatively few shrubs and trees found only in riparian habitats. Landscapes that naturally would be grassland have been extensively modified by human activities, mostly for agricultural crops and grazing. Thus, relatively little of the original grassland ecosystems continue to exist, and these have largely been depleted of their original large herbivores.

As with other ecosystems, the effects of potential acute climatic stresses associated with nuclear war are first considered. The major grasslands of the Northern Hemisphere are at the latitudes of potential nuclear war targets, and they are in areas where the maritime influence on the climate is minimal. Thus, these ecosystems could experience rapid onset of severe climatic disturbances. In addition, being concentrated in the continental, nuclear war zone, these ecosystems would likely be subject to additional stresses such as radiation, fire, pyrotoxins, air pollutants, and human exploitation.

Following a *winter* nuclear war, the effects of reduced temperature and light levels during the acute phase would not initially reduce primary productivity, which is low or nonexistent during this season. However, delayed effects, such as a reduction in average temperatures extending into the following summer months, could delay or inhibit plant productivity. The effects of immediate temperature reduction on the large mammals could be severe, with perhaps 25–75% mortality because of cold temperatures, potentially increased initial snowfall, and reduced access to forage. Small mammal mortality would not be nearly so large because of aestivation. Resident birds would be severely affected. However, the soil subsystem would remain essentially intact. In general, the impact on the plant community, even in southern grasslands, would be far less than the impacts on the large mammal and bird populations.

---

[3] This section is based in part on discussions of the ecosystem working group at the Toronto conference, L.C. Bliss chairman. The section on simulation modelling of grasslands under simulated post-nuclear war conditions was largely written by J.K. Detling and J.D. Hanson.

Following a Northern Hemisphere *summer* nuclear war, grasslands throughout North America (i.e., from Alberta and Saskatchewan to New Mexico and Arizona), as well as grasslands throughout the U.S.S.R. and Asia, could be severely affected if low temperatures and limited light occurred during the peak of the growing season. Essentially all aboveground portions of grasses and shrubs would be killed to ground level, and belowground components could experience significant mortality (perhaps 20–50%), depending on the intensity of cold events and their duration. Grasses are well adapted to tolerating drought conditions during the growing season (Wilson and Sarles, 1978; Redmann, 1971), but not freezing episodes.

All large herbivore populations would be severely reduced by the low temperatures and loss of food supplies, especially if plant biomass was covered by snow or ice. Small mammals and bird populations would also be eliminated or reduced to very low densities. The possible sudden onset of cold would not allow animals that normally aestivate to attain the level of cold tolerance typical of winter conditions. Invertebrates would suffer high mortalities among adults, but most species would survive through their egg and larval stages.

2.2.3.2 Vulnerabilities to Chronic Climatic Disturbances

In the case of possible chronic climatic stresses, reduced precipitation, light, and temperature would lead to reduced primary production. Laboratory studies of North American grass species indicate that a 5°C shift in daytime temperature may result in anything from a negligible change in production to a doubling or halving in production. Similar trends regarding the effects of temperature on above- and belowground production of *B. gracilis* (C_4) and *Agropyron smithii* (C_3) from the shortgrass prairie were reported by Kemp and Williams (1980). Thus, relatively small changes in temperature could have profound effects on total plant production and hence food availability and forage quality, as well as total protein yield available.

The seed bank in grassland soils is adequate to permit reestablishment of most species. Ruderal species are less abundant in grassland ecosystems than in forest ecosystems, therefore, plant succession dominated by pioneer species is less important than in forests. With the disruption in agriculture, the large tracts of previously cultivated lands would be dominated by weedy annuals for a number of years .

2.2.3.3 Results from Modelling Studies

Ongoing modeling studies at USDA-ARS in Fort Collins, Colorado and laboratory experiments in the Natural Resource Ecology Laboratory at Colorado State University were used to evaluate potential sensitivities to reductions in temperature and light. The initial simulations were done to evaluate the potential effects of chronic stresses following a nuclear war, i.e., conditions following the first few months. The direct effects of a possible extreme acute phase were *not* included in the initial simulations. Other runs that did include acute effects are reported later. These model results should not be interpreted as predictions of post-war grassland conditions, but as analyses of sensitivities to the stresses considered.

A recently developed grassland model, SPUR (Simulation of Production and Utilization of Rangelands), was used to evaluate the potential effects of several combinations of reductions in light and temperature on primary production and plant standing crops for a shortgrass prairie site. As depicted in Figure 2.6, the SPUR model (Hanson et al., 1983) simulates the flow of carbon and nitrogen from the atmosphere through rangeland plants.

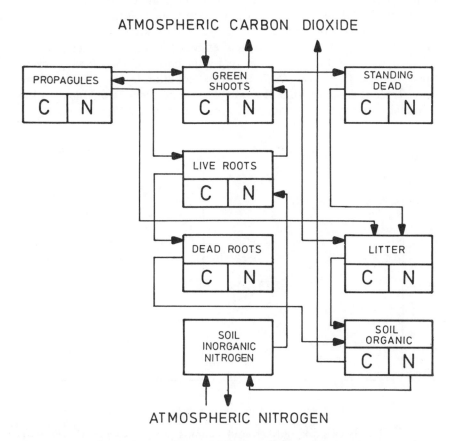

Figure 2.6 Carbon (C) and nitrogen (N) flow diagram for the plant growth component of the SPUR grassland model. Based on Hanson et al. (1983)

The initial set of simulations consisted of running the model for an entire year, using one of four different light levels (normal solar radiation and 25%, 50%, or 75% reductions), and four different temperature combinations (normal maximum and minimum daily temperatures, and 3°C, 6°C, or 9°C reductions in these values), based on weather data from the Pawnee Site in north-central Colorado for 1972. No changes in precipitation were included in these simulations.

The sensitivity of primary productivity to temperature decreases (Figure 2.7) is considerably less than seen for deciduous forests, as shown by the FORNUT simulations, described previously. The result using the SPUR model for grasslands is quite consistent with the results reported in Cooper et al. (1979), where 6% reduction in primary productivity was projected for each degree C reduction in temperature over the range of 0–4°C reductions. The decreased soil moisture stress in grasslands under reduced temperature conditions and associated reduced rates of evapotranspiration mitigated somewhat the effects of reduced temperatures on photosynthesis rates. The model results suggest that the principal effect of a decrease in temperature of 5°C (Figures 2.8 and 2.9) would be a shortening of the growing season for both C_3 and C_4 grasses. A 2–3 month reduction in the length of time that live (green) grasses would be available to consumers would have serious consequences for animal production, winter survival, and fecundity.

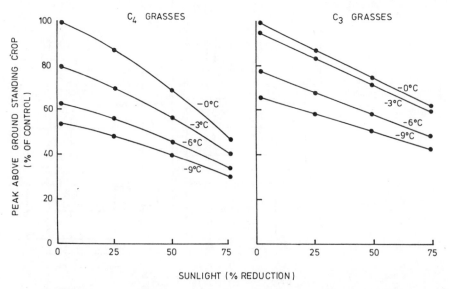

Figure 2.7 Simulated peak aboveground standing crop of C_3 and C_4 grasses at various reductions in temperature and light from observed values. Hanson et al., unpublished

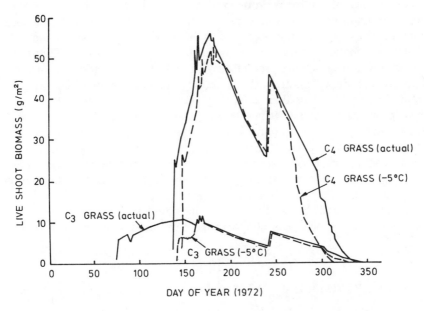

Figure 2.8 Simulated live shoot biomass dynamics of C₃ and C₄ grasses under actual measured temperatures for 1972 and with a 5°C decrease in temperature at the Pawnee grassland site

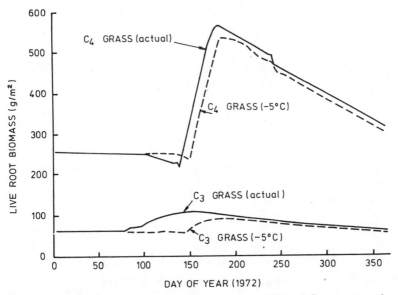

Figure 2.9 Simulated live root biomass dynamics of C₃ and C₄ grasses under conditions specified in Figure 2.8

A great deal of caution must be exercised in evaluating the results of these initial simulations. For example, no attempt was made to simulate increased plant death, which might be expected to be particularly high should episodes of severe climatic disturbances occur during the growing season. That is, the reductions in productivity predicted by these SPUR simulations occurred as a result of reduced photosynthetic activity for each plant rather than the actual loss of plants or their offspring. Also, as many models of perennial grass growth have shown (e.g., Detling et al., 1979), production in a given year is highly dependent upon the size of the perennating live biomass (e.g., crowns, stolons, rhizomes). In these simulations, no reductions in the primary producer state variables were made; hence, annual productivity might well be far less than predicted in the model runs. The set of simulations discussed below in part accounts for these factors.

Results of the first-year simulations indicated that a nuclear war on 1 January could reduce peak aboveground live standing crop more than an

TABLE 2.2

PEAK ABOVEGROUND LIVE PLANT STANDING CROP (g BIOMASS m^{-2})[a]

PLANT FUNCTIONAL GROUP	NOMINAL SITUATION	ACUTE ON DAY 1	ACUTE ON DAY 182
YEAR 1			
C_4 Grasses	37.8	38.0	37.8
C_3 Grasses	12.6	4.7	12.6
Warm Season Forbs	3.8	11.6	3.8
Cool Season Forbs	10.3	0.7	10.3
Dwarf Shrubs	16.1	13.1	16.1
TOTAL	80.6	68.1	80.6
YEAR 2			
C_4 Grasses	46.0	38.5	31.0
C_3 Grasses	11.9	7.2	9.1
Warm Season Forbs	10.9	9.5	9.2
Cool Season Forbs	9.6	3.2	2.8
Dwarf Shrubs	13.0	11.5	9.8
TOTAL	91.4	69.9	61.9

[a] From simulations by J.K. Detling and J.D. Hanson using the SPUR model.

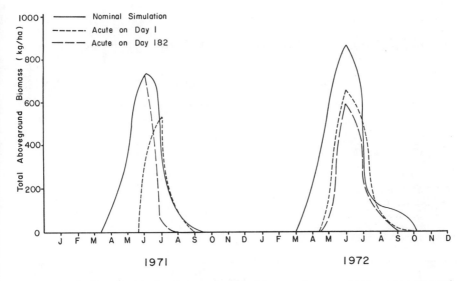

Figure 2.10 Simulated aboveground plant biomass for grassland under normal conditions and with climatic perturbations beginning on 1 January and 1 July. Simulations by Detling and Hanson using SPUR model

exchange conducted on 1 July (Table 2.2 and Figure 2.10). This result is somewhat misleading, however, because the peak biomass during 1971 was attained prior to 1 July (nearly all photosynthesis had occurred before that date [Table 2.3]) as a result of the extended summer drought and, thus, occurred *before* the climatic disturbances from a summer-onset nuclear war was assumed to begin. More importantly, as Figure 2.10 indicates, the aboveground live biomass immediately fell to near zero levels in the aftermath of a summer-onset nuclear war because of plant mortality. These near-zero levels remained until the second growing season. By contrast, the SPUR simulations suggest that primary productivity could recur during the first growing season after the winter-onset nuclear war.

In these nuclear war scenarios, the period of time during which live aboveground biomass was present was greatly reduced (Figures 2.10, 2.11, 2.12). This reduction in the growing season duration would be of particular significance to surviving grazing animals whose nutritional needs could best be met by consuming nutritionally superior live forage. Also, in years in which normal weather patterns would have favored a greater amount of late season growth, such growth would likely be completely eliminated following a mid-summer nuclear exchange and reduced following a mid-winter exchange.

The abiotic section of the SPUR model simulates soil erosion losses on the

TABLE 2.3

ANNUAL ABOVEGROUND NET PHOTOSYNTHESIS (g BIOMASS m^{-2})[a]

Plant Functional Group	Nominal Situation	Acute on Day 1	Acute on Day 182
		Year 1	
C$_4$ Grasses	197	240	193
C$_3$ Grasses	93	7	92
Warm Season Forbs	4	28	4
Cool Season Forbs	24	1	24
Dwarf Shrubs	58	39	57
Total	376	315	370
		Year 2	
C$_4$ Grasses	266	155	129
C$_3$ Grasses	73	46	16
Warm Season Forbs	27	9	19
Cool Season Forbs	11	6	2
Dwarf Shrubs	17	12	2
Total	394	228	168

[a] From simulations by J.K. Detling and J.D. Hanson using the SPUR model.

8000-hectare Pawnee Site. Following a simulated nuclear exchange, soil erosion losses from the site were estimated to be from 22 to 27 times greater during the year of the nuclear war than in nominal simulations. During the second year following the simulated nuclear war, the soil erosion losses continued to be greater than in the nominal simulation, but they were considerably less than the soil erosion losses of the first year. Soil losses were markedly greater in the second year following a summer-onset nuclear war than following a winter-onset nuclear war.

As with other simulation models, the results from these analyses need to be treated carefully. For example, this model is unable to simulate changes in species composition within any of the individual plant functional groups. It is possible that one species in a functional group might be largely replaced

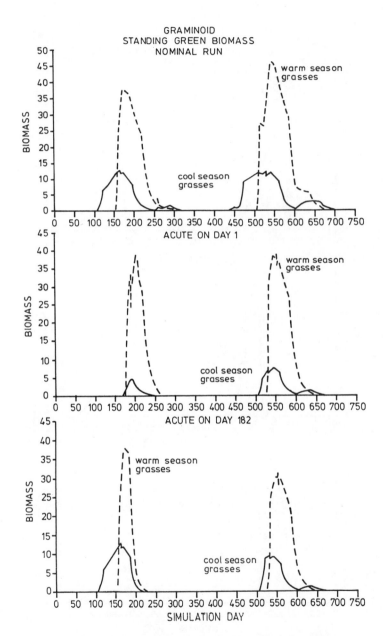

Figure 2.11 Simulated aboveground biomass for grassland ecosystem warm season and cool season grasses under normal conditions and with climatic perturbations beginning on 1 January and 1 July. Simulations by Detling and Hanson using SPUR model

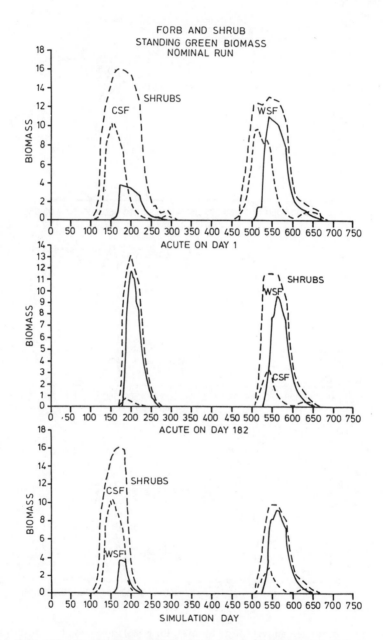

Figure 2.12 Simulated aboveground biomass for grassland ecosystem forbs and shrubs under normal conditions and with climatic perturbations beginning on 1 January and 1 July. Simulations by Detling and Hanson using SPUR model

by another less nutritional or desirable species. The model does not purport to handle the animal populations with the degree of reliability as the plant components. Changes occurring indirectly as a result of other factors (e.g., fire enhancement, human activities, loss of herbivores, loss of insect predators, and many other examples) could translate back into effects on primary production and community composition in ways not addressed by the simulations. Additionally, indications are that how the reduction in the average temperature over a growing season is imposed in a simulation can have a large effect on the results of the simulation. For example, a 3°C reduction in every daily maximum and minimum is likely to give quite different results from having most days with a lesser reduction, but a few days with much colder episodes. This issue was found to be very important for the simulations of agricultural productivity (Chapter 4), but for grassland ecosystems the effects of such temporal climatic variability have not yet been simulated.

2.2.4 Potential Effects on Arid and Semi-arid Ecosystems [4]

2.2.4.1 Introduction

The arid and semi-arid ecosystems of the temperate regions of the Northern Hemisphere include a wide variety of types, ranging from arctic to subtropical in distribution (Whittaker, 1975). Arctic-alpine semi-arid ecosystems occur above the timberline limited by latitude or elevation; these systems have been included in previous discussions. Cool semi-arid ecosystems are typified by the landscapes of the Great Basin in the United States, between the Cascade and Rocky Mountains, and in broad reaches of central Asia such as the Gobi. They are characterized by drab gray scrub, with the most widespread communities dominated by sagebrush (*Artemisia* spp.) and perennial grasses.

In more southerly areas, warm semi-arid ecosystems occur, characterized by open scrub of creosote bush (*Larrea divaricata*) with smaller shrubs and cacti. These ecosystems are widespread in North America, and through large areas in Northern Africa, the Arabian Peninsula, and India. In the warm semi-arid ecosystems, there has not been the convergence to a dominant plant form, as is the case for the cool semi-arid regions and other biomes (Whittaker, 1975). Animals in these ecosystems include a relatively rich diversity of reptiles (especially lizards and snakes), small mammals, and birds, and these ecosystems are often utilized to support large herds of beef

---

[4] This section is drawn primarily from the discussions of the ecosystems working group at the Toronto conference, chaired by L.C. Bliss.

cattle, sheep, or goats. By contrast, true deserts are characterized by very low species diversity of animals, and occur primarily in subtropical regions. Essentially no plant community exists for those regions where the precipitation is less than 2 cm per year, and sparse vegetation occurs between 2 and 5 cm of precipitation per year. True deserts are characterized by the nature of the ground surface (e.g., sand, stony desert pavements, salt crust, and barren rock). These ecosystems occur in the Northern Hemisphere in Northern Africa, the Arabian Peninsula, and in parts of the Southwestern United States.

2.2.4.2 Vulnerabilities to Potential Acute Climatic Disturbances

Considering first the vulnerability of these ecosystems to an acute climatic response to a nuclear war that occurred in the *winter*, in the cool semi-arid regions it is expected that reductions in temperature would not have a great impact on the plant communities, since these systems usually experience cold temperatures, with some snow, each winter. The shrubs and grasses in these ecosystems are cold hardened, probably to levels similar to tundra ecosystems, since the lack of a deep snow cover subjects the plants to more extreme temperatures than would be experienced under a snowpack. The hot deserts, however, could be significantly affected by climatic alterations in the winter, since many of the constituent plants in these ecosystems are not cold hardened. Nobel (1982) reported on the low temperature tolerance and cold hardiness of cacti, including 14 species in North America and 4 species from South America. Cacti from southern Arizona and California are cold hardy to $-6°C$ to $-9°C$; cacti from high, semi-arid grasslands in Wyoming are cold hardy to $-20°C$. This suggests that cacti could survive temperature reductions of $5°C$ to $15°C$ in the winter, and might be able to cope with subfreezing temperatures even in the summer. Some shrubs would survive, although mortality could exceed 75%.

Large animals would be reduced in numbers, and most birds would die. Small mammals in the warm semi-arid ecosystems would suffer, since they would have reduced food supplies and since they do not aestivate, unlike their cool desert counterparts. Most invertebrates, and other species in the soil subsystems, would survive in either the cool or warm semi-arid ecosystems.

In the event of a *summer*-onset nuclear war, subfreezing temperatures and light reductions occurring in an acute phase would result in very large effects on either cool or warm semi-arid ecosystems. High plant mortality would occur. If temperatures did not reach below the freezing point, plants could probably survive, but photosynthesis would be substantially reduced. Animal populations would suffer high mortality initially from extreme temperatures, and recovery would be impeded because of insufficient food availability resulting from the loss of primary production. The soil subsystem would remain intact. In subsequent periods, when temperatures returned to near-normal levels, nutrients would be released in a pulse, as decomposition and recycling processes would suddenly increase because of the increased substrate. Plants would eventually resprout or would grow from germination within the seed bank, which would be largely unaffected by the acute perturbations. Annual species are common, but a group of true successional, ruderal species is quite limited. Plant reestablishment is largely limited to perennial grasses, shrubs, and cacti.

2.2.4.3 Vulnerabilities to Potential Chronic Climatic Disturbances

The vulnerability of semi-arid ecosystems to the chronic effects of a nuclear war would be dominated by effects on precipitation rather than effects on temperature. For these ecosystems, the results reported in Cooper et al. (1979) suggest that reducing temperature by a few degrees gives an effect similar to the mechanism seen in grasslands, where productivity reductions were found to be less than for other types of ecosystems because of the reduced levels of evapotranspiration associated with reduced temperatures. However, in the case of the semi-arid ecosystems, reduction in evapotranspiration and concomitant reduction in moisture stress typically more than compensates for reduction in temperature, so that there would likely be a net increase in primary production in response to the reduction in temperature by a few degrees. The analyses reported in Cooper et al. (1979) indicated that about a 3% increase in primary production would occur per degree decrease in average temperature over the range of $+3$ to $-3°C$ difference from normal temperatures. On the other hand, if a reduction in precipitation of 25% to 50% also occurred, as believed to be possible after a nuclear war, then reduced primary production would ensue. However, even in those circumstances, the major ecosystem components would survive, since these ecosystems are largely adapted to prolonged periods of drought, and most of the organisms would compensate by shifts in the timing of their life cycles.

Ecosystems of arid lands contain few plant species that are truly successional and thus changes in species composition following major climatic disturbances would relate to shifts in the relative importance of species. Semi-arid ecosystems should be less sensitive to episodes of extreme temperature, since the biota often experience large drops in temperature during a single diurnal cycle in the summer months and, thus, are better adapted to brief temperature excursions than, e.g., forests. Therefore, the way in which an average temperature reduction would be imposed (i.e., uniformly versus episodic) would cause less sensitive effects for deserts and semi-arid ecosystems than for most other ecosystems.

2.3 POTENTIAL EFFECTS ON AQUATIC ECOSYSTEMS

2.3.1 Effects on Marine and Estuarine Ecosystems [1]

2.3.1.1 Introduction

Marine ecosystems cover the major portion of the Earth's surface (71%, Sverdrup et al., 1942), and, thus, are tremendously diverse and spatially extensive. For our purposes, marine ecosystems include: open ocean ecosystems, including surface pelagic and deep pelagic ecosystems; deep ocean and continental shelf benthic ecosystems; near-shore marine ecosystems; littoral ecosystems, including coral reefs, mud flats, and sandy beaches; and estuarine ecosystems. Vulnerability effects are separately considered for marine ecosystems in the Northern Hemisphere, in the tropics, and in the Southern Ocean. In each case, there are different levels of potential nuclear war-induced perturbations to consider, different sensitivities and resiliences of the ecosystems, and different degrees of importance to humans of consequences on the ecosystems.

An initial consideration is simply that much less is known about marine ecosystems than about terrestrial ecosystems, having both fewer data and a poorer understanding of basic processes. There have not been the sorts of experimental manipulations of most types of marine ecosystems as with their terrestrial counterparts, and observations in the field are more difficult and expensive to make. Existing ecosystem models of marine systems, although useful in characterizing what is known and what information is needed to understand these ecosystems, have limited predictive capabilities, even within more normal ranges of physical parameters than would be the case after a nuclear war. Moreover, there has to be a translation of the effects of nuclear war on the atmosphere into effects on the physical conditions of aquatic ecosystems. This is necessary in part because such changes in the physical conditions of bodies of water with significant water masses would be mediated and subject to a considerable time delay compared to the atmospheric conditions. And it is necessary in part because in coastal regions, the influxes of cold air, freshwater runoff, and sediment loadings from land areas are likely to be highly variable in intensity, spatial extent, and duration; these influxes alter the hydrodynamic features of vertical mixing and advective transport of fluids and suspended matter, which in turn affect temperature and light distributions. Nevertheless, enough is understood so

---

[1] The discussions in this section are based on the marine working group considerations at the Toronto conference, J.R. Kelly rapporteur, and on discussion papers developed for SCOPE-ENUWAR by J.M. Teal; A. Seymour; D.W.H. Walton; A. Spitzy, V. Ittekkot, and E.T. Degens; and by G.J. Kelly and S.W. Jeffrey. The Narragansett Bay Model simulations were conducted by J. McKenna.

that initial estimates of the effects on marine systems of nuclear war can be made, with more known about near-shore than open-ocean ecosystems.

Many types of marine ecosystems are light limited, so that reductions in solar insolation may be more important to primary production than in terrestrial ecosystems. Some marine ecosystems are also nutrient limited, so that alterations in nutrient cycling processes can be quite consequential. The trophic structures of marine ecosystems are typically based on unicellular plants with rapid turnover in individuals and in their constituent elements, the same elements often recycling many times within the producer communities. These factors should be kept in mind in the following discussion.

2.3.1.2 Vulnerability of Open Ocean Ecosystems to Potential Climatic Disturbances

In this section, effects on pelagic and benthic ecosystems are considered. Pelagic systems contain plankton and larger swimming animals. Oceanic phytoplankton account for about 90% of total ocean primary production. Light and nutrients are limiting, and both must be co-located for photosynthesis to proceed at significant levels (Figure 2.13; Bunt, 1975).

The deep pelagic ecosystem is totally heterotrophic, dependent on food from outside sources, especially settling plankton and particulates from near-surface pelagic ecosystems. The deep pelagic systems contain distinctive ani-

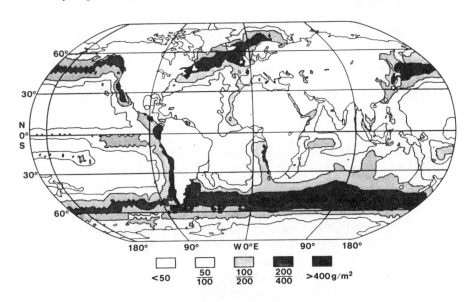

Figure 2.13   Primary productivity pattern of the oceans. Ranges mapped in g dry matter m^{-2} yr^{-1}. After Bunt (1975)

mal populations, including colonial protozoans, carnivorous crustaceans, and larger vertebrates. Benthic communities are also heterotrophic and cover the continental shelf and deep ocean. They consist of bacteria and animals living on or in the ocean bottom mud, and, on continental shelves, extensive algal communities supporting abundant herbivores and associated carnivores.

The first consideration of the potential effects of nuclear war on open ocean ecosystems is that they are well buffered against temperature changes. It might be possible for the sea-surface temperatures to be decreased by a degree or two in response to prolonged nuclear war-induced climatic perturbations, but larger water temperature reductions are not anticipated for the open oceans. Laboratory experiments indicate that phytoplankton would continue to grow under such temperature reductions (Figure 2.14). The nektonic (i.e., swimming) organisms in the pelagic oceans would not experience any major effects from a few degrees reduction in temperature, except that where behavioral patterns were finely tuned to ambient temperatures, some effects might occur.

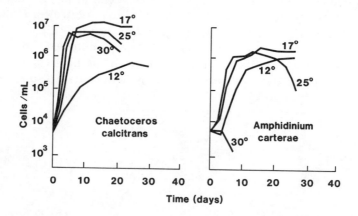

Figure 2.14   Growth in culture of two unicellular marine algae at various temperatures. Similar temperature tolerances were observed with seven other examined species. From Wilson, M.K., Kelly, G.J., and Jeffrey, S.W., unpublished

These projected minor temperature changes for the open ocean water would not extend very deeply into the water column, certainly not down to the level of the benthos. The animals in the lower water and benthic regions are also not sensitive to small reductions in temperatures, even if these could occur in response to climatic changes. Thus, one would not expect *any* direct effects from water temperature changes for either the pelagic or benthic biological communities in the open oceans. The potential for indirect effects, especially changes in ocean currents and in thermocline depths and stability (see Luyten et al., 1983a,b), however, does warrant further consideration.

Reduction in light levels, on the other hand, could significantly affect the primary productivity of pelagic ecosystems. Phytoplankton exist at depths to which irradiance is reduced to 1–10% of surface levels, in the range of 10 to 200 μ Einsteins m^{-2} sec–1 (Richardson et al., 1983). If this were reduced by 95% or more for a period lasting up to several weeks, growth for most algal species would effectively cease, since the remaining irradiance would fall below the light compensation point. That value is defined as the amount of light input at which photosynthetic carbon dioxide fixation is just sufficient to compensate for the loss of carbon dioxide through respiration by the plant organism (Figure 2.15). With a 95% reduction in incident solar radiation at the surface, the light compensation point, which normally occurs at the lower boundary of the euphotic zone, would be raised much closer to the surface (Figure 2.16). Consequently, light would not be limiting above the new compensation point. However, nutrients, which are relatively homogeneously mixed within the water column above the thermocline, would not be available at the depths to which light penetrated; e.g., in Figure 2.16, the depth to the compensation point would decrease from 110 m to about 10 m, reducing the water volume and associated nutrients available for photosynthesis by an order of magnitude. This much thinner layer of light availability would require an additional influx of nutrients, such as from upwelling, to maintain the levels of primary productivity.

Recent work suggests that significant levels of photosynthesis can continue for some species in the open ocean when the light levels are greatly reduced, even down to the extreme levels postulated for the post-nuclear

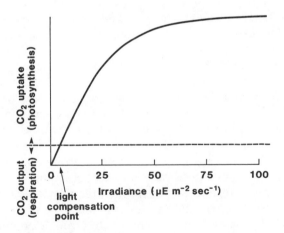

Figure 2.15   Idealized curve for effect of solar irradiance on phytoplankton growth. The light compensation point is about 5μE m^{-2} sec^{-1}. From Wilson, M.K., Kelly, G.J., and Jeffrey, S.W., unpublished

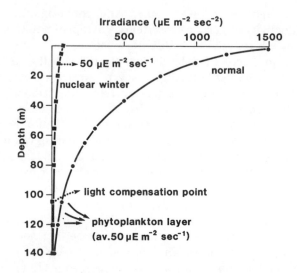

Figure 2.16   Light penetration and phytoplankton growth in the ocean. The 'normal' curve is for relatively transparent waters of the Coral Sea (Jeffrey et al., 1982), where depth profiles of phytoplankton Chlorophyll *a* are maximal at about 100–120 m (Jeffrey, S.W., and Hallegraeff, G.M., unpublished). The 'nuclear winter' curve is constructed using solar irradiance values equal to 5% of those on the normal curve

war situation (Jenkins and Goldman, 1985). However, it is not clear how widespread this phenomenon is and whether or not it could compensate for the reduction in primary productivity associated with plankton that require higher intensities of incident sunlight. Thus, potential for a compensatory mechanism does exist, but would require replacement of much of the phytoplanktonic community by low-light tolerant species of phytoplankton, which may be present locally. In general, reducing solar input by 95% for periods of weeks or more would greatly reduce phytoplankton photosynthesis and reproduction, and the biomass of the primary producers would largely disappear, as their cells would not be replenished even though grazing and mortality would continue, perhaps even at higher than usual rates.

Whether or not particular phytoplankton populations would survive would depend on their capability to exist heterotrophically, to photosynthesize at low-light levels, or to become encysted until more favorable environmental conditions returned. At the most extreme light reduction scenarios, e.g., reduction to 1% of normal lasting for months, the phytoplankton standing crop would be insufficient to support heterotrophic populations, and the question of species survival rather than just population size would become central. Survival of diatoms for three months in darkness has been recorded (Garrison, 1984), and the formation of spore or cyst stages that can survive for months or even years has been documented for several groups, including diatoms and dinoflagellates. Indeed, polar species have for millenia survived darkness that lasts for months. Thus, it is probable that plankton communities would recover (i.e., not go extinct) after light levels returned to normal, with a relative increase in low-light tolerant species, species that encysted, and populations that were transported by currents into the depleted regions.

If the phytoplankton biomass in the pelagic regions of the Northern Hemisphere were severely depleted following an acute reduction in insolation, it is probable that the zooplankton that feed on phytoplankton would decrease in numbers, as would the larval fish that feed on the zooplankton. This is because these relatively small organisms do not have the energy reserves to carry them for long periods of time without food inputs; baleen whales, on the other hand, which feed on phytoplankton and zooplankton, would not likely suffer mass mortality if the plankton populations recovered over the space of several months.

It is not clear how intermediate-sized heterotrophic populations, such as the pelagic fishes, would respond to a loss of the primary producer base. If the plankton food sources were lost for a long enough period, mortality of fish from insufficient food might occur. However, many of these species might find alternative food sources, and many could endure prolonged periods without food. One factor to consider is the potential for feedback between limited phytoplankton resources and increased herbivory by the zooplankton. In coastal waters, this could lead to increased loss of phytoplankton populations (i.e., those that survived the physiological problems of insufficient light might be subject to an increased rate of consumption by herbivores); however, in open ocean ecosystems, zooplankton populations tend to starve to death, in large part because of the lower density of plankton populations.

If fish larval life stages were eliminated but the adults did not experience substantial direct mortality, then the overall population impacts would depend on the longevity of the species and the number of years for which adults are reproductively viable. Projections of fish population responses are highly uncertain; current models are not good predictors of fish population size based on estimating effects of the physical environment on recruitment, since the relationships between larval survival and adult recruitment are poorly understood. Some generalities can be identified, however. Species such as cod, which ordinarily produce significant year classes every year, would suffer a relatively small reduction in total population, since individual adults are long-lived, on the order of 10 years. Thus, complete loss of an age class would constitute only a 10% reduction in the total population. On the other hand, species such as haddock, which produce a significant year class only every 7–10 years (i.e., essentially only once in the adult population's life cycle), could either not be affected (i.e., if the perturbations occurred in a year for which there were not a major production of new juveniles), or could be devastated (i.e., if the nuclear-war induced perturbations eliminated the total new year class). In that case, the species itself could be in jeopardy, depending on the spatial extent of the larval die-off. In general, however, ocean fisheries would not experience total elimination from climatic perturbations; indeed, many species might actually experience significant increases in numbers following a reduction in the human fishing pressure, which is now the principal cause of mortality for the adult fish of many species. Such an increase in fish populations occurred during the years of World War II, apparently for this reason (Cushing, 1975; Gulland, 1974).

The impacts on pelagic ecosystems from a potential *chronic* reduction in light levels by 5–20% and air temperatures by one degree or so do not appear to be significant. Once light levels returned to a substantial fraction of normal, the phytoplankton and zooplankton populations would recover rather quickly, albeit perhaps with different dominant species. The populations of larger animals of the euphotic and deep pelagic regions would survive essentially intact. Thus, long-lasting acute effects, if any, would not extend into the chronic period, and the potential levels of stress at that time are considered to be insufficient to cause substantial reductions in primary or secondary production by direct mechanisms.

On the other hand, indirect effects from altered oceanic circulation patterns could substantially alter the spatial distribution of upwellings and, therefore, of high productivity. For example, the recent El Niño was associated with alterations in oceanic circulation patterns that resulted in decreased upwelling off the coast of Peru, resulting in a collapse of that nation's anchovy fishery. El Niño is a good example of how relatively small sea surface temperature changes can be linked to a decrease in the strength of trade winds. Much larger alterations in wind strengths and directions would likely be possible in the chronic phase of a post-nuclear war world in response to differential temperature effects between the Northern and Southern Hemispheres, and between oceanic and continental regions. Thus, ocean fisheries are vulnerable to indirect effects, mediated via changes in oceanic circulation, both with respect to their magnitude and variability, and with respect to the predictability of location of this potential food source by human survivors. Moreover, disturbances of ocean currents have been known to last for years and to interfere with fisheries for years or decades thereafter.

Effects of climatic alterations on the benthic ecosystems well away from continents would be minimal. During the acute or the chronic periods, there would be no change in the light regime experienced by benthic biota, since they already exist in the dark. There would also be no change in the temperatures at the bottom, since the upper water mass would totally absorb these temperature changes before they could be felt by the benthos. Thus, effects on benthic ecosystems would be limited to indirect effects propagated by changes in the biological productivity of the upper pelagic systems.

Mortality of plankton in an acute period could lead to a temporary increase in food inputs to the benthos; however, the standing crop of plankton is small relative to total annual production. Therefore, receiving the brief, small pulse of additional organic inputs from planktonic die-off would be more than compensated for by the decrease in inputs in subsequent periods. Another factor is that fine particles in the upper layers of the ocean have settling velocities that are too slow to overcome turbulent mixing in the waters. These do not accumulate in the water column, however, since there is a biologically mediated formation of aggregates heavy enough to sink. Two mechanisms are involved: 1.) fecal pellet formation by zooplankton; and 2.) formation of organic-rich flocs, consisting of minerals glued together by organic matter derived from metabolic activities of phytoplankton (Kranck and Milligan, 1980; Honjo, 1982; Deuser et al., 1983). Mass mortality in planktonic populations could substantially alter this source of sedimentation to the benthos.

It is not clear how much reduction in the total resource base inputs (i.e., direct plankton and plankton-mediated inputs) would actually be felt by demersal fish and benthic invertebrates, nor what their capability is to withstand temporary reductions in food. Since the energy for benthic ecosystems comes seasonally from the surface, with rapid enough response so that that seasonality can be seen in the benthos (Deuser et al., 1983), one could expect that these organisms are adapted to surviving periods without food inputs and, therefore, would be essentially unaffected by nuclear-war induced perturbations.

2.3.1.3 Vulnerability of Coastal Ocean Ecosystems to Potential Climatic Disturbances

Pelagic and benthic regions closer to the continents are different from open ocean systems because of the proximity to terrestrial systems. The pelagic systems are more influenced by nutrients, sediments, and other inputs from terrestrial systems, and are thereby generally of higher productivity than their more open ocean counterparts. They are also more subject to anthropogenic influences. The coastal benthos is subject to considerably less constancy than deep ocean benthos, with fluctuations in light, temperature, and particulate and other organic inputs.

In the context of the potential consequences of nuclear war, the coastal pelagic ecosystems are subject to the same sorts of light limitations and effects as discussed for open oceans. In addition, however, the near-shore pelagic ecosystems could experience a greater temperature effect, because of the shallowness of the water and because of influence of runoff from freshwater systems. Moreover, coastal systems could experience increased storminess and thereby experience turbulence, increased sedimentation, and increased mixing. The sediment load could add to light limitation problems; increased mixing and turbulence, along with enhanced nutrient inputs from terrestrial systems and from near-shore upwelling, would tend to increase primary productivity where sufficient light was available.

Coastal production in normal winter is apparently quite large and proceeds most rapidly at low light levels (Glibert et al., 1985), including levels typical of what is projected for atmospheric disturbances. Primary production, in that case, would not be as adversely affected if the phytoplankton populations could adapt to the unusual timing of an apparent winter. The animal populations would survive as long as the food remained sufficient. Thus, there is the potential for greater resistance to the stresses associated with climatic alterations than is the case for open oceanic pelagic ecosystems.

Tropical coastal marine ecosystems are much more sensitive to changes in both light and temperature. In general, the range of temperature tolerances in tropical waters is narrow, only about one-half the range found in temperate regions. These tropical ecosystems do not have an elevated maximum temperature; the upper limits are typically not much higher than in the temperate counterparts. Rather, the minimum temperature limits are usually at higher values, and tropical marine species have reduced cold tolerance (Zieman, 1975). For example, coral reefs are ecosystems that are restricted to the warmer oceans of the world where winter temperatures do not drop below 20°C and where depths typically do not exceed 50 m (Moore, 1966). Some corals depend on their symbiotic relationships with zooxanthellae for survival, and these corals have been shown to die after only about 30 days in the dark; other coral reefs recovered after exposure to dark for 60 days, and still others are not light sensitive at all (i.e., not dependent on the algae) (Franzisket, 1970; Lang, 1971). Coral reefs can also be damaged by temperatures of about 15°C , which was seen to kill staghorn corals in the Persian Gulf after only a 9-hr exposure (Shinn, 1976). In addition, corals are especially sensitive to increased levels of UV-B radiation, particularly those corals exposed or nearly exposed to the air at low tides (Harriott, 1985), as well as increased sedimentation. In short, it is probable that effects on coral reefs from nuclear-war induced perturbations would be among the most widespread and severe for marine ecosystems. Similarly, shallow-water tropical seagrass ecosystems are quite vulnerable to temperature reductions (Zieman, 1975, 1982).

The coastal benthic ecosystems that are partially autotrophic would likely have that source of production eliminated, as insufficient light would reach the bottom because of atmospheric darkening and water murkiness. It has been discovered that attached benthic algae live and grow at depths where less than 0.1% of the surface light penetrates (Littler et al., 1985); since these plants are close to the limits of tolerance, they would seem to have only a limited ability to withstand additional reduction in light. Strictly heterotrophic benthic ecosystems would experience the same types of effects as seen in open ocean benthic ecosystems, specifically the temporary loss of organic inputs from the pelagic systems above. Direct effects from light and temperature changes would not be noticed on the benthic systems. However, increased sediment loadings from terrestrial runoff could reach the benthos, carrying with it increased inputs of organics, toxic chemicals, and radionuclides.

Truly coastal areas such as beaches, mud flats, and salt marshes would be subject to much greater extremes of perturbations than the other ocean systems, especially with respect to temperature reductions, perhaps experiencing subfreezing temperatures for periods of time. Intertidal areas could likewise experience subfreezing temperatures at regular intervals (i.e., when exposed to the air). The consequences of extremes of temperatures would depend on the season, location, salinity, and tide strength. In winter in high latitude coasts, these conditions are normally accommodated, but most mid- and low- latitude coastal zones do not experience subfreezing temperatures; in that situation, mortality of surface-dwelling organisms would be likely, but those organisms that routinely burrow into sand or sediments would be at least partially protected. As another example, mangrove ecosystems which form the tropical protection for soft-sediment coastlines are unable to withstand freezing even briefly, although they would have sufficient energy reserves to withstand prolonged periods without solar light. (See discussion in Section 2.4.2.6). Mangroves and other coastal ecosystems are also especially vulnerable to intense coastal storms, which can move sediments and coastline profiles on a large scale (Kuhn and Shepard, 1981, 1983; Emery and Kuhn, 1982).

Fish populations in coastal waters that do not normally experience cold temperatures are vulnerable to substantial mortality from brief episodes of cold temperatures. Subfreezing episodes in coastal waters of Florida and Texas provide clear examples of this effect on low- and mid-latitude areas throughout the year, and, perhaps, on more northerly ecosystems in the summer. A 5-day freezing episode in Texas left many adult fish killed, with an apparent correlation between the extent of mortality and the rapidity of onset of freezing (Gunter and Hildebrand, 1951; see also, Storey and Gudger, 1936; Storey, 1937; Gunter, 1941). In the Florida Keys, an unusually cool month of January, with minimum air temperatures in the range of 4–10°C, led to widespread fish mortality across many species (Miller, 1940; Galloway, 1941); another cold event in Tampa Bay, Florida, with air temperatures rapidly falling to $-7°C$ and water temperatures down to 10°C, resulted in a fish kill, especially for subtropical and tropical species (Rinckey and Saloman, 1964). In most cases, adult fish mortality seems to occur at a greater rate for the larger species and larger individuals within a species (Snelson and Bradley, 1978) and for the shallower water areas (Dahlberg and Smith, 1970). This evidence suggests that near-shore fisheries in tropical and sub-tropical waters, and in temperate waters in the summer, are substantially vulnerable to episodes of cold temperatures, especially in bays and other shallow-water bodies that would be most directly accessible to human survivors. An additional factor to consider is that for many commercial fish species, their eggs or larvae live near the surface, and, thus, would experience increased stresses related to temperature, UV-B, radiation, toxic chemicals, and other stresses.

2.3.1.4 Vulnerability of Estuarine Ecosystems to Potential Climatic Disturbances

For those saline ecosystems that are more closely linked to freshwater and terrestrial ecosystems, i.e., estuarine ecosystems, many of the same considerations apply as discussed for the near-shore coastal waters; however, estuarine ecosystems would likely be subject to even greater stresses, particularly with respect to temperatures and surface runoff. One aspect not previously thought to be of significance for marine ecosystems discussions is the effect of potentially reduced precipitation, resulting in decreased inputs of fresh water into estuaries and, therefore, leading to increased salinities in the upper sections of these ecosystems.

Considering first salt marshes and intertidal wetlands, these ecosystems are dominated in their plant community by a few species of grasses, especially *Spartina*. This is a C_4 plant, adapted to high light levels; primary productivity decreases essentially in direct proportion to decreased insolation. In addition, survival of the plants in the summer can be a problem in the dark; the plants can survive for only a few weeks if the underground part of the marsh system, with its warm sediments, continues to respire rapidly while temperature and light effects prevent the aboveground portions from photosynthesizing (Hartman, 1984). The effect would depend on the precise timing of the onset of climatic perturbations, with a summer occurrence of extreme climatic disturbances resulting in a large-scale die-off of the plant community.

Such a die-off would propagate to the animal community and would lead to increased sediment load being exported from the marsh ecosystems. This sedimentation, along with increased resuspension associated with potentially increased storminess, would cause smothering of shellfish and other benthic organisms before the waters cooled sufficiently for these organisms to become dormant and, therefore, resistant to suffocation. The increased sediment load would inhibit light penetration, further reducing photosynthesis. Fish that depend on the wetlands for nursery areas could suffer loss of the year class; waterfowl and shorebirds could be affected by the loss of food as well as by the physical environmental stresses.

Other estuaries are also vulnerable to climatic perturbations. Most estuaries in the Northern Hemisphere are closely associated with human populations, and therefore could experience fallout and other direct effects from local nuclear detonations in combatant countries. Increased run-off in the early periods, associated with fires, habitat destruction, an initial pulse of precipitation, and other factors, would carry a substantial load of pollutants, which tend to accumulate in estuaries (Meade, 1972). Current anthropogenic pollutants, such as aromatic hydrocarbons, are transported into estuarine and near-shore sediments (Hoffman et al., 1984), and benthic organisms accumulate these compounds (Farrington et al., 1980), and their partial metabolic products (McElroy, 1985). Increases in these inputs would reduce the value of shellfish and other fisheries in these areas of closest proximity to humans, although tidal wetlands themselves are relatively resistant to pollution damage (Valiela et al., 1984).

Since it appears that estuarine ecosystems are both more vulnerable to nuclear war effects than other marine ecosystems and of greater importance to humans, a simulation model was used to look more closely at the responses of a major estuarine ecosystem, the Narragansett Bay in Rhode Island. The Narragansett Bay Model (Kremer and Nixon, 1978) simulates the flows of energy and materials among the compartments of the Bay, as shown in Figure 2.17 (see Chapter 2 appendix for model description).

Harwell (1984) reviewed simulations using the Narragansett Bay Model reported in Kremer and Nixon (1978) (i.e., simulation runs not done to simulate nuclear war climatic disturbances) for implications about those conditions. These simulations showed that the model ecosystem is sensitive to alterations in the seasonal patterns of water temperatures, that rapid reduction in primary and secondary production would follow from reductions in sunlight, and that rapid recovery of plankton production would occur when the physical conditions ameliorated.

In the present analyses, the Narragansett Bay Model was used to simulate the Bay under physical conditions of climatic perturbations. A series of simulations was conducted to represent: 1.) the acute onset of air temperature reductions of 5°C and 10°C lasting for two months, coupled with 90% reductions in insolation; nuclear war-induced climatic disturbances occurring in January and in July were simulated, and in another simulation, a July onset of acute climatic disturbances (lasting two months) was directly followed by the onset of chronic conditions (3°C /13% light reduction); and 2.) a chronic climatic perturbation period, with air temperatures and light levels reduced for the entire simulation period by 1°C /5%, 3°C /13%, and 5°C /16%, respectively. The simulations were conducted on the entire Bay, but results reported only for the area in the upper reaches of the Bay.

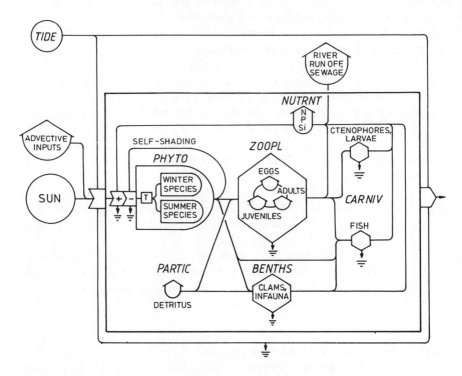

Figure 2.17 Energy flow diagram and conceptual framework for the simulation model of the Narragansett Bay ecosystem. After Kremer and Nixon (1978)

Figures 2.18a,b show how the water temperature and light levels were applied to the two acute scenarios. (The slight difference in second and third year temperatures are an artifact of the air/water temperature conversion process.) These represent the forcing functions for the simulations shown in Figures 2.18c,d. The phytoplankton production graph (representing net primary productivity) shows that phytoplankton production is vulnerable to a summer disruption in climate. By contrast, a January simulation resulted in an initial time lag in the development of the initial phytoplankton bloom during the spring, but by summer, when the temperature and light levels had returned to normal in this simulation, there were no effects on the phytoplankton production or dynamics. By the second and third year, no effects were seen to carry over from simulated acute stresses which lasted two months in the first year. (Note: The increased rates of phytoplankton production in the second and third years reflect an artifact in the modelled increase in temperature during that part of the simulation, and, therefore, they do not represent a nuclear war-induced response.)

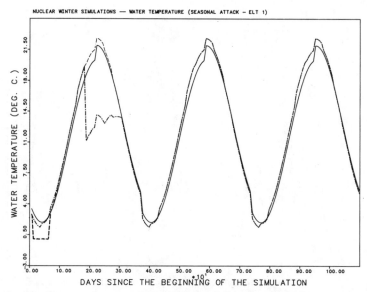

Figure 2.18a Water temperatures used in the Narragansett Bay Model simulations for normal (solid line), winter (dashed line), and summer (dash–dot line) acute climatic alterations. Temperatures were reduced by 5°C and 10°C for two months for winter and summer simulations respectively. Simulations conducted by J. McKenna

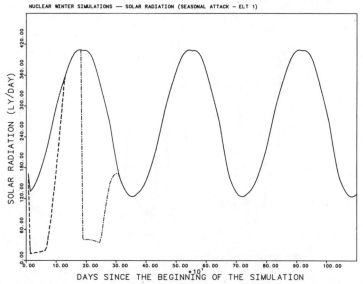

Figure 2.18b Solar insolation used in the Narragansett Bay Model simulations for normal (solid line), winter (dashed line), and summer (dash–dot line) acute climatic alterations. Light levels were reduced by 90% for two months

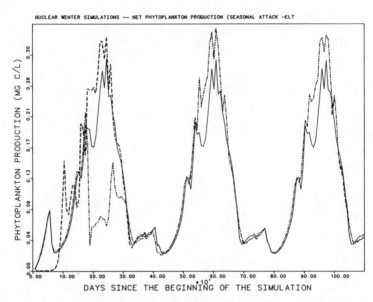

Figure 2.18c Simulated phytoplankton biomass (expressed as mg C l^{-1}) for Narragansett Bay Model. Simulations of normal (solid line), winter (dashed line), and summer (dash–dot line) acute climatic alterations

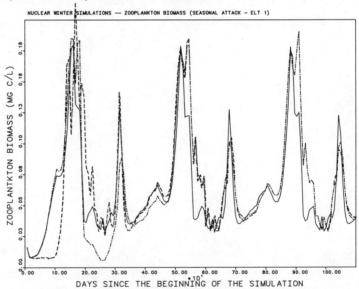

Figure 2.18d Simulated zooplankton biomass (expressed as mg C l^{-1}) for Narragansett Bay Model. Simulations of normal (solid line), winter (dashed line), and summer (dash–dot line) acute climatic alterations

For this simulation, the zooplankton population experienced a considerably less marked effect during the first year, and no effect in subsequent years (again after accounting for the temperature discrepancies). Climatic disturbances beginning in the winter were seen to delay the growth of the zooplankton populations the following spring, reflecting the delay in phytoplankton blooms; an initiation of climatic effects in the summer resulted in a time delay from its normal pattern before the zooplankton population reduction in the fall, and a more substantial drop in the population levels at the minimum periods the following winter.

It is clear from these simulations that the recovery rates after acute stress would be very rapid, and that there is no carryover effect into following years. The simulations of the chronic period, however, show that effects last as long as the stresses are imposed. Figures 2.19a,b illustrate the water temperature and light regimes imposed during the simulation for three levels of a chronic condition, as described above. The effects on the phytoplankton production are shown in Figure 2.19c. From this it can be seen that there is only a slight difference from the mild chronic case (1°C /5%) compared with the control run, but the middle and high chronic runs resulted in significant reductions in primary productivity, with rates at maximum production

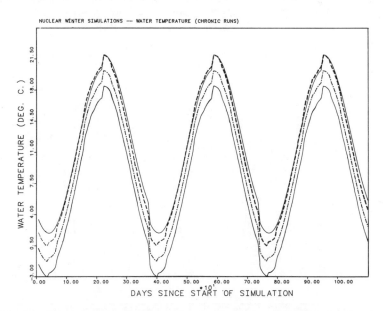

Figure 2.19a   Water temperatures used in the Narragansett Bay Model simulations for chronic climatic alterations for normal air temperatures (solid line), and for air temperatures reduced by 1°C (dashed line), 3°C (dash–dot line), and 5°C (thin solid line)

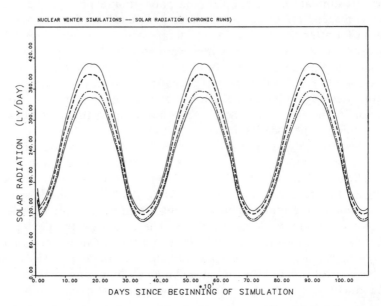

Figure 2.19b   Solar insolation used in the Narragansett Bay Model simulations for chronic climatic alterations for normal (solid line), and for solar insolation reduced by 5% (dashed line). 13% (dash–dot line), and 16% (thin solid line)

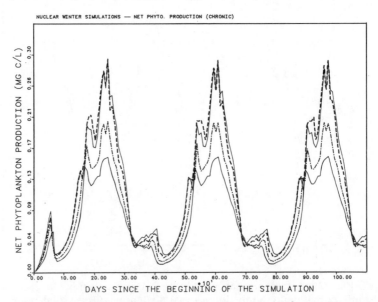

Figure 2.19c   Simulated phytoplankton biomass (mg C l^{-1}) for chronic simulations of Narragansett Bay Model specified in Figures 2.19a, b

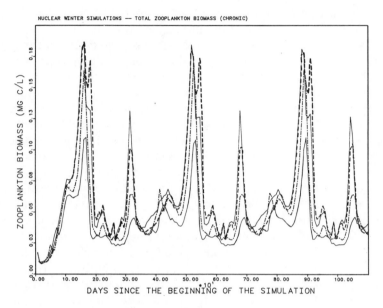

Figure 2.19d Simulated zooplankton biomass (mg C l⁻¹) for chronic simulations of Narragansett Bay Model specified in Figures 2.19a, b

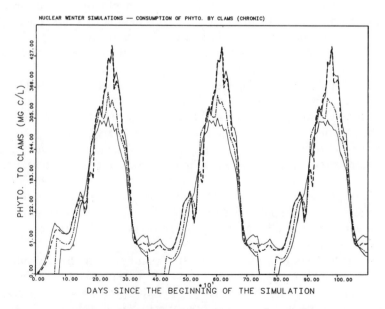

Figure 2.19e Simulated consumption rate (mg C l⁻¹ day⁻¹) of phytoplankton by clams for chronic simulations of Narragansett Bay Model specified in Figures 2.19a, b

being decreased by one-third to one-half, respectively. Note that there are no effects on the seasonality of the primary production; this is because the sinusoidal patterns of temperatures and light are maintained in the chronic runs. However, the timing of the initiation of population growth is delayed under chronic stresses, and the onset of the fall decline in production is accelerated.

Zooplankton population levels again show little sensitivity to a mild chronic case (Figure 2.19d), and while there is a noticeable effect in the medium chronic case, the effect is much greater in the high chronic case, indicating a nonlinear response to increased perturbation. Seasonality does not appear affected, but the same effect on the duration of the high biomass periods is seen as in the case of the phytoplankton. An interesting aspect is that the normal second population growth period in the late fall is more sensitive to the chronic stresses than the summer growth period.

Figure 2.19e shows how the consumption rate for clams feeding on phytoplankton is affected by the chronic conditions. This reflects primarily the temperature-dependent function that controls clam filtration rates, as illustrated by the nonlinear response during the winter for the medium and chronic case; this is because of a threshold in the model for a minimum temperature for clam activity. Comparison of this graph with Figure 2.19c indicates that the reduction in phytoplankton production does not translate into a proportional decrease in clam feeding on phytoplankton; however, that may be an artifact of the particular formulation of clam consumption in the model as controlled by abiotic versus biotic factors.

The final set of Narragansett Bay Model simulations involved an acute perturbation beginning in July and lasting two months, and followed by a high chronic perturbation (Figures 2.20a,b). For the phytoplankton, the first year (Figure 2.20c) followed very closely the pattern seen in the previous acute climatic simulation imposed in July (Figure 2.18c). By the second year, the phytoplankton production rates followed very closely the rates seen in the high chronic simulation (Figure 2.19c). Likewise, the zooplankton population levels in the first year (Figure 2.20d) were the same as in the July acute case (Figure 2.18d), then followed quite closely the zooplankton biomass response seen in the high chronic only simulation (Figure 2.19d). These results clearly show no carryover effect across time from an acute to a chronic phase, again indicating a very rapid recovery response for the estuary ecosystem as a whole.

Some caution should be used in extrapolating from these simulations. While the model is reasonably well validated against real data for the Narragansett Bay (Kremer and Nixon, 1978), it is site specific and, therefore, may not reflect conditions in other estuaries, particularly those at different latitudes. Secondly, the model did not include the additional stresses on the Bay that could ensue from nearby detonations, increased sedimentation loading,

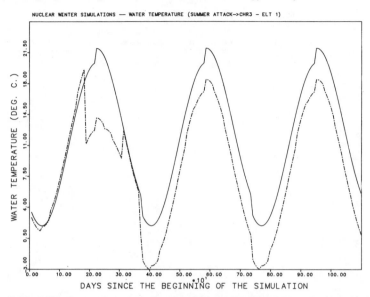

Figure 2.20a   Water temperatures used in the Narragansett Bay Model simulations for the acute-chronic case, with acute (10°C) decrease in air temperatures beginning 1 July for two months, then chronic decrease by 3°C (dashed line). Normal water temperatures shown by solid line

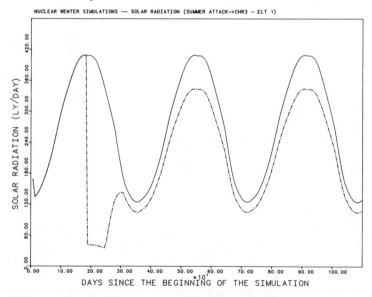

Figure 2.20b   Solar insolation used in the Narragansett Bay Model simulations for the acute-chronic case, with acute decrease by 90% beginning 1 July for two months, then chronic decrease by 13% (dashed line). Normal solar insolation shown by solid line

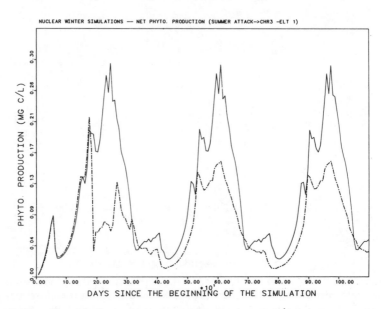

Figure 2.20c   Simulated phytoplankton biomass (mg C l⁻¹) for the acute-chronic
simulation specified in Figures 2.20a, b

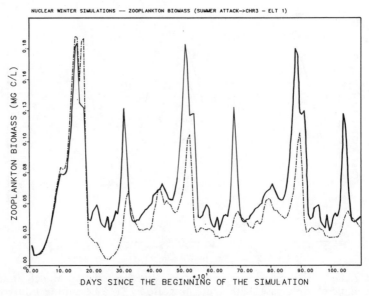

Figure 2.20d   Simulated zooplankton biomass (mg C l⁻¹) for the acute-chronic
simulation specified in Figures 2.20a, b

burdens of toxic chemicals, increased coastal storminess, and other physical disturbances. These could alter the response patterns, especially the recovery processes. Nevertheless, these simulations are instructive in evaluating the potential vulnerability of estuarine ecosystems to nuclear war.

2.3.2 Potential Effects on Freshwater Ecosystems [1]

2.3.2.1 Vulnerabilities to Potential Climatic Disturbances to Surface Water Systems

Freshwater ecosystems include lentic ecosystems (i.e., ponds and lakes) and lotic ecosystems (i.e., streams and rivers). These ecosystems range in scale from very small farm ponds to the Great Lakes, and from intermittent streams to the Amazon River. Figure 2.21 illustrates the major changes that could occur to the terrestrial hydrologic cycle in response to possible atmospheric changes following a nuclear war. In general, both reduced temperatures and reduced precipitation would lead to early reductions in the amount of liquid water stored at the surface in rivers and lakes. Groundwater would be much slower to change, and any alterations would be much slighter. Groundwater might be used as a drinking water source for humans, but only if there continued to be energy available to pump groundwater to the surface. Freezing of more readily available surface waters is, therefore, a very important question for humans and for other animals. It is useful to divide attention between those lakes and streams that normally experience freezing annually versus those freshwater ecosystems that never freeze over. Lakes store most of the Earth's fresh surface water; river channels contain relatively little water at any one time (Table 2.4); therefore, this discussion will concentrate on lakes.

The characteristics of lakes depend on their size, nutrient inputs, substrate, bedrock, surrounding watershed, precipitation, and a host of other factors. A discussion of the physical and chemical attributes of lakes is given in Rawson (1961); Brylinsky and Mann (1973); Margalef (1978); Forsberg and Ryding (1980); and Kalff and Knoechel (1978). The relationships between the physicochemical characteristics and the constituent biological communities are discussed in Jonasson (1970); Larkin and Northcote (1970); and Colby et al. (1972). Similar characterizations for stream ecosystems are presented in Horwitz (1978); Moyle and Li (1979); and Payson (1982).

The key issue for freshwater ecosystem responses to climatic disturbances is the possible reduction in temperature and, secondarily, the reduction in

---

[1] The discussions in this section are based on the freshwater working group at the Toronto conference, J.R. Kelly rapporteur, and on a discussion paper prepared by A. Keast. Model simulations were performed by V.M. Ponomarev, V.V. Ivanishchev, and V.V. Mikhailov.

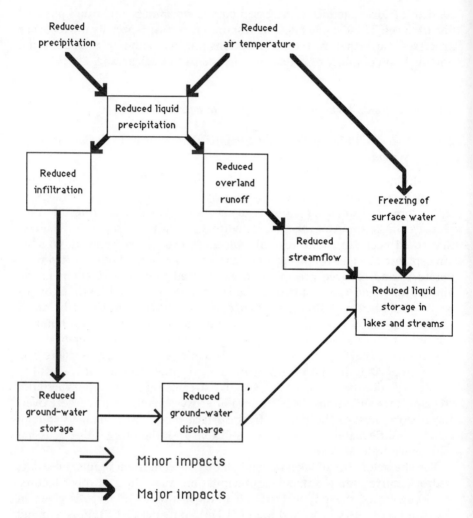

Figure 2.21 Potential mechanisms for climatic disturbance effects on the hydro-logic cycle

insolation. Temperature alterations are dampened considerably from the changes experienced by terrestrial ecosystems because of the high specific heat of water, especially for large bodies of freshwater. However, freshwater ecosystems are subject to potential adverse temperature impacts, unlike the situation in the open ocean ecosystems. It is instructive first to examine the temperature changes and responses of the normal ecosystems.

Air temperatures below freezing for long periods of time can produce a thick layer of ice. The thicker the ice, the greater the difficulty in breaking

TABLE 2.4

SELECTED COMPONENTS OF THE NORTHERN HEMISPHERE
WATER BALANCE[a]

COMPONENT	EUROPE	ASIA	NORTH AMERICA
Average water stored, rivers (km^3)	80	565	250
Inputs (km^3yr^{-1})			
from overland runoff	2090	10,660	5290
from ground water	1120	3750	2160
Outputs (km^3yr^1)	3210	14,410	7450
Average water stored, lakes (km^3)	2027	27,782	25,623
Average water stored, reservoirs (km^3)	422	1350	950

[a] From U.S.S.R. Committee for the International Hydrologic Decade (1977, 1978).

it and the longer the duration of the ice cover, restricting human access and potentially leading to anoxia under the ice cover, which could be lethal to some aquatic organisms. Thick ice on a shallow lake can tie up a significant fraction of its volume; this is another important measure of the impact of ice on freshwater ecosystems.

Soviet scientists have compiled statistics about lake sizes, which include surface area and total volume information, summarized in Table 2.5 (U.S.S.R. Committee 1977, 1978). One pattern to note is that the largest number of lakes, and, therefore, the most widely distributed and accessible to humans, is the category of the smallest and shallowest lakes, which would be most subject to having a substantial proportion of the volume tied up in ice. Table 2.6 shows calculated lake area and volume statistics.

This discussion focuses on lakes that routinely freeze over as instructive in how these ecosystems respond to freezing, and treats the other category of lakes in terms of sensitivity to freezing as similar to the summer lakes of northern climates. The characteristics of the lakes of eastern Ontario are noted as representative of temperate lakes, since the ranges of physical, chemical, and biological conditions among lakes globally are far too diverse for consideration in this study.

TABLE 2.5

DISTRIBUTION OF FRESHWATER LAKE AND RESERVOIR
VOLUMES AND AREAS[a]

AREA CLASS (km^2)	EUROPE			ASIA			NORTH AMERICA		
	No.	(km^2)	(km^3)	No.	(km^2)	(km^3)	No.	(km^2)	(km^3)
>10000	1	17,700	908	4	92,670	23,200	8	327,280	24,322
1000 - 10,000	26	74,989	995	21	67,070	3128	22	73,185	1258
100 - 1000	23	9618	479	36	16,760	520	17	7252	214

[a] Data summarized from U.S.S.R Committee for the International Hydrologic Decade
(1977, 1978);   Tamrazyan (1974); and Bowen (1982).

TABLE 2.6

DISTRIBUTION OF LAKE VOLUME BY DEPTH
FOR DIFFERENT SIZE CLASSES

LAKE AREA	PERCENTAGE OF TOTAL VOLUME[a] ABOVE GIVEN DEPTH					PERCENTAGE OF HEMISPHERE[b]	
Size Class Lake (km^2)	0.5m	1.0m	1.5m	2.0m	2.5m	Area	Volume
>10^4	0.5%	0.9%	1.3%	1.8%	2.2%	22%	86%
10^3- 10^4	2.0%	4.0%	5.8%	7.6%	9.2%	11%	10%
10^2- 10^3	1.4%	2.8%	4.2%	5.5%	6.8%	2%	2%
10 - 10^2	14%	27%	38%	49%	58%	12%	0.8%
1 - 10	28%	50%	68%	81%	91%	19%	0.6%
<1	56%	88%	100%	100%	100%	35%	0.5%

[a] Calculations were made by assuming that lakes are shaped like elliptic sinusoids, whose volume is
stated by: V = 1.456 abz; a and b = radii, z = maximum depth.
[b] Size statistics summarized from U.S.S.R. Committee for the International Hydrologic Decade (1977)
for lakes over 100 km^2 area; from Tamrazyn (1974) and Bowen (1982) for smaller lakes.

Northern lake ecosystems are subject to an extensive cover of ice (1.5–2.0 m), extending from November or December until April or May, alternating with periods of open water. Most of the biological activity, including photosynthesis, feeding, growth, reproduction, and decomposition occur during the open water period. Those activities that do continue through the winter months tend to operate at much reduced rates. With spring ice melt, water warming is accelerated until it reaches a maximum in August, from which it returns to freezing by the end of the year. Plant growth commences in May, with the greatest biomass being achieved from late July until early September (Craig, 1976). The spring and summer period is also characterized by rapid buildup in the animal populations, with fluctuations in population levels thereafter.

Fish populations typically begin breeding in the spring and continue through the summer. There is a marked temporal component to this, with different species undergoing reproduction at different times, thereby reducing direct competition for food among the young of the year. Breeding times are determined by temperature and day lengths (Keast, 1977). All fish species in these Northern lakes follow a consistent metabolic pattern, however. The annual cycle requires that they restore body energy reserves following the winter period of low food availability and low temperatures; feed, grow, and reproduce during the summer; and lay down body fat as energy reserves for the succeeding winter. There is probably little resistance to changes in the physical parameters controlling the development of these stages.

Disruption in any of the life history phases would lead to at least the loss of a new age class, and severe perturbations would lead to the loss of adults. The consequences of the former depend on the longevity of the adults and the number of age classes in the population at any point in time; for instance, if a fish lives and reproduces for 5 years, then the loss of a new age class would not devastate the population, whereas loss of an age class in a shorter-lived species or in one that only reproduces once, would have far more serious effects. Likewise, stresses that result in direct mortality of the adults could lead to at least local extermination of a population.

Biological impacts would follow from freezing of the water in freshwater ecosystems during the spring-summer for temperate lakes, or any time for more southerly lakes. Thus, the extent of freezing likely to be experienced is one factor in analyzing the potential effects of climatic disturbances on freshwater ecosystems. Calculations performed by Pacenka, reported in Harwell (1984), indicate that freshwater ecosystems of the Northern Hemisphere would freeze in response to climatic disturbances associated with a large-scale nuclear war, with ice thicknesses forming to 0.5–1.2 m, depending on the specific scenario of nuclear war. However, these calculations were based on a hemispherically and annually averaged temperature and, therefore, did not account for the effects of seasonality, either of the temperature reduction itself, or of the base normal temperature to which the decrements were applied. Further, the calculations did not account for differences across latitudes or in mid-continental versus coastal areas. Therefore, the actual extent of freezing that would be experienced following a climatic disturbance requires further analysis.

One basis for evaluating potential effects on lake ecosystems is the study by Ponomarev et al. (1984), done for the SCOPE–ENUWAR project. These researchers used the Lake Ecosystem Simulation Model developed at the U.S.S.R. Academy of Sciences Leningrad Research Computer Center. This model is being developed and validated for evaluating the dynamics of lake ecosystems and their constituent species, the relationships between lakes and their watersheds, and the effects of industrial development on lakes. The model consists of three biotic compartments (phytoplankton, zooplankton, and detritus) linked to nitrogen, phosphorus, sediment, dissolved oxygen, air temperature, insolation, and radiation factors (Figure 2.22). The simulation of severe climatic perturbations was done by reducing air temperatures by 15°C within 20 days, returning to a 5°C deficit by about the 120th day after a nuclear war occurring in either February or July; concomitant reductions in insolation were imposed in the simulations.

Results from the February nuclear war are shown in Figure 2.23, where the normal and hypothetical climatic alteration curves are shown for water temperature, insolation, phytoplankton biomass, zooplankton biomass, detritus biomass, and mineral-to-organic nitrogen ratio. The phytoplankton population in these ecosystems demonstrates a rapid decrease from a rather high normal level in the winter; this population recovers rapidly after insolation levels return to normal by the end of the summer, even though temperature levels at that time are still significantly depressed. This suggests that phytoplankton biomass is more sensitive to light level reductions than to temperature reductions. The zooplankton population suffers an immediate decline and does not recover within a year, presumably because of the loss of food resources. The development of anoxia in the water is predicted in the model to occur from an increase in the detritus, which contributes to increased respiration rates and depletion of dissolved oxygen at a time when photosynthesis is suppressed.

Effects from climatic alterations imposed on the July simulation are more dramatic and long-lasting (Figure 2.24). The recovery of temperatures and insolation would occur in this scenario just at the onset of the normal winter period, thereby prolonging the total period of low light and temperature levels. This results in the essential loss of phytoplankton activity for an entire year, with associated loss of zooplankton. However, the model results indicate rapid recovery of phytoplankton and zooplankton populations upon resumption of insolation at normal levels the following summer.

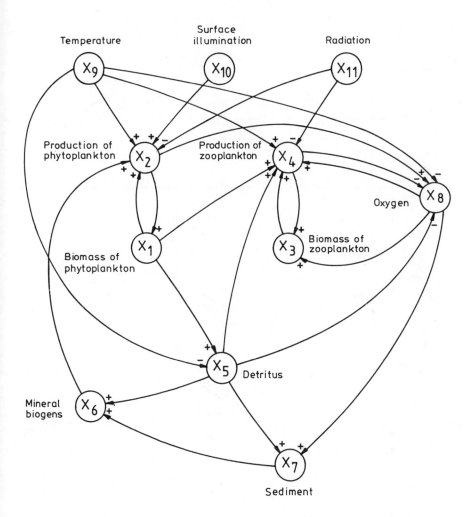

Figure 2.22 Conceptual framework for the Soviet lake ecosystem model. After Ponomarev et al. (1984)

These simulations are instructive for characterizing the response of lake ecosystems with respect to energetics and material flow. A simulation that takes into account the populational responses of primary and secondary producers, including the life cycle dynamics of fish and other fauna, has not been done. These considerations, by necessity, were addressed in the ENUWAR workshops in qualitative discussions among appropriate experts. The pattern of biological responses developed by these groups follows.

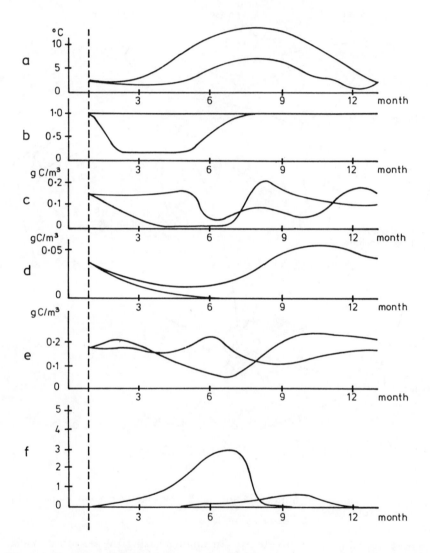

Figure 2.23 Dynamics of major lake ecosystem components after a February war. a—mean lake water temperature; b—relative surface insolation level; c, d, e—biomass of phytoplankton, zooplankton, and detritus (g C m^{-3}; f—mineral to organic nitrogen ratio. After Ponomarev et al.(1984)

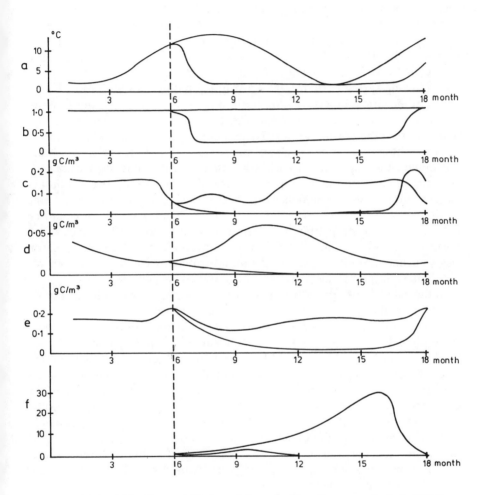

Figure 2.24   As in Figure 2.23 for a July war. After Ponomarev et al. (1984)

If nuclear war-induced climatic disturbances were to occur in the winter in regions where the lakes normally were near freezing, ice cover thickness could increase. With minimal temperature decrease, this might have no effect, but in greater temperature declines, the increased ice thickness, especially coupled with lower insolation levels, could reduce ongoing photosynthesis and associated oxygen levels to the point where phytoplankton could die and the ecosystem could become anoxic. In shallow lakes, freezing could occur to the bottom, killing most of the biota in the lake. In streams that normally experience some freezing, a winter-onset war could result in the formation of anchor ice, i.e., ice forming at the bottom even though the entire water column was not frozen. Such a situation could also result in death to many of the stream organisms. A winter acute disturbance affecting freshwater ecosystems that do not normally freeze over could lead to marked biological effects, as the species present would not be adapted to such conditions. The duration of freezing for those lakes would extend into the following spring period, totally disrupting biological activities.

A chronic climatic perturbation beginning in the spring, or the carryover effect from a winter-onset nuclear war, could delay melting of the ice remaining from the normal winter. There would be a delay in the initiation of photosynthesis and the life cycles of many animals. For example, fish would not initiate their spawning cycles, since these are dependent on increasing both the photoperiod and temperature (de Vlaming, 1972). If they did begin spawning, it would be delayed so that there would be insufficient time for life cycle completion prior to the following winter, and there would be greatly enhanced competition for limited resources across fish species which normally did not overlap in their timing but for whom the available season was shortened. Similar delays and timing problems would occur even for those lakes in the southern regions which did not experience freezing.

In the case of late spring freeze, or a freezing event for southern lakes at any time of the year, there would likely be wholesale elimination of biota from the direct effects of temperature and light reductions. Plants would cease photosynthesis and animals cease feeding. The active areas in the littoral zones of larger lakes would be especially affected, including the areas where much of the reproductive cycle would be underway, and at least the new age class, and perhaps the total populations, of most species would be eliminated. If freezing occurred in summer, however, effects would possibly be less immediately deleterious, since many of the sensitive life stages would have been completed; the effect would depend on the extent of freezing as to whether adult organisms suffered direct mortality. However, the outlook for those who did survive the initial period would be poor, since insufficient feeding would likely have occurred to store enough body fat to get through the following winter. The duration of effects would be particularly important the following spring.

Climatic disturbances during the fall would appear to be the least consequential for northern freshwater ecosystems, since the organisms would have passed the reproductive stages and feeding requirements of the current year and would have already initiated acclimation to winter conditions (Weiser, 1973). For more southerly lakes and streams, however, the effects would still be severe, because those ecosystems would not have begun winter acclimation.

The longer-term factors affecting freshwater ecosystem recovery include the potential loss of fish species in individual lakes, for which recolonization is a large problem because of isolation from other sources. The invertebrate, phytoplankton, and decomposer populations, however, even if they had suffered widespread mortality, should recover once the climatic conditions returned to near normal. Nevertheless, the ecosystem as a whole could continue to show residual effects for long periods of time, including the possibility of some irreversible effects.

2.4 POTENTIAL EFFECTS ON TROPICAL ECOSYSTEMS [1]

2.4.1 Introduction

The potential responses of tropical ecological and agricultural systems to climatic disturbances after nuclear war were discussed at the SCOPE-ENUWAR tropical workshop. Though there was a focus on American tropical and sub-tropical systems, it was felt that many of the discussions and conclusions could be extrapolated to tropical systems in Asia, Australia, and Africa.

In order to have a framework for considering effects on tropical systems, probable responses of a number of key tropical ecosystems were examined. Similar to the temperate ecosystem analyses, a set of perturbations was considered to establish the *vulnerability* of tropical ecosystems to the types of climatic alterations possible after a nuclear war, rather than analyzing a single particular scenario. Vulnerability to reduced temperature was examined for a severe acute phase, characterized by freezing temperatures occurring for brief periods, and for chronic temperature declines of 1°C to 5°C for extended periods of time. Precipitation declines of 25%, 50%, or more were considered. The effects of light reductions of up to 90% in an acute phase and 1% to 10% in a chronic phase were considered. For each of these physical disturbances, no prediction is made that it necessarily would occur at a particular location or in a particular time period.

Since many tropical systems have seasonal rains, climatic perturbations occurring both in wet and dry seasons were examined. Temperature and light seasonality in the tropics would be of limited significance because of the even daylight-night hours and the general limited temperature fluctuations on a monthly or annual basis. Near sea level, the mean monthly air temperature at most tropical stations is between 20°C to 30°C in every month of the year. Mean temperature fluctuates from day to day around the monthly mean in response to local synoptic weather patterns, but the changes are less

---

[1] This section is based primarily on the tropical ecological working group discussions at Caracas, Venezuela, chaired by T.C. Hutchinson.

frequent and less abrupt in the tropics than in temperate latitudes. Diurnal temperature fluctuations are even further reduced within the forest than out in the open or above the canopy. The diurnal fluctuations in temperature may be larger and more important to plant growth and animal activity than monthly fluctuations in temperature. The adaptation to this constancy of temperature makes biotic systems more vulnerable to extreme episodic temperature excursions. These are nearly always declines, and in the case of the friagems extending into Amazonia they can cause severe damage.

Major mountain ranges are found in the tropics, especially in South and Central America, and at sufficiently high altitudes these have either ice or snow fields. The decrease in temperature attributable to altitude is about 0.6 °C per 100 m, in the lowest 1.5 km (Monteith, 1977). At the higher altitudes frosts are often a daily event (e.g., in Mount Kilimanjaro in Africa or in the puna and paramo regions of the Andes). The altitudinal zonation of vegetation on these mountains in general parallels the latitudinal zonation.

The annual range in daily solar insolation is much smaller in the tropics than in temperate latitudes. Annual insolation ranges from about 8GJ m^{-2} on the margins of the subtropical deserts to 5GJ m^{-2} in wet equatorial regions. Daylength is just over 12 hours throughout the year at the equator and ranges from 10.6 to 13.7 at latitude 25°. While the range of daylength is also much less than in temperate regions, the development of tropical crops and native vegetation is nevertheless related to changes in day length.

Rainfall may be uniform and high (e.g., in coastal regions of evergreen forests or in central continental regions such as Zaire and Amazonia), or it may be strongly seasonal (e.g., the extreme seasonality of the monsoons of Asia and Africa). In some higher altitude forests, much precipitation occurs by contact with clouds and fogs, allowing the development of cloud forests. Seasonal droughts are characteristic of tropical grasslands, savannahs, and deciduous forests. Deciduous trees are numerous in the rainforests in all parts of the tropics and are present even in climates with an almost uniformly distributed rainfall (e.g., in Singapore and in the New Hebrides) (Richards, 1966). As the precipitation limit of the rainforest is approached, the proportion of deciduous species gradually increases, first in the upper, then in the lower stories.

The following sections focus on several ecosystem types occurring in the tropics. The estimates of potential vulnerabilities are based primarily on the direct effects of climatic disturbances on the ecosystems. It should be kept in mind for ecosystems in general, and particularly for tropical ecosystems, that indirect effects would likely be widespread, affecting species not vulnerable to direct effects and extending ecosystem effects over time. Further, the potential for synergisms is very high, but predictions are very tenuous. Consequently, the vulnerability of tropical ecosystems to specific perturbations is likely to be greater than projected here.

2.4.2 Vulnerabilities of Tropical Ecosystems to Potential Climatic Disturbances

2.4.2.1 Evergreen Tropical Rainforest

The evergreen tropical rainforest is characterized by a lack of seasonality in temperature, rainfall, light intensity, and photoperiod. Light intensity declines sharply through the canopy strata to ground level. These forests have a very uniform environment and great species richness and diversity in both plants and animals. The three major evergreen rainforest areas are in: 1.) South and Central America and the Caribbean, 2.) the Indo-Malayan region, and 3.) central Africa. Perennial plants dominate, and annuals are very rare. Soil types differ considerably, but are often deep, ancient soils leached by high rainfall and with a poor nutrient status. Major nutrients are often deficient in the soils, and nutrient turn-over and litter decomposition are very rapid. Epiphytes are abundant, increasing in frequency at higher altitudes as relative humidity rises. Pollination is predominantly by insects or birds, rather than the wind-pollination typical for temperate trees. Many animals are arboreal.

In considering the vulnerabilities of these ecosystems to near- or sub-freezing episodes, it was felt that *all* photosynthetic aboveground plant tissues would be killed rapidly, as tropical plants are very sensitive to chilling. They neither chill- nor frost-harden as do temperate plants, nor do they have the genetic-physiological capacity to acclimate to such extremes. In contrast, reductions of a few degrees in a chronic situation would not likely have major impacts on these ecosystems. The critical phenomenon for tropical lowland ecosystems would be the occurrence of episodes of low temperatures.

If a freezing event were short, i.e., up to a week, then *some* limited recovery could be expected through aboveground sprouting, coppicing, or production of adventitious buds on the trunks and stems. The position of the apical meristems of tropical species well above the ground put them in a most exposed position (phanerophytes), and protective bud scales are absent. Many tropical palms would be killed also because of their exposed meristem, though some of the palms would be able to regenerate from underground rhizomes. Bamboo and other species that sprout from below or near the ground would be better able to survive and regenerate because of the insulation provided to their meristems.

Most forest trees and shrubs in evergreen tropical forests have limited seed banks, and those seeds that are present are primarily of the current year and lack a dormant phase. These seeds are often fleshy or contained within fleshy fruit. Seeds in the soil could be killed because they are not deeply buried or covered with a thick litter layer. The drought- and cold-resistant seeds typical of grasslands, savannahs, and temperate systems are largely absent. Instead of a seed bank, the forest floor often contains a seedling bank. Seedlings and saplings are cold sensitive, so that future reserves would be killed by freezing episodes along with the parent trees.

Those seeds that might survive brief extremes of temperatures belong to pioneer species. Secondary species occur in small numbers in natural openings, such as where large trees have fallen and opened the canopy (Richards, 1966). Such naturally weedy species have adaptations that enable them to exploit open situations, and they often can regenerate from rootstocks. Palms with hard seeds may also be able to regenerate even if the parents are killed. The amount of moisture available for seed imbibition could be important. If the seeds were at low temperatures in wet soils, then their viability would decrease considerably.

The limited regeneration after an acute temperature decline would yield only a small fraction of the former species diversity. For example, Chevalier (1909) reported that the secondary forests of the Ivory Coast, after clearance and burning, consisted of about 30 species of trees, while that of the virgin forest consisted of 250–300.

When extensive clearing occurs in evergreen tropical forests, recovery can be very slow. For example, savannah occurs in extensive areas adjacent to evergreen forests for which the climate is appropriate for evergreen forests (e.g., Sumatra and Venezuela), but such forests do not occur because fire prevents successional development. Similarly, in Guiana and Belize, thorn forests and dwarf forests are believed to be secondary as a result of ancient human interference. These successional forests are composed of fast-growing but short-lived species, which would add to the instability of the recovery process.

Most of the secondary forest species would be at an advantage in a recovery phase after a nuclear-war induced climatic disturbance, since they can regenerate in high light conditions, whereas many of the virgin forest species require low light levels. Since most evergreen tree and shrub species would be killed in a freezing episode, there would be high light intensities at the forest floor and a substantial accumulation of dead wood and organic matter.

Reliable models are lacking for predicting animal responses during an acute freezing phase. The effects of freezing or chilling would be severe on animals that are accustomed to warm, constant environments. Since most rainforest animal species are arboreal, they would not survive in areas experiencing total devastation of the forest trees. Generally, larger animals would be most vulnerable to cold temperatures. Large carnivores are the most likely to survive during the short term, since there would be plenty of meat (carcasses) available. Hibernating animals do not have an advantage since hibernation is physiologically complex and cannot be induced without the proper environmental cues. Most soil-dwelling insects or those that are not food specialists might survive even extreme temperatures. Fruit-eating bird species, comprising the majority of the rainforest avifauna, have high metabolic requirements and would die where their food source was destroyed. Bird species that occur or are able to migrate to coastal areas, where the temperature extremes are not expected to be as severe, would have better survival rates. Migratory birds would have the capability of moving to a better climate, though this response is felt to be tenuous as migratory instincts might miscue.

2.4.2.2 Deciduous (Seasonal) Forests

Tropical deciduous forests occur at the margins of evergreen rainforest, where seasonal rains prevail, and in areas experiencing monsoons. Such rainforests occur in India, Burma, Indochina, East Africa, North Australia, and South America. Annual drought, characteristic of such forests, affects the vegetation in a number of ways. Most trees lose their leaves during the dry season. The duration of this leaf loss depends upon soil moisture; for example, along river banks where moisture is plentiful, leaf loss is reduced. Even in the deciduous forest, a number of evergreen species occur (Vickery, 1984). These evergreen species have small, leathery leaves, which are often are highly toxic to consumers and which are similar to leaves on Mediterranean species, in contrast to the large leaf forms of the deciduous species. In Australia, where this forest is extensive inland in the northeast, merging into savannah and thornscrub, the ground flora is often of tussocky C_4 grasses with high root:shoot ratios (3:1 to 10:1), and forest species include large evergreen *Eucalyptus* species. In South America in the zone between the deciduous and evergreen forests, the upper tree story is made up of deciduous thick-trunked *Bombidaceae*, while the lower stories are still evergreen, so that the forests can be termed tropical semi-evergreen (Walter, 1973).

The stratification of the canopy is simpler, and since more light reaches the ground, the shrub layers are thicker than for rainforests. Most herbs produce their leaves and flowers during the wet season, and survive the drought period in dormancy, often as bulbs, corms, or tubers. Annuals complete their life cycle in the wet season, and their seeds lie dormant in the soil through the drought. Many of the deciduous forest trees flower at the end of the dry season, enabling ripening of fruit and seeds to occur when water is plentiful. Bird and insect pollination predominates. Epiphytes are much less common than in the evergreen forests.

During the dry season tropical deciduous forests are very susceptible to fire. Most trees have evolved thick and often deeply fissured bark as an adaptation to fire.

Extreme temperature reductions during the wet season would be as devastating for seasonal forests as they would be at any time for evergreen tropical rainforests. If cold temperatures occurred during the dry season, many tree species would be dormant and without leaves. Herbaceous species might survive as underground perennating organs. Thus, overall effects of freezing would not be as great as during the wet season, but extinction of sensitive species could still occur. If the freeze were prolonged or repeated during the growing season, there could be death of virtually all existing vegetation. For the chronic period, the deciduous forest species are expected to be more hardy than those of the evergreen forest because temperature and drought fluctuations are both greater in these systems. With a drop of a few degrees, most plant species would survive intact, but at more extreme chronic temperature reductions, some species would grow very poorly and might experience chill damage.

Recovery would be more rapid in deciduous tropical forests than in evergreen forests because of better seed survival, a larger seed bank, and better sprouting ability. If frosts occurred when the trees were flowering at the end of the dry season, an entire seed year could be lost, along with the pollinators. There are features of drought tolerance which would also enhance frost (or chilling) tolerances (Ivory and Whiteman, 1978a, 1978b). Many of the grasses would have intact seed banks, and the trees have deep tap roots, especially on sandy soils. Similarly, thick, fire-tolerant bark would enhance frost-tolerance. In areas which experience ground fires frequently, the vegetation would be better pre-adapted to the acute phase of climatic disturbances. Recovery, as a result of re-sprouting, coppicing, adventitious shoots, and stolons, would occur as it does for many species in the post-fire phase. The deep roots of the deciduous trees and shrubs would also provide some protection and enhance recovery.

Animals would suffer a high mortality from chilling and freezing events, especially if they occurred in the wet season when species would be active and arboreal. In the dry season, many animals stay closer to the water and would be less vulnerable. Some, such as armadillos and a few rodents, would be protected by burrowing. Homoiothermic animals might die from chilling if they became wet before freezing occurred. Long-term continuation of reduced temperatures could lead to gradual replacement of animal species.

Birds inhabiting the deciduous rainforest could suffer the same stresses as those in the evergreen forest. The omnivorous, wide-ranging species, such as vultures, would have the best chance of survival. The insects of the deciduous forest would have a better chance of survival than in tropical rainforests, since in the dry season their eggs are able to survive low temperatures and the metabolic activity of the adults can slow down.

Vulnerability to reduced light levels is much less than the vulnerability to temperature reductions, so that even a large decrease in light accompanying acute temperature reductions would be merely an additional stress factor for vegetation. A maximum light reduction of 10% during a chronic perturbation probably would not result in major effects.

Tropical deciduous forest ecosystems are often fire-adapted. Germination of many seeds are favored by fires, and the longevity of the seed bank is greater than in the evergreen forest. In South America, for example, palms are fairly long lived and produce drought-tolerant, thick-walled seeds. If fires occurred in the growing season, the seed bank would lose one year of input, which for some species could be a very high percentage. If most vegetation were killed in an extreme temperature episode, the subsequent fuel load would be high. If the precipitation were also reduced, then fires would be a certainty. Such fires could be much more severe than those normally experienced, eliminating the remaining aboveground surviving shoots and seedlings. High temperatures at the soil surface could destroy the seed bank. If fires occurred after a chronic temperature phase, the fuel load on the ground would be much less. Fires under these circumstances would be similar to those occurring normally in the deciduous forests, and the fire adaptation of the plants would enable many or most to survive.

An extreme situation of prolonged periods of very low levels of precipitation could turn the deciduous forest into a desert within a few years. A smaller decrease in precipitation might allow for some acclimation of species, but with considerably slower growth and with xeric species being favored. The distribution of precipitation is an important consideration, both spatially and temporally. Lower precipitation would be less of a factor here than a similar percentage drop in evergreen forest.

2.4.2.3 Montane–Cloud Forest

Orographic precipitation occurs as air masses ascend mountainous areas. Dry seasons occurring in the lowlands become shorter with increasing altitude, or disappear altogether. Also, temperature decreases, and clouds and fog drift through the trees on a daily basis, maintaining a very high humidity. These conditions result in montane–cloud forests, characterized by a two-story structure. Cloud forests are found between 1000 m and 2500 m, but up to 3400 m in some regions.

The continuous fogs cause low direct light intensities, so the ground flora are not as rich as in the evergreen lowland forest. Temperature is lower but almost constant. Such climate conditions encourage the growth of epiphytes. Bamboos in Asia and Africa are the dominant species of the wet low slopes of cloud forests, while *Selaginella* covers open ground. Tree ferns are also numerous in South America, southern Asia, and New Zealand. Walter (1973) notes that in many tropical mountain regions, the wettest altitudinal belt is characterized by palms or dense bamboo stands.

In the montane–cloud forest, the great majority of the trees are evergreen, and rather few are buttressed. Some trees are very large, especially at lower altitudes. At very high altitudes, the trees become dwarfed and gnarled with twisted branches, forming elfin forests. At higher altitudes, conifers enter the community. As the trees are eliminated, a shrub zone occurs, narrow in altitudinal range. The treeline may be determined by precipitation or the occurrence of frost at high elevations, where temperatures can drop below freezing point at night for a few hours (Walter and Medina, 1969).

An extreme temperature drop to below freezing would be devastating. Most trees and shrubs would be killed within a few days as the cold penetrated the trunks and caused ice formation in the tissues. The shallow roots of many species could be killed by the cold. However, leaf litter is greater in these forests than in evergreen forest, so that some soil protection might be provided. Erosion on steep slopes would be substantial. The upper slope parts of these forests are likely to be more cold-adapted than lower areas and also better adapted to reduced precipitation and humidity. Species with coppicing potential and those with seeds having a thick protective coat would be at an advantage in regeneration.

The consequences of ambient drops in temperature during the chronic phase of climatic disturbances would most impact root systems. The length of the chronic phase and its severity would ultimately determine the amount of altitudinal destruction of forest taking place because of soil mean temperature effects alone. At the timberline, roots require a soil temperature of 7–8°C. If an ambient drop of 5°C occurred, treeline species would die. For those mid-altitude cloud forest species which require root-soil temperatures of 10°C–12°C, then clearly more dramatic declines would be expected in the forests.

For montane-cloud forest systems under chronic perturbations, there could be severe damage at timberline even if the ambient temperature were reduced by less than 5°C. The timberline would probably shift down by 800 m with a 5°C decrease in temperature. Since light would likely be decreased along with temperatures, many of the plants requiring insolation for heating the rocks and soils in which they live would suffer from further decreases in their ambient temperature. Further from the timberline, species would not suffer such extremes. However, erosion on steep slopes could be severe.

Many animal species in these ecosystems are quite vulnerable to subfreezing temperatures; e.g., in Central and South America, no monkeys occur above 2500 m, suggesting thermal intolerance to low temperatures. Burrowing animals such as the agouti would probably survive if the acute phase were not prolonged. Large predators, such as the ocelot and jaguar, could be able to migrate to more favorable conditions. Tree-dwelling animals such as sloths and monkeys would be particularly vulnerable, just as in evergreen forests. Birds in the cloud forest are fairly specialized, often feeding on fruit and restricted in altitudinal range. If their food supplies were destroyed by frost and cold, many birds would perish.

Since a 30–40% decrease in precipitation is within the normal variability of this ecosystem type, vegetation can tolerate a decrease of 30% for up to a year. The epiphytic community would be the most vulnerable. A 30% decrease in incidence of fog could have a significant effect in a dry cloud forest, since it is dependent on frequent episodes of moisture. A long-term reduction in temperature by a few degrees coupled with reductions in precipitation would result in significant damage within one or two years and a drastic change in species composition over longer periods.

Greater decreases in precipitation would increase the risk of fire. The frequency of fires would increase as a result of human activities. Fires would cause large-scale erosion on slopes and loss of seed banks.There is a high percentage of plants with fleshy fruit in the tropical cloud forest and their seed would be destroyed by fire. Further, the seedling bank, which is relied upon for recovery processes, is particularly vulnerable to fires.

The recovery of the cloud forest after extensive fires would be most rapid in the valleys because of increased moisture availability. Erosion on the slopes would favor the invasion of grasses and shrubs rather than cloud forest species, which require greater soil depths. Palms would not re-sprout, though the ability of their seeds to survive might be high.

2.4.2.4 Tropical Alpine Systems

In the wet tropics, the alpine region (páramo) is almost perpetually wet, misty, and cold, with frequent night frosts and seasonal precipitation. The plants are adapted to continuous freezing and thawing cycle, primarily relying on supercooling. During the flowering season, the upper soil layers warm during the day to temperatures above the annual mean. A rocky habitat is more favorable for this than a wet, cold soil.

Tropical alpine ecosystems would not be totally devastated by an acute phase reduction in temperatures; some of the vegetation might be able to withstand up to a 7–8°C drop. Those species that presently tolerate a 15°C diurnal cycle through cold-temperature avoidance mechanisms would be able to survive a 10–15°C drop. Those plant species that supercool could not withstand these temperature drops. The duration of the temperature drop would have to be brief for plants to survive; for instance, after three days, the meristems would suffer because they are adapted to daily freezing or thawing, not to continuous freezing.

If precipitation were severely reduced, fires could occur, as they now do on occasion in the lower páramo. However, fuel loads would be low, and fires are less likely in tropical alpine ecosystems than in almost any other tropical ecosystem. The puna and lower pramo might recover in some areas from fires, because most of the reproductive organs are in the soil.

Tropical alpine areas would not suffer greatly during the chronic phase in terms of survival, since supercooling ability of plants increases with lower availability of resources, though growth rate may be decreased. Aggressive, weedy alpine species might be able to colonize areas where other vegetation was lost. If much vegetation were lost, the possibility of landslides and avalanches increases. Freezing of the alpine watershed could occur with a temperature drop of 10°C at high altitudes.

It is anticipated that many endemic animals (e.g., vicuña, alpaca, llama, chinchilla, and vizcacha) would migrate from areas of temperature extremes. However, the specialization in feeding behavior of these animals might limit their survival in areas with a different plant composition. For example, condors, which are found from sea level to 5000 m, should be able to migrate to areas with accessible food; on the other hand, high-altitude flamingos, giant coots, and plovers might be able to move down, but they require open water for feeding and would not survive for more than a few days without food.

2.4.2.5 Tropical Grasslands and Savannahs

Tropical grasslands and savannahs are widely distributed in South America, Australia, Africa, and Indo-Malaysia. The transition from open forest with grassy undergrowth (savannah-woodland) to true savannah is gradual. In many cases savannahs and grasslands are of anthropogenic origin from grazing, burning, and shifting cultivation; some are quite ancient. Indeed, the ease of burning and clearance for agriculture currently results in an expansion of these ecosystems.

Annual rainfall in the tropical grasslands varies from 75 mm to over 1500 mm and is generally seasonal. Grasses can utilize the water of the wet season very effectively. At the end of the rainy season when water becomes scarce, transpiration continues until the leaves and usually the entire aerial shoot system dies. Only the root system and the terminal growing point of the shoot survive. This intercalary meristem (between the root and the shoot) is well protected during the ensuing drought by the many layers of dried-out leaf sheaths. The high rainfall of many savannahs, such as the llanos of Venezuela, is more characteristic of deciduous tropical forests. Trees are present in natural savannahs if there remains sufficient water at the end of the rainy season to support maintenance of tree and shrubland roots through the following dry season. In some areas where savannah occurs, but where the climate is typical of deciduous tropical forests, the determining factor in savannah establishment is soil type. This is the case in the very extensive llanos area of Venezuela and Colombia, where a hard lateritic crust is formed between 30–80 cm depth, cemented by ferric hydroxide.

The mean temperature of the tropical grasslands varies between 22–28°C, with greater seasonal fluctuations than in the forested regions. In higher altitude grasslands, such as in East Africa and Australia, cool or cold nights are common. In Australia, the presence of woody species (*Acacia* and *Eucalyptus*) offers a more forested appearance than occurs elsewhere in the world under similar climatic conditions because of the tolerances to drought and fire of these genera.

Grazing by livestock in tropical grasslands reduces foliar leaf area, thereby reducing evapotranspiration and increasing soil moisture content. This allows shrubs and trees to colonize. Since thornbushes are able to tolerate grazing, grazed grasslands have a strong tendency to change to secondary thornscrubs, as in Australia, Africa, and South America, as well as in warm temperate regions such as Texas in the southern U.S. If a higher human population density occurs in these areas, the bush is often used for fuel, and overuse eventually leads to desert conditions.

Other factors affecting the composition of the grasslands and savannahs are grazing by large herbivores, such as the wildebeest and antelopes of East Africa and kangaroos in Australia, and the frequent occurrence of fires in the dry season. Deliberate annual fires set just before the wet season have a large influence on species composition of tropical grasslands, especially when this is followed immediately by cattle or sheep grazing.

A few days of sub-freezing temperature during the wet season would kill aboveground plant tissues. The dominant C_4 grasses are unable to tolerate temperatures much below freezing, and some suffer chilling injury at $+2°C$ to $+4°C$ (Ivory and Whiteman, 1978a, 1978b). As temperatures ameliorated, herbs and grasses would re-sprout from rhizomes and crowns, and the trees and shrubs by coppicing. If the freezing occurred in the dry season, damage to grasses might be very limited because of protected and insulated meristems. If the freezing or severe chilling were to occur for more than a few days, then all vegetation could be expected to die. Some regeneration could be expected from seed banks. These systems are much more vulnerable to temperature variations than to changes in light, so that acute decreases in light levels are not likely to add to effects on these ecosystems.

Large mammals, especially grazing animals, could die from loss of heat (body chilling) and lack of food if severe temperature decreases occurred during the wet, growing season. Carnivores would have a better food supply, consisting of carcasses, than herbivores. If acute temperature decreases did not last more than a few weeks, carnivores might survive. However, if heavy rains occurred at temperatures near freezing point, then chilling effects might predominate. Adult insects would die from subfreezing episodes, but survival of the eggs and diapausing insects in the dry season would be likely. Reptiles, amphibia, and many birds would die in an acute phase. If more favorable areas are within reach, then mobile species might survive.

Because of the potential support to surviving human populations by grasslands, the sensitivity of Serengeti grassland ecosystems to potential chronic phase temperature and light reductions was simulated with a previously developed computer model (Coughenour et al., 1984). These simulation results apply only to grasslands not severely damaged by acute phase climatic disturbances. The results must not be interpreted as predictions of post-nuclear war productivity levels in Serengeti grasslands, but should be used in conjunction with other judgments of potential responses.

Baseline production in the simulated grassland is about 350 gC m^{-2} yr^{-1}, with 900 mm of annual precipitation. The combined effects of reducing mean temperature 5°C or less and reducing insolation 6–22% below normal were seen in the simulations to *increase* primary productivity. This pattern was observed whether or not grazing was included in the model. These simulated climatic alterations tend to decrease moisture stress, but decreased precipitation levels could greatly reduce productivity.

In most savannahs, water supply is the limiting factor. A reduction in overall annual precipitation of 25%, 50%, or more would cause substantial reduction in primary production. If seasonality were lost but overall amounts of precipitation were maintained, production would still be reduced, as endogenous dormancy reduces the ability to benefit from dry season rains. Shrubs and trees would benefit, but grasses would suffer. If this occurred, the system would move towards a desert ecosystem, especially if 50% or greater reduction in precipitation occurred. The last decade in the Sahel of North Africa demonstrate this effect of decreased precipitation. In grasslands and savannahs with greater than 1000 mm rainfall per year, the effects of decreased precipitation would be less. Maintenance of reduced rains for a number of years would have major effects, causing changes in species composition and ultimately threatening survival of the ecosystem.

Subtropical grasslands and savannahs in Africa and South America might be the least affected of the terrestrial ecosystems, because plants are more cold tolerant and drought resistant, and there is a reservoir of C_3 plants which can maintain net production under cooler, lower light conditions (McNaughton and Medina, 1985). The sensitivity of tropical grasslands is substantially larger, but the dry season adaptations and the temperature fluctuations, especially in higher altitude ecosystems such as in East Africa, enhance their probability of survival. Grassland-savannah ecosystems in general are more robust to climatic stresses than are evergreen tropical forests, montane–cloud forests, or mangroves.

Tropical grasslands often have a history of burning by humans and are adapted to fire. The frequency of natural tropical grassland fires initiated by lightning is much rarer than in the temperate ecosystems because of the high precipitation which usually accompanies storms (Rundel, 1981). Decreased precipitation, if occurring post-nuclear war, would increase the fuel combustability of grasslands, and the probability of large-scale burns would be high. These fires, however, would be cooler than forest fires, protecting the belowground tissues from damage. Recovery would be initiated by perennial grasses, which are extremely fire resistant because they renew growth from the protected leaf bases of old leaves. Fire resistant seed germination would be the second step in the process of recovery.

A severe drop in chronic temperatures could cause chilling and even frost damage to occur in some seasons, and C_4 grasses would have reduced rates of photosynthesis. Respiration might not be so reduced. Consequently, a moderate to severe reduction in net primary production could occur, leading to collapse of the trophic food web. As a consequence, subsequent rains would allow species to regenerate from the seed bank, but there would be an increase in ruderal species. In all chronic phases, some animals would survive, but overall diversity and biomass would be drastically reduced.

2.4.2.6 Mangroves

Mangrove swamps are a striking feature of tropical and sub-tropical coastal systems, occurring from about 35°N to 38°S in all parts of the world. Generally, they develop on sediments deposited in sheltered estuaries, inlets, and bays, especially in the leeward side of islands and off-shore reefs. They are subject to periodic flooding by tidal waters and are usually intersected by a dendritic creek system. Mangrove swamps are woody communities dominated by the stilt-rooted and pneumatophore-bearing mangrove shrubs and trees. They are the equivalent of the salt marshes of the temperate regions. Productivity in mangroves is normally very high.

More than 50 different mangrove species occur, with members of the genera *Rhizophora* and *Avicennia* being the most widespread. A zonation occurs as one moves from open water towards the coast. The sediment gradually rises in elevation, and changes in species accompany this rise (Macrae, 1968). Salinity, light, exposure and nutrient status alter along this sequence. Because of evaporation, the most saline habitats are at the in-shore edge of the swamps. Most mangrove species have unusual morphological and physiological adaptations to their extreme habitat, which include special organs that assist in oxygen supply in the anaerobic sediments; the production of viviparous, specialized shoots which are finger-like seedlings detached from the mangroves; and the ability to grow by anchoring in mud. The roots of mangroves are able to exclude most of the salt, and the little that enters is stored in vacuoles and excreted through the roots. The plants are succulent, have high internal osmotic pressures in their cells, and contain aerenchymatous tissues.

Mangrove swamps are very important feeding and nursery grounds for shellfish and fish, and their waters teem with life. They also export large amounts of carbon to the sea in the form of detritus (Heald, 1969; Odum, 1969), which is essential in the food chains of estuarine and commercial fisheries. Mangrove swamps are also important feeding areas for birds and numerous crustaceans and are the home of many species of fiddler crabs and aquatic mammals, such as manatee.

Towards the latitudinal margins for mangrove swamps, the species diversity of plants is reduced. For example at the northerly limit in Florida, it is reduced to one species (*Avicennia nitida*), while in temperate Australia, it is reduced to two species (Rodriguez, 1975).

Pannier and Pannier (1977) pointed out that the southern limits of mangrove ecosystems is about 4°S on the Pacific coast of South America, while it is about 28°S on the Atlantic coast. They found that while temperature tolerance was a key factor in this, the pressure of an annual rainy season in the Atlantic was critical.

Four factors are involved in mangrove distributional limits and occurrences. These are: 1.) thermal tolerance; 2.) photoperiodic sensitivity; 3.) precipitation fluxes; and 4.) impact of storms (Pannier, 1985). The distribution of mangroves is thermally limited worldwide. Many species are unable to withstand any frost, and many are susceptible to chilling injury. Annual temperatures of 24.5°C to 26.5°C are normal. *Avicennia nitida* can tolerate temperatures to -4 or -5°C for short periods, while the lower limit for *Rhizophora racemosa* is 19°C, below which temperature the salt-root barrier breaks down and chloride concentration instantly increases in the roots. Mangroves favor a 12-hour photoperiod. If exposed to long days, the root-salt barrier is broken, allowing high salt levels to develop in the roots, killing them. A number of studies on the temperature tolerances of particular species have emphasized the inability of all species except *Avicennia nitida* to tolerate any frost at all, and the general extreme sensitivity of mangroves to low temperature (Pannier and Pannier, 1977; McMillan, 1975, 1979; Lugo and Zucca, 1977). Temperature is also important to the induction of roots on the new shoots and for epicotylar bud development. Roots need to be formed very quickly to anchor the stick- or finger-like seedlings or they will be washed away. At lower temperatures, seedling establishment may fail, since lower temperatures cause an increase in root induction time, as well as lowering the percentage of bud development of the seedlings.

Annual rains are necessary to allow seedling establishment. The importance of adequate rainfall for mangroves (1700–2000 mm year^{-1}) was noted by Pannier and Pannier (1977). Jennings and Bird (1967) ascribe Australia's lack of extensive swamps and marshes to the general aridity of Australian estuaries and to low run-off coefficients and the few perennial rivers, which flood only spasmodically, releasing less fluvial sediments than elsewhere. Any decrease in precipitation would decrease the input from rivers, so that salinities would increase, which could adversely affect all species. *Avicennia nitida* would be least affected by this, but this is uncertain as there are reports of temperature decreases lowering salinity tolerances of several species (Lugo and Zucca, 1977). If in an acute or chronic phase after a nuclear war precipitation were reduced by 25% to 75%, this would prevent re-establishment of damaged or devastated mangrove swamps.

Two main factors are responsible for the destruction of mangroves during coastal storms: 1.) the physical destruction and uprooting of the outer zones of the mangroves; and 2.) increase in sedimentation. Both sudden heavy sedimentation or removal of sediments can kill mangroves. In Florida, damage from a storm which struck the Everglades in 1934 is still visible after 50 years. If the coastal storms were to be increased in intensity after a nuclear war, mangrove ecosystems would be very much at risk, irrespective of reduced temperature and rainfall. A key factor in recovery is the occurrence of the floating regenerative viviparous units. Without these, recovery is not possible.

Mangroves have burned in southern Florida during droughts, such as in 1985. They are replaced by herbaceous vegetation and recovery is slow, with encroachment from the periphery of the burned areas. During severe droughts, the organic soils may also burn.

During a chronic phase of climatic perturbations, mangrove ecosystems might well be the most sensitive of tropical systems to temperature decreases, enhanced coastal storm activity, and reductions in precipitation. Mangrove species cannot cold harden, and they are thus especially susceptible to frost. They do not have seed banks, nor do they have dry, thick-coated seeds. Many species are dependent on water levels, sedimentation, and precipitation for production of live regenerative viviparous propagules, which are very vulnerable to frost and cold. This vulnerability makes recovery unlikely or, at best, very slow. The mangrove systems in the tropics grow in low stress areas with respect to temperature. If the temperature falls on average 5–10°C, this would have a very severe impact at all latitudes, with some fish kills and disruption of food chains. In an acute phase with temperatures falling to near- or sub-zero for a few days, there would be complete mortality for low latitude mangroves, even at temperatures as high as at +5°C. At higher latitudes and at the latitudinal extremes of distribution of mangroves, there would be general die-back, except for *Avicennia* which might survive if the freeze is for just a few days. There would be widespread mortality of fish, shellfish, and plankton in the shallow waters. *Avicennia* might be able to resprout from any living basal wood. If the temperature fell 1–3°C from ambient, then there would be a reduction in productivity, and some species would be adversely affected, especially as regards reproduction.

The susceptibilty of the mangrove ecosystems to reduced precipitation, with the resulting changes in salinity, would affect reproduction and the ability of mature mangroves to survive. Increased storms would cause extensive damage and allow flooding of low-lying coastal areas. This would be accentuated by the occurrence of weakened plants following temperature declines. Mangrove ecosystems, if disturbed on a large scale by severe perturbations, tend to have slow recovery rates, as evidenced by the current devastated state of mangrove ecosystems in Vietnam over a decade after cessation of military applications of herbicides (Netter, 1985).

2.5 POTENTIAL EFFECTS ON SOUTHERN HEMISPHERE ECOSYSTEMS

2.5.1 Vulnerability of Terrestrial Ecosystems to Climatic Disturbances [1]

2.5.1.1 Introduction

Northern Hemisphere and tropical ecosystems might experience nuclear war-induced climatic effects from a war occurring any time of the year, although seasonality is believed to be an important consideration. For the Southern Hemisphere, the importance of seasonality is more marked, with current projections of acute effects occurring in the Southern Hemisphere only following a nuclear war initiated in the Northern summer. A Northern winter-onset nuclear war, on the other hand, does not appear to offer the potential for altered atmospheric circulation patterns to result in significant transport of particulates into the Southern Hemisphere (see Volume I of this report; see also, Pittock, 1985; Pittock and Nix, 1985a).

Another important difference between the Southern and Northern Hemisphere potential climatic effects is the reduced intensity of both acute and chronic stresses, a result of two factors: 1.) the nuclear war is hypothesized to occur largely or totally in the Northern Hemisphere and, thus, the smoke and soot would be initially limited to Northern latitudes; and 2.) the Southern Hemisphere has a much larger proportion of its area covered by ocean (about 80%), so that temperature buffering from the high specific heat of water is much greater. Further, because the transport of the smoke clouds across hemispheres would require alteration of atmospheric circulation patterns on a massive scale and the movement of particulates across several thousands of kilometers, there could be a noticeable time lag before effects occurred. The final difference in potential climatic effects that should be kept in mind is the possibility of changes in monsoonal circulation patterns, a factor noted to have potentially devastating effects on tropical systems.

The net effect of these considerations is the projections of possible acute

---

[1] The information in this section is primarily based on the biological working group discussions at the Melbourne conference, M.J. Salinger, chairman, and on the synopses of the discussions prepared by Salinger and by N. Cherry.

and chronic stresses on the Southern Hemisphere following a summer- and winter-onset nuclear war, as indicated in Table 2.1. These projections have a great deal of uncertainty associated with them; thus, all estimations of the effects on Southern Hemisphere ecosystems must be treated as preliminary and tentative. This is especially true for the projections of precipitation anomalies, which appear to be a very important potential effect for Southern Hemisphere ecosystems. In evaluating the vulnerability of ecosystems to these types of stresses, as in the Northern Hemisphere evaluations, possible climatic disturbances have been categorized to include brief periods of subfreezing temperatures, along with reduced sunlight (described as an acute situation), and to include a few degree reduction in average temperatures, with associated 5–20% reductions in insolation. The vulnerability to large (up to 50%) reductions in precipitation was also considered. As previously, such perturbations are *not* projected to occur at any particular probability level or over any particular spatial extent; rather, these are chosen for understanding the vulnerability of Southern Hemisphere ecosystems to classes of perturbations after a large-scale nuclear war, categorized on the basis of biological importance.

The land areas that fall in this region include southern Africa, southern South America, Australia, and New Zealand. Our deliberations focused on the latter two countries as the topic of the Melbourne, Australia, workshop. It is believed that the environmental stresses and responses in southern Africa would be similar to those experienced in Australia, but extra-tropical ecosystems of Africa or South America have not been specifically analyzed.

2.5.1.2 Potential Vulnerabilities of Australian Ecosystems

Considering Australia as representing effects on continental areas, it is clear that the important concerns for the Southern Hemisphere extra-tropics are dominated by grasslands/rangelands, discussed in detail in the agricultural section (Chapter 4), and by oceans, discussed below. Only the effects on forests, deserts, and freshwater ecosystems are briefly considered here.

Terrestrial ecosystems in Australia are largely xerophytic, i.e., the plant and animal communities are adapted to periods of low water availability. Trees and other forest plants typically have sclerophyll leaves, characterized as being tough, evergreen, relatively small, and broad. The warm semi-arid scrub ecosystems in Australia, having evolved in isolation, do not have the succulents of parallel ecosystems on other continents; spiny tussock grasses (spinifex, *Triodia*) predominate. Other terrestrial ecosystems in Australia include the cool semi-arid deserts and true, extreme deserts.

It is felt that none of these ecosystems would be sensitive to brief periods of reduced temperatures and light levels in an acute period and that none is vulnerable to longer, milder climatic disturbances of a chronic phase. This is supported by research on the transportability of several Australian plant species considered for export in cool storage on ocean-going ships (Brunsdon et al., 1984). This research indicated that many such plant species could withstand low temperatures (1°C to 10°C) if simultaneously kept in dark containers, with survival significantly greater at the 10°C level.

The effects of prolonged periods of reduced precipitation, such as possible in the chronic phase after a nuclear war, were also felt to be within the bounds of what the forests and semi-arid and arid ecosystems could absorb without significant effect, since these ecosystems routinely are subjected to prolonged periods of reduced precipitation.

Effects on freshwater ecosystems in Australia would also appear to be limited, in that the temperature reductions do not seem likely to remain below freezing for long enough periods for these ecosystems to freeze. Water availability for humans and other animals might become limiting in the case of prolonged periods of precipitation being reduced by half, but this would not be a problem in the short term because of the current water storage capacity in reservoirs.

2.5.1.3 Potential Vulnerabilities of New Zealand Ecosystems

Effects on the ecosystems of New Zealand and Tasmania could be more marked with respect to temperature reductions. Many of New Zealand's indigenous species are both drought- and frost-sensitive. It is felt that brief temperature excursions near or below freezing could result in plant mortality on a substantial scale. The probability of such events would seem to be diminished in general for New Zealand compared to Australia, because of a greater influence on the weather and climate by the ocean, and, therefore, a dampening of temperature excursions; however, the greater range of altitudes and the more temperate climate of New Zealand suggest that a smaller decrease in average temperatures would be needed to attain near freezing conditions. Clearly, the effects of acute temperature reductions in New Zealand cannot be projected without better resolution of the physical stresses likely to be encountered.

Effects of reduced precipitation on New Zealand ecosystems would become a problem in those areas where precipitation fell below 100 cm annually, with a reduction in primary production likely in those circumstances. Freshwater streams in particular would be adversely affected by major reductions in precipitation. However, precipitation in New Zealand is largely controlled by the direction of winds from the ocean, with a strong orographic component to the distribution of rainfall across the landscape. Knowing the direction and intensity of the on-shore winds in the aftermath of a markedly altered atmosphere is below the level of resolution of climatic projections currently available, and again predictions of ecological effects on New Zealand are tentative. New Zealand ecosystems would appear to be as vulnerable to subfreezing temperatures, half-normal precipitation, and other more extreme climatic perturbations as are comparable ecosystems in the Northern Hemisphere (New Zealand Ecological Society, 1985; Royal Society of New Zealand, 1985); however, the extremes of climatic disturbances do not currently seem plausible to occur in New Zealand after a Northern Hemisphere nuclear war.

2.5.2 Potential Effects on the Southern Ocean and Antarctica [2]

The Southern Hemisphere global weather patterns are dominated by two features—a vast expanse of ocean and the Antarctic continent with its associated sea ice cover. It is the Antarctic and the winter sea ice which seem likely to be the critical feature in any response to nuclear war-induced climatic disturbances in the region.

The Antarctic ice sheet, with an area of about 14×10^6 km^2, contains about 90% of the global freshwater (Walton, 1984). Any major long-term changes in its mass balance would have world-wide effects on sea level and more local effects on Southern Hemisphere heat balance and weather system dynamics.

The Southern Ocean surrounding the continent supports a biologically rich marine ecosystem, and it is significant both in its likely role as an atmospheric CO_2 sink and in its interactions with temperate and tropical ocean waters to the north. Antarctic bottom water, formed in the Southern Ocean, influences deep oceanic temperatures on a global scale. Each winter a large part of the Southern Ocean is covered by seasonally formed sea ice, which is at a minimum in February and increases five-fold in area to a maximum in October. This increases the total ice cover (i.e., including Continental ice) in the Southern Hemisphere from about 17×10^6 km^2 to about 34×10^6 km^2. Sea ice cover shows considerable annual variation, both in extent and duration. Changes in either would have a major effect on marine communities in the Southern Ocean.

An attempt was made by Budd (1975) to relate sea ice changes to air temperatures. Using 60°S as the mean position of the maximum extent of sea ice, Budd suggested that a decrease of 1°C in mean annual air temperature would shift the limit north by about 1° latitude. Using the longest run of Antarctic meteorological data (from Laurie Island, South Orkney Islands) to estimate local temperature effects on ice duration, it was calculated that a decrease of 1°C in mean annual temperature would increase sea ice longevity by about 70 days at that latitude (70°S). However, more recent analyses of these temperature data and sea ice extent (Raper et al., 1984) suggest that the

---

[2] This section was primarily written by D.W.H. Walton.

relationship is more complex and that continental Antarctic sea ice trends cannot be reliably inferred from the Laurie Island data.

Recent studies by Takahashi et al. (1984) suggest that the Southern Ocean waters south of the Antarctic Convergence may well act as a sink for over 30% of global industrial CO_2. Gordon (1979) suggested that the area of ocean and sea ice south of the Antarctic Convergence may act as the heat exchanger for the entire Earth's oceans, providing a major area for heat loss to balance heat inputs elsewhere. A crucial feature of this is the area of cold open water within the sea ice in winter, since this accounts for the highest rates of cooling and gas exchange. Large polynya (i.e., open water areas within ice formations) are therefore of considerable importance to global dynamics. Current satellite photographs indicate that at least 25% open water exists within the sea ice even in late winter and up to 60% open water within the ice pack in summer (Keys, 1984), in sharp contrast to the Arctic Ocean, where over 95% is generally frozen.

If the Southern Ocean is defined as the area from the Antarctic continent north to the subtropical convergence (about 49°S), it has an area of about 36×10^6 km^2 and encompasses about 10% of the total world oceanic area. Within this area, ice-free land is very limited (the Antarctic has only 1–2% ice-free areas), and all terrestrial ecosystems are closely marine related. The marine trophic food webs may be much simpler than elsewhere, with Antarctic krill occupying the critical position in many areas, and copepods in others. There are relatively few predator species, primarily marine mammals, and land biota are very depauperate because of the combination of long-range dispersal problems and extreme climatic stress. Nutrient transfer from sea to land is principally by birds and aerosols, and nutrients may be limiting to survival of terrestrial biota.

The Antarctic marine flora, like that of other major oceans, consist almost entirely of phytoplankton (Heywood and Whitaker, 1984). Ice-associated species of phytoplankton are important, being found throughout the whole depth of ice in the Weddell Sea, and forming dense and rich communities beneath the fast ice. Many of the phytoplankton are well adapted to low light levels, down to 0.1% of incident noon insolation (about 0.25 W m^{-2}). This level of light occurs to depths of 40–200 m of ocean water and about 2 m of sea ice. Most species are obligate psychrophiles, with a sharp metabolic fall-off above 10°C, although they seem to be operating at suboptimal temperatures in the Southern Ocean environment. Limited available evidence suggests that primary production is no greater than in other oceans, with the exception of the Arctic Ocean.

Because of the nature of the trophic structure, organisms and processes initially most critically affected by changes in sea ice dynamics following a nuclear war would be phytoplankton and krill (Everson, 1984). If reductions in temperature and insolation were to reach the Southern Ocean in the austral summer, and if these were substantial, the sea ice growth in the fall could begin earlier and extend farther north than normal. Duration of sea ice could, in a positive feedback mechanism, lead to a minimal summer season the following year and further enhance winter conditions. However, if temperature effects were to reach the Southern Ocean in the austral winter, only a slight increase in sea ice cover would be expected, and the end of the following summer might see a return to normal sea ice conditions.

The effects of prolonged sea ice cover would likely be complex. If the proportion of open water within the sea ice pack were substantially below normal, the Antarctic Convergence would be shifted north, and the open water period in summer would be reduced. These could lead to a northward shift of cold water between the Antarctic and Subtropical Convergences, possibly with a reduction in the width of this zone. In the worst case, there could be a reduction in the Antarctic penguin and seal populations because of a loss of breeding grounds and a reduction in food supply, and a shift in the habitat of petrel and albatross populations to areas further north. However, since these animals are long-lived, the maximum impact would likely be loss of an age class rather than of the entire population. Only extreme prolonged climatic changes would result in the loss of a substantial portion of the adult population

It is not yet clear what the physical stresses on the ecosystems in the most southern parts of the Earth would be in the aftermath of a nuclear war, but the range of possible perturbations outlined in Volume I does not imply that a sufficiently long temperature depression would ensue that would permanently alter the Southern Ocean and Antarctic ecosystems, because of: 1.) rapid recovery times of effects on plankton and krill; 2.) the resistance, longevity, and spatial extent of the populations of the larger organisms; and 3.) the adaptations of many organisms to low light and temperature levels. Antarctica and the Southern Ocean seem likely to survive nuclear war-induced climatic disturbances largely unscathed. However, the role of the Southern Ocean and its sea ice cover in global dynamics does offer the possibility of longer-term and larger-scale effects on other parts of the Earth.

APPENDIX

The Narragansett Bay Model (Kremer and Nixon, 1978) simulates the flows of energy and materials among the compartments of the Bay, as shown in Figure 2.17. A hydrodynamical model is necessary as an input to the ecological model, since many of the important parameters for the latter are controlled by the hydrodynamics. In the model, solar input is the driving energy source for the phytoplankton primary producer compartment, using a daily time step and including effects of the diel cycle.

Primary production is calculated based on a function of maximal potential growth, which is decremented in response to less-than-optimal physical parameters. The relationships with light are based on a time and depth integration of a photosynthesis/light response that includes surface inhibition and self-shading. Nutrient limitations are based on a Michaelis-Menten (1913) function assuming the most-limiting nutrient only; the nutrients simulated include ammonia, oxidized forms of nitrogen, phosphate, and silicate.

The primary producers are split into two physiological groups, with specific values for each for temperature and nutrient responses, half-saturation constants, nutrient content, and nutrient:carbon ratios. The zooplankton compartment consists primarily of herbivorous copepods found in the Bay, and is separated into compartments for eggs, juveniles, and adult life stages. Adults consume phytoplankton, detritus, and zooplankton eggs and juveniles in a density-dependent manner as a function of temperature. Egg release and development are functions of temperature. Seasonality is imposed on predators, especially involving ctenophore and fish populations. A benthos compartment is included, which receives inputs from the plankton; clams actively filter the water at a temperature-dependent rate. Benthos also regenerate nutrients into the water column by releasing ammonia, phosphate, and silicate at temperature-dependent rates. Finally, a chemical nutrient compartment is incorporated in the model, providing a critical feedback loop connecting all other compartments and adding inputs from anthropogenic sources.

Water temperatures were calculated as a function of the assigned reduction in air temperatures, according to a linear regression analysis of the air/water temperature relationships seen in Narragansett Bay from a 20-yr record of weekly mean water temperatures and climatological data from Newport, RI, for the same periods. The relationships applied were:

$$T_w = 1.34736 + 0.880516\, T_a \qquad (r^2 = 0.974) \qquad \text{warming period}$$
$$T_w = 3.24267 + 0.868082\, T_a \qquad (r^2 = 0.982) \qquad \text{cooling period}$$

where:

$$T_w = \text{water temperature (°C)}$$
$$T_a = \text{air temperature (°C).}$$

The high r^2 values indicate a close correlation between air temperatures and water temperatures; the shift in warming versus cooling period relationships was instituted on 1 August of the simulated years.

These temperature analyses and the model simulations were done by J. McKenna, of the Graduate School of Oceanography, University of Rhode Island, for the SCOPE–ENUWAR project.

REFERENCES

Addison, P.A., and Bliss, L.C. (1984). Adaptations of *Luzula confusa* to the polar semi-desert environment. *Arctic,* **37**, 121–132.

Andrews, J.T., Davis, P.T., and Wright, C. (1976). Little Ice Age permanent snow-cover in the Eastern Canadian Arctic: Extent mapped from Landsat-1 Satellite Imagery. *Geografiska Annaler.,* **58**(A1–2), 71–81.

Black, R.A., and Bliss, L.C. (1980). Reproductive ecology of Picea mariana at tree line near Inuvik, Northwest Territories, Canada. *Ecol. Mgr.,* **50**, 331–354.

Bliss, L.C. (1977). General summary, Truelove Lowland ecosystem. In Bliss, L.C. (Ed.). *Truelove Lowland, Devon Island, Canada: A High Arctic Ecosystem.* University of Alberta Press, Alberta: 714 pages.

Bliss, L.C. (1985). Estimated ecological impacts of a nuclear winter in the subarctic and arctic. Unpublished discussion paper for the SCOPE–ENUWAR Workshop, Toronto, Canada.

Bowen, R. (1982). *Surface Water.* Wiley-Interscience, New York: 290 pages.

Brunsdon, P.H., Derera, N.F., and Granville, N.S. (1984). *Integrated Nursery System Project.* Stage II. Phase A. Plant Environment Investigation. Report by Burns, Philp, and Co., Ltd., Sydney, for the Australia Department of Science and Technology, Canberra: 297 pages.

Brylinsky, M., and Mann, K.H. (1973). An analysis of factors governing productivity in lakes and reservoirs. *Limnol. Oceanogr.,* **18**, 1–14.

Budd, W.F. (1975). Antarctic sea ice variations from satellite sensing in relation to climate. *J. Glaciology,* **15**, 417–428.

Bunt, J.S. (1975). Primary productivity of marine ecosystems. In Leith, H., and Whittaker, R.H. (Eds.). *Primary Productivity of the Biosphere.* Springer-Verlag, New York.

Chevalier, A. (1909). Growth and regeneration of old forests of tropical Africa. *C.R. Acad. Sci., Paris,* **149**, 458–461. (in French).

Colby, P.J., Spangler, G.R., Hurley, D.A., and McCombie, A.M. (1972). Effects of eutrophication on salmonid communities in oligotrophic lakes. *J. Fish. Res. Board Can.,* **29**, 975–983.

Cooper, C.F., Blasing, T.J., Fritts, H.C., The Oak Ridge Systems Ecology Group, Smith, F.M., Parton, W.J., Schreuder, G.F., Sollins, P., Zich, J., and Stoner, W. (1979). Simulation models of the effects of climatic change on natural ecosystems. In: Shugart, H.H., and O'Neill, R.V. *Benchmark Papers in Ecology.* Volume 9. Systems Ecology. Dowden, Hutchinson, and Ross, Stroudsburg, Pennsylvania: 367 pages.

Coughenour, M.B., McNaughton, S.J., and Wallace, L.L. (1984). Modelling productivity of perennial graminoids–uniting physiological processes and morphometric traits. *Ecol. Modelling,* **23**, 101–134.

Craig, S.R. (1976). *Seasonal Development of Structure in Two Macrophytic Communities in Lake Opinicon, Ontario.* M.S. Thesis. Queen's University, Kingston, Ontario: 104 pages.

Cushing, D.H. (1975). *Marine Ecology and Fisheries.* Cambridge University Press, Cambridge: 278 pages.

Dahl, E. (1985). Effects of nuclear winter on forest ecosystems. *Ambio,* **14**, 63.

Dahlberg, M.D., and Smith, F.G. (1970). Mortality of estuarine animals due to cold on the Georgia coast. *Ecology,* **51**(5), 931–933.

Detling, J.K. (1979). Processes controlling blue grama production on the shortgrass prairie. In French, N.R. (Ed.). *Perspectives in Grassland Ecology.* Springer-Verlag, New York.

Detling, J. K., Parton, W.J., and Hunt, H.W. (1979). A simulation model of *Bouteloua gracilis* biomass dynamics on the North American shortgrass prairie. *Oecologia*, **38**, 167–191.

Deuser, W.G., Brewer, P.G., Jickells, T.D., and Commeau, R.D. (1983). Biological control of the removal of abiogenic particles from the surface ocean. *Science*, **219**, 388–391.

de Vlaming, V.L. (1972). Environmental control of teleost reproductive cycles: A brief review. *J. Fish. Biol.*, **4**, 131–140.

Dyke, A.S. (1978). Indications of neoglacierization on Somerset Island, District of Franklin. Scientific and technical notes. Current Research. *Geol. Surv. Can. Paper*, 78–1B, 215–217.

Dyke, A.S. (1979). Glacial and sea-level history of southwestern Cumberland peninsula, Baffin Island, N.W.T., Canada. *Arctic and Alpine Research*, **11**(2), 179–202.

Emery, K.O., and Kuhn, G.G. (1982). Sea cliffs: Their processes, profiles, and classification. *Geological Society of America Bulletin*, **93**, 644–654.

Everson, I. (1984). Marine interactions. In Laws, R.M. (Ed.). *Antarctic Ecology*. Academic Press, New York.

Forsberg, C., and Ryding, S. (1980). Eutrophication parameters and trophic state indices in 30 Swedish water-receiving lakes. *Arch. Hydrobiol.*, **89**, 189–207.

Franzisket, L. (1970). The atrophy of hermatypic reef corals maintained in darkness and their subsequent regeneration in light. *Int. Revue ges. Hydrobiol.*, **55**, 1–12.

Fuller, W.A., Martell, A.M., Smith, R.F.S., and Speller, S.W. (1977). Biology and secondary production of *Dirostonyx groenlandicus* on Truelove Lowland. In Bliss, L.C. (Ed.). *Truelove Lowland, Devon Island, Canada: A High Arctic Ecosystem*. University of Alberta Press, Edmonton, Alberta: 714 pages.

Galloway, J.C. (1941). Lethal effect of the cold winter of 1939-40 on marine fishes at Key West, Florida. *Copeia*, **2**, 118–119.

Garrison, D.L. (1984). Plankton diatoms. In Steidinger, K.A., and Walker, L.M. (Eds.). *Marine Plankton Life Cycle Strategies*. CRC Press, Florida.

Glibert, P.M., Dennett, M.R., and Goldman, J.C. (1985). Inorganic carbon uptake by phytoplankton in Vineyard Sound, Mass.: I. Measurements of the photosynthesis-irradiance response of winter and early spring assemblages. *J. Exp. Mar. Biol. Ecol.*, (in press).

Gordon, A. (1979). Meridional heat flux in the Southern Ocean. *WHOI Tech. Report*, Woods Hole, Massachusetts.

Gulland, J.A. (1974). *The Management of Marine Fisheries*. University of Washington Press, Seattle: 198 pages.

Gunter, G. (1941). Death of fishes due to cold on the Texas Coast, January, 1940. *Ecology*, **22**(2), 203–208.

Gunter, G., and Hildebrand, H.H. (1951). Destruction of fishes and other organisms on the South Texas Coast by the cold wave of January 28-February 3, 1951. *Ecology*, **32**(4), 731–736.

Hanson, J. D., Parton, W.J., and Skiles, J.W. (1983). SPUR plant growth component. In. Wright, J.R. (Ed.). *SPUR–Simulation of Production and Utilization of Rangelands: A Rangeland Model for Management and Research*. U.S. Dept. Agric., Misc. Publ. No. 1431, Washington, D.C.

Harriott, V.J. (1985). Mortality rates of scleractinian corals before and during a mass bleaching event. *Mar. Environ. Sci.*, (in press).

Hartgerink, A.P., and Mayo, J.M. (1976). Controlled environment studies on net assimilation and water relations of *Dryas integrifolia*. *Can. J. Bot.*, **54**, 1884–1895.

Hartman, J.M. (1984). *The Role of Wrack Disturbance in the Vegetation of a New*

England Salt Marsh. Ph.D. Dissertation, University of Connecticut, Storrs: 130 pages.
Harwell, M.A. (1984). *Nuclear Winter: The Human and Environmental Consequences of Nuclear War.* Springer-Verlag, New York: 179 pages.
Harwell, M.A., and Weinstein, D.W. (1982). *Modelling the Effects of Air Pollution on Forested Ecosystems.* ERC Report 6. Ecosystems Research Center, Cornell University, Ithaca, NY.
Heald, E.J. (1969). *The Production of Organic Detritus in a South Florida Estuary.* Ph.D. Dissertation. University of Miami, Miami: 111 pages.
Heywood, R.B., and Whitaker, T.M. (1984). The marine flora. In Laws, R.M. (Ed.). *Antarctic Ecology.* Academic Press, New York.
Hoffman, E.J., Mills, G.L., Latimer, J.S., and Quinn, J.G. (1984). Urban run-off as a source of polycyclic aromatic hydrocarbons to coastal waters. *Environ. Sci. Tech.,* **18**. 580–587.
Honjo, S. (1982). Seasonality and interaction of biogenic and lithogenic particulate flux at Panama Basin. *Science,* **218**, 883–884.
Horwitz, R.J. (1978). Temporal variability patterns and the distribution patterns of stream fishes. *Ecol. Monogr.,* **48**, 307–321.
Ivory, D.A., and Whiteman, P.C. (1978a). Effects of environment and plant factors on freezing resistance in tropical grasses. I. *Austral. J. Agric. Res.,* **29**, 243–259.
Ivory, D.A., and Whiteman, P.C. (1978b). Effects of environment and plant factors on freezing resistance in tropical grasses. II. *Austral. J. Agric. Res.,* **29**, 261–266.
Jenkins, W.J., and Goldman, J.C. (1985). Seasonal oxygen cycling and primary productivity in the Sargasso Sea. *J. Mar. Res.,* (in press).
Jennings, J.N., and Bird, E.C.F. (1967). Regional geomorphological characteristics of some Australian estuaries. In Lauff, G.H. (Ed.). *Estuaries.* 121–128. American Association for the Advancement of Science, Washington, D.C.
Jonasson, P.M. (1970). Bottom fauna and eutrophication. In *Eutrophication: Causes, Consequences, and Correctives.* National Academy of Sciences, Washington, D.C.
Kalff, J., and Knoechel, R. (1978). Phytoplankton and their dynamics in oligotrophic and eutrophic lakes. *Ann. Rev. Ecol. Syst.,* **9**, 475–495.
Keast, A. (1977). Diet overlaps and feeding relationships between the year classes in the yellow perch (*Perca flavescens*). *Environ. Biol. Fish.,* **2**, 53–70.
Kemp, P. R., and Williams, G.J., III. (1980). A physiological basis for niche separation between *Agropyron smithii* (C$_3$) and *Bouteloua gracilis* (C$_4$). *Ecology,* **61**, 846–858.
Keys, J.R. (1984). *Antarctic Marine Environments and Offshore Oil.* New Zealand Commission for the Environment, Wellington: 180 pages.
Kranck, K., and Milligan, T. (1980). Macroflocs: Production of marine snow in the laboratory. *Mar. Ecol. Progr. Ser.,* **3**, 19–24.
Kremer, J.N., and Nixon, S.W. (1978). *A Coastal Marine Ecosystem: Simulation and Analysis.* Springer-Verlag, Berlin: 217 pages.
Kuhn, G.G., and Shepard, F.P. (1981). Should Southern California build defenses against violent storms resulting in lowland flooding as discovered in records of the past century. *Shore and Beach,* **49**(4), 3–11.
Kuhn, G.G., and Shepard, F.P. (1983). Beach processes and sea cliff erosion in San Diego County, California. In Komar, P.D. (Ed.). *CRC Handbook of Coastal Processes and Erosion.* 267–284. CRC Press, Inc., Boca Raton, FL.
Lang, J.C. (1971). Interspecific aggression by scleractinian corals. I. The rediscovery of Scolymia cubensis. *Bull. Mar. Sci.,* **21**, 952–959.
Larkin, P.A., and Northcote, T.G. (1970). Fishes and indices of eutrophication.

In *Eutrophication: Causes, Consequences, and Correctives*. National Academy of Sciences, Washington, D.C.

Littler, M.M., Littler, D.S., Blair, S.M., and Norris, J.M. (1985). Deepest known plant life discovered on an unchartered seamount. *Science*, **227**, 57–59.

Lugo, A.E., and Zucca, C.P. (1977). The impact of low temperature stress on mangrove structure and growth. *Tropical Ecol.*, **18**, 149–161.

Luyten, J., Pedlosky, J., and Stommel, H. (1983a). The ventilated thermocline. *J. Physical Oceanography*, **13**(2), 292–309.

Luyten, J., Pedlosky, J., and Stommel, H. (1983b). Climatic inferences from the ventilated thermocline. *Climatic Change*, **5**, 183–191.

Macrae, W. (1968). A general account of the fauna and flora of mangrove swamps and forests in the Indo-West Pacific region. *Adv. Mar. Biol.*, **6**, 73–270.

Margalef, R. (1978). Life-forms of phytoplankton as survival alternatives in an unstable environment. *Oceanol. Acta.*, **1**, 493–509.

Mayo, J.M., Harter, J.E., Nelson, S., and Davis, G. (1980). Plant physiology. In Bliss, L.C., and Mayo, J.M. (Eds.). *An Ecophysiological Investigation of the Jack Pine Woodland with Reference to Revegetation of Mined Sands*. Alberta Oil Sands Environmental Research Program, Edmonton: 124 pages.

McElroy, A.E. (1985). *Benz(a)anthracene in Benthic Marine Environments: Bioavailability, Metabolism, and Physiological Effects on the Polychaete*, Nereis virens. Ph.D. Dissertation. MIT/WHOI Joint Program, Woods Hole, Massachusetts.

McMillan, C. (1975). Adaptive differentiation to chilling in mangrove populations. In Walsh, G.E., Snedaker, S.C., and Teas, H.J. (Eds.). *Proceeding of the International Symposium on the Biology and Management of Mangroves*. 62–68. IFAS, University of Florida, Gainesville, FL.

McMillan, C. (1979). Differentiation in response to chilling temperatures among populations of three marine spermatophytes. *Amer. J. Bot.*, **66**, 810–819.

McNaughton, S.J., and Medina, E. (1985). *Tropical grasslands and savannahs*. Unpublished manuscript contributed to SCOPE–ENUWAR.

Meade, R.H. (1972). Sources and sinks of suspended matter on continental shelves. In Swift, O.J., Duane, D.B., and Pilkey, O.H. (Eds.). *Shelf Sediment Transport*. Dowden, Hutchinson, & Ross, Inc., Stroudsburg, Pennsylvania.

Michaelis, L., and Menten, M.L. (1913). Der Kinetic der Inverteinwirkung. *Biochem. Z.*, **49**, 333–369. (in German).

Miller, E.M. (1940). Mortality of fishes due to cold on the Southeast Florida coast, 1940. *Ecology*, **21**(3), 420–421.

Miller, F.L., Russell, R.H., and Gunn, A. (1975). The decline of peary caribou on Western Queen Elizabeth Islands of arctic Canada. *Polarforschung*, **45**, 17–21.

Miller, P.C., and Tieszen, L. (1972). A preliminary model of processes affecting primary production in the arctic tundra. *Arctic and Alpine Research*, **4**, 1–18.

Monteith, J.L. (1977). Climate. In Alvim, P.de T., and Kozlowski, T.T. (Eds.). *Ecophysiology of Tropical Crops*. 1–28. Academic Press, New York.

Moore, H.B. (1966). *Marine Ecology*. John Wiley & Sons, New York: 492 pages.

Moyle, P.B., and Li, H.W. (1979). Community ecology and predator-prey relations in warm water streams. In Stroud, R.H., and Clepper, H. (Eds.). *Predator–Prey Systems in Fisheries Management*. Sport Fishing Institute, Washington, D.C.

Netter, T.W. (1985). Vietnam's deforestation brings new alarm. *New York Times*, 21 May 1985.

New Zealand Ecological Society. (1985). *The Environmental Consequences to New Zealand of Nuclear Warfare in the Northern Hemisphere*. A Statement of Concern by the Council of the New Zealand Ecological Society (Inc.). NZES, Wellington:

24 pages.

Nobel, P.S. (1982). Low-temperature tolerance and cold hardening of cacti. *Ecology*, **63**, 1650–1656.

Odum, E.P. (1969). The strategy of ecosystem development. *Science*, **164**, 262–270.

Opler, P.A., Baker, H.G., and Frankie, G.W. (1977). Recovery of tropical lowland forest ecosystems. In Cairns, J., Dickson, K.L., and Herricks, E.E. (Eds.). *Recovery and Restoration of Damaged Ecosystems*. University of Virginia Press, Charlottesville: 531 pages.

Pannier, F. (1985). *The potential effects of climatic changes on mangrove ecosystems.* Discussion paper prepared for SCOPE–ENUWAR Tropical Workshop, Caracas, Venezuela.

Pannier, F., and Pannier, Y.R.F. (1977). Physiological interpretation of the distribution of mangroves on the South American coast. *Interciencia*, **2**(3), 153–162. (in Spanish).

Payson, P.D. (1982). *Fish Assemblages in Medway Creek Relative to Prey Resource Background and Habitat Availability: Are the Assemblages Structured?* M.S. Thesis, Queen's University, Kingston, Ontario: 352 pages.

Pittock, A.B. (1985). Australia and nuclear winter. *Search*, **15**(11–12), 332–338.

Pittock, A.B., Ackerman, T.A., Crutzen, P., MacCracken, M., Shapiro, C., and Turco, R.P. (1985). *The Environmental Consequences of Nuclear War.* Volume I: Physical. SCOPE 28a. John Wiley & Sons, Chichester.

Pittock, A.B., and Nix, H.A. (1985a). Effects of nuclear winter scenarios on Australian biomass productivity. (Abstr.). *Abstracts*, Australia and New Zealand Environmental Effects of Nuclear War Workshop, Melbourne, Australia.

Pittock, A.B., and Nix, H.A. (1985b). The effect of changing climate on Australian biomass production: A preliminary study. *Climatic Change* (in press).

Ponomarev, V.M., Ivanishchev, V.V., and Mikhailov, V.V. (1984). *Lake ecosystem simulation under extreme forcing.* Discussion paper for SCOPE–ENUWAR Conference. U.S.S.R. Academy of Sciences Research Computer Center, Leningrad.

Raper, S.C.B., Wigley, T.M.L., Mayes, P.R., Jones, P.D., and Salinger, M.J. (1984). Variations in surface air temperature. Part 3: The Antarctic, 1957–1982. *Monthly Weather Rev.*, **112**, 1341–1353.

Rawson, D.S. (1961). A critical analysis of the limnological variables used in assessing the productivity of northern Saskatchewan lakes. *Verh. Internat. Verein Limnol.*, **14**, 160–166.

Redmann, R.E. (1971). Caribou dioxide exchange by native Great Plains grasses. *Can. J. Bot.*, **49**, 1341–1344.

Richards, P.W. (1966) *The Tropical Rainforest.* Cambridge University Press, Cambridge: 450 pages.

Richardson, K., Beardall, J., and Raven, J.A. (1983). Adaptation of unicellular algae to irradiance: An analysis of strategies. *New Photologist*, **93**, 157–191.

Rinckey, G.R., and Saloman, C.H. (1964). Effect of reduced water temperature on fishes of Tampa Bay, Florida. *Quart. Jour. Florida Acad. Sci.*, **27**(1), 9–16.

Robinson, J.P. (1979). *The Effects of Weapons on Ecosystems.* UNEP Studies, Vol. I. Pergammon Press, Oxford, U.K.: 70 pages.

Rodriguez, G. (1975). Some aspects of the ecology of tropical estuaries. In Golley, F.B., and Medina, E. (Eds.). *Tropical Ecological Systems*, Ecology Series II: 313–333. Springer-Verlag, New York.

The Royal Society of New Zealand. (1985). *The Threat of Nuclear War: A New Zealand Perspective.* The Royal Society of New Zealand Miscellaneous Series 11, Wellington: 83 pages.

Rundel, P.W. (1981). Fire as an ecological factor. In Lange, O.L., Nobel, P.S., Osmond, C.B., and Ziegler, H. (Eds.). *Encyclopedia of Plant Physiology* Vol. 12A: Physiological Plant Ecology I. Responses to the Physical Environment. Springer-Verlag, New York.

Sakai, A., and Otsuka, K. (1970). Freezing resistance of alpine plants. *Ecology*, **51**, 665–671.

Savile, D.B.O. (1972). *Arctic Adaptations in Plants.* Monograph No. 6, Canada Department of Agriculture, Ottawa: 81 pages.

Shinn, E.A. (1976). Coral reef recovery in Florida and the Persian Gulf. *Environ. Geol.*, **1**, 241–254.

Snelson, F.F., Jr., and W.K. Bradley, Jr. (1978). Mortality of fishes due to cold on the East Coast of Florida, January, 1977. *Florida Scientist*, **41**, 1–12.

Somers, D.E. (1981). *An Investigation into the Environmental Control of Cold Acclimation in High Arctic Populations of* Salix arctica *and* Saxifraga oppositifolia. M.S. Thesis. University of Alberta, Edmonton.

Storey, M. (1937). The relation between normal range and mortality of fishes due to cold at Sanibel Island, Florida. *Ecology*, **18**(1), 10–26.

Storey, M., and Gudger, E.W.(1936). Mortality of fishes due to cold at Sanibel Island, Florida, 1886–1936. *Ecology*, **17**(4), 640–648.

Sverdrup, H.U., Johnson, M.W., and Fleming, R.H. (1942). *The Oceans. Their Physics, Chemistry, and General Biology.* Prentice-Hall, Inc., Englewood Cliffs, N.J: 1087 pages.

Svoboda, J. (1982). Due to the Little Ice Age climatic impact, most of the vegetative cover in the Canadian High Arctic is of recent origin. A hypothesis. (Abstr.) *Proceedings 33 Alaska Science Conference*, Science in the North. Fairbanks, Alaska.

Svoboda, J., and Taylor, H.W. (1985). *Nuclear winter and the Northern ecosystem.* Unpublished discussion paper for the SCOPE–ENUWAR Workshop, Toronto, Canada.

Takahashi, T. et al. (1984). *Seasonal study of the* CO_2 *and tracer distribution in the high latitude North and South Atlantic Oceans.* Unpublished manuscript.

Tamrazyn, G.P. (1974). Total lake water resources of the planet. *Bull. Geol. Soc. Finland*, **46**, 23–27.

Timin, M.E., Collier, B.D., Zich, J., and Walters, D. (1973). A Computer Simulation of the Arctic Tundra Ecosystem Near Barrow, Alaska. *U.S. Tundra Biome Report 73–1*, University of Alaska, Fairbanks: 82 pages.

U.S.S.R. Committee for the International Hydrologic Decade. (1977). *Atlas of World Water Balance.* UNESCO Press, Paris.

U.S.S.R. Committee for the International Hydrologic Decade. (1978). *World Water Balance and Water Resources of the Earth.* UNESCO Press, Paris: 663 pages.

Valiela, I., Teal, J.M., Cogswell, C., Allen, S., Goehringer, D., Van Etten, R., and Hartmen, J. (1984). Some long-term consequences of sewage contamination in salt marsh ecosystems. In *Proceedings of the Workshop on Wetlands Treatment on Municipal Wastewater*, University of Massachusetts, (in press).

van Zindern Bakker, E.M. (1974). *An Ecophysiological Study of Black Spruce in Central Alberta.* Ph.D. Dissertation. University of Alberta, Edmonton.

Vickery, M.L. (1984). *Ecology of Tropical Plants.* John Wiley & Sons, Chichester: 170 pages.

Walter, H. (1973). *Vegetation of the Earth.* Springer-Verlag, New York: 273 pages.

Walter, H., and Medina, E. (1969). Die Bodentemperatur als aussschlaggebebder Faktor für die Gliederrung der subalpinen und alpinen Stufe in den Anden Venezuelas. *Ber. Dtsch. Bot. Gez.*, **82**, 275–281. (in German).

Walton, D.W.H. (1984). The terrestrial environment. In Laws, R.M. (Ed.). *Antarctic Ecology.* Academic Press, New York.

Warren, S.G., and Wiscombe, W.J. (1985). Dirty snow after nuclear war. *Nature,* **313**(7), 467– 469.

Weinstein, D.A. (1983). A User's Guide to FORNUT. *ERC Report No. 28,* Ecosystems Research Center, Cornell University, Ithaca, NY.

Weinstein, D.A., and Shugart, H.H. (1983). Ecological modelling of landscape dynamics. In Mooney, H., and Godron, M. (Eds.) *Disturbance and Ecosystems.* 29– 46. Springer-Verlag, New York.

Weiser, W. (Ed.). (1973). *Effects of Temperature on Ectothermic Organisms.* Springer-Verlag, New York.

Whittaker, R.H. (1975). *Communities and Ecosystems.* MacMillan Publishing Co., New York: 385 pages.

Wilson, A.M., and Sarles, J.A. (1978). Quantification of growth, drought tolerance and avoidance of blue grama seedlings. *Agron. J.,* **70**, 231–237.

Zieman, J.C. (1975). Seasonal variation of turtle grass, *Thalassia testdinum,* with reference to temperature and salinity effects. *Aq. Bot.,* **1**, 107–123.

Zieman, J.C. (1982). *The Ecology of the Seagrasses of South Florida: A Community Profile.* FWS/OBS-82/25. U.S. Fish and Wildlife Service, Washington, D.C.

Environmental Consequences of Nuclear War Volume II:
Ecological and Agricultural Effects
Edited by M.A. Harwell and T.C. Hutchinson
© 1985 SCOPE. Published by John Wiley & Sons Ltd

CHAPTER 3

Additional Potential Effects of Nuclear War on Ecological Systems

THOMAS C. HUTCHINSON, MARK A. HARWELL,
WENDELL P. CROPPER, JR., AND HERBERT D. GROVER

Primary Contributions by: C. C. Harwell, M. Havas, K. Limburg,
D. W. H. Walton, R. C. Worrest

3.1 INTRODUCTION

In the event of a major nuclear war, ecological systems would be exposed to unprecedented levels and combinations of radiation, toxic materials, and climatic stresses. It is difficult to specify probable biological responses to such conditions because of variability and uncertainty in the potential exposure levels, and lack of experimental evidence comparable to a post-nuclear war environment.

Ecosystem responses to nuclear war-induced climatic stresses were discussed in Chapter 2. In this chapter, we initially summarize biological and ecosystem responses to enhanced UV-B, air pollutants, radiation, and fire. The concentrations and biological responses associated with these perturbations are based on current experience and experimentation. Additional research is needed to quantify probable post-nuclear war exposures and potential responses.

Many of these stresses would be experienced at significant levels only in restricted regions. For example, significant acid rain and acid fogs and elevated air pollutant exposures would probably be restricted to quite localized regions associated with burning urban and industrial targets. However, these localized exposure zones could be widely distributed in North America, Europe, and Asia, as well as in other targeted regions. The effects of enhanced UV-B could be felt throughout the Northern Hemisphere and perhaps the entire Earth. The most serious radiation exposure would probably be limited to areas of high dose-rate local fallout, rather than involving areas that experienced only global fallout. Nevertheless, such local fallout areas could cover significant fractions of the landscape (5%–20%) in North America, Europe, and the U.S.S.R. with lethal levels of radiation. The total areas that might be covered by one or more of these stresses could be enormous, and the effects, especially in combination, might be devastating for agriculture and human populations.

The latter part of Chapter 3 provides a summary of all of the potential effects of nuclear war on the variety of the Earth's ecosystems, including perturbations from climatic alterations, radiation, pollutants, and UV-B. This section, then reflects all of the considerations in Part I of this volume.

3.2 RESPONSES AND EFFECTS OF UV-B [1]

3.2.1 Introduction

Potential stratospheric ozone perturbations following a nuclear war would be highly dependent on the yield of the individual explosions. The scenario involving mainly high-yield nuclear weapons described in Volume I yields a maximum ozone column depletion of 44% after six months. Scenarios involving lower yield weapons (e.g., Ambio, 1982) would produce little stratospheric ozone reduction. As calculated with simple one-dimensional models assuming an unperturbed climate, maximum ozone depletion would be reached in 6 to 12 months, and a depletion of at least 10% could persist for about three to six years for the high-yield scenario. The effectively instantaneous meridional and longitudinal spreading that occurs in the one-dimensional model utilized in these calculations may underestimate ozone reduction in the Northern mid-latitudes for the first few months, when the injected NO_x would remain peaked over the involved areas. Increases in ultraviolet flux at the surface would depend on latitude and season, and absorption by intervening clouds of smoke and other species. Until the smoke substantially cleared, the UV-B flux could not significantly increase at the surface, even for large ozone reductions. Changes in stratospheric ozone concentrations by chemical reactions with nitrogen oxides and by smoke-induced temperature and circulation changes could affect the recovery time of the atmosphere, even after smoke particles were removed (Pittock et al., 1985).

Stratospheric ozone currently functions effectively as an ultraviolet screen by filtering out solar insolation in the ultraviolet wavelengths as it passes through the stratosphere, thus allowing only small amounts of the longer wavelengths of UV radiation to leak through to the surface of the Earth. Although currently this radiation comprises only a minute fraction (less than 1%) of the total solar spectrum, it can have a major impact on biological systems because of its actinic nature. There would be several biospheric consequences of increased levels of solar UV-B radiation (i.e., light in the 280 – 320 nm band) reaching the surface of the Earth.

---

[1] This section written by R. Worrest.

Many organic molecules, most notably DNA and proteins, absorb UV-B radiation, which can initiate photochemical reactions. Most of the known biological effects of UV-B radiation are damaging, and the defense mechanisms that serve to protect both plants and animals from current levels of UV-B radiation are quite varied. These mechanisms might not suffice under conditions of the extreme levels of UV-B radiation that could follow a nuclear war. It should also be remembered that UV-B levels differ both latitudinally and altitudinally, with the highest exposures at the tropics or at high altitudes. The current difference between the extremes of exposures is about 3- to 6-fold, but biota are presently adapted to the levels that are normally experienced at their locations.

3.2.2 Biological Sensitivity Functions

The biological response to ultraviolet radiation can be very wavelength dependent. This wavelength specificity makes it necessary to develop weighting functions to express ultraviolet radiation in biologically meaningful terms (Caldwell, 1981). Biological action spectra normally serve as the basis for these weighting functions.

A generalized equation to describe the use of a biological weighting function is:

$$I_c = \int I_\lambda \cdot E_\lambda \cdot d\lambda \qquad (3.1)$$

where:

I_c = effective irradiance

I_λ = spectral irradiance

E_λ = relative effectiveness of irradiance at wavelength

λ to elicit a particular biological response.

The weighting function is normally taken as an action spectrum for a particular biological response. Several action spectra have been developed describing the response of biological systems to UV-B radiation (Figure 3.1). Examples are a representation of a DNA response as described by Setlow (1974), a generalized plant response (Caldwell, 1968), an erythemal action spectrum (Nachtwey and Rundel, 1981), and a photoinhibition response for plant photosynthesis (Jones and Kok, 1966).

Based on an analytic characterization of ultraviolet skylight by Green et al. (1980), a 40% ozone reduction at 45°N latitude would only result in a 5% increase in total solar ultraviolet (between 290 nm and 360 nm) daily flux. This would be of minimal consequence if radiation throughout the 290–360 nm waveband were of equal biological effectiveness. However, when the biological weighting functions based on the action spectra are

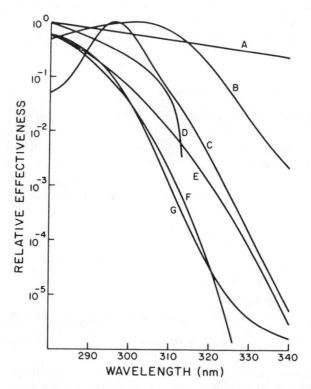

Figure 3.1   Plots of several action spectra used as weighting function for assessing the biological impact of UV-B radiation. From Worrest (1983). A. Photoinhibition action spectrum (Jones and Kok, 1966); B. Robertson–Berger Meter; C. erythema; D. Caldwell's (1968) generalized plant action spectrum; E. A721, used at the University of Florida; F. A79, used by the U.S.D.A. Agricultural Research Center. Beltsville, MD; G. generalized DNA action spectrum (Setlow, 1974)

employed, a very different picture emerges. Based on the DNA response described by Setlow (1974), a 40% ozone decrease would result in a 213% increase in biologically effective radiation (DNA damage). The generalized plant response would increase by 132% (plant damage) (Table 3. 1).

TABLE 3.1

RELATIONSHIP BETWEEN OZONE DEPLETION

AND BIOLOGICAL EFFECTIVENESS OF INCREASED UV-B[a]

Ozone Decrease	Ultraviolet Increase		Increase in Biological Effectiveness	
	290-320 nm	320-360 nm	DNA	Plant
10%	8%	0.4%	28%	21%
20%	17%	0.8%	67%	49%
30%	27%	1.2%	125%	85%
40%	38%	1.6%	213%	132%

[a] Increase in absolute and biologically effective ultraviolet daily irradiance at the surface of the Earth associated with various levels of stratospheric ozone depletion. Absolute irradiance is based on a model by Green et al. (1980) [45°N latitude at the summer solstice; 20-year average ozone thickness at this latitude and date = 0.338 cm]. DNA action spectrum based on Setlow (1974), and plant action spectrum based on Caldwell (1968). Action spectra referenced to 300 nm = 1.00

3.2.3 Effects on Terrestrial Plants

Terrestrial plants (in non-arid zones) have evolved to maximize exposure of their photosynthetic tissues. Therefore, these tissues are concomitantly exposed to the potential stress of solar ultraviolet radiation. Many studies have demonstrated that photosynthesis is inhibited by UV-B radiation. In addition, it has been shown that UV-B radiation can affect leaf expansion, abscisic acid content, pigment concentrations, plant growth, carbohydrate metabolism, fruit growth and yield, pollen germination, and pollen tube growth (Caldwell, 1981; Teramura, 1982; Teramura, 1983).

Of primary importance to humans in the months following a nuclear war could be the effect of ultraviolet radiation on total yield of crop species.

The effect of UV-B radiation on the yield of several crop species has been studied. One series of experiments relevant to the ozone depletion problem is the research by Teramura (1983). Although the results were variable across years, significant reductions in crop yield following exposure to UV-B radiation simulating 16% and 25% ozone depletion were found for two cultivars of soybean (range of reductions, 14–25%). Not only was the total yield reduced but protein concentrations declined by as much as 5% in one cultivar during two years of the study, and seed lipid concentrations were reduced by 3–5% in another cultivar.

As the atmospheric particulates were gradually removed in the weeks and months following a major nuclear war, plants would become exposed to enhanced levels of UV-B radiation. Because of the long recovery time of the ozone layer, the ratio of UV-B radiation to photosynthetically active radiation would be far greater than normal as the atmosphere cleared. In studies involving soybean plants, it was found that supplemental UV-B radiation adversely affected net photosynthesis and some growth parameters when the exposure occurred concurrently with low levels of photosynthetically active radiation (Teramura, 1980; Biggs et al., 1981; Teramura, 1982).

There are other problems that arise in plants following exposure to high levels of UV-B radiation. Flint and Caldwell (1984) found that 2- to 3-fold increases in biologically effective ultraviolet radiation were sufficient to inhibit pollen germination. A more subtle effect of UV-B radiation might be on the timing of the flowering of plants. The results of recent experiments have demonstrated that UV-B radiation can have either an inhibitory or stimulatory effect on flowering, depending on plant species, growth conditions, and other factors (Caldwell, 1968; Biggs and Basiouny, 1975; Biggs and Kossuth, 1978; Mirecki and Teramura, 1984). Whether UV-B radiation directly influences flowering events or plays an indirect role through changes in photosynthate reserves is not yet known.

Some plant species apparently acclimatize to enhanced levels of UV-B radiation. Although the ozone thickness in the tropics is significantly less than at temperate latitudes and ambient levels of UV-B irradiance are much higher, temperate-zone alpine species exist at high elevations in the tropics (Robberecht et al., 1980; Caldwell et al., 1980). Such species are exposed to a wide range of UV-B levels over their geographical ranges. There are inherent differences in sensitivity of the photosynthetic system to UV-B radiation damage that have been demonstrated for species of the same genus, or even races of the same species, which occur in different locations on the latitudinal gradient of the arctic-alpine life zone (Caldwell et al., 1982). If acclimatization to environments with high ultraviolet exposure levels is merely a phenotypic response, the plants might be able to cope with small increases in UV-B irradiance. If, on the other hand, acclimatization involves genotypic change for some species, the heterogeneity of the gene pool would influence the population-level adaptability to the enhanced UV-B following a nuclear war.

Plant resistance to a change in an environmental parameter is, in part, a genotypically controlled, species-specific characteristic (Levitt, 1980). An alteration of an environmental stress could thus lead to a change in the competitive balance of the plant community resulting from inherent differences in plant resistance. Many plants have been shown to exhibit a wide range of sensitivity to enhanced UV-B radiation (Teramura, 1983). Since UV-B radiation can be considered as an environmental stress, any increase in UV irradiance could lead to changes in competitive ability within plant communities through differential resistance of the competing species (Caldwell, 1977). Competition could occur within the same species (intraspecific) or between different species (interspecific).

Intraspecific competition becomes increasingly important in monospecific communities such as agricultural systems. On the other hand, in natural ecosystems with high species diversity, interspecific competition predominates. In agricultural systems, interspecific competition could also be important between a crop and weed species. Total harvestable yield, as well as its quality, can be altered by the presence of weeds. Because of the subtle nature of UV-B-radiation stress, an enhancement of solar UV-B radiation might alter the competitive balance of plants indirectly more than directly, permanently reducing ecosystem primary productivity. The results of Gold and Caldwell (1983) and Fox and Caldwell (1978) support this hypothesis.

In natural ecosystems, although the total productivity might not be permanently altered as a consequence of increased UV-B radiation, a shift could occur in species composition. Because of the shifts in competitive balance, increasing solar UV-B radiation would pose a considerable risk both to agricultural as well as natural ecosystems. In agricultural systems, any increase in weed competitiveness would certainly result in reduction in actual harvestable crop yields, a lowering of crop quality, or an alteration in disease or pest sensitivity. Presumably, more UV-B-tolerant species would proliferate at the expense of the sensitive ones. Changes in the competitive balance of native species could also have profound effects on natural ecosystems. Even very subtle differences in sensitivity could result in large changes in species composition over time and possibly affect ecosystem function.

3.2.4 Effects on Marine Ecosystems

The euphotic zone, i.e., those depths with light levels sufficient for net photosynthesis to be positive, is frequently taken as the water column down to the depth at which there is 1% of the surface photosynthetically active radiation. In marine ecosystems, UV-B radiation penetrates approximately the upper 10% of the coastal euphotic zone before it is reduced to 1% of its surface irradiance (Jerlov, 1976). Penetration of UV-B radiation into natural waters is a key variable in assessing the potential impact of this light on any aquatic ecosystem. The calculations of the penetration of UV-B radiation and biologically effective dose rates in natural waters has been described in detail (Smith and Baker, 1982; Baker and Smith, 1982a,b). Based on the data, it has been calculated that near the surface of the ocean, enhanced UV-B radiation simulating a 25% reduction in ozone concentration would cause a decrease in production by about 35% (Smith and Baker, 1982). The estimated reduction in production for the whole euphotic zone would be about 10%. These calculations were based on attenuation lengths, i.e., the product of depth in the water column and the diffuse attenuation coefficient of the water. Therefore, waters of various turbidities and absorption characteristics could be compared, a factor that must be considered when dealing with the turbid environment of coastal areas caused by potential post-war storms.

The amount of UV-B radiation reaching the ocean's surface has long been suspected as a factor influencing primary production (Steeman-Nielsen, 1964; Jitts et al., 1976; Lorenzen, 1979; Smith et al., 1980; Thomson et al., 1980; Worrest et al., 1980). Research shows convincingly that ultraviolet radiation, at present levels incident at the surface of natural bodies of water, has an influence on phytoplankton productivity. If one assumes that current phytoplankton populations sense and control their average vertical position in such a way as to limit UV-B exposure to a tolerable level, then a 10% increase in solar UV-B exposure would necessitate a downward movement of the average position, thereby reducing the average UV-B exposure by 10%. There would be a corresponding reduction of light available for photosynthesis at the increased depths, and the magnitude of visible light loss would be proportional to the ratio of the absorption coefficient of photosynthetically active radiation (PAR) divided by the absorption coefficient of UV-B radiation. The percentage loss of PAR would always be less than the percentage change in UV-B radiation. The loss of PAR in many locations might not be significant. However, in some very productive areas, especially high latitude ocean areas, PAR is the primary limiting factor on marine productivity (Russell-Hunter, 1970). From optical measurements, Calkins (1982) estimated the PAR loss to be in the range of 2.5–5% for a 10% UV-B increase.

In addition, the sensitivity of various species of phytoplankton to UV-B radiation differs; a difference that would result in shifts in community composition following changes in exposure to UV-B radiation (Worrest et al., 1981a,b). One effect of enhanced levels of UV-B radiation would be to alter the size distribution of the component producers in a marine ecosystem. Increasing or decreasing the size of the representative primary producers upon which consumers graze can significantly increase the energy allotment required for consumption, thereby reducing the feeding efficiency of the consumer. In addition, the food quality of the producers is altered by exposure to UV-B radiation. Döhler (1982) demonstrated that protein content, dry weight, and pigment concentration are all depressed by enhanced levels of UV-B radiation.

The impact on marine fisheries as a food supply to humans would be significant if the species that adapted to enhanced UV-B radiation were of different nutritional value (i.e., if they altered growth and fecundity of the consumers or different accessibility to human survivors). If the indirect impact of suppression upon consumers were linear, a 10% reduction of primary production would result in a 10% reduction in fish production. A question still under investigation is whether the trophodynamic relationships might be non-linear. For example, there may be an amplification factor involved that results in a relatively greater impact at higher trophic levels than at the primary-producer level. In the type of example described by Worrest (1983), a 10% reduction in energy transfer efficiency would result in a 27% reduction in fish-food production.

Zooplankton are critical components in typical aquatic food webs which lead to larger animals, including those comprising human food fisheries. Zooplankton contain nearly all groups of aquatic animals, at least for some phase in their life history, such as the egg or larval stage. Many zooplankton species normally live very close to the surface, even in daylight, while others occupy the near-surface layer during only part of their life cycle. The near-surface layer is a very important zone in the interactions of the physical/chemical/biological components of aquatic systems. Investigators have reported that the effect of increased UV-B radiation on some marine zooplankton (e.g., copepods, shrimp larvae, crab larvae) is to increase the mortality of the organisms and to decrease the fecundity of the survivors (Karanas et al., 1979; Damkaer et al., 1980; Damkaer et al., 1981; Karanas et al., 1981; Damkaer and Dey, 1983). Regardless of the cellular-level responses to ultraviolet irradiation, it is usually noted that up to some level of exposure, there is no apparent effect on the organism. However, once this threshold is exceeded, either the repair systems themselves become inactivated by the radiation, or the damage to the general tissues is beyond the capacity of the repair systems. The apparent thresholds are near current incident ultraviolet levels.

Damkaer et al. (1981) compared the estimated effective ultraviolet daily doses under various ozone reductions with survival thresholds. A 40% ozone reduction significantly reduces the window of safety at the beginning of the zooplankton near-surface season. Whether or not the populations could endure a drastically reduced time at the near-surface waters is not known. Success of any year-class depends on the timing of a great number of other events in addition to levels of exposure to UV-B radiation.

The direct effect of UV-B radiation on food-fish larvae closely parallels the effect on zooplankton. There is an implication in some review papers (e.g., Hunter et al., 1981, 1982; NRC, 1984) that UV-B damage would be overcome by the maximally functioning photo-repair mechanism. Up to some level (daily-dose threshold) this is probably true, but near-surface exposure levels would exceed threshold levels following the washout of particulate material caused by a nuclear war. Hunter et al. (1982) realized that information is required on seasonal abundances and vertical distributions of fish larvae, vertical mixing, and penetration of UV-B into appropriate water columns before effects of incident or increased levels of exposure to UV-B radiation can be predicted. For March through October, with the larvae described by Hunter et al. (1981) and with a 10 m mixing layer, a 10% increase in incident UV-B radiation would not exceed threshold doses in less than 20 days. With a 20% increase in incident UV-B radiation, however, the depth of the threshold dose-rate is increased. In the dose/dose-rate threshold model, all of the larvae within a 10 m mixed layer in April and August would be killed after 15 days. It was calculated that about 8% of the annual larval population throughout the entire water column would be directly killed by a 20% increase in exposure to UV-B radiation. For models with increased mixing, to 15 m, there is no predicted effect until UV-B radiation increases by 50%, and no additional loss beyond that level with a 60% increase.

3.2.5 Effects on Human Health

Human health is influenced by UV radiation in many ways; for example, by the formation of vitamin D, sunburn, eye diseases, immunological changes, photoallergic reactions, and skin diseases, including skin cancer. Skin cancer stands out as one problem that increases with increased UV-B radiation. The severity of the health and other biological effects of radiation depend on its spectral composition, irradiance, and exposure time. UV-B radiation has been demonstrated, in many instances, to be several orders of magnitude more biologically effective than UV-A radiation.

Epidemiological studies have shown that the incidence of non-melanoma skin cancer correlates with exposure to sunlight. While non-melanoma skin cancers occur in people of all skin types, the incidence is highest in light-skinned people. In patients with *Xeroderma pigmentosum* (a rare recessive genetic disorder), who have increased susceptibility to skin cancer, there is reduced repair of DNA damage caused by UV-B radiation. Animal experiments have revealed that UV-B radiation is the most effective wavelength region for carcinogenesis by UV radiation. These data indicate that increased incidence of non-melanoma skin cancer could be expected from increased UV-B irradiance.

Non-melanoma skin cancer is exceptional among the biological effects of UV-B in that statistics are available. Studies indicate that, apart from the radiation amplification, biological amplifications exist for the particular biological effects. Specifically, with unchanged exposure habits, for every 1% decrease in total ozone, the incidence of basal cell carcinomas increases by 2% to 4% and the incidence of squamous cell carcinomas increases by 3% to 8%. Although the incidence of squamous cell carcinoma is only about 20% of the total, it is more invasive and lethal than basal cell carcinoma. While these conditions can usually be treated effectively if medical help is available, they currently still result in thousands of deaths per year. In the United States, there are approximately 500,000 new cases of non-melanoma skin cancer per year, and the total annual number of deaths, about 5000, is comparable to the annual total for malignant melanoma. Mortality rates would be higher in the absence of medical attention, a likely situation after a large-scale nuclear war.

There are several indications that sunlight may also be one of the causative factors in the pathogenesis of malignant melanoma, which affects people of all skin types. These indications come from epidemiological and clinical observations which, because they deal with exposure to total sunlight, do not point to any particular wavelength range in the solar spectrum. In cases where UV-B radiation is involved, a decrease in stratospheric ozone might be expected to increase the incidence of melanoma. In some types, such as *Lentigo melanoma* and in melanoma arising in patients with *Xeroderma pigmentosum*, the relationship to sunlight is relatively clear. In other cases, the evidence is circumstantial. The incidence of malignant melanoma in patients with *Xeroderma pigmentosum* suggests that, at least in these cases, UV-B radiation is involved.

UV-B radiation has been shown to alter several responses of the immunological system. UV-B radiation has been reported to depress delayed hypersensitivity responses in human skin. It causes reduction in the number of Langerhans cells in human skin, and induces alterations in the distribution and function of subpopulations of circulating lymphocytes in humans. Effects of UV-B radiation on the immunological system diminish the ability of a mouse to reject a transplanted tumor induced by UV-B radiation in another mouse. UV-B radiation also impedes the ability of a mouse to reject tumors initiated by UV-B radiation in its own skin. The doses of UV-B radiation causing these immunological changes are much smaller than the doses which induce tumors. A primary concern is the possibility that these immunological changes may contribute to the development of malignant melanoma in humans, especially as the immunological changes are caused mainly by the shortest wavelengths in sunlight.

Overall, although the effects of enhanced exposures to UV-B would not be as severe as the effects of acute climatic disturbances on agricultural and natural ecosystems, it seems likely that significant, adverse biological effects would occur. In marine ecosystems, there could be substantial effects on phytoplankton and zooplankton productivity and composition. Human health effects could also be expected, including increased incidences of eye disease and various forms of skin cancer.

3.3 ATMOSPHERIC POLLUTANTS

3.3.1 Introduction

As a consequence of a major nuclear war, large quantities of various gases and particulate pollutants would be generated, both from the bursts themselves and from the burning of cities, fuel depots, and natural vegetation and crops over a period of days to weeks (Volume I). These pollutants would include various oxides of nitrogen, sulphur dioxide, ozone, hydrochloric acid, cyanides, photochemical oxidants, pyrotoxins, and hydrocarbons. Carbon monoxide would also be generated in large quantities from low temperature, persistent fires. Around the edge of the particulate-laden smoke clouds, oxidation of hydrocarbons with NO_x could result in the production of photochemical oxidants, such as peroxy acetylnitrate (PAN). Massive amounts of particulate matter could be transported from centers of combustion, and the expanding forest and grassland fires could add to this load for weeks. The dust and bomb debris deposited from nuclear weapon bursts would deposit radioactive material both locally and, eventually, globally. Particulates from combustion would deposit soot, hydrocarbons, sulphates, ammonia, and elements from burning vegetation and fuels. Large quantities of manganese, cadmium, copper, cobalt, nickel, and arsenic would be transported from cities and eventually be deposited in downwind locations.

The quantities and distribution of pollutants over time are dealt with to some extent in Volume I, and by Crutzen and Birks (1982) and NRC (1985). Svirezhev et al. (1985) considered a worst-case scenario, suggesting that large quantities of NO_x would be produced, as well as SO_2 and sulphate. They suggested that rain events of pH 2.4 could continue for a number of weeks over mid-latitudes in the Northern Hemisphere. Volume I authors, using a much less severe scenario, suggested perhaps two weeks of rains of approximately pH 3.0. NO_x, O_3, and photooxidants would be released from combustion, and smoldering fires would generate large quantities of CO.

In the discussion that follows, we assume that the Northern Hemisphere, especially in the mid-latitudes, would be exposed to elevated levels of these pollutants, recognizing that there are very large uncertainties as to concentrations and spatial and temporal patterns of each of the pollutants. Relatively little attention has yet been paid to quantification of them and even less to exposures that would be experienced by human survivors and by agricultural crops, livestock, and natural ecosystems. This is an area requiring further research and clarification in order for the biological effects to be more precisely characterized.

3.3.2 Dust Effects on Vegetation

Significant dust deposition on vegetation following a nuclear war would probably be limited to localized regions associated with surface bursts. The effects of inert dust alone (i.e., ignoring the effects of radioactivity associated with dust) can be estimated from the Mt. St. Helens volcanic eruption in the State of Washington in May, 1980. This eruption deposited layers of ash 0.5 to 20 cm thick on a large area of forest to the northeast of the mountain. Ash remained on the foliage despite wind and 10 cm of rain in the two months following the eruption (Seymour et al., 1983). The dust was largely inert and silicaceous, but significant damage occurred to the pre-1980 foliage after the eruption. Recovery of native vegetation initially was from coppicing and from underground shoots; later invasions by weedy species has occurred. Following a nuclear war, however, the effects of dust deposition of the magnitude of Mt. St. Helens would be very limited in extent, duration, and significance.

3.3.3 Asbestos

NRC (1985) indicated that 5 million tons of asbestos could be released into the atmosphere by nuclear war from city destruction. This would probably substantially elevate exposure to human survivors in the local fallout areas and beyond, with the health effects from asbestos being added to the other threats to humans. Such asbestos-related carcinomas as mesothelioma, and lung cancer have incubation times from 10–35 years; short-term effects would not be obvious from such asbestos exposure.

For plants, asbestos fibers are inert and would be merely part of the dust component. Asbestos dispersal as a result of nuclear war has only recently been recognized, and it needs further attention. It is unlikely, however, to have significant ecological impacts, and its effects on humans would likely not be major compared with the direct effects of nuclear detonations or indirect effects on climate and societal systems.

3.3.4 Oxides of Nitrogen

Volume I describes the enormous quantities of NO_x which a large-scale nuclear war would produce. Urban, industrial, and forest and grassland fires could also yield very large quantities. The NO_x would be mixed through a broad depth of atmosphere. Total production of NO_x following a nuclear war could be equal to the total current annual production from automobile and industrial combustion processes. The distribution of NO_x horizontally and vertically is a matter that needs further study. An increase in exposure to humans and ecosystems would be expected (Svirezhev et al., 1985), but concentrations are unlikely to reach 1 ppm, except very locally.

NO_x alone is not as phytotoxic as O_3 or SO_2. Considerable evidence shows that NO_x acts synergistically with SO_2 and O_3, increasing the total phytotoxicity. Altman and Dittmer (1966) reported that for 11 species tested for their susceptibility to NO_2 as seedlings, all showed some effects at 20 ppm when exposed for 4 hours. These species included such diverse plants as sunflower, french bean, and kale. Longer term but lower concentration exposures were examined by Taylor and Eaton (1966), who exposed tomato seedlings continuously for 10–22 days and found a significant growth suppression. This study, and others, suggest that it is very unlikely that NO_x levels below 1ppm would be phytotoxic. Thus, based on initial estimates of the concentrations and extent of NO_x following a nuclear war, it is concluded that the ecological and human effects would be insignificant.

3.3.5. Ozone

While ozone levels in the lower troposphere could continue to increase after a nuclear war as a result of oxidation of hydrocarbons in air with NO_x, it is suggested that levels would not exceed 1 ppm and that this would take some time to be achieved (Volume I). We need therefore to consider the sensitivity of crops and ecosystems to ozone in general, especially at concentrations of about 1 ppm.

Ozone is a potent phytotoxic gas, which is currently responsible for large crop losses in the United States and elsewhere, especially for salad crops in California. It has been stated that ozone and other oxidants cause crop losses of approximately 15% in eastern North America. It also has been shown to be a toxic gas to forests in the southwestern U.S. (Miller, 1983; McLaughlin, 1985), where ponderosa pine and Jeffery pine are especially sensitive. Recently ozone has been put forward as a factor in forest decline in eastern North America. It is also suggested that increases in ozone levels in central Europe are a major factor in the decline and dieback of trees in the West German, Swiss, and Austrian forests (McLaughlin, 1985; Ashmore et al., 1985). In central Europe, it is generally agreed that a number of factors combine to cause the rapid spread of forest decline. Ozone levels have increased more than 3-fold in southern Germany since 1960. Annual mean values of ozone vary from 50 to $100 \mu g \cdot m^{-3}$ (i.e., 25 to 50 ppb), with annual maxima typically from 140 to $320 \mu g \cdot m^{-3}$. In California's San Bernadino Mountains, where ozone damage has been severe, ozone has been recorded at up to $1160 \mu g \cdot m^{-3}$, with 34% to 45% of summer hours being over 100 ppb O_3 (Miller, 1983). In the San Bernadino and San Gabriel mountains, pines showed foliar injury, premature leaf fall, decreased photosynthetic capacity, and reduced radial growth. In the rural northeastern U.S., where annual averages of O_3 are 100 $\mu g \cdot m^{-3}$, with hourly maxima of 250 $\mu g \cdot m^{-3}$ (125 ppb), growth of tree seedlings and biomass of native herbaceous species are reduced. Of additional relevance to post-nuclear war studies are the findings that ozone-weakened trees show reduced carbohydrate production, increasing the susceptibility to pine bark beetles, increasing mortality, and changing species composition in heavily impacted areas (Miller, 1983).

Table 3.2 shows the ozone sensitivity of a large number of agricultural species. It is apparent that exposures to less than 0.5 ppm for a few hours will cause damage to most species, including maize (*Zea mays*), potato (*Sloanum tuberosum*), pinto beans, wheat (*Triticum aestivum*), and barley (*Hordeum vulgare*).

Although the tropospheric ozone levels that would be experienced following a nuclear war are very uncertain, it seems that ozone would be more likely to cause damage to vegetation than NO_x. Better resolution of the tropospheric concentrations of ozone after a nuclear war is needed. The potential effects of *reduced* stratospheric ozone (increasing UV-B exposures) are discussed in Section 3.2.

3.3.6 Sulphur Dioxide

Sulphur dioxide is perhaps the best known phytotoxic gas, having caused death of forests very extensively around point sources, such as smelters where ores containing large amounts of sulphur are processed. The devastation can be seen for more than 20 km from the sources at Sudbury, Canada; Ducktown, Tennessee; Wawa, Canada; and at smelter sites in Poland, Czechoslovakia, and Sweden (Hutchinson and Whitby, 1974; Gorham and Gordon, 1960; Thomas, 1961; Materna, 1984; Freedman and Hutchinson, 1980). Concentrations of $\geq$ 1–2 ppm maintained for a number of hours during episodic fumigation can be lethal to both woody and herbaceous species. Sulphur dioxide from coal burning and industrial activity has also contributed to erosion of buildings, to health problems, and to the paucity of lichens and mosses near urban or point-source areas.

Svirezhev et al. (1985) suggested that SO_2 would be produced after a nuclear war from oxidation of sulphur compounds in burning of fossil fuels and cities. Concentrations in the atmosphere would undoubtedly increase, and locally, at least, they could be phytotoxic. Both SO_2 and NO_x in the atmosphere would add to atmospheric acidity and, when scrubbed out by precipitation or dry deposition, would provide a source of acidity to soils and vegetation. Volume I suggests that rain acidity could reach pH 3.0 locally, while a worst-case scenario in Svirezhev et al. (1985) suggested that pH 2.4 could occur for a few weeks in local areas, and pH 4.2 to 4.6 elsewhere

TABLE 3.2
SUSCEPTIBILITY OF SPERMATOPHYTES TO OZONE DAMAGE[a]

SPECIES (SYNONYM)	OZONE CONCENTRATION (ppm)	DURATION OF EXPOSURE (hr)	BIOLOGICAL EFFECT
Allium cepa	0.4	2	necrosis
	0.48	2	none
Arachis hypogaea	0.1-0.3	8	necrosis
Avena sativa	0.13	2	none
	0.23	2	chlorosis
Begonia sp.	0.41	2	necrosis
Beta macrorhiza (B. vulgaris macrorhiza)	0.3-1.0	8	necrosis
B. vulgaris	0.13	2	none
	0.20	4	necrosis
	0.41	2	chlorosis
B. vulgaris cicla (B. chilensis)	0.50	8	none
Brassica oleracea	0.25	2	chlorosis
B. rapa	0.35	2	chlorosis
Capsicum frutescens	0.20	4	chlorosis
	1.0	8	none
Chrysanthemum sp.	0.1-0.3	8	necrosis
	0.41	2	necrosis
Cichorium endivia	0.20	4	necrosis
	0.35	2	necrosis
Citrus limon	0.5	48	necrotic stipple
Coleus blumei	0.1-0.3	8	necrosis
	0.41	2	none
Cucumis sativus	0.41	2	none
Dactylis glomerata	0.35	2	chlorosis
Daucus carota	0.35	2	chlorosis
Fragaria sp.	0.3-1.0	8	stipple
Fuchsia sp.	0.41	2	necrosis
Geranium sp.	0.34	2	none
	0.41	2	necrosis
Gladiolus sp.	1.0	8	none
Gossypium hirsutum	0.35	35	chlorosis
	0.35	72	abscission
	0.41	2	none
Hordeum vulgare	0.13	2	none
	0.23	2	chlorosis
Hypericum sp.	0.1-0.3	8	necrosis
Impatiens sp.	0.40	2	none
Ipomoea batatas	0.3-1.0	8	necrosis
Kalanchoe sp.	1.0	8	none
Lactuca sativa	0.41	2	none
	0.50	8	necrosis
Lycopersicon esculentum	0.1	8	necrosis
	0.13	2	none
	0.25	2	chlorosis

[a] Data from Altman and Dittmer (1966).

SPECIES (SYNONYM)	OZONE CONCENTRATION (ppm)	DURATION OF EXPOSURE (hr)	BIOLOGICAL EFFECT
Medicago sativa	0.1-0.3	8	necrosis
	0.13	2	none
	0.21	2	chlorosis
Mentha piperita	0.3-1.0	8	necrosis
Mimosa pudica	0.3-1.0	8	necrosis
Nicotiana tabacum	0.1	8	necrosis
	0.1-0.3	8	necrosis
	0.16	2	none
	0.24	2	necrosis
	0.25	18	necrosis
Pastinaca sativa	0.35	2	chlorosis
Persea americana	0.3-1.0	8	stipple
Petroselinum crispum	0.13	2	none
latifolium (P. hortense)	0.28	2	chlorosis
Petunia hybrida	0.34	2	chlorosis
Phaseolus vulgaris			
Black Valentine	0.1	8	necrosis
	0.13	2	none
	0.25	2	necrosis
Pinto	0.1	4	chlorosis
	0.12	40	necrosis
	0.13	2	none
	0.25	2	necrosis
	0.4	0.33	necrosis
Pinus strobus	0.1	2	necrosis
Piqueria trinervia	0.1-0.3	8	necrosis
Pisum sativum	0.20	4	necrosis
	0.50	4	chlorosis
Poa annua	0.13	2	none
	0.20	4	chlorosis
	0.64	2	chlorosis
Polygonum sp.	0.1	8	necrosis
Prunus persica	0.28	2	chlorosis
Raphanus sativus	0.35	2	chlorosis and necrosis
Solanum pseudocapsicum	0.3-1.0	8	necrosis
S. tuberosum	0.1	8	necrosis
Spinacia oleracea	0.1	8	necrosis
	0.13	2	none
	0.23	2	chlorosis
Tolmiea menziesi	1.0	8	none
Triticum aestivum	0.13	2	none
	0.23	2	chlorosis
Verbena sp.	0.3-1.0	8	necrosis
Vitis vinifera	0.3-1.0	8	necrosis
	0.34	2	necrosis
	0.5	3	necrosis and abscission
Zea mays	0.13	2	none
	0.25	2	chlorosis and necrosis

(see discussion of acid precipitation below). Sulphur dioxide levels are not referred to directly in these studies, but SO_2 often reaches 0.1 ppm or more locally where high sulphur sources burn.

Continuous exposure to 0.1 ppm SO_2 for a number of days or weeks would cause destruction of chlorophyll, breakdown of cell membranes, and death of tissues or entire plants for many species. Exposure to such levels in combination with soot and particulates in damp, acidic atmospheres of industrial centers in Britain and western Europe has caused substantial human health problems in the past. Many plants were unable to survive in such inner city areas. Table 3.3 compares SO_2 susceptibility in 130 plant species; the species differed substantially in their sensitivity. Leaf necrosis (i.e., death of an area of tissue followed by collapse of cells and appearance of white, then brown patches) occurs at SO_2 levels of 1.5 to 8.0 ppm for 1 hour for most species. An important crop legume used extensively in pastures, *Medicago sativa*, is especially susceptible, with damage occurring at 0.3 ppm SO_2 for 8 hours, 1 ppm for 3 hours, or 2 ppm for 1.5 hours. This concentration-time interaction is a very common plant response to SO_2. Sustained exposure to 0.1 ppm could thereby cause damage as severe as that from a short-term episode of 1 ppm. The privet hedges common even in the most polluted European cities early this century are accounted for by the remarkable tolerance of privet (*Ligustrum vulgare*) to even 18.7 ppm SO_2.

One report of potential importance to nuclear war studies is that of Taylor et al. (1985), who examined the effect of temperature during exposure to SO_2. At higher temperatures (up to 35°C), they found that SO_2 uptake of three woody species was enhanced, and detrimental effects were greater than at lower temperatures. This is in agreement with the general responses of plants to phytotoxic gaseous pollutants; their greatest effect is when metabolic activity is highest, both diurnally and seasonally. Furthermore, stomatal closure at night, preventing the entry of gases, and lower night temperatures decrease vulnerability, as does dormancy during the winter and during seasonal droughts.

It follows that during potentially lowered temperature phases following a nuclear war, especially during the acute phase of exposures to gaseous pollutants, air pollutants would have less effects on crops and ecosystems than would otherwise be the case (i.e., if temperatures were normal). The effects of an acute exposure to air pollutants commencing in the summer growing season would be much more severe than those of an acute phase commencing in winter. Thus, in temperate ecosystems, dormant-season exposures to air pollutants would be much less effective than growing-season exposures (see Rapport et al., 1985).

The role of stomatal closure in reducing sensitivity to SO_2 toxicity is emphasized by the work of Winner and Mooney (1985) on the effects on native plants of SO_2 emissions from a Hawaiian volcano. They emphasized the large differences in SO_2 sensitivity among species and the role of SO_2 in selection of populations and species for SO_2 tolerance. The sensitive leaves or species did not close their stomata when exposed to elevated atmospheric SO_2 concentrations.

Winner, who has also worked on SO_2 tolerance of species in Nicaragua from volcanic and thermal areas, feels that, in general, tropical evergreen forest plants and those from deciduous tropical forests in the wet season would be particularly sensitive to SO_2 and NO_2 because of their high uptake capacity and high metabolic activity. However, from the standpoint of a nuclear war scenario, elevated SO_2 levels would be anticipated for Northern Hemisphere mid-latitudes but not the tropics. The highest SO_2 levels would likely be local and occur simultaneously with atmospheric cooling. Under these conditions, vegetation is less susceptible to SO_2 damage, and, in any event, much more damage would result from acute temperature drops. In comparing ecosystem sensitivity to SO_2, it seems that desert ecosystems (Wood and Nash, 1976) are much less sensitive than are deciduous and coniferous forest ecosystems (Gorham and Gordon, 1960; Hutchinson and Whitby, 1974; Buchauer, 1973).

3.3.7 Pollutant Interactions

It is not possible to predict accurately the concentrations of pollutants that would occur at any specific location following a nuclear war. It is clear, however, that organisms could experience an unprecedented burden of pollutants and stress factors during a relatively short time period. Without additional information on concentrations and combinations of pollutants that would occur (and perhaps additional experimental evidence), it is also not possible to specify biological responses. The potential types of pollutant interactions can be illustrated, based on experimental data.

Interactions between pollutants can be additive, synergistic, or antagonistic, with respect to biological response. A synergistic interaction implies that the presence of one pollutant amplifies the toxicity of other pollutants present. An antagonistic interaction could occur, if, for example, one pollutant causes closure of plant stomata, limiting the internal exposure to other gases. The following examples are presented as illustrations of pollutant interactions, not as predictions of post-nuclear war effects.

Runeckles (1984) noted that as ambient concentrations of NO_2 rarely approach the injury threshold for plants, concern over the presence of NO_2 in air stems largely from its potential interactions with other pollutants, particularly SO_2. Tingely et al. (1971) showed that SO_2 and NO_2 could act synergistically in causing leaf injury to soybean, radish, tobacco, oats, tomato, and various beans. In contrast, with 87 native species indigenous to

TABLE 3.3
SUSCEPTIBILITY OF SPERMATOPHYTES TO SO$_2$ DAMAGE[a]

SPECIES (SYNONYM)	CONCENTRATION (ppm)	DURATION OF EXPOSURE (hr)	EFFECT
Acer sp.	4.1	1	necrosis
A. negundo	4.1	1	necrosis
Allium cepa	4.8	1	necrosis
A. porrum	2.8	1	necrosis
Amaranthus retroflexus	2.1	1	necrosis
Apium graveolens	8.0	1	necrosis
Asclepias sp.	5.8	1	necrosis
Avena sativa	1.6	1	necrosis
Beta macrorhiza (B. vulgaris	2.0	1	necrosis
macrorhiza)	2.0	1.3	necrosis
B. vulgaris	1.6	1	necrosis
B. vulgaris cicla	1.9	1	necrosis
Betula pendula	3.0	1	necrosis
Brassica nigra	2.1	1	necrosis
B. oleracea acephala	2.9	1	necrosis
B. oleracea botrytis	2.0	1	necrosis
B. oleracea capitata	2.5	1	necrosis
B. oleracea gemmifera	1.6	1	necrosis
B. oleracea italica	1.6	1	necrosis
B. rapa	1.9	1	necrosis
Bromus tectorum	1.2	1	necrosis
Canna generalis	3.2	1	necrosis
Capsella bursa-pastoris	3.8	1	necrosis
Catalpa bignonioides	2.4	1	necrosis
Chenopodium album	2.2	1	necrosis
Chrysanthemum sp.	7.9	1	necrosis
Cichorium endivia	1.2	1	necrosis
Citrus sp.	8.4	1	necrosis
C. aurantium	2.5	2	silvering
	2.5	4	necrosis
C. sinensis	2.5	2	necrosis
Cosmos bipinnatus	1.4	1	necrosis
Cucumis melo	9.6	1	necrosis
C. sativus	5.2	1	necrosis
Cucurbita sp.	6.5	1	necrosis
C. pepo	1.6	1	necrosis
Dactylis glomerata	2.0	1	necrosis
Daucus carota	1.9	1	necrosis
Distichlis spicata	5.8	1	necrosis
Fagopyrum sagittatum (F. esculentum)	1.6	1	necrosis
Gladiolus hortulanus	3.2	1	necrosis
Gossypium hirsutum	1.2	1	necrosis
Helianthus annuus	1.7	1	necrosis
Hibiscus grandiflorus	4.6	1	necrosis
Hordeum vulgare	1.2	1	necrosis
Hygrangea macrophylla	2.8	1	necrosis
Iris sp.	3.0	1	necrosis
Lactuca sativa	1.5	1	necrosis
Larix laricina	1.9	1	necrosis
Lathyrus odoratus	1.4	1	necrosis
Ligustrum vulgare	18.7	1	necrosis

a Data from Altman and Dittmer (1966).

TABLE 3.3 continued

SPECIES (SYNONYM)	CONCEN-TRATION (ppm)	DURATION OF EXPOSURE (hr)	EFFECT
Lolium perenne	1.8	1	necrosis
Lonicera sp.	4.4	1	necrosis
Lycopersicon esculentum	1.9	1	necrosis
Malus sylvestris	2.2	1	necrosis
Malva parviflora	1.4	1	necrosis
Medicago sativa	0.3	8	none
	0.4	8	necrosis
	1.0	3	none
	1.2	1	necrosis
	1.5	0.2	necrosis
	2.0	1.5	necrosis
Melilotus sp.	2.4	1	necrosis
Nicotiana glauca	1.2	1	necrosis
Phaseolus vulgaris	1.6	1	necrosis
Philadelphus grandiflorus	4.4	1	necrosis
Pinus ponderosa			
spring growth	2.0	1	necrosis
autumn growth	3.0	1	necrosis
Pisum sativum	2.6	1	necrosis
Plantago sp.	1.6	1	necrosis
Polygonum sp.	2.2	1	necrosis
Portulaca oleracea	3.2	1	necrosis
Prunus armeniaca	2.9	1	necrosis
P. cerasus	3.2	1	necrosis
P. domestica	3.1	1	necrosis
Pseudotsuga taxifolia	2.9	1	necrosis
Quercus agrifolia	17.5	1	necrosis
Rhus sp.	3.5	1	necrosis
Ribes rubrum	1.6	0.835	none
	1.6	6	necrosis
R. uva-crispa (R. grossularia)	2.6	1	necrosis
Ricinus communis	4.0	1	necrosis
Rumex crispus	1.5	1	necrosis
Secale cereale	1.2	1	necrosis
	1.6	0.25	none
	1.6	0.5	necrosis
Sisymbrium altissium	3.0	1	necrosis
S. officinale	2.6	1	necrosis
Solanum melongena	2.1	1	necrosis
S. nigrum	2.5	1	necrosis
S. tuberosum	3.8	1	necrosis
Spinacia oleracea	1.5	1	necrosis
Syringa vulgaris	5.0	1	necrosis
Taraxacum officinale	2.0	1	necrosis
Thuja occidentalis	9.8	1	necrosis
Tilia americana	2.9	1	necrosis
Triticum aestivum	1.9	1	necrosis
Ulmus americana	3.0	1	necrosis
Viburnum opulus	7.3	1	necrosis
Vitis vinifera	3.2	1	necrosis
Wistera sinensis	4.1	1	necrosis
Xanthium orientale (X. canadense)	2.9	1	necrosis
Zea mays	5.0	1	necrosis

the southwestern U.S., Hill et al. (1984) found no evidence of more than additive effects.

Synergistic interactions in suppressing tree growth have been reported by Kress and Skelley (1982), who studied the response of several North American eastern forest species to chronic doses of ozone and NO_x (0.1 ppm of each). Runeckles et al. (1978) also found the gaseous combination caused reduced dry matter accumulation of leaves and roots of radish, bush bean, and wheat.

A number of studies have shown that for crops, deciduous and coniferous trees of temperate regions, and herbaceous species, SO_2 and O_3 act synergistically (Reinert, 1984; Runeckles, 1984; MacDowall and Cole, 1971; Menser and Heggestad, 1966). They also found that, dependent upon species, the gaseous interactions could be antagonistic. In studies on eastern U.S. forests, Costonis (1973) showed that sequential exposures of white pine (*Pinus stobus*) to the individual gases one day prior to exposure to a mixture of the gases predisposed plants to greater injury. Runeckles (1984) suggested that synergism is widespread and involves stomatal function and membrane permeability.

Reinert et al. (1982) studied three-way interactions of O_3, SO_2, and NO_2. The combined 3-gas mixture caused maximum damage to the radish. Ozone damage was increased by SO_2, NO_2, or both. It appears that if the plant develops repair mechanisms against O_3 stress, this repair function is impaired with the simultaneous stress of SO_2, O_3, and NO_2.

It has again to be emphasized that we do not have reliable estimates of the levels of gaseous pollutants after a nuclear war, but it does seem certain that agricultural and ecological systems already stressed by light reductions, temperature reductions, and enhanced radiation, would also have to contend with air pollutant mixtures, at least on a localized scale This is a currently unquantified, additional stress, likely to produce adverse responses.

3.3.8 Acid Rain and Low Temperature Acid Mists

It is suggested for some of the nuclear exchange scenarios that the large quantities of NO_x generated from the fireball and from subsequent fires would spread through the atmosphere and eventually be scrubbed out through deposition processes. The SO_2 and HCl generated from fires would add to the acid potential in the atmosphere. A cold, smoke-laden, and acidic mist could envelop low ventilation, mid-latitude areas (e.g., in river valleys) in regions of smoldering fires, with a reducing atmosphere containing large loads of particulates, similar to the London smogs which prevailed up to the 1950s. The visibility could be quite restricted, to 50 to 200 m (Volume I).

Rains would begin to clear the atmosphere but in these regions might produce very dirty and acidic rain (or snow) in the acute phase. Rains of pH

3.0 occurring over weeks to months would have a severe effect on exposed foliage. The Soviet model for a worst-case scenario suggested even lower pH levels (Svirezhev et al., 1985).

The possible role of acid mists in the decline of higher altitude forests in the Adirondacks of the U.S. and in southern West Germany has been suggested recently. The pH of such mists and clouds is often more acidic than of the rains which fall. Fogs of pH 2.0 have been reported near Los Angeles, and fogs of pH 3.0 and less in the Adirondacks. It is believed that such pervasive acidic fogs could damage cuticles, leach nutrients from cells, and encourage infections by pests (McLaughlin, 1985; Johnson et al., 1983; Tukey, 1970; Abrahamsen et al., 1976; Jacobson, 1980; Ulrich, 1983; Shriner, 1977).

The vegetation exposed to such an acid mist would accumulate potentially toxic and acid-corrosive deposits on its leaves. Foliar leaching of bases and other essential elements could occur (e.g., Ca, Mg, and K). However, since this acid mist would be worst at Northern Hemisphere mid-latitudes, the predicted acute phase after a major nuclear war might have already destroyed much of the photosynthetic parts of the plants. Until atmospheric clearing allowed temperatures to rise in the chronic phase, the acid mist would be largely on the soil or adsorbed onto dead or dying foliage.

The remaining healthy foliage of many crop plants would be severely damaged by a series of rain events of about pH 3.0. To put this in perspective, in the acid precipitation affected areas of northern Europe and America, rain events as low as pH 3.0–3.5 are rare, occurring generally at a frequency of less than 1% of rains. Prolonged rains of such a pH would severely damage sensitive lichens and mosses of the boreal and deciduous temperate forests. Direct foliar damage could be expected, and photosynthesis would be reduced.

For most soils and for most ecosystems, acid pulses reaching the soil as a result of even a few weeks of strongly acidic precipitation would not cause significant decreases in pH of soil or the upper litter surface, since these are strongly buffered by inorganic and organic buffers. Even 10–15 years of rains of pH 3.8 to 4.2 have had virtually imperceptible effects on soil pH in Scandinavia and Canada. However, if nuclear war-caused acidic rains were maintained for long periods, i.e., months, then adverse effects could be expected, with accompanying increases in such toxic elements as Al, Mn, and eventually Fe. Such effects have been described in soils in the immediate vicinity of major smelters emitting high levels of SO_2 over a number of years (Hutchinson and Whitby, 1974), and most recently in Sweden from regional acidic precipitation over the past 20 years (C.O. Tamm, unpublished). Such severe effects seem unlikely as a result of atmospheric pollution in the form of acidic deposition following a nuclear exchange. However, the postulated acid mist certainly could damage plants. In addition, if acidic rains fell on frozen ground, then run-off would carry into surface water bodies both the elevated acidity and contaminants in the precipitation (e.g., radionuclides, acid-soluble metals and elements, sulphates, chlorides, and nitrates). This could cause additional contamination of groundwater and surface water systems.

3.4 BIOLOGICAL RESPONSES TO IONIZING RADIATION

3.4.1 Introduction

One of the most important potential consequences of nuclear war involves the production and distribution of radioactivity. Ionizing radiation constitutes a relatively small fraction of the energy of nuclear detonations (Glasstone and Dolan, 1977), but that energy is so effective in causing biological damage that it can comprise a disproportionate share of consequences. There are two types of ionizing radiation associated with nuclear detonations: initial and residual. Initial ionizing radiation consists of the fast neutrons and gamma rays emitted from the fireball within about one minute after the detonation (Glasstone and Dolan, 1977). This radiation caused injury at Hiroshima and Nagasaki (see Chapter 6), but it would not constitute a hazard for modern strategic nuclear warhead detonations, since the lethal area for this type of radiation is substantially smaller than the lethal areas of blast and thermal radiation, for warheads of 100 kT or greater yield (Glasstone and Dolan, 1977).

The other category of ionizing radiation (residual) primarily includes the radiation in local and global fallout. In Volume I of the SCOPE–ENUWAR report (Pittock et al., 1985) are presented assessments of the intensity and spatial extent of fallout, as summarized in the following sections.

Most fallout consists of fission products from the splitting of each atom of uranium or plutonium. Most of these products are radioactive and decay primarily by beta emissions, with some gamma rays. Table 3.4 shows the major fission products. The half-lives vary from fractions of seconds to millions of years for the 300 radionuclides of 36 elements identified. An inverse relationship exists between the radionuclide activity $(Ci \cdot g^{-1})$ and its half-life. The activity of initial fallout is very high and drops rapidly with time as the short half-life nuclides decay leaving a mixture of nuclides with longer half-lives. An example of the yields of several important radionuclides per MT of fission is shown in Table 3.4. Of the large array of fission products, a few are of particular biological importance. Those factors that make certain fission products particularly important include high yield, a reasonably long half-life, energetic radiation, and chemical characteristics that permit their transport through food chains and deposition in biological tissues (Whicker and Schultz, 1982).

TABLE 3.4

MAJOR FISSION PRODUCTS[a]

Fission product	Fission yield (%)	Radiation type	Half-life
^{140}Barium	5.7	Beta, gamma, X-ray	12.8 d
^{144}Cerium	4.9	Beta, gamma, X-ray	284.3 d
^{134}Cesium	6.6	Beta, gamma, X-ray	2.06 yr
^{135}Cesium	6.0	Beta	2.3×10^6 yr
^{137}Cesium	6.2	Beta	30.2 yr
^{129}Iodine	0.9	Beta, gamma, X-ray	1.6×10^7 yr
^{131}Iodine	3.2	Beta, gamma, X-ray	8.04 d
^{147}Promethium	2.4	Beta	2.62 yr
^{103}Ruthenium	6.6	Beta, gamma, X-ray	39.4 d
^{105}Ruthenium	2.7	Beta	368 d
^{89}Strontium	2.9	Beta	50.6 d
^{90}Strontium	3.2	Beta	28.6 yr
^{99}Technetium	6.3	Beta	2.1×10^5 yr
^{133}Xenon	5.5	Beta, gamma, X-ray	5.25 d
^{91}Yttrium	5.8	Beta	58.5 d
^{93}Zirconium	6.4	Beta	1.5×10^6 yr
^{95}Zirconium	6.3	Beta, gamma	64.0 d

[a] From Harwell (1984).

The other major source of radioactive fallout is from neutron activation of previously stable materials in the soil, air, water, and other materials surrounding the nuclear detonation. Neutron-activation radionuclides generally differ from the principal fission products. Many neutron activation-produced radionuclides are isotopes of major or minor nutrients, and thus are incorporated into organisms and into food chains. But the fission products generally dominate doses to humans.

Once fallout particulates are deposited, their behavior and fate are determined to a large extent by their deposition location, solubility, and chemical properties. Relatively soluble nuclides cycle quite readily through food chains within both aquatic and terrestrial ecosystems. Insoluble constituents of fallout accumulate in soil or sediments quite rapidly or are sorbed on the foliage of plants. These radioactive elements can give biological doses in two categories: external and internal doses. External doses are especially associated with gamma rays and typically involve whole-body exposures of plants and animals. Most of the analyses of Volume I relate to such external doses.

Following a large-scale nuclear war, the radiation doses to biota and humans would initially be dominated by external doses. Over longer time periods, internal doses would become relatively more important, eventually dominating. Internal doses result from ingestion or inhalation of radionuclides into organisms. Whereas alpha- (and to a substantial extent beta-) radiation do not give biologically significant external doses because they are absorbed in thin layers of epidermis or cuticle, they do constitute a hazard once incorporated into organisms. This is particularly true for alpha particles, since these have a high relative biological effectiveness.

In order to understand the biological significance of radiation, a few terms require clarification. Radiation results in biological damage through the dissipation of energy absorbed in tissues, specifically involving the creation of ions and radicals in the absorbing medium. These ions are reactive chemically, and subsequent chemical transformations can result in adverse biological effects on cells, tissues, and the entire organism.

To measure the energy in radiation-matter interactions, the *radiation exposure* is defined as the ability of a given quantity of radiation to create ion pairs in air. This is measured in *roentgen* (R), defined as the quantity of gamma- or X-rays that produces a charge of 1 coulomb in 1 kg of air at standard temperature and pressure; this involves 2×10^9 ion pairs per cm^3 of air. Many monitoring instruments measure in R.

The value of more relevance, however, is the *radiation dose*, i.e., the amount of energy absorbed in tissues. One measure of dose is the *rad*, defined as absorption of 100 $erg \cdot g^{-1}$ of material. It is important to note that the rad level depends on the absorbing medium as well as the nature and intensity of the radiation. Whereas no simple translation from R to rad exists for all media, for gamma rays in air, 1 R $\approx$ 0.87 rad, but in water (and, therefore, in soft biological tissues), 1 R $\approx$ 1 rad.

To estimate biological effects, however, the rad is insufficient alone, since different types of radiation cause different amounts of damage per unit of absorbed energy. This is because some radiation disperses its energy very quickly, being slowed down and stopped within small distances in tissues; in that case, the energy per unit distance would be high and damage concentrated. This relationship is referred to as the *linear energy transfer* (LET), where high LET relates to high biological damage. The ratio of LET for a high-LET radiation (e.g., alpha particles) compared to low-LET radiation (e.g., gamma rays) is the *relative biological effectiveness* (RBE). Thus, biological damage can be measured as a *dose equivalent*, where the unit *rem* is defined as the *rad* × *RBE*. RBE factors are 1 for beta radiation, gamma rays and X-rays; 10–20 for alpha particles; and for neutrons, 1 for acute effects and 4–10 for long-term effects (Harwell, 1984). Thus, for example, one rad of alpha dose would cause the same damage as 10 to 20 rads of gamma rays.

The levels of absorbed dose that can cause biological effects are discussed in Section 3.4.3.

3.4.2 Distribution and Levels of Fallout

3.4.2.1 Local Fallout

Local fallout is the early deposition (within 24 to 48 hr) of larger radioactive particles that have been lofted into the troposphere during a detonation whose fireball contacts the ground surface. About 50% of the total fallout from a surface burst would occur as local fallout (Rotblat, 1981). Despite the term local, as opposed to regional or global, the areas affected by significant local fallout following a major nuclear war could be rather large. For example, using a 450 rad, 48 hour dose as lethal to most humans, and based on the scenario assumed in Volume I, the KDFOC$_2$ computer model estimated that about 5% of the land surface in the United States, Europe, and the U.S.S.R. would be covered by such local fallout. (Refer to Volume I for details of these estimates and those for other than a full baseline exchange; see also Harwell, 1984; Rotblat, 1981; Ambio, 1982).

The extent and significance of local fallout would be particularly dependent upon the actual target strategies used in the event of a major nuclear war. When different scenarios are analyzed (e.g., surface bursting weapons over cities), the area affected by lethal levels of local fallout could increase several fold. We could anticipate large areas of lethal (for humans) local fallout downwind of missile silos and other hardened targets, where ground bursts would likely be used. The possibility, and severe consequences in terms of radioactive contamination, of strikes aimed at nuclear power plant facilities were also considered in Volume I; spent fuel and nuclear wastes would be especially amenable to dispersal by nuclear detonations. Other analyses (Ambio, 1982; Harwell, 1984; Rotblat, 1981; Ramberg, 1978) have illustrated that the targeting of such facilities could very substantially increase the area and long-term doses associated with local fallout.

One important factor potentially ameliorating local fallout effects is the shielding of individuals, which is difficult to estimate, but could decrease the effective lethal areas significantly. Local fallout is anticipated to occur for targeted nations, but could also be expected to affect adjacent non-targeted nations; for example, Ambio (1982) suggests that all countries in Europe could be blanketed with local fallout. Weather conditions, such as rainfall or snowfall events, would be a major factor in causing substantial unevenness in the distribution of radiation on the ground from local fallout. For example, the area receiving an accumulated dose from local fallout of greater than 450 rads from a 500 kT detonation varies by a factor of more than three between wind speeds of 16 to 72 km hour^{-1}. As wind speeds increase, the airborne debris is dispersed. Particulate residues become mixed and deposited unevenly if rain originates above or within the mushroom cloud, causing local fallout hot spots.

It is clear from several studies that local fallout estimates are highly variable. Some of the uncertainties are related to the specific targeting scenario assumed, and, thus, these uncertainties cannot be eliminated, since scenarios would remain uncertain until a large-scale nuclear war actually occurred. Other components of the range of estimates involve differences in modelling methodologies and extrapolations from simulations of single warhead detonations to estimations of areal coverage from overlapping plumes associated with multiple nuclear detonations. The latter issues can be addressed by further analyses, and sophisticated simulations of alternative multiple-detonation scenarios are needed in order to define more precisely the range of potential local fallout estimates. As will become clear in the discussions in this section, local fallout has the potential for widespread, severe biological consequences, unlike the situation for global fallout.

3.4.2.2 Global Fallout

Global fallout consists of the fine particulate matter and gases that are injected by nuclear explosions into the atmosphere, especially the upper level. This fallout could continue for years. Volume I also identifies intermediate fallout as the material initially injected into the troposphere, which is principally removed within the first month. Scenarios using fewer high-yield weapons have increased the importance of intermediate fallout because of the reduced proportion of injection into the stratosphere from ground bursts of smaller yield weapons. The other component of global fallout is long-term deposition. This component of the finest particles gradually re-enters the troposphere, where the particles are scavenged by wet precipitation or dry deposition.

Volume I analyses of global fallout using the GLODEP$_2$ model compare two baseline nuclear war scenarios. These scenarios assume an atmosphere with normal circulation patterns (i.e., unperturbed by nuclear war), which occurs in either the winter or the summer. The Northern Hemisphere average dose is estimated to be 13.1 to 19.1 rads over 50 years. For the Southern Hemisphere, the equivalent 50-year dose is 0.3 to 0.7 rads. GLODEP$_2$ estimates doses of 19.1 rads for the total Northern Hemisphere and 41.7 rads for the 30°N to 50°N latitudinal band. Another analysis of the intermediate- and long-term fallout using similar scenarios (Turco et al., 1983) estimated corresponding doses of 20 rads and about 40 to 60 rads, respectively.

When a perturbed atmosphere is used in the models based on the same nuclear war scenarios, but with an atmosphere altered by the injected smoke from the nuclear war, the latitudinally averaged predicted dosages are as given in Table 3.5. These calculations indicate that the estimates for the dose from a perturbed atmosphere are only about 15% lower than the figures for the unperturbed atmosphere in the Northern Hemisphere. However, doses from global fallout occurring in the Southern Hemisphere were estimated to be increased somewhat because of altered atmospheric circulation patterns.

TABLE 3.5

GLOBAL FALLOUT DOSES FOLLOWING A LARGE-SCALE NUCLEAR WAR[a,b]

Latitudinal Band	Scenario A (no smoke)	Scenario A (smoke)	Scenario B (no smoke)	Scenario B (smoke)
70-90°N	7.8	6.4	8.2	5.8
50-70°N	21.3	17.2	24.6	18.0
30-50°N	22.3	20.1	23.9	20.4
10-30°N	7.6	7.5	7.2	7.2
10°N-10°S	1.3	1.6	1.0	1.4
10-30°S	0.6	0.8	0.4	0.6
30-50°S	0.7	0.8	0.4	0.5
50-70°S	0.5	0.5	0.3	0.3
70-90°S	0.2	0.2	0.1	0.1
Area averaged:				
Northern Hemisphere	12.8	11.5	13.7	11.5
Southern Hemipshere	0.7	0.8	0.4	0.6
Earth	6.8	6.1	7.1	6.1

[a] From Volume I (Pittock et al., 1985).

[b] Global fallout dose using three-dimensional GRANTOUR model for a summer nuclear war scenario and a post-nuclear war atmosphere with and without perturbation by nuclear war-induced smoke. Doses are in rads. Both tropospheric and stratospheric contributions are included. Two scenarios are analyzed, involving a 5300 MT nuclear war (Scenario A) and a 5000 MT nuclear war (Scenario B).

'Hot spots' are localized areas of sharply higher radiation levels caused by uneven deposition of fallout from the atmosphere. The most common cause would be local rainfall, either induced by the nuclear clouds themselves or natural rains. A localized rain shower falling through an atmosphere of radioactive dust can create a hot spot; for example, in 1953, 36 hours after a nuclear explosion at the Nevada test site in the U.S., a significant fraction of the radioactivity in a debris cloud was washed out by a violent thunderstorm around Troy, New York, 2,300 miles (3,700 km) from the site of the explosion. Geiger counter readings of 5 mR hour^{-1} were recorded in the downtown area, and hot spots as high as 120 mR hour^{-1} were found, compared to normal background levels of 0.015 mR hour^{-1}.

The 3-dimensional GRANTOUR simulations in Volume I show global fallout hot spots that typically are about a factor of 6–8 higher than the Northern Hemisphere average global fallout dose, with hot spots of up to 80 rads occurring in a latitudinal belt from 30°N–60°N. The resolution of this model is limited by the grid size, in this case 10^6 km^2. Thus, a 'local hot spot' as characterized by this model covers a relatively large area. More localized hot spots would likely be higher than those averaged over a 10^6 km^2 area. The dimensions of the hot spots that would actually occur from global fallout cannot be predicted with confidence, but it is clear that hot spots would occur and that they would be a function of local meteorological conditions and of the patterns of nuclear detonations. In fact, neither the plumes nor the dose could be expected to be uniform. Meteorological conditions could substantially affect fallout patterns, including the areas that could receive a dose lethal to humans. It seems probable that some hot spots from global fallout following a major nuclear war could exceed the human lethal dose in localized areas, and would add to the large local fallout area with such levels.

3.4.2.3 Deposition and Retention on Plants

In natural ecosystems, most fallout would first be intercepted by vegetation. Airborne radionuclides readily contaminate plant surfaces. The nature of the plant surface is important in determining the amounts of radioactive particulates deposited and retained and the ease with which contaminated leaves could be cleansed of these particulates. Rainfall is very important in the deposition and removal of radioactive particles from plants. The dominating mechanisms for dry deposition are gravitational settling for large particles and eddy turbulence and diffusion for gases. Large particles are more easily washed or blown off leaves, whereas fine particles of $< 20\ \mu$m are often quite difficult to remove. For crops with edible leaves, washing would be necessary to reduce surface contamination, especially in areas affected by local fallout, if such crops remained otherwise edible.

Waxy fruits and leaves, such as tomatoes and cabbage, are easily and effectively cleaned, but others, such as kale, lettuce, and spinach, retain particulates more effectively. Cataldo and Vaughan (1980) showed that small particles were less available for leaching with increasing residence time on the leaves of bush bean and sugar beet. More than 90% of the foliar plutonium deposits were found to be firmly held on to the leaf surface. Cataldo and Vaughan (1980) reported retention half-times of 10 to 24 days for particles of $10-200\ \mu$m.

Some foliar-deposited radionuclides could be absorbed and enter the plant tissues and be translocated to the roots (Chamberlain, 1970). Romney et al. (1973) experimentally demonstrated that in plants at the Nevada test site, 87% of the ^{90}Sr, 81% of the ^{137}Cs, and 73% of the ^{144}Ce in forage plant tissues were derived from foliar contamination.

Molchanov et al. (1968) and Aleksahkin et al. (1970) reported that the retention of radionuclides by aboveground foliage relative to overall deposition may be quite high. However, over time, as the foliage dies and falls onto the soil, the radionuclides eventually enter the soil, often being retained on the organic litter layer which, in turn, becomes a major source for radionuclides to be uptaken by plants via the root system (Svirezhev et al., 1985).

Accumulation of radionuclides in soil is affected by a range of factors. The degree of retention depends on the concentrations of the nuclide and competitive ions, soil organic matter content, soil mineral type, the presence of chelating agents, and the physicochemical characteristics of the particular nuclide, such as solubility. Most radionuclides accumulate in the top few cm of soil or sediments or are retained in the films of water on particulate surfaces, adsorbed onto humus, or incorporated into the crystal lattice of soil minerals. Nuclides can also occur in solution, as cations or anions retained on mineral or organic particles, in colloidal form, as complexes with minerals and organic matter, and as glassified particulate matter.

Some plants are especially effective at intercepting and removing particulates from the air. Lichens and mosses are examples of this, as are epiphytes in general. In tundra regions, the ability of lichens to accumulate radionuclides directly from the air has been widely reported (Hanson, 1971; Holm and Persson, 1975; Hutchinson-Benson et al., 1985; Tuominen, 1967). This effectiveness, combined with strong retentive properties, leads to these plants becoming sinks for anticipated global fallout from a major nuclear war, as they were for fallout from atmospheric tests in the 1950s and 1960s. The biological half-time of ^{137}Cs in lichens was calculated to be >10 years, compared with that of ^{90}Sr, which was 1.0 to 1.6 years (Eberhardt and Hanson, 1969).

Foliar retention of radionuclides depends largely upon the length of time the leaves themselves are retained by the plants. For grasslands and herbaceous layers of forests, this is a single growing season for most species. The same applies to retention by deciduous tree species, for which radionuclides would be deposited on the ground as the leaves fall in the autumn. For boreal coniferous species, needle retention is typically for two to four years, while for tundra cushion plants (e.g., lichens and mosses, which are long-lived perennials), leaf retention may be for many years. Even dead leaves are retained on many arctic and alpine plants as insulation. Leaf-retention factors would influence rates of cycling of radionuclides, their availability to be grazed from leaf surfaces directly, and the speed with which they became available in the soil for further uptake into microorganisms, plants, and animals.

3.4.3 Effects of Ionizing Radiation on Plants and Animals

3.4.3.1 Introduction

In order to assess the responses of individual plants and animals to radiation, including domestic animals, crops, and natural ecosystems, we need to know their sensitivity to a range of radiation doses. We also need to know the fate and transport of radionuclides in ecosystems, especially the propensity for plants to take up radionuclides from the soil and from water bodies.

Effects of radiation on biological systems are affected by the dose *rate*, i.e., the duration over which a dose is absorbed. Acute doses (i.e., absorbed within a few hours or days) tend to be more consequential per unit dose absorbed than chronic doses. Most of the discussions in the following sections relate to acute exposures.

3.4.3.2 Sensitivity of Plants to Radiation

Not only do plant species differ in their ability to intercept and retain particulates containing radionuclides, but species also differ considerably in their sensitivity to radiation. Woodwell and Sparrow (1965) have shown a general relationship between interphase chromosome volume of a species and its radiation sensitivity. The smaller the chromosome volume, the less sensitive the plants are to radiation effects (Table 3.6).

Some general patterns are apparent. The coniferous genera (e.g., *Pinus*, *Picea*, *Abies*, *Pseudotsuga*) are quite sensitive to ionizing radiation because they have large interphase chromosome volumes (which represent targets for absorption of radiation). These trees are somewhat inhibited in growth at exposures of 150 to 300 roentgen. The lethal dose for most conifers listed lies between 400 and 950 roentgen. *Thuja plicata* is an exception in its tolerance to radiation within the Pacific conifer group, but it has an exceptionally small chromosome volume. In contrast, deciduous tree species generally are growth inhibited at exposures of 1500 to 4000 roentgen, and they are killed at exposures of 3500 to 10,000+ roentgen. These species have interphase chromosome volumes approximately 10 to 20 times smaller than the coniferous species (Table 3.6). The table also lists the sensitivity of the prairie grass (*Andropogon scoparius*), wheat (*Triticum*), and maize (*Zea mays*). All of these monocots are similar to deciduous trees in their tolerance to ionizing radiation.

On the basis of these limited data, it would seem that conifer-dominated forests, such as the boreal and northern mixed forests, have a predominance of radiation-sensitive species, while deciduous forest species are considerably more tolerant. Cereal crops and other native grasses are also relatively tolerant of radiation.

Other factors which have been determined to be of importance in determining radiosensitivity in plants are in Table 3.7. Polyploid organisms, with perhaps redundant DNA, are more resistant to radiation damage and seem to be more resistant to other forms of stress. Polyploidy is particularly common among plants in harsh environments, such as in tundra ecosystems.

Non-flowering (i.e., lower) plants seem to be much more radiation resistant than angiosperms (flowering plants). Steere (1970) found this was the case with mosses in the irradiated forest at El Verde, Puerto Rico, and ascribed it to the very small size of their chromosomes. Since mosses are haploid (only one set of chromosomes) compared with the diploid (duplicate set of chromosomes) flowering plants, this is somewhat surprising since presumably duplicate (i.e., extra) DNA is limited.

In a separate study of mosses and liverworts from temperate woodland and bog sites in the U.K., Woollon and Davies (1981) showed a close correlation between chromosome volume and gamma radiation sensitivity. The correlation was so good they feel it to be predictive for radiation sensitivity of other bryophytes. Some bryophytes were only killed at levels of 100,000 + rads, whereas crop plants such as wheat, barley, oats, potatoes, and sugarbeet are killed at less than 10,000 rads.

3.4.3.3 Sensitivity of Seeds to Radiation

Generally, dry seeds in dormant condition are very tolerant of high radiation doses. This may assist recovery process in soils that have accumulated fallout and that have substantial seed banks (e.g., boreal and deciduous forests, grasslands). The sensitivities of seeds from a number of species are shown in Table 3.8. Exposures to $10-60 \times 10^3$ roentgens are necessary for many species, to reduce seed survival by 50%. The response can be altered, in some cases strikingly, by such factors as: genotype within a species, age and moisture content of seeds, the gaseous atmosphere during irradiation, time from irradiation to germination, and stress during the growing period.

There is a general relationship between metabolic activity and radiation sensitivity, and between moisture content of tissues and sensitivity. Actively dividing cells are more sensitive than non-dividing or quiescent cells. Thus, any seeds or dormant plants in the dry season are markedly more tolerant than seeds that have imbibed water, or leaves growing actively in the wet season. This is a striking parallel with the degree of cold- and drought-hardiness of these tissues.

3.4.3.4 Sensitivity of Animals to Radiation Effects

It is generally accepted from a wide range of experiments and observations that mammals are the most sensitive to radiation and that microorganisms are generally the most resistant to radiation. Substantial variation in sensitivity occurs within each major group, and genetic differences occur among individuals of the same species, including humans. Svirezhev et al. (1985) pointed out that the degree of radiation damage is affected by abiotic factors such as pollution, injury to plants, non-optimal weather, and other environmental conditions, which tend to increase the extent of radiation damage. Consequently, synergistic interactions are likely to occur.

TABLE 3.6

SENSITIVITY OF MAJOR ECOSYSTEMS TO IONIZING RADIATION[a]

MAJOR ECOSYSTEM AND VEGETATION TYPES	SPECIES	SOMATIC CHROMOSOME NUMBER	INTERPHASE CHROMOSOME VOLUME	ROENTGENS CAUSING: SLIGHT GROWTH INHIBITION	100% MORTALITY
CONIFEROUS FOREST[b]					
Boreal	Abies balsamea	24	33.4	270	700
	Picea glauca	24	39.7	220	590
Subalpine	Abies lasiocarpa	24	33.5	270	700
(Rocky Mts)	Picea engelmanni	24	26.8	330	880
Montane					
(Rocky Mts)	Pinus ponderosa	24	36.7	240	640
	Pseudotsuga menziesii	26	28.5	310	820
(Sierra-Cascades)	Abies concolor	24	23.3	380	1010
	Pinus jeffreyi	24	48.1	190	490
	P. lambertiana	24	57.8	150	410
	P. ponderosa	24	36.7	240	640
	Pseudotsuga menziesii	26	28.5	310	820
(Pacific conifer)	Abies grandis	24	33.2	270	710
	Thuja plicata	22	8.6	1040	2730
	Tsuga heterophylla	24	23.7	377	990
DECIDUOUS FOREST[c]					
Mixed mesophytic	Acer saccharum	26	3.2	2800	7360
	Fagus grandifolia	24	2.3	3810	10000
	Liriodendron tulipifera	38	6.4	1400	3680
	Magnolia acuminata	76	4.8	1850	4840
	Quercus alba	24	6.6	1350	3550
	Tilia americana	82	2.5	3520	9230

[a] Adapted from Altman and Dittmer (1966). Data apply to an acute exposure of one-half to several days. Estimates for species are based on correlations between radiosensitivity and interphase chromosome volume. Variability introduced by the measurements of nuclear volumes alone is approximately 30% ± of the means listed. Other uncontrolled intrinsic and environmental factors increase the potential variability. Sensitivity of ecosystems estimated from empirical data on radiation effects and from chromosome volumes of dominant species.

b Minor damage estimated from exposure to 200 r; severe damage at doses exceeding 2000r.

c Minor damage estimated from exposure to 200 r; severe damage at doses exceeding 10,000r

TABLE 3.6 continued

Major Ecosystem and Vegetation Types	Species	Somatic Chromosome Number	Interphase Chromosome Volume	Roentgens Causing: Slight Growth Inhibition	Roentgens Causing: 100% Mortality
Beech-maple, maple-basswood	Acer saccharum	26	3.2	2800	7360
	Fagus grandifolia	24	2.3	3810	10000
	Tilia americana	82	2.5	3520	9230
	Tsuga canadensis	24	21.3	420	1100
Hemlock-hardwood	Acer saccharum	26	3.2	2800	7360
	Betula lutea	84	2.2	3860	10120
	Pinus resinosa	24	43.2	210	540
	P. strobus	24	46.5	190	500
	Tsuga canadensis	24	21.3	420	1100
Oak-chestnut	Castanea dentata	24	4.7	1900	5000
	Pinus rigida	24	48.3	190	490
	Quercus coccinea	24	3.6	2490	6530
	Q. prinus	24	6.1	1470	3870
Oak-hickory	Carya cordiformis	32	1.8	5090	13370
	C. laciniosa	32	2.6	3470	9110
	C. ovata	32	2.5	3560	9340
	C. tomentosa	64	1.8	5080	13350
	Pinus taeda	24	52.6	170	450
	Quercus alba	24	6.6	1350	3550
	Q. marilandica	24	3.3	2690	7060
	Q. rubra	24	5.5	1620	4250
	Q. stellata	24	4.4	2040	5350
	Q. velutina	24	3.2	2830	7430
Grasslands[d] Grass	Andropogon scoparius	40	6.4	2330	9200
Agricultural[e] Field crop	Triticum aestivum	42	14.6	1020	4020
	Zea mays,	20	14.0	1060	4200

d Minor damage estimated from exposure to 200 r; severe damage at doses exceeding 20,000r; herbaceous successional ecosystems suffer minor damage at 4000r, severe damage at doses exceeding 70,000 r.
e Minor damage to agricultural ecosystems and urban ecosystems estimated for exposure to 200 r.

TABLE 3.7

FACTORS AFFECTING PLANT SENSITIVITY TO RADIATION[a]

FACTORS INCREASING SENSITIVITY	FACTORS INCREASING RESISTANCE
Large nucleus (high DNA)	Small nucleus (low DNA)
Large nucleus:nucleolar volume ratio	Small nucleus:nucleolar volume ratio
Much heterochromatin	Little heterochromatin
Large chromosomes	Small chromosomes
Acrocentric chromosomes	Metacentric chromosomes
Normal centromere	Polycentric or diffuse centromere
Uni-nucleate cells	Multi-nucleate cells
Low chromosome number	High chromosome number
Diploid or haploid	High polyploidy
Sexual reproduction	Asexual reproduction
Slow rate of division	Fast rate of cell division
Long dormant period	Short dormant period
Meiotic stages present at dormancy	Meiotic stages not present at dormancy
Slow meiosis and premeiosis	Fast meiosis and premeiosis
Low concentration of protective chemicals (e.g., ascorbic acid)	High concentration of protective chemicals

[a] Adapted from Whicker and Schultz (1982).

O'Brien and Wolfe (1964) found that insects are insensitive to radiation compared to vertebrates, since much of the developmental processes of insects takes place in the well-protected egg or pupal stages. After they hatch, very little cell division occurs during the larval life. However, certain cells do divide in the adult (e.g., the cells of the gonads), and these cells are very sensitive to radiation. Juvenile forms of insects are more sensitive than adults as a result of having greater number of dividing cells. Willard and Cherry (1975) concluded from a study of 37 species of 8 insect orders that large, long-lived adults are more sensitive than small, short-lived adults.

The radiation sensitivity of reptiles is greater than for insects. For example, Cosgrove (1971) reported the lethal dose for several species of snakes is 300–400 R, and for a turtle species is about 1000 R. In another study, Tinkle (1965) exposed free-ranging lizards in a 1 hectare enclosure to 450 R prior to the breeding season. After 2 years, a 50% decline in natality was observed in the irradiated individuals.

Studies with birds have shown progressive stunting of growth when eastern bluebirds were given from 300 R to 2000 R total exposure at 2 and 16 days of age. Birds of the 2 day-old exposure group were able to leave the nest box at the normal times, but their weakened condition and inferior flying ability made them more vulnerable to predation during this critical fledgling period (Willard, 1963). Garg et al. (1964) exposed starlings to gamma radiation of 300 to 3000 rads. Approximately 1000 rads was found to be the lethal dose, but extensive damage of bone marrow, spleen, and duodenum occurred at lower levels. Birds appear to be rather sensitve to ionizing radiation, as noted in Figure 3.2. For example, lethal doses for three duck species ranged from about 500 R to about 900 R. The anticipated doses of greater than 500 R would likely be damaging to birds in areas of high levels of local fallout. This would include domesticated birds used for human food sources (e.g., chickens, ducks, and geese). In the outer fringes of local fallout areas, where dosages of 100–300 rads might occur, bird populations could be expected to show effects in breeding success and in growth and vigor. The proposed doses from global fallout should be low enough to have no significant effects.

Whicker and Schultz (1982) reported lethal dose values for a large number of small mammals exposed to a ^{60}Co source (Table 3.9). At high doses, weight losses and other symptoms of radiation injury occurred in all species.

Blair (1958) studied deer mice after irradiation of males whose gonads were exposed to 500 R of X-rays. After introduction into the field, reductions in litter size were noted that were maintained through 4 years of irradiation. Blair concluded from this and similar work on a toad (*Bufo valliceps*) that natural populations are capable of surviving substantial genetic damage without impairing their success in natural environments. Both species share a high attrition of the large number of young produced each generation; this provides a mechanism for intensive selection. It was also concluded that

TABLE 3.8

SENSITIVITY OF DORMANT SEEDS TO RADIATION[a]

Species	Measurement	Exposure (kR)	Effectiveness (% of control)
Acer rubrum	survival	10	88
A. saccharum	survival	10	1
Aesculus octandra	survival	10-50	30
Allium cepa	germination	21.5	97
Alopecurus myosuroides	survival	20	50
A. pratensis	survival	26	20-30
Amaranthus retroflexus	survival	> 64	20-30
Antirrhinum majus	survival	< 10	20-30
Avena fatua	survival	18	50
A. sativa	survival	15	4
Beta vulgaris	survival	40	8
Brassica kaber	survival	67	50
B. napus	survival	35	30
B. nigra	survival	115	30
B. rapa	seedling growth	26-100	50
Cannabis sativa	survival	7.5	20-30
Carya ovata	survival	10	4
Chenopodium album	survival	15	50
Cosmos bipinnatus	seedling growth	10	50
Dactylis glomerata	germination	30	3
Daucus carota	seedling dry	57-66	50
Glycine max	germination	11	50
Hordeum vulgare	germination	18	50
	seedling height	55	50

[a] Data from Altman and Dittmer (1966).

recessive mutants would be eliminated through inbreeding in future generations.

Laboratory results may overestimate the radiation resistance of free-ranging small mammals. For instance, O'Farrell et al. (1972) found that irradiated pocket-mice (*Perognathus parvus*) released to the field survived for a shorter time than irradiated individuals kept in the laboratory and than non-irradiated ones left in the field.

3.4.3.5 Effects of External Beta Radiation on Biota

The discussions thus far have concentrated on external radiation from gamma rays. Other radiation that could lead to an external dose includes beta radiation, emitted by many fission product radionuclides. Despite the lim-

TABLE 3.8 continued

Species	Measurement	Exposure (kR)	Effectiveness (% of control)
Juglans nigra	survival	10-50	30
Lactuca sativa	seedling growth	< 20	50
Liquidambar styraciflua	survival	10-50	30
Lotus corniculatus	survival	30	27
Lupinus luteus	seedling growth	40	50
Lycopersicon esculentum	seedling height	21	58
Medicago lupulina	survival	80	50
Nyssa sylvatica	survival	10	28
Oryza sativa	seedling height	26	50
Phalaris canariensis	survival	7.5	50
Phaseolus vulgaris	survival	10	89
Picea abies	survival	1	50
Pinus sp.	germination	< 10	50
P. rigida	survival	10	0
P. sylvestris	survival	1	50
Pisum sativum	growth	5-15	50
Platanus occidentalis	survival	10	61
Quercus alba	survival	10	0
Q. prinus	survival	10	0
Q. velutina	survival	10	27
Robina pseudoacacia	survival	10	23
Secale cereale	survival	15	19
Sorghum nitidum	survival	26	50
Triticum aestivum	germination	14-25	50
	fertility	15	70
	survival	15	61
T. durum	seedling	50	50
Zea mays	seedling height	37	50
	germination	22	100

ited penetrating ability of beta radiation, Murphy and McCormick (1971a,b) showed experimentally that this should not be construed as an indication that beta-emitters in fallout are biologically unimportant. In granite-outcrop plants exposed to 3500 rads and 5000 rads of the beta-emitter ^{90}Y, aberrant flowering heads increased almost 2- to 3-fold above control levels, with abnormal flowers producing 38% fewer seeds than normal heads. These seeds also showed a substantial delay in time of germination and reduction in total germination. This suggests that beta irradiation, even introduced as an external, acute dose, is capable of altering the morphology of plant reproductive structures and subsequent flowering biology under field conditions.

Whicker and Schultz (1982) suggested that beta particles may contribute significantly to the total external dose received by small or thin organisms from environmental radioactivity. One noted external beta radiation prob-

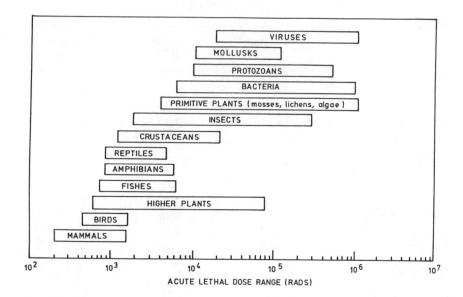

Figure 3.2 Approximate acute lethal dose ranges for various taxonomic groups. From Whicker and Schultz (1982)

lem with animal grazers, such as livestock, is damage to the mouth parts (e.g., mucosa of lips, gums, and oral cavity) from grazing on beta-contaminated plants (Bell, 1971). Bell also found synergistic effects of beta and gamma doses applied simultaneously to animals.

Svirezhev et al. (1985) emphasized beta exposures as being particularly consequential after a nuclear war, potentially giving eight times the dose of gamma rays in fallout. More studies are needed on the potential effects of beta radiation on such ecosystem components as soil microorganisms, plant reproductive and perennating parts, and animal grazers. The problem of external exposures from alpha particles, on the other hand, would be insignificant because of their extremely low penetration of external tissues. Alpha-emitters would constitute a major hazard from internal doses, however, especially for long-term radiation effects

3.4.3.6 Effects of External Radiation on Terrestrial Ecosystems

Research on the effects of radiation on ecosystems has involved studies of plant communities in the vicinity of nuclear bomb tests, including temperate and tropical, terrestrial and aquatic ecosystems, and studies of intact ecosystems exposed to intense point sources of radiation at known radiation exposures for given time periods. The study on the effects of chronic gamma

TABLE 3.9

LETHAL RADIATION DOSES FOR SMALL MAMMALS AND BIRDS[a]

SPECIES	$LD_{50/30}$ (RADS)[b]
Small rodents	300-600
Goat	350
Raccoon	580
Lynx	580
Gray fox	710
Rabbit	750-820
Linnet	400
Bramble finch	500
Goldfinch	600
Greenfinch	600
House sparrow	625
Pigeon	920

[a] Data from Whicker and Schultz (1982).
[b] $LD_{50/30}$ is the dose in rads that kills 50% of the exposed population within 30 days.

irradiation on an oak–pine forest at Brookhaven National Laboratory is one of the best known and most comprehensive, including plants, animals, microorganisms, and detritivores and examining successional aspects (Woodwell, 1967; Woodwell and Rebuck, 1967; Woodwell and Sparrow, 1965). A further study examined effects of a gamma irradiation source on old-field succession. The effects of a short-term, 3-month gamma irradiation on the El Verde rainforest in eastern Puerto Rico provided much information on responses of a highly structured ecosystem (Odum, 1970). A deciduous forest in the northern Georgian piedmont was exposed to neutron-gamma exposures from an air shielded reactor (Platt, 1965). A Mediterranean ecosystem, consisting of trees, scrubby growth, and vegetated clearings, was studied by Fabries et al. (1972), and a short-grass ecosystem in Colorado was studied by Fraley and Whicker (1973). Granite outcrop ecosystems were exposed to simulated beta fallout by Murphy and McCormick (1971b). Desert communities were examined after Nevada bomb tests by various groups, including Rickard and Shields (1963), Rhoades et al. (1971), and Romney et al. (1971). Clearly, in the United States at least, a large number of systems have been exposed to irradiation or to contamination by radionuclides after bomb tests.

The general responses of ecosystems to radiation exposure are given in Table 3.10. The coniferous forests are considered likely to be the most injured directly by radiation, the tropical evergreen rain forests are substantially less susceptible, and temperate mixed and deciduous forests are intermediate in response. For moderate to high damage to any of the ecosystems, only the northern coniferous forest is likely to be susceptible to 1000–2000 rad, while other plant communities would require 5000 rad to as high as 40,000 to 100,000 rad before community disruption would occur as a result of radiation alone. Svirezhev et al. (1985) cited similar ecosystem sensitivities.

TABLE 3.10

SENSITIVITY OF PLANT COMMUNITIES TO RADIATION[a]

	Dose (10^3 rads)		
COMMUNITY TYPE	LOW DAMAGE	MODERATE DAMAGE	HIGH DAMAGE
Coniferous forest	0.1 - 1	1 - 2	> 2
Mixed forest	1 - 5	5 - 10	10 - 60
Tropical rain forest	4 - 10	10 - 40	> 40
Shrub community	1 - 5	5 - 20	>20
Grassland community	8 - 10	10 - 100	> 100
Moss and lichen community	10 - 50	50 - 500	> 500
Lichen community	60 - 100	100 - 200	> 200

[a] Data from Whicker and Schultz (1982).

This being the case, it is probable that following a major nuclear war, of the plant communities which dominate major ecosystems, only those occurring within the area of high levels of local fallout would likely be seriously disrupted by radiation levels alone. Many factors could alter this general picture, however. Just as the location and protection of meristematic tissues in buds and root tips are important to tolerances to cold and drought, they are also important to exposure and effects from radiation. Age, structure, physiological state, metabolic activity, and nucleus and chromosome variables are all likely to influence responses.

Radiation-damaged cells have the capability of repair, provided that the damage is not too great. Understanding how entire ecosystems might recover requires major extrapolation from observations around point sources or around nuclear detonation sites. In a modern nuclear war, the areas of devastation could be enormous, and extrapolations to attempt to predict recovery are poorly based. Nevertheless, some generalizations can be made (Platt, 1965; Whicker and Fraley, 1974):

1.) Plant communities would recover from radiation damage, but the rate and pattern of such recovery would be highly dependent on many variables, and is not generally predictable without their specification.

2.) Recovery by surviving irradiated individual plants could occur, provided some propagative tissues were left intact and soil and climatic conditions were favorable for plant growth following the stress.

3.) Plant communities might recover following ordinary successional processes, if propagules were sufficiently available and edaphic and climatic conditions sufficiently favorable.

3.4.4 Fate and Transport of Radionuclides in Ecosystems

3.4.4.1 Biomagnification of Radionuclides in Terrestrial Ecosystems

The biomagnification of various radionuclides in terrestrial and aquatic food chains has been known for several decades. Ecosystem processes can channel seemingly insignificant quantities of fallout into significant concentrations in higher organisms, including humans. Relatively simple ecosystems that have evolved under stressed climatic or nutrient-poor conditions especially tend to conserve essential elements. Fallout radionuclides in these ecosystems are concentrated into a relatively small array of species and a relatively small biomass. The behavior of radionuclides in arctic ecosystems, which provides clear examples of biomagnification, reflects many important functional processes of ecosystems. Factors such as climate, vegetation, and the food-chain relationships of consumers are important (Whicker and Schultz, 1982).

Examples have been reported of contamination of tundra ecosystems by global fallout from nuclear weapons testing. Linden (1961) reported measurements of human body burdens of radionuclides in Scandinavia. People who had eaten large amounts of reindeer meat had much higher levels of ^{137}Cs than those who had not, with up to 50-fold increases in some individuals. Wolves feeding on caribou in Alaska had ^{137}Cs levels twice that of the caribou (Hanson, 1967). Reindeer meat from northern Sweden contained 28 nCi of ^{137}Cs per kg, while beef from Lund had only 0.1 nCi of ^{137}Cs per kg. The source of the radionuclide to the reindeer was found to be principally lichens, which accumulated fallout. Hanson (1966) found high levels of ^{137}Cs in Alaskan lichens in 1959–1962. Human body burdens of caribou-eating Alaskan Inuit were found to be comparable to those of the reindeer-eating Lapps. Both reindeer and caribou feed on lichens, mosses, and sedges on the tundra. Similar findings were reported for Finland (Miettenen and Hasanen, 1967) and the U.S.S.R. (Nevstrueva et al., 1967).

A key factor in the lichen–reindeer–human food chain is that lichens in arctic and sub-arctic regions are prostrate or mat-like, and obtain a large proportion of their nutrients from the atmosphere. They are very effective at interception and adsorption of elements in precipitation. Gorham (1959) reported on the occurrence of higher concentrations of radioactive materials in plants having persistent aboveground parts, while Hanson and Eberhardt (1969) found that the effective half-life for ^{137}Cs in Alaskan lichens exceeds 10 years. Rickard et al. (1965) and Potter and Barr (1969) showed that lichens retain radionuclides for much longer periods and accumulate concentrations roughly two- to ten-times higher than flowering plants in the same area.

Other examples of ecosystems in which food-chain biomagnification of radionuclides produced by atmospheric testing of nuclear weapons has been studied are the temperate mountainous areas of Colorado. Here, as elsewhere, fallout deposition generally increases with elevation in mountain areas; associated concentrations of ^{137}Cs for soils, litter, vegetation, and animals increase with elevation. Fallout following a nuclear war would likely show this same effect.

Increased precipitation seems to be the key factor in this increase, which can be up to three-fold over an elevational increase of 1500 m (Whicker and Schultz, 1982). The eastern versus western exposure of mountainous slopes often show differences in precipitation, which are reflected in differences in fallout burdens. Snow is an important factor in this, in that stratospheric debris enters the upper troposphere in the Northern Hemisphere to the greatest extent in spring, when snowfalls are still frequent and heavy.

In mountain ecosystems, radionuclides are initially present in the vegetation, but soon move to the soil. Most eventually reside in the litter and upper soil horizons, where they bind strongly to litter, humus, and small inorganic particles such as clay.

Whicker et al. (1965, 1967) studied body burdens in mule deer, which are principal grazers in the high alpine summer meadows. Maximum concentrations occurred in the summer when deer were at higher altitudes, and minimum values occurred in winter, when deer feed at lower altitudes.

Whicker et al. (1968) reported that deer tissues in Colorado in 1962–1964 contained five to ten times the concentration of ^{137}Cs burdens in humans. After the 1962 test ban treaty, the levels of radionuclides in deer gradually declined, similar to the situation for arctic reindeer and caribou.

Mountain lions in Colorado were reported to show a three-fold increase in ^{137}Cs over the mule deer. ^{90}Sr and ^{131}I would not significantly enter humans from deer consumption since these radionuclides accumulate in bone and thyroid, but consumption of deer liver (or caribou liver) could cause increased internal dosage of ^{144}Ce, ^{137}Cs, and ^{106}Ru.

In warmer terrestrial ecosystems, the accumulation and residence times of radionuclides in biota seem to be reduced compared with the examples listed above because of more rapid metabolic activity and more rapid rates of litter decomposition. Lichens, mushrooms, and ferns were reported to have the highest levels in lower coastal plain communities. Johnson and Mayfield (1970) reported that the high ^{137}Cs levels in white-tailed deer in Florida could be accounted for by their eating mushrooms frequently enough to cause increased body burdens. Whicker and Schultz (1982) reported that seasonal changes in food habits were indicated by fluctuating body burdens in deer. High values in muscle tissues related to high vegetation levels of Cs and to low K levels in vegetation, a situation favoring Cs absorption and retention.

While food chain accumulation in terrestrial ecosystems subjected to radionuclide fallout strongly suggests that a significant increase in internal dose to humans could occur following a major nuclear war from eating a high dietary content of wild animal meat, the actual biomagnification shown to occur in terrestrial ecosystems is generally not more than a few hundred- to a thousand-fold. In part, this is because of the short food chains involved. In aquatic ecosystems, however, biomagnification has been found to be substantially greater (see below).

3.4.4.2 Fate and Transport of Radionuclides in Freshwater Ecosystems [1]

Freshwater ecosystems comprise lakes, ponds, rivers, streams, and groundwater. Pollution of surface water by radionuclides following a nuclear war could be caused by direct deposition from contaminated precipitation and dry deposition, by surface runoff, and by infiltration into the soil and subsequent subsurface transport into freshwater ecosystems. Some of the radionuclides in surface water bodies would be adsorbed onto sediments. Once the initial peak of pollutants passed through the system, some of the adsorbed ions would be remobilized. Sediments can also be remobilized during periods of high flow. The consequence is prolonged pollution of surface waters.

---

[1] This section largely prepared by M. Havas and D. W. H. Walton.

   The major radionuclides produced during detonation of nuclear warheads
are listed in Table 3.4. A number of the radionuclides, particularly the activation products, are relatively short-lived and are likely to have a local
rather than a world-wide distribution. In contrast, some of the long-lived
radionuclides (^{14}C, ^{60}Co, ^{90}Sr, ^{106}Ru, ^{45}Ca) would likely be distributed globally. Attention will therefore be focused on these longer-lived radionuclides,
their fate and transport within different freshwater ecosystems, their bioaccumulation, and their toxicity to aquatic plants and animals.

   The processes that affect the fate and transport of radionuclides within
ecosystems can be quite complex. Figure 3.3 shows the principal routes of
radionuclides into soil/water systems and their likely pathways through the
biota. Retention times in some compartments can be very long, such as in
lake sediments and in the organic-litter layers of forested ecosystems.

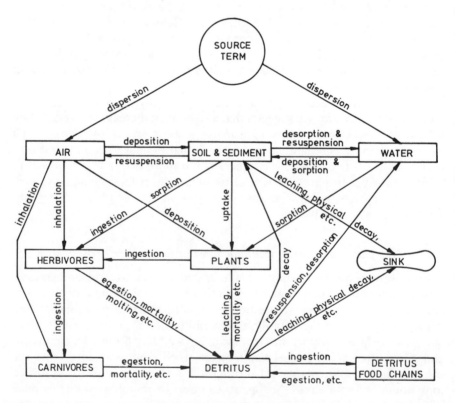

Figure 3.3 Major processes which affect radionuclide transport in ecosystems.
Boxes represent ecosystem components while arrows represent flow of materials
through functional processes. From Whicker and Schultz (1982)

Freshwater ecosystems are likely to be less sensitive to external radiation than terrestrial ecosystems because of the attentuation of radiation by water, and more sensitive than marine ecosystems because of more limited dilution. The significance of any radionuclide as a pollutant of freshwater systems is based on its persistence in these systems, either within bottom sediments or within organisms, and is derived from its physical and biological half-lives, its abundance in fallout, and its toxicity. The radionuclides of most concern are ^{89}Sr, ^{90}Sr, ^{106}Cs, and ^{131}I. Uranium and plutonium nuclides would less likely be significant contaminants, since they are usually present in insoluble form.

Groundwater contamination would likely be minimal in the short term, since most of the radionuclides would be absorbed by the overlying soils. The time it would take radionuclides to reach many groundwater sources would likely exceed the life of most of the short-lived isotopes. Relatively long-lived isotopes, such as Cs, Pu, and Am, have a strong binding affinity with soil, and their transport to groundwater would be substantially delayed. Acid precipitation could produce significant pulses of enhanced leaching from contaminated soil. Once groundwater became contaminated, it would remain contaminated for much longer periods than streams and lakes because of longer retention times; depending on the characteristics of the aquifers, including recharge and flow rates, contamination by long-lived radionuclides could last for decades.

Many radionuclides in fallout are not particularly soluble. They would likely find their way into sediments, where they would persist for long periods. The sediments, therefore, would provide a short-term sink and a long-term source to the overlying water. Since attenuation of gamma radiation, as well as alpha and beta particles, is quite substantial in water, the major route of exposure would likely be via food (i.e., internal radiation). Since the highest exposures would likely be in sediments, bottom feeders would be at a greater risk than pelagic forms. The primary routes of bioaccumulation would be via absorption and adsorption into aquatic plants and subsequent ingestion by aquatic animals.

Uptake of radionuclides is similar to the uptake of their chemical analogs. The bioconcentration factor (BF) is defined as the concentration of the element or radionuclide in the organism (μ Ci•g^{-1} fresh weight) divided by the concentration in the water (μ Ci•g^{-1}). Bioconcentration factors can vary from less than 1 to greater than 10,000. Despite a substantial body of information for different species in a variety of habitats, few generalizations about bioconcentration can be made. It is apparent, however, that filter-feeding zooplankton would likely accumulate substantial burdens of particulate-borne radionuclides compared with the concentrations in the water column; also, water-soluble radionuclides could accumulate and biomagnify through aquatic trophic webs.

Some environmental factors that would affect bioconcentration of radionuclides in surface waters include the water chemistry, water-sediment interactions, nutrient status, mineral content, and the concentration of suspended solids in the water (Vanderploeg et al., 1975) and in the short term the chemical form of the discharged radionuclide can have a profound effect on its assimilability. High turbidity would reduce the potential bioconcentration by binding the radionuclides to suspended particulates, particularly clays and organic matter. High mineral content of the water can reduce the bioconcentration for Ru, Ra, U, and Pu two- to ten-fold. Bioconcentration of ions from solution in nutrient-rich water is lower than in nutrient poor environments, presumably because of competition for sorption sites.

Two of the most important fission products, ^{90}Sr and ^{137}Cs, have bioconcentration factors in fish which range over four orders of magnitude. The bioconcentration factor for ^{90}Sr is inversely correlated with the Ca content of the water, whereas the BF for ^{137}Cs is inversely correlated with the K content of the water (Ophel, 1978). Adsorption of radionuclides on suspended or deposited sediments could prevent or reduce its assimilation by organisms; in other cases, sediment-sorbed radionuclides could have an increased availability to filter-feeding or bottom-dwelling organisms.

Ophel and Fraser (1973) determined the bioconcentration factors for ^{60}Co which entered a small, soft-water dystrophic–eutrophic lake in eastern Canada. In the same lake, Ophel et al. (1971) reported on the bioconcentration of ^{90}Sr. Representative bioconcentration factors found for these two radionuclides are shown in Table 3.11.

Strontium-90 behaves like calcium in biological tissue. Adsorption of ^{90}Sr onto sediments is a function of the cation exchange capacity of the sediments, pH, Ca, Mg, and Na ion concentrations, although the sediments are not the ultimate sink for Sr as they are for some other radionuclides. Strontium-90 is readily accumulated by aquatic organisms. Bioconcentration factors for Sr vary from 0.7 in omnivorous fish to greater than 700 in benthic invertebrates. The bioconcentration of ^{90}Sr is negatively correlated with the Ca^{2+} concentration in the water (Figure 3.4). Concentrations in fish bone may be 100 times higher than in fish flesh. Concentrations of Sr^{2+} are typically 100- to 2000-times higher in biota from freshwater than from salt water (NCRP, 1984). The highest concentrations are found in benthic invertebrates, filamentous algae, and aquatic macrophytes. Phytoplankton, zooplankton, and planktivorous fish have significantly lower concentrations of Sr. Transfer of Sr from phytoplankton to zooplankton appears to be 85% efficient in marine environments (NAS, 1971). Strontium has a high retention time (years) in biota.

Cesium-137 resembles potassium and exists as a monovalent cation in freshwater. Bioaccumulation of Cs is affected by competing ions, especially sodium and potassium. The uptake of Cs does not appear to be reversible in

TABLE 3.11

REPRESENTATIVE COBALT AND STRONTIUM BIOCONCENTRATION
FACTORS (BF) FOR BIOTA[a]

ORGANISM/COMPONENT	^{60}Co BF
freshwater clam	
shell	290
tissues	330
snail	440
crayfish (Cambarus sp.)	1600
bullfrog (Rana catasbina)	
adult	30
tadpole	250
snapping turtle	90
yellow perch	18
black-nose shiner	20
brown bullhead	63

ORGANISM/COMPONENT	^{90}Sr BF
6 fish species	450 - 1250
22 aquatic plant species	30 - 1300
beaver bone	1300
muskrat bone	3500
bottom sediments	180

[a] Data from Ophel and Fraser (1973); Ophel et al. (1971); and Ophel (1963). Bioconcentration factor = concentration in tissues ÷ concentration in lake water solution.

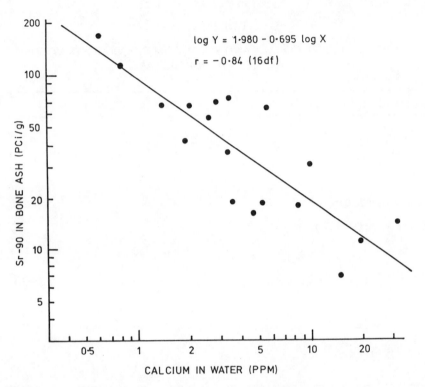

Figure 3.4   Strontium-90 concentrations in bone samples of trout from 18 mountain lakes in Colorado vs. dissolved calcium concentrations in water samples. From Whicker and Schultz (1982)

freshwater systems as it is in marine environment (NCRP, 1984). Maximum uptake of Cs^+ occurs in nutrient-poor water low in K^+ and suspended solids. Bioaccumulation of Cs^+ is 100 times greater in freshwater than in salt water (Whicker and Schultz, 1982). Bioconcentration of Cs in freshwater varies from 100 to greater than 10,000. The lowest concentrations are found in zooplankton and aquatic macrophytes. Concentrations in non-piscivorous fish are lower than in piscivorous fish.

Iodine-131 is highly active initially after its release, and could affect surface waters. Pathways of ^{131}I need to be considered only for a few weeks after its release into the environment because of its relatively short half-life (8 days). By contrast, [129]I has a half-life exceeding 10 million years. Iodine-129 occurs as a monovalent anion or in combination with oxygen (IO_3-). Adsorption onto sediments is quite low, although iodine can be co-valently bound to organic compounds. Uptake by sediments is related to the clay and silt contents of the sediments. In biological material, ^{129}I replaces stable iodine and accumulates in thyroid tissue. Invertebrates and algae have the highest concentrations in freshwater, while fish have the lowest concentrations. Bioconcentration factors are similar in freshwater and salt water, ranging from 8 to 570. Biological retention of I varies from weeks to months.

Cobalt-60 is one of the longer-lived activation products produced during the detonation of a nuclear warhead, but should only be present in significant amounts if salted bombs were used. In neutral solutions, ^{60}Co is not particularly water soluble and will readily adsorb onto suspended particulates. In acidic solutions, cobalt is soluble. The highest concentrations have been found in macrophytes and herbivores. There is no evidence for biomagnification; e.g., piscivorous fish have the lowest concentrations of cobalt. Transfer of Co from phytoplankton to zooplankton appears to be 30% efficient (NAS, 1971). Bioaccumulation in saltwater may be slightly higher than in freshwater (Whicker and Schultz, 1982). Cobalt is found at moderate concentrations in the gastointestinal tract but at low concentrations in other parts of the body (Whicker and Schultz, 1982). Biological retention times for ^{60}Co are in the order of days (Whicker and Schultz, 1982).

Ruthenium-106 exists in non-ionic form in water and is readily adsorbed by soil and sediment. Bioconcentration ranges from 0.2 in piscivorous fish to 57 in algae. There is no known analog for Ru. Biological retention time in the body is short (days).

The bioconcentration of tritium varies from 0.8 to 1.22 for aquatic biota. Tritium has a uniform distribution and a low retention time in the body (days). It has little significance in aquatic systems because of its enormous isotopic dilution by stable hydrogen associated with water molecules.

Carbon-14 is another activation product readily incorporated into inorganic and organic compounds, but, like tritium, is subject to substantial isotopic dilution. Its bioconcentration factor approaches one. Carbon-14 can accumulate in plant structural tissues and in dead organic matter. It has a low retention time (days) (Whicker and Schultz, 1982).

3.4.4.3 Fate and Transport of Radionuclides in Marine Ecosystems [2]

The vertical and lateral distributions of fallout radionuclides in ocean water and sediments would be governed by physical, chemical, and biological processes. Radionuclides enter the ocean as solutes, colloids, or particulates. Solutes or colloids would be transported laterally by advective movement of the water and would be slowly transferred to deep water by mixing and diffusion processes. Some solutes and colloids could become associated with particulates by biological or physicochemical processes. Insoluble particulates with densities greater than seawater would sink relatively rapidly.

---

[2] Based on Seymour (1982) and discussion of the Marine Working Group at the SCOPE Toronto meeting.

Mixing of fallout throughout the surface layer (5–200 m) could occur as rapidly as a few days or weeks for some of the fallout radionuclides. The pycnocline (i.e., the surface-deep water boundary) provides a temporary barrier to downward movement; its effectiveness for soluble elements is indicated by the half-residence time of 3.5 yr for ^{3}H in surface water. Below the pycnocline, the downward movement of soluble radionuclides would be even slower, with a turnover time on the order of decades or centuries. Residence times for deep ocean waters are a relative measure of water exchange rates, and values of 100–400 years for Atlantic Antarctic Intermediate Water, 600 years for North Atlantic Deep Water, and 1000–1300 years for Pacific and Indian Ocean Deep Water have been reported (Pritchard et al., 1971).

Radionuclides can be transported vertically by upwelling, sinking of surface water, diurnal plankton migrations, or sinking of fecal pellets. In areas of upwelling, radionuclides in water of moderate depths (approximately 300 m) can be brought to the surface. Cold surface water at high latitudes sinks and moves toward the equator, potentially carrying surface fallout radionuclides. Hence, the sources of fallout radionuclides in deep water at mid- and low latitudes could be the overlying water or the high-latitude surface waters.

Plankton accumulates radionuclides from water by sorption and particulate filtration; the diurnal migration by some species from deep water through the pycnocline can provide a vector for both upward and downward movement of radionuclides. Fecal pellets of organisms living in the surface layer provide an effective mechanism for scavenging particulates from surface waters.

The bioconcentration of radionuclides in marine systems is considerably less than in freshwater systems, especially because of competition of radionuclides with the much more concentrated stable isotopes present in the saline marine system. The strikingly large differences in concentration in biota compared with the amount present in the water are shown in Table 3.12. For example, the bioconcentration factors for Cs in crustaceans and fish muscle are several thousand-fold, whereas in marine systems, they are 23 and 15, respectively. A similar pattern, but with lowered bioconcentration factors, is shown for ^{90}Sr. Note that molluscs and crustaceans, which include many filter feeders, are capable of considerable concentration of radionuclides, as well as of many other toxic chemicals. Since marine shellfish are especially harvested in shallow coastal water, which would be subject to substantial contamination by run-off from land, these sources of human food might be contaminated to an unacceptable and even dangerous extent following a large-scale nuclear war.

The potential importance of internal dose for marine biota exposed to a variety of radionuclides in the water column following a major nuclear war is indicated by comparing internal and external radiation doses to selected

TABLE 3.12.

TYPICAL BIOCONCENTRATION FACTORS
FOR CS AND SR IN AQUATIC ORGANISMS[a]

ELEMENT	ECOSYSTEM	MOLLUSCS	CRUSTACEANS	FISH MUSCLE
		Bioconcentration factors		
Cesium	Freshwater	600	4000	3000
	Marine	8	23	15
Strontium	Freshwater	600	200	200
	Marine	1	3	0.1

[a] Data from Whicker and Schultz (1982).

biota from natural sources (Table 3.13). It can be seen that for surface waters especially, internal dose predominates, but at mid-depths and in the deepest waters external dose predominates. However, the groups of organisms differ substantially. For crustaceans and molluscs, external dose predominates at all ocean depths, while for algae and fish, external dose is the main source of radiation.

Both ^{90}Sr and ^{137}Cs remain soluble in seawater, but a small fraction attaches to fine particles. Strontium-90 concentrates in structural tissues (e.g., bone, shell, and fish scales). Cesium-137 concentrates in soft tissues, including muscle. Because ^{90}Sr is mostly deposited in non-edible tissues of seafoods and its concentration in seawater would be less, ^{137}Cs would offer the greater hazard to humans. Iodine-129 is unique because of its extremely long half-life. However, it is produced in small quantities (Table 3.4), is significantly diluted by stable iodine in the ocean, and decays by emission of low energy radiation. The other three important long-lived radionuclides are transuranic elements (^{238}Pu, ^{239}Pu, ^{241}Am), which are mostly insoluble in seawater and are transported relatively rapidly to the bottom sediments. However, it appears that a portion of the Pu on sinking particles could be resolubilized. These radionuclides would be most available to benthic organisms and to animals that feed on the bottom-living organisms.

Direct evidence of the horizontal movement of soluble radionuclides comes from the radioactivity deposited in the North Equatorial Current System from the 1 March 1954, 15 MT detonation at Bikini Atoll. During the subsequent 18 months, the maximum observed ^{90}Sr value in water

TABLE 3.13

WHOLE-BODY DOSES TO MARINE BIOTA
FROM 10,000 MT NUCLEAR WAR[a]

| | | DOSES IN MRAD•YR^{-1} | |
ORGANISM	INTERNAL	EXTERNAL	TOTAL
Northern latitude - surface			
Fish	0.8	0.01	0.8
Crustacea	2	70	70
Mollusc	2	70	70
Birds (plant diet)	50	0.007	50
Birds (fish diet)	4	0.007	4
Northern latitude - mid-depth			
Fish	0.3	0.005	0.3
Crustacea	1	30	31
Mollusc	1	30	31
Algae	8	0.01	20
Northern latitude - deep water			
Fish	0.4	0.006	0.4
Crustacea	1	30	30
Mollusc	1	30	30
Algae	20	0.02	20

[a] Data from NAS (1975).

decreased from 194 to 0.5 pCi•l^{-1}. From these data, the horizontal eddy diffusion coefficient and lateral rates of advance were calculated to be 14.8 and 7.7 km day^{-1} at two months and one year, respectively. By comparison, vertical transport is about 5 m per year in deep ocean water of the Pacific (Pritchard et al., 1971).

The best available empirical data on the biological effects of nuclear detonations in an oceanic environment are from the U.S. Pacific Test Site. There were numerous detonations at Bikini and Eniwetok Atolls between 1946 and 1952. Measurements of environmental contamination and biological accumulation of radionuclides were made on numerous occasions. The predominant radionuclides in marine organisms from the lagoons were neutron-activated radionuclides (e.g., ^{65}Zn, ^{60}Co, and ^{54}Mn), whereas the predominant radionuclides in the terrestrial forms were fission products (e.g., ^{137}Cs, ^{90}Sr). Large fish kills were not observed, but the removal rate of injured or dead fish by predators was not known. There was extensive destruction of habitat in some areas from the deposition of sediment.

Although there are limited observational data on the oceanic distribution of global fallout radionuclides, the behavior of ^{90}Sr and ^{137}Cs in the North Atlantic Ocean 10 or more years after fallout has been well documented (Kupferman, et al., 1979). These data provide a model for reliable predictions of the depth and latitudinal distribution of soluble fallout radionuclides. After 10 years, 73% remained above 1000 m, 25% below 1000 m, and 2% in sediments or shelf water. The latitudinal distributions of ^{90}Sr on land and in the ocean closely parallel each other, but a difference of about 25% suggests that either fallout on land has been underestimated or fallout into the ocean is greater than on land (Kupferman et al., 1979).

The observed distribution of a relatively insoluble radionuclide, Pu, in the central and north Pacific Ocean was unexpected. Truly non-soluble nuclides would be expected to be found only near the bottom; however, Pu was also found in a shallow subsurface layer (450 m) at concentrations exceeding the near-bottom values. The likely explanation for the presence of the shallow layer is resolubilization of Pu from sinking particles. For Pu that had already reached the ocean floor in near-shore areas, the observed concentrations in bottom sediments probably resulted from Pu transported on a mixed population of particles, for which the annual rates of descent were 70 m for 30%, 140 m for 40%, and 392 m for the remaining 30% of the particulates.

3.4.5 Internal Dose and Pathways to Humans

The analyses thus far have largely concerned external doses, especially of gamma-emitters. The other major category of radiation doses is internal doses, i.e., resulting from radionuclides incorporated into the body of an organism through inhalation or ingestion. This type of dose is particularly important to human health effects because: 1.) Internal doses involve the longer-lived beta- and alpha-emitters; the latter have very high relative biological effectiveness values. 2.) These radionuclides are especially deleterious to the tissues of the lungs and the gastrointestinal tract, through which they enter the body, and to organs in which they often concentrate; thus, doses can be focused on particular components of the body rather than diluted throughout. 3.) Since internal doses result from consumption of contaminated food and water, in a world with insufficient food resources (Chapters 4 and 5), survivors might have to choose between Scylla and Charybdis; whereas food surfaces contaminated in the early periods could often be cleansed of radiation, over the longer term, as radionuclides become incorporated into the food itself, there would be no mechanism for ready decontamination and no counterpart to active shielding against external doses. 4.) Internal doses would typically be chronic, and health effects could involve the protracted development of cancers, the reduced immunity to disease, and the opportunity for synergistic interactions with many other chronic period stresses on survivors. Such human health effects are outside the scope of this study; the reader is referred to the World Health Organization study (Bergstrom et al., 1983), and to Gofman (1981), Middleton (1982), Ishikawa and Swain (1981), Rotblat (1981), Leaning (1984), and Glasstone and Dolan (1977).

Pathways for internal dose to humans follow two basic routes: 1.) ingestion or inhalation of radionuclide-borne particulates directly; and 2.) consumption of food or water that was itself internally contaminated. The first would predominate in the early time periods, as fallout reached the surface and as contaminated soils and aerosols were resuspended and transported by air. This would also involve consumption of foods that were contaminated on the surface. Damage from this category of sources could be partially mitigated by careful attention to active avoidance (e.g., by washing food carefully).

The second category involves consumption of food into which bioavailable radionuclides had been incorporated. This could occur from agricultural crops, in which uptake through the roots or foliar surfaces of the plants occurred for particulate and, especially, dissolved forms of radionuclides. Soil type, soil pH, fallout levels, climatic factors, and many other variables could affect such biouptakes. Further, rates of assimilation of radionuclides differ considerably among crop species, with some plants bioconcentrating radionuclides, just as they do with stable analogs. Root crops are especially prone to accumulation through soil uptake, whereas leafy crops, such as lettuce and spinach, are liable to accumulate particulate radionuclides through openings in the leaves. Generally, waxy fruits (e.g., tomatoes, apples, cucumbers, and pumpkins) are low accumulators.

A second route for consumption of contaminated food would be consumption of domestic animal meat and milk products from animals that grazed on pastures contaminated internally or on the surface (e.g., from cattle, sheep, and goats). The absorption of fission products by grazing animals depends on the solubility of the radionuclides as they passed through the gastrointestinal tract. These animals also ingest or inhale considerable amounts of soil and dust in grazing, providing a direct route for uptake of fallout. Milk in particular can concentrate Cs and Sr (Romney et al., 1963), as seen from vastly smaller inputs associated with atmospheric tests. For example, Burton et al. (1960) estimated that about 80% of the ^{90}Sr in milk in England and Wales during 1958 was derived from fallout-contaminated foliage. Radio-iodine is another potential problem from contaminated milk, especially ^{131}I during the first few weeks after a nuclear war. Unlike Cs and Sr, however, survivors could actively protect themselves from ^{131}I by prior consumption of stable iodine, saturating the thyroid glands; it is questionable, however, that such active measures would occur on a massive scale following a nuclear war.

These isotopes, along with ^{59}Fe, ^{35}S, ^{60}Co, ^{65}Zn, ^{32}P, ^{3}H, ^{14}C, and others, would also affect drinking water, initially from surface water sources and potentially, over the longer term, from contaminated groundwater sources. Should groundwater become significantly contaminated, it could remain hazardous for decades; however, it is unlikely that groundwater would on a large scale become contaminated with radiation at levels of importance to human health effects, and, in any case, specific activities in surface waters would generally be much higher than in groundwater.

As with internally contaminated food, water is not readily decontaminated. For example, simple boiling, which can make bacterially contaminated water safe for drinking, would not remove radionuclide contaminants. More sophisticated methods do exist (e.g., ion exchange resins), but their large-scale availability and use after a nuclear war is doubtful.

The third major route of internally contaminated food involves the uptake and transport through natural ecological food chains, a mechanism discussed in previous sections. This offers the potential for significant bioconcentration of radioactivity into consumable food, especially for food taken from freshwater, estuarine, and marine ecosystems. In general, filter-feeding organisms (e.g., clams and mussels) and higher carnivores (e.g., piscivorous fish) have the potential for significant contribution to human internal doses. Fruits, berries, seeds, and animals from terrestrial ecosystems would also be potential sources of human internal dose.

Internal radiation doses to humans have not been calculated in the SCOPE–ENUWAR analyses. Existing computer models are available for making such calculations; however, there are no reported studies using these sophisticated models for analyzing the human internal doses that would ensue from local and global fallout of a large-scale nuclear war. The two major issues that would need to be resolved are the extent and intensity of fallout patterns and the alterations that could occur in human dietary patterns in the aftermath of a nuclear war.

The internal dose models that are available primarily rely on bioconcentration factors in aquatic and terrestrial ecosystems for various radionuclides, on estimates of surface contamination of food products and water, and on estimates of inhalation of aerosols and particulates. The latter can include inhalation of the fallout directly or inhalation of resuspended materials, such as wind-blown agricultural soils, aerosols near coasts, drift from irrigation spray, and so on. The models also include radioactive decay to other radioactive isotopes (daughter products), which may have their own assimilation and bioconcentration factors. The models account for elimination of radiocontaminants from biota, including humans. Examples of the methodologies used in such models are given in Baker et al. (1976), Soldat et al. (1974), and Harwell et al. (1982). Since the potential for fallout is significant and the potential for radionuclide transport to humans via ingestion and inhalation is large, this is clearly an area of research that needs to be undertaken.

3.4.6 Summary of Direct Effects of Fallout on Biota

In view of the projected *global* fallout levels given in Table 3.5 from Pittock et al. (1985), which include doses of a few tens of rads in the latitudinal band of 30°N–70°N, it is important to note that virtually all organisms require an acute dose well in excess of 100 rads before significant prompt mortality could be expected (Whicker and Schultz, 1982). Effects on animal or plant populations would probably not occur in ecosystems receiving fallout doses of 50 rads or less per year. Genetic effects might occur, but large population sizes, rapid generation times, and intensive competition among individuals would result in minimal effects at the population level. Most ecological communities are likely to require in excess of 1000 rads in order for significant effects on key components to occur. These very high doses would only likely be found within areas of *local* fallout or within very limited hot spots. Before the effects of global radionuclide fallout on ecosystems are dismissed as inconsequential, however, we need to recognize two additional factors:

1.) More subtle, but possibly significant effects, such as impairment of reproduction or growth, might occur at sub-lethal doses. Whicker and Schultz (1982) suggested that these could occur over the range of 10% to 100% of the lethal dose. Very low doses (i.e., less than 1% of the lethal dose) would not likely produce measurable pertubations in populations or communities. At the individual level, however, low levels of radiation could produce a range of low probability effects. These include induction of carcinomas, genetic mutations, and the shortening of lifespan. These effects increase in frequency as dosage is increased. The cumulative population doses for humans could be very large, since global fallout could expose much of the world's population to radioactivity.

2.) Food chain bioaccumulation of radionuclides can occur, often resulting in a substantial biomagnification at higher trophic levels. This biomagnification can lead to concentration factors of several thousand along a food chain that ultimately includes humans.

Both for local and global fallout, the emphasis in Volume I is on external gamma dose, with an external dose of approximately 450 rads taken as lethal for healthy humans. Several factors need to be considered in estimating the impact of such doses on humans and other biota:

1.) The effects from 450 rad external doses are estimates for healthy, and presumably un-traumatized, adult human populations; but this is highly unlikely for many of the survivors of the immediate aftermath of a major nuclear war. While variation would exist among individuals, the effect of such traumatic and physiological stresses as shock, psychological stress, contamination of water supplies and food, decreases in food availability, injury from flying debris, blast, burns, and inhalation of potential toxic fumes from burning, would all decrease the radiation dose necessary to cause fatalities. Such lower lethal doses would extend the areas of fatal radiation dosage, perhaps substantially, dependent upon the patterns of fallout.

2.) The *internal* dose would be in addition to effects caused by external dose. Inhalation of radioactive dust and air with radioactive gases would be one such source of internal dose, as would ingestion of contaminated food and water (see Section 3.4.5).

3.) The recent Soviet report (Svirezhev et al., 1985) focused considerable attention on beta doses, which were not estimated in Volume I. These doses were estimated to be approximately 8-times higher than gamma doses, although the depth of penetration of beta as an external dose is very limited. For humans, external beta dose can cause skin burns (as seen as a result of the Marshallese and Lucky Dragon episodes [Conard,1975]), but external beta does not give a whole-body dose comparable to gamma rays. On the other hand, external beta dose could be significant for the perennating tissues of plants, as seen following nuclear tests in Nevada (Rhoads et al., 1971; Rickard and Shields, 1963).

4.) Estimates of the area covered by local fallout vary substantially, in part dependent upon the specific nuclear war scenario but also on the specific model used. Volume I suggests that lethal areas of local fallout could increase several fold using different scenarios (e.g., surface bursting weapons on cities, attacks on nuclear power plant facilities). The baseline scenario of Volume I was estimated to lead to about 5% of the land mass of Europe, U.S.S.R., and U.S. being affected by lethal levels of local fallout. Other analyses suggest the land area covered in combatant countries could exceed 25% (Ambio, 1982; Harwell, 1984; Rotblat, 1981).

5.) Different models give different local fallout predictions. For instance, the model used in the Volume I analyses estimated about one-half the lethal area coverage for one benchmark calculation compared to the estimate using the Glasstone and Dolan (1977) model.

6.) Local fallout estimates are sensitive to assumptions concerning overlap of fallout patterns from multiple nuclear detonations. For example, calculations of no overlap versus total overlap for one scenario differed by a factor of about two, with the no-overlap calculations giving the larger area (Volume I). However, a simulation allowing intermediate levels of overlap determined by actual placement of local fallout plumes associated with specific targets gave a lethal area about three times larger than the no-overlap case (i.e., six-times larger than the total-overlap simulation). Further research is needed in order to characterize more adequately the spatial extent of lethal and damaging levels of local fallout from a large-scale nuclear war.

The lethal dose for humans of 450 rads is taken for short-term exposure within the first 48 hours after a detonation, while for longer term (two-week) exposure, 600 rads is taken as the human lethal dose, and about 1350 rads, based on a protection factor of 3 for reduction in external dose by shielding, after the first two days after nuclear war (Rotblat, pers. comm.). Harwell (1984) suggested that 1350 rads short-term exposure is an appropriate lethal dose to use in estimating human casualties, since shelter would be sought, while 600 rads was suggested as the lethal dose for longer-term exposure, as people would move out of shelters to seek food, relatives, etc. Using a severe nuclear war scenario, Leaning and Keyes (1983) estimated 67 million fatalities would result from local fallout radiation exposure for the United States, while Harwell (1984) suggested 12 million fatalites in the early post-war period and 50 million over the longer term from radiation, based on a scenario similar to that in Ambio (1982). Additional non-lethal radiation sickness would affect many more millions, assuming a dosage for this of 200 rads.

Rotblat (1981) suggested local fallout from a severe nuclear war in the U.S., western Europe, and the western U.S.S.R. to cover more than 25% of the land surface with greater than 450 rads; using the OTA (1979) scenario, it was suggested that casualties in the U.S.S.R. and U.S. could be 265 million, with a further 133 million injured and unlikely to receive proper medical attention. The OTA scenario further estimated possible total radiation-induced casualties in the U.S. and U.S.S.R. as 14.8 million from cancer, 18.4 million from thyroid cancers and nodules, 14 million abortions, and an additional 21.5 million casualties listed as possible in other countries on a long-term basis as a direct result of the nuclear war. No account was taken of starvation, epidemics, fatalities from fires, toxic smoke fumes, etc., nor was the nuclear attack postulated for countries other than the U.S. and U.S.S.R. Clearly, scenarios are legion and an actual war circumstance cannot be predicted, but the casualty estimates are enormous from immediate and longer-term direct consequences alone. Local fallout and radiation exposure play a large role in these effects. Even the minimal estimate (5%)

for land coverage for local fallout could cause millions of deaths, especially in Europe where population densities are high.

In the area affected by local fallout, there would be agricultural crops and natural ecosystems as well as human populations. Some areas would be affected by very extensive fires. High radiation levels in these areas would undoubtedly act synergistically to inhibit the rate of recovery of natural ecosystems. Equally important, the high level of radioactivity in soils would have an influence on the ability of land to grow crops with acceptable levels of radioactive contamination. Agriculture would undoubtedly be attempted, in any event, since the area of local fallout might be very extensive in many crop growing areas, such as in the midwestern U.S. or the Ukraine. Crop uptake of radionuclides, use of contaminated land, and sensitivity of plants and animals to radiation would be important factors after a nuclear war, as discussed previously and in Whicker and Schultz (1982), Kulikov and Molchanova (1982), and Svirezhev et al. (1985).

To put the consequences of radiation exposures into perspective for human populations within areas of local fallout, we need to consider overall casualty estimates from a nuclear conflict. Studies by WHO (Bergstrom et al., 1983) for a severe nuclear war in which most cities in the world were targeted suggested 1.1 billion deaths and 1.1 billion additional injuries worldwide; in the Ambio studies, Middleton (1982) estimated 750 million deaths worldwide; less severe scenarios would lead to several hundred million direct fatalities from a nuclear war. A large portion of these estimates is attributed to the effects from local fallout. It is with this perspective that we need to consider the sensitivities of biota other than humans to ionizing radiation, and to recognize that locally contaminated areas, which could cover large overall areas of the mid-latititude Northern Hemisphere, would be contaminated by radionuclides for long periods of time, especially if destruction of nuclear power and fuel storage facilities were to occur, considerably extending the longevity of this contamination and significantly adding to overall doses.

Thus, the direct effects of fallout on humans would likely far exceed the indirect effects resulting from destruction or disturbance of ecological systems. We have seen that much higher levels of radiation would be needed to cause devastation of most ecosystems, involving doses in excess of 1000 or even 10,000 rad. The areas of ecological damage would be considerably less extensive than areas of lethal effects on humans. Nevertheless, even sub-lethal levels of radiation can have significant and long-lasting effects on ecosystems, especially if occurring in concert with other environmental stresses. Radiation effects from local fallout would constitute one additional, and significant, stress on the post-nuclear war environment, reducing its capacity for supporting humans, retarding its recovery from a multitude of perturbations, and providing important routes for internal doses to humans.

3.5 ECOLOGICAL EFFECTS OF FIRE

3.5.1 Introduction

There is an extensive literature on fire ecology, including the ecological effects of wildland fires (e.g., Kozlowski and Ahlgren, 1974; Boerner, 1982; Wein and MacLean, 1983). The objective of this discussion is to draw attention to the variables that are unique to nuclear weapons and war and that could determine the expanse of nuclear war-induced fires, their abiotic and biotic consequences, and conditions under which recovery would occur in the post-nuclear war period. Included also is a discussion of the potential for secondary fires as a result of vegetation dieback from other environmental effects of nuclear war (e.g. reduced temperature, reduced light, or increased ionizing or ultraviolet radiation).

Nuclear weapon detonations in a large-scale war would start numerous fires in areas surrounding targets. It is also possible that the frequency of secondary fires in devastated ecosystems would greatly increase over time. Considerable uncertainty exists regarding the estimated extent of initial wildland and cropland fires (Table 3.14). Both the NRC (1985) and the Crutzen et al. (1984) studies considered as baseline cases that 0.25×10^6 km^2 of forest would burn, while other calculations yield estimates from as low as 0.03×10^6 km^2 to as high as 4.0×10^6 km^2 (Svirezhev et al., 1985). Assump-

TABLE 3.14

ESTIMATED CROPLAND AND WILDLAND FIRES
CAUSED BY NUCLEAR WAR

SOURCE	AREA ($\times 10^6$ KM^2)	COMMENTS
NRC (1985)	0.25	global
Crutzen et al. (1984)	0.25	global
Crutzen and Birks (1982)	1.0	global
Turco et al. (1983)	0.50	global
Grover in Harwell (1984)	0.18 - 0.20	U.S. only
Ayers (1965)	0.05 - 0.41	U.S. only
Svirezhev et al. (1985)	1.0 - 4.0 0.072	global no war - forest fire only
Small and Bush (1985)	0.03 - 0.19	global

tions regarding fuel flammability and targeting strategy accounts for most of the large disparity between these numbers.

Fuel flammability would affect the areal extent of fires primarily through affecting fire initiation and spread. Some authors suggested that 50% of the non-urban fuels in the U.S. are medium to highly flammable during summer months (Grover, 1985); other evaluations suggested that fuel conditions are highly variable, and that conditions for extensive cropland and wildland fires may be uncommon to rare and highly seasonal (Small and Bush, 1985).

Svirezhev et al. (1985) classified forest fires as: 1.) lower, in which forest litter, lichens, and other surface materials are consumed; 2.) upper, in which canopy involvement occurs; and 3.) underground, in which organic soil horizons such as peat are consumed. Lower forest fires generally constitute 76–84% of all fires, and canopy and peat fires represent about 16–24% and 0.1%, respectively. In dry years, this relationship can change. For example, in 1938, about 6% of all fires in the U.S.S.R. were peat fires, whereas 51% were surface fires.

Climatic data can be used to calculate fire probabilities. The effects of local weather on fire intensity and spread can be predicted using the burning index, B (Chandler et al., 1963) summarized in Table 3.15. Representative fire probabilities and burning index values are given in Table 3.16. These values indicate that boreal forests are at a low risk of fire for much of the year, with fire probabilities exceeding about 25% only during the summer months. Even during high risk periods, burning index values indicate that only surface fires could be sustained.

TABLE 3.15

BURNING INDEX AND FIRE INTENSITIES[a]

FIRE INTENSITY	BURNING INDEX
creeping fire	1 - 19
surface fire	20 - 39
running fire with some crown involvement	40 - 59
hot running fire with spotting	60 - 79
crown fire	≥ 80

[a] Data from Chandler et al. (1963).

TABLE 3.16

REPRESENTATIVE FIRE PROBABILITIES AND BURNING INDEX
VALUES FOR NORTHERN HEMISPHERE ECOSYSTEMS[a]

Ecosystem type	January		February		March		April		May		June	
	pbty.	B	pbty.	B	pbty.	B	pbty.	B	pbty.	B	pbty.	B
BOREAL CONIFEROUS												
USSR	0	0	0	0	0	10	0	19	0	29	0.02	32
Canada	0	0	0	0	0	0	0	0	0	17	0.24	22
TEMPERATE												
mixed conifer/hardwood												
France	0	0	0	1	0	4	0	0	0.24	0	0.44	4
US (East)	0	0	0	1	0	5	0	11	0.3	15	0.54	11
deciduous												
US (East)	0	13	0	15	0	24	0	26	0.14	15	0.36	20
woodland/grassland												
USSR	0	0	0	0	0	0	0.53	9	0.57	11	0.67	20
US (Great Plains)	0	17	0	19	0	42	0.35	45	0.33	27	0.45	32
US (Southwest)	0	17	0	21	0	39	0	48	0	71	0.57	99
brushland												
Spain	0.65	17	0.57	21	0.65	24	0.57	29	0.69	37	0.85	37
Greece	0	8	0.06	5	0.35	17	0.64	19	0.77	29	0.86	42
US (California)	0	32	0.07	36	0.45	34	0.63	31	0.87	37	0.96	48
desert												
US (California)	0	48	0	59	0.22	85	0.72	99	0.88	107	0.95	117

[a] Data from Chandler et al. (1963).

TABLE 3.16 continued

ECOSYSTEM TYPE	JULY		AUGUST		SEPTEMBER		OCTOBER		NOVEMBER		DECEMBER	
	pbty.	B	pbty.	B	pbty.	B	pbty.	B	pbty.	B	pbty.	B
BOREAL CONIFEROUS												
USSR	0.53	24	0.64	17	0.45	9	0	2	0	0	0	0
Canada	0.48	20	0.52	17	0.25	5	0	0	0	0	0	0
TEMPERATE												
mixed conifer/hardwood												
France	0.52	3	0.28	4	0	2	0	2	0	1	1	1
US (East)	0.75	20	0.76	15	0.37	10	0	3	0	1	0	0
deciduous												
US (East)	0.44	22	0.54	27	0.56	27	0.33	27	0	22	0	15
woodland/grassland												
USSR	0.53	22	0.72	20	0.57	12	0.71	4	0	0	0	0
US (Great Plains)	0.54	37	0.58	37	0.6	46	0.53	37	0.44	36	0	19
US (Southwest)	0.34	45	0.37	45	0.46	54	0.36	54	0	39	0	24
brushland												
Spain	0.96	43	0.97	25	0.69	24	0.62	22	0.16	26	0.36	15
Greece	0.94	43	0.93	40	0.84	29	0.53	17	0	2	0	2
US (California)	0.99	63	0.97	58	0.97	60	0.93	54	0.67	54	0.24	51
desert												
US (California)	0.97	117	0.97	119	0.93	115	0.87	98	0.66	77	0	57

Temperate forests are at somewhat greater risk from about May until September or October, but even during this period, only surface fires would likely predominate. Woodland and grassland areas show a potential for fire from about April to October, with running fires possible in some areas for a substantial portion of this period. Brushland areas (i.e., chaparral) around the Northern Hemisphere are at risk for fire in all months of the year. Additionally, relatively intense surface fires and running fires can occur in brushland areas during 8–10 months of the year, depending on the region. Deserts reflect a high probability for fire (exceeding 25% for 9 months), and a high potential fire intensity (B > 40 during all months), but sufficient plant biomass to carry fire is generally lacking.

Fire probabilities and burning indices are based on the same variables used to define various biome types (e.g., humidity, maximum and minimum temperatures). Thus, the sequence of fire susceptibility (deserts > brushland > woodland/grassland > mixed conifer/deciduous forest > boreal coniferous forest) reflects a continuum of hot–dry to cold–moist conditions. This sequence is misleading, however, because fuel availability limits the occurrence of fire in many ecosystem types, especially those of lesser productivity (e.g., deserts).

Thus, fuel loading is a variable of special importance to calculating cropland and wildland fire effects of nuclear war. Typical surface and fine fuel loadings range from about 0.015 to 0.1 $g \cdot cm^{-2}$ for grasslands and old fields, to about 2 $g \cdot cm^{-2}$ for forests (Table 3.17). Natural fires of moderate intensity can consume 25% of the fuels in forests, with greater proportions (50%–75% or more) consumed in grasslands, old fields, and other ecosystems dominated by herbaceous vegetation or containing larger quantities of fine fuels (e.g., brushlands). More intense fires (burning index > 30–35) could consume all fuels on the ground surface, as well as canopy fuels (foliage and branch materials) if torching and canopy involvement resulted.

Small and Bush (1985) summarized the burned fuel loadings used in several studies, reporting a range of 0.55 $g \cdot cm^{-2}$ to 0.01 $g \cdot cm^{-2}$. The value Small and Bush used in their analyses for forested ecosystems was 0.17 $g \cdot cm^{-2}$, which is the lowest estimate anyone has used in analyses of effects of nuclear war.

The potential for firespread once ignition occurred is important to calculating the total area of fire involvement following a nuclear war. However, some calculations suggest that firespread would be a relatively small component of total areal involvement when the ignition zones of multiple nuclear weapon detonations are summed (see calculations by Grover in Harwell, 1984). Fire behavior models were used by Small and Bush (1985) to derive this component of their estimate, but it is not clear in their report whether a central ignition zone was included in their calculations.

In addition to fire probabilities and intensities, the area of potential fire-

TABLE 3.17

REPRESENTATIVE FUEL LOADINGS FOR
NORTHERN HEMISPHERE ECOSYSTEMS[a]

Ecosystem Type	Fuel (g·cm^{-2})
boreal coniferous forest	0.79 - 1.1[b]
coniferous forest	1.3 - 1.8[b]
deciduous forest	0.31 - 0.71[b]
chaparral	1.0 - 3.0
grasslands	0.015 - 0.1
old fields	0.04
maize	0.16 - 0.26
wheat	0.11 - 0.18
alfalfa	0.22
soybean	0.05 - 0.09

[a] Compiled by Grover (1985).
[b] Low value represents litter plus understory; high value represents litter, understory, foliage, and branches.

spread following a nuclear war is also a matter of interest. Haines et al. (1975) compiled data on wildfires during the period 1960–1969 in the national forests of the northeastern and north-central regions of the United States. Large fires (those involving 4 ha or more) represented only 14% of the total number of fires for which data were available. Data on Canadian fires from 1968–1977 revealed an expected seasonal pattern in fire occurrence (Table 3.18), with the greatest number of fires occurring in the summer months. Although fire size data were not reported, average fire size ranged from about 1 ha for February fires, to greater than 290 ha for June fires, again reflecting seasonal pattern. Examination of the fire data reported above also reveals an earlier peak in fire frequency for the U.S., with the greatest number occurring in April and May. Nonetheless, as concluded by Ayers (1965), and Grover (in Harwell, 1984), the ignition zone of potential nuclear bursts is the principal variable of interest for these calculations. Weapon yield and targeting scenarios, coupled with a thorough analysis of fuel types and fuel loadings, take on great importance when projecting cropland and wildland fire involvement.

TABLE 3.18

AVERAGE FIRE DISTRIBUTION AND SIZE DURING 1968 - 1977 IN CANADA[a]

Month	# of Fires	Total Area (ha)	Average Size (ha)
January	13	30	2.3
February	6	7	1.2
March	45	540	12
April	650	21,000	32
May	2,000	166,000	83
June	1,500	440,000	295
July	1,900	370,000	195
August	1,800	150,000	83
September	500	15,000	30
October	225	4,500	20
November	45	1,700	38
December	6	10	1.7
Total	8,690	1.2×10^6	

[a] Data compiled by Grover (1985).

3.5.2 Fire Ignition

Radiant exposures of $5-7$ cal$\cdot$cm^{-2} are generally considered sufficient to ignite many kindling fuels (Glasstone and Dolan, 1977). Most studies that quantify the fire effects of multiple nuclear weapon detonations use radiant exposures of $10-20$ cal$\cdot$cm^{-2} to define ignition thresholds (e.g., Ayers, 1965; NRC, 1985; Harwell, 1984). For a weapon in the 200 kT yield range, the area contained within the 10 cal$\cdot$cm^{-2} isopleth is about 100 km^2; for 1 MT this area is about 480 km^2. In studies using an ignition threshold of 20 cal$\cdot$cm^{-2}, an areal involvement of 250 km^2 per MT of yield is generally assumed. Considering that the strategic installations (e.g., ICBM silo fields) that are presumed to be targeted in a nuclear war number in the thousands, estimates on the order of 10^6 km^2 involved in cropland and wildland fires are readily obtained.

3.5.3 Potential for Fires

All of the major biomes of the Northern Hemisphere are represented by the range of ecosystem types likely to be targeted in a nuclear war. In the United States, short-grass prairie and agricultural mosaics are at greatest risk because of the placement of ICBM silo fields in the Great Plains states

(Table 3.19). In fact, calculations by Ackerman and Stenback (pers. comm.) (Table 3.20) reveal that up to 94% (Grand Forks AFB, SD), and no less than 20% (Ellsworth AFB, SD), of the area in which U.S. ICBM silos are located are involved in agriculture, while the rest of these areas are dominated by short-grass and mixed grass prairies. An analysis of the distribution of an additional 68 military installations in the U.S. (Table 3.21) reveals that southeastern ixed deciduous forest, oak–hickory–pine forests in the central U.S., annual grasslands in central California, coastal sage and chaparral in southern California, and northern hardwood forests in the northeastern U.S. are at significant risk, with 6 or more targets identified in each of these vegetation types. Boreal coniferous forests and steppe vegetation dominate the interior of the U.S.S.R., where many of their strategic installations are located.

Based on regional climate, fire probabilities in boreal coniferous forests are highest in July, August, and September (0.53, 0.64, and 0.45, respectively) (see Volume I; also Chandler et al., 1963; Harwell, 1984; Wein and Maclean, 1983). In the eastern U.S., fire probabilities in the range 0.14 to 0.54 can occur during the months of May through October; however Haines

TABLE 3.19

POTENTIAL VEGETATION ASSOCIATIONS FOR MAJOR
MILITARY INSTALLATIONS IN THE US[a]

INSTALLATION	POTENTIAL VEGETATION
Warren AFB Cheyenne, WY	Short-grass prairie
Grand Forks AFB Grand Forks, ND	Tall-grass prairie
Maelstrom AFB Great Falls, MT	Short-grass prairie
Whiteman AFB Knob Norster, MO	Oak-hickory savanna
Minot AFB Minot, ND	Mixed-grass prairie
Ellsworth AFB Rapid City, SD	Mixed-grass prairie

[a] From Grover (1985).

TABLE 3.20

MAJOR LAND USE CATEGORIES FOR U.S. ICBM INSTALLATIONS[a]

INSTALLATION	AGRICULTURE	RANGELAND	CONIFEROUS FOREST	DECIDUOUS FOREST	SURFACE WATER
Warren AFB	45	54	<1	0	<1
Grand Forks AFB	94	3	0	3	<1
Maelstrom AFB	40	48	12	0	<1
Whiteman AFB	83	<1	0	15	<1
Minot AFB	73	22	0	<1	5
Ellsworth AFB	20	71	5	4	<1

[a] Compiled by Ackerman and Stenback (pers. comm.). Data listed as % of land area.

et al. (1975) found that the majority of large fires in this region and the upper midwestern U.S. occur in April and May. Woodland and grassland areas in the U.S., and the steppe regions of the U.S.S.R., can experience high fire probabilities (0.35 to 0.72) during the months of April to November. Mediterranean shrub zones (chaparral) in the southwestern U.S. and southern Europe can be highly susceptible to fire initiation year-round, but most natural fires in these areas occur during the summer and early fall. Croplands surrounding targeted areas would be most susceptible to fire for a short period (about 2 weeks) prior to harvest, and perhaps for an equal period after harvest if crop residues were left in the fields. Thus, all ecosystems in which prime military targets are located would not be highly susceptible to fire at the same time. However, where dry conditions prevail, the late spring, summer, and early fall months present the greatest potential for intensive fires and firespread. Also, many of the most intensively targeted ecosystem types (e.g., the grasslands of the interior U.S.) generally experience similar climatic conditions at the same time, and therefore would be equally vulnerable at the time of an attack.

3.5.4 Abiotic Effects

The principal abiotic effects of fire on ecosystems concern the redistribution of inorganic elements, either directly through combustion of organic

TABLE 3.21

POTENTIAL VEGETATION ASSOCIATIONS
SURROUNDING U.S. MILITARY INSTALLATIONS[a]

Vegetation	# of installations
Forests	
Western Ponderosa Pine	1
Western Mixed Conifer	1
Northwestern Mixed Conifer	3
Great Lakes Pine	1
Oak-Hickory-Pine	7
Northeastern Oak-Pine	1
Northeastern Hardwood-Spruce-Fir	6
Eastern Mixed Oak	4
Southeastern Mixed Pine-Hardwood	10
Southern Floodplain	1
Transition Woodlands	
California Oak Woodlands	1
Oak-Hickory-Savanna	2
Shrub-Oak-Grassland	2
Grasslands	
Tall-Grass Prairie	1
Mixed-Grass Prairie	3
Short-Grass Prairie	2
Arid Grassland	2
Annual Grassland	7
Coastal Sage-Chaparral	6
Arid Lands	
Desert Scrub	4
Sagebrush-Steppe	3

[a] Data compiled by Grover (1985).

materials and entrainment of ash elements in smoke plumes, or indirectly through soil erosion following the initial fire. Increased soil temperatures induced by fire are a function of the kind and amount of fuel present and the condition (i.e., flammability) of the fuel at the time of burn. Grassland fires are somewhat cooler than forest fires (by about 50°C–100°C), while shrubland fires are characteristically the hottest. Although these values are for natural or anthropogenic fires, there is no evidence to suggest that nuclear war-induced fires would demonstrate differences in relative intensity or surface temperatures.

Prolonged abiotic effects include a warmer soil microclimate associated with darker, exposed soils. Removal of vegetation and decreased evapotranspiration can result in both increased runoff across the soil surface, and increased infiltration into the soil, depending on fire intensity. Following severe hot fires in which all organic material is lost from the soil surface, runoff may exceed percolation and may result in severe erosion (Boerner, 1982). For example, soil erosional loss from several eastern Washington watersheds increased from undetectable levels before burning to 41–127 m^3 following fire. Other studies have documented erosional loss from sliding, surface creep, and wind erosion (see Boerner, 1982). There is also evidence for some soils (especially in chaparral) that hydrophobic organic constituents in fuels may be formed that result in reduced water infiltration, soil drying, and increased surface runoff and erosion (Debano and Conrad, 1978).

Loss of elements from burning ecosystems varies as a function of the composition of aboveground vegetation and other fuels, and the intensity and duration of the fire. More than half of the ash elements (e.g., Ca, Mg, and K) but less than half of the nitrogen from burned vegetation and litter may be returned to the soil. Although loss of nitrogen and phosphorus can be quantitatively significant (e.g. Christensen, 1977), increased remobilization and availability of plant macronutrients in the soil are often associated with fire. Ash element remobilization is often manifested by an increase in soil pH of up to one unit in some forested ecosystems, whereas in grasslands and chaparral, soil pH changes may be 0.25 units or less.

3.5.5 Biological Effects

Although fire can be detrimental to an ecosystem over the short term, many ecosystem types are fire adapted, and a change in species composition and ecosystem function may occur with the absence of fire (see examples in Kozlowski and Ahlgren, 1974; Wein and MacLean, 1983). Indeed, there is ample evidence to show that fire has been a major evolutionary force in shaping the composition of the biosphere.

The severity with which fire may impact an ecosystem may be roughly surmised from the frequency with which fires normally occur. Table 3.22 summarizes data from Grover (1985) to indicate that many portions of landscapes in most of the Northern Hemisphere experience fire on a cycle of 25 years or less. Similarly, there are ecosystems that experience fire very infrequently, i.e., at intervals measured in hundreds of years. Not surprisingly, those ecosystems that experience fire at less than 100-year intervals are generally dominated by fire-adapted vegetation. Fire adaptation in plants is often expressed in the form of thickened, fire resistant bark (e.g., *Sequoia* spp.), serotinous cones for seed protection and storage (e.g., *Pinus rigida*), or propagules protected at or near the soil surface (e.g., root sprouting shrubs, seeds requiring fire scarification, grasses).

TABLE 3.22

REPRESENTATIVE FIRE FREQUENCIES
IN DIFFERENT ECOSYSTEMS[a]

Ecosystem type	Fire Frequency (average yr between fires)
Tundra	300 - 1000+
Boreal Forest	50 - 200
High Elevation Coniferous Forest	25 - 1000+
Low Elevation Coniferous Forest	10 - 350
Moist Temperate Forest	3 - 300
Dry Temperate Forest	5 - 100
Grasslands	1 - 25
Chaparral	20 - 100
Tropical Forest	several hundred

[a] Data compiled by Grover (1985); see also Wein and MacLean (1983).

3.5.6 Recovery Potential

Much of the previous discussion applies to the effects of natural fires on ecosystems variously adapted to their occurrence. Fires initiated by nuclear weapon detonations might be qualitatively different in their short-term and long-term effects. For example, assuming that the ignition zone from nuclear detonations extended to about the 10–15 $cal \cdot cm^{-2}$ radiant exposure isopleth, winds associated with the blast wave at this distance from the epicenter could exceed 60–70 mph (Glasstone and Dolan, 1977). In forests, winds of this magnitude could cause canopy blow down of 30% or more, changing the fuelbed configuration and intensifying the fire.

In the case of surface bursts, canopy destruction would be of secondary importance; deposition of local fallout with doses on the order of 10^4 rads would be of overriding biological significance in the immediate vicinity and for many kilometers downwind of the blast epicenter.

The studies of recovery at nuclear test sites suggest that within the zone denuded by blast, and within the zone in which fire would remove or kill existing vegetation, recovery of some plant species could occur within a few months or years by root sprouting of radiation-resistant species and by invasion of some opportunistic species. However, it is important to note that recovery in these cases has proceeded under normal climatic conditions; reduced temperatures and reduced sunlight, coupled with residual ionizing radiation and enhanced ultraviolet radiation during the weeks and months following a nuclear war, could severely limit biological activity. Prolonged exposure of soils denuded by blast effects or fire would increase the probability for significant soil erosion, thereby compromising even further the ability of plants to reestablish.

In heavily targeted regions (e.g., ICBM bases in the Great Plains of the U.S.), the cumulative area directly affected by weapon blast, fire, and radiation effects could act to slow recovery. Odum (1965) first recognized that the scale of disturbances associated with nuclear war may be one of the most unique and important factors to consider. Although the area assumed to be ignited by a single 1 MT nuclear weapon is not extensive (on the order of 250 km^2), the total area affected by a massive attack on one ICBM base could be on the order of 10^4–10^5 km^2. On an ecological time scale, disturbances of this size are rare, certainly in the short-grass prairie.

In the taiga forests of the north and northwestern U.S.S.R., paludification of burned areas could be an important phenomenon (Svirezhev et al., 1985). Between 60°N latitude and the Arctic Circle, two subzones of taiga forests occur: the northern taiga subzone of gley-podzol soils, and the middle taiga subzone of podzol soils. Gley-podzol soils are characterized by a groundwater saturated zone at about 40–60 cm, with deposition of reduced forms of iron and other elements. Paludification describes further water-logging of the soil profile, leading to bog formation, when the water table rises to within about 40 cm of the surface. Calculations by Svirezhev et al. (1985) indicated that if as little as 20% of the tree cover were removed, increased water infiltration through the soil and decreased evapotranspiration could lead to paludification and subsequent conversion of large areas to bog-type systems. In contrast to the U.S.S.R., soil conditions in the North American boreal forests would be conducive to paludification in only a few areas (e.g., Hudson Bay).

3.5.7 Secondary Fires

As indicated previously in this discussion and preceding chapters, the climatic and environmental effects of nuclear war could be devastating to large regions of the Northern Hemisphere and to portions of the equatorial and southern latitudes as well. Recurring freezes and chronic exposures to ultraviolet radiation and residual ionizing radiation could kill exposed vegetation over large areas. Other indirect effects of a stressed environment (e.g., insect outbreaks on physiologically weakened vegetation) could contribute further to the buildup of readily ignitable dead or dying vegetation.

Svirezhev et al. (1985) suggested that the total area burned annually by natural fires in the aftermath of nuclear war could eventually be double the current rate (about 0.3% of forested areas, or 1.4×10^9 km^2). This report also suggested that peat bogs could increase in significance. Peat fires could be important to atmospheric conditions if sufficiently extensive, because of high levels of nitrogen and sulphur in the fuel materials and the low intensity with which they burn.

The scale effects, discussed earlier, could be an important determinant of recovery, as would depletion of seed banks and other propagule reserves by the short-term environmental effects of nuclear war. Confounding changes in the environment, and subsequent changes in the species pool present following secondary fires, make it very difficult to assume that post-fire recovery patterns would resemble those documented under current conditions.

3.5.8 Summary

The total area of croplands and wildlands involved in fire as a direct result of nuclear war could range from 10^5 to 10^6 km^2. Firespread would likely be less important than the cumulative area ignited directly by thermal emissions from nuclear detonations. Although most targeting strategies suggest that the Great Plains of North America and portions of the boreal coniferous forests and steppes of interior Eurasia are at greatest risk, a substantial number of potential military targets are located in other highly flammable vegetation associations (e.g., chaparral). The direct abiotic and biotic effects of nuclear war-induced fires would be comparable to those documented for natural fires. However, residual ionizing radiation, deposited as local fallout on burned areas, could prolong recovery and alter the assemblage of plant and animal species present. Moreover, climatic and other environmental effects of nuclear war would selectively deplete the species pool available for eventual recovery of these and other directly disturbed areas. The probability of secondary fires would increase with time, as dead or dying vegetation dried and increased in flammability. These fires could be more intense and of greater areal involvement than natural fires under current conditions. Ecosystem recovery from these secondary fires is impossible to predict from existing knowledge because of the confounding climatic and environmental effects of nuclear war and other indirect ecosystem-level effects.

3.6 SUMMARY OF EFFECTS ON ECOLOGICAL SYSTEMS

3.6.1 Introduction

In the preceding sections of this chapter, and in the analyses of Chapter 2, we have examined the individual effects on ecosystems of the variety of environmental perturbations that could occur after a large-scale nuclear war. The purpose of this section is to recapitulate these effects and to consider them in combination and across ecosystem types. We also examine briefly the potential for natural ecosystems to support human populations and the implications for a post-nuclear war world.

Much of the previous discussions focused on the direct effects on ecological systems, especially the various effects on the dominant species in each ecosystem. For example, in most of the discussion on potential climatic effects, the perturbations were often sufficiently severe that more subtle, indirect consequences could be ignored in making estimates of the major responses of ecosystems to those perturbations. We have also focused on effects on plant species, reflecting the fundamental role of the primary producers in ecosystem processes. However, effects on ecosystems cannot be projected simply from direct effects on the dominant plant species; rather, ecosystems, by their nature as interactive complexes of biological populations linked to the abiotic environment, are subject to indirect effects involving those interactions and linkages.

Mechanisms for propagation of effects across species center on species interactions, including: 1.) mutualism, in which each species relies on the other for survival; 2.) competition, in which each species attempts to acquire the same resources; and 3.) predation and parasitism, in which one species feeds on another. In the first case, reduction or elimination of one population would adversely affect the other population, even if the latter did not experience direct effects from the perturbation. In the second case, reduction in one competitor could allow others to have increased resources, thereby enhancing those populations. In the third case, elimination of the prey would adversely affect the predator, whereas reduction in the predator population alone could enhance the situation for the prey species. Other combinations of these types of interactions occur in ecosystems, including different degrees of dependency on species interactions, but for the purposes here, the key elements of species interactions are the potential for effects to be propagated across species and often with prolongation of the time of effects. One analysis performed in this study that did explicitly include effects mediated through altered competitive interactions, i.e., the FORNUT simulations discussed in Chapter 2, clearly showed the potential for prolonged and indirect effects on the community composition of forests.

Biological populations are also linked intimately with the abiotic components of the environment, such that effects on biota can translate into effects on abiotic and biotic processes, and vice versa. Again, different species react differently to changed abiotic conditions; as one example, loss of nutrients in an ecosystem could result in the loss of one species because of insufficient resources for survival, but another species might increase its abundance in response to the different competitive regime.

Other issues of ecosystems processes are important (Levin et al., 1984). For instance, critical species are those species that occupy a particularly important position in trophic structures, such that loss of that species could adversely affect the structure of the community as a whole. Often there exist only a few biological taxa that perform essential functions in ecosystems, and the simultaneous loss of these species would result in a change in the functional characteristics of the ecosystem. How many species that perform similar functions and how closely they are related provides a measure of the functional redundancy of an ecosystem; low functional redundancy means an ecosystem would be more vulnerable to disruption of that function. In general, disruptions in ecosystem processes and functions would result in substantial propagation of that disruption to the biotic components of the ecosystem.

Another factor of importance is the spatial scale of the ecosystem, its populations, and the perturbation affecting it. This would be a particularly important factor after a large-scale nuclear war, in that perturbations that an ecosystem might well be capable of accommodating, if at a relatively small scale, could be devastating if occurring over a broad landscape. The issues of scale are especially important to the rates and prospects for recovery. Similarly, the potential for nonlinearities in response to perturbations is great, and often thresholds are seen in the stress-response relationships of individual species as well as whole ecosystems. Thus, perturbations that are routinely accommodated by ecosystems can become devastating if thresholds are exceeded in the intensity or frequency of the stress.

Because of these and a host of other factors that result from the complex and interactive nature of ecosystems, it is not possible to predict the full range of consequences to follow from nuclear war-induced perturbations. The potential for propagation of effects beyond stresses directly affecting particular species, extending effects across the trophic structure and across time, is clearly very high; but the particular pathways that such reverberations would follow cannot be specified because of uncertainties in our understanding of: 1.) the stress-response relationships of individual species to individual perturbations; 2.) these relationships for individual species subjected simultaneously to multiple, often synergistic perturbations; 3.) all of the species–species interactions in ecosystems; and 4.) the timing, intensity, and spatial extent of the various physical disruptions from a large-scale nuclear war. Many of these uncertainties can be reduced by continued research in ecosystems ecology, especially in stress ecology and particularly for the types of perturbations anticipated from a large-scale nuclear war; other uncertainties can never be eliminated. It is clear, however, that assessing ecological effects of nuclear war primarily on the basis of direct effects on plant species, as we have done in Part I of this volume, consistently gives *underestimates* of ecological effects, effects that would be extended in both intensity and duration by inclusion of the synergistic and indirect responses to nuclear war.

3.6.2 Summary of Consequences

A synopsis of the potential effects of nuclear war on ecological systems is presented in Table 3.23. Included are the major biomes, discussed previously in Part I, and agricultural systems, discussed in detail in Part II of this volume. The table reflects both acute and chronic phase effects on ecological and agricultural systems.

This table represents the generalizations that can currently be drawn concerning ecosystem-level responses to nuclear war, including the following:

1.) The climatic alterations that could follow a large-scale nuclear war offer the greatest potential for severe, widespread, and unprecedented effects on ecological systems. Terrestrial ecosystems are particularly vulnerable to acute, severe decreases in temperature; aquatic ecosystems are especially vulnerable to disruptions in insolation. Chronic decreases in precipitation could lead to significant effects on terrestrial and lotic ecosystems.

2.) Seasonality would be very important to the vulnerability of ecosystems to climatic alterations. For instance, temperate ecosystems would respond adversely to temperature decreases in the spring–summer period of the year, but much less so to such decreases in the other half of the year. On the other hand, tropical ecosystems would be adversely affected irrespective of the time of year in which the temperature perturbations occurred. The life-stages of the species exposed to perturbations often are quite important in determining the nature of the response; an example of this is the discussion on the climatic effects on freshwater ecosystems in Chapter 2.

3.) Radiation from global fallout would not constitute a significant hazard to ecological systems. Local fallout, however, could occur at levels exceeding thresholds for severe ecological disruptions from external radiation. The major uncertainty in projecting ecosystem responses to local fallout relates to the spatial coverage of such intense levels of radioactivity. It is clear that coniferous ecosystems would be most vulnerable to radiation damage. Not shown in the table of ecological impacts of radiation is the considerable potential for ecosystems to provide a vector for internal doses to humans, especially from radionuclides transported through aquatic food chains. Thus, the ecological importance of radiation from fallout exceeds its ecosystem-level damage.

4.) Ultraviolet radiation (UV-B) would be the most spatially extensive of

TABLE 3.23

SUMMARY OF CONSEQUENCES FOR ECOLOGICAL SYSTEMS[a]
STRESS/RESPONSES

SYSTEM TYPE	temp.	light	ppt.	rad.	UV-B	air pollutants	fire
agriculture	••••	•	•••	••	•	••	•
tundra/alpine	♦ ◊	• ◊	• ○	• ○	• ○	• ○	• ○
boreal forests	•• ○	• ○	• ○	•• ○	• ○	• ○	• ○
temperate forests deciduous	•• ○	• ○	•• ○	•• ○	• ○	•• ○	•• ○
coniferous	•• ○	• ○	•• ○	••• ○	• ○	• ○	•• ○
tropical forests	••• ○○○	• ○	•• ○○	• ○	•• ○○	• ○	•• ○○
grasslands	•• ○	• ○	•• ○	• ○	• ○	• ○	•• ○
lakes and streams	•• ○	•• ○	•• ○	• ○	•• ○○	• ○	♦ ◊
estuaries	•• ○	••• ○○	• ○	• ○	•• ○	•• ○	♦ ◊
marine	♦ ◊	••• ○○	♦ ◊	♦ ◊	•• ○○	♦ ◊	♦ ◊

[a] Highly generalized representation of consequences of various physical stresses on biological systems resulting from nuclear war. Includes both acute and chronic stresses and reflects large-scale effects rather than localized situations.   Stresses are:

temp.	air temperature reductions	UV-B	increased uv-B from ozone depletion
light	incident sunlight reductions	air pollutants	toxic gases (e.g., O_3, SO_2, NO_x)
ppt.	precipitation reductions	fire	initiated by nuclear detonations or
rad.	fallout radiation		from increased frequency later.

Symbols in the chart reflect both the extent of the stress on the specified system and the vulnerability of that system to the specified stress. Open symbols represent consequences if stresses occurred in winter, closed symbols for stresses in summer. Symbols are:

summer	winter	
♦	◊	essentially no effect
•	○	low effect
••	○○	medium effect
•••	○○○	large effect
••••	○○○○	extremely large effect

the non-climatic stresses following a large-scale nuclear war. However, significant ecological impacts would most likely be limited to aquatic ecosystems.

5.) Air pollution would be rather localized, and, thus, not constitute a major large-scale effect from nuclear war; however, the potential for transport of toxic chemicals from coastal urban areas to estuaries could be important, especially as a vector for consumption of toxics by humans who exploited nearby coastal and estuarine systems for food.

6.) Fire could affect large areas of ecosystems near nuclear detonation targets, especially for military sites away from urban areas; however, these systems are largely fire-adapted, and long-term effects would not be anticipated. On the other hand, should precipitation be reduced for substantial periods of time in a chronic climatic perturbation phase, the potential for fires in ecosystems not adapted to them, such as tropical forests, could be important, and could result in long-term damage.

7.) The potential for simultaneous exposure to more than one of these physical perturbations is quite high for most of the ecosystems of at least the Northern Hemisphere. Such concurrent stresses could act antagonistically (i.e., effects in combination being less than the simple addition of effects); however, in general, the propensity for synergistic responses is much greater for ecosystems, and it could be anticipated that the total consequences from multiple stresses would be *greater* than the estimations made for individual stresses.

The consensus from the SCOPE–ENUWAR analyses, then, is that ecological systems could experience disturbances on a scale and intensity of unprecedented magnitude following a large-scale nuclear war. These disturbances could result in the simplification of ecosystems over large areas in at least the Northern Hemisphere, and probably extending through the tropics, effected through the differential elimination of populations sensitive to the direct effects of the stresses and of populations affected indirectly through impacts on other biota or on ecosystem processes. Although some species could become extinct if the area of devastation exceeded the species range, others would only become locally or regionally extirpated. Yet other species could actually prosper because of changes in interspecific interactions, such as release from competitive or predator pressures. In this way, the biotic composition of ecosystems, and the genetic components of the populations, could be substantially altered in seriously affected regions.

3.6.3 Recovery Processes

Once a severe disturbance to ecological systems has taken place, the issue of importance is the rate, and indeed the possibility, of recovery. Recovery is used here to mean the processes that would follow after the ecological damage and alteration had reached some maximum point and the system began to reorganize its components and reestablish its processes. This does not imply that a precise return to the pre-disturbance state would ever occur, but, rather, than an ecosystem of similar structure and function eventually would develop at a location.

The specific routes of recovery for each ecosystem are also not predictable because of uncertainties in the levels of stress, the individual stress responses of species, and the indirect effects that would reverberate through the ecosystem. Nevertheless, there are again some general principals that can be drawn:

1.) Recovery would be quite affected by the spatial scale of the perturbation. If the scale is small, there is the ready opportunity for ecological redevelopment to be assisted by imports of biota and resources from adjacent ecological areas; on the other hand, disruption on a landscape scale could greatly prolong, or even preclude, recovery.

2.) One key factor to recovery of plant communities is the regenerative base for those species. The presence of a seed, seedling, or spore bank that could survive extreme perturbations that killed adult populations would ensure redevelopment of the community; on the other hand, the reliance on regenerative bases that themselves are vulnerable to perturbations, such as the seedling banks of tropical rainforests, makes the recovery of the ecosystem very questionable.

3.) Related to this is the ability of the species, both plant and animal, to recolonize disrupted or denuded areas, which in turn is a function of rates of dispersion of propagules and ability to establish in an abiotically controlled environment.

4.) Functional recovery might occur sooner or more completely than compositional recovery. Thus, for example, forests might reestablish their previous leaf area indices relatively quickly, through the rapid growth of opportunistic plants, and thereby resume near-previous levels of primary productivity, even though the plant species would little resemble the components of the pre-nuclear war forest.

5.) The extent of extinctions and associated reduced genetic diversity could substantially affect recovery by limiting the options available for ecological re-development.

6.) Factors that would retard or preclude recovery include: increased incidences of fire; continued climatic perturbations, especially with respect to chronic reductions in temperature and precipitation; presence of long-lived fallout at intense levels; depletion of soil nutrient status; biological reverberations, such as outbreaks of pest species on large scales; and overexploitation of the environment by animals seeking resources.

7.) With regard to the last item, the possibility of human overexploitation of the environment in the aftermath of a nuclear war, and its associated disruption in agricultural and societal systems (as discussed in Parts II and III), would be a major factor in the recovery of ecological systems. The current human-environmental catastrophe in much of Africa is a strong case in point, where climatic disruptions in ecosystems are prolonged and exacerbated by pressures on those systems by humans trying to survive. In light of the importance of natural ecosystems to human support, and the feedback to the recovery of those natural systems, the next section briefly examines the potential for ecosystems, even healthy ones, to support human populations.

3.6.4 Ecosystem Carrying Capacities for Humans

The current human population of almost 5 billion can be maintained only in conjunction with the efficient food production and distribution capabilities of modern agriculture. These agricultural systems are vulnerable to widespread losses of productivity following a large-scale nuclear war (Chapter 4), causing a potential food crisis of unprecedented magnitude (Chapter 5). In regions with large-scale food shortages, the human population would attempt to use natural resources for alternate or supplemental food sources, just at the time when climatic perturbations, radiation, air pollutants, fire, and other unprecedented disturbances from a nuclear war would reduce the productivity of natural, i.e., non-agricultural ecosystems. If agricultural productivity and distribution were to be severely decreased in response to a large-scale nuclear war, an eventuality that seems highly likely considering the combination of physical and societal disturbances projected to occur (as discussed in Parts II and III), then the surviving human population would likely increase its demands on natural ecosystems for support. However, even in ecosystems unperturbed by climatic and other stresses associated with a nuclear war, the human population could be maintained at only a very small fraction of pre-nuclear war levels in the absence of any agricultural support.

We do not project that agricultural and societal systems would be totally demolished by even a large-scale nuclear war; however, the unique potential for a global nuclear war to cause global disturbances to those vulnerable systems mandates consideration of the ultimate vulnerability of the world's human population to the loss of its support base. This entails the consideration of the outer bounds of that vulnerability, i.e., sole reliance on natural ecological systems for sustenance. In subsequent chapters, the sensitivity of the global agricultural production and distribution systems to nuclear war-induced perturbations will be more closely examined. This discussion concentrates on the potential for natural ecosystems to supplant agricultural systems.

The size or density of population that could be indefinitely sustained by food from a natural, non-agriculturalized region is called the 'carrying capacity' (Zubrow, 1975). This carrying capacity is directly related to consideration of human nutritional requirements. With no agricultural production available, food would be limited to the small fraction of the natural biota that could be harvested and digested. It should be emphasized that the principal limitation to non-agricultural carrying capacity is the relatively low production rates of usable food energy.

In order to estimate potential human carrying capacities of natural ecosystems, historical and anthropological information can be drawn upon for analogs. It is clear that the complete absence of agricultural support is associated with very low densities of human population. The human population densities that can be supported in different ecosystem types are quite variable (Table 3.24), with the highest levels associated with coastal or floodplain environments. In these environments, both aquatic and terrestrial resources could be harvested. In contrast, many of the potentially most supportive ecosystems, particularly the oceans (Figure 3.5), could not be fully exploited by survivors of a nuclear war. In a forested ecosystem, most of the organic material is in the form of undigestable fiber (wood) and unpalatable or toxic foliage of little nutritive value. Considerable skill and experience would be required to exploit natural resources to maintain populations near the carrying capacity. Even assuming that this skill would be widely available, because of the limitations of utilizable energy flow through the ecosystems, the human population density would have to be reduced to levels comparable to those of hunter-gatherer societies (cf. Table 3.24, upland and lowland forest population densities, with Table 3.25, non-agriculture, hunter/gatherer densities).

This fundamental limitation to human populations also applies to other animals, upon which humans might rely for food. The net annual production of animals is only a small fraction of the net primary productivity of ecosystems, the energy fixed by plants (Figure 3.5). This illustrates that only a small fraction of net primary productivity is available for net animal productivity, and, of course, only small fractions of this actually could be utilized in sustaining human populations. Thus, even under the most favorable circumstances, only small human populations could be maintained totally by harvesting wild animals. Low human population densities are typical of hunting communities, and even simple hand-powered agriculture greatly increases the density of population supported (Table 3.25). Aboriginal population densities were much lower than those associated with modern agriculture (Table 3.24). For example, Bliss (1985) described Alaskan and Canadian

TABLE 3.24

PRE-COLONIAL POPULATION ESTIMATES FOR THE AMAZONS[a]

Habitat	Area (10^3 km^2)	Estimated Density (individuals km^{-2})
Floodplain	103	14.6
Coastal	105	9.5
Upland Forest	1,473	0.8
Lowland Forest	5,038	0.2
Central Savanna	2,178	0.5
Northern Savanna	395	1.3
Lowland Savanna	180	2.0

[a] Data from Denevan (1976).

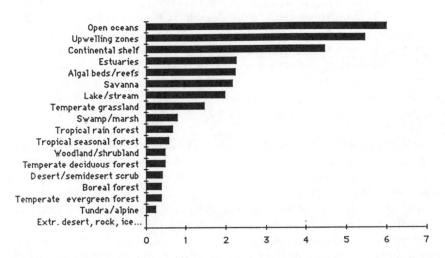

Figure 3.5   Ratios of net animal production to net primary productivity for major ecosystems of the world (as %). Data from Whittaker (1975)

TABLE 3.25

POPULATION DENSITY ESTIMATES
FOR SELECTED NON-INDUSTRALIZED POPULATIONS[a]

POPULATION	SUBSISTENCE PATTERN	DENSITY (individuals km^{-2})
NON-AGRICULTURAL		
Eskimos, Alaska	Hunting, fishing	0.008 [b]
!Kung bushmen, Botswana	Hunter/gatherer	0.2
Hazda, Tanzania	Hunter/gatherer	0.5
LOW-LEVEL AGRICULTURAL		
Raipu Enga, New Guinea	Intensive root cultivation, pig husbandry	96.0
Kofyar, Nigeria	Intensive dryfield cultivation	112.0
Pul Eliya, Sri Lanka	Irrigated and dry field cultivation	227.0
Yaruro, Venezuela	Manioc swiddens	41.0

[a] Data from Bliss (1985); Ellen (1982).
[b] Estimated carrying capacity.

communities that rely mainly on hunting terrestrial and marine mammals, fish, and birds. Five communities within the arctic (approximately 210,000 km^2) harvested an average of 422 kg of meat person^{-1} year^{-1}, sufficient to maintain about 4–8 persons per 1,000 km^2. Even these communities import food produced from agricultural systems.

While there are no clearcut relationships between ecosystem net primary productivity and human carrying capacity, it is evident that only very small fractions of the current human population could be maintained solely on natural ecosystems. Analyses of the past 3000-year record suggest that prior to the rapid agricultural/industrial development of the last few centuries, the human population was maintained at one to two orders of magnitude below current levels, even including considerable support from contemporary agricultural systems (Whittaker, 1975). The record from China illustrates how human population increased in response to agricultural developments; nevertheless, as the vulnerable agricultural support bases experienced various perturbations, a series of overpopulations experienced severe reductions. This record is illustrative of the problems associated with overexploitation of natural and agricultural systems.

In summary, a first approximation is that the human population support capacity of very low-level agriculture is about one order of magnitude reduction from current levels, and support capacity by natural ecosystems alone is approximately another order of magnitude reduction. Disruptions in natural ecological productivity that might occur following a large-scale nuclear war would reduce the human support capacity even further. Again, it must be emphasized that projections are not being made of such a situation taking place after a nuclear war; rather, it is being suggested that the current human population levels are potentially very vulnerable to the loss of agricultural support systems if they were to be disrupted on a global scale. The following chapters examine these issues.

REFERENCES

Abrahamsen, G., Sjors, K., and Horntvedt, R. (1976). Effects of acid precipitation on coniferous forests. In Braeke, F.H. (Ed). *Impact of Acid Precipitation on Forest and Fresh Water Ecosystems in Norway.* 37–63. Research Report No. 6, SNSF Project, Oslo, Norway.

Aleksakhin, R.M., Tikhomirov, F.A., and Kulikov, N.V. (1970). The state and goals of forest radioecology. *Ekologiya*, 1. (in Russian).

Altman, P.L., and Dittmer, D.S. (1966). *Environmental Biology.* Fed. Amer. Soc. Expt. Biol., Bethesda, Maryland: 694 pages.

Ambio. (1982). Nuclear War: The Aftermath. *Ambio* Volume 11, No. 2–3. Pergamon Press, New York.

Ashmore, M., Bell, N.G.B., and Rutter, J. (1985). The role of ozone in forest damage in West Germany. *Ambio.* 14, 81–87.

Ayers, R. (1965). *Environmental Effects of Nuclear Weapons.* HI-518-RR. Hudson Research Institute, Harmon-on-Hudson, New York.

Baker, D.A., Hoenes, G.R., and Soldat, J.K. (1976). *Food—An Interactive Code to Calculate Internal Radiation Doses from Contaminated Food Products.* BNWL-SA-5532. Battelle Pacific Northwest Laboratories, Richland, WA.

Baker, K.S., and Smith, R.C. (1982a). Bio-optical classification and model of natural waters. 2. *Limnol. Oceanogr.*, **28**, 500–509.

Baker, K.S., and Smith, R.C. (1982b). Spectral irradiance penetration in natural waters. In Calkins, J. (Ed.). *The Role of Solar Ultraviolet Radiation in Marine Ecosystems.* 23–246. Plenum, New York.

Bell, M.C. (1971). Radiation effects on farm animals: A review. In Bensen, D.W., and Sparrow, A.H. *Survival of Food Crops and Livestock in the Event of Nuclear War.* 656–669. U.S. Atomic Energy Commission CONF-700909. NTIS, Springfield, VA.

Bergstrom, S., Black, D., Bochkov, N.P., Eklund, S., Kruisinga, R.J.H., Leaf, A., Obasanjo, O., Shigematsu, I., Tubiana, M., and Whittembury, G. (1983). *Effects of a Nuclear War on Health and Health Services.* Report of the International Committee of Experts in Medical Sciences and Public Health, WHO Pub. A36.12. Geneva, Switzerland: 176 pages.

Biggs, R.H., and Basiouny, F.M. (1975). *Plant growth responses to elevated UV-radiation under growth chamber, greenhouse, and solarium conditions.* CIAP Monog. 5: 4197–4249. U.S. Department of Transportation, Washington, D.C.

Biggs, R.H., and Kossuth, S.V. (1978). Impact of solar UV-B radiation on crop productivity. In *Final Report of UV-B Biological and Climate Effects Research, Non-Human Organisms.* USEPA Report No. EPA-IAG-D6-0618: II-1 to II-79. U. S. Environmental Protection Agency, Washington, D.C.

Biggs, R.H., Kossuth, S.V., and Teramura A.H. (1981). Response of 19 cultivars of soybeans to ultraviolet-B irradiance. *Physiol. Plant.,* **53**, 19–26.

Blair, W.F. (1958). Effects of x-irradiation on a natural population of the deermouse (*Peromysus maniculatus*). *Ecology,* **39** (1), 113–121.

Bliss, L.C. (1985). *Nuclear winter and human carrying capacity of northern ecosystems.* Unpublished manuscript contributed to SCOPE–ENUWAR.

Boerner, R.E.J. (1982). Fire and nutrient cycling in temperate ecosystems. *Bio-Science,* **32**, 187–192.

Buchauer, M.J. (1973). Contamination of soil and vegetation near a zinc smelter by zinc, cadmium, copper and lead. *Environ. Sci. Technol.,* **7**, 131–135.

Burton, J.D., Millbourn, G.M. and Russell, R.S. (1960). Relationship between the rate of fallout and the concentration of ^{90}Sr in human diet in the United Kingdom. *Nature,* **185**, 498–500.

Caldwell, M.M. (1968). Solar ultraviolet radiation as an ecological factor for alpine plants. *Ecol. Monogr.,* **38**, 243–268.

Caldwell, M.M. (1977). The effects of solar UV-B (280-315 nm) on higher plants: Implications of stratospheric ozone reduction. In *Research in Photobiology.* 597–607. Plenum, New York.

Caldwell, M.M. (1981). Plant response to solar ultraviolet radiation. In Lange, O.L., Nobel, P.S., Osmond, C.B., and Ziegler, H. (Eds.). *Encyclopedia of Plant Physiology,* New Series, Physiological Plant Ecology I, 12A: 170–197. Springer-Verlag, Berlin.

Caldwell, M.M., Robberecht, R., and Billings, W.D. (1980). A steep latitudinal gradient of solar ultraviolet-B radiation in the arctic-alpine life zone. *Ecology,* **61**, 600–611.

Caldwell, M.M., Robberecht, R., Nowak, R.S., and Billings, W.D. (1982). Differential photosynthetic inhibition by ultraviolet radiation in species from the arctic-alpine life zone. *Arctic Alp. Res.,* **14**, 195–202.

Calkins, J. (1982). Modeling light loss versus UV-B increase for organisms which control their vertical position in the water column. In Calkins, J. (Ed.). *The Role of Solar Ultraviolet Radiation in Marine Ecosystems.* 539–542. Plenum, New York.

Cataldo, D.A. and Vaughan, B.E. (1980). Interaction of airborne plutonium with plant foliage. In Hanson, W.C. (Ed.). *Transuranic Elements in the Environment.* 288–299. U.S. Department of Energy, Washington, D.C.

Chamberlain, A.C. (1970). Interception and retention of radioactive aerosols by vegetation. *Atmospheric Environment,* **4**, 57–58.

Chandler, C.C., Storey, T.G., and Tangren, C.D. (1963). *Prediction of Fire Spread following Nuclear Explosions.* U.S. Forest Service Res. Paper PSW-5. Pacific Southwest Forest Range Experiment Station, Berkeley, CA.

Christensen, N.L. (1977). Fire and soil-plant nutrient relationship in a pine-wiregrass savanna on the coastal plain of North Carolina. *Oecologia,* **31**, 27–44.

Conard, R. (1975). *A Twenty-Year Review of Medical Findings in a Marshallese Population Accidentally Exposed to Radioactive Fallout.* U.S. Energy Research and Development Administration. Washington, D.C.: 154 pages.

Cosgrove, G.E. (1971). Reptilian radiobiology. *J. Am. Vet. Med. Assoc.*, **159** (11), 1678–1683.

Costonis, A.C. (1973). Injury of eastern white pine by SO_2 and O_3 alone and in mixtures. *Env. J. For. Path.*, **3**, 50–55.

Crutzen, P.J. and Birks, J.W. (1982). The atmosphere after a nuclear war: Twilight at noon. *Ambio*, **11**, 114–125.

Crutzen, P.J., Galbally, I.E., and Bruhl, C. (1984). Atmospheric effects from post-nuclear fires. *Climatic Change*, **6**, 323.

Damkaer, D.M., Dey, D.B., Heron, G.A., and Prentice, E.F. (1980). Effects of UV-B radiation on near-surface zooplankton of Puget Sound. *Oecologia (Berl.)*, **44**, 149–158.

Damkaer, D.M., Dey, D.B., and Heron, G.A. (1981). Dose-rate responses of shrimp larvae to UV-B radiation. *Oecologia (Berl.)*, **48**, 178–182.

Damkaer, D., and Dey, D. (1983). UV damage and photoreactivation potentials of larvel shrimp, *Pandalus platyceros*, and adult euphausids, *Thysanoessa raschii. Oecologia*, **60**, 169–175.

Debano, L.F., and Conrad, C.E. (1978). Effects of fire on nutrients in a chaparral ecosystem. *Ecology*, **59**, 489–497.

Denevan, W.M. (1976). The aboriginal population of Amazonia. In Denevan, W.M. (Ed.). *The Native Population of the Americas in 1492*. 205–234. University of Wisconsin Press, Madison, WI.

Dhler, G. (1982). Effect of UV-B radiation on the marine diatom *Bellerochea yucatanensis*. In Bauer, H., Caldwell, M.M., Tevini, M., and Worrest, R.C. *Biological Effects of UV-B Radiation*. 211–215. Gesellschaft fur Strahlen-und Umweltforschung mbH, Munich.

Eberhardt, L.L., and Hanson, W.C. (1969). A simulation model for the arctic food chain. *Health Phys.*, **17**, 793–806.

Ellen, R. (1982). *Environment, Subsistence, and System: The Ecology of Small-Scale Social Formations*. Cambridge University Press, Cambridge: 324 pages.

Fabries, M., Grauby, A., and Trichain, J.L. (1972). Study of a Mediterranean-type phytocoenose subjected to chronic gamma irradiation. *Radiat. Bot.*, **12**, 125–132.

Flint, S.D., and Caldwell, M.M. (1984). Partial inhibition of in vitro pollen germination by simulated solar ultraviolet-B radiation. *Ecology*, **65**, 792–795.

Fox, F.M., and Caldwell, M.M. (1978). Competitive interaction in plant populations exposed to supplementary ultraviolet-B radiation. *Oecologia (Berl.)*, **36**, 173–190.

Fraley Jr., L., and Whicker, F.W. (1973). Response of shortgrass plains vegetation to gamma radiation. I. Chronic irradiation. *Radit. Bot.*, **13**, 242–348.

Freedman, W., and Hutchinson, T.C. (1980). Long-term effects of smelter pollution at Sudbury, Ontario, on surrounding forest communities. *Can. J. Bot.*, **58**, 2123–2140.

Garg, S.P., Zajanc, A., and Bankowski, R.A. (1964). The effects of cobalt-60 on starlings (*Sturnus vulgaris vulgaris*). *Avian. Dis.*, **8** (4), 555–559.

Glasstone, S., and Dolan, P. (1977). *The Effect of Nuclear Weapons* (3rd Ed.) U.S. Government Printing Office, Washington, D.C.: 653 pages.

Gofman, J.W. (1981). *Radiation and Human Health*. Sierra Club Books, San Francisco: 908 pages.

Gold, W.G., and Caldwell, M.M. (1983). The effects of ultraviolet-B radiation on plant competition in terrestrial ecosystems. *Physiol. Plant.*, **58**, 435–444.

Gorham, E. (1959). A comparison of lower and higher plants as accumulators of radioactive fallout. *Can. J. Bot.*, **37** (2), 327–335.

Gorham, E., and Gordon, A.G. (1960). Some effects of smelter pollution northeast of Falconbridge, Ontario. *Can. J. Bot.*, **38**, 307–312.

Green, A.E.S.. Cross, K.R., and Smith, L.A. (1980). Improved analytic characterization of ultraviolet skylight. *Photochem. Photobiol.*, **31**, 59–65.

Grover, H.D. (1985). *Ecological effects of nuclear war-caused wildland fires.* Unpublished manuscript contributed to SCOPE–ENUWAR.

Haines, D.A., Johnson, V.L., and Main, W.A. (1975). *Wildfire Atlas of the Northeastern and North Central States.* General Tech. Report NC-16. U.S.D.A. Forest Service, Washington, D.C.

Hanson, W.C. (1966). Fallout radionuclides in Alaskan food chains. *Am. J. Vet. Res.*, **27** (116), 359.

Hanson, W.C. (1967). Radioecological concentration processes characterizing arctic ecosystems. In berg, B., and Hungate, F.P. (Eds.). *Radioecological Concentration Processes.* 183. Pergamon Press, New York.

Hanson, W.C. (1971). Fallout radionuclide distribution in lichen communities near Thule. *Arctic*, **24**, 269–276.

Hanson, W.C., and Eberhart, L.L. (1969). Effective half-times of radionuclides in Alaskan lichens and Eskimos. In Nelson, D.J., and Evans. F.C. (Eds.). *Symposium on Radioecology.* U.S.A.E.C. Rep. CONF-670503. U.S. Atomic Energy Commission, Washington, D.C.

Harwell, M.A. (1984). *Nuclear Winter: The Human and Environmental Consequences of Nuclear War.* Springer-Verlag, New York: 179 pages.

Harwell, M.A., Brandstetter, A., Benson, G.L., Raymond, J.R., Bradley, D.J., Serne. R.J., Soldat, J.K., Cole, C.R., Deutsch. W.J., Gupta, S.K., Harwell, C.C., Napier, B.A., Reisenauer, A.E., Prater, L.S., Simmons, C.S., Strenge. D.L., Washburn. J.F., and Zellmer, J.T. (1982). *Reference Site Initial Assessment for a Salt Dome Repository.* PNL-2955, Vol. I and II. Battelle Pacific Northwest Laboratories. Richland, WA.

Hill, A.C., Hill. S., Lamb, C., and Barrett, T.W. (1974). Sensitivity of native desert vegetation to SO_2 and to SO_2 and NO_2 combined. *J. Air Pollut. Control Assoc.*, **24**, 153–157.

Holm, E., and Persson, R.B.R. (1975). Fallout plutonium in Swedish reindeer lichens. *Health Phys.*, **29**, 43–51.

Hunter, J.R., Kaupp, S.E., and Taylor, J.H. (1981). Assessment of effects of UV radiation on marine fish larvae. In Calkins, J. (Ed.). *The Role of Solar Ultraviolet Radiation in Marine Ecosystems.* 549–498. Plenum, New York.

Hunter, J.R., Kaupp, S.E., and Taylor, J.H. (1982). *Assessment of effects of UV radiation on marine fish larvae.* NATO Conf. Ser., Mar. Sci., 7: 459–497. North Atlantic Treaty Organization, Geneva.

Hutchinson-Benson, E.A., Svoboda, J., and Taylor, H.W. (1985). The latitudinal inventory of ^{137}Cs in vegetation and top soil in Northern Canada, 1980. *Can. J. Bot.*, **63**, 784–791.

Hutchinson, T.C., and Whitby, L.M. (1974). Heavy metal pollution of the Sudbury mining and smelting region of Canada. I. Soil and vegetation contamination by nickel. copper and other metals. *Environ. Conserv.*, **1**, 123–132.

Ishikawa, E., and Swain, D.L. (1981). *Hiroshima and Nagasaki. The Physical, Medical, and Social Effects of the Atomic Bombings.* Basic Books, New York: 706 pages.

Jacobson, J.S. (1980). The influence of rainfall composition on the yield and quantity of agriculture crops. In Droblos, D., and Tollan, A. (Eds.). *Ecological Impact of Acid Precipitation*. 41–46. Proc. Intern. Conf., SNSF Project, Oslo, Norway.

Jerlov, N.G. (1976). *Marine Optics*. 127–150. Elsevier Scientific, Amsterdam.

Jitts, H.R., Morel, A., and Saijo, Y. (1976). The relation of oceanic primary production to available photosynthetic irradiance. *Aust. J. Mar. Freshwater Res.*, **27**, 441–454.

Johnson, W., and Mayfield, C.L. (1970). Elevated levels of Cs-137 in common mushrooms with possible relationship to high levels of Cs-137 in whitetail deer, 1968–69. *Health Data Rep.*, **11** (10), 527.

Johnson, D.W., Richter, D.D., Van Migroet, H., and Cole, D.W. (1983). Contributions of acid deposition and natural processes to cation leaching from forest soils: A review. *J. Air Pollut. Control Assoc.*, **33**, 1036–1052.

Jones, L.W., and Kok, B.(1966). Photoinhibition of chloroplast reactions. I. Kinetics and action spectra. *Plant Physiol.*, **41**, 1037–1043.

Karanas, J.J., Van Dyke, H., and Worrest, R.C. (1979). Midultraviolet (UV-B) sensitivity of *Acartia clausii* Giesbrecht (Copepoda). *Limnol. Oceanogr.*, **24**, 1104–1116.

Karanas, J.J., Worrest, R.C., and Van Dyke, H. (1981). Impact of UV-B radiation on the fecundity of the Copepod *Acartia clausii*. *Mar. Biol.*, **65**, 125–133.

Kocher, D. (1981). *Radioactive Decay Tables—A Handbook of Decay Data for Application to Radiation Dosimetry and Radiological Assessments*. US Dept. of Energy, DOE-TIC-11026. NTIS, Springfield, VA.: 228 pages.

Kozlowski, T.T., and Ahlgren, C.E. (1974). *Fire and Ecosystems*. Academic Press, New York.

Kress, L.W., and Skelly, J.M. (1982). Responses of several eastern forest tree species to chronic doses of ozone and nitrogen dioxide. *Plant Dis.*, **66**, 1149–1152.

Kulikov, N.V., and Molchanova, I.V. (1982). *Continental Radioecology*. Plenum Press and Nauka Pub., Moscow: 174 pages.

Kupferman, S.I., Livingston, H.D., and Bowen, V.T. (1979). A mass balance for ^{137}Cs and ^{90}Sr in the North Atlantic Ocean. *J. Marine Res.*, **37**, 157–199.4

Leaning, J. (1984). An ill wind: Radiation consequences of nuclear war. In Leaning, J., and Keyes, L. (Eds.). *The Counterfeit Ark*. 183–230. Ballinger, Cambridge, MA.

Leaning, J., and Keyes, L. (Eds.) (1983). *The Counterfeit Ark*. Ballinger, Cambridge, MA: 337 pages.

Levin, S.A., Kimball, K.D., McDowell, W.H., and Kimball, S.F. (1984). New perspectives in ecotoxicology. *Environmental Management*, **8**, 375–442.

Levitt, J. (1980). *Responses of Plants to Environmental Stresses*. Vol. 1: 497. Vol. 2: 606. Academic Press, New York.

Linden, K. (1961). Cesium-137 burdens in Swedish Laplanders and reindeer. *Acta Radiol.*, **56** (3), 237.

Lorenzen, C.J. (1979). Ultraviolet radiation and phytoplankton photosynthesis. *Limnol. Oceanogr.*, **24**, 1117–1120.

MacDowall, F.D.H., and Cole, A.F.W. (1971).Threshold and synergistic damage to tobacco by ozone and sulfur dioxide. *Atmos. Environ.*, **5**, 553–559.

Materna, J. (1984). Impact of atmospheric pollution on natural ecosystems. In Treshow, M. (Ed.). *Air Pollution and Plant Life*. 397–416. John Wiley & Sons, Chichester.

McLaughlin, S.B. (1985). Effects of air pollution on forests. *J. Air Pollut. Control Assoc.*, **35**, 512–534.

Menser, H.A., and Heggestad, H.E. (1966). Ozone and sulphur dioxide synergism: Injury to tobacco plants. *Science*, **153**, 424–425.

Middleton. H. (1982). Epidemiology, the future is sickness and death. *Ambio*, **11**, 100-105.

Miettenen, J.W., and Hasanen, E. (1967). [137]Cs in Finnish Lapps and other Finns in 1962-66. In berg, B., and Hungate, F.P. (Eds.). *Radioecological Concentration Processes*. 209. Pergamon Press, New York.

Miller, P.R. (1983). Ozone effects in the St. Bernadino National Forest. In David. D.D., Miller. P.R., and Dochinger, L. (Eds.). *Air Pollution and the Productivity of the Forest*. 161-198. Issac Walton League of America, Arlington, Virginia.

Mirecki, R.M., and Teramura, A.H. (1984). Effects of UV-B irradiance on soybean. V. The development of plant sensitivity on the photosynthetic photon flux density during and after leaf expansion. *Plant Physiol.*, **74**, 475-480.

Molchanov, A.A., Fyodorov, E.A., Aleksakhim, R.M., Aleksakhina, M.M., Mishenkov, N.N., Naryshkin, M.A., Tyumenev, L.N., Ukhanova, V.A., and Yulonov, V.P. (1968). Some regularities in the distribution of radioactive fission products from the global fallouts in forest vegetation. *Lesovedenye*, No. 6. (in Russian).

Murphy, P.G., and McCormick, J.F. (1971a). Effects of beta radiation from simulated fallout on the reproductive potential of a dominant plant species in a natural plant community. In Nelson, D.J. (Ed.). Radionuclides in Ecosystems. *Proc. Third Nat. Symp. on Radioecology*. USAEC Report CONF 710501. Oak Ridge Nat. Lab., Oak Ridge, TN.

Murphy, P.G., and McCormick. J.F. (1971b). Ecological effects of acute beta irradiation from simulated fallout particles of a natural plant community. In Benson, D.W., and Sparrow, A.H. *Survival of Food Crops and Livestock in the Event of Nuclear War*. 454-481. U.S. Atomic Energy Commission CONF-700909. NTIS, Springfield, VA.

Nachtwey, D.S., and Rundel, R.D. (1981). A photobiological evaluation of tanning booths. *Science*. **211**, 405-407.

Nachtwey, D.S., and Rundel, R.D. (1982). Ozone change: Biological effects. In Bower, F.A., and Ward, R.V. (Eds.). *Stratospheric Ozone and Man*. Vol. II: 81-121. CRC Press, West Palm Beach, FL.

Nakagoshi, N. (1984). Buried viable seed populations in forest communities on the Hiba Mountains, Southwestern Japan. *J. Sci. Hiroshima Univ*. Series B, Div. 2 (Bot.), **19**, 1-56.

NAS. (1971). *Radioactivity in the Marine Environment*. Prepared by the Panel on Radioactivity in the Marine Environment. National Academy of Sciences, Washington, D.C.: 272 pages.

NAS. (1975). *Long-Term Worldwide Effects of Multiple Nuclear-Weapons Detonations*. National Academy of Sciences, Washington, D.C.: 213 pages.

National Council on Radiation Protection and Measurement (NCRP). (1984). *Radiological Assessment: Predicting the Transport, Bioaccumulation, and Uptake by Man of Radionuclides Released to the Environment*. NCRP Report 76, Bethesda, MD.: 300 pages.

National Research Council (NRC). (1984). *Causes and Effects of Changes in Stratospheric Ozone: Update 1983*. National Academy Press, Washington, D.C.

National Research Council (NRC). (1985). *The Effects on the Atmosphere of a Major Nuclear Exchange*. National Academy Press, Washington, D.C.: 193 pages.

Nevstrueva. M.A., Ramzaev, P.V., Moiseer, A.A., Ibatullin, M.S., and Teplykh, L.A. (1967). The nature of ^{137}Cs and ^{90}Sr transport over the lichen-reindeer food chain. In berg, B., and Hungate, F.P. (Eds.). *Radioecological Concentration Processes*. 209. Pergamon Press, New York.

Nobel, P.S. (1980). Influences of minimum stem temperatures on ranges of cacti in southwestern United States and Central Chile. *Oecolgia*, **47**, 10–15.

O'Brien, R.D., and Wolfe, L.S. (1964). Nongenetic effects of radiation. In O'Brien, R.D., and Wolfe, L.S. (Eds.). *Radiation, Radioactivity and Insects.* 23–54. Academic Press, New York.

Odum, E.P. (1965). Summary. In Woodwell, G.M. (Ed.). *Ecological Effects of Nuclear War.* 69–72. BNL 917, Brookhaven National Laboratory. NTIS, Springfield, VA.

Odum, H.T. (1970). *A tropical rain forest: A study in irradiation and ecology at El Verde, Puerto Rico.* Odum, H.T., and Pigeon, R.F. (Eds.). USAEC Report TD24270 CPR NC-138. U.S. Atomic Energy Commission, Washington, D.C.: 1230 pages.

O'Farrell, T.P., Hedlund, J.D., Olson, R.J., and Gilbert, R.O. (1972). Effects of ionizing radiation on survival, longevity and reproduction in free-ranging pocket mice *Perognathus parvus. Radiat. Res.,* **49** (3), 611–617.

Ophel, I.L. (1963). The fate of radiostrontium in a freshwater community. In Schultz, V., and Klement Jr., A.W. (Eds.). *Radioecology.* 213–216. Reinhold, New York.

Ophel, I.L. (1978). Aquatic food chain transport of radionuclides. In *Proc. Workshop on Evaluation of Models Used for the Environmental Assessment of Radionuclide Releases.* 73–84. Oak Ridge Nat. Lab. CONF 770901.

Ophel, I.L., and Fraser C.D. (1973). The fate of cobalt-60 in a natural freshwater system. In Nelson, D.J. (Ed.). *Proc. Nat. Symp. on Radioecology.* Vol. 1: 323–327. CONF 710501-P1, U. S. Atomic Energy Commission.

Ophel, I.L., Fraser C.D., and Judd, J.M. (1971). Strontium concentration factors in biota and bottom sediments of a freshwater lake. In *Proc. Internat. Symp. on Radioecology Applied to the Protection of Man and His Environment.* 510–530. Atomic Energy Commission Ltd. Canada, AECL-4475.

OTA. (1979). *The Effects of Nuclear War.* U.S. Congress, Office of Technology Assessment, Washington, D.C.: 151 pages.

Pittock, A.B., Ackerman, T.A., Crutzen, P., MacCracken, M., Shapiro, C., and Turco, R.P. (1985) *The Environmental Consequences of Nuclear War.* Volume I: Physical. SCOPE 28a. John Wiley & Sons, Chichester.

Platt, R.B. (1965). Ionizing radiation and homeostasis of ecosystems. In Woodwell, G.M. (Ed.). *Ecological Effects of Nuclear War.* 39–51. U.S. AEC Rep. BNL-917(C-43). Brookhaven National Lab., Upton, New York.

Potter, L.D., and Barr, M. (1969). Cesium-137 concentrations in Alaskan tundra vegetation 1967. *Arctic Alpine Res.,* **1** (3), 147.

Pritchard, D.W., Reid, R.O., Okubo, A., and Carter, H.H. (1971). Physical processes of water movement and mixing. In *Radioactivity in the Marine Environment.* 90. Panel on Radioactivity in the Marine Environment, Nat. Acad. Science, Washington, D.C.

Ramberg, B. (1978). *Destruction of Nuclear Energy Facilities in War—The Problem and the Implications.* Lexington Books, Lexington, MA: 203 pages.

Rapport, D.J., Regier, H.A., and Hutchinson, T.C. (1985). Ecosystem behavior under stress. *Amer. Naturalist,* **125**, 617–640.

Reinert, R.A. (1984). Plant responses to air pollutant mixtures. *Ann. Rev. Phytopath.,* **22**, 421–442.

Reinert, R.A., Shriner, D.S., and Rawlings, J.O. (1982). Response of radish to all combinations of three concentrations of nitrogen dioxide, sulphur dioxide and ozone. *J. Environ. Qual.,* **11**, 52–57.

Rhoads, W.A., Ragsdale, H.L., Platt, R.B., and Romney, E.M. (1971). Radiation doses to vegetation from close-in fallout at Project Schooner. In Bensen, D.W., and Sparrow, A.H. (Eds.). *Survival of Food Crops and Livestock in the Event of Nuclear War.* U.S. Atomic Energy Commission, CONF- 700909. NTIS, Springfield, VA.

Rickard, W.H., Davis, J.J., Hanson, W.C., and Watson, D.C. (1965). Gamma emitting radionuclides in Alaskan tundra vegetation 1959–1961. *Ecology,* **46** (3), 352–361.

Rickard, W.H., and Shields, L.M. (1963). An early stage in the plant recolonization of a nuclear target area. *Radiat. Bot.,* **3**, 41–44.

Robberecht, R., Caldwell, M.M., and Billings W.D. (1980). Leaf ultraviolet optical properties along a latitudinal gradient in the arctic-alpine life zone. *Ecology,* **61**, 612–619.

Romney, E.M., Lindberg, R.G. Hawthorne, H.A., Bystrom, B.G., and Larson, K.H. (1963). Contamination of plant foliage with radioactive fallout. *Ecology,* **44**, 343–349.

Romney, E.M., Rhoads, W.A., Wallace, A., and Wood, R.A. (1973). Persistence of radionuclides in soils, plants and small mammals in areas contaminated with radioactive fallout. In Nelson, D.J. (Ed.). Radionuclides in Ecosystems. 70–176. *Proc. Third Nat. Symp. in Radioecology.* U.S. AEC Report CONF-710501. Oak Ridge Nat. Lab., Oak Ridge, TN.

Romney, E.M., Wallace, A., and Childress, J.D. (1971). Re-vegetation problems following nuclear testing at the Nevada test site. In Nelson, D.J. (Ed.). Radionuclides in Ecosystems. 1015–1022. *Proc. Third Nat. Symp. in Radioecology.* U.S. AEC Report CONF-710501. Oak Ridge Nat. Lab., Oak Ridge, TN.

Rotblat, J. (1981). *Nuclear Radiation in Warfare.* Stockholm International Peace Research Institute. Oelgeschlagev, Gunn and Hain, Cambridge, MA.: 149 pages.

Runeckles, V.C. (1984). Impact of air pollutant combination on plants. In Treshow, M. (Ed.). *Air Pollution and Plant Life.* 239–258. John Wiley & Sons, Chichester

Runeckles, V.C., Palmer, K., and Giles, K. (1978). *Effects of sequential exposures to NO_2 and O_3 on plants.* 343. Abstracts, Third Int. Congr. Plant Path., Munich.

Russell-Hunter, W.D. (1970). *Aquatic Productivity.* Macmillan, New York: 306 pages.

Setlow, R.B. (1974). The wavelengths in sunlight effective in producing skin cancer: A theoretical analysis. *Proc. Natl. Acad. Sci. (U.S.A.),* **71**, 3363–3366.

Seymour, A.H. (1982). The impact on ocean ecosystems. *Ambio,* **11**, 132–137.

Seymour, V.A., Hinckley, T.M., Morikawa, Y., and Franklin, J.F. (1983). Foliage damage in coniferous trees following volcanic ashfall from Mt. St. Helens. *Oecologia (Berlin),* **59**, 339–343.

Shriner, D.S. (1977). Effects of simulated acid rain, acidified with sulphuric acid on host-parasite interactions. *Water, Air and Soil Pollut.,* **8**, 9–19.

Small, R.D., and Bush, B.W. (1985). Smoke production from multiple nuclear explosions in non-urban areas. *Science,* (in press).

Smith, R.C., and Baker, K.S. (1982). Assessment of the influence of enhanced UV-B on marine primary productivity. In Calkins, J. (Ed.). *The Role of Solar Ultraviolet Radiation in Marine Ecosystems.* 509–538. Plenum Press, New York.

Smith, R.C., Baker, K.S., Holm-Hanson, O., and Nelson, R. (1980). Photoinhibition of photosynthesis in natural waters. *Photochem. Photobiol.,* **31**, 585–592.

Soldat, J.K., Robinson, N.M., and Baker, P.A. (1974). *Models and Computer Codes for Evaluating Environmental Radiation Doses.* BNWL-1754. Battelle Pacific Northwest Laboratories, Richland, WA.

Steeman-Nielson, E. (1964). On a complication in marine productivity work due to the influence of ultraviolet light. *J. Cons. Int. Explor. Mer.*, **20**, 130–135.

Steere, W.C. (1970). Bryophyte studies on the irradiated and control sites in the rain forest at El Verde. In Odum, H.T. (Ed.). *Tropical Rain Forest.* 213–225. U.S. AEC Tech. Inform. Center, Oak Ridge TN.

Svirezhev, Y.M., Alexandrov, G.A., Arkhipov, P.L., Armand, A.D., Belotelov, N.V., Denisenko, E.A., Fesenko, S.V., Krapivin, V.F., Logofet, D.O., Ovsyannikov, L.L., Pak, S.B., Pasekov, V.P., Pisarenko, N.F., Razzevaikin, V.N., Sarancha, D.A., Semenov, M.A., Schmidt, D.A., Stenchikov, G.L., Tarko, A.M., Vedjushkin, M.A., Volkova, L.P., and Voinov, A.A. (1985). *Ecological and Demographic Consequences of Nuclear War.* Computer Centre of the U.S.S.R. Academy of Sciences, Moscow: 275 pages.

Taylor, G.E. Jr., Selvidge, W.J., and Crumbly, I.J. (1985). Temperature effects on plant response to sulphur dioxide in *Zea mays, Liriodendron tulipifera* and *Fraxinus penslyvanica. Water, Air and Soil Pollut.*, **24**, 405–418.

Taylor, O.C., and Eaton, F.M. (1966). Suppression of plant growth by nitrogen dioxide. *Plant Physiol.*, **41**, 132–135.

Teramura, A.H. (1980). Effects of ultraviolet-B irradiance on soybean. I. Importance of photosynthetically active radiation in evaluating ultraviolet-B irradiance effects on soybean and wheat growth. *Physiol. Plant.*, **48**, 333–339.

Teramura, A.H. (1982). The amelioration of UV-B effects on productivity by visible radiation. In Calkins, J. (Ed.). *The Role of Solar Ultraviolet Radiation in Marine Ecosystems.* 367–382. Plenum, New York.

Teramura, A.H. (1983). Effects of ultraviolet-B radiation on the growth and yield of crops. *Physiol. Plant.*, **58**, 415–427.

Thomas, M.D. (1961). Effects of air pollution on plants. In *World Health Organization Monograph 46.* 233–278. Columbia University Press, New York: 442 pages.

Thomson, B.E., Worrest, R.C., and Van Dyke, H. (1980). The growth response of an estuarine diatom (*Melosira nummuloides* 'Dillw.' Ag.) to UV-B (290–320 nm) radiation. *Estuaries*, **3**, 69–72.

Tingely, D.T., Reinert, R.A., Dunning, J.A., and Heck, W.W. (1971). Vegetation injury from the interaction of nitrogen dioxide and sulphur dioxide. *Phytopathology*, **61**, 1506–1511.

Tinkle, D.W. (1965). Effects of radiation on the natality, density and breeding structure of a natural population of lizards *Uta stansburiana. Health Phys.*, **11** (12), 1595.

Tukey, H.B. (1970). The leaching of substances from plants. *Ann. Rev. Plant Physiol.*, **21**, 305–322.

Tuominen, Y. (1967). Studies on the strontium uptake of the *Cladonia alpestris* thallus. *Ann. Bot. Fenn.*, **4**, 1–28.

Turco, R.P., Toon, O.B., Ackerman, T.A., Pollack, J.P., and Sagan, C. (1983). Nuclear winter: Global consequences of multiple nuclear explosions. *Science*, **222**, 1283–1292.

Ulrich, B. (1983). A concept of forest ecosystem stability and of acid deposition as a driving force for destabilization. In Ulrich, B., and Pankrath, J. (Eds.). *Effects of Accumulation of Air Pollutants in Forest Ecosystems.* 621–628. Reidel Pub. Co., Boston.

Vanderploeg, A.A., Parzyck, D.C., Wilcox, W.H., Kerchev, J.R., and Kaye, S.V. (1975). *Bioaccumulation factors for radionuclides in freshwater biota.* Oak Ridge National Laboratory Report ORNL-50002. Oak Ridge Nat. Lab., Oak Ridge, TN.

Wein, R.W., and MacLean, D.A. (1983). *The Role of Fire in Northern Circumpolar Ecosystems.* SCOPE 18. John Wiley & Sons, Chichester: 322 pages.

Whicker, F.W., Farris, G.C., and Dahl, A.H. (1967). Concentration patterns of ^{90}Sr, ^{137}Cs, and ^{131}I in a wild deer population and environment. In Aberg, B., and Hungate, F.P. (Eds.). *Radioecological Concentration Processes.* 621. Pergamon Press, New York.

Whicker, F.W., Farris, G.C., and Dahl, A.H. (1968). Wild deer as a source of radionuclide intake by humans and as indicators of fallout hazards. In Snyder, W.S. (Ed.). *Radiation Protection.* Part 2:1105. Pergamon Press, New York.

Whicker, F.W., Farris, G.C., Remmenga, E.E., and Dahl, A.H. (1965). Factors influencing the accumulation of ^{137}Cs in mule deer in Colorado. *Health Phys.,* **11** (12), 1407.

Whicker, F.W., and Schultz, V. (1982). *Radioecology: Nuclear Energy and the Environment.* Vol. 1:212. Vol. 2: 228. CRC Press Inc., Boca Raton, FL.

Whittaker, R.H. (1975). *Communities and Ecosystems.* Macmillan, New York: 385 pages.

Willard, W.K. (1963). Relative sensitivity of nestlings of wild passerine birds to gamma radiation. In Schultz, V., and Klement Jr., A.W. (Eds.). *Radioecology.* Reinhold, New York: 345 pages.

Willard, W.K., and Cherry, D.S. (1975). Comparative radiosensitivity in the class Insecta. *J. Theor. Biol.,* **52** (1), 149.

Winner, W.E., and Mooney, H.A. (1985). Ecology of SO2 resistance. V. Effects of volcanic SO_2 on native Hawaiian plants. *Oecologia (Berlin)* (In press).

Wood Jr., C.W., and Nash III, T.N. (1976). Copper smelter effluent effects on Sonoran desert vegetation. *Ecology,* **57**, 1311–1316.

Woodwell, G.M. (1967). Radiation and the patterns of nature. *Science,* **156**, 461–467.

Woodwell, G.M., and Rebuck, A.L. (1967). Effects of chronic gamma radiation on the structure and diversity of an oak-pine forest. *Ecol. Monogr.,* **37**, 53–82.

Woodwell, G.M., and Sparrow, A.H. (1965). Effects of ionizing radiation on ecological systems. In Woodwell, G.M. (Ed.). *Ecological Effects of Nuclear War.* 20–30. U.S. AEC Rep. BNL-917 (C-43), Brookhaven National Lab., Upton, New York.

Woollon, F.B.M., and Davies, C.R. (1981). The response of bryophytes to ionizing radiation. *Environ. Expt. Bot.,* **21**, 89–93.

Worrest, R.C. (1983). Impact of solar ultraviolet-B radiation (290–320 nm) upon marine microalgae. *Physiol. Plant.,* **58**, 428–434.

Worrest, R.C., Brooker, D.L., and Van Dyke, H. (1980). Results of a primary productivity study as affected by the type of glass in the culture bottles. *Limnol. Oceanogr.,* **25**, 360–364.

Worrest, R.C., Thomson, B.E., and Van Dyke, H. (1981a). Impact of UV-B radiation upon estuarine microcosms. *Photochem. Photobiol.,* **33**, 861–867.

Worrest, R.C., Wolniakowski, K.U., Scott, J.D., Brooker, D.L., Thomson, B.E., and Van Dyke, H. (1981b). Sensitivity of marine phytoplankton to UV-B radiation: Impact upon a model ecosystem. *Photochem. Photobiol.,* **33**, 223–227.

Zubrow, E.B.W. (1974). *Prehistoric Carrying Capacity: A Model.* Cummings Publishing Co., Menlo Park, CA: 143 pages.

PART II

Agricultural Effects

Part II examines the vulnerabilities of agricultural systems to nuclear war-induced climatic perturbations and to other, indirect effects of nuclear war. Discussion is included of the dependency of agricultural production on technological inputs and the effects of loss or reduction of these inputs in a post-nuclear war world.

Environmental Consequences of Nuclear War Volume II:
Ecological and Agricultural Effects
Edited by M.A. Harwell and T.C. Hutchinson
© 1985 SCOPE. Published by John Wiley & Sons Ltd

CHAPTER 4

Potential Effects of Nuclear War on Agricultural Productivity

MARK A. HARWELL AND WENDELL P. CROPPER, JR.

Primary Contributions by: J. A. Clark, C. C. Harwell, R. Herrera,
R. L. Myers, D. Pimentel, J. Porter, S. J. Risch, T. Sinclair,
R. B. Stewart, P. B. Tinker, Z. Uchijima, M. H. Unsworth,
M. Verstraete

Additional Contributions by: Essex Workshop participants,
Caracas Agricultural Working Group participants,
Melbourne Biology Working Group participants

4.1 INTRODUCTION

The current human population on Earth is nearly 5×10^9 individuals, and the population continues to grow at least exponentially. Humans are almost totally dependent on biological activity for food and other sustenance, yet the human population now far exceeds the capacity of the natural ecosystems for support. Indeed, without any agricultural productivity, at least 90% to 99% of the current human population could not be maintained indefinitely, an issue discussed in more depth in Chapters 3 and 7.

Agricultural plants are largely derived species that evolved in tropical or subtropical areas, species capable of high seed production. They are especially sensitive to even brief periods of cold temperatures, to insufficient water availability, to insufficient nutrient supply, and to disruptions in their life cycles. Humans establish an artificial environment for most crop plants; this includes: 1.) reduction in competition against other plant species (e.g., through cultivation, weed removal, and applications of herbicides); 2.) supplements of nutrients and moisture (e.g., through fertilization, crop rotations to refurbish soil nutrient levels, and irrigation); 3.) protection against herbivory and disease (e.g., through applications of insecticides and fungicides); 4.) development of optimal genetic constitution (e.g., through artificial selection and controlled mixing of genomes); and 5.) protection from the vagaries of nature (e.g., by optimal timing of sowing to coincide with the weather conditions extant at a particular location). These, and many other, subsidies by humans for agricultural systems allow the high levels of productivity that are presently attained.

Humans, of course, cannot yet reliably control the weather, so the particular vulnerability of agriculture to adverse weather provides a constant back-drop to the production of substantial yields each year. But based on experience and selective breeding, the distribution of particular agricultural crops across the landscape reflects a deliberate reduction in the risk of failure, and, thus, indirectly provides protection of the crops from variations in the physical environment. Those years in which the conditions are adverse for crop production differ among crop species and locations; thus, there are few instances where disruptions in climate occur simultaneously on a global scale. Local- or regional-scale disruptions in productivity are usually compensated for via the economic system, involving trade from other areas (although this is not always the case for the poorer regions of the world). This complex interaction between human and biological systems, then, is largely successful in maintaining the modern human population, at least up to current population levels, because the scale of disruptive perturbations is relatively small compared to the total, global scale of the agricultural system, probably within $\pm 5\%$ globally in any single year.

But the possibility for global-scale disruptions in climate and the high probability for global-scale disruptions in human economic and societal systems resulting from a large-scale nuclear war for the first time offer the scale of perturbations that simultaneously could disrupt agricultural productivity world-wide. No other anthropogenic perturbation to the environment has this disruptive potential; consequently, little previous scientific investigation of the impacts of global disruptions on the agricultural system has been done. Previous work has focused on the possibility of an increase in global average temperatures by a few degrees in response to anthropogenically induced increases in atmospheric CO_2, and some work on small reductions in temperature has been done in the context of possible alterations in atmospheric ozone from human activities and the potential for general climate cooling at northern latitudes. However, these situations would develop gradually, with time for feedbacks from the human systems at least partially to compensate for climatic changes. Moreover, projections of these stresses do not invoke simultaneous, massive disruptions of societal systems. Therefore, while we will draw from these studies somewhat, there is essentially no precedent to the consideration of the types and scales of stresses potentially associated with nuclear war.

Previous assessments of the global environmental effects of nuclear war (e.g., Woodwell, 1963; Ayres, 1965; NAS, 1975; OTA, 1979; ACDA, 1979; UN, 1968, 1979, 1980, 1981; Lewis, 1979; Katz, 1982) and studies specific to agricultural effects of nuclear war (e.g., Brown and Pilz, 1969; Brown et al., 1973; Bensen and Sparrow, 1971; Haaland et al., 1976; Hill and Gardiner, 1979; FEMA, 1982; Hjort, 1982, 1984) did not consider the potential for large-scale climatic alterations. In many of these studies, agricultural effects were limited to consideration of radiation, since fallout was considered to be essentially the only global-scale stress requiring consideration. Many of the agricultural effects studies did consider some aspects of disruption of societal systems in their role of providing support to food production and distribution, but almost all examined only effects on the United States, often based upon a highly optimistic scenario of the post-nuclear war world. Katz (1982) and Hjort (1982, 1984) presented a more balanced picture of the societal constraints on post-nuclear war food production and distribution, and Hjort (1984) did extend the considerations to the global scale. Nevertheless, reading of the extensive literature on the effects of nuclear war that was prepared prior to considerations of climatic disturbances would not lead one to believe that agricultural effects were likely to be dominant.

In Ehrlich et al. (1983) the suggestion was made of the potential vulnerability of food production on a global scale following a nuclear war. This was examined more closely in Harwell (1984), and the conclusion was reached that globally the greatest vulnerability of humans to a nuclear war may be that associated with food availability. Here we will investigate the issue in considerably more depth, drawing upon a variety of information sources in order to make the best estimates of nuclear war-induced reductions in food production and availability. The approach is to examine first the vulnerability of world agricultural productivity to the potential climatic changes, including both acute and chronic stresses and considering effects on different crops and different parts of the Earth. We then consider, in the absence of climatic alterations, the effects on productivity from the loss of human subsidies to agriculture. These combined effects lead to at least the possibility of little or no agricultural productivity on up to a hemispheric scale during the acute phase response to a large-scale nuclear war, and to the severe reduction in agricultural productivity extending into the chronic period and beyond. The obvious next issue is the existence, availability, and duration of food stores on a global basis; this issue is examined in detail in Chapter 5 in order to translate the effects of nuclear war into effects on the large fraction of the human population that would not be victimized by the nuclear detonations directly.

4.2 VULNERABILITY OF AGRICULTURAL PRODUCTIVITY TO CLIMATIC PERTURBATIONS

4.2.1 General Issues Concerning the Effects of Climatic Perturbations on Agricultural Productivity

The SCOPE–ENUWAR team investigating the atmospheric and climatic responses to a major nuclear war (Volume I, Pittock et al., 1985) has estimated possible changes in air temperature, solar insolation, and precipitation that could occur on hemispheric or global scales (Table 2.1). There remains significant uncertainty in the specific projections (see also, NRC, 1985), and the projections differ considerably across locations and across seasons.

It is not possible for those of us examining the biological effects of climatic and other potential nuclear war-induced perturbations to select a single physical environmental scenario to be analyzed. This is because of 1.) the uncertainties in the physical analyses; 2.) the evolving nature of the detailed physical projections, as new analyses continue to be performed by the physical scientists; 3.) the complexity of the distribution of physical environmental conditions across the global landscape; and 4.) the complexity of distribution of biological systems and associated stress-response relationships across the global landscape.

For the purposes of the agricultural assessments in the present study, the possible climatic changes were categorized into groups of types of stresses based on their likely significances to biological systems and on the most appropriate methodology for use in making an assessment of those stress responses. Each of these categories has different implications for agricultural productivity, and different approaches to evaluating their effects were undertaken. The categories were not selected to represent the most likely outcome of a nuclear war, nor is there any implication in selecting these categories of the level of probability associated with their occurrence at any particular location or any particular point in time. Such estimations of probabilities and extent of occurrence of climatic disturbances are needed for more specific biological assessments to be conducted, but these remain for the physical scientists yet to resolve. The categorization used in the present analyses was: 1.) a climatic disturbance identified as being 'acute', characterized by transient, average land-surface air temperature extremes near or below freezing, and associated average light reductions of 90–99% below normal; 2.) a 'chronic' phase climatic disturbance, characterized by average annual land-surface air temperature reductions of a few degrees below normal ($1°C$, $3°C$, $5°C$, or even $10°C$); and 3) an acute or chronic phase climatic disturbance characterized by precipitation reductions that could be 50% or greater below normal. Because the issue of patchiness in the post-nuclear war environment, e.g., having acute-type perturbations intermixed with more normal conditions, has not yet been resolved by the physical scientists, this issue was not analyzed explicitly; nevertheless, it is recognized that such an eventuality might lead to greater biological consequences than could follow from a single acute perturbation or from a monotonic, gradual decrease in temperatures, for which acclimatization might be possible.

We wish to emphasize again that the issue of probability for any or all of these climatic disturbances to occur at a particular location or region is not considered here. Thus, as an example, analyses of the potential effects on wheat production in Canada in response to an average growing-season temperature decrease of 3°C are presented in order to illustrate the vulnerability of that agricultural system to that level of perturbation. The specific level of temperature disturbance in those analyses is within the range of outcomes considered to be plausible based on Volume I; however, we are not predicting it would necessarily occur nor are we implying any specific level of probability of occurrence. By utilizing a systems vulnerability approach, the analyses presented in this volume should remain instructive, even as there continue to be adjustments in the projections of the physical scientists concerning the environmental responses to nuclear war. These cautions apply throughout the analyses in this chapter and the rest of this volume.

If an acute decrease in average temperatures down to near or below freezing were to occur during the growing season, the consequences on crop yields can be inferred from the types of physiological information discussed in Chapter 1. However, the other stresses require a closer examination for the potentially associated agricultural responses; we addressed these issues using physiological-level considerations, analyzing empirical data on crop-weather relationships, examining historical analogs, and utilizing simulation models. Each of these approaches is incorporated in the following sections. But we first need to examine the context of climatic changes on agriculture.

One key issue is the difference between average climatic conditions and actual weather experienced at a location and at a point in time. Except for the possibility of initial, transient 'quick freeze' phenomena, the projections from the atmospheric/climatic studies are for *average conditions*. For most of the analyses, these are averaged over diurnal cycles, over long periods of time, including seasonal cycles, and over large expanses of landscape. However, the understanding of the response of crops to the physical environment is based on far smaller scales of time and space. While it is important to know what the cumulative reduction in temperature over a growing season would be (i.e., the thermal time discussed below) at a particular location, a value that can be calculated from average climate predictions, it is also critical to know what the range of temperature variations and the incidence of brief cold events during the growing season would be. The average temperature drop may well define what crop yields would be, because a reduction in the available energy over the growing season translates into a reduction in crop yields. Averaged over time, this in large part determines what crops should be planted in specific regions. But it is the occurrence of short-duration episodes of low minimum temperatures that can lead directly to the death of plants or to the irreversible interference with maturation of the crop, i.e., can lead to total crop loss for that growing season. Both of these processes operate in the relationship between climatic alterations and crop productivity.

Consider a hypothetical example case, in which a projected chronic decrease in average temperature of, say, 3°C, occurred by having each and every daily maximum and minimum temperature decreased by 3°C. Over a growing season of, say, 100 days, that would translate into a loss of 300 degree-days, a value that could be used to estimate the yield responses of different crop species. Additionally, an average decrease in which the variance and autocorrelation of daily variance were unchanged would reduce the length of the growing season, if defined as the frost-free period, by an amount determined by the seasonal rate of warming in the spring and cooling in the autumn; i.e., if the average daily temperatures at the beginning of the growing season in our example are increasing at a rate of, say, 0.5°C per day, then a scenario having a 3°C reduction in average daily temperatures would correspond to an average delay in the onset of the growing season by 6 days.

The issue of changed variance in association with a nuclear war-induced change in average temperatures is an issue that has not been clarified to date. Changes in the variation of daily temperatures and the variation over diurnal cycles are possible in a nuclear war-altered climate. Suggestions have been made that the diurnal and monthly variance might decrease under a nuclear war-altered atmosphere for the mid-latitudes in mid-continental regions, and that variations at the periphery of a nuclear war-induced smoke cloud, such as at coastal zones and in tropical regions, might increase from current patterns (Volume I, Pittock et al., 1985). However, there does not appear to be a solid basis for such suggestions nor any quantification yet done. Thus, unless otherwise noted, the climatic analyses in the present volume were accomplished assuming no changes in weather variance after a nuclear war. It is clear that if an average cooling were to occur with an associated change in climatic variance over time, then the relationship between an average decrease in temperature and a reduction in the length of the growing season might differ from the pre-nuclear war situation. Likewise, if there were a differential reduction in temperature over a growing season, even without a change in the total variance, the reduction in the length of the growing season as a function of altered average conditions could be different from the estimates based on uniform application of a temperature decrease across the growing season, either extended or compressed in time.

As one method to estimate the present relationship between the reduction in the average temperature and the length of the frost-free season, a study that examined the potential effects from a 2°C reduction in global annual average temperature included an analysis of gradients of temperatures across latitude in comparison with the length of the growing season. Based on these assessments (Dale et al., 1975), it was reported that a 1°C change in the mean growing season temperature would result in reduction in the frost-free period by 10 days. Again, this assessment took no account of a change in the local weather variance or autocorrelation in daily temperatures.

We have performed similar evaluations by examining weather data from 38 stations across the continental United States to determine the relationship within a single year between the mean growing season temperatures and the length of the frost-free period, defined as the number of consecutive days with the minimum temperature above 0°C (Figure 4.1a) or above −2°C (Figure 4.1b). Two other plots were made for several weather stations over *different* years (Figures 4.1c,d). In all four situations, the estimate of about 10 days per 1°C average change in temperature was consistent.

In another set of evaluations performed in order to investigate this topic, a set of five stations was selected from a large climatological data base at the National Center for Atmospheric Research, which includes information recorded for weather stations throughout the United States and Canada. Each station has at least a 40-year record, and often many more years are covered by the data base. The long-term daily mean minimum temperatures for the selected stations were computed and subjected to harmonic analysis in a study performed by M. Verstraete for the SCOPE–ENUWAR project. This involved the decomposing of the seasonal temperature traces into Fourier components.

This procedure expresses the variance in the original records as a superpositioning of sine and cosine elementary signals, each with a particular amplitude, phase, and frequency. Since the annual temperature cycles are well defined for most of the stations in the survey, the first few components of the analysis accounted for most of the variance; over 99% of the total variance of the seasonal signal can be reconstructed from the first five harmonics. Therefore, it is possible to obtain for each station an analytical expression that very accurately reflects the long-term average seasonal cycle of the daily minimum temperatures.

This approach was used for examining the dates at which the daily minimum temperatures in May and September finally or initially crossed the threshold temperature of −2°C by analyzing the time derivative of the analytical expression at those points in time. The analysis is based on the seasonality component of the time series, with all other characteristics of the time–temperature signal, such as variance and autocorrelation, assumed to remain unchanged. The calculated slope value, as discussed above, represents the rate at which a change in average temperature translates into a change in the length of the frost-free period. For the selected weather

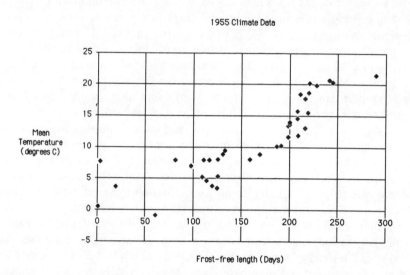

Figure 4.1a   Consecutive days above 0°C for selected continental U.S. weather stations in 1955

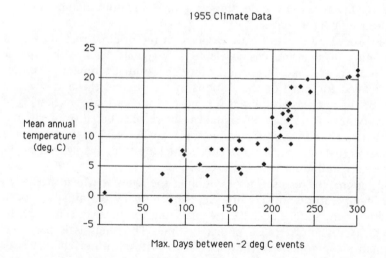

Figure 4.1b   Consecutive days above − 2°C for selected continental U.S. weather stations in 1955

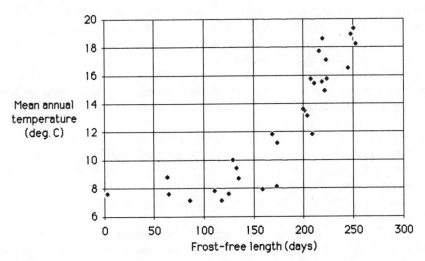

Figure 4.1c   Consecutive days above 0°C for selected continental U.S. weather stations in 1955, 1965, and 1975

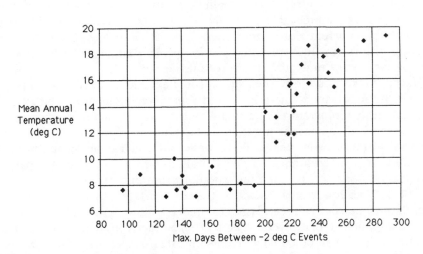

Figure 4.1d   Consecutive days above −2°C for selected continental U.S. weather stations in 1955, 1965, and 1975

stations analyzed in the mid-latitudes, the sensitivity of the length of the growing season, as defined as the number of consecutive days during which the mean daily temperature remained above $-2°C$, was found to be approximately 10 to 12 days per degree C change in the mean temperature.

With respect to the sensitivities at other latitudes, stations in southern regions, especially into subtropical and tropical regions, never experience freezing, and this analysis is not applicable. More northerly stations were seen in this analysis to have a more marked seasonal cycle, reducing the sensitivity to this kind of change somewhat. However, Bollman and Hellyer (1974), in another analysis, concluded that the reduction in frost-free period per degree is greater in more northerly latitudes, i.e., the rate of change increases with shorter growing season. In Canada, they predicted that a 1 °C change translates into a 20 day reduction in the frost-free period, again assuming present average temperature-variance relationships. Their result, however, is contrary to the results from the wheat and barley productivity models analyzed by Stewart, as discussed in a later section.

Thus far, we have discussed the effect of decreasing temperatures by the same amount each day of the growing season; but there is another way in which a hypothetical chronic 3°C reduction in average temperature could occur: an increase in the frequency, intensity, and/or duration of cold episodes occurring within an otherwise normal growing season. This again relates to the variance in climate after a nuclear war, an issue for which we have little guidance from the climate analysts. On the one hand, it would seem that variance in temperature under a nuclear war-altered atmosphere would be decreased, because diurnal cycles might be dampened and because the atmosphere might be more stable vertically; on the other hand, the considerable disruption in current global atmospheric circulation patterns could possibly lead to historically unprecedented disruptions in weather patterns, increasing variance over time; also, those regions near the edge of a nuclear war-induced smoke cloud (e.g., the tropics) could experience increased temporal variability in weather. There is a strong spatial component involved here; e.g., monthly temperatures at a single location vary much more on a year-to-year basis than does the monthly temperature averaged over the entirety of the Northern Hemisphere. Thus, while one could establish the normal variation in temperatures on a global scale to be within 1°C in comparing growing seasons across years, the variation from one year to the next at a particular location is typically much greater. Clark (1985) also discussed in depth the importance of scale issues for understanding agricultural responses to climate, noting that several orders of magnitude differences in time and spatial scales are all potentially involved in stress-response characterization.

As a simple illustration of the spatial and temporal components of temperature variance, consider the hypothetical situation depicted in Figure 4.2. In Case 1, some perturbation is applied to the normal pattern for an entire

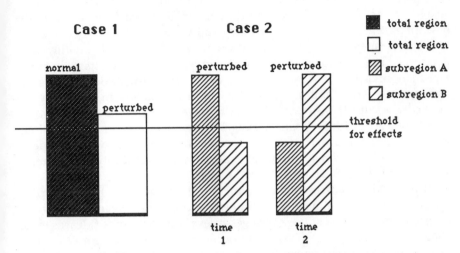

Figure 4.2   Idealized representation of effect of spatial and temporal scale on evaluating effects from average conditions. See text for discussion

region. In Case 2, the total region is subdivided into two halves. Twice as intense a perturbation occurring over half the area would give the same regionally averaged value as the first case. Alternatively, to add a temporal component, consider two time periods in Case 2, where one half of the region experiences the perturbation for half the time, followed by the other half being perturbed for the other half of the time. Again, the time- and region-averaged perturbation would be the same as in Case 1. However, if there is a threshold for effects, then the actual consequences would be quite different from the averaged case to the more local-scale situation. As an example, in the regionally average case of Figure 4.2, no effects at all would be predicted, since the threshold would never have been exceeded. In the other case, 50% or even 100% of the area could suffer total effects, depending on the time pattern of imposing the perturbation (e.g., having half the region perturbed for the total time, or having each half of the region perturbed for half the time). Thus, if exceeding some threshold for brief periods of time can result in an impact, then a spatially and temporally averaged picture of the perturbation cannot reliably predict the consequences that would be felt. And that is precisely the situation with respect to agricultural impacts from climatic changes. For example, in the acute period there is the possibility of experiencing sudden freezes that move across large areas of landscape, even though only a relatively small area would be perturbed at any one point in time; likewise, in a chronic period, episodes of extreme temperatures could be a part of a generalized reduction in average temperatures.

   One approach to dealing with these issues is to identify the probability of experiencing conditions exceeding the threshold for effects. A detailed analysis of agricultural success and failure in southern Scotland over the past three centuries was done by Parry and Carter (1985). They characterized the frequency of failure of oat crops as a function of monthly temperatures. The conclusion was that the importance of the episodic event, especially occurring in extreme years, was a key factor in determining the probability of crop failure. The shift in the risk of failure in cool years was markedly greater than the shift in the average temperature alone. Thus, as noted by Parry (1985), spatial changes in temperature (or precipitation), which are often approximately linear in the rate of change with latitude or altitude, result in strongly nonlinear changes in the probability of occurrence of extreme events. Further, the relationship between changes in mean temperatures and the corresponding change in the frequency of occurrence of extreme events is nonlinear, and relatively small average changes sometimes translates into relatively large changes in event probabilities (Mearns et al., 1985; Warrick, in press). This might occur even if there were no change in the variance–average temperature relationship, such as after a nuclear war compared to the present. This will have implications in our later discussions of the post-nuclear war chronic period with respect to the planting strategies by survivors in order to reduce the probabilities of crop failure in an uncertain environment.

Another aspect of the disturbed climate projections is a measure of the magnitude of the stresses. For instance, a 1°C change in average temperatures over a growing season may seem relatively small, yet major climatic consequences can follow from global average temperatures that are below normal by smaller or even nonexistent levels The average annual Northern Hemisphere temperature has been within about ±0.75°C over the past century, and differences between current hemispheric temperatures and the warmest interglacial periods of the last half million years are only about 2–3 °C (IIASA, 1981). In 1816 killing frosts continued through the summer in much of North America and Europe (Stommel and Stommel, 1979), even though there was probably less than 1°C or 2°C difference in global temperature. As another example, consider the extreme weather responses to the most recent El Niño episode, in which large regions experienced record-breaking low or high temperatures, and extremes of rainfall or drought; changes in global average temperatures were essentially irrelevant to this large, regionally important anomaly.

Similarly, projections of precipitation possibly being reduced on a regional scale by 25% or 50% need to be perceived within the context of normal year-to-year variation. Figure 4.3 shows the current rainfall variability on Earth (IIASA, 1981, citing Petterssen, 1969). Large portions of the agriculturally productive areas of North and South America, Europe, and Asia experience annual rainfall deviations from normal of less than

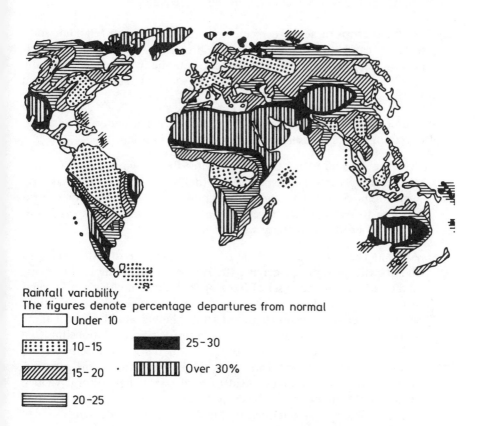

Rainfall variability
The figures denote percentage departures from normal

☐ Under 10

▦ 10-15   ■ 25-30

▨ 15-20 ·   ▥ Over 30%

▤ 20-25

Figure 4.3   Annual variability of rainfall. After IIASA (1981)

20%, according to this reference, and only the more arid regions of Africa, the Arabian Penisula, Australia, the Arctic, and the deserts of America and Central Asia experience deviations of 30% of more, reflecting a general trend of greater variation occurring in areas of lower average precipitation. Thus, changes in precipitation of the magnitude projected as potentially occurring over at least a regional scale following a large-scale nuclear war are unprecedented for those regions for which agricultural productivity is high.

4.2.2 Summary

These preceding considerations guide us in our approach to evaluating the agricultural effects of nuclear war. The potential responses of agricultural productivity to altered climatic conditions may involve one or more of the following factors, discussed in detail in the subsequent sections:

1.) Effects on crops of acute, extreme changes in temperature and/or solar insolation can be most appropriately addressed by physiological considerations. The extreme climatic stresses potentially associated with the acute period are outside the bounds of analyses based on historical records or simulation models.

2.) Chronic effects and less extreme acute climatic perturbation effects must be examined more closely, with the following in mind:

   • Average reductions in temperature alter the growing season as characterized by the total thermal time (degree-days); i.e., optimal crop yields require sufficient energy integrated over time for primary production to be high, and thresholds of total thermal time exist below which no crop productivity would occur.

   • Average reductions in temperature may also relate to a shortening of the growing season by delaying the last date of freezing in the spring and/or advancing the onset of freezing in the autumn; this would occur if there were no change in the average temperature-variance relationships that exist in an unperturbed atmosphethis would occur if there were no change in the average temperature-variance relationships that exist in an unperturbed atmosphere and if the average temperature reduction extended uniformly over the entire period. This growing-season reduction factor can lead to total loss of agricultural yield if insufficient time exists for the crop to reach maturity, even if the total thermal time as characterized by the degree-days is adequate.

   • The reduction in average temperatures over a growing season typically results in a reduction in the rate of the crop maturation processes; this tends to extend in time the length of a growing period required for completion of crop maturation, thereby exacerbating the effect of shortening the growing season.

   • Episodes of extreme temperatures are often associated with changes in the average temperatures over a growing season; thus, within a growing season there is an increased probability of crop failure on a regional scale resulting from even a brief period of extreme weather;

   • Because agricultural plants have distinct thresholds for survival and/or production of a usable crop, exceeding the threshold can lead to non-linear effects that are irreversible for that growing season;

- Precipitation on at least a regional scale might be changed by unprecedented amounts following a large-scale nuclear war; most grain crops, the major basis for human support, are grown in water-limited areas under normal precipitation patterns, so they are especially vulnerable to reductions in precipitation.

In the following sections we examine the effects of nuclear war-induced climatic perturbations on agricultural production in the Northern Hemisphere, in the tropics, and in the Southern Hemisphere. Our primary emphasis is on the grain crops as providing the most important component globally in the human diet. Secondary consideration is given to animal productivity, especially in those areas (e.g., New Zealand) where animals provide a major food resource.

4.3 POTENTIAL VULNERABILITY OF NORTHERN TEMPERATE AGRICULTURE

4.3.1 Response to Acute Extreme Climatic Perturbations

The mid-latitudes of the Northern Hemisphere are highly productive agriculturally, providing a large fraction of the grain production in the world. Of particular interest here is the production of wheat, maize (corn), and rice. Figures 4.4 a–c illustrate the current distribution of the growing areas for these three grains in North America, the U.K., and Eurasia. These growing areas are the region potentially most subject to the direct and the climate-induced indirect effects of nuclear war. Based on the discussions in Volume I, it is likely that the Northern mid-latitudes would have the highest probability of any region on Earth of experiencing acute climatic perturbations, particularly from a summer-onset nuclear war. With respect to the biological analyses, the acute, extreme climatic perturbation of at least brief periods of near- or sub-freezing temperatures, with concomitant light level reductions, is instructive for examining the vulnerability of Northern temperate agricultural to the potential effects of a large-scale nuclear war.

The response of crop plants to freezing events during the growing season is discussed in Chapter 1. A synopsis of some of the minimum temperatures that various crops can endure without either death or the irreversible interruption in the production of yield is listed in Table 4.1. It is apparent from these data that any of the crops of substantial value for human food production would be killed outright or the yield considerably reduced or even lost for a growing season in which freezing occurred.

By considering this simple, direct response at the physiological level, the response of agriculture in the Northern mid-latitudes to the potentially extreme temperature excursions of the acute period of nuclear war-induced

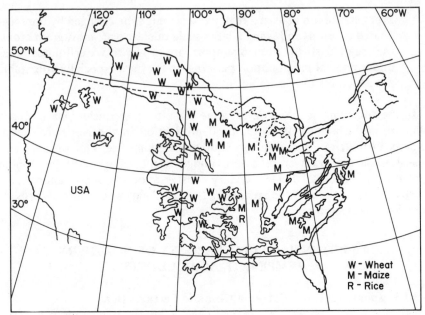

Figure 4.4a   Current growing areas for wheat (W), maize (M), and rice (R) in North America. Maps prepared by J. Porter

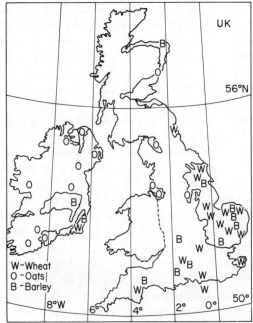

Figure 4.4b   Current growing areas for wheat (W), oats (O), and barley (B) in the U.K.

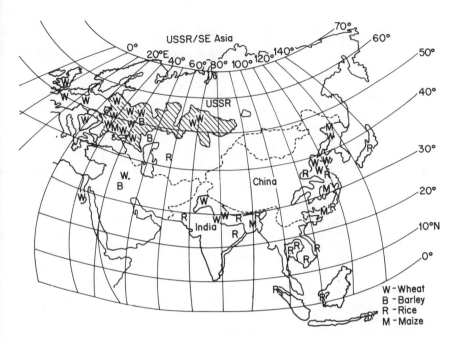

Figure 4.4c   Current growing areas for wheat (W), rice (R), barley (B), and maize (M) in Eurasia

climatic disturbances can be determined by knowing the spatial extent of such freezing episodes. The best information from the climatic analyses is that most inland continental areas of the Northern mid-latitudes could experience subfreezing minimum temperatures after a summer- or a winter-onset nuclear war of sufficient magnitude to inject about 2×10^8 tonnes of smoke into the atmosphere, and by inference following such a war at other times of the year. For example, Table 4.2 illustrates the mean minimum daily temperature during June at a number of locations above 30°N latitude, indicating the vulnerability of those locations to a drop of 15°C below the daily minimum levels. If such a temperature excursion were to occur below average normal June conditions, each location would be near or below freezing and, thus, subject to the types of chilling or freezing effects discussed in Chapter 1. Likewise, if a climatic perturbation induced by a nuclear war were to occur in the spring, summer, or early autumn, then any subfreezing episodes that did occur would coincide with the growing season, and essentially no agricultural crop production in that location would occur that year. In short, a transient acute, extreme climatic perturbation would lead to the loss of a crop for the year for all Northern temperate areas in which such an event

TABLE 4.1

RESISTANCE OF SELECTED CROPS TO FROST IN DIFFERENT
DEVELOPMENTAL STAGES[a]

Temperature (°C) harmful to plant in phases of:

	Germination	Flowering	Fruiting
HIGHEST RESISTANCE			
Spring wheat	-9	-1	-2
Oats	-8	-1	-2
Barley	-7	-1	-2
Peas	-7	-2	-3
LOW RESISTANCE			
Corn	-2	-1	-2
Millet	-2	-1	-2
Sorghum	-2	-1	-2
Potatoes	-2	-1	-1
NO RESISTANCE			
Buckwheat	-1	-1	-0.5
Cotton	-1	-1	-2
Rice	-0.5	-0.5	-0.5
Peanuts	-0.5	------	------
Tobacco	0	0	0

[a] Data from Oliver (1973).

occurred. In the case of a major, hemispheric-scale transient acute cooling response to nuclear war, such as the higher ranges of the possible outcomes projected from Volume I, agricultural productivity in the Northern temperate regions would be lost if a nuclear war occurred in about a six-month window of vulnerability, during the spring/summer/early autumn.

In the event of a war occurring in the autumn immediately after harvesting of the previous summer's crops, then the issue with respect to responses to acute perturbations is one of the duration of the acute period. If the acute period were to extend into the following growing season, then the same effect would apply, and no production could occur the following summer. However, based on Volume I, it seems more likely that the acute period would already be passed prior to the onset of the following summer months; thus, the potential effects on agricultural productivity can be assessed using the approaches for the chronic period, discussed in detail in the following sections.

TABLE 4.2

SUSCEPTIBILITY TO SUBFREEZING TEMPERATURES BASED ON A 15°C
DECREASE IN MEAN TEMPERATURES IN JUNE FOR SELECTED NORTHERN
HEMISPHERE LOCATIONS[a]

Weather Station	Latitude	Mean June Minimum Temp. (°C)	Mean June Minimum Temp. -15°C (°C)
Irkutsk, U.S.S.R.	52°N	-1	-16
Vladivostok, U.S.S.R.	43°N	+7	-8
Krasnovodsk, U.S.S.R.	40°N	+16	+1
Rome, Italy	42°N	+13	-2
Brno, Czechoslovakia	49°N	+6	-9
Munich, F.R. Ger.	48°N	+5	-10
Madrid, Spain	40°N	+9	-6
London, U.K.	51°N	+7	-8
Osaka, Japan	34°N	+12	-3
Nanking, China	32°N	+16	+1
Oak Ridge, TN, U.S.	36°N	+17	+2
Fort Wayne, IN, U.S.	41°N	+16	+1
Bismark, ND, U.S.	47°N	+11	-4

[a] Data from Rudloff (1981).

The consensus, then, reached among the large number of agricultural scientists considering this issue, is that, on the basis of temperature perturbations alone, the initial growing season in the Northern Hemisphere mid-latitudes following a nuclear war in which major climatic perturbations ensued would have essentially no agricultural productivity for a nuclear war occurring within, at a minimum, a several month period. Further, significant productivity might be unlikely for a large-scale nuclear war occurring at any other time of the year, again considering only the effects of transient, acute reductions in temperature.

Added to this could be the effect of reduced solar insolation. As discussed in Chapter 1, the net photosynthetic response of a single plant is typically for saturation to be reached at levels of light input well below full sunlight;

however, an entire crop canopy's light levels often do not reach saturation. This is because the leaves in a crop canopy are an assemblage of leaves at different ages, different physiological states, and different degrees of shading. The plant leaves in the context of the rest of the canopy receive but a fraction of full sunlight, and many of the leaves may photosynthesize at rates below that of respiration (i.e., have no net photosynthesis). This response means that reduction in insolation often leads to a direct decrease in productivity.

During periods in the acute phase of potential nuclear war-induced climatic disturbances, if sunlight levels at the top of the crop canopy were reduced by 90% or more, insufficient sunlight would reach the canopy as a whole for the crop system to be above the light compensation point. If this circumstance were prolonged, the crop would essentially starve to death as the carbohydrate energy reserves became depleted by respiration. The length of period required for this to occur is not easily determined, but would be a function of the crop type, the level of maturation reached prior to the onset of reduced light, and interactions with the effects of temperature. With respect to the latter, if conditions were not so extreme that the temperature killed the plants (e.g., after a relatively mild nuclear war-induced climatic disturbance, at the margins of a nuclear war-induced smoke cloud, or in the chronic period at some point later in time), then reduced temperatures would reduce respiration rates and perhaps compensate somewhat for the effect of reduced light levels.

The other stresses that could be associated with nuclear war-induced climatic disturbances, specifically, areas of reduced precipitation and perhaps increased storminess, would appear to be much less significant with respect to reductions in agricultural productivity during the acute period than the potential reductions in temperature and light. If temperature minimums were not so extreme, such as following a nuclear war that resulted in less disturbance to the atmosphere, then precipitation could become limiting to crop production, as discussed in more depth in the sections on chronic responses.

4.3.2 Responses to Potential Chronic Climatic Perturbations

4.3.2.1 Analytical Approaches

The projections for the chronic phase of nuclear war-induced climatic stresses include the possibility of average temperatures over the growing season being decreased below normal levels by 1°C, 3°C, 5°C, or even 10°C. The light levels assumed to have induced these temperature reductions are projected to be, respectively, approximately 5%, 13%, 16%, and 26% below normal insolation at the surface. The Volume I analysts also suggest that at least on a regional scale, there could be precipitation decreases of 25% to 50% for at least the Northern Hemisphere continental regions, although the uncertainties on these estimates are larger. than for the other physical parameters and local increases in precipitation are possible, especially on windward coasts. In order to evaluate the potential consequences of these stresses on agricultural productivity, a number of approaches are utilized.

One basis is historical precedent, examining the past years of extreme low temperatures or precipitation levels for effects on crop yields. While it is clear that there are no historical precedents to the acute onset of extreme nuclear war-induced climatic disturbances, the potential conditions of a chronic phase or a particularly mild climatic disturbance during the acute period may appropriately be analyzed by limited extrapolation and predictions based on the historical record. This approach tends to be anecdotal, and the issues of scale become important, as years in which there were poor yields in some regions may have had good yields elsewhere. In addition, historical extreme years typically had environmental conditions less severe than most of the range of perturbations projected to be possible for even the chronic period after a nuclear war. For example, a decrease in the hemispherically averaged temperature of 3°C or higher is essentially unprecedented within the historical record (Budyko, 1982).

The second approach is to use statistical models, i.e., also to look at the historical record, but to look across years for patterns and relationships rather than at a single year's situation. Again, this approach is limited by the range of physical parameters actually encountered in the past, as much of the variation of possible nuclear war-induced climatic disturbances is unprecedented, and, therefore, is outside the bounds of a statistical approach. Nevertheless, this does provide one additional line of reasoning as a part of the collective analyses.

Another approach is to use empirically based models of plant metabolism in response to environmental parameters, such as ambient temperature, light availability, and moisture stress. This approach is based primarily on laboratory experiments conducted to examine the physiological responses of plants, especially crop species, and follows much of the considerations presented in Chapter 1. Where in the discussions of the consequences of extreme climatic disturbances in an acute case, we relied on the physiological response of crop plant death or crop yield loss in response to near- or sub-freezing temperatures, the physiological approach here uses other indicators of metabolic activity, such as rates of photosynthesis.

The fourth approach is to use simulation modelling, based on models that have been constructed from mechanistic and empirical principles relating the various factors controlling primary production to physical parameters and that have been subsequently validated against actual crop yield data. This approach goes beyond the simple physiological approach by placing the crop plant in the context of the total environment, and, thus, provides a technique to examine multiple perturbations simultaneously. This method also has its limitations, however, especially at the outer bounds of the physical parameters for which the model is appropriate; nevertheless, these simulation models can be very instructive in projecting chronic agricultural responses.

4.3.2.2. Historical Approach

The first consideration for chronic effects of nuclear war-induced climatic disturbances on temperate agriculture is the historical approach. One instance of particular relevance is the year without a summer, 1816, on the food production in the Northeastern United States, Canada, and Western Europe. A detailed account of the consequences is given in Stommel and Stommel (1979) and in Post (1977). These authors examined the temperature records for several locations in the Northeast U.S., with evidence of abnormal cold on average over the summer months. For example, New Haven, Connecticut, had a mean monthly temperature in June, 1816, that was about 3°C below the normal level experienced over the first third of the 19th Century. This translated into a considerable delay in the onset of summer conditions, with the occurrence of several frosts in May. However, warm temperatures at the beginning of June were followed by an extreme cold episode lasting for about a week, during which killing frosts occurred.

The same pattern was seen twice more that summer, with warm periods being abruptly terminated by cold episodes and nighttime frosts in early July and in late August. Inspection of the *average* daily temperatures, however, shows these values did not go below 11°C in June, 14°C in July, and 13°C in August. Nevertheless, the occurrence of frosts during brief periods at night was sufficient to lead to severe impacts on crop yields. Most of the crops that had germinated in late May were killed by the June episode, and much of the subsequently planted crops were killed by the July episode. In many locations, crops that had survived the initial frosts succumbed to the August episode; for instance, it was said that maize production in the region was eliminated in all but the most protected locations because of the effectively two-week early termination of the growing season.

Maize was apparently most affected among the grains, with wheat less severely impacted. Plants grown for hay fared better with respect to temperature decreases, but the reduction in precipitation that occurred simultaneously apparently reduced yields by one-half. On the other hand, those hay yields that were harvested were qualitatively better than normal because of better curing in the drier weather. One important synergistic effect was that the reduced temperatures on average over the growing season prolonged the time required for crop maturation, especially the filling and ripening of the grains; this made the effect worse when the early onset of frost occurred, since the crops were in a less mature, and therefore, less consumable state.

The net effect of the climatic perturbations is difficult to quantify based on anecdotal information. However, one objective measure of the effects was the market price of the food commodities and the incidence of famine. The prices for grains, potatoes, hay, and livestock were reported to increase by factors of two to six, although meat prices fell precipitously because of farmers' killing off their stock for meat rather than try to maintain the herds in the face of high feed prices. Food shortages were not reported for the North American regions that were impacted, since the economic and agricultural systems extant there were adequately buffered; however, urban areas in Europe, such as in Switzerland and France, did suffer famine and associated societal disruptions. This resulted because much of Europe was still stressed from the recently ended Napoleonic Wars, and the societal systems' resistance to perturbation was low (Stommel and Stommel, 1979; Post, 1977). The potential similarity here to a post-nuclear war situation hardly needs further emphasis.

Another set of historical analogs is found in the period known as the 'Little Ice Age'. This period extended from the late 16th Century through the end of the 17th Century, with dendrochronological evidence indicating prolonged periods of regional-scale adverse weather during the 1590s, 1620s, 1640s, 1650s, and 1690s (Parker, 1980). Parker reports that this climatic change is reflected in the vineyard records in France, and in written records from observers at the time. A large variety of anecdotal pieces of information support the general response to an estimated 1°C reduction in average summer temperatures, including shifts in the ranges of crops (e.g., citrus production being eliminated in south China), lower snow lines in mountainous areas, extension of glaciers, and increased incidences of drought. It is estimated by Parker (1980) that the average growing season was reduced in length by three or four weeks. In response, grain yields fell by up to 75% in parts of Europe over the period, and human population growth, which had been rapid for the previous century, was reportedly slowed or even reversed into a population decline for many areas. The mechanism by which the reduced yields translated into human population impacts was apparently largely economic, in which the prices of grains increased substantially during the periods of low harvests, making food beyond the economic resources of the poorer constituents of society, a pattern seen consistently seen in historical and modern famines. It also seems likely that there was a linkage between the reduced food support for humans and the epidemic outbreaks of diseases, such as the bubonic plague, as well as interactions between limited resources and warfare.

4.3.2.3 Statistical Approaches

As an example of the use of statistical models to relate agricultural productivity to climatic change, Björnsson and Helgadottir (1984) examined in detail the record of hay production in Iceland on the same experimental plots that have been studied for the past five decades. The fertilizer treatments were constant over the experimental period, although there were differences in cutting treatments that had to be compensated for statistically. Yields and seasonal mean temperatures were found to be linearly related with a slope of about a 10% reduction in yield per decrease of 1°C for the Akureyri site in Northern Iceland (loss of about 600 kg ha^{-1} °C^{-1}), with greater losses in more southerly locations in Iceland (up to 1100–1200 kg ha^{-1} °C^{-1} at Skriduklaustur). In similar studies, Bergthorsson (1985) reported on a statistical model of hay yield in relation to temperature averaged over the year. The result, corrected for fertilizer differences, is a curvilinear relationship between the annual average temperatures of 1.5°C to 5°C (Figure 4.5). From about 4.5°C to 2.5°C, yields fell about 25%; however, another 1°C decrease in temperature would result in an additional loss of 25%, illustrating the nonlinearity of the response.

The use of linear statistical models based on historical data was explored in detail in the analyses of the Climate Impact Assessment Program (U.S. Department of Transportation, 1975). This study was designed to examine the potential effects of an average temperature reduction or increase of 3°C and

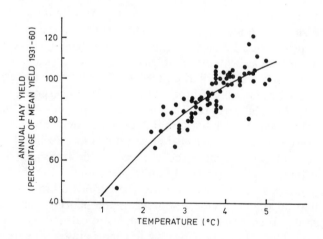

Figure 4.5   Hay yields in Iceland in 1901–1975 as percent of average yields (1931–1960) as a function of average air temperature at Stykkisholmur during October–April. After Bergthorsson (1985)

±30% change in precipitation in the Northern Hemisphere associated with hypothesized impacts from anthropogenic disturbance to the ozone layer in the stratosphere. Variance in temperature and precipitation was assumed not to change, allowing the researchers to use the historical record for relationships between climate and agricultural productivity (see Thompson, 1969a, 1969b, 1970). These statistical models were based on multiple regressions relating crop yield to mean monthly climate data over the growing season. Account was made in time trends for the increased yields attained historically in response to improvements in agricultural technology and energy subsidies. Because the regression models are based on high-energy agricultural production, their applicability for a post-nuclear war world is limited. (See the discussion of the potential effects from the loss of human subsidies to agricultural production, Section 4.6.)

The statistical models of wheat yield indicated a variable response to climatic change. Lower temperatures ($1°C$ or $2°C$ below normal) were shown actually to *increase* production in those areas normally experiencing limitations of precipitation. This relationship, to be seen again in the results from simulation models and in the discussions of ecosystems effects, reflects a reduced rate of evapotranspiration under reduced temperature, and, therefore, a reduction in soil moisture stress. Since this, rather than low temperatures, is a limiting factor for grain production in many areas, decreasing soil moisture stress allows primary production and crop yields to increase. These statistical models also indicated that in other areas, relatively small decreases in temperatures decreased projected wheat yields; however, the greatest sensitivity to changes in the physical parameters was to precipitation, with reduced precipitation resulting in marked reductions in wheat yields (Thompson, 1975). Similar results were reported for statistical analyses of maize production in the United States (Thompson, 1969a; U.S. Department of Transportation, 1975).

The use of statistical crop yield models to predict the agricultural consequences of climatic change has been strongly criticized. For example, Katz (1977) points out that statistical crop yield models are limited by the small amount of reliable historical data available. Further, these models use a large number of predictor variables, none of which have a high impact if acting in isolation. The multiple linear regression models used in the CIAP evaluation of potential climatic change consist of a number of coefficients relating mean monthly variables, such as temperature and precipitation, as well as technology trends to crop yield. However, it is clear from much evidence that crop yield responses to these and other environmental parameters are not linear; therefore, model extrapolations of climatic changes beyond the narrow limits of the historical data base are tenuous at best (Katz, 1977). Consequently, these types of statistical models are not relied upon for the present analyses.

4.3.2.4 Physiological Analysis Approach

The third approach to evaluating the effects of chronic stresses on agricultural production relies on empirical relationships determined primarily by laboratory experimentation. This mechanistic approach has the particular advantage of relating crop plant development to physical parameters acting independently and under controlled conditions. The qualitative responses of crops to altered light and temperature regimes can then be deduced from simple physiological relationships and the known requirements of the plants. An example of this approach is found in Clark (1985a), who pointed out that for most crop plants that have been studied in detail, the responses of growth and development to temperature can be diagrammatically represented by Figure 4.6. A measure of the rate of growth (e.g., the rate of increase in leaf length in mm hr^{-1}) or the rate of development (e.g., the inverse of the time period required for an event to occur, such as germination) increases essentially linearly with temperature above some minimum threshold value (T_{min}) up to some optimum value (T_{opt}). Above T_{opt} there is a sharper, but also approximately linear, decrease in the rate of growth or development, back down to the zero level above some maximum threshold level (T_{max}). Clark reports that for crops of tropical origin (e.g., rice), $T_{min} \approx 10°C$; $T_{opt} \approx 35°C$; $T_{max} \approx 45°C$. For crops of temperate systems (e.g., wheat and barley), $T_{min} \approx 0°C$; $T_{opt} \approx 25°C$; $T_{max} \approx 35°C$. In the case of a nuclear war-induced climatic disturbance imposed on temperate climates, we are only interested in the lower levels of these ranges, i.e., below optimum conditions and perhaps below minimum levels.

One characterization of this response is the concept of degree-days (or Day-Degrees of Thermal Time in the terminology of Monteith, 1981). This suggests that the development time of a plant is a function of the duration and the magnitude of temperature above the minimum level; specifically,

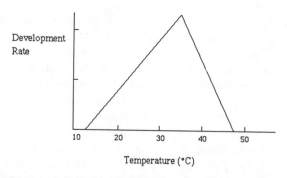

Figure 4.6   Idealized representation of effect of temperature on plant development rates. See text for discussion

the rate of growth or development is directly proportional to $(T-T_{min})$, but that the rate is zero below T_{min}. If temperatures are warm, the rate of development and growth are high; if they are low, it takes longer for the crop to complete its life cycle. This reproductive cycle for crops in the U.K., and for much of the rest of the Northern mid-latitudes, takes between 1000 and 2000 degree-days; below that there is insufficient time for the crop to reach maturity. As an example of this approach in describing the limits of crop ranges, Clark examined the temperature values for a station in the low Midlands of the U.K. The mean minimum monthly temperature in January and February is about 3°C, reaching a level of about 17°C in July. The mean annual thermal time above 10°C is just under 1000 degree-days; consistent with this, crops of tropical origin are marginal at this location. Thermal time above 0°C is about 3500 degree-days, sufficient for all temperate crops to be grown.

In an analysis based on the mechanistic approach, Clark (1985a) predicted the effects of chronic reductions in temperature on agricultural productivity in the U.K. A 7°C decrease in average temperature over the growing season was projected to produce a climate in the U.K. similar to Iceland, with a mean thermal time above 0°C of only about 1000 degree-days; consequently, only grasses and the shortest season cereal crops could be grown at low altitudes, and then only marginally. A 3°C decrease in temperature over the growing season would preclude yields from tropical and vegetable crops. In the English lowlands, the thermal time above 0°C would still be large enough (about 2500 degree-days) to support most temperate crops, but in northern and upland areas, the thermal time would be insufficient. Consequently, a 3 °C reduction in temperature would reduce the crop ranges of the temperate crops, according to the physiological approach. Finally, a 1°C drop was projected to be near the range of normal variation in the U.K., with little or no effect on the ability of temperate crops to reach maturity. It may be that a 1°C decrease, in the absence of any other perturbations, could result in an increase in yields, not because of reducing evapotranspiration rates, as the case for moisture-limited grain production in North America, but because the metabolic activity of the crops would be slowed down somewhat, making the crop more efficient in capturing solar energy into a useful form (i.e., biomass).

The mechanistic approach can also be used to examine the effect of reduced light levels on crop productivity. As discussed previously, whereas light is not limiting for individual leaves in sunlight, within the context of a crop canopy, photosynthesis is not light-saturated, and reductions in insolation can lead to reductions in productivity. At the higher levels of insolation, the reduction would not be directly proportional, and a 10% reduction in insolation would produce less than a 10% reduction in photosynthesis and in yield. In the middle ranges of the response curve, the relationship would be approximately linear, so that a 50% reduction in sunlight would give about a 50% reduction in productivity. At the lower levels of insolation, threshold levels are reached, specifically the light compensation point, at which level photosynthesis just matches respiration. Clark (1985a) suggests that point for most crops is at about the 10% level of normal light. Light reductions below the compensation point would lead to crop plant death from exhaustion of the carbohydrate reserves if maintained for a prolonged amount of time.

In the context of the present consideration, i.e., the climatic perturbations that might occur during chronic period of the post-nuclear war environment, the mechanistic, physiological approach suggests that the projected reductions in insolation by 5–25% would not reduce crop yields more than proportionately and, therefore, would seem to be minor compared to the corresponding temperature reductions. However, other considerations discussed below indicate that a nonlinear response could occur at less severe light reductions because of insufficient total sunlight time for crop maturation processes to be completed.

4.3.2.5 Simulation Model Approach

4.3.2.5.1 Canadian wheat and barley simulations

The final approach used in evaluating the potential chronic climatic disturbances that could follow a large-scale nuclear war is the utilization of simulation models. As with other methodologies, there are limits to this approach, specifically extending projections beyond the range to which the model reliably predicts the response of the real system; the limitations of input data to the model; the propagation through the model of uncertainties associated with those data; the site-specificity versus site-generality of the models and, therefore, the potential for extrapolation to other locations or other crops; and the ability of the model to consider other physical parameters that could affect crop yield predictions. Nevertheless, insofar as validated models can be identified that are sensitive to the changes of temperature, precipitation, and light levels being projected, this approach does offer promise for analyzing the chronic period.

With this in mind, we selected the simulation model of Agriculture Canada for analysis of wheat and barley production in the western provinces of Canada. This work, under the direction of R.B. Stewart, relied on a model developed initially by FAO (1978) and later modified by Stewart (1981) for Canadian conditions. This model is based on the de Wit (1965) methodology for estimating net biomass production. The model was used to evaluate long-term crop production capability under optimum management practices; this means that effects on agricultural productivity from disruptions in human subsidies and other factors leading to less-than-optimal management would result in further reductions in yields from those predicted by the model. Input data include monthly averages of temperature, precipitation, solar insolation, wind speed, and vapor pressure. A photosynthesis equation describes constraint-free yields, i.e., yields under optimal conditions, with a sigmoidal cumulative growth curve incremented up to the number of days required for the crop to mature. Net biomass production is calculated by taking into account the gross biomass production capacity of the crop as influenced by this temperature- and insolation-dependent photosynthesis term, subtracting the respiration losses resulting from another temperature-dependent function. A description of the model is provided in the appendix to this chapter.

The scenarios simulated using the Agriculture Canada model included:

1.) Changes in temperature by 1°C, 2°C, 3°C, 4°C, and 5°C, and changes in precipitation by ±25% respectively. This was done by decreasing the daily minimum and maximum temperatures uniformly by the specified amount. As discussed previously, this has the effect of reducing the length of the growing season by delaying the initiation of the frost-free period and enhancing the onset of the first freeze in the autumn. However, the relationship inferred from the statistical relationships of growing season length as a function of average temperature, discussed previously, was not explicitly incorporated into the model. Rather, the model generated its own growing season length stochastically by having the probability of a freezing event occurring increase substantially when the average daily temperature fell below a threshold value. Changes in precipitation were made to the monthly values, i.e., assuming the pattern of precipitation was unchanged over the growing season.

2.) Changes in seasonal temperatures by the same amounts, but holding the growing season length fixed; that is, the growing season average temperatures were reduced by the appropriate amount, but the daily temperature on the days beginning and ending the growing season were not changed (Figure 4.7).

3.) Changes in temperatures, insolation, and daylength to simulate the passing of a nuclear war-induced smoke cloud; for this scenario, the seasonal monthly values for temperature and insolation (intensity and daylength) were below normal by amounts that decreased over a three-month period.

To estimate the overall effect on Canadian wheat production, the total areal extent of spring wheat and barley production was estimated based on model-calculated changes from the actual ranges for the past two decades; crop yields per area were calculated by the model.

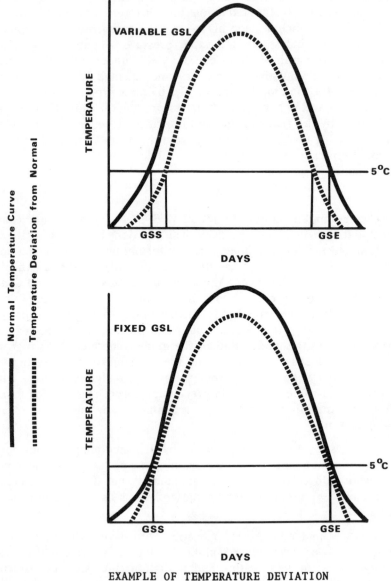

EXAMPLE OF TEMPERATURE DEVIATION
FROM NORMAL FOR VARIABLE AND FIXED
GROWING SEASON LENGHTS

Figure 4.7 Representation of two approaches to reducing temperatures with variable- and fixed-length growing seasons used in the Agriculture Canada wheat and barley simulations. From Stewart. 1985

4.3.2.5.2 Effects of reductions in average growing season temperature

The results from the first set of simulations are presented in Figures 4.8a and 4.8b, and the data are summarized in Tables 4.3 and 4.4. Figure 4.8a illustrates that for wheat production in Canada, a 1°C decrease in annual temperature does not substantially change the area in which wheat can be grown; however, the model predicts that a 2°C decrease in mean growing season temperature would eliminate all of the potential area for wheat production in Alberta and most of the area in Saskatchewan and Manitoba. A 3°C reduction would totally eliminate wheat production in Canada. Barley is not quite as sensitive, with little areal reduction for a 1°C or 2°C decrease in average temperatures; however, by 4°C, almost all barley production would be eliminated in Canada.

The reduction in the areal extent of potential grain production follows from two factors: 1.) The decrease in temperatures applied to every daily maximum and minimum value results in a shortening of the growing season at a rate of about 7 to 10 days per °C; this is the same rate seen from several sources of estimation, as discussed previously; 2.) The decrease in average temperature reduces the rate of crop development and growth, also as discussed previously; here, the model predicts that the time required to reach maturation is increased by 3 to 5 days per °C decrease in temperature. It is the combination of these two factors that results in the nonlinear response to decreased temperatures.

In the model simulations for either the base or alternate period, total crop production losses associated with the sudden decrease in the range over which the grain crops could be grown were partially compensated for at the lower temperature values by increased yields per hectare on those areas in which the grain could reach maturity. This resulted because of the reduction in the evapotranspiration rate and, therefore, a reduction in the soil moisture stress, which is important to productivity in precipitation-limited areas. This sensitivity to precipitation levels is highlighted by Table 4.4 for the 0°C difference case. The simulations indicate that crop yields would decrease by about 50% for wheat and 40% for barley in response to a 25% reduction in precipitation. Also, there is a disproportionately greater effect by reducing precipitation by 25% versus increasing it by 25%, suggesting a nonlinear response. This has implications for the effects from a greater decrease in precipitation, in that crop yields may decrease even more than would be estimated by mere extrapolating from the 25% case; i.e., there is the potential for the essential elimination of wheat production in Canada in response to a 50% reduction in growing season precipitation.

4.3.2.5.3 Effects of reducing thermal time only

In order to test the effect on crop yields of reducing only the thermal time

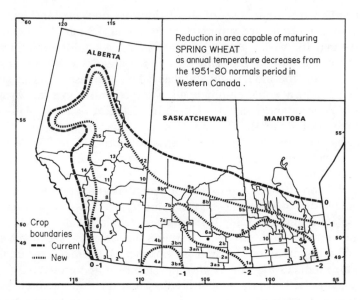

Figure 4.8a   Reduction in area capable of maturing spring wheat as average temperatures are reduced by 1°C and 2°C from normals of 1951–1980. Based on Agriculture Canada model simulations by Stewart (1985)

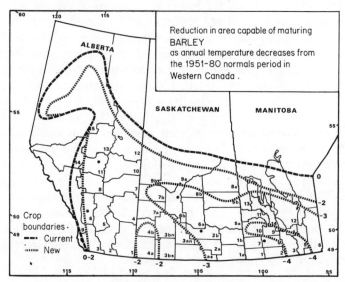

Figure 4.8b   Reduction in area capable of maturing barley as average temperatures are reduced by 1°C and 2°C from normals of 1951–1980. Based on Agriculture Canada model simulations by Stewart (1985)

TABLE 4.3

PERCENT OF 1961-1981 AVERAGE WHEAT AREA AND PRODUCTION BASED ON TEMPERATURE DECREASES OF 1°C, 2°C, AND 3°C; PRECIPITATION LEVELS OF 75%, 100%, AND 125% OF THE 1951-1980 NORMALS[a]

	Normals			-1°C			-2°C			-3°C		
PRECIPITATION	75	100	125	75	100	125	75	100	125	75	100	125
MANITOBA												
Area	100	100	100	97	97	97	94	94	94	0	0	0
Production	68	100	136	82	120	149	103	150	169	0	0	0
SASKATCHEWAN												
Area	100	100	100	83	83	83	25	25	25	0	0	0
Production	56	100	137	63	106	140	27	41	56	0	0	0
ALBERTA												
Area	100	100	100	98	98	98	0	0	0	0	0	0
Production	56	100	137	73	123	164	0	0	0	0	0	0
TOTAL												
Area	100	100	100	88	88	88	28	28	28	0	0	0
Production	58	100	137	68	112	147	32	45	57	0	0	0

[a] Based on simulations by R.B. Stewart using the Agriculture Canada model.

TABLE 4.4

PERCENT OF 1961-1981 BARLEY AREA AND PRODUCTION BASED ON GROWING SEASON TEMPERATURE DECREASES OF 1°C, 2°C, 3°C, AND 4°C; PRECIPITATION LEVELS OF 75%, 100% AND 125% OF THE 1951-1980 NORMALS[a]

	Normals			-1°C			-2°C			-3°C			-4°C		
Precipitation	75	100	125	75	100	125	75	100	125	75	100	125	75	100	125
MANITOBA															
Area	100	100	100	100	100	100	94	94	94	94	94	94	45	45	45
Production	64	100	130	79	120	140	95	130	140	118	142	148	69	78	78
SASKATCHEWAN															
Area	100	100	100	100	100	100	97	97	97	45	45	45	0	0	0
Production	62	100	133	78	122	154	101	144	173	61	87	101	0	0	0
ALBERTA															
Area	100	100	100	100	100	100	97	97	97	0	0	0	0	0	0
Production	62	100	125	77	115	140	93	132	154	0	0	0	0	0	0
TOTAL															
Area	100	100	100	100	100	100	96	96	96	29	29	29	6	6	6
Production	62	100	128	78	118	145	96	135	158	35	47	52	9	10	10

[a] Based on simulations by R.B. Stewart using the Agriculture Canada model.

(i.e., *not* including the effects of a reduced growing season acting against an increased maturation requirement), a sensitivity analysis was completed by holding the growing season length constant, but imposing the same average decrease in temperatures within the growing season. This scenario is not considered to be likely in the aftermath of a nuclear war, if the relationship between reduced average temperature and the reduction in the frost-free period, which has been demonstrated for a non-perturbed atmosphere, is assumed to remain after a nuclear war. Nevertheless, it is instructive to understanding the relative importance on crop productivity of the two major factors, growing season sufficiency versus thermal time sufficiency.

Results are shown in Figures 4.9 and 4.10 and Tables 4.5a,b and 4.6a,b for wheat and barley, respectively, indicating a decreased sensitivity to the reduction in average temperatures. For wheat, a 2°C change does not reduce the area of wheat production, and a 3°C reduction does not affect the area of barley production. But another 1°C reduction or so eliminates production of both crops, again indicating a strong nonlinearity in response. These results suggest that both the thermal time and the growing season length factors are important in determining the response of Canadian agriculture to climatic disturbances.

4.3.2.5.4 Effects of transient climatic perturbations

The final set of simulations using the Agriculture Canada model were designed to test the sensitivity of the model predictions to changes in insolation and to simulate the temporal response of a passing nuclear war-induced smoke cloud. These computer runs simulated the movement of a debris cloud by assuming that temperatures were reduced by 5°C the first month, 3°C the second month, and 1°C the third month, beginning at various times between April and August. Corresponding to these temperature reductions, solar insolation and day length were decreased by 22%, 15%, and 8%, in one simulation and by 11%, 8%, and 3% in another. All other climatic input data, including precipitation, were consistent with the 1951–1980 levels. Tables 4.7a–c show the impact on the area capable of maturing spring wheat based on production averages for 1961–1980. The months listed in the table indicate the month the transient effects are assumed to begin. For each month, it is assumed that the smoke cloud moves rapidly into the region, with gradual reduction of effects over the subsequent three months. Results are based on: 1.) effects of temperature reductions alone; 2.) effects of light and daylength reductions alone; and 3.) combined temperature, light, and daylength effects.

Temperature reductions alone are seen to cause substantial impacts on spring wheat, except for the case of initiation of the perturbation in April. For all areas except Manitoba, temperature reductions beginning at

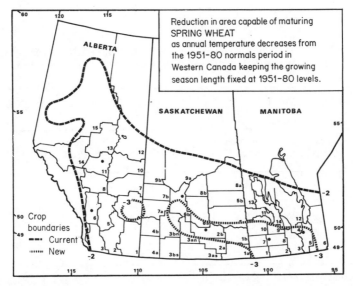

Figure 4.9 Reduction in area capable of maturing spring wheat as average temperatures are reduced by 1°C, 2°C, and 3°C from normals of 1951–1980 but keeping growing season length fixed. Based on Agriculture Canada model simulations by Stewart (1985)

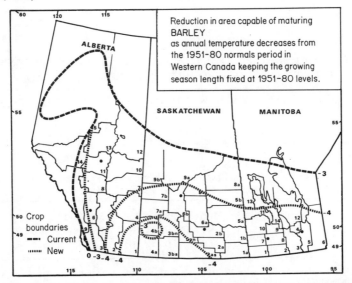

Figure 4.10 Reduction in area capable of maturing barley as average temperatures are reduced by 3°C and 4°C from normals of 1951–1980 but keeping growing season length fixed. Based on Agriculture Canada model simulations by Stewart (1985)

TABLE 4.5a

THE EFFECT OF CHANGING TEMPERATURE AND GROWING SEASON LENGTH
ON SPRING WHEAT PRODUCTION IN WESTERN CANADA[a]

DECREASING TEMPERATURE AND FIXING THE GROWING SEASON LENGTH
AT THE 1951-1980 NORMALS LEVEL

Temp. Normal	Manitoba[b] Area	Prod.	Saskatchewan Area	Prod.	Alberta Area	Prod.	Prairies Area	Prod.
-1°C	100	122	100	122	99	121	99	121
-2°C	97	146	77	117	88	130	82	124
-3°C	83	156	20	38	10	14	25	47
-4°C	0	0	0	0	0	0	0	0

[a] Based on simulations by R.B. Stewart using the Agriculture Canada model. Area and production are expressed in terms of percent of the 1961-1981 average.

[b] Area and production figures represent the 1961-1976 average. A change in the crop district boundaries in 1977 does not allow comparison of production data beyond 1976.

TABLE 4.5b

THE EFFECT OF CHANGING TEMPERATURE AND GROWING SEASON LENGTH
ON SPRING WHEAT PRODUCTION IN WESTERN CANADA[a]

DECREASING TEMPERATURE AND VARYING THE GROWING SEASON
LENGTH

Temp. Normal	Manitoba[b] Area	Prod.	Saskatchewan Area	Prod.	Alberta Area	Prod.	Prairies Area	Prod.
-1°C	97	120	83	106	98	123	88	112
-2°C	94	150	25	41	0	0	28	45
-3°C	0	0	0	0	0	0	0	0

[a] Based on simulations by R.B. Stewart using the Agriculture Canada model. Area and production are expressed in terms of percent of the 1961-1981 average.

[b] Area and production figures represent the 1961-1976 average. A change in the crop district boundaries in 1977 does not allow comparison of production data beyond 1976.

TABLE 4.6a

THE EFFECT OF CHANGING TEMPERATURE AND GROWING SEASON LENGTH
ON BARLEY PRODUCTION IN WESTERN CANADA[a]

DECREASING TEMPERATURE AND FIXING THE GROWING SEASON LENGTH
AT THE 1951-1980 NORMALS LEVEL

Temp. Normal	Manitoba[b] Area	Prod.	Saskatchewan Area	Prod.	Alberta Area	Prod.	Prairies Area	Prod.
-1°C	100	115	100	112	100	121	99	121
-2°C	100	130	100	131	100	130	82	124
-3°C	100	144	99	156	97	14	25	47
-4°C	94	158	50	113	8	0	0	0

[a] Based on simulations by R.B. Stewart using the Agriculture Canada model. Area and production are expressed in terms of percent of the 1961-1981 average.
[b] Area and production figures represent the 1961-1976 average. A change in the crop district boundaries in 1977 does not allow comparison of production data beyond 1976.

TABLE 4.6b

THE EFFECT OF CHANGING TEMPERATURE AND GROWING SEASON LENGTH
ON BARLEY PRODUCTION IN WESTERN CANADA[a]

DECREASING TEMPERATURE AND VARYING THE GROWING SEASON
LENGTH

Temp. Normal	Manitoba[b] Area	Prod.	Saskatchewan Area	Prod.	Alberta Area	Prod.	Prairies Area	Prod.
-1°C	100	121	100	122	100	115	100	117
-2°C	94	130	97	144	97	132	96	135
-3°C	94	142	44	87	0	0	29	47
-4°C	45	78	0	0	0	0	6	10
-5°C	0	0	0	0	0	0	0	0

[a] Based on simulations by R.B. Stewart using the Agriculture Canada model. Area and production are expressed in terms of percent of the 1961-1981 average.
[b] Area and production figures represent the 1961-1976 average. A change in the crop district boundaries in 1977 does not allow comparison of production data beyond 1976.

any other time (May through August) would devastate crop production (Table 4.7a); Manitoba seems only sensitive to an event initiated in June. For an episode beginning in that month, essentially all areas that normally grow wheat in Canada would be precluded from any crop production. Clearly, there are strong seasonality components to the response of crops to temperature excursions.

The reductions in light and daylength levels are seen not to cause major yield reductions at the lower levels (11% peak decrease) (Table 4.7b) for anywhere in Western Canada, although larger light reductions essentially eliminates yields if initiated in the mid-growing season. The marked difference between results of light and daylength reductions of 11% versus 22% suggests that the growing season as defined as cumulative hours of incident sunlight within the frost-free period can be a critical parameter. This is further indicated by the data on the combination of effects, which indicate strongly synergistic responses.

The results for barley production (Tables 4.8a–c) show considerably more resistance to temperature or light effects when applied independently, but the synergism of the combined perturbations leads to much greater impacts of some combinations of temperature, light, and daylength reductions. Again, a strong seasonality is apparent, and the occurrence of peak events in June would be devastating, according to the simulations.

TABLE 4.7a

EFFECTS ON AREA CAPABLE OF MATURING WHEAT AND TOTAL PRODUCTION IN WESTERN CANADA CORRESPONDING TO SEQUENTIAL MONTHLY TEMPERATURE REDUCTIONS OF -5°C, -3°C, AND -1°C RESPECTIVELY, BEGINNING IN THE MONTH INDICATED[a]

Month	Manitoba Area	Manitoba Prod.	Saskatchewan Area	Saskatchewan Prod.	Alberta Area	Alberta Prod.	Total Area	Total Prod.
April	100	101	94	97	99	102	96	100
May	97	100	53	59	17	21	51	55
June	0	0	0	0	0	0	0	0
July	95	110	33	39	0	0	34	39
August	94	99	20	22	0	0	25	26

[a] Based on simulations by R.B. Stewart using the Agriculture Canada model. Percent of 1961-1981 average production; all climatic input other than temperature was held constant at the 1951-1980 levels.

TABLE 4.7b

EFFECT ON AREA CAPABLE OF MATURING WHEAT AND TOTAL PRODUCTION
IN WESTERN CANADA CORRESPONDING TO SEQUENTIAL MONTHLY SOLAR
INSOLATION AND DAYLENGTH REDUCTIONS OF I.) -22%, -15%, AND -8%;
AND II.) -11%, -8%, AND -3% RESPECTIVELY, BEGINNING IN THE MONTH
INDICATED[a]

I.) INSOLATION AND DAYLENGTH (-22%, -15%, -8%)

MONTH	Manitoba Area	Prod.	Saskatchewan Area	Prod.	Alberta Area	Prod.	Total Area	Prod.
April	100	102	100	101	100	101	100	100
May	97	102	87	93	99	106	91	97
June	11	15	0	0	0	0	1	2
July	0	0	0	0	0	0	0	0
August	94	89	66	66	81	82	73	72

II.) INSOLATION AND DAYLENGTH (-11%, -8%, -3%)

MONTH	Manitoba Area	Prod.	Saskatchewan Area	Prod.	Alberta Area	Prod.	Total Area	Prod.
April	100	100	100	100	100	100	100	100
May	100	103	96	99	99	101	97	100
June	97	101	82	88	99	105	87	94
July	97	99	82	87	99	104	87	92
August	100	98	96	96	99	.98	97	96

[a] Based on simulations by R.B. Stewart using the Agriculture Canada model. Percent of 1961-1981 production average; all other climatic inputs than solar insolation and daylength were held constant at the 1951-1981 level.

TABLE 4.7c

EFFECT ON AREA CAPABLE OF MATURING WHEAT AND TOTAL PRODUCTION IN WESTERN CANADA CORRESPONDING TO SEQUENTIAL MONTHLY TEMPERATURE DECREASES OF -5°C, -3°C, AND -1°C AND SOLAR INSOLATION AND DAYLENGTH REDUCTIONS OF I.) -22%, -15%, AND -8%, AND II.) -11%, -8%, AND -3% RESPECTIVELY, BEGINNING IN THE MONTH INDICATED[a]

I.) INSOLATION AND DAYLENGTH (-22%, -15%, -8%)

MONTH	Manitoba Area	Prod.	Saskatchewan Area	Prod.	Alberta Area	Prod.	Total Area	Prod.
April	97	97	94	98	99	105	95	101
May	52	61	0	0	0	0	6	8
June	0	0	0	0	0	0	0	0
July	0	0	0	0	0	0	0	0
August	92	92	38	39	0	0	36	37

II.) INSOLATION AND DAYLENGTH (-11%, -8%, -3%)

MONTH	Manitoba Area	Prod.	Saskatchewan Area	Prod.	Alberta Area	Prod.	Total Area	Prod.
April	100	102	94	99	99	103	96	100
May	96	103	38	43	0	0	37	40
June	0	0	0	0	0	0	0	0
July	53	65	13	16	0	0	15	18
August	94	97	33	34	0	0	34	34

[a] Based on simulations by R.B. Stewart using the Agriculture Canada model. Percent of 1961-1981 average production; all other climatic input was held constant at the 1951-1980 level.

TABLE 4.8a

EFFECT ON AREA CAPABLE OF MATURING BARLEY AND TOTAL
PRODUCTION IN WESTERN CANADA CORRESPONDING TO SEQUENTIAL
MONTHLY TEMPERATURE REDUCTIONS OF -5°C, -3°C, AND -1°C,
RESPECTIVELY, BEGINNING IN THE MONTH INDICATED[a]

MONTH	Manitoba Area	Prod.	Saskatchewan Area	Prod.	Alberta Area	Prod.	Total Area	Prod.
April	100	103	99	104	100	102	100	103
May	100	102	97	102	97	100	97	101
June	94	99	26	28	0	0	22	22
July	94	104	83	94	66	73	76	84
August	94	94	95	93	97	90	96	92

[a] Based on simulations by R.B. Stewart using the Agriculture Canada model. Percent of 1961-1979 average production; all climatic input other than temperature was held constant at the 1951-1980 level.

TABLE 4.8b

EFFECT ON AREA CAPABLE OF MATURING BARLEY AND TOTAL
PRODUCTION IN WESTERN CANADA CORRESPONDING TO SEQUENTIAL
MONTHLY SOLAR INSOLATION AND DAYLENGTH REDUCTIONS OF I.) -22%, -
15%, AND -8%, AND II.) -11%, -8%, AND -3% RESPECTIVELY, BEGINNING IN
THE MONTH INDICATED[a]

A) INSOLATION AND DAYLENGTH (-22%, -15%, -8%)

MONTH	Manitoba Area	Prod.	Saskatchewan Area	Prod.	Alberta Area	Prod.	Total Area	Prod.
April	100	101	100	101	100	98	100	99
May	100	104	100	103	100	102	100	103
June	100	108	97	105	100	105	99	106
July	100	97	99	99	100	96	100	97
August	100	99	100	98	100	96	100	97

B) INSOLATION AND DAYLENGTH (-11%, -8%, -3%)

MONTH	Manitoba Area	Prod.	Saskatchewan Area	Prod.	Alberta Area	Prod.	Total Area	Prod.
April	100	100	100	100	100	98	100	99
May	100	102	100	101	100	99	100	100
June	100	103	100	102	100	101	100	101
July	100	101	100	100	100	98	100	99
August	100	100	100	100	100	98	100	99

[a] Based on simulations by R.B. Stewart using the Agriculture Canada model. Percent of 1961-1981 average production; all other climatic input was held constant at the 1951-1980 level.

TABLE 4.8c

EFFECT ON AREA CAPABLE OF MATURING BARLEY AND TOTAL
PRODUCTION IN WESTERN CANADA CORRESPONDING TO SEQUENTIAL
MONTHLY TEMPERATURE DECREASES OF -5°C, -3°C, AND -1°C AND SOLAR
INSOLATION AND DAYLENGTH REDUCTIONS OF I.) -22%, -15%, AND -8%,
AND II.) -11%, -8% AND -3% RESPECTIVELY, BEGINNING IN THE MONTH
INDICATED[a]

A) INSOLATION AND DAYLENGTH (-22%, -15%, -8%)

Month	Manitoba Area	Manitoba Prod.	Saskatchewan Area	Saskatchewan Prod.	Alberta Area	Alberta Prod.	Total Area	Total Prod.
April	100	103	99	105	100	102	100	103
May	94	97	95	105	90	98	92	100
June	0	0	0	0	0	0	0	0
July	94	100	56	61	60	69	64	71
August	94	94	95	94	97	90	96	92

B) INSOLATION AND DAYLENGTH (-11%, -8%, -3%)

Month	Manitoba Area	Manitoba Prod.	Saskatchewan Area	Saskatchewan Prod.	Alberta Area	Alberta Prod.	Total Area	Total Prod.
April	100	103	99	104	100	102	97	103
May	100	103	95	101	95	99	96	100
June	94	106	12	14	0	0	17	18
July	94	101	68	75	63	71	69	76
August	94	94	95	93	97	90	96	92

[a] Based on simulations by R.B. Stewart using the Agriculture Canada model. Percent of 1961-1981 average production; all other climatic input was held constant at the 1951-1980 level.

4.3.2.5.5 Conclusions from Canadian grain analyses

These simulations suggest the following conclusions:

- Chronic (growing season) reductions in average temperatures of slightly more than 2°C for spring wheat and 4°C for barley would result in the total elimination of those crops from production in Western Canada, irrespective of any changes in light or precipitation.

- The growing season decreases at a rate of 7–10 days per °C decrease in average temperature at the same time that the maturity requirements for wheat and barley are increased by 4–6 days.

- For those areas remaining in crop production, reduced temperatures, if imposed alone, could result in increased yields per hectare in response to reduced soil moisture stress. However, in almost all cases, the area in which crops can mature decreases more substantially than the per hectare yields increase, resulting in a net reduction in total production.

- Analyses of transient episodes indicate high sensitivity to temperature reductions at particular times of initiation of the episode; the specifics of the sensitivity to temperature or light reductions also depend on location.

- There is a high sensitivity to reduction in solar inputs (insolation and daylength) if these exceed a threshold, resulting in no losses at 10% reductions and total losses (depending on timing) at 20% reductions. The light sensitivity apparently relates to having enough hours of daylight for crop maturation;

- Combinations of temperature and light reductions are synergistic, with the combined sensitivities being highly dependent on location and timing of the onset of a climatic perturbation.

These results provide the most convincing evidence thus far of the tremendous potential agricultural consequences from the occurrence of even the milder cases of a nuclear war-induced climatic disturbance. This reflects on the conclusions for the acute period, in that if the acute perturbations occurred in the part of the year immediately after the autumn harvest, we previously were unable to state unequivocally that the following summer's crop would be essentially eliminated, because of not knowing precisely enough from the climatic analysts how long the acute period would last. However, we can now see that relatively mild continued repercussions of climate in the first growing season following a nuclear war could also lead to the substantial or complete loss of crop yields, based on the physical environmental constraints alone (i.e., not considering the effects on the agricultural system itself, discussed later).

4.3.2.6 Soybean Simulation Analyses

Another major crop of particular interest for the effects of nuclear war is soybeans (*Glycine max*); this crop is potentially of enhanced importance after a nuclear war, because its cultivars are self-pollinating inbreds, i.e., not requiring commercial sources for hybrid seed stocks. Soybean is a legume, and therefore does not require nitrogen fertilization. It has high content of both protein and oil, potentially providing a major source of protein in replacement of the potential loss of animal sources.

A physiologically based simulation model was used by Sinclair (1985a) for simulation of a nuclear war-induced climatic perturbation. The model uses climatic information, including daily minimum and maximum temperatures, solar insolation, and precipitation, to calculate carbon and nitrogen accumulation. These elements were apportioned between vegetative tissue and seeds; physiological response is limited by soil moisture stress. The model has been verified against field observations with respect to both seasonal development and total seed yield (Sinclair, 1985b; Muchow and Sinclair, 1985).

The normal temperature values were selected to be representative of the soybean production area in the midwestern United States, based on a sine function fixed with a 180 day freeze-free period, a peak summer average diurnal maximum of 20°C, and a daily range of temperatures set at 12 °C. Perturbed simulations were based on a 2°C, 4°C, or 6°C reduction in the daily maximum and minimum values throughout the growing season. The model simulations began after the unifoliate leaves emerged, and crop growth began 10 days following the attainment of a daily minimum temperature of 10°C (approximately day 40 of the normal simulation), following the physiological evidence that soybeans exhibit a 10°C minimum temperature for most growth processes (Da Moto, 1978). Other temperature thresholds were incorporated into the model; for instance, soybean pods are not formed if the minimum temperature falls below 13°C (Hume and Jackson, 1981), so the simulations were terminated if this condition was met at the critical time. Carbon fixation and nitrogen assimilation rates were set to zero if the minimum temperature fell below 7°C, and the simulations were terminated if temperatures reached 0°C.

Solar inputs were also reduced in these simulations by 10%, 20%, and 30% for the 2°C, 4°C, and 6°C cases, respectively. Moisture stress was simulated by additional runs, in which drought was imposed for either three weeks in July (simulation days 80 to 100) or in August (simulation days 110 to 130); otherwise, the soil was assumed to be fully charged with water. Crop maturation times reflecting different cultivars were imposed in the model at 40 days, 50 days, and 60 days, with 50 days being the normal value.

Results are shown in Table 4.9. For the shortest season crops and a July drought, temperature reductions increased yields, as seen previously in re-

TABLE 4.9

SIMULATION RESULTS OF POTENTIAL SOYBEAN YIELD WHEN SUBJECTED
TO CLIMATIC PERTURBATIONS OF DIFFERING SEVERITIES[a]

	Yield (g m^{-2})			
Drought	Normal	T -2°C	T -4°C	T -6°C
	Termination of Leaf Growth on Day 40			
None	336	304	238[b]	146[c]
July	260	283	236[b]	146[c]
August	310	284	230[b]	144[c]
	Termination of Leaf Growth on Day 50			
None	445	378[b]	265[b]	NPS[d]
July	385	366[b]	265[b]	NPS
August	357	328[b]	250[b]	NPS
	Termination of Leaf Growth on Day 60			
None	556[b]	417[b]	246[c]	NPS
July	525[b]	412[b]	246[c]	NPS
August	415	352[b]	239[c]	NPS

[a] Based on simulations by T. Sinclair.

[b] Crop subjected to temperatures less than 7°C

[c] Crop subjected to end-of-season temperatures less than 0°C.

[d] NPS = No pod set because of temperatures less than 13°C.

sponse to reduced soil moisture stress, since the drought period coincided with the maximum leaf area development and, therefore, the maximum evapotranspiration rates. In all other simulations, yields decreased in response to temperature decreases. The yield reductions in the absence of precipitation changes were 10% to 25% for the different season length cultivars under the 2°C simulation, and 30% to 55% under the 4°C simulation. At 6°C reductions, either the pods did not set or freezing was experienced prior to the end of the required growing season, implying crop loss.

Sinclair (1985a) concluded that soybean production during the acute phase of a nuclear war-caused climatic perturbation would be impossible, and temperatures would have to return to within 4°C of normal for there to be any production at the modelled locations. Having shorter-season cultivars would be necessary for production at those temperatures, so that in double-cropped areas, it might be possible for production to occur in a 4°C temperature reduction scenario if a single crop was grown over the warmest period and if seed sources were available. However, actual yields would be more sensitive than even this shows because of uncertainty in optimal planting time, the possibility of extreme cold events during the growing season, and the loss of subsidies to agriculture, as discussed in a later section.

In a different study, another simulation model was used to examine the effects of climatic perturbations on soybean production. To assess the potential impacts of temperature diverging from normal levels by ±2°C, Curry and Baker (1975) used the SOYMODI model for three sites in the midwestern United States; their model was subject to only limited validation for the three sites. This model is also physiologically based, including plant development factors as functions of the physiological day, analogous to the thermal time of Monteith (1981), i.e., based on the integrated heat units above 10 °C and below 30°C. The results of these simulations, which were not done with the nuclear war-induced climatic disturbances in mind, indicated that a 2°C decrease in average growing season temperatures would reduce yields in the majority of years simulated. Using climatic data from 1971 to 1974 for an Ohio site, Curry and Baker (1975) found reduced yields predicted by SOYMOD I for both a 1°C and a 2°C reduction, except for the simulation based on 1974 climatic data. In this case, yield increases were predicted to result from a 1°C or 2°C decrease in air temperatures because that year was subject to particularly hot conditions; therefore, the response was again seen of soil moisture stress being reduced by lowered temperatures and thereby increasing yields.

These two sets of soybean simulations again reflect the great sensitivity of crops to reductions in temperature. Whereas the Canadian situation was more thoroughly analyzed, it alone is not sufficient evidence of crop sensitivity in warmer agricultural regions. However, the simulations with the soybean models suggest the high vulnerability of warm-climate crops to a reduction in a few degrees of average growing season temperatures. This sensitivity is seen to be even greater for the crop that is of greatest importance to global food supplies, rice, as discussed in the tropical agricultural section later.

4.3.3 Consensus of Temperate Agricultural Workshop

The SCOPE–ENUWAR project convened a workshop at the University of Essex to address the issues associated with the potential effects of nuclear war on the agricultural systems of the Northern mid-latitudes. This workshop focused on agricultural productivity effects in response to acute and chronic scenarios of climatic perturbations. Many of the crops discussed at the workshop were subsequently further analyzed, and the resultant discussions appear in previous sections of this chapter. In the present section is presented a synopsis of expected impacts on temperate agriculture for those crops not previously discussed.

Consideration was given to the major crops and farm animals of the Northern Hemisphere, including tropical and subtropical regions; the latter are reported on in a later section. Crops in marginal areas were distinguished from their counterparts nearer the center of the crop distribution, where crops would presumably have increased resistance to climatic disturbances. For each case, consideration was given to how climatic changes would alter the areas where traditional crops could grow and how the productivity of those crops might alter. No consideration was given to substantial replacement of crops by other crops in the aftermath of a large-scale nuclear war, since it was the consensus of the workshop participants that in the Northern midlatitudes, the area most likely to be directly affected by nuclear devastation, it was unlikely that seed or expertise would be available in the first years after a nuclear war. The group wished to emphasize that the *potentials* for crop growth and production were assessed, but that there are many factors that could combine to ensure that these potentials could not be attained, and that total production of major crops would be but a small fraction of current levels, even under the most benign of climatic disturbances, primarily in response to disruptions in societal systems and subsidies to agriculture, a topic discussed in Section 4.6.

The group concentrated on temperature and precipitation reductions, although the lack of detailed information from the climatic scientists concerning precipitation levels and patterns, temperature variances, atmospheric circulation alterations, and duration of effects limited the discussions. Reductions in insolation were not considered to be of primary importance, except that under relatively small temperature reductions, cold hardiness could interact with reduced light levels; likewise, radiation and air pollutants were considered to be important only for combatant zones, but on a global scale would not be the limiting factor on food productivity.

Tables 4.10 and 4.11 summarize the results of the group evaluations. It was concluded that a nuclear war causing significant climatic perturbations during the period of February to August would probably eliminate any useful crop yields from Northern temperate zones. A nuclear war-induced climatic perturbation after August might produce climatic alterations after the crops had been harvested, but the possibility of continued reduced temperatures the following spring, if they were to occur, would limit potential production the subsequent growing season.

For wheat and barley, the previous discussions apply. In addition, it is felt likely that seasonal average temperatures of 1–2°C below normal are within

TABLE 4.10

CROP AND ANIMAL RESPONSES TO ACUTE CLIMATIC PERTURBATIONS
OCCURRING IN JANUARY

ZONE	
Northern Temperate:	Winter wheat would survive all except extreme temperatures (e.g., -50°C in Canada or U.S.S.R.), especially if snow-covered, but low average temperatures in the growing season would not allow grain to develop except at a few low latitudes (e.g., N. India, N. Africa, Southern U.S., provided that there was adequate rainfall). Yields might also be possible in coastal areas if mean temperatures there were warmer (e.g., W. Europe). Spring sowings of wheat, barley, and maize might be possible, but, except in coastal zones, seasonal mean temperatures would be too low for grain to form. Most crops of these cereals in N. America, U.S.S.R., and China would fail. Rice in Japan and China would fail. Potatoes would produce no yield (e.g., Europe, U.S.S.R.). Rye in E. Europe would survive cold but would fail because of season length. Spring sown soybeans at low latitudes (e.g., Southern U.S.) would have the potential to yield effectively provided that there was adequate rainfall. Grasslands would survive the cold with some leaf damage. Intensively housed animals would not survive failure of mechanical ventilation and feeding. Most healthy adult ruminants would survive the cold outdoors; food and water would be limiting factors for their potential survival. Young animals would die of cold stress. Low light levels could affect the fertility of animals such as sheep.
Tropics:	Rice, maize, sorghum, and millet would be killed if even short cold spells occurred during susceptible stages. Better estimates of temperature means and variations are necessary to improve conclusions. Staple crops of semi-arid zones (millet, sorghum in Africa and India) would fail if rainfall decreased substantially. Maize currently planted at the lower limit of its rainfall requirement ($\approx$500 mm) would also be susceptible to drought (parts of Central Africa, Central and S. America). Tropical grasslands would also be cold sensitive but recovery would be likely when temperatiure and rainfall reached adequate levels. Animals would survive cold periods and their ultimate survival would depend on food availability. Changes in the general circulation, as well as influencing temperature and rainfall, would also modify the range of major migratory pests. Possibilities of more than one crop in a year in the humid tropics would probably be lost.
Southern Hemisphere:	Lack of clear climatic predictions limits the ability to estimate effects.

TABLE 4.11

CROP AND ANIMAL RESPONSES TO ACUTE CLIMATIC PERTURBATIONS
OCCURRING IN JULY

ZONE	
Northern Temperate:	Some winter and spring-sown <u>cereals</u> would have been harvested by July (e.g., in India, China, N. Africa, U.S.), but harvest operations in Canada, U.S.S.R., and W. Europe would be severely affected. Cold and darkness would cause <u>maize</u>, <u>soybeans</u>, <u>potatoes</u>, and <u>rice</u> to fail. Adult ruminants would survive, but young <u>animals</u> and shorn sheep would die of cold. <u>Grasslands</u> would probably be killed by cold although recovery later might occur.
Tropics:	All <u>crops</u> are susceptible to cold. Areas where agriculture is closely linked to timing of monsoon rains (e.g., India, Indonesia) would be strongly affected by alterations in general circulation. Effects in N. tropics would be likely to be more severe than in the January scenario because of the timing of planting of <u>millet</u>, <u>sorghum</u>, and <u>rice</u> in June-July. Multiple crop possibilities in one year in the humid tropics would probably be lost.
Southern Hemisphere:	Cold would lengthen the period for maturation of <u>wheat</u> and <u>maize</u> in Australia, S. Africa, and S. America, and would slow growth of <u>grasslands</u>, but water would be more likely to limit production. <u>Animal</u> production would be limited by food availability, but would not be significantly affected directly by temperature decreases.

the range of natural variation, and any effect on yields to be seen would probably relate to increased yields in response to reduced moisture limitations. However, even that level of temperature reduction would shorten the growing season, based on present temperature variance relationships, while increasing the crop maturation times. At the margins of these grain crops, such as in Canada and the U.S.S.R., this could have a marked effect on potential crop ranges. A reduction of 2°C or more would reduce the area for which wheat could develop by perhaps 50%; a 5°C reduction would adversely affect essentially all wheat-producing regions of the Northern Hemisphere, and grain production everywhere would be extremely low.

Effects of shifts in rainfall patterns could also be considerable. Increases of rainfall in combination with cooler temperatures could lead to increased crop loss to disease; decreased precipitation, of the order of 50%, would lead to substantial crop failures in wheat growing areas of the U.S. and U.S.S.R., where rainfall is already limiting.

Maize production could be difficult because only limited supplies of hybrid seeds would probably be available after a nuclear war, forcing many to use open-pollinated seeds which have increased variation in productivity. For those fields with adapted, pure line seeds, the general response of maize to a chronic climatic alteration would be similar to other grains, with slight increases in yields for 2°C reductions associated with no change in precipitation in many areas, but reduction in productivity in regions nearer the margins of the normal range. Greater temperature reductions, 2°C to 5°C, would decrease yields in virtually all areas, with total crop failures in northern regions, but with high yield potential remaining in the southern extremities.

About 80% of the total potato production annually occurs in Northern Europe and the U.S.S.R. Calculations were performed using a model developed by Ingram and McCloud (1984) for climates in two regions: the Northwest U.S. and the Midlands of England. A 5°C reduction in England was found to result in about a 50% reduction in production, with other physical parameters left unchanged, and 2°C reductions could occur without any major impact. In the U.S.S.R. and Poland, where potatoes grow nearer their temperature limit, it is estimated that a few degrees reduction in temperature would severely reduce production, and that a 5°C reduction would eliminate yields. Because potatoes are vegetatively propagated, it is unlikely that stocks would be available if the previous year's crop were lost in an acute, extreme climatic disturbance following a nuclear war. Potato limitations in North America would likely be more related to reductions in human subsidies than to changes in climatic conditions in a chronic period.

4.4 POTENTIAL VULNERABILITY OF TROPICAL AGRICULTURE

4.4.1 General Considerations

Tropical agroecosystems are vulnerable to the same types of perturbations that could impair temperate agricultural production following a nuclear war. Tropical agriculture, however, requires special consideration because of the unique crops and climates within this region and because of differences in the magnitudes of stresses that would be experienced. Further, the disproportionate fraction of humans surviving the immediate consequences of a large-scale nuclear war would likely be in tropical and subtropical regions.

The following section is primarily based on contributions to, and conclusions of, the agricultural working group of the ENUWAR tropical workshop.

4.4.2 Temperature Stresses

Direct experience of freezing conditions in lowland tropical agroecosystems is very limited. It is possible to predict some of the consequences of temperature reduction for tropical crops based on laboratory determinations of physiological tolerances (Chapter 1), and from records of exposures of tropical plants growing in climates that experience freezing events. The Florida peninsula of the United States is an example of a subtropical region with documented frost events that damage plants of tropical origin. Although freezing occurs at low frequencies in southern Florida, those episodes that do occur are responsible for severe damage to citrus, tropical fruits, and sugar cane. Five major freezing events in Florida between 1977 and 1985 caused huge losses of vegetable crops and fruit, with a period of several years required for recovery of damaged trees (Myers, 1985).

Tropical tree crops would not exhibit the cold acclimation exhibited by Florida citrus trees. Even acclimated plants of the most cold-tolerant varieties are killed by temperatures below $-10°C$ (Davies et al., 1981; Wiltbank and Oswalt, 1983). These cultivars are not grown in tropical regions.

The major tropical and subtropical agricultural plants are quite sensitive to chilling injury, and are killed by brief periods of freezing (Chapter 1). Rice, the principal grain crop in many tropical countries, is damaged by exposures to temperatures as high as $15°C$ during certain phenological-stages (an extensive discussion of rice and climatic stress is found in Section 4.4.6). The tropical workshop group on agricultural effects concluded that climatic events of brief duration, producing minimum daily temperatures of $10°C$ to $15°C$, would substantially reduce yields of most crops grown in the tropics. Additional temperature decreases would eliminate the possibility of producing others. Some cultivars of potato, barley, and rye were considered to be the most cold tolerant, but there are generally grown at high elevations in the tropics.

Temperature decreases throughout the growing season were also considered. Mean temperature reductions between $3°C$ and $10°C$ would cause widespread yield decreases, and could reduce the area of land suitable for certain crops. Brazil is an example of a tropical country that could experience serious perturbations to its agricultural system following a mean temperature decrease of $3°C$. Lopes et al. (1985) considered the production of soybeans, coffee, and sugar cane during the potential climatic alterations for the chronic post-nuclear war period. Based on consideration of current climate-production relationships and limits on these crops, Lopes et al. (1985) calculated that as much as 165 million km^2 would be lost from the area capable of producing these crops.

4.4.3 Vulnerability to Precipitation Stress

Although many weather stations in tropical regions report annual rainfall levels between 2 and 4 meters, precipitation reductions following a nuclear war are a potential problem. Even the wettest regions often exhibit a highly seasonal distribution of precipitation, and altering the initiation and duration of rainy seasons could result in the planting of crops unable to mature. Arid and semi-arid tropical regions are of course particularly vulnerable to decreased precipitation, as evidenced by the poor agricultural production found in the Sahel. Long-term changes in atmospheric and oceanic circulation patterns could lead to impacts as severe as desertification. The climatic changes associated with El Niño events demonstrate the vulnerability of tropical agriculture to even small temporary changes in circulation patterns.

4.4.4 Energy Subsidy Losses

Many tropical countries, particularly those dependent on imports, would experience impaired agricultural production as a result of diminished energy subsidies following a nuclear war. (A more thorough discussion is presented in Section 4.6, and analyses of representative countries are in Chapter 5.) Some of the acute phase disruptions would decrease yields for an extensive time period. Many tropical countries require large inputs of draught animal power for agricultural production. If these animals were consumed as food during an acute-phase crisis, potential crop production would be reduced to that maintained in handpowered agricultural systems. In the seasonal tropics, many of the most important crops are grown during the dry season under irrigation. Shortages of power and maintenance capability for irrigation could cause massive crop failures. Loss of international trade in petroleum products, machinery, and inorganic fertilizers could not be easily compensated for in many tropical countries.

4.4.5 Potentially Ameliorating Factors

Broad geographical and climatic diversity within tropical regions ensure that some type of agriculture would be possible under most of the nuclear war scenarios considered. In regions with high temperatures and precipitation, nuclear war-induced climatic stresses might produce climates similar to sub-tropical or temperate regions. Although productive agriculture would be possible in these regions, matching the correct crops and farming practices to the new climate could be quite difficult. Similarly, transporting seed or rootstock and new cultural knowledge needed for planting and preparing crops from high-elevation or temperate regions to affected tropical farmers could be difficult.

Following climatic shifts, tropical farmers might increase the use of intercropping. Crop failures involving only one species would not be as serious with an intercropping system. It would also be possible to compensate for reduced yields by increasing the land area used for food crops. Many tropical countries use a substantial fraction of their arable land for the production of non-food and export crops (Table 4.12a). This additional land represents a potential for greatly increased food production levels under conditions of adequate temperature and precipitation. Assuming the climate allows any agriculture, flexible responses are possible to these stresses; however, the time lag before successful implementation would be significant, and societal responses could determine the extent of such implementation.

TABLE 4.12a

AREAS UNDER CURRENT PRODUCTION OF SELECTED CROPS

	(x 1,000 ha)[a]		
	Food Crops[b]	Sugar Cane	Export Crops[c]
Brazil	32,851	3,370	10,667
Costa Rica	220	51	1,159
Indonesia	15,431	24,531	13,281
Philippines	7,248	480	4,395

[a] Source: FAO Production Yearbook (1983).
[b] Cereals, pulses, roots and tubers, soybeans.
[c] Coffee, tea, cocoa, bananas, cotton and other fibers, tobacco, hops, coconuts.

TABLE 4.12b

CRITICAL TEMPERATURES FOR RICE DEVELOPMENT[a]

Growth Stage	Minimum	Maximum	Optimum
		Temperatures (°C)	
Germination	16-19	45	18-40
Seedling Emergence	12-25	35	25-30
Rooting	16	35	25-28
Leaf Elongation	7-12	45	31
Tillering	9-16	33	25-31
Panicle Initiation	15	--	--
Panicle Differentiation	15-20	30	--
Anthesis	22	35-36	30-33
Ripening	12-18	>30	20-29

[a] Data from De Datta (1981).

4.4.6 Vulnerability of Rice to Climatic Perturbations

4.4.6.1 General Characteristics of Rice Production

The responses of rice production to the effects of climatic change and other stresses require separate attention because of the important role rice plays in world food balances. More than 4×10^8 metric tons of rice are produced annually (FAO, 1982), and rice currently supplies over one-half the energy requirements and an important part of the protein intake, in the diets of more than a billion people. After a nuclear war, a disproportionate fraction of the survivors would probably exist initially in the areas of current rice production; therefore, if rice could be grown under the post-nuclear war conditions, it would probably provide the major cereal crop for survivors in non-combatant countries. Because of this tremendous potential for human support after a nuclear war, it is necessary to evaluate its particular vulnerability to the environmental perturbations projected to occur.

Rice is currently grown under irrigation and as a rainfed crop. The rainfed upland rice constitutes about 10% of the world production, and rainfed lowland rice another 30% (De Datta, 1981). Irrigated, deepwater, and floating rice constitute 45%, 11%, and 4%, respectively. Paddy rice is the dominant type in the U.S., the U.S.S.R., Japan, China, Egypt, Indonesia, and Southeast Asia; upland rice is common in South America (particularly Argentina, Brazil, Columbia, and Paraguay) and in Africa. However, all of Latin America's areas under rice cultivation are less than Bangladesh's, and West Africa's rice land constitutes only 1.4% of the world's area under rice cultivation (De Datta, 1981). Clearly, Asia's rice production is the most important in terms of area, crop production, and human support.

Climatic conditions largely control rice production. For upland rice crops, such as in West Africa and South America, the amount and annual distribution of precipitation are of critical importance. Because of the lack of adequate irrigation facilities, most of the rice here is grown as a wet-season crop, and no production is possible in other parts of the year. The development of monsoonal rains is the key to crop production in many upland rice regions. In many rice-growing regions, especially in South and Southeast Asia, there is a strong seasonality in precipitation, and rice is grown in the wet season; in these situations, rice production is typically rainfall limited. Rainfall in the dry season is insufficient for rice production, so those times of the year and locations must have irrigation for production of a dry-season crop.

Variability in rainfall is also the primarily controlling factor for rainfed rice in Asia, which constitutes about 80% of the rice grown in that area (De Datta, 1970, 1981). Most of tropical SE Asia receives about 2000 mm of rain per year, which is adequate for one rice crop if the precipitation is evenly distributed over the year; if rainfall is more seasonal, such as monsoonal areas, as little as 1200–1500 mm of rain per year is adequate for a single crop. However, the two largest rice-growing countries in the world, India and China, receive less than this amount of rainfall; in the case of China, almost all rice is grown under irrigation; India often has too little, or too much, rainfall, and crop production is frequently adversely affected. In Thailand, widespread crop failure from either drought or excessive flooding occurred during 8 of the 58 years between 1907 and 1965, and at least 10% of the crop area was not even harvestable in 24 of the 58 years (i.e., over 40% of the time) (Yoshida, 1981).

Variability in the onset of the monsoon season determines the time of planting for transplanted rainfed rice; to reduce the effects of this uncertainty, many farmers hold water in the fields by bunds, with concomitant loss of seedlings and with lodging in the later stages of crop development reducing productivity. If rainfall extremes coincide with critical periods in the rice life cycle, yield reductions can be severe. For upland rice, rainfall variability is even more important than for lowland cultivation, and moisture stress often kills plants that receive large amounts of rain in one day and none for the subsequent few weeks. Varieties of rice that can mature in less than 100 days are an advantage in mitigating the effects of precipitation variability.

The availability of sunlight is also important to rice maturity and yields, although not nearly as critical as precipitation. The correlation between insolation and grain yield in the tropics has been found to be highly significant, especially during the last 30 days of rice growth (De Datta and Zarate, 1970). The amount of insolation received from panicle initiation until the later stages of crop maturation is particularly important (Stansel, 1975; De Datta, 1981).

Of considerable importance to the production of rice in many areas is the temperature regime. Mean growing season temperatures, temperature sums (e.g., degree-days), temperature ranges and extremes, seasonal distribution of temperatures, and diurnal ranges have each been shown to be correlated with rice yields (Moomaw and Vergara, 1965; De Datta, 1981). Critical temperatures for germination, tillering, inflorescence initiation and development, dehiscence, and ripening have been empirically derived (Table 4.12b)(De Datta, 1981). In northern areas, rice is sown when temperatures are low, and the crop begins its growth cycle in a period of rising temperatures; after flowering, maturation occurs during the period of declining temperatures. In lower latitudes, sowing occurs at high temperature periods, with slowly declining levels until maturation; near the equator, little temperature change occurs annually. In tropical regions, slightly lower temperatures during the ripening period increase yields in response to slower ripening and longer time for grain filling (De Datta, 1981).

Growing seasons, and the number of crops per year, vary among countries. In Japan, the growing season typically is May to September. Southern China and Taiwan have two rice crops each year, April to September and October to December. The latter crop in particular is affected by climatic conditions because of the marginality of growing conditions under the climate and variability of that time period. Indonesia is a major example of a location where rice is grown essentially year-round, but here seasonality in precipitation often limits yields. Such continuous cropping countries, more often occurring in tropical regions, are less subject to temperature fluctuations than more northerly latitudes; however, the crops in the tropical regions are more sensitive to those temperature excursions that do occur (Uchijima, pers. comm.).

Cold-temperature injury to rice occurs in many temperate and tropical regions, and rice is clearly more temperature sensitive than the other grains considered in this report. Rice production in northern latitudes in particular is limited by low temperatures; e.g., low rice yields from low temperatures often occur in Korea (Chung, 1979). In California, seedling establishment and vigor have been reduced in response to temperatures under 18°C; sterility has been found following night-time temperatures below 15°C if within two weeks of heading (Rutger and Peterson, 1979).

Japanese rice production provides a substantial data base for estimating temperature effects on rice production, since its crops are frequently reduced considerably in yields because of cool weather. For example, for 25% of the years over the last century in Hokkaido, rice yields have been low because of cool temperatures during the growing season (Satake, 1976), and this district, along with the Tohoku district, frequently suffer yield losses in excess of 50% (Horie, in press). These districts in good years account for 40% of the total Japanese crop. In 1980 as a result of only about a 0.5°C reduction in average temperatures over the growing season, the overall Japanese rice yield averaged about 5,100 kg ha^{-1}, compared to an average yield for the 1974–1976 period of 5,850 kg ha^{-1} (FAO, 1982). In some regions during 1980, the July and August temperatures were reduced by less than 2°C, but one-third reduction in rice yields occurred (Horie, in press). In general, historical data indicate that a 1°C to 2°C decrease in temperatures averaged over the growing season result in rice crop failure, and that any brief temperature excursions below about 15°C would result in the loss of at least one-third of the crop (Uchijima, pers. comm.).

Meiosis is a phase in the rice life cycle that is particularly susceptible to reductions in temperature. Sterility can occur at temperatures falling below 15°C–17°C in the highly cold-tolerant varieties, and 17°C–19°C in the cold-sensitive varieties, a result primarily of injuries occurring in anthesis (Satake, 1976; De Datta, 1981). Cool temperatures can also lead to poor germination, slow growth, stunted growth, delayed heading, incomplete panicle exsertion, prolonged flowering periods because of irregular heading, degeneration of spikes, irregular maturity, and formation of abnormal grains (Kaneda and Beachell, 1974; De Datta, 1981). Often effects that lead to a loss of rice yield will not kill the plant outright, but since rice is an annual rather than a perennial, loss of the grains means that crop will never produce a usable yield.

Sensitivity to temperature varies among the major cultivars of rice. Japonica cultivars are primarily the ones used in Japan and other temperate regions, and the temperature minima listed above relate particularly to this type (Uchijima, pers. comm.). A more tropical cultivar, Indica, grown in SE Asia and India, would have significant yield reductions at temperatures a few degrees higher than those for Japonica (Uchijima, pers. comm.). Javanica rice, grown in Indonesia, is intermediate between the two in temperature sensitivity, but on a global scale its production is not as important as the others.

A final physical effect often limiting to rice production is the presence of winds. A gentle wind improves grain yields by increasing turbulence in the canopy, replenishing the CO_2 supply before it becomes depleted (De Datta, 1981). However, strong winds can dessicate panicles, increasing floret sterility; strong winds enhance certain bacterial leaf diseases; they can dessicate and cause mechanical damage to rice leaves, reducing photosynthetic capability; and, if occurring after heading, strong winds can cause severe lodging and shattering (De Datta, 1981).

4.4.6.2 Potential Vulnerability of Rice to Nuclear War-Induced Climatic Perturbations

In considering the potential impacts of a nuclear war-induced climatic disturbance on rice production in the world, it is clear from the above discussions that brief episodes of subfreezing temperatures during the growing season would kill the rice outright, and even with temperature minima well above freezing, there still would be the loss of the current growing season's crop. In short, it can be stated that during the acute period of a significant nuclear war-caused climatic event, rice production would be essentially eliminated in at least the Northern Hemisphere, and the Southern Hemisphere could experience the same fate, depending on the nature of the temperature excursions in that part of the world.

In the potential climatic disturbances associated with a chronic phase, the effects of temperature reductions would also cause severe or total rice crop loss. Having a mean growing season temperature below 15°C would be expected to preclude rice production (Stansel and Huke, 1975). The critical mean growing season temperature for Japan, below which yields would be reduced, is 19°C–25.5°C, depending on the regional variety of the rice (Uchijima, 1981). These results follow from having insufficient thermal time over the growing season (Uchijima 1981, 1982; Yoshida, 1981), and are in addition to the effects that would result from brief temperature reductions over a day or more during the growing season.

A simulation model has been developed based on dynamic crop-weather relationships using daily solar insolation and temperature data to simulate rice growth and yield (Horie, in press). This model was validated to simulate final crop biomass dry weight and rice yield to within 10% of actual values for most cases of different locations, seasons, and climate. Importantly, the model was found to be accurate in simulating rice production in the northern limits of production in Japan, where annual yield variation is large, and where severe crop losses occur approximately once every three or four years (Horie, in press). Using this model for simulations of reducing temperatures over the growing season by an average of 2°C lead to a loss of 70% of the rice yield in an area calibrated to Sapporo, Japan.

Based on the model and the mechanistic-physiological considerations discussed above, it is concluded that a chronic average decrease in growing season temperatures by 2°C–3°C would likely result in the loss of rice production over the Northern Hemisphere through the combined effect of the loss of thermal time and of the occurrence of cold temperature episodes. The rice-growing areas of the Southern Hemisphere are dominated by upland rice cropping, as noted above. These are the more sensitive to changes in temperature and precipitation. Therefore, those rice-growing areas of lesser climatic perturbations are also the areas of greater sensitivity to such climatic alterations, and would also appear to be vulnerable to the temperature effects of nuclear war.

With respect to the issue of possible reductions in precipitation, in those areas where irrigation systems are sophisticated, such as in Japan, a reduction in precipitation during the chronic period would not result in reductions in rice production because the water stores in the system is sufficient to last a year, especially if water demand were reduced by having a loss of industrial activity. Timing of the nuclear war would be important, e.g., as in the case of Japan, the rains come primarily in June, providing the charging to the water storage system; if the nuclear war were to happen prior to that and if there were a subsequent major reduction in precipitation, insufficient recharging of the s9stem would occur and insufficient water would be available for crop production. Over a longer period, precipitation decreases of 50% or more would be expected to be the point at which the irrigation system would have insufficient water, and crop yields would suffer (Uchijima, pers. comm.). For countries with less sophisticated or non-existent irrigation systems, such as in Africa, reductions in precipitation would translate directly into crop yield losses, as there is essentially no buffer against water loss. Those areas in which rainfed upland rice is grown would also be directly sensitive to reductions in precipitation, and a 50% reduction in precipitation would be expected to reduce yields by an even greater amount (i.e., >50%).

Light reductions would not seem to be significant in causing loss of yields from having too short a photoperiod, as was felt to be the case for other grains, discussed previously. However, prolonged periods of reduced light levels would result in comparable reductions in total rice production, based on the highly significant correlation of grain yields to light levels (De Datta and Zarate, 1970). The effects of light reductions, however, would likely be secondary to the effects of temperature and precipitation reductions.

4.5 POTENTIAL VULNERABILITIES OF EXTRA-TROPICAL SOUTHERN HEMISPHERE AGRICULTURE[1]

4.5.1 Introduction

The potential effects of climatic disturbances following a nuclear war on the agricultural productivity of the Southern Hemisphere was a topic of consideration at the SCOPE–ENUWAR workshop in Melbourne, Australia. As in the case of the ecological effects, the emphasis at this workshop was on extra-tropical Australia and New Zealand as representing the Southern Hemisphere continental and large island situations Those issues associated with tropical agricultural systems are discussed in the section on the tropics (Section 4.4). Those issues associated with temperate agriculture in Africa and South America have not explicitly been addressed, but it was felt among the workshop participants that the situation in southern Africa would most be analogous to Australia.

The projected perturbations to the physical environment in the Southern Hemisphere are substantially different from those projected potentially to occur in the Northern Hemisphere after a Northern Hemisphere nuclear war. This difference relates to several key factors: 1.) isolation from the particulate inputs to the atmosphere from the major fires and dust that would result from nuclear detonations in the Northern Hemisphere; this isolation is because of the spatial separation of the areas and, particularly, because of the limited exchange of the troposphere across the equator; 2.) few, if any, nuclear detonations in the Southern Hemisphere; 3.) much greater expanse of the hemisphere being covered by ocean as opposed to continental areas.

As discussed in Volume I (Pittock et al., 1985), there is an increased assurance from recent atmospheric analyses that the particulate inputs to the atmosphere in the Northern Hemisphere could be elevated to high altitudes, almost irrespective of the initial height of injection of the smoke plumes. This could tend to increase transport into the Southern Hemisphere atmo-

---

[1] This section was written by M.J. Salinger and is primarily based on the biological working group discussions at the Melbourne conference, with input from N. Cherry, H. Hughes, N. Nicholls, B. Pittock, and D. Potter.

sphere because of the much greater exchange across the equator by the stratosphere than by the troposphere. Further, other analyses indicate that for a Northern Hemisphere summer-onset nuclear war, the strong differences in absorptive properties of the Northern Hemisphere atmosphere in the early period after the nuclear war compared to the Southern Hemisphere could establish altered global atmospheric circulation patterns. The current inhibitions against trans-hemispheric transport could be reduced or eliminated, and a new circulation pattern that includes atmospheric circulation extending from the Northern mid-latitudes down to 30°S latitude or so could become established. In this circumstance, climatic perturbations following a summer-onset nuclear war could extend through the tropics of the Southern Hemisphere and perhaps to even more southerly latitudes. Such an atmospheric response would apparently not occur if the nuclear war were to occur in the Northern winter, unless the particulates were to remain in the atmosphere in sufficient quantities so that on the following summer the altered circulation patterns would then become established.

For our purposes, these possibilities suggest that there is a great deal of uncertainty concerning the environmental perturbations that could be experienced in the Southern temperate regions. There also might be an increase in the variance about whatever climatic effects were felt there, in that the boundary of a nuclear war-induced cloud could tend to have periods of obscuration alternating with periods of clearing of the skies. These factors also suggest a particularly strong seasonality effect for the timing of the nuclear war as affecting the Southern Hemisphere environment, more so than for other parts of the Earth. Finally, the predominance of ocean areas in the region would mean lessened intensities of temperature drops, but there might be more effects on precipitation in response to relatively subtle changes in ocean currents and sea-surface temperatures. That the latter substantially controls periods of drought in at least Australia was demonstrated by Nicholls (in press). Because of these uncertainties, the approach taken for the Australian and New Zealand estimations was to consider the sensitivities of these agricultural systems to the various climatic disturbances, rather than concentrate on one or a few specific climatic disturbance scenarios.

The land areas that fall into this region include southern Africa, southern South America, Australia, and New Zealand. The Melbourne, Australia workshop focused discussions on the latter two countries. It is believed that southern Africa's agricultural responses would be similar to those experienced in Australia, but these have not been specifically analyzed. Southern Hemisphere extra-tropical agricultural systems differ from those in comparable latitudes in the Northern Hemisphere by the emphasis placed on pastoral agriculture for meat and wool production. The emphasis is demonstrated by the percentage of agricultural land devoted to this activity. Although grain crops, especially wheat, are important in Argentina and Australia, pastoral farming is still the dominant agricultural activity.

There are several different features of Southern Hemisphere grassland agricultural systems compared with equivalent Northern Hemisphere systems. They are not based upon indigenous species, but largely utilize exotic species that have either been introduced from the Northern Hemisphere or are cultivars that have been selected from breeding programs. Another difference is that in many of the Southern Hemisphere countries (e.g., New Zealand), the pasture swards introduced by the European settlers have replaced the indigenous vegetation, including grassland and bush. On the basis of the above differences of the pastoral ecosystems of the Southern Hemisphere and the specialized management of this system that is practiced, the grassland ecosystems here are considered under agriculture, rather than in the ecosystem chapter. This also recognizes the importance placed on livestock production, a characteristic of agriculture in this hemisphere.

4.5.2 Vulnerabilities to Possible Acute Climatic Effects

Extra-tropical Southern Hemisphere agricultural systems are unlikely to experience severe acute climatic effects according to modelling studies (Volume I). As most of the smoke would be injected in Northern latitudes, the initial circulation state of the atmosphere, where the circulation of both hemispheres only meets in the tropics, prevents any immediate atmospheric effects from spreading rapidly south. However, with the lofting of smoke plumes into the upper troposphere and lower stratosphere, and under favorable circulation, smoke streamers might travel south for short durations and must be considered as possible consequences, especially for the north of this zone (Covey et al., 1984). The incidence of frosts in the growing season (usually September to May, depending on the latitude) could be very damaging to some aspects of agriculture. Such an event, especially at a critical crop growth stage, could decimate the current year's production of frost-sensitive crops. However, the grassland systems which dominate are largely resistant even to such an extreme event.

4.5.3 Vulnerabilities to Potential Chronic Climatic Effects

The greatest potential effects seen for Southern Hemisphere extra-tropical agriculture would be in the chronic time period. In order to evaluate vulnerabilities to a potential chronic climatic disturbance, the effects of a few degree reduction in average temperature (1°, 2°, or 5°C, depending on location), with associated 5–20% reductions in insolation, and the potential for large (up to 50%) reductions in precipitation were considered.

Given that much of Australian rangeland and cereal cropping activities are inland from the coast, the environmental stresses would be akin to that of continental Southern Hemisphere areas. The bulk of agricultural production is from pastoral farming and cereal cropping activities. Several studies are relevant to potential chronic phase stresses. As a first-order investigation of the sensitivity of Australian biological systems to such effects, Pittock and Nix (1985) ran the 'Miami Model' of net primary production for various disturbed climate scenarios. Because the Miami Model uses non-linear regression relationships between mean temperature, annual precipitation, and net primary production at any one place, it assumes that whichever relationship gives the lowest primary production is the limiting factor (Lieth, 1975). Therefore, the model has limitations, discussed below. However, it is still useful in providing indications of responses to stresses lasting through one or more growing seasons.

The results pertinent to this study are the scenarios of 2°C and 5°C temperature reductions with 50% of normal precipitation. As might be expected, the major effects occur in response to a 50% reduction in precipitation. Biomass was predicted to be reduced by 25% in high rainfall zones, 33% in subhumid zones, and 50% in arid zones. Temperature reductions were seen to have very little effect north of 30°S, but a 5°C degree temperature drop could cause up to a 20% reduction in production in the coldest parts of Australia, according to the model.

Production estimates based on the Miami model, as with other regression models, should be used with caution. Although this technique can be used to illustrate the potential sensitivity of an ecosystem type to climatic change, the model does not represent a mechanistic description of physiological processes or vegetation dynamics. The Miami model was developed using data collected from the dominant or "climax" vegetation at a large number of locations. The relationships between geographical variation in annual climate and predicted productivity are not analogous to responses of plants to rapid or severe climatic change. In addition, predictions using normal climatic parameters may be inaccurate at any specific unperturbed location. The Miami model can be used as a first-order approximation of relative sensitivity to climatic change, but it probably underestimates the actual sensitivity of vegetation to the rapid climatic perturbations that could follow a nuclear war.

In another analysis, Harris and Stapper (1985) found it difficult to detect possible effects of climatic change on wheat yields because of inherent variability in yields. However, their methods did not adjust yield data for trends. The workshop discussions identified rainfall as the critical determinant of wheat yield as it is required in the sowing stage in autumn and again during the grain filling period in spring. Other studies support these conclusions. Wigley and Tu (1984) identified precipitation as the main determinant of wheat yields in the inland areas of Western Australia. Such a conclusion is further strengthened by the work of Nicholls (1985a,b). The El Niño–Southern Oscillation phenomenon is an important mode of climatic variation affecting the Australasian region; therefore, inter-annual fluctuations of some Australian crops might be expected to be closely related to this phenomenon. Nicholls demonstrated that total production anomalies of all cereal crops, once allowance is made for trends, is significantly related to an index of the Southern Oscillation index. A typical wheat yield is 1.2 t hectare^{-1}, so anomalies of up to 0.5 t hectare^{-1} represent substantial inter-annual variability in yield. A drought index was further defined by Nicholls, representing rainfall in inland New South Wales, Victoria, and southern Queensland, for June to November. This index had both high correlations with the total value of Australian crop production over a 32-year period ($r = 0.72$) and El Niño–Southern Oscillation indices ($r = -0.76$ for Darwin pressure) over a 47-year period.

A final piece of evidence relating grass growth to aspects of rainfall and water balance comes from New Zealand studies. Maunder (1974) demonstrated that pasture growth over the warm season in New Zealand is determined by precipitation through soil moisture levels.

Therefore, it is reasonable to conclude from all these studies, and because present day Australian agricultural activities are located in climatic zones where temperature reductions would not likely be a significant factor, that nuclear war-induced reduction in precipitation, if that occurred, would be the dominant effect on Australian pastoral and cereal cropping production. Similar conclusions can be extrapolated to South Africa and the northern agricultural areas of Argentina. Depending on what the precipitation reduction would be, the workshop tentatively estimated that grassland and cereal production could drop from between 0 and 50% at the beginning of a chronic phase. Persistence into the chronic phase would cause a further decrease with loss of fertilizer support. If stresses were to last only a year, then production would return to normal, followed by a decline when agricultural systems lost their fertilizer support. However, adaptation would likely occur, and Australia could still be a net food producer, though with dramatically lower production.

In contrast, effects in New Zealand would be more in response to possible temperature reductions in the chronic phase than to possible changes in precipitation. In New Zealand and Tasmania, there are areas which are precipitation limited, and reductions in precipitation would produce proportionate drops in yield. Maunder (1974) demonstrated that monthly dairy production in New Zealand is related to weighted indices of water deficit. However, better understanding of regional airflow is required, because wind direction fundamentally determines topographic precipitation patterns. Temperature effects on productivity would be more important in the chronic phase. If effects are assumed to persist through at least one and possibly more growing seasons, in contrast to the hotter continental climate of Australia where plants are often heat stressed, in the cooler maritime climates of the islands, plants are more often closer to their threshold temperature for growth. Thus, yield is temperature limited and colder temperatures would significantly reduce yields.

This point is illustrated by Salinger (1985) in a study examining the effect of various temperature decrease scenarios on the length and intensity of the New Zealand growing season for various start times. Chronic phase scenarios modelled ranged from a temperature reduction of 3°C for six months, then 1°C for another six months, to a 1°C reduction for twelve months (Table 4.13). For Ruakura, a location typical of agricultural areas in northern New

TABLE 4.13

EFFECT OF DIFFERENT TEMPERATURE SCENARIOS
ON THE GROWING SEASON IN NEW ZEALAND

	SCENARIOS			
	-3°C 6 mo. -1°C 6 mo.	-3°C 3 mo. -1°C 9 mo.	-1°C 12 mo.	-1°C 6 mo.
STARTING TIME				
September	828[a] ••[b,c] 67[d]	1003[a] ••[b,c] 33[d]	1113[a] 40[c] 22[d]	1215[a] 27[c] 17[d]
November	783 •• 80	942 •• 39	1113 40 22	1200 32 13
December	808 •• 44	938 •• 40	1113 40 22	1211 23 10
March	957 •• 15	983 12 14	1113 40 22	1274 3 0
May	977 •• 22	1087 40 14	1113 40 22	1289 6 3
June	977 •• 32	1087 40 14	1113 40 22	1278 9 7

[a] GDD above 10°C. Average during normal climate is 1376 growing degree days (GDD) above 10°C.

[b] •• indicates that the crop would not reach maturity.

[c] Reduction in the growing season (days) for the time period over which crops requiring 1000 GDD would be grown.

[d] Reduction in the growing season (days) for the time period over which crops requiring 700 GDD would be grown.

Zealand, almost 1400 growing degree-days are normally accumulated above 1°C. The largest change scenario gave reductions in growing degree-day accumulations to 800–900. This represents a reduction in growing season length by 3 to 5 weeks for plants requiring 700 growing degree-days to mature. Thus, plants requiring 1000 growing degree-days for maturity would not mature under this scenario. Even the smallest temperature reduction scenario (Table 4.13 and Figure 4.11) gave a reduction in length of the growing season by 1 to 3 weeks.

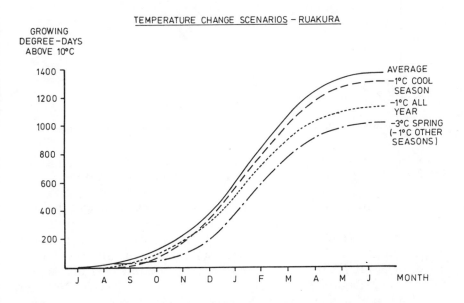

Figure 4.11   Effect of different temperature reduction scenarios at Ruakura, New Zealand, on growing degree-days above 10°C. From Salinger, 1985

This study also demonstrated the significance of timing of the effects of climatic disturbances from a nuclear war. For the 3°C reduction for three months, followed by a 1°C reduction for nine months (Table 4.13 and Figure 4.12), the maximum impact occurred when effects occurred in spring or early summer. In this case, 3 to 4 weeks were lost from the growing season, and many crops would be unable to reach maturity because of insufficient thermal time. However, a war producing such effects in autumn or winter would have much less impact. Warm weather crops would be able to reach maturity, and the reduction in growing season length was predicted to be about two weeks.

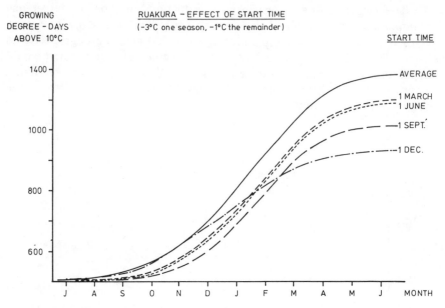

Figure 4.12   Effect of different temperature reduction initiation times at Ruakara, New Zealand, on growing degree-days above 10°C. From Salinger, 1985

Grassland production responds to mean temperature changes, but it is probably not subject to frost damage. Yield reductions can be directly estimated from the results seen from the SPUR grassland model simulations, reported in Chapter 2. The results suggest a reduction in production of C_4 grasses by about 7% per degree decrease in temperature over the range of 0°C–6°C and about a 3% per degree reduction for C_3 grasses. However, in drylands precipitation would also be a significant factor. Lower temperatures and reduced pasture yield would limit livestock carrying capacity. At the present, the summer excess in pasture production is harvested and stored for winter feed (Levy, 1970). This could be lost for at least one season following climatic perturbations from a nuclear war, leading to moderate-to-severe winter livestock feeding problems. Cold stress on newborn lambs, exacerbated by food shortages, could reduce animal numbers.

Effects on New Zealand cropping and horticultural activities are illustrated by growing degree-day reductions for two scenarios calculated by Salinger (1985). In the greater temperature reduction scenario (reductions of 3°C in spring, and 1°C for other seasons), thermal time accumulations would decline by 200 to 470 growing degree-days (Figure 4.12 and Table 4.14). Crops requiring 1000 growing degree-days or more would be unable to reach maturity in much of the North Island, areas where they currently

TABLE 4.14

EFFECT ON GROWING SEASON LENGTH AND
GROWING DEGREE-DAYS OF CHRONIC SCENARIO

	GROWING DEGREE-DAYS(GDD) ABOVE 10°C		REDUCTION IN GROWING SEASON LENGTH (DAYS)	
	Normal	Perturbed[a]	1000 GDD[b]	700 GDD[c]
North Island[d]				
Kerikeri	1441	970	••[e]	25
Tauranga	1215	796	••	27
Ruakura	1003	630	••	••
New Plymouth	916	604	••	••
Gisborne	1183	786	••	27
Havelock North	969	621	••	••
Waingawa	917	691	••	••
Palmerston North	929	564	••	••
Levin	907	539	••	••
South Island				
Appleby	865	530	••	••
Christchurch Airport	781	495	••	••
Blenheim	1066	825	••	17
Ashburton	714	439	••	••
Oamaru	569	319	••	••
Earnscleugh	644	399	••	••
Roxburgh	677	408	••	••
Otautau	381	177	••	••

[a] Scenario 1 includes a 3°C reduction in average temperature during the spring, 1°C reduction for all other seasons.

[b] Reduction in length of growing season for the time period in which 1000 GDD crops are normally grown.

[c] Reduction in length of growing season for the time period in which 700 GDD crops are normally grown.

[d] Locations arranged in order of increasing latitude from north to south.

[e] •• indicates that the crop would be unable to reach maturity under the chronic perturbation because of insufficient GDD.

can mature. For crops requiring only 700 growing degree-days, as is the case for many cereals, maturation would be from 4 to 6 weeks later, and in the south, crops would be unable to reach maturity. In the case of a less severe reduction of 1°C for 12 months, growing season reductions by 2–4 weeks would cause delayed maturation of crops, and some heat-demanding crops would not reach maturity in northern New Zealand. Other considerations are important for cereal crops. Wheat is the main crop grown in the South Island. Frosts during emergence, low temperatures delaying germination, shortening of the growing season, and low temperatures during grain formation all cause severe problems for the production of wheat (and other cereals), with growing season drops of 2°C or more.

Because of the dominant contribution of grasslands, food production in New Zealand could drop by around 20 to 50%, depending on the severity of temperature drop and frost occurrence in New Zealand (with similar declines probable in Tasmania). Since New Zealand agriculture presently supports over twice its population, it would continue to be able to support its present population through the first and subsequent years with such reductions. However, critical to continuing effects would be the length of the chronic phase, an aspect which is of great importance to all the Southern Hemisphere extra-tropical agricultural systems.

4.6 POTENTIAL EFFECTS ON AGRICULTURE OF ALTERATIONS IN HUMAN SUBSIDIES

4.6.1 Introduction

Many agricultural production systems could be altered dramatically or even eliminated for a period of several years following a nuclear war. Possible climatic stresses, the direct effects of nuclear weapon detonations, and the disruption of economic and societal systems would be some of the principal problems in the first post-nuclear war year. In subsequent years, redevelopment of agricultural production in combatant countries, and adjustment of production levels in non-combatant countries, could continue to be affected by climatic disturbances. In addition, agricultrual production could be affected in varying levels of intensity by a reduction of the technological and energy subsdies that could be delivered. Impairment of most of the industrial and transportation systems of major exporting countries, as well as fundamental alterations of the current international economic structure, would likely leave the survivors of a nuclear war with destabilized food production capabilities. The climatic disturbances could cause significant decreases in world-wide agricultural yields, but even with no climatic perturbations, technological simplification and reduced fossil fuel subsidies would lower production levels. The vulnerability of agricultural productivity to technological simplification and reduction of energy subsidies of agriculture is considered in this section as *independent* of any potential climatic stresses.

Agricultural production technologies that depend on high energy inputs are characteristic of developed nations such as Canada, United Kingdom, Australia, and U.S.S.R. In the U.S. about 6% of total energy in the economy is used for food production, about 6% for processing and packaging, and 5% for distribution and preparation. This represents 17% of total U.S. energy, or about 1500 liters (400 gals) of fuel per person annually.

Other agricultural systems, particularly in developing countries, are not nearly so dependent on high energy subsidies for production. On an areal comparison basis, they are not as productive, but their lowered reliance on largely imported subsidies in the form of direct energy inputs, and indirect inputs through manufacture of machinery, fertilizers, and pesticides, renders them less susceptible to large alterations in levels of productivity in the context of post-nuclear war pertubations.

Petroleum refineries, ports, railroad facilities, and oil fields could all be severely damaged in major nuclear war. This destruction would not only impair agricultural production in combatant countries, but also in developing countries that depend on energy imports. In addition to crop production, industrial fishing fleets, food transportation and storage capability, and timber harvesting would be severely affected by the destruction associated with nuclear war. Refrigeration of food could be a limiting factor in combatant countries and countries highly dependent on energy imports.

It is through examination of the various levels and types of subsidies that an interpretation can be made of the relative vulnerabilities of agricultural production systems and crops to the types of disturbances that could be experienced in the aftermath of a large-scale nuclear war.

4.6.2 Fossil Fuel Energy Subsidies of Agricultural Production

The new technologies that have been adopted by agriculture during the last century depend primarily upon fossil energy subsidies. Examination of potential effects of massive alterations in agricultural production systems from the effects of a major nuclear war should focus on how these energy inputs affect current agriculture and, therefore, how vulnerable the system is to disruption of that process.

Direct fossil fuel use and indirect energy subsidies, such as through the production and transportation of fertilizers and pesticides, in particular, are strongly related to the increased agricultural yields experienced during the past 45 years. In developed countries, yields have increased 3- to 4-fold since 1940 and have increased about 2-fold in developing countries.

One of the obvious areas for possible severe disruption in a post-nuclear war agricultural production system would be in the supply of fossil fuel products. These are used currently, in a direct form, to run and lubricate the machinery which aids in the planting, cultivation, and harvesting to produce crops on a large scale. The amount of diesel fuel currently consumed per hectare in raising grain crops in developed countries is approximately 100 liters ha^{-1} (Pimentel, 1985). During the past two decades, liquid fuel inputs have declined somewhat as larger, more energy efficient farm machinery came into use.

In combatant countries, once local centers of supply became depleted, it could be difficult to obtain fuel for agricultural purposes. In non-combatant regions, supplies of fuel which were traditionally imported from the combatant regions would be imperiled; where supplies originated from within a region not directly affected on a large scale by nuclear detonations, availability would be dependent on a number of factors external to the actual agricultural system.

Direct energy subsidies to agricultural production in the form of fuel for use in agricultural machinery are relatively easy to trace. In contrast, the indirect energy subsidies to agricultural production are less visible; they are, however, key factors in the production levels of agriculture which allow the support of the current world population. The energy-intensive agriculture of developed countries is particularly vulnerable to reductions in the level of subsidies available following a nuclear war. Combatant countries suffering direct destruction, as well as other countries dependent on imports from them, would be affected. Widespread yield declines are possible, independent of any potential climatic effects. A detailed analysis of each country or region is required to describe the specific responses and redevelopment potentials (see Chapters 5 and 7).

Though direct fuel inputs to farming in developed countries have fallen somewhat in the last years, fossil enery inputs for farm machinery construction have risen as larger farm equipment is used. Large farm equipment can till, plant, and harvest more efficiently and over larger areas than small equipment. One area of vulnerability for redeveloping agricultural systems would be the continuing availability of equipment and replacement parts, which would be dependent on the availability of energy for use in manufacture and repair, among many other considerations.

The use of fertilizers in crop production is extremely important in determining the levels of productivity in regions to high energy subsidy of agriculture, i.e., largely the developed countries. For example, in 1983, nitrogen application rates for maize grown in the U.S. had reached a high of 152 kg ha^{-1}, typical of developed countries (Table 4.15). Application rates of phosphorus, potassium, and lime were also high, but these inputs do not require as much fossil energy in production as nitrogen. Wheat and rice production also received relatively heavy applications of fertilizers.

TABLE 4.15

ENERGY INPUTS IN U.S. MAIZE PRODUCTION IN 1983[a]

INPUTS	QUANTITY HA^{-1}	KCAL HA^{-1}
Labor	9.88 hr	--------
Machinery	56.1 kg	1,025,781
Fuel	112.3 liters	1,264,798
Manure	1.12 ton	--------
Nitrogen	151.6 kg	3,216,770
Phosphorus	75.2 kg	475,544
Potassium	95.4 kg	241,506
Lime	426.6 kg	134,447
Seeds	21.3	522,850
Insecticides	2.8 kg	301,261
Herbicides	7.9 kg	806,682
Irrigation	--------	2,265,682
Drying	3332.3 kg	664,766
Electricity	99,590 kcal	99,590
Transport	323.3 kg	89,631
TOTAL		11,109,308
OUTPUTS		
Corn Yield	6,539 kg	26,207,214
KCAL OUTPUT/KCAL INPUT = 2.36		

[a] Data from Pimentel (1985).

About 10% of the total energy employed in developed nations' maize production is involved in the use of pesticides (Table 4.15), with slightly lower proportions of pesticides used in wheat and rice production; in all cases, herbicides dominate the pesticide inputs. When maize is harvested as grain directly, it contains 25% to 30% moisture. The maize must be dried and cannot contain more than 13% to 15% moisture before being placed in storage. About 0.7×10^6 kcal of energy is required to dry 6,500 kg of maize (Table 4.15). Harvesting maize as cobs and then drying it in maize cribs by wind or solar energy has been calculated to use 33% less fossil energy than harvesting the maize as grain and drying it using fossil energy (Hudson, 1984).

There has been a steady increase in the application of irrigation water for maize and other grain production in developed countries. The quantity of water used is now slightly more than 2.2×10^6 liters per hectare and requires an energy input of 2.3×10^6 kcal for pumping. During 1945, less than 1% of the maize area was irrigated; now an estimated 18% is irrigated (Table

4.15). Rice production often requires a significant fuel input for moving water. Gravity-fed irrigation systems require less energy for pumping, but do use energy inputs for construction and maintenance.

Although argicultural systems in many developing countries are relatively low levels of indirect fossil fuel subsidies, major production systems of developing countries currently have high input levels. In China, for example, the level of fertilizer application per hectare exceeds the average for developed countries (FAO, 1982). For Indian paddy rice production, more energy can be used in one season for nitrogen fertilizer (2.0×10^6 kcal ha^{-1}) than for human labor and bullock power combined (0.95×10^6 kcal ha^{-1}) (Hameed and Parimanam, 1983).

Rice production in developing countries is often based on energy-intensive inputs, particularly of N-fertilizer, resulting in a doubling of yield since 1950 (Figure 4.13). There is an approximately linear relationship between crop yields and energy (fertilizer) inputs (Greenwood, 1981; Schlichter et

TABLE 4.16

ENERGY INPUTS FOR RICE PRODUCTION IN DAWA COUNTY
LIAONING PROVINCE, CHINA[a]

INPUTS	QUANTITY HA^{-1}	KCAL HA^{-1}
Labor	3,045 hr	--------
Horses	332 hr	1,517,173
Tools	4.50 kg	93,204
Machinery	14.6 kg	263,160
Diesel	72.9 liters	832,195
Electricity	122 kw hr	348,914
Nitrogen	191 kg	2,292,600
Phosphorus	96.7 kg	290,190
Insecticides	0.90 kg	78,219
Herbicides	1.88 kg	187,831
Seeds	164 kg	482,800
Irrigation	184 cm	1,170,013
Transportation	81.1 kg	720,840
TOTAL		7,577,139
OUTPUTS		
Rice Yield	8,094 kg	23,906,477

KCAL OUTPUT/KCAL INPUT = 3.16

[a] Annual average for 1979-1981; data from Wen Dazong and Pimentel (1984).

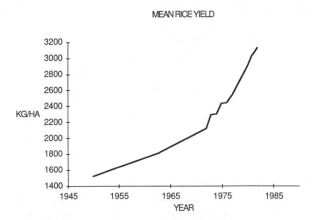

Figure 4.13   Average rice yields (kcal • ha⁻¹) for China, India, the Philippines, and Indonesia. Data from FAO Production Yearbooks, 1950–1983

al., 1985), particularly for low- to intermediate-subsidy levels. Almost one-third of the total world fertilizer consumption occurs in developing countries (Greenwood, 1981). In Central American agriculture, fertilizer inputs account for more than 50% of the energy subsidies, and essentially all of the inorganic fertilizers, pesticides, farm machinery and fuels are imported (Schlichter et al., 1985).

Loss of nitrogen fertilizer would not be immediately catastrophic in areas with fertile soils or a long history of prior fertilization. Simulations of wheat production in the U.K under post-nuclear war climatic alteration conditions indicate that reduced levels of crop growth and nitrogen mineralization rates are expected with temperatures 5°C–10°C lower than normal; under that circumstance, soil nitrogen supplies would be adequate without additional fertilization (Addiscott and Whitmore, 1985). In general, however, the nutrients supplied by unfertilized soild are a small fraction of the requirements for maximum growth, and most arable soils in the world can supply fewer nutrients than soils in the United Kingdom (Greenwood, 1981).

In sum, the current productivity levels of agricultural systems worldwide are heavily dependent on the use of indirect sources of energy, particularly through application of fertilizers and pesticides. Disruption or cessation of such subsidies would force a fundamental alteration in the methodologies of agriculture and the resultant outputs.

4.6.3 Human and Animal Labor Inputs to Production

The use of engine power has made tremendous differences in developed societies as well as elsewhere in the world. This can be illustrated by analyzing the human labor equivalent present in a gallon of fuel. One gallon (3.79 liters) of fuel fed to a small gasoline engine will provide 20% of the heat energy produced in the form of mechanical energy. Thus, from about 31,000 kcal in a gallon of fuel, about 6200 kcal of mechanical energy can be produced. This is the equivalent of about 10 horse power-hours or 100 human power-hours of power (Pimentel and Pimentel, 1979). Thus, 1 gal of gasoline can provide about 2.5 weeks of human power equivalents. This is part of the reason for the dramatic reductions in labor inputs that have occurred in agricultural production in industrialized nations (Pimentel and Wen Dazong, 1985).

With the current heavy mechanization of agriculture in developed countries, the labor input in maize production is about 10 hr per hectare (Table 4.15). This is less than 1% of the input required to produce maize by hand (Pimentel, 1985); however, this does not take into account all the indirect labor inputs that go into agricultural production. If these are taken into consideration, then, for example, current U.S. maize production uses about 2% of the labor input for hand-grown maize. This is still a dramatic reduction in total amount of labor required to produce maize compared with producing maize by hand.

In most industrialized nations today, insufficient human labor exists to subsitute for the tractor power that is present on farms. Even if the human labor were available, this labor is inexperienced in crop agriculture. The most productive agricultural systems would be most vulnerable to the disruptions and energy input losses expected after a nuclear war.

In some countries like China and India, both draft animals and small tractors supplement human labor, though the labor input in these systems is still quite high, ranging from 700 to 1252 hr ha^{-1}, which is similar to some hand-produced maize systems (Pimentel and Pimentel, 1979). Rice is an example of an often labor-intensive agricultural system (e.g., 3,045 hrs ha^{-1} in Liaoning Province, China).

Although most food crops in the world are produced using tractor or draft animal power, a significant quantity of food crops (estimated to be 10%–15%) are produced using only humanpower. Over 90% of the global agricultural labor force is in developing countries (Figure 4.14)(FAO, 1982). The hand labor required to produce a hectare of maize, wheat, and rice crops by hand is approximately 1200 hrs of labor per hectare (Pimentel and Pimentel, 1979). About one-third of the labor is required to till the soil for planting, and about half of the labor is for weeding. The remaining 17–20% is for harvesting. Overall, about 100- to 120-fold more labor is required to produce a grain crop by hand than using heavy mechanization.

The technological and fossil fuel inputs used in hand-powered agriculture are usually a small fraction of the total energy inputs (Tables 4.17, 4.18). Although fertilizer and other subsidies are sometimes used in these systems,

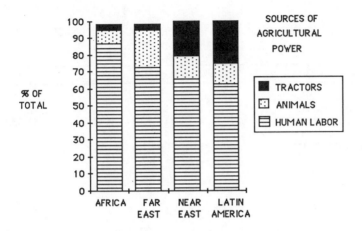

Figure 4.14   Sources of agricultural power (tractors, animals, and human labor). Data from FAO, 1982a

TABLE 4.17

ENERGY INPUTS FOR RICE PRODUCTION BY THE IBAN OF BORNEO USING ONLY HUMANPOWER[a]

INPUTS	QUANTITY HA^{-1}	KCAL HA^{-1}
Labor	1,186 hr	-------
Axe and hoe	16,570 kcal	16,570
Seeds	108 kg	392,040
TOTAL		408,610
OUTPUTS		
Rice Yield	2,016 kg	7,318,080
KCAL OUTPUT/KCAL INPUT = 17.91		

[a] Data from Pimentel and Pimentel (1979).

TABLE 4.18

ENERGY INPUTS FOR MAIZE PRODUCTION IN NIGERIA
USING ONLY HUMANPOWER[a]

INPUTS	QUANTITY HA^{-1}	KCAL HA^{-1}
Labor	620 hr	-------
Axe and hoe	16,570 kcal	16,570
Nitrogen	11 kg	161,700
Phosphorus	4 kg	12,000
Potassium	6 kg	9,600
Seeds	10.4 kg	36,608
OUTPUTS		
Corn Yield	1,004 kg	3,564,200
KCAL OUTPUT/KCAL INPUT = 15.07		

[a] Data from Pimentel and Pimentel (1979).

the quantities are minimal and relatively little yield reduction would occur
if these were removed.

4.6.4 Veterinary Subsidies

Many countries rely on imported veterinary expertise and supplies or imported feedstocks for domestic production of medicines. The direct effects
of a nuclear war, and the associated disruptions in societal systems and the
physical environment, could be expected to reduce severely the supplies and
availability of critical veterinary support.

As an example of the potential vulnerability of loss of veterinary support, consider the case in Africa of rinderpest, a potentially devastating disease of livestock. This disease is currently under substantial control through
the institution of an intensive inoculation program (McNaughton, 1985).
However, prior to the use of attenuated-virus inoculations in the extensive program initiated in mid-1960s, rinderpest virtually eliminated pastoral
agriculture throughout the Serengeti plains. Rinderpest continues to remain
endemic in many wild animal species of the Serengeti (McNaughton, 1985),
and there thus remains a serious vulnerability to large-scale losses from this
disease in the instance of loss of veterinary support.

It seems highly likely that many other diseases that currently are well
controlled by intensive veterinary regimes also offer high vulnerability to
loss of such support.

4.6.5 Conclusions

Considerable quantitative and qualitative changes in energy dependence have evolved over the period of modern agricultural development. Clearly, without the technological inputs of diesel and gasoline fuel, fertilizers, pesticides, and hybrid seed, agriculture in both developed and developing countries would be severely altered. Technologies in developed countries would suffer disproportionately more because they are more sophisticated and are more heavily dependent on fossil fuels than the technologies in developing countries. In developed countries, about 1000 liters of oil equivalents are used to raise one hectare of food, whereas in a developing country employing primarily hand labor, only about 10 liters of fuel per hectare are used. Labor inputs for grain production in developed countries average about 10 hours ha^{-1}, but in developing countries it often averages 1200 hours ha^{-1} for hand-produced grain.

Considering *only* the perturbations of the disruption or severing of supplies of fuel and fuel-based agricultural subsidies, it is clear that agricultural systems in countries that currently experience high levels of energy inputs would be extremely vulnerable to such perturbations. Their adaptability over the long run would be variable in different situations and would depend on many factors, including the suitability of the soil type to different types of crops and different methods of cultivation, the availability of different types of seeds in response to altered agricultural methodologies, and the availability and efficacy of draft animal and human labor to replace machines and methodologies when there would not be adequate energy inputs to maintain prior production activities.

In areas of the world that would not have their supplies and sources of energy destroyed or severely impaired, agricultural production could continue to be subsidized by fuel and fuel-produced applications. In those regions that are not now heavily dependent on high energy subsidies, agricultural practices could revert to prior methodologies, though with a concomitant lowering of productivity. It seems clear that both of the latter areas would be less vulnerable to the loss of human subsidies to agriculture than would energy-intensive combatant countries.

APPENDIX

Model Descriptions

4A.1 Canadian Wheat and Barley Model

The model used to analyze the effects on yields of wheat and barley in Canada was developed initially by FAO (1978) and later modified by Stewart

(1981) for Canadian conditions; it is currently implemented at Agriculture Canada under the guidance of R.B. Stewart. This model is based on the de Wit (1965) methodology for estimating net biomass production under optimum management practices. Input data include monthly averages of temperatures, precipitation, solar insolation, wind speed, and vapor pressure. A photosynthesis equation describes constraint-free yields, i.e., yields under optimal conditions, with a sigmoidal cumulative growth curve incremented up to the number of days required for the crop to mature. Net biomass production is calculated by taking into account the gross biomass production capacity of the crop as influenced by this temperature- and insolation-dependent photosynthesis term, subtracting the respiration losses resulting from another temperature-dependent function. This relationship is:

$$B_n = 0.36 B_{gm}(1/N + 0.25 C_T)^{-1} \qquad (4A.1)$$

where:

B_n = net biomass production

B_{gm} = gross biomass production

N = number of days required for the crop to mature

C_T = maintenance respiration coefficient

The value for N was based on the biometeorological time scale (Robertson, 1968), and C_T follows an expression developed by McCree (1974). Crop dry matter yield is then derived as:

$$B_y = B_n H_i \qquad (4A.2)$$

where:

B_y = crop dry matter yield

H_i = harvest index.

The harvest index is defined as that fraction of the net biomass production that is economically useful. Here H_i is based on Major and Hamman (1981), who calculated the index for Neepawa wheat at a location in Alberta, Canada. They found that H_i is inversely related to moisture availability, such that under moisture-limiting conditions, a greater percentage of the biomass is converted into yield than under moist conditions. In the current simulations, the moisture stress was indicated by the ratio of actual evapotranspiration to potential evapotranspiration (AET/PET) (calculated as outlined in Stewart, 1981), and the value for H_i was set as follows:

If (AET/PET) $\geq$ 0.75, then H_i = 0.35; if (AET/PET) $\leq$ 0.36, then H_i = 0.52; for (AET/PET) between the two limits, a linear interpolation of H_i was done between 0.35 and 0.52.

Values of B_y computed by equation 4A.2 are for constraint-free (i.e., genetic potential) yields, neglecting the effects of physical stresses, presence of weeds or pests, field condition, etc. For this study, correction was made for a moisture-stress yield reduction factor:

$$B_{ye} = B_y \text{MSF} \tag{4A.3}$$

where:

$$B_{ye} = \text{estimated dry matter biomass corrected for}$$
$$\text{moisture stress}$$
$$\text{MSF} = \text{moisture stress factor.}$$

This factor was derived using an expression relating the relative yield decreases to relative evapotranspiration deficit as:

$$Y_a = Y_p(1 - K_y(1 - \text{AET}/\text{PET})) = Y_p\text{MSF} \tag{4A.4}$$

where:

$$Y_a = \text{actual yield}$$
$$Y_p = \text{potential yield}$$
$$K_y = \text{empirically derived crop yield response factor to moisture}$$
$$\text{deficits} = 1.10 \text{ (based on Doorenbos and Kassram, 1979).}$$

The planting date is defined as the date at which the mean minimum temperature exceeds 5°C, representing the average date (50% probability) for the last spring killing frost calculated by the technique of Sly and Coligado (1974) from the 30-yr climatic normals data (Atmospheric Environment Service, 1982). After the planting date, the biometeorological time scale of Robertson (1968) was used to estimate the length of time required to reach maturity based on minimum and maximum air temperatures and daylength.

The climatic data were based on the record for 1951–1980, computed as monthly averages for the crop districts of three western provinces, using the procedure of Stewart (1981). Daily information for all climatic parameters except precipitation were generated from these monthly data by the technique of Brooks (1943). Precipitation data were converted to weekly averages, distributed as 60%, 30%, and 10%, respectively, for the first three days of the week, with none thereafter.

The model was validated against the data of Major and Hamman (1981) and Onofrei (pers. comm.) for seven locations in Manitoba and Alberta;

predicted results were generally within 15% of actual yields. It should be reemphasized that the model results are for optimal conditions, not for those conditions actually experienced commercially; therefore, the results are normalized to the average yields reported for 1961–1980.

REFERENCES

ACDA. (1979). *Effects of Nuclear War.* U.S. Arms Control and Disarmament Agency, Washington, D.C.: 26 pages.

Addiscott, T.M., and Whitmore, A.P. (1985). *Possible effects of long term change in rainfall and soil temperature on soil mineral nitrogen and growth and nitrogen uptake by winter wheat.* Presented at SCOPE–ENUWAR Agricultural Workshop, Essex, U.K. Unpublished manuscript.

Atmospheric Environment Service. (1982). *Canadian Climate Normals 1951–1980.* Vol. 1–6. Environment Canada, Downsview, Ontario.

Ayers, R. (1965). *Environmental Effects of Nuclear Weapons.* Parts I, II, III. HI-518-RR. Hudson Research Institute, Harmon-on-Hudson, NY.

Bensen, D., and Sparrow, A. (Eds.). (1971). *Survival of Food Crops and Livestock in the Event of Nuclear War.* U.S. Atomic Energy Commission, Washington, D.C.: 754 pages.

Bergthorsson, Pall. (1985). Sensitivity of Icelandic agriculture to climatic variations. *Climatic Change,* **7**, 111–127.

Björnsson, H., and Helgadottir, A. (1984). *Climatic variability and grass growth: An experimental approach.* Discussion paper at IIASA Task Force Meeting, Assessment of Climatic Impacts on Agriculture and Forestry in High-Latitude Regions, April, 1984, Laxenburg, Austria.

Bollman, F. and Hellyer, G. (1974). *The economic consequences of projected temperature changes in climatically sensitive wheat-growing areas of the Canadian prairie.* Development and Resources Corp., Sacramento, California.

Brooks, C.E.P. (1943). Interpolation tables for daily values of meteorological elements. *Quart. J. Roy. Met. Soc.,* 69(300), 160–162.

Brown, S.L., and Pilz, U.F. (1969). *U.S. Agriculture: Potential Vulnerability to Nuclear War.* Stanford Research Institute, Prepared for the U.S. Defense Civil Preparedness Agency, Washington, D.C.

Brown, S.L., Lee, H., Mackin, J.L., and Moll. K.D. (1973). *Agricultural Vulnerability to Nuclear War.* Stanford Research Institute, Prepared for the U.S. Defense Civil Preparedness Agency, Washington, D.C.

Budyko, M.I. (1982). *The Earth's Climate: Past and Future.* Academic Press, New York.

Chung, G.S. (1979). The rice tolerance program in Korea. In *International Rice Research Institute. Report of a Rice Cold Tolerance Workshop.* Los Baños, Philippines.

Clark, J.A. (1985a). *Agricultural effects of nuclear winter.* Discussion paper for the SCOPE–ENUWAR Workshop on Temperate Agricultural Effects of Nuclear War, Essex, U.K.

Clark, W.C. (1985b). Scales of climatic impact. *Climatic Change.* **7**. 5–27.

Covey, C., Schneider, S.H., and Thompson. S.L. (1984). Global atmospheric effects of massive smoke injections from a nuclear war: Results from general circulation model simulations. *Nature,* **308**, 21–25.

Curry, R.B., and Baker, C.H. (1975). Climatic change as it affects soybean growth and development. In *Impacts of Climatic Change on the Biosphere*. U.S. Department of Transportation, Washington, D.C.

Dale, R.F., Holtan, H.N., Jensen, R.E., Ramirez, J.M., and Ritchie, J.T. (1975). Interpretation of induced climatic variables. In *Impacts of Climatic Change on the Biosphere*. U.S. Department of Transportation, Washington, D.C.

Da Moto, F.S. (1978). *Soya Bean and Weather*. World Meteorological Organization Tech. Note No. 160, Geneva, Switzerland.

Davies, F.S., Buchanan, D.W., and Anderson, J.A. (1981). Water stress and cold hardiness in field-grown citrus. *J. Amer. Soc. Hort. Sci.*, **106**, 197–200.

De Datta, S.K. (1970). The environment of rice production in tropical Asia. In *Rice Production Manual*, University of the Philippines College of Agriculture, Los Baños.

De Datta, S.K. (1981). *Principles and Practices of Rice Production*. John Wiley & Sons, New York.

De Datta, S.K., and Zarate, P.M. (1970). Environmental conditions affecting growth characteristics, nitrogen response and grain yield of tropical rice. *Biometeorology*. **4**, 71–89.

de Wit, C.T. (1965). Photosynthesis of Leaf Canopies. *Agricultural Research Report 663*, Center for Agricultural Publications, Wageningen.

Doorenbos, J., and Kassam, A.H. (1979). *Yield Response to Water*. Food and Agriculture Organization, Rome, Italy.

Ehrlich, P.R., Harte, J., Harwell, M.A., Raven, P.H., Sagan, C., Woodwell, G.M., Berry, J., Ayensu, E.S., Ehrlich, A.H., Eisner, T., Gould, S.J., Grover, H.D., Herrera, R., May, R.M., Mayr, E., McKay, C.P., Mooney, H.A., Myers, N., Pimentel, D., and Teal, J.M. (1983). Long-term biological consequences of nuclear war. *Science*, **222**, 1293–1300.

FAO. (1978). Report on the Agro-Ecological Zones Project: Vol. 1. Methodology and Results for Africa. *World Resources Report 48*, Food and Agriculture Organization, Rome, Italy: 158 pages.

FAO. (1982). *FAO Production Yearbook*. Food and Agriculture Division, United Nations, Rome, Italy.

FAO. (1983). *FAO Production Yearbook*. Food and Agriculture Division, United Nations, Rome, Italy.

FEMA. (1982). *Food Vulnerability Briefing*. Unpublished briefing of the U.S. Cabinet Council by the Federal Emergency Management Agency, Washington, D.C.

Greenwood, D.J. (1981). Fertilizer use and food production: World scene. *Fertilizer Research*, **2**, 33–51

Haaland, C.M., Chester, C.V., and Wigner, E.P. (1976). *Survival of the Relocated Population of the U.S. After a Nuclear Attack*. ORNL-5041, U.S. Defense Preparedness Agency, Washington, D.C.

Hameed, P.S., and Parimanam, M. (1983). Energetics of paddy production in Tamilnada. *Tropical Ecology*, **24**, 29–32

Harris, C.H., and Stapper, M. (1985). *Assessment of climatic impact on Australian wheat yields*. Unpublished manuscript contributed to SCOPE-ENUWAR.

Harwell, M.A. (1984). *Nuclear Winter: The Human and Environmental Consequences of Nuclear War*. Springer-Verlag, New York: 179 pages.

Hill, G., and Gardiner, P. (1979). *Managing the U.S. Economy in a Post-Attack Environment*. Federal Emergency Management Agency, Washington, D.C.

Hjort, H.W. (1982). The impact on global food supplies. *Ambio*, **11**(2–3), 153–157.

Hjort, H.W. (1984). The good Earth: Agricultural productivity after nuclear war.

In Leaning, J., and Keyes, L. (Eds.). 231–246. *The Counterfeit Ark.* Ballinger, Cambridge, Massachusetts.

Horie, T. (in press). Simulated rice yields under changing climatic conditions. In Parry, M.L. (Ed.). *Assessment of Climatic Impact on Agriculture in High Latitude Regions.* D. Reidel Publishing Co., Dordrecht, The Netherlands.

Hudson, W.J. (1984). Biomass, energy and food–conflicts? In Pimentel, D., and Hall, C.W. (Eds.) *Food and Energy Resources.* 207–236. Academic Press, New York.

Hume, D.J., and Jackson, K.H. (1981). Pod formation in soybeans at low temperatures. *Crop Sci.,* **21,** 933–937.

IIASA. (1981). *Life on a Warmer Earth. Possible Climatic Consequences of Man-Made Global Warming.* International Institute for Applied Systems Analysis, Laxenburg, Austria: 66 pages.

Ingram, K.T., and McCloud, D.E. (1984). Simulation of potato crop growth and development. *Crop Science,* **24,** 21–27.

Kaneda, C., and Beachell, H.M. (1974). Response of indica-japonica rice hybrids to low temperatures. *SABRAO J.,* **6,** 17–32.

Katz, A. (1982). *Life After Nuclear War—The Economic and Social Impacts on the United States.* Ballinger, Cambridge, Massachusetts: 422 pages.

Katz, R.W. (1977). Assessing the impact of climatic change on food production. *Climatic Change,* **1,** 85–96.

Lieth, H. (1975). Modeling the primary productivity of the world. In Leith, H., and Whittaker, R.H. (Eds.). *Primary Productivity of the Biosphere.* Springer-Verlag, New York.

Levy, E.B. (1970). *Grasslands of New Zealand.* 3rd ed. Government Printer, Wellington: 374 pages.

Lewis, K.N. (1979). The prompt and delayed effects of nuclear war. *Sci. Amer.,* **241,** 35–47.

Lopes, E.S., Pedro, Jr., M.J., and Alfonsi, R.R. (1985). *Effects of nuclear winter on some tropical crops in Brasil.* Presented at SCOPE–ENUWAR Tropical Agricultural Workshop, Caracas, Venezuela. Unpublished manuscript.

Major, D.J., and Hamman, W.M. (1981). Comparison of sorghum with wheat and barley grown on dry land. *Can. J. Plant Sci.,* **61,** 37–43.

Maunder, W.J. (1974). The prediction of monthly dairy production in New Zealand through the use of weighted weather indices of water deficit. *New Zealand Meteorological Service Tech. Note No. 277:* 1–7. New Zealand Met. Service, Wellington.

McCree, K.J. (1974). Equations for the rate of dark respiration of white clover and grain sorghum, as functions of dry weight, photosynthetic rate and temperature. *Crop. Sci.,* **14,** 509–514.

McNaughton, S.J. (1985). *The propagation of disturbances through grassland food webs.* Unpublished manuscript contributed to SCOPE–ENUWAR.

Mearns, L.O., Katz, R.W., and Schneider, S.H. (1985). Extreme high temperature events: Changes in their probabilities with changes in mean temperature. *J. Climatology and Applied Meteorology,* (in press).

Montieth, J.L. (1981). Climatic variation and the growth of crops. *Quart. J. Roy. Met. Soc.,* **107,** 749–774.

Moomaw, J.C., and Vergara, B.S. (1965). The environment of tropical rice production. In *International Rice Research Institute. The Mineral Nutrition of the Rice Plant.* The Johns Hopkins Press, Baltimore, Maryland.

Muchow, R.C., and Sinclair, T.R. (1985). Water and nitrogen limitations in soybean grain production. II. Field and model analyses. (Submitted to *Agronomy J.*).

Myers, R.L. (1985). *Florida's freezes: An analog of short-duration nuclear winter events in the tropics.* Presented at SCOPE–ENUWAR Tropical Agricultural Workshop, Caracas, Venezuela. Unpublished manuscript.

NAS. (1975). *Long-Term Worldwide Effects of Multiple Nuclear-Weapons Detonations.* National Academy of Sciences, Washington, D.C.: 213 pages.

NRC. (1985). *The Effects on the Atmosphere of a Major Nuclear Exchange.* National Academy Press, Washington, D.C.: 193 pages.

Nicholls, N. (1985a). Impact of the Southern Oscillation on Australian crops. *Journal of Climatology,* **5**.

Nicholls, N. (1985b). Towards the prediction of major Australian droughts. *Australian Meteorological Magazine,* (in press).

Oliver, J.E. (1973). *Climate and Man's Environment.* John Wiley & Sons, New York: 517 pages.

OTA. (1979). *The Effects of Nuclear War.* U.S. Congress, Office of Technology Assessment, Washington, D.C.

Parry, M.L. (1985). Estimating the sensitivity of natural ecosystems and agriculture to climatic change—guest editorial. *Climatic Change,* **7**, 1–3.

Parry, M.L., and Carter, T.R. (1985). The effect of climatic variations on agricultural risk. *Climatic Change,* **7**, 95–110.

Parker, G. (1980). *Europe in Crisis 1598–1648.* Harvester Press, Ltd., Sussex, U.K.

Petterssen, S. (1969). *Introduction to Meteorology.* McGraw-Hill, New York.

Pimentel, D. (1985). *Technological changes in agricultural production after a nuclear war.* Unpublished manuscript contributed to SCOPE–ENUWAR.

Pimentel, D., and Wen Dazong (1985). *Technical changes in energy use in U.S. agricultural production.* Unpublished manuscript.

Pimentel, D., and Pimentel, M. (1979). *Food, Energy and Society.* Edward Arnold Ltd., London: 165 pages.

Pittock, A.B., Ackerman, T.A., Crutzen, P., MacCracken, M., Shapiro, C., and Turco, R.P. (1985). *The Environmental Consequences of Nuclear War.* Volume I: Physical. SCOPE 28a. John Wiley & Sons, Chichester.

Pittock, A.B., and Nix, H. (1985). Effects of nuclear winter scenarios on Australian biomass productivity. (Abstr.). *Abstracts, Australia and New Zealand Environmental Effects of Nuclear War Workshop,* Melbourne, Australia.

Post, J.D. (1977). *The Last Great Subsistence Crisis in the Western World.* Johns Hopkins University Press, Baltimore, Maryland.

Robertson, G.W. (1968). A biometeorological time scale for a cereal crop involving day and night temperatures and photoperiod. *International Journal of Biometeorology,* **2**, 191–223.

Rudloff, W. (1981). *World-Climates with Tables of Climatic Data and Practical Suggestions.* Wissenschaftliche Verlagsgellschaft, Stuttgart: 632 pages.

Rutger, J.N., and Peterson, M.L. (1979). Cold tolerance of rice in California. In *International Rice Research Institute. Report of a Rice Cold Tolerance Workshop.* Los Baños, Philippines.

Salinger, M.J. (1985). Nuclear winter: Scenarios of impacts on the New Zealand growing season. (Abstr.). *Abstracts, Australia and New Zealand Environmental Effects of Nuclear War Workshop,* Melbourne, Australia.

Satake, T. (1976). Sterile-type cool injury in paddy rice plants. In *International Rice Research Institute. Climate and Rice.* Los Baños, Philippines.

Schlichter, T., Hall, C.A.S., Bolanos, A., and Palmieri, V. (1985). *Energy and Central American agriculture: Analysis for Costa Rica and possibilities for regional independence.* Unpublished manuscript.

Sinclair, T.R. (1985a). *Soybean production during a nuclear winter.* Unpublished manuscript.

Sinclair, T.R. (1985b). Water and nitrogen limitations in soybean grain production. I. Model development. (Submitted to *Agronomy J.*).

Sly, W.K., and Coligado, M.C. (1974). Agroclimatic Maps for Canada Derived Data: Moisture and Critical Temperatures Near Freezing. *Tech. Bull. No. 81*, Research Branch, Agriculture Canada, Ottawa: 31 pages.

Stansel, J.W. (1975). Effective utilization of sunlight. In *Six Decades of Rice Research in Texas.* Texas Agricultural Experiment Station Res. Monogr. 4.

Stansel, J., and Huke, R.E. (1975). Rice. In *Impacts of Climatic Change on the Biosphere.* U.S. Department of Transportation, Washington, D.C.

Stewart, R.B. (1981). Modeling Methodology for Assessing Crop Production Potentials in Canada. *Tech. Bull. No. 96*, Research Branch, Agriculture Canada, Ottawa: 29 pages.

Stewart, R.B., and Stewart, D.W. (1984). *Two methods for evaluating the impact of climate change on spring wheat production in Saskatchewan.* Discussion paper at IIASA Task Force Meeting, Assessment of Climatic Impacts on Agriculture and Forestry in High-Latitude Regions, April, 1984, Laxenburg, Austria.

Stewart, R.B. (1985). *The impact of climatic cooling on spring wheat and barley production in Western Canada.* Unpublished manuscript contributed to SCOPE–ENUWAR.

Stommel, H., and Stommel, E. (1979). The year without a summer. *Sci. Amer.*, **240**, 176–183.

Thompson, L.M. (1969a). Weather and technology in the production of corn in the U.S. corn belt. *Agronomy J.*, **61**, 453–456.

Thompson, L.M. (1969b). Weather and technology in the production of wheat in the United States. *J. Soil Water Conserv.*, **24**, 219–224.

Thompson, L.M. (1970). Weather and technology in the production of soybeans in the central United States. *Agronomy J.*, **62**, 232–238.

Thompson, L.M. (1975). Weather variability, climatic change, and grain production. *Science*, **188**, 535–541.

Uchijima, Z. (1981). Yield variability of crops in Japan. *Geo. Journal*, **5**, 151–164.

Uchijima, Z. (1982). Microclimate and rice production. *Korean J. Crop Sci.*, **27**, 314–339.

UN. (1968). *Effects of the Possible Use of Nuclear Weapons and the Security and Economic Implications for States of the Acquisition and Further Development of These Weapons.* United Nations, New York: 76 pages.

UN. (1979). *The Effects of Weapons on Ecosystems.* United Nations Environment Programme, New York: 70 pages.

UN. (1980). *Nuclear Weapons.* Autumn Press, Brookline, Massachusetts: 223 pages.

UN. (1981). *Comprehensive Study on Nuclear Weapons.* United Nations, New York: 172 pages.

U.S. Department of Transportation. (1975). *Impacts of Climatic Change on the Biosphere.* U.S. Department of Transportation, Washington, D.C.

Warrick, R. (1985). *Assessing the agricultural impacts of nuclear winter.* Unpublished manuscript contributed to SCOPE–ENUWAR.

Wen Dazong, and Pimentel, D. (1984). Energy inputs in agricultural systems of China. *Agriculture, Ecosystems and Environment*, **11**, 29–35.

Wigley, T.M.L., and Tu, Q. (1983). Crop climate modeling using spatial patterns of yield and climate. 1. Background and an example from Australia. *Journal of Climate and Applied Meteorology*, **22**, 1831–1841.

Wiltbank, W.J., and Oswalt, T.W. (1983). Laboratory determination of the killing temperature of citrus leaves during the 1981–1982 and 1982–1983 low temperature periods. *Proc. Florida State Hort. Soc.,* **96**, 31–34.

Woodwell, G.W. (Ed.). (1963). *The Ecological Effects of Nuclear War.* Brookhaven National Laboratory BNL-917 (C-43). NTIS, Springfield, Virginia.

Yoshida, S. (1981). *Fundamentals of Rice Crop Science.* International Rice Research Institute. Los Baños, Philippines.

PART III

Human Effects

Part III concentrates on the human effects of a major nuclear war. Chapter 5 delineates the current food stores in a number of countries and discusses the vulnerabilities of food supplies to decreases in agricultural production and loss of food imports. Chapter 6 examines historical information on effects of the detonations on Hiroshima and Nagasaki and describes an extrapolation of those effects to quantify the consequences of a 1 MT detonation on a city such as Hiroshima. Comparisons with effects of other major natural disasters are examined. Chapter 7 synthesizes and integrates all of the information from Volume II to describe the consequences to human survivors of a world after nuclear war.

Environmental Consequences of Nuclear War Volume II:
Ecological and Agricultural Effects
Edited by M.A. Harwell and T.C. Hutchinson
© 1985 SCOPE. Published by John Wiley & Sons Ltd

CHAPTER 5
Food Availability After Nuclear War

WENDELL P. CROPPER, JR. AND MARK A. HARWELL

Additional Contributions by : C. C. Harwell

5.1 INTRODUCTION

Many studies have been published describing the potential consequences of nuclear war on scales spanning local to global effects. Most of these analyses have concentrated on the immediate and short-term effects of blast, fire, and fallout. There is no doubt that a large-scale nuclear war would produce unprecedented and disastrous death and destruction from such effects. It has not been clear, however, that the consequences of nuclear war would be equally disastrous for several billion survivors in non-combatant countries. It is evident from the discussions in Chapter 4 that one of the major problems that many survivors could face is food shortages.

Food shortages during the first few years following a nuclear war could be the result of disruption of the international economy and trade, climatic stress to agricultural systems, and the associated societal disruption that would follow (Harwell, 1984; Scrimshaw, 1984). The vulnerability of the global human population to such changes must be assessed on the basis of defining the human population that could be supported by the resulting agricultural and food distribution system. Hjort (1982) and Harwell (1984) describe many of the processes that could cause decreased food availability following nuclear warfare. These problems include direct destruction of food crops and stores, radioactive contamination, uncontrollable fires, loss of fertilizers and pesticides, reduced fuel supplies, and destruction of major ports and facilities of the global food distribution network. The United States and Canada are major food exporters that would probably suffer severe and widespread destruction in a large-scale nuclear war, and probable elimination of the means and incentives to export additional food. Other exporting countries would be faced with an international economic system disrupted to such an extent that large scale food shipments might be greatly reduced.

The projected responses of agroecosystems would greatly depend on the timing and intensity of the nuclear war, and on the assumed magnitude of climatic alteration. The temperature and precipitation reduction estimates derived from climatic modelling and analysis could be sufficient to eliminate agricultural production in most of the Northern Hemisphere and much of the Southern Hemisphere for at least one year (see Volume 1 and Chapter 4, Volume 2). Even in the absence of climatic perturbations, food production might be reduced beyond the acute effects of the first year in response to disruptions in agricultural subsidies; therefore analysis of chronic effects extending several years after a war must also be included.

The amount of food in storage is a critical issue to be resolved in an analysis of the vulnerability to an acute phase agricultural disruption. This poorly measured and poorly documented quantity is not limited to storage facilities controlled by central governments. Unless there were no time lag between food harvest and consumption, there would be food stores in farms, transportation facilities, food processing plants, and other locations. Analysis of food storage, and other critical variables, is difficult on a global basis. Nuclear war impacts would be quite different for combatant Northern Hemisphere countries and non-combatant or Southern Hemisphere countries.

Because it would be difficult to examine all countries in sufficient detail,

TABLE 5.1

1983 POPULATION DATA[a]

COUNTRY	TOTAL POPULATION (10^6)	AGRICULTURAL POP. (10^6)	% AGR.
Argentina	28.0	3.4	12
Australia	15.0	0.8	5
Brazil1	31.1	47.0	36
Canada	24.9	1.1	4
China	1,033.7	591.2	57
Costa Rica	2.4	0.8	33
India	725.5	442.1	61
Indonesia	155.6	87.9	56
Japan	119.3	10.7	9
Kenya	18.6	14.1	76
Nigeria	85.2	43.0	50
Phillipines	53.2	23.2	44
U.K.	56.3	1.0	2
U.S.	234.2	4.4	2
U.S.S.R.	272.3	39.6	14
WORLD TOTAL	4,669.7	2,075.9	43

[a] Data from FAO Production Yearbook (1983).

we have concentrated on 15 representative countries (Table 5.1), selected to include a wide spectrum of population levels, agricultural productivities, and economic and social structures. These 15 countries make up about 63% of the total world population. We have also used simplified models to provide estimates of potential food impacts on an additional 120 countries. These calculations are presented to be illustrative of potential global effects, but more research needs to be done on a national basis to properly assess this problem. The results of these analyses indicate that food problems could be the single most significant contributor to human mortality following a nuclear war. This conclusion results from a consideration of the potential global-scale disruptions in societal and agricultural systems. This vulnerability is an aspect not currently a part of the understanding of nuclear war; not only are the major combatant countries in danger, but virtually the entire human population is being held hostage to the large scale use of nuclear weapons.

5.2 METHODS AND ASSUMPTIONS

5.2.1 Introduction

Calculations of food production, stores, and consumption rates were based on energetic (caloric) equivalents (Table 5.2). Energy intake is only one aspect of diet; nutritional problems other than insufficient energy might also be important following a nuclear war, but these limitations are difficult to quantify. The resistance of individuals to vitamin and food shortages depends greatly on the initial state of health and nutrition. Shifts in dietary consumption patterns are to be expected following a nuclear war, but we

TABLE 5.2

ENERGETIC EQUIVALENTS FOR MAJOR FOOD TYPES[a]

	$KCAL \cdot KG^{-1}$
Cereals	3,420
Pulses (Legumes)	3,350
Cow meat and organs	2,400

[a] Data from Chatfield (1954).

assume that an average consumption rate of 2,000 kcal·person^{-1}·day^{-1} is necessary to sustain people with normal activity levels, based on analyses of minimum dietary requirements for humans.

The major category of interest for food impact analyses is cereal grains. Cereals make up about 70% of the total world food energy intake (Bender and Bender, 1982). Maintaining sufficient energy intake alone would not assure survival in a food crisis; it is also necessary to consider other food types, particularly when calculated food energy supplies seem sufficient. We have also included pulses (legumes) and meat in our calculations, food types more likely to be available than fruits and vegetables. Maintaining stores of starch-rich root crops and fruits and vegetables can be very difficult; post-harvest losses of these crops are often 50–80% in tropical regions (Cross, 1985).

5.2.2 Dietary Assumptions

The normal dietary consumption pattern, classified by major food types (Table 5.3), would probably be greatly altered following a large-scale nuclear war. The average caloric intake necessary to sustain human life depends on

TABLE 5.3

DIETARY COMPOSITION[a]
(KCAL·PERSON^{-1}·DAY^{-1})

COUNTRY	CEREALS	ROOTS/ TUBERS	SUGAR/ HONEY	PULSES	NUTS/ OILSEEDS	VEGE- TABLES	FRUITS	ANIMAL PRODUCTS	TOTAL[b]
Argentina	997	143	398	17	26	53	117	1,056	3,358
Australia	837	94	572	7	21	52	103	1,330	3,400
Brazil	903	243	464	164	21	18	122	415	2,521
Canada	704	128	494	22	60	63	103	1,415	3,345
China	1,547	209	41	104	62	40	8	237	2,362
Costa Rica	876	32	611	99	19	16	149	413	2,487
India	1,233	42	177	142	28	32	29	91	1,889
Indonesia	1,405	214	134	17	117	11	26	50	2,115
Kenya	1,209	197	167	149	29	14	49	234	2,141
Japan	1,312	63	269	26	127	68	62	533	2,848
Nigeria	932	680	42	75	62	25	61	80	2,219
Phillipines	1,310	121	205	10	27	18	73	221	2,128
U.K.	693	175	537	27	34	50	62	1,255	3,311
U.S.	615	111	562	29	69	64	120	1,300	3,539
U.S.S.R.	1,365	234	446	37	21	54	56	938	3,443

[a] Data from FAO food balance sheets; 1975-1977 averages.
[b] Total includes input from other sources.

a number of factors, including population age distribution, activity levels, and climate. All of these factors, as well as what food is available and can be maintained in stores, might be influenced by nuclear war. Based on inspection of FAO calculated food energy requirements (FAO, 1982a), we assume that a minimum of 2,000 kcal•person^{-1}•day^{-1} is necessary to sustain life for an extended period of time. For the purpose of illustrating potential food problems, we have assumed a diet of 1,500 kcal•person^{-1}•day^{-1} of cereals, 500 kcal•person^{-1}•day^{-1} of animal products, and pulse consumption rates at current levels (Table 5.3). This dietary pattern represents the largest relative changes for developed-industrialized countries. Many countries in this category would be probable combatants in a large-scale nuclear war and would suffer destruction and disruption of the energy intensive food distribution system currently supplying more than 3,000 kcal•person^{-1}•day^{-1}.

5.2.3 Calculation Methods: Vulnerability in the Acute Phase

The climatic consequences of nuclear war include the possibility, in the acute phase, of the elimination of agricultural production in large regions of the Northern Hemisphere temperate zone, and perhaps tropical regions in both hemispheres (see Chapter 4). In such circumstances, food storage would be a critical item controlling human survival following nuclear war induced climatic disturbances. Even with minor climatic perturbations, many countries would be expected to suffer severe food shortages in the acute phase because of probable disruption or elimination of imports.

Food storage levels differ greatly among and within countries and fluctuate significantly during the course of year. Therefore, the timing of a nuclear exchange directly relates to the potential severity of food shortages. An attack immediately after the harvest period would coincide with food storage levels much higher than one immediately before the harvest period. To account for the range of food storage levels possible within a year, we calculated food supplies three ways, representing a range of food available immediately after nuclear war:

1). Carryovers only are available. This case represents the low point in food stores. Carryover levels tend to be much higher in countries that are major grain exporters or importers (Table 5.4). We have assumed that carryovers are equal to 10% of production (the mean of measured levels in India, China, and Brazil) for Costa Rica, Indonesia, Kenya, Nigeria, and the Philippines. For the United Kingdom we have assumed that carryovers are 23% of production. Pulse carryover levels were assumed to be the same fraction of production as in cereals for all countries.

TABLE 5.4

CEREAL CARRYOVERS[a]
(10^6 TONS)

Country	Cereal Production	Carryovers	Carryovers as % Prod.
Argentina	18.47	1.1	6
Australia	16.38	5.0	31
Brazil	33.22	1.3	4
Canada	41.48	14.3	34
China	280.40	53.0	19
India	140.50	10.8	8
Japan	13.19	10.6	80
U.S.	270.00	78.1	29
U.S.S.R.	182.70	16.0	9

[a] Data from FAO (1982a); 1980 data.

2). A median case includes carryovers, a fraction of annual imports, and a fraction of a full production, weighted for the number of harvests. The equation used to calculate the median case is:

$$F_a = 0.5 \cdot (P + C) \cdot H^{-1} + C + I/12 \qquad (5.1)$$

Where:

F_a = stored food available (kcal)

P = full harvest (kcal)

H = number of harvests per year

C = Carryovers (kcal)

I = annual imports (kcal)

3). Full production, but no imports are available. Because of variations in import levels, dietary consumption rates, and animal feeding on grains, the full production calculation may indicate support of either less than or more than the current population.

It should be clearly understood that none of these sets of assumptions reflect a prediction of the specific situation after a large-scale nuclear war. Rather, these assumptions were selected to illustrate the range of vulnerability of the human population to societal and agricultural system disruptions.

The three levels of food availability are illustrated with two hypothetical countries, each with 96×10^6 tons of cereal production. In the first case (Figure 5.1), there is only one major harvest per year (typical of many temperate countries). In this situation, maximum food storage is approximated by full annual production. Assuming a monthly consumption rate of 1/12 of annual production, the median value (disregarding imports) is midway between full production and the lowest value (carryovers). In the second case (Figure 5.2), there are two principal harvests within the year, yielding a maximum storage value half of that for the single harvest situation. The median value can be calculated as $(0.5 \cdot (P+C) \cdot H^{-1})$, or midway between one full harvest and the low point. In each case, carryovers and 1/12 of annual imports are added to the calculated median value to provide a conservative estimate.

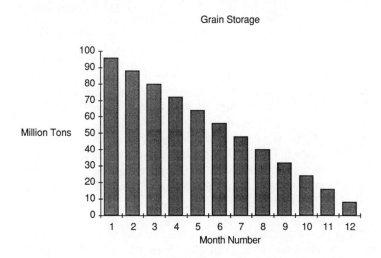

Grain Storage

Figure 5.1 Hypothetical monthly variation of grain stores for a country with one major harvest period. Annual production (full harvest) = 96×10^6 tons; median value = 52×10^6 tons; carryover level = 8×10^6 tons

There are several major assumptions associated with the food storage calculations outlined above. The significance of some of these assumptions can be tested with sensitivity analysis, that is, varying parameter values and calculation methods and assessing the effect on the final answers. The principal assumptions, in addition to those already discussed are:

1.) No animals are fed on grain. Any feeding of animals reduces the potential support capacity to humans of grain stores and production.

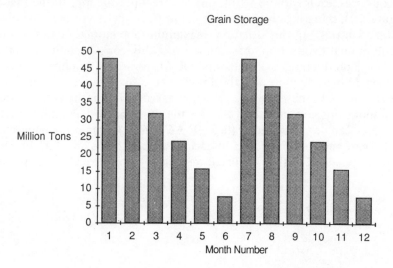

Figure 5.2 Hypothetical monthly variation of grain stores for a country with two major harvest periods. Annual production $= 96 \times 10^{6}$ tons; one full harvest $= 48 \times 10^{6}$ tons; median value $= 26 \times 10^{6}$ tons; carryover level $= 8 \times 10^{6}$ tons

2.) Food stores and population are destroyed in equal proportions in combatant countries. The level of destruction assumed in the principal combatant countries varied from 25 to 75% of pre-war levels. The level of destruction is highly scenario-dependent, and the vulnerability of food stores needs additional research.

3.) Optimal food distribution within a country occurs, so that the maximum number of people survive given the dietary assumptions. This is an highly unlikely situation following a nuclear war considering the current food maldistribution and historical analogs (Chapter 6). This assumption also requires that no food is used by those people who cannot be supported for a full year; although this assumption is very conservative, it is impossible to predict accurately the level of food hoarding, destruction, and maldistribution that would occur in any country. We have addressed this issue with sensitivity analyses of food distribution patterns, which show that more realistic assumptions would lead to significant reductions in the number of survivors.

4.) Most of the food stored would be in the form of major cereal crops. Any large stores of other foods, such as root crops and vegetables, would increase the population support capacity within a country.

5.) No predictions are ventured as to how the behavior of people as individuals and in groups would be modified by the experience of nuclear war or by the anticipation of the explosions and subsequent events.

We have used two methods of calculating human support capability of food stores in the acute phase. Assuming no agricultural production or imports for one year, the duration of support of the full surviving population is calculated, as is the total storage support in person-years.

These calculations reflect the vulnerability of the Earth's population to the loss of agricultural productivity. Based on the assumptions listed above, these values are intended to represent the physically limited, maximum number of humans that could be supported with no agricultural production. The equation used to calculate the duration of full population support is:

$$T = F_\mathrm{a}/N \cdot D \qquad (5.2)$$

Where:

T = duration (days) before food stores are depleted

F_a = total food (kcal) available (either full production, median value, or carryovers only)

N = population size

D = per capita consumption rate (kcal $\cdot$ person$^{-1} \cdot$ day^{-1})

A similar equation is used to calculate food storage support capacity in person-years:

$$Y = F_\mathrm{a}/(D \cdot 365) \qquad (5.3)$$

The person-year values calculated from this equation can be interpreted as the maximum number of people that could be maintained by food at the consumption rate specified (D) for one year. Of course more people could be supported at lower consumption rates, but energy shortfalls significantly below 2,000 kcal $\cdot$ person$^{-1} \cdot$ day^{-1} would have to be made up by other food sources. Another interpretation of this calculation could be that half the population (Y) could be supported for twice as long (two years). Given the assumption of optimal distribution noted above, it is highly unlikely that this maximum support figure could be realistically maintained in a food crisis.

For the countries (of the 15 listed in Table 1) considered to be possible combatants or targets in a major nuclear war (Australia, Canada, China, Japan, U.K., U.S.A., U.S.S.R.), the immediate effect of nuclear weapon detonations would alter food supply requirements. A critical issue concerns possible differential destruction of food stores and population. Although the distribution of food storage capacity within some countries is well known, the distribution and annual variation of actual stores is poorly known. For the combatant countries, we have assumed that food stores and population are reduced by the same fraction. In this case, food stores (assuming no agricultural production) would last as long as the pre-war levels, as in the non-combatant countries, i.e. the number of people assumed to die from the direct effects of nuclear war would have no bearing on the ultimate duration of food stores as calculated here. Calculated values for grain stores (person-years) can be easily adjusted for other assumptions. The actual vulnerability of food stores to destruction in a nuclear war, and the annual variation in stores remain an important research question.

In addition to the detailed analyses of the 15 countries (Table 5.1) outlined above, a simpler data set and model were used to assess potential food shortages in 120 other countries. Carryovers were assumed to be 10% of annual production for all countries, and only one harvest per year was assumed.

The acute phase analyses were designed to illustrate the vulnerability of each country to losses of agricultural productivity. Although the climatic analysis of Volume 1, and consideration of agricultural responses (Chapter 4, Volume 2), indicate that widespread crop losses are possible following a major nuclear war, we cannot predict the precise conditions that would be experienced in any region. If acute phase climatic disturbances permitted some agricultural production, the chronic phase analyses that follow would apply to the first post-war year also.

5.2.4 Calculation Methods: Vulnerability in the Chronic Phase

In the chronic case we assume that after the first year at least some agricultural production might be possible. Population support capacity is calculated using an equation analogous to Equation 5.3.

$$S = F_a/(D \cdot 365) \qquad (5.4)$$

In this case F_a represents a sustained level of annual agricultural production, and not a storage level. The calculated value of S then, is a steady-state carrying capacity associated with the production level F_a. The actual level of production that would be realized during a chronic time-frame would be dependent on climate change and sensitivity, economic and social disruption, and losses of technological support and inputs for agriculture. These analyses are restricted to the 15 countries listed in Table 5.1 and presented as a range of possibilities, since no single most probable scenario can be identified.

The level of agricultural production and food supply in the chronic phase would depend on a number of factors. Even with 100% of pre-war production, the loss of food imports could seriously reduce population support capabilities in some countries. Climatic disturbances severe enough to impair agricultural production might occur in the chronic phase. It is not possible to predict the precise climate that would be experienced in any region during the chronic phase; therefore, we have treated this analysis as an evaluation of a range of effects from no change in climate to that of severe climatic stress (a decrease of up to 5°C in mean temperature or a 50% decrease in annual precipitation).

The potential effects of disruptions in agricultural subsidies and international trade are considered for the range of the climatic conditions postulated. The chronic phase analysis reflects the fundamental vulnerability of food supply systems to nuclear war but can only be presented as a range of possibilities.

Figure 5.3 represents the approach taken to illustrate that range of possibilities, in this case for Argentina. Six levels of production (10%, 25%, ··· 100%) are shown with their corresponding capability to support the human population, characterized as the fraction of current population. Many countries (particularly food exporters) produce more food than is necessary to feed the entire pre-war population (indicated by the bold 100% line in Figure 5.3). In Argentina, for example, the entire population could be supported by less than half of the current agricultural production. For chronic-phase impact analysis, three scenarios of agricultural production are considered, with post-war production estimates derived from a qualitative

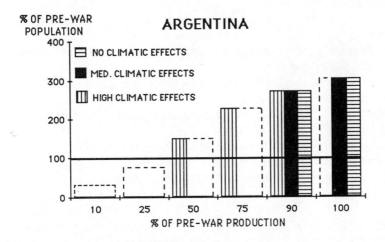

Figure 5.3   Wheat yield in Argentina. (FAO production yearbooks)

assessment of the vulnerability of the country's agriculture to climatic disturbances and losses of energy subsidies. If, for example, Argentina experienced no chronic-phase climatic disturbances, agricultural production could be maintained at near normal levels (here estimated at 90–100% of current production, Figure 5.3). If climatic disturbances also occurred (e.g., a decrease of up to 5°C in mean annual temperature, or up to a 50% decrease in precipitation), agricultural production could be further reduced (e.g., for Argentina we estimate production could decrease to levels of about 50% to 90% of pre-war production, Figure 5.3). Other analyses may more accurately refine the level of agricultural production that would occur; these may readily be viewed in terms of potential human population levels by selecting the appropriate production value from the figure. Open dashed bar graphics illustrate the production/population relationships for levels of production not considered likely to occur, based on the current estimates of possible climatic perturbations and import dependency of the country's agricultural production.

5.3 RESULTS: ANALYSIS OF 15 REPRESENTATIVE COUNTRIES

5.3.1 Introduction

A comprehensive analysis of the consequences of nuclear war requires consideration of stresses and responses on a local and regional basis, as well as on a global basis, because of the climatic, social, and economic heterogeneity that exists. We have initiated this approach using the 15 representative countries listed in Table 5.1. The analysis of each country includes a description of population support capabilities of stored food, reflecting the vulnerability to an acute phase loss of agricultural production, and of the factors influencing agricultural production for several years following a nuclear war (chronic phase).

We cannot know the climate that any country would actually experience following a nuclear war. The uncertainties discussed in Volume 1 preclude a precise analysis of agricultural responses. However, widespread and significant climatic disturbances could occur, and it is important to assess the vulnerability of agricultural systems under these circumstances.

The detailed consideration for each country (discussed below) of potential climatic disturbances and other post-war agricultural stresses has led to the following major conclusions:

1.) Most countries in the world would suffer severe food shortages and mass starvation if agricultural production were eliminated for a single growing season. Food exporting countries would normally have adequate food stores, but many of these countries could be targets of nuclear weapons. Climatic disturbances of sufficient magnitude to produce these effects might be possible over large areas of the Northern Hemisphere, and some regions of the Southern Hemisphere (see Chapter 4).

2.) If international food trade were eliminated following a nuclear war, those countries that import a large fraction of their food requirements would experience severe food shortages, even with no climatic disturbances.

3.) Agricultural production in most of the world would probably be impaired for a period of at least several years after a major nuclear war. Climatic disturbances and disruptions in world trade and production of fossil fuel, machinery, fertilizers and other agricultural subsidies could reduce the level of production maintained in the chronic phase.

Careful consideration of the assumptions should be employed when considering the descriptions of potential food and agricultural problems that follow. The climatic disturbances discussed do not represent predictions of actual post-war climates, but are discussed in order to characterize the vulnerability of each country.

5.3.2 Argentina

The impacts of a Northern Hemisphere nuclear war on Argentina would probably be much less severe than for most of the other countries analyzed. As a Southern Hemisphere temperate country, the climatic disturbances might be insignificant. If there were climatic effects, they would probably be quite variable within the country, because of the large altitudinal and latitudinal range involved. In the very severe scenarios, mean temperature decreases of a few to 15°C are possible. Additionally, significant precipitation decreases are possible. Under these conditions, mean summer temperatures (Nov.–Feb.) could be 10°C or less in most of the country. If this severe case occurred, agriculture would be significantly impaired, and only marginal crop production would be possible during the first year following a war. Animal grazing systems are an important part of agriculture in Argentina, and these pastoral regions would probably be more resistant to climatic disturbances.

Stored food shortages could become critical if production were eliminated. Although we do not have access to data on the actual monthly variation of food stores, our calculations were designed to illustrate a range of possibilities, as well as a median case. Again, we are not implying that elimination of all agriculture for one year is probable in Argentina, but we are examining the country's vulnerability to such conditions.

As a major grain exporter, Argentina has much more food on hand shortly after harvest than is necessary to feed the full population (Table 5.5). The large number of cattle (twice the human population) also provides a margin of safety. The timing of the nuclear war could be a critical factor. The level of carryovers in Argentina relative to production is unusually small for a food exporting country (Table 5.4), and if only carryovers were available, only a relatively small proportion of the population could be maintained with stores. In these circumstances, $1,000$ kcal $\cdot$ person^{-1} $\cdot$ day^{-1} would have to be provided from other sources or mass starvation would result.

TABLE 5.5

ARGENTINA
ACUTE PHASE FOOD SUPPORT

	DURATION OF SUPPORT (DAYS)		
	Full Harvest	Median Case	Carryovers
Cereals	1,105	586	66
Pulses	------	734	------
Beef	------	1,391	------

	PERSON-YEARS (10^6) (% OF 1980 POPULATION)		
	Full Harvest	Median Case	Carryovers
Cereals	82 (303%)	43 (161%)	5 (18%)
Pulses	------	54 (201%)	------
Beef	------	103 (381%)	------

During the first few years following a large-scale nuclear war, Argentina, along with all other countries, would probably be affected by the disruption of the international economy and trade, even if no additional climatic impacts were experienced. Argentina is relatively independent in terms of energy production; however, coal imports represent a potential vulnerability (Table 5.6). Another potential problem area is imports of nitrogen fertilizer, which is strongly related to agricultural yields (Greenwood, 1981). Wheat yields have increased considerably in Argentina during the last 30 years (Figure 5.4), and some yield declines could be associated with fertilizer limitation in the early chronic phase. Additional climate problems are also possible in the chronic phase, if mean temperatures 5 to 10 degrees

TABLE 5.6

ARGENTINA 1982[a]

FUEL	PRODUCTION	NET IMPORTS	IMPORTS AS % PRODUCTION
Crude Oil (1,000 MT)	25,196	728	3
Hard Coal (1,000 MT)	515	730	142
Gasoline (1,000 MT)	5,111	-15	0
Diesel Fuel (1,000 MT)	7,569	-480	0

ELECTRICAL GENERATION	10^6 KWH	% OF TOTAL
Hydroelectric	17,586	44
Thermal	20,348	51
Nuclear	1,870	5
Geothermal	-------	---
TOTAL	39,804	100

N-FERTILIZER (1,000 MT)	PRODUCTION	IMPORTS	IMPORTS % OF PRODUCTION
	25,124	26,049	104

TRACTORS	IN USE (1980)	IMPORTS (1980)	IMPORTS % OF PRODUCTION
	166,700	4,750	3

LAND USE	IRRIGATED (1,000 HA)	TOTAL ARABLE (1,000 HA)	IRRIGATED % OF TOTAL
	1,620	35,800	5

[a] Data from FAO Production Yearbook (1982); FAO Trade Yearbook (1982); U.N. Energy Statistics Yearbook (1983).

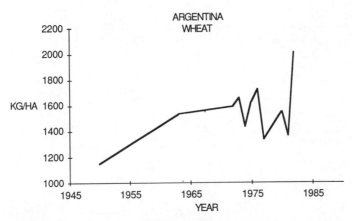

Figure 5.4   Chronic phase population support in Argentina

below normal as well as precipitation decreases of up to 50% of normal occurred.

The principal ameliorating factor for Argentina is the strength of its agricultural production system. Argentina is currently producing much more food than is needed domestically, and unless production were reduced by a factor of two, the full population should be easily supported (Figure 5.3). This figure shows a range of agricultural production and steady-state population support for three scenarios. Each case includes the energy, economic and societal disruptions that might influence agricultural production, within three levels of climatic effects.

5.3.3 Australia

Australia, as a Southern Hemisphere major food exporting country, would not be catastrophically damaged by a nuclear war fought in the Northern Hemisphere. There is a possibility, however, that Australia itself could be a target of nuclear weapons in a major war, leading to significant direct impacts (Ambio, 1982). Climatic stresses associated with nuclear war-induced atmospheric disturbances could also affect Australian agriculture (Chapter 4). Mean temperature reductions of the order of a few degrees C might lead to yield increases as a result of reduced evapo-transpiration and moisture stress, but larger decreases or freezing episodes during the growing season could cause significant crop losses. Precipitation decreases would also cause reduced crop yield in much of Australia. The potential vulnerability of

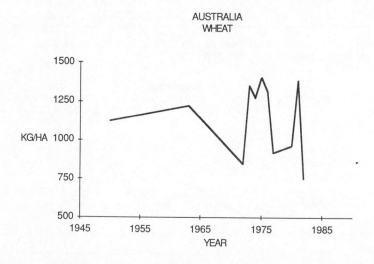

Figure 5.5   Wheat yield in Australia. (FAO production yearbooks)

Australian wheat production to climatic change is illustrated by Figure 5.5. Although Australian agriculture is energy-intensive and mechanized, there is no evidence of increased wheat yields during the last 30 years. A large fraction of the year-to-year variability of Australian crop yields (60–80%) is attributable to weather variability (Russell, 1973). Precipitation decreases of 50% would be expected to cause significant yield declines.

As a net food exporter, with large numbers of sheep and cattle, even complete elimination of agricultural production for one year would not necessarily lead to acute food shortages for the Australian population (Table 5.7). Pastoral agriculture is very important in Australia, and would be more resistant to climatic disturbances than wheat production.

TABLE 5.7

AUSTRALIA
ACUTE PHASE FOOD SUPPORT

| | DURATION OF SUPPORT (DAYS) | | |
	Full Harvest	Median Case	Carryovers
Cereals	1,856	1,211	566
Pulses	------	3,233	------
Beef	------	1,219	------

| | PERSON-YEARS (10^6) (% OF 1980 POPULATION) | | |
	Full Harvest	Median Case	Carryovers
Cereals	37 (254%)	24 (166%)	11 (78%)
Pulses	------	64 (443%)	------
Beef	------	24 (167%)	------

Nuclear weapon detonations might have significant impacts on Australian agriculture. Of course, we cannot know the actual level of mortality and destruction that would be experienced in Australia. One major variable would be the number of targets, if any, associated with urban areas. For this analysis, a more critical assumption is that food stores and population are destroyed in equal proportions, an issue that needs additional study.

The estimates of population support from food stores, assuming 50% destruction, are the same as the no-casualty scenario because the same fraction was used to reduce stores and population; however, the estimates in person-years should be doubled to calculate the carrying capacity of pre-war stores. In either case, there would potentially be enough food stored to feed the

TABLE 5.8

AUSTRALIA 1982[a]

FUEL	PRODUCTION	NET IMPORTS	IMPORTS AS % PRODUCTION
Crude Oil (1,000 MT)	18,700	9,000	48
Hard Coal (1,000 MT)	96,786	(-53,000)	0
Gasoline (1,000 MT)	10,500	150	1
Diesel Fuel (1,000 MT)	7,200	(-100)	0

ELECTRICAL GENERATION	10^6 KWH	% OF TOTAL	
Hydroelectric	15,000	14	
Thermal	89,890	86	
Nuclear	-------	---	
Geothermal	-------	---	
TOTAL	104,890	100	

N-FERTILIZER (1,000 MT) PRODUCTION		IMPORTS	IMPORTS % OF PRODUCTION
	206,000	52,000	25

TRACTORS	IN USE (1980)	IMPORTS (1980)	IMPORTS % OF PRODUCTION
	332,000	21,331	6

LAND USE	IRRIGATED (1,000 HA)	TOTAL ARABLE (1,000 HA)	IRRIGATED % OF TOTAL
	1,700	46,544	4

[a] Data from FAO Production Yearbook (1982); FAO Trade Yearbook (1982); U.N. Energy Statistics Yearbook (1983).

entire surviving population for one year with no agricultural production (Table 5.7). This would be true regardless of the timing of the war.

The principal factors associated with agricultural impairment in the chronic phase are similar to those considered with the acute phase. The effects of disruption of agricultural technology and losses of energy subsidies could be significant, even in developed Southern Hemisphere nations. The international economic and trade relations of every country would probably be affected by a large-scale nuclear war. Australia is an example of a country that would seem relatively immune to nuclear war effects (if not targeted),

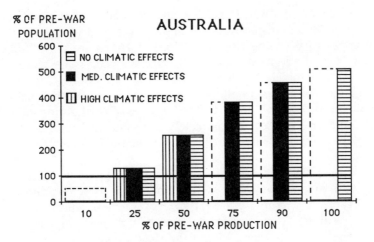

Figure 5.6 Chronic phase population support in Australia

but serious impairments of agricultural production could occur. Although Australia is a net energy exporter (Table 5.8), the liquid fuels required for crop production, lubrication, and food processing and transportation are imported in significant amounts.

Australia is also dependent on overseas raw material for the production of fertilizers. Most of the herbicides, pesticides, and veterinary medicines used in Australian agriculture are currently imported from countries likely to be combatants in a major nuclear war. Although raw materials and alternative technologies could be developed to replace interrupted supplies of imports, there might be a significant time lag for complete replacement.

Decreased precipitation is the potential climatic stress of the chronic phase to which Australian agriculture is most vulnerable. Although increased precipitation is possible in the coastal areas during the chronic phase, substantial decreases could occur inland. The wide range of climatic possibilities and the possibility of a range of targeting intensities produces a wide range of potential agricultural responses during the chronic phase (Figure 5.6). If Australia were not targeted, and if the climatic changes were small, little direct impact on production would be expected. Unless production decreased below 25% of pre-war levels the surviving population could be easily supported. Thus, Australia appears to be among the least vulnerable of countries to post-war food shortages.

5.3.4 Brazil

Although Brazil spans both equatorial and Southern Hemisphere latitudes, and is not considered likely to be a nuclear target, severe impacts are possible following a nuclear war. Brazil is a diverse country climatically, ranging from tropical to sub-tropical and from very wet to drier steppe climates. Mean temperatures in the tropical regions of Brazil are typically 25°C in May–Aug. and are approximately 27°C in Nov.–Feb.; more temperate regions are approximately 10–20°C in May–Aug. and 20–25°C in Nov.–Feb. Much of Brazilian food agriculture is in temperate and sub-tropical regions. Mean temperatures below 10°C, and/or episodes of frost during the growing season, could be expected to completely eliminate agricultural production for one growing cycle. Thus, Brazil is quite vulnerable to even brief episodes of cold temperatures.

Brazil does not have sufficient stored food to support its full population for one year of no production, except under the most favorable circumstances (Table 5.9). The median or carryover cases indicate that human mortality resulting from insufficient food could occur, depending on the timing of the war. Less severe climatic impacts would cause less severe mortality in a food crisis, but a large fraction of current production is needed to support the current population. A large-scale food crisis and mortality would be an unprecedented catastrophe for Brazil, and would be expected to add to the societal and economic disruption caused by nuclear warfare.

In the chronic phase of a few years following a nuclear conflict, several factors indicate a substantial potential for agricultural impairment. Brazil imports large amounts of oil, coal, N-fertilizer, and grain (Table 5.10). Brazilian agriculture is subsidy dependent, with significant yield gains during the past 30 years (Figure 5.7). Although Brazil produces most of its electricity from hydroelectric plants, the other energy vulnerabilities could decrease production. Chronic phase temperature decreases of several °C and precipitation

TABLE 5.9

BRAZIL
ACUTE PHASE FOOD SUPPORT

| | DURATION OF SUPPORT (DAYS) | | |
	Full Harvest	Median Case	Carryovers
Cereals	433	233	17
Pulses	------	174	------
Beef	------	557	------

| | PERSON-YEARS (10^6) (% OF 1980 POPULATION) | | |
	Full Harvest	Median Case	Carryovers
Cereals	145 (119%)	78 (64%)	6 (5%)
Pulses	------	58 (48%)	------
Beef	------	187 (153%)	------

TABLE 5.10

BRAZIL 1982[a]

FUEL	PRODUCTION	NET IMPORTS	IMPORTS AS % PRODUCTION
Crude Oil (1,000 MT)	12,622	38,709	307
Hard Coal (1,000 MT)	6,400	4,406	69
Gasoline (1,000 MT)	8,841	(-1,149)	0
Diesel Fuel (1,000 MT)	16,268	(-825)	0

ELECTRICAL GENERATION	10^6 KWH	% OF TOTAL	
Hydroelectric	141,224	93	
Thermal	10,865	7	
Nuclear	--------	---	
Geothermal	--------	---	
TOTAL	152,089	100	

N-FERTILIZER (1,000 MT) PRODUCTION	IMPORTS	IMPORTS % OF PRODUCTION
349,400	319,100	91

TRACTORS	IN USE (1980)	IMPORTS (1980)	IMPORTS % OF PRODUCTION
	330,000	1,000	0.3

LAND USE	IRRIGATED (1,000 HA)	TOTAL ARABLE (1,000 HA)	IRRIGATED % OF TOTAL
	2,000	74,670	3

[a] Data from FAO Production Yearbook (1982); FAO Trade Yearbook (1982); U.N. Energy Statistics Yearbook (1983).

decreases of 25 to 50% of normal could also cause problems, however there are possible methods of compensation. Brazil uses more than 10^6 ha for non-food and export crops. In the environment of a post-war economy, this land could be shifted to food production. In addition, the climatic diversity of Brazil indicates that at least some parts of the country would be suitable for agriculture, even if chronic climatic disturbances occur. Finding the appropriate crops and locations could, however, be a difficult operation for most farmers.

A range of possibilities for agricultural production in chronic phase Brazil is illustrated in Figure 5.8. Some agricultural impairment seems likely, even

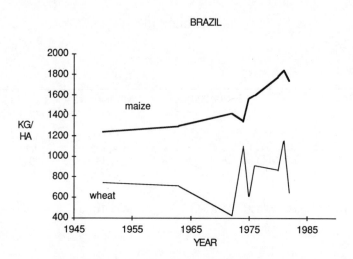

Figure 5.7   Maize and wheat yields in Brazil. (FAO production yearbooks)

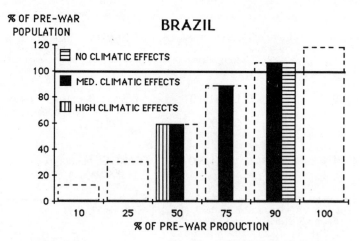

Figure 5.8   Chronic phase population support in Brazil

with no climatic impacts, due to the heavy import dependence of Brazil. Additional agricultural effects due to climatic stresses could reduce production below the levels necessary to support the current population.

5.3.5 Canada

Canadian agriculture would suffer severe consequences in a major nuclear war as a result of possible climatic disturbances and, perhaps, targeting. As

TABLE 5.11

CANADA
ACUTE PHASE FOOD SUPPORT

| | DURATION OF SUPPORT (DAYS) | | |
	Full Harvest	Median Case	Carryovers
Cereals	2,866	1,935	988
Pulses	------	808	------
Beef	------	347	------

| | PERSON-YEARS (10^6) (% OF 1980 POPULATION) | | |
	Full Harvest	Median Case	Carryovers
Cereals	95 (393%)	64 (265%)	33 (135%)
Pulses	------	27 (111%)	------
Beef	------	11 (48%)	------

a member of NATO, heavy destruction of industrial and urban areas associated with targets of military significance could greatly disrupt the complex system that supports current agriculture. In addition, Canadian agriculture is very sensitive to temperature declines, with the majority located between 44 and 55°N latitude. Simulation studies (Chapter 4) indicate that mean temperature decreases of a few degrees C could completely eliminate wheat

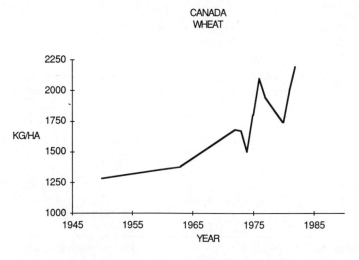

Figure 5.9 Wheat yield in Canada. (FAO production yearbooks)

production in Canada. Mean temperatures of approximately 15°C (May–Aug.) are common in the Canadian continental interior. Even relatively mild climatic disturbances could virtually eliminate Canadian agriculture for a single growing season, and in the worst cases, for a number of years.

However, the consequences to humans of the severe climatic stresses predicted for Canada are not necessarily as severe as in most other countries. The high levels of agricultural production relative to population size indicates that all survivors could be fed on stored food for an extended time period (Table 5.11). These calculations assume that the survivors would have

TABLE 5.12

CANADA 1982[a]

FUEL	PRODUCTION	NET IMPORTS	IMPORTS AS % PRODUCTION
Crude Oil (1,000 MT)	62,163	6,915	11
Hard Coal (1,000 MT)	22,379	(-331)	0
Gasoline (1,000 MT)	24,796	(-370)	0
Diesel Fuel (1,000 MT)	19,404	(-711)	0

ELECTRICAL GENERATION	10^6 KWH	% OF TOTAL	
Hydroelectric	261,055	67	
Thermal	91,084	24	
Nuclear	35,321	9	
Geothermal	-------	---	
TOTAL	387,460	100	

N-FERTILIZER (1,000 MT) PRODUCTION		IMPORTS	IMPORTS % OF PRODUCTION
	1,750,000	126,000	7

TRACTORS	IN USE (1980)	IMPORTS (1980)	IMPORTS % OF PRODUCTION
	657,400	76,763	12

LAND USE	IRRIGATED (1,000 HA)	TOTAL ARABLE (1,000 HA)	IRRIGATED % OF TOTAL
	615	46,180	1

[a] Data from FAO Production Yearbook (1982); FAO Trade Yearbook (1982); U.N. Energy Statistics Yearbook (1983).

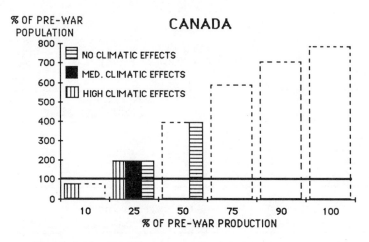

Figure 5.10   Chronic phase population support in Canada

the information and means to deliver food to the entire population. Given such assumptions, an acute phase food crisis need not occur in Canada.

The principal factors promoting recovery during the chronic phase are Canadian import independence and the potential strength of the agricultural system. Although Canada can produce the major energy sources and subsidies necessary for agriculture (Table 5.12), targeting of industry and refineries could seriously diminish this capacity for an extended time period. Yield decreases of 1,000 kg·ha^{-1} could occur with the implementation of a less subsidy-dependent agricultural system. Climatic stresses during the chronic phase could also reduce agricultural production. Only a small fraction of pre-war agricultural production would be necessary to support the full population of Canada (Figure 5.10), but the combined effects of these stresses could reduce production to insignificant levels.

5.3.6 China

The Chinese agricultural and food supply system is vulnerable to severe disruption and damage following a nuclear war, even if China were not a direct target. A high level of production must be maintained to feed 1,000 million people, an unlikely possibility given the possible post-nuclear war climatic disturbances. Because of its mid-latitude, continental location, China could experience mean temperatures 10 to 35°C below normal following a major nuclear war, with smaller reductions possible for an extended time period. Even temperature reductions at the mild end of this range would bring mean temperatures near the tolerance limits for rice in much of China, and would produce minimum temperatures that could eliminate rice production.

TABLE 5.13

CHINA
ACUTE PHASE FOOD SUPPORT

| | DURATION OF SUPPORT (DAYS) | | |
	Full Harvest	Median Case	Carryovers
Cereals	456	274	86
Pulses	------	130	------
Beef	------	40	------

| | PERSON-YEARS (10^6) (% OF 1980 POPULATION) | | |
	Full Harvest	Median Case	Carryovers
Cereals	933 (94%)	559 (56%)	176 (18%)
Pulses	------	265 (27%)	------
Beef	------	81 (8%)	------

Elimination of agricultural production would result in a food crisis in China under all but the most favorable circumstances (Table 5.13). If full annual production were in storage, adequate food for one year might be available, but median or carryover levels would support only a fraction of the current population. These calculations assume that both population and food stores would be destroyed as a direct effect of nuclear weapons, but

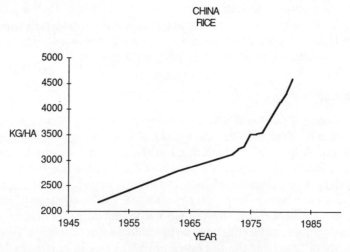

Figure 5.11   Rice yield in China. (FAO production yearbooks)

TABLE 5.14

CHINA 1982[a]

Fuel	Production	Net Imports	Imports as % Production
Crude Oil (1,000 MT)	102,120	(-14,560)	0
Hard Coal (1,000 MT)	635,000	(-4254)	0
Gasoline (1,000 MT)	11,140	(-980)	0
Diesel Fuel (1,000 MT)	17,460	(-1,475)	0

Electrical Generation	10^6 KWH	% of Total
Hydroelectric	74,400	23
Thermal	253,280	77
Nuclear	--------	---
Geothermal	--------	---
Total	327,460	100

N-Fertilizer (1,000 MT)	Production	Imports	Imports % of Production
	10,106,600	1,430,600	14

Tractors	In Use (1980)	Imports (1980)	Imports % of Production
	745,315	4,198	0.6

Land Use	Irrigated (1,000 HA)	Total Arable (1,000 HA)	Irrigated % of Total
	44,770	100,891	44

[a] Data from FAO Production Yearbook (1982); FAO Trade Yearbook (1982); U.N. Energy Statistics Yearbook (1983).

the results are not greatly improved if no stores are destroyed. In the worst cases, a majority of the Chinese population could suffer mortality related to food shortages. A disaster of this magnitude would multiply the societal disruption caused by a large-scale nuclear war.

Chronic-phase recovery would also present many problems for Chinese agriculture. The societal damages associated with targeting and/or an acute phase food crisis would make agricultural recovery much more difficult. Chinese agriculture is energy and subsidy intensive (see Chapter 4), and rice yields would be expected to decline significantly at low subsidy levels

(Figure 5.11). Although China currently produces most of the energy and subsidies necessary for modern agriculture (Table 5.14), the disruptions of communications, transportation, and industrial capacity associated with the acute phase could substantially eliminate the subsidies. An example of a potential vulnerability is irrigation. A large fraction of Chinese agricultural land is currently irrigated (Table 5.14), and requires significant amounts of labor and energy to maintain the system.

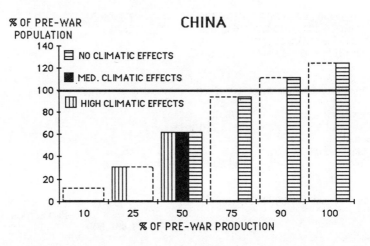

Figure 5.12   Chronic phase population support in China

A wide range of levels of Chinese agricultural production in the chronic phase seem possible (Figure 5.12). If China were not a target of nuclear weapons, and if climate effects were small or nonexistent, little reduction of agricultural production might occur. This is largely a reflection of the import independence of China. Direct nuclear attacks and climatic disturbances could reduce production levels substantially below those required to support the current population. China is particularly vulnerable to climate effects in the chronic phase, because of the importance of rice, a highly cold-sensitive plant.

5.3.7 Costa Rica

Agriculture and food distribution in Costa Rica, a tropical Northern Hemisphere country, could be seriously impaired by a major nuclear war. In the first several weeks following nuclear war, patchy occurrences of low temperatures could occur, although the Costa Rican climate is moderated greatly by the nearby marine influence. As a tropical country, mean temperatures vary little over the annual cycle, and generally range from 20 to 30°C at different locations. Extended periods 10 to 20°C below normal would cause large scale crop losses. Coastal areas might experience milder temperatures, and less severe impacts. Temperature reductions of several degrees could occur in the months following a nuclear war, with possible agricultural effects. Precipitation reductions, and shifts in timing, also might have potential agricultural consequences. Although precipitation increases are possible in coastal areas, decreases of up to 50% might occur in the interior regions as convective precipitation activity became suppressed. Precipitation decreases of up to 50% would not necessarily reduce crop production potential, particularly coupled with decreased temperatures (annual rainfalls of 2 to 3 meters are common). These changes might, however, require shifts of crop types and location by individual farmers, based on little or no climatic predictability.

Extended periods of crop failure and elimination of food imports would lead to food shortages in Costa Rica (Table 5.15). Even cereal stores equaling the full annual harvest would not be sufficient to feed the entire population for one year. In these circumstances, grain that is currently used to feed animals could be shifted to human consumption to replace imported grain. This assumption was made for the calculations in Table 5.15. Pulses might also be in short supply with no production, but cattle and other animals could be used to provide some of the missing calories. We have assumed that cow products are consumed at rates of 500 kcal $\cdot$ person^{-1} $\cdot$ day^{-1}. Higher consumption rates would reduce population support, and it is not clear whether

TABLE 5.15

COSTA RICA
ACUTE PHASE FOOD SUPPORT

| | DURATION OF SUPPORT (DAYS) | | |
	Full Harvest	Median Case	Carryovers
Cereals	224	135	23
Pulses	------	101	------
Beef	------	745	------

| | PERSON-YEARS (10^6) (% OF 1980 POPULATION) | | |
	Full Harvest	Median Case	Carryovers
Cereals	1.4 (61%)	0.8 (37%)	0.1 (6%)
Pulses	------	0.6 (28%)	------
Beef	------	4.5 (204%)	------

TABLE 5.16

COSTA RICA 1982[a]

FUEL	PRODUCTION	NET IMPORTS	IMPORTS AS % PRODUCTION
Crude Oil (1,000 MT)	0	450	---
Hard Coal (1,000 MT)	---	---	---
Gasoline (1,000 MT)	80	50	62
Diesel Fuel (1,000 MT)	140	200	143

ELECTRICAL GENERATION	10^6 KWH	% OF TOTAL	
Hydroelectric	2,430	97	
Thermal	70	3	
Nuclear	------	---	
Geothermal	------	---	
TOTAL	2,500	100	

N-FERTILIZER (1,000 MT)PRODUCTION		IMPORTS	IMPORTS % OF PRODUCTION
	42,000	12,600	30

TRACTORS	IN USE (1980)	IMPORTS (1980)	IMPORTS % OF PRODUCTION
	5,950	515	9

LAND USE	IRRIGATED (1,000 HA)	TOTAL ARABLE (1,000 HA)	IRRIGATED % OF TOTAL
	26	635	4

[a] Data from FAO Production Yearbook (1982); FAO Trade Yearbook (1982);
U.N. Energy Statistics Yearbook (1983).

other food stores would be available to compensate for insufficient stored grain.

Costa Rican agriculture is vulnerable in the chronic phase following a nuclear war for a variety of reasons. If severe food shortages developed during the first year, recovery of production would be more difficult as a result of social disruption. As with grain, Costa Rica depends on imports for many items of agricultural significance (Table 5.16). Energy-intensive inputs are responsible for the recent large yield increases (Figure 5.13) in Costa Rican crops, leading to an unstable agricultural system (Schlichter et

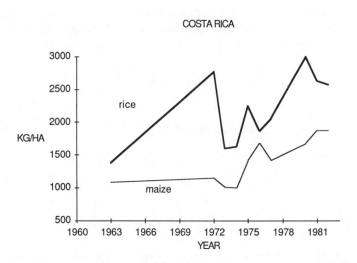

Figure 5.13   Rice and maize yields in Costa Rica (FAO production yearbooks)

al 1985). Ameliorating factors in the chronic phase include the large land area ($>10^6$ ha) used to produce export crops, and the large fraction of electricity produced in hydroelectric facilities. The wide range of climatic impacts, and the potential compensations for nuclear war stresses, lead to a wide range of potential productivities in the chronic post-war environment (Figure 5.14).

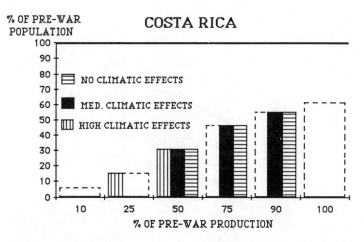

Figure 5.14   Chronic phase population support in Costa Rica

5.3.8 India

India could suffer consequences of nuclear war as severe as those faced by the major combatant countries. India is extremely vulnerable to decreases in the level of agricultural production; food shortages would surely follow

TABLE 5.17

INDIA
ACUTE PHASE FOOD SUPPORT

| | DURATION OF SUPPORT (DAYS) | | |
	Full Harvest	Median Case	Carryovers
Cereals	185	113	28
Pulses	------	170	------
Beef	------	200	------

| | PERSON-YEARS (10^6) (% OF 1980 POPULATION) | | |
	Full Harvest	Median Case	Carryovers
Cereals	347 (51%)	213 (31%)	53 (8%)
Pulses	------	319 (47%)	------
Beef	------	374 (55%)	------

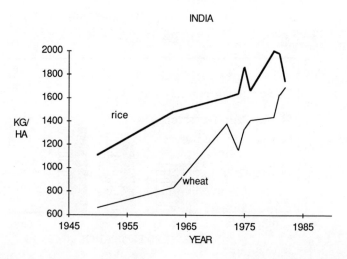

Figure 5.15   Rice and wheat yield in India. (FAO production yearbooks)

a post-war climatic disturbance covering the Northern Hemisphere. India spans a wide latitude range (approximately 10–35°N latitude) and has a wide range of climates. Annual rainfall ranges from less than 500 to more than 3,000 mm, and mean annual temperatures from about 15 to 30°C. Acute-phase reductions in mean temperature could range from relatively mild in some coastal regions to severe in dry inland regions with dense smoke cover. One of the critical considerations would be the timing of a war. Over longer periods, temperature decreases might be less, but the monsoon could be largely absent even for relatively small temperature decreases. Mean temperature reductions of 15°C or more would be expected

TABLE 5.18

INDIA 1982[a]

Fuel	Production	Net Imports	Imports as % Production
Crude Oil (1,000 MT)	19,734	12,936	66
Hard Coal (1,000 MT)	128,320	1,160	1
Gasoline (1,000 MT)	1,750	0	0
Diesel Fuel (1,000 MT)	10,468	2,412	23

Electrical Generation	10^6 KWH	% of Total	
Hydroelectric	52,675	38	
Thermal	82,792	60	
Nuclear	3,210	2	
Geothermal	-------	---	
Total	138,677	100	

N-Fertilizer (1,000 MT) Production	Imports	Imports % of Production
3,143,300	1,055,100	34

Tractors	In Use (1980)	Imports (1980)	Imports % of Production
	418,116	34	---

Land Use	Irrigated (1,000 HA)	Total Arable (1,000 HA)	Irrigated % of Total
	40,600	169,540	24

[a] Data from FAO Production Yearbook (1982); FAO Trade Yearbook (1982); U.N. Energy Statistics Yearbook (1983).

to eliminate agricultural production in India, as would large precipitation decreases associated with failure of the monsoons.

The consequences to India of diminished or eliminated production would be enormous. There is little capacity to feed the population on stored food (Table 5.17). Since there are two major grain harvests in India, even having a full harvest in storage would not support the population for one year. In the worst cases, most of the Indian population would suffer mortality related to food shortages. Although we have assumed India would not be a target of nuclear weapons for the purposes of these calculations, it is possible that India would be targeted, and that would increase the severity of acute phase impacts.

Indian agriculture could be affected by nuclear war for an extended period during the chronic phase. Severe acute-phase effects would slow agricultural recovery, even with no additional climatic impacts. Chronic-phase precipitation reductions could significantly reduce agricultural production. Rainfall in India tends to be highly seasonal, and alterations of rainfall patterns or failure or shifting of monsoons could produce extended difficulties. Chronic phase temperature decreases could produce problems for rice cropping in much of India. Indian agriculture relies on a number of energy inputs and subsidies (Hameed and Parimanam, 1983) to produce high grain yields (Figure 5.15). Without additional climatic disturbances, India might be able to compensate for losses of imported oil and fertilizers (Table 5.18), but with severe disruptions, and possible targeting, yields would be expected to decline.

India is currently independent of food imports, but there is little excess

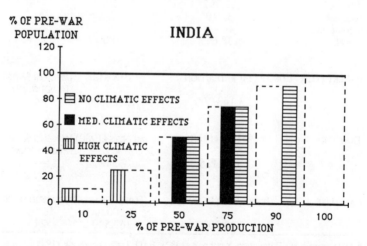

Figure 5.16   Chronic phase population support in India

agricultural production available (Figure 5.16). Given severe climatic scenarios, only a small fraction of the current population could be supported by the diminished agricultural system. Even with no nuclear weapon detonations in India, and no significant climatic stresses, some impact on agriculture could occur as a result of the massive disruption of the international economy and trade expected after a major nuclear war.

5.3.9 Indonesia

The effects of nuclear war on Indonesia are difficult to predict, and depend to a large extent on the severity of climate stresses that would be experienced in equatorial islands. Temperature reductions in the Indonesian tropical lowlands could be moderated by the surrounding ocean. Temperature decreases of a few degrees C would probably not seriously impair agriculture in regions with mean temperatures of 25 to 30°C. Temperature decreases in the range of 5 to 15°C could have a major impact on Indonesian agriculture.

TABLE 5.19

INDONESIA
ACUTE PHASE FOOD SUPPORT

| | DURATION OF SUPPORT (DAYS) | | |
	Full Harvest	Median Case	Carryovers
Cereals	67	67	37
Pulses	------	227	------
Beef	------	32	------

| | PERSON-YEARS(10^6) (% OF 1980 POPULATION) | | |
	Full Harvest	Median Case	Carryovers
Cereals	27 (18%)	27 (18%)	15 (10%)
Pulses	------	92 (62%)	------
Beef	------	13 (9%)	------

Food storage could be a serious problem in the chronic phase if production were eliminated for more than a few months (Table 5.19). Temperature variations are small in the tropical climate of Indonesia, and agricultural production is normally possible throughout the year. The calculations in Table 5.19 are based on the assumption that 1/12 of annual production would be available in storage at any time. The median and full harvest cases

TABLE 5.20

INDONESIA 1982[a]

FUEL	PRODUCTION	NET IMPORTS	IMPORTS AS % PRODUCTION
Crude Oil (1,000 MT)	65,853	(-51,887)	0
Hard Coal (1,000 MT)	481	(-208)	0
Gasoline (1,000 MT)	1,971	1,394	71
Diesel Fuel (1,000 MT)	4,855	275	6

ELECTRICAL GENERATION	10^6 KWH	% OF TOTAL	
Hydroelectric	1,560	21	
Thermal	5,805	79	
Nuclear	------	---	
Geothermal	------	---	
TOTAL	7,365	100	

N-FERTILIZER (1,000 MT)	PRODUCTION	IMPORTS	IMPORTS % OF PRODUCTION
	966,443	183,620	19

TRACTORS	IN USE (1980)	IMPORTS (1980)	IMPORTS % OF PRODUCTION
	13,000	5,149	40

LAND USE	IRRIGATED (1,000 HA)	TOTAL ARABLE (1,000 HA)	IRRIGATED % OF TOTAL
	5,450	19,600	28

[a] Data from FAO Production Yearbook (1982); FAO Trade Yearbook (1982); U.N. Energy Statistics Yearbook (1983).

are both based on this level of food storage. If no other food were available, a massive food crisis would result from the severe climate scenarios.

The significance of potential chronic phase agricultural impacts also depends largely on the severity of climatic impacts experienced. Indonesia is a major energy exporter (Table 5.20), and although there are significant imports of refined energy products and machinery, relatively small impacts are expected independent of climatic stress. High-yield, energy-intensive rice (Figure 5.17) is the major cereal crop in Indonesia. In the severe scenarios for chronic phase temperature and precipitation reductions, annual rice

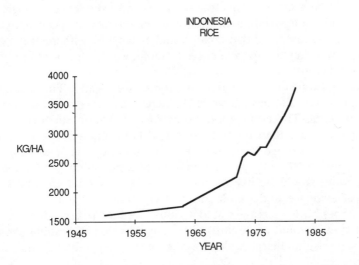

Figure 5.17 Rice yield in Indonesia. (FAO production yearbooks)

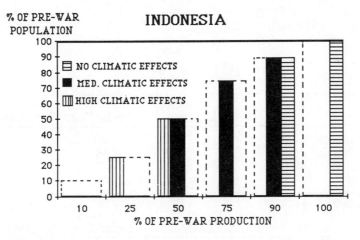

Figure 5.18 Chronic phase population support in Indonesia

production levels might not be substantially reduced, but large changes in precipitation levels or patterns could cause serious problems.

5.3.10 Japan

Japan would be likely to suffer devastating impacts following a major nuclear war, with·vulnerabilities in all of the categories we have analyzed.

Japan could be a target of nuclear weapons and experience damage to the industry and transportation necessary to maintain a modern agricultural system. We have assumed that Japan would be targeted with nuclear weapons in a major war, but the consequences to Japan would also be severe if there were no direct attack.

Japan imports more grain than it produces annually. The median case food support calculations (Table 5.21) include carryovers and a fraction of annual imports. Therefore, food stores for population support is greater in the median case than for full harvest without imports. For none of the calculated food storage levels would there be enough food to support the entire population for a year. Elimination of agricultural production for a year or more would be likely from even relatively mild climatic stresses. Historical evidence and simulation studies indicate that a 3 to 5 degree mean temperature decrease would seriously reduce rice production, and a larger decrease would make Japanese rice production impossible. An acute-phase food crisis and large-scale mortality would be possible in such circumstances.

TABLE 5.21

JAPAN
ACUTE PHASE FOOD SUPPORT

| | DURATION OF SUPPORT (DAYS) | | |
	Full Harvest	Median Case	Carryovers
Cereals	190	201	153
Pulses	------	99	------
Beef	------	28	------

| | PERSON-YEARS(10^6) (% OF 1980 POPULATION) | | |
	Full Harvest	Median Case	Carryovers
Cereals	30 (26%)	32 (28%)	24 (21%)
Pulses	------	16 (14%)	------
Beef	------	5 (4%)	------

Chronic-phase impacts on Japan following a nuclear war could interfere with agricultural recovery. Temperature decreases could continue to inhibit Japanese agricultural production for a year or more following a war, since it is downwind of a large continental area that might have temperatures well below normal. In the worst scenarios, rice production would be impossi-

TABLE 5.22

JAPAN 1982[a]

FUEL	PRODUCTION	NET IMPORTS	IMPORTS AS % PRODUCTION
Crude Oil (1,000 MT)	397	177,455	44,699
Hard Coal (1,000 MT)	17,606	79,066	499
Gasoline (1,000 MT)	26,348	0	0
Diesel Fuel (1,000 MT)	34,979	1,486	4

ELECTRICAL GENERATION	10^6 KWH	% OF TOTAL
Hydroelectric	84,039	14
Thermal	393,405	68
Nuclear	102,430	18
Geothermal	1,273	0.2
TOTAL	581,147	100

N-FERTILIZER (1,000 MT)	PRODUCTION	IMPORTS	IMPORTS % OF PRODUCTION
	1,032,000	48,000	5

TRACTORS	IN USE (1980)	IMPORTS (1980)	IMPORTS % OF PRODUCTION
	1,471,400	5,348	0.4

LAND USE	IRRIGATED (1,000 HA)	TOTAL ARABLE (1,000 HA)	IRRIGATED % OF TOTAL
	3,230	4,829	67

[a] Data from FAO Production Yearbook (1982); FAO Trade Yearbook (1982); U.N. Energy Statistics Yearbook (1983).

ble indefinitely. Even with no climatic impacts, the heavy Japanese reliance on imported energy (Table 5.22) would seriously impair the current energy-intensive system. With reduced subsidies, yield declines of up to 1,000–2,000 kg·ha^{-1} could occur (Figure 5.19). Chronic phase impacts are summarized in Figure 5.20. Because of Japan's import dependence, even 100% of current production could not sustain the current population at steady state. The additional impacts of nuclear detonations, climatic stress, and energy shortages could each significantly reduce Japanese agriculture. The combined impacts of all of these stresses would be devastating.

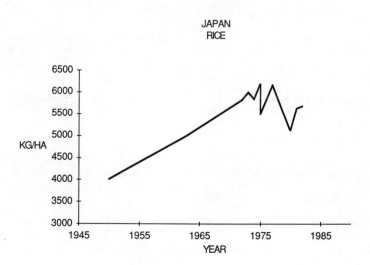

Figure 5.19   Rice yield in Japan. (FAO production yearbooks)

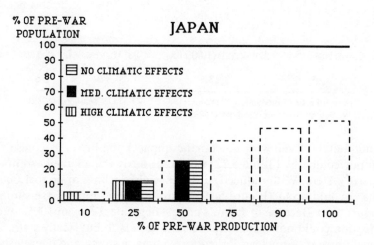

Figure 5.20   Chronic phase population support in Japan

5.3.11 Kenya

Although Kenya is unlikely to be a direct target of nuclear weapons, significant indirect effects could be experienced following a major nuclear conflict. Climatic stresses in the acute phase could reduce agricultural productivity, particularly in the uplands. Large precipitation decreases are possible in the acute phase and might continue into the chronic phase if the monsoons were altered. Transient freezing could also occur in the initial weeks under dense smoke clouds. A nuclear war occurring in the Northern Hemisphere spring or summer would have greater potential for agricultural damage, but yield reductions could also occur after an autumn or winter war.

Kenya would be vulnerable to an acute phase food crisis if cereal production were eliminated for a year or more (Table 5.23). The median and carryover cases indicate that only a fraction of the Kenyan population could be supported for one year on stored food alone. Kenya's cereal imports were 17% of domestic production (1980), and even if the full annual production were in storage, there might be insufficient food for the entire population. Three-quarters of Kenya's population is classified as agricultural (Table 5.1), and its farmers make extensive use of household gardens, an ameliorating factor in a food crisis when compared to more urbanized countries in the same circumstances. The duration and severity of climatic stresses experienced are the principal variables controlling the probability of a food crisis in Kenya.

In the chronic phase, a number of factors could extend nuclear war im-

TABLE 5.23

KENYA
ACUTE PHASE FOOD SUPPORT

| | DURATION OF SUPPORT (DAYS) | | |
	Full Harvest	Median Case	Carryovers
Cereals	251	141	25
Pulses	------	172	------
Beef	------	500	------

| | PERSON-YEARS (10^6) (% OF 1980 POPULATION) | | |
	Full Harvest	Median Case	Carryovers
Cereals	11 (69%)	6 (39%)	1 (7%)
Pulses	------	8 (47%)	------
Beef	------	23 (137%)	------

pacts for several years. Climatic alterations could continue in this period and influence agriculture. Mean temperature decreases of several degrees C and precipitation decreases could reduce yields, increase the time necessary for crop maturity, and require shifts in crop systems and locations. Even with no climatic alterations, a major nuclear war would produce problems in Kenya as a result of disruptions of the international economy and trade. Kenya imports all of it's crude oil, coal, and N-fertilizer, as well as significant amounts of machinery (Table 5.24). The elimination or reduction of these imports could be expected to reduce yields by as much as 1,000 kg·ha^{-1} (Figure 5.21). If climatic stresses were added to import deficiencies of food, energy, and machinery, agricultural production in Kenya could fall to levels much smaller than current (Figure 5.22).

TABLE 5.24

KENYA 1982[a]

Fuel	Production	Net Imports	Imports as % Production
Crude Oil (1,000 MT)	0	2,426	---
Hard Coal (1,000 MT)	0	32	---
Gasoline (1,000 MT)	322	-69	0
Diesel Fuel (1,000 MT)	464	-101	0

Electrical Generation	10^6 KWh	% of Total	
Hydroelectric	1,397	77	
Thermal	311	17	
Nuclear	------	---	
Geothermal	96	5	
Total	1,804	100	

N-Fertilizer (1,000 MT) Production	Imports	Imports % of Production
0	33,900	---

Tractors	In Use (1980)	Imports (1980)	Imports % of Production
	6,546	5,752	88

Land Use	Irrigated (1,000 ha)	Total Arable (1,000 ha)	Irrigated % of Total
	50	2,388	2

[a] Data from FAO Production Yearbook (1982); FAO Trade Yearbook (1982); U.N. Energy Statistics Yearbook (1983).

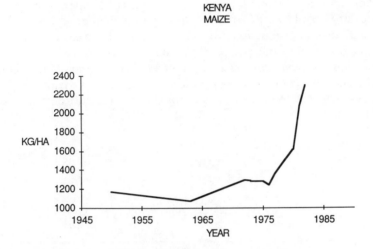

Figure 5.21   Maize yield in Kenya. (FAO production yearbooks)

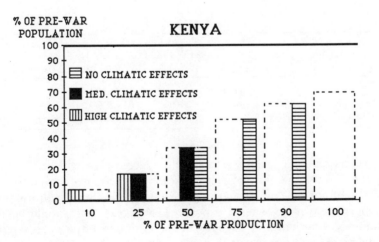

Figure 5.22   Chronic phase population support in Kenya

5.3.12 Nigeria

Nigeria is potentially vulnerable to the climatic disturbances that might follow a nuclear war. These climatic stresses would affect the coastal mangrove and rainforest region differently from the savannahs and arid regions in the north. In the severe case, prolonged periods of temperatures depressed by 10 to 20°C could be experienced throughout the country, seriously affecting agricultural production. Mean temperature decreases of less than 5°C might improve yields, but any precipitation decreases during the first postwar year could be very serious and might extend for years if the monsoon were affected. In the event of a prolonged period of no agricultural production or imports, the food stores could not support the entire population for one year (Table 5.25).

TABLE 5.25

NIGERIA
ACUTE PHASE FOOD SUPPORT

| | DURATION OF SUPPORT (DAYS) | | |
	Full Harvest	Median Case	Carryovers
Cereals	241	137	25
Pulses	------	288	------
Beef	------	119	------

| | PERSON-YEARS (10^6) (% OF 1980 POPULATION) | | |
	Full Harvest	Median Case	Carryovers
Cereals	51 (66%)	29 (37%)	5 (7%)
Pulses	------	61 (79%)	------
Beef	------	25 (33%)	------

Climatic stress, particularly precipitation decreases, might be the most serious concern for the chronic phase. Prolonged periods of rainfall at levels 25 to 50% of normal could lead to significant declines in agricultural production. Nigeria is a major energy exporter (Table 5.26) and should be able to maintain some agricultural subsidies at current rates. Imports of N-fertilizer and machinery are significant, but crop yields (Figure 5.23) are currently low. Elimination of imports could reduce the amount of marginal land used for agriculture. With no climatic effects, current levels of agricultural production could probably be maintained (Figure 5.24).

TABLE 5.26

NIGERIA 1982[a]

FUEL	PRODUCTION	NET IMPORTS	IMPORTS AS % PRODUCTION
Crude Oil (1,000 MT)	63,800	(-56,900)	0
Hard Coal (1,000 MT)	210	0	0
Gasoline (1,000 MT)	2,600	20	1
Diesel Fuel (1,000 MT)	1,900	-20	0

ELECTRICAL GENERATION	10^6 KWH	% OF TOTAL	
Hydroelectric	4,000	53	
Thermal	3,500	47	
Nuclear	------	---	
Geothermal	------	---	
TOTAL	7,500	100	

N-FERTILIZER (1,000 MT)	PRODUCTION	IMPORTS	IMPORTS % OF PRODUCTION
	0	96,700	---

TRACTORS	IN USE (1980)	IMPORTS (1980)	IMPORTS % OF PRODUCTION
	8,600	2,950	34

LAND USE	IRRIGATED (1,000 HA)	TOTAL ARABLE (1,000 HA)	IRRIGATED % OF TOTAL
	30	30,435	0.1

[a] Data from FAO Production Yearbook (1982); FAO Trade Yearbook (1982); U.N. Energy Statistics Yearbook (1983).

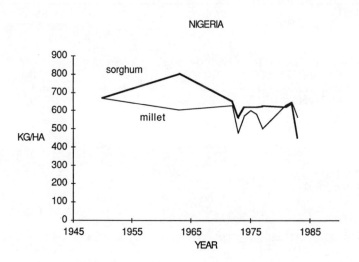

Figure 5.23   Millet and sorghum yields in Nigeria. (FAO production yearbooks)

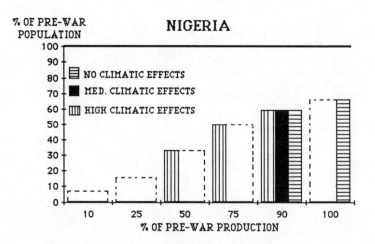

Figure 5.24   Chronic phase population support in Nigeria

5.3.13 Philippines

The Philippine islands cover a wide latitude range within the Northern Hemisphere tropical zone. Coastal environments in the acute phase could expect mean temperature decreases of about 5 degrees or less. Temperature

TABLE 5.27

PHILIPPINES
ACUTE PHASE FOOD SUPPORT

| | DURATION OF SUPPORT (DAYS) | | |
	Full Harvest	Median Case	Carryovers
Cereals	179	119	36
Pulses	------	195	------
Beef	------	29	------

| | PERSON-YEARS (10^6) (% OF 1980 POPULATION) | | |
	Full Harvest	Median Case	Carryovers
Cereals	24 (49%)	16 (33%)	5 (10%)
Pulses	------	26 (53%)	------
Beef	------	4 (8%)	------

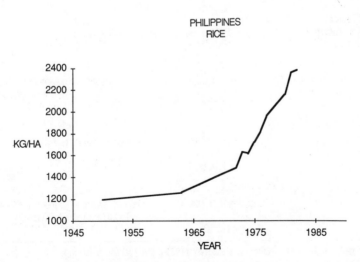

Figure 5.25   Rice yield in the Philippines. (FAO production yearbooks)

changes of this magnitude would not eliminate agriculture because mean temperatures between 25 and 30°C are typical in the Philippine lowlands. Short-term episodes of somewhat larger temperature decreases might occur in the acute phase as the result of the passage of dense smoke clouds or from colder air masses moving off of the Asian continent. Rice production in the Philippines would be very vulnerable to such episodes of chilling temperatures.

The Philippines are vulnerable to a food shortage crisis with no agricultural production for an extended time period (Table 5.27), but the current climatic analysis (Volume 1) indicates that such conditions are not likely. The chronic-phase nuclear war impacts on the Philippines could be diverse.

TABLE 5.28

PHILIPPINES 1982[a]

Fuel	Production	Net Imports	Imports as % Production
Crude Oil (1,000 MT)	463	9,636	2,081
Hard Coal (1,000 MT)	558	4	1
Gasoline (1,000 MT)	1,231	(-20)	0
Diesel Fuel (1,000 MT)	2,325	1,450	62

Electrical Generation	10^6KWh	% of Total	
Hydroelectric	3,773	19	
Thermal	12,093	62	
Nuclear	-------	---	
Geothermal	3,540	18	
Total	19,406	100	

N-Fertilizer (1,000 MT) Production		Imports	Imports % of Production
	40,200	187,000	465

Tractors	In Use (1980)	Imports (1980)	Imports % of Production
	17,000	1,703	10

Land Use	Irrigated (1,000 ha)	Total Arable (1,000 ha)	Irrigated % of Total
	1,370	11,800	12

[a] Data from FAO Production Yearbook (1982); FAO Trade Yearbook (1982); U.N. Energy Statistics Yearbook (1983).

Port facilities and U.S. military bases could be targets of nuclear weapons, imports of energy and N-fertilizer could be reduced, and climatic changes could affect the rice production system.

Philippine agriculture is high-yield (Figure 5.25) and energy intensive. High levels of oil and N-fertilizer imports relative to domestic production (Table 5.28) indicates that Philippine agriculture may be vulnerable to indirect reductions as a result of import elimination. Rice is the principal cereal crop in the Philippines, and is very sensitive to reduced temperatures (Chapter 4). Mean temperatures in the Philippines are generally between 25 and 30°C, and small temperature decreases in the chronic phase might not additionally reduce agricultural production (Figure 5.26). Decreased precipitation, or alterations of timing and duration of rainy periods could affect Philippine agricultural production.

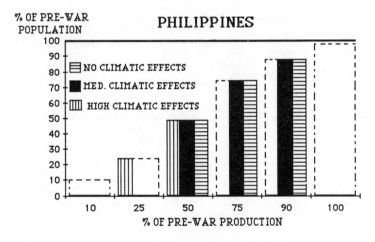

Figure 5.26 Chronic phase population support in the Philippines

5.3.14 United Kingdom

The major impacts of nuclear war on the United Kingdom would be associated with the effects of nuclear detonations. Openshaw et al. (1983) estimated that 20 to 90% of the U.K. population would be casualties in attacks ranging from 40 to 350 megatons of total yield. In addition to massive human casualties, Openshaw et al. described the destruction of large parts of the energy, fuel, and water supply systems, as well as much of industry and transportation.

A large-scale nuclear attack on the U.K. would also cause serious problems for food supply and agriculture. Destruction of food shops and warehouses in urban areas, and the electrical system necessary to maintain frozen food stores, could exacerbate the difficulties of providing food to survivors. If 75% of the population and food supplies were destroyed in a nuclear attack, there might be an adequate amount of food for the survivors (Table 5.29), but food distribution problems would increase difficulties. Mean temperature decreases of 5 to 10°C would be severe enough to eliminate additional agricultural production in the first year following the war.

TABLE 5.29

UNITED KINGDOM
ACUTE PHASE FOOD SUPPORT

| | DURATION OF SUPPORT (DAYS) | | |
	Full Harvest	Median Case	Carryovers
Cereals	600	382	136
Pulses	------	352	------
Beef	------	161	------

| | PERSON-YEARS (10^6) (% OF 1980 POPULATION) | | |
	Full Harvest	Median Case	Carryovers
Cereals	23 (41%)	15 (26%)	5 (9%)
Pulses	------	14 (24%)	------
Beef	------	6 (11%)	------

Many of the problems of the acute phase would continue to impair the recovery of U.K. agricultural production in the chronic phase. Climatic stresses of decreased temperature and precipitation would decrease potential yields, as well as the effects of destruction of the industrial system supporting modern agriculture in the United Kingdom. Residual radioactivity from local fallout could contaminate a substantial fraction of the arable land. Although the United Kingdom is a net energy exporter (Table 5.30), destruction of refineries, transportation facilities, and electrical generators would make it difficult to maintain the high yields typical of pre-war agriculture (Figure 5.27). The combined effects of these stresses and destruction would be to reduce the support capacity of U.K. agriculture to a small fraction of pre-war levels (Figure 5.28).

TABLE 5.30

UNITED KINGDOM 1982[a]

FUEL	PRODUCTION	NET IMPORTS	IMPORTS AS % PRODUCTION
Crude Oil (1,000 MT)	103,647	(-26,465)	0
Hard Coal (1,000 MT)	124,711	(-3,448)	0
Gasoline (1,000 MT)	19,135	(-1,302)	0
Diesel Fuel (1,000 MT)	20,598	(-2,918)	0

ELECTRICAL GENERATION	10^6 KWH	% OF TOTAL
Hydroelectric	5,637	2
Thermal	222,553	82
Nuclear	43,972	16
Geothermal	---------	---
TOTAL	272,162	100

N-FERTILIZER (1,000 MT)	PRODUCTION	IMPORTS	IMPORTS % OF PRODUCTION
	1,270,000	222,000	17

TRACTORS	IN USE (1980)	IMPORTS (1980)	IMPORTS % OF PRODUCTION
	512,494	12,924	3

LAND USE	IRRIGATED (1,000 HA)	TOTAL ARABLE (1,000 HA)	IRRIGATED % OF TOTAL
	152	6,978	2

[a] Data from FAO Production Yearbook (1982); FAO Trade Yearbook (1982); U.N. Energy Statistics Yearbook (1983).

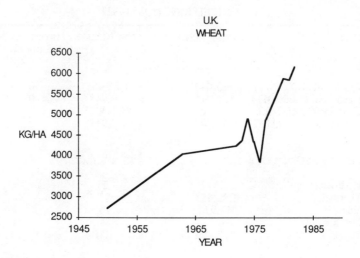

Figure 5.27   Wheat yield in the United Kingdom. (FAO production yearbooks)

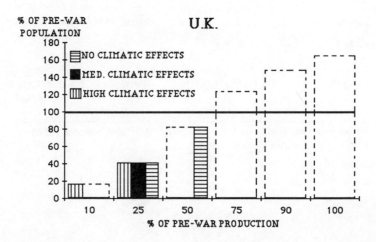

Figure 5.28   Chronic phase population support in the United Kingdom

5.3.15 U.S.A.

The effects of blast, fire, and local fallout "hotspots" would seriously impair the agricultural system of the United States following a major nuclear war. Human casualties of between 50 and 150 million, as well as destruction of most of the industrial system supporting agriculture, would decrease production levels (Harwell, 1984). The subsequent climatic disturbances could essentially eliminate agricultural production in the U.S.A. for at least one year. Mean temperature decreases up to 20 to 40°C and short-term precipitation decreases of up to 100% are possible during the first few weeks. Climatic stresses of half this magnitude could essentially eliminate an entire growing season of production. These impacts would not be confined to the production of grains. Only a small fraction of the current levels of production of animal products and other crops would occur in the first year following a nuclear war (Harwell, 1984).

TABLE 5.31

U.S.
ACUTE PHASE FOOD SUPPORT

| | DURATION OF SUPPORT (DAYS) | | |
	Full Harvest	Median Case	Carryovers
Cereals	2,000	1,290	579
Pulses	------	487	------
Beef	------	329	------

| | PERSON-YEARS (10^6) (% OF 1980 POPULATION) | | |
	Full Harvest	Median Case	Carryovers
Cereals	312 (137%)	201 (88%)	90 (40%)
Pulses	------	76 (33%)	------
Beef	------	51 (23%)	------

The U.S.A. is a major food exporter, with large amounts of stored grain. After an extensive nuclear war it is unlikely that the ability to continue food exports from the remaining stores would exist. This could propagate food shortages to non-combatant countries. As a massive food producer, there are potentially enough food stores to feed the entire surviving United States population for a period of several years (Table 5.31). Serious difficulties in the remaining food distribution and transportation systems could reduce effective food supplies significantly for urban area survivors.

The societal disruptions of a major nuclear attack on the United States would probably continue to impair agricultural recovery for a number of years. In addition, climatic stresses could be significant for up to a few years. Chronic-phase mean temperatures 5 to 10 degrees below normal are possible the first year, as well as precipitation decreases of up to 50% below normal. In the severe chronic climatic cases, agricultural production in the United States would remain difficult for several years. Even milder climatic changes could cause additional disruption of the production system. Mean temperature shifts of only a few degrees could alter the locations where specific crops could be grown. Planting times and frost probabilities could shift enough to make previous experience useless.

The current agricultural system of the United States is energy intensive and high yield (Figure 5.29). Yield decreases of 1,000 to 5,000 kg•ha^{-1} could

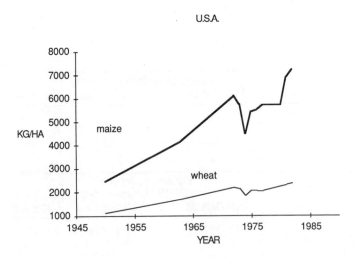

Figure 5.29   Wheat and maize yields in the U.S.A. (FAO production yearbooks)

occur if energy subsidies were cut off. Although the United States has the capability to supply the energy required for modern agriculture (Table 5.32), this capability would be reduced after a major nuclear war (Harwell 1984). Even a relatively small fraction of current agricultural production would support the pre-war population (Figure 5.30), but production decreases in the chronic phase might be reduced below this level.

TABLE 5.32

U.S. 1982[a]

Fuel	Production	Net Imports	Imports as % Production
Crude Oil (1,000 MT)	425,591	161,529	38
Hard Coal (1,000 MT)	707,226	(-95,692)	0
Gasoline (1,000 MT)	272,153	7,602	3
Diesel Fuel (1,000 MT)	131,579	956	1

Electrical Generation	10^6 KWh	% of Total	
Hydroelectric	310,788	13	
Thermal	1,705,807	74	
Nuclear	282,773	12	
Geothermal	4,843	1	
Total	2,304,211	100	

N-Fertilizer (1,000 MT) Production		Imports	Imports % of Production
	10,513,000	2,296,000	22

Tractors	In Use (1980)	Imports (1980)	Imports % of Production
	4,740,000	93,035	2

Land Use	Irrigated (1,000 ha)	Total Arable (1,000 ha)	Irrigated % of Total
	20,582	190,624	11

[a] Data from FAO Production Yearbook (1982); FAO Trade Yearbook (1982);
U.N. Energy Statistics Yearbook (1983).

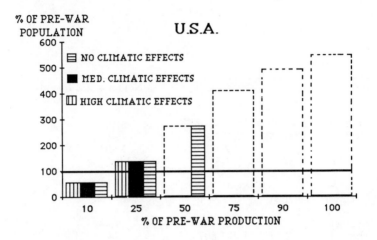

Figure 5.30   Chronic phase population support in the U.S.A.

5.3.16 U.S.S.R.

Agriculture in the Soviet Union is vulnerable to major disruption and reduction following a large-scale nuclear war. Climatic stresses and the effects
of nuclear weapon detonations are the principal dangers to Soviet agricul-

TABLE 5.33

U.S.S.R.
ACUTE PHASE FOOD SUPPORT

	DURATION OF SUPPORT (DAYS)		
	Full Harvest	Median Case	Carryovers
Cereals	1,113	622	98
Pulses	------	1,179	------
Beef	------	292	------

	PERSON-YEARS(10^6) (% OF 1980 POPULATION)		
	Full Harvest	Median Case	Carryovers
Cereals	202 (76%)	113 (43%)	18 (7%)
Pulses	------	214 (81%)	------
Beef	------	53 (20%)	------

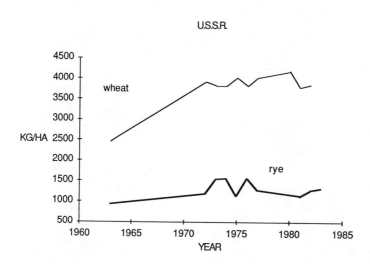

Figure 5.31   Wheat and rye yields in the U.S.S.R. (FAO production yearbooks)

ture. The destruction of a large fraction of the industrial and urban areas associated with military targets would have the additional effect of disrupting the complex system that supports current agriculture.

The Soviet Union is a large, diverse country containing every type of climate, except tropical. Much of the agricultural production in the Soviet Union is associated with mean annual temperatures below 15°C. These areas would be especially vulnerable to the effects of climatic disturbances. As in Canada, Soviet agriculture could be completely eliminated by temperature and precipitation decreases in the first post-war year. The Soviet Union has a strong agricultural system, and stored food could probably support the survivors if distribution systems were intact (Table 5.33). If the war occurred during annual minimum food storage levels (the carryover case), however, food shortages could be a problem even with an intact distribution system.

In the chronic-phase, Soviet agriculture would continue to be vulnerable to climatic stresses and to the effects of massive destruction caused by nuclear weapons. Chronic-phase temperature decreases of even several degrees, coupled with precipitation decreases up to 50% of normal, might be possible for an extended time period. These, or smaller magnitude stresses, could significantly reduce agricultural production. Even with no climatic stresses, agricultural recovery in the Soviet Union would be impaired by the disruption of the industrial and transportation system necessary for modern agriculture. Wheat yields could decline by one-third or more if energy subsidies were eliminated (Figure 5.31). Although the Soviet Union is an

TABLE 5.34

U.S.S.R. 1982[a]

Fuel	Production	Net Imports	Imports as % Production
Crude Oil (1,000 MT)	612,600	(-120,000)	0
Hard Coal (1,000 MT)	488,022	(-11,131)	0
Gasoline (1,000 MT)	77,000	(-7,500)	0
Diesel Fuel (1,000 MT)	121,000	(-22,400)	0

Electrical Generation	10^6 KWh	% of Total	
Hydroelectric	175,277	13	
Thermal	1,111,823	81	
Nuclear	80,000	6	
Geothermal	----------	---	
Total	1,367,100	100	

N-Fertilizer (1,000 MT) Production	Imports	Imports % of Production
10,581,000	32,700	0.3

Tractors	In Use (1980)	Imports (1980)	Imports % of Production
	2,562,000	6,000	0.2

Land Use	Irrigated (1,000 ha)	Total Arable (1,000 ha)	Irrigated % of Total
	18,608	232,266	8

[a] Data from FAO Production Yearbook (1982); FAO Trade Yearbook (1982); U.N. Energy Statistics Yearbook (1983).

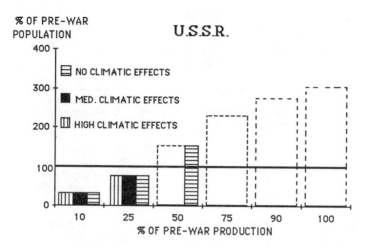

Figure 5.32   Chronic phase population support in the U.S.S.R.

energy exporter (Table 5.34), it would not likely be capable of using and delivering these resources for agricultural production for an extended period. With no climatic stresses, the steady-state carrying capacity of Soviet agriculture could be large enough to support the entire pre-war population (Figure 5.32), but prolonged climatic stresses could reduce production to a small fraction of current levels.

5.4 SENSITIVITY ANALYSES

The calculations of acute-phase food support in each country depend on a number of assumptions. Many of our assumptions were intended to provide a *maximum* estimate of the number of people that could live one year on stored food. Several of these assumptions have been tested with sensitivity analyses.

We have assumed that no animals are fed on stored grain. Animals would be available for direct consumption, and if adequate food were otherwise available, herds could persist at reduced levels through grazing. Consumption of grain directly is more energy efficient, and larger human populations could be maintained on a shorter food chain. We have also assumed a dietary consumption rate of 1,500 $kcal \cdot person^{-1} \cdot day^{-1}$ for cereals. Cereals are currently the largest dietary component in most of the countries considered (Table 5.3). We have assumed this level of cereal consumption because it is not clear that other food stores would be available to provide the minimum requirement of approximately 2,000 $kcal \cdot person^{-1} \cdot day^{-1}$ (based on FAO calculations).

TABLE 5.35

FOOD DISTRIBUTION: SENSITIVITY
CARRYOVERS

Usage Rate (KCAL·PERSON⁻¹·DAY⁻¹)	Person-Years (10⁶)	Distribution Assumption
1,233	82	optimal
1,500	67	optimal
1,233	54	2% of population uses or stores 3,000 kcal person⁻¹ day⁻¹
1,233	56	full population supported 14 days, then optimal.

The importance of dietary consumption rates can be tested through sensitivity analysis. Using the India data as an example (Table 5.35), it is clear that a dietary consumption rate of $1,233$ kcal·person⁻¹·day⁻¹ (based on FAO food balance sheet averages) would still result in only a small fraction of the current population supported by carryovers. We have also compared consumption rates of $1,000$ and $1,500$ kcal·person⁻¹·day⁻¹ for both median and carryover cases (see section 5.5) on a global basis. These calculations indicate that the same pattern of vulnerability to food shortages demonstrated by the analysis of 15 countries holds true even at lower consumption rates. If only $1,000$ kcal·person⁻¹·day⁻¹ were available, other food stores would have to be found to provide long-term population support. Proper nutrition requires more than the minimum energy requirements we have assumed. Fruit and vegetable production would be vulnerable to the climatic effects of nuclear war, and the survivors could be seriously malnourished in terms of Vitamins A, B_{12}, C, and riboflavin (Harwell, 1984).

One of the most critical assumptions of the food calculations is that of optimal distribution pattern. An optimal distribution maximizes the number of survivors in a food crisis. An optimal system implies that the first response must be to deprive a large segment of the population from access to food stores. This dilemma can be illustrated for India. If agricultural production were eliminated for a year or more and only stored food were available, there would be insufficient food for the entire population to survive for one year (Table 5.17). If only carryovers were available, the full population could be supported for less than one month. An optimal distribution system would feed *only* people that could ultimately survive. Diverting food to others would have the result of decreasing the possible number of survivors. Another aspect of the optimal distribution assumption is that no one could store or use more than the minimum share. Any additional consumption or hoarding would reduce the number of survivors. For example, if only 2% of the Indian population used and stored cereals at the rate of 3,000 kcal $\cdot$ person$^{-1}\cdot$day^{-1}, the number of survivors after one year would be reduced by 28 million (Table 5.35). Similarly if implementation of an optimal scheme was delayed by 2 weeks, the number of survivors would be reduced by 26 million. The number of survivors would be even lower at higher per capita consumption rates.

5.5 SUMMARY AND GLOBAL ANALYSIS

The analysis of acute-phase food shortage vulnerabilities for 15 countries clearly indicates that in many countries massive levels of malnutrition and starvation are a possible outcome of a major nuclear war. The principal direct cause of such food shortages would be the climatic disturbances and societal disruptions during the initial post-war year. Even without climatic disturbances, import-dependent countries could suffer food shortages. Many of the countries with the highest levels of agricultural production and storage would probably be targets of nuclear weapons. It seems unlikely that food exports would continue from severely damaged countries, thus propagating effects to non-combatant countries. A similar analysis of food storage vulnerability in 130 countries (Figure 5.33), indicates that a majority of people live in countries with inadequate food stores for such major perturbations.

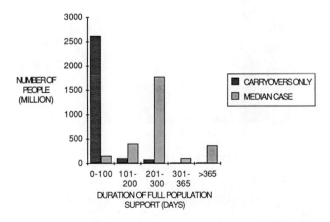

Figure 5.33 Global population at risk of food shortages following a nuclear war

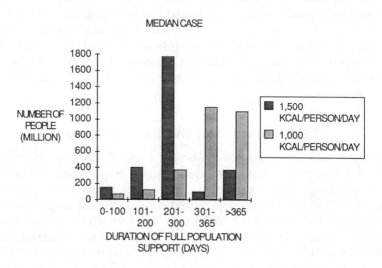

Figure 5.34   Global population at risk of food shortages following a nuclear war, median case.

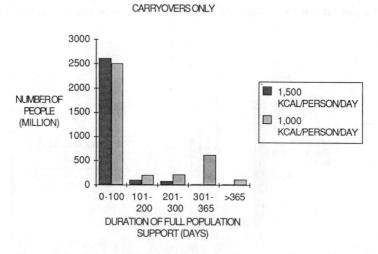

Figure 5.35   Global population at risk of food shortages following a nuclear war, carryovers only.

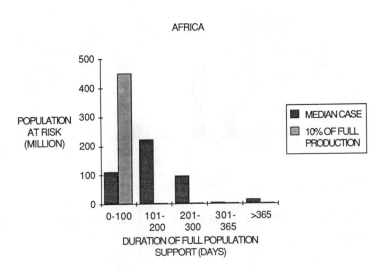

Figure 5.36   African population at risk of food shortages following a nuclear war

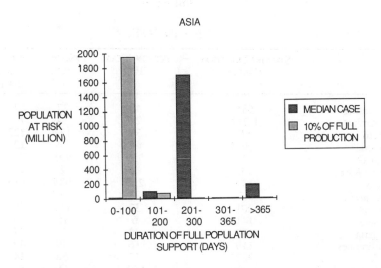

Figure 5.37   Asian population at risk of food shortages following a nuclear war

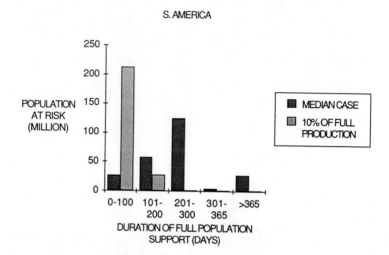

Figure 5.38   South American population at risk of food shortages following a nuclear war

TABLE 5.36

MEDIAN CASE

	Support Duration (Days)	Person-Years (10⁶)	1980 Pop. (10⁶)	Initial Survivors (10⁶)
Argentina	586	43	27	27
Australia[a]	1,211	24	14	7
Brazil	233	78	122	122
Canada[a]	1,935	64	24	12
China[a]	274	559	995	746
Costa Rica	135	1	2	2
India	113	213	685	685
Indonesia	67	27	148	148
Japan[a]	201	32	117	58
Kenya	141	6	16	16
Nigeria	137	29	77	77
Philippines	119	16	49	49
U.K.[a]	382	15	56	14
U.S.A.[a]	1,290	201	228	57
U.S.S.R.[a]	622	113	266	66

[a] Assumed targets, population, and grain stores destroyed in equal proportions.

This is true even if consumption rates of 1,000 kcal·person^{-1}·day^{-1} are assumed rather than 1,500 kcal·person^{-1}·day^{-1} (Figures 5.34 and 5.35).

This vulnerability is particularly severe in Africa (Figure 5.36), Asia (Figure 5.37) and, South America (Figure 5.38). Even though most of the countries of these continents have no nuclear weapons and are not likely to be targeted, the human consequences of a major nuclear war could be nearly as severe as in the principal combatant countries. Few countries would have sufficient food stores for their entire population (Table 5.36), and massive mortality would result if only pre-harvest levels were available (Table 5.37).

TABLE 5.37

CARRYOVERS ONLY

	SUPPORT DURATION (DAYS)	PERSON-YEARS (10^6)	1980 POP. (10^6)	INITIAL SURVIVORS (10^6)
Argentina	66	5	27	27
Australia[a]	566	11	14	7
Brazil	17	6	122	122
Canada[a]	988	33	24	12
China[a]	86	176	995	746
Costa Rica	23	0.1	2	2
India	28	53	685	'685
Indonesia	37	15	148	148
Japan[a]	153	24	117	58
Kenya	25	1	16	16
Nigeria	25	5	77	77
Philippines	36	5	49	49
U.K.[a]	136	5	56	14
U.S.A.[a]	579	90	228	57
U.S.S.R.[a]	98	18	266	66

[a] Assumed targets, population, and grain stores destroyed in equal proportions.

These conclusions represent an aspect of nuclear war that has only been recently realized. The possibility of climatic disturbances following a large nuclear war has introduced a new element to the global consequences expected. Not only are the populations of the major combatant countries at risk in a nuclear exchange, but also most of the global human population. Further, the stresses and problems of the agricultural and food supply systems are not limited to first year following a war. Many countries could experience decreased levels of production, even with no additional climatic effects (Table 5.38).

A similar conclusion was reached in an independent Soviet analysis of

TABLE 5.38

VULNERABILITY OF AGRICULTURAL PRODUCTION
DURING THE CHRONIC PHASE[a]

(ALL CASES INCLUDE ENERGY-SUBSIDY FACTORS)

	NO CLIMATE EFFECTS	MODERATE CLIMATE EFFECTS	SEVERE CLIMATE EFFECTS
Argentina	N-L	N-L	L-M
Australia	N M-H[b]	L	M
Brazil	L	L-M	M
Canada	M-H[b]	H	H-VH
China	N-L M[b]	M	H-VH
Costa Rica	L-M	L-M	M-H
India	L-M	M	H-VH
Indonesia	N-L	L-M	M-H
Japan	M M-H[b]	M-H	H-VH
Kenya	L-M	M-H	H-VH
Nigeria	N-L	L	L-M
Philippines	L-M	L-M	M-H
U.K.	M-H[b]	H	H-VH
U.S.A.	M-H[b]	H	H-VH
U.S.S.R.	M-H[b]	H	H-VH

[a] N = None; L = Low; M = Moderate; H = High; VH = Very High Effects.
[b] Assuming nuclear targets.

chronic phase post-war food supply problems (Svirezhev et al., 1985). This analysis was based on losses of energy subsidies (technological simplification) and altered patterns of international trade. Assuming a minimal caloric supply rate of 1,900 kcal·person^{-1}·day^{-1}, the post-war population support potential of developing countries would be reduced substantially. Africa for example, could only support 67% of the 1980 population following a nuclear war (Svirezhev et al., 1985). This conclusion supports the analysis and ranges presented for chronic-phase population levels in Nigeria and Kenya. As the population and levels of agricultural energy subsidies continue to increase during the remainder of the century, food supply vulnerabilities will increase in developing countries (Svirezhev et al., 1985). If in addition to the import and subsidy losses, climatic disturbances of the chronic phase were severe, only a small fraction of the current world population could expect to survive a few years after a nuclear war.

REFERENCES

Ambio Advisory Group. (1982). Reference scenario: How a nuclear war might be fought. *Ambio*, 1, 94–99.

Bender, A.E., and Bender, D.A. (1982). *Nutrition for Medical Students.* John Wiley & Sons, Chichester.

Chatfield, C. (1954). *Food Composition Tables.* Food and Agriculture Organization of the United Nations, Rome, Italy.

Cross, M. (1985). Waiting for a green revolution. *New Scientist*, 106(1450), 36–40.

FAO (1982a). *The State of Food and Agriculture 1982.* Food and Agriculture Organization of the United Nations, Rome, Italy.

FAO (1982b). *FAO Fertilizer Yearbook.* Food and Agriculture Organization of the United Nations, Rome, Italy.

FAO (1982c). *FAO Production Yearbook.* Food and Agriculture Organization of the United Nations, Rome, Italy.

FAO (1982d). *FAO Trade Yearbook.* Food and Agriculture Organization of the United Nations, Rome, Italy.

FAO (1983). *FAO Production Yearbook.* Food and Agriculture Organization of the United Nations, Rome, Italy.

Greenwood, D.J. (1981). Fertilizer use and food production: World scene. *Fertilizer Research*, 2, 33–51

Hameed, P.S., and Parimanam, M. (1983). Energetics of paddy production in Tamilnada. *Tropical Ecology*, 24, 29–32

Harwell, M.A. (1984). *Nuclear Winter: The Human and Environmental Consequences of Nuclear War.* Springer-Verlag, New York: 179 pages.

Hjort, H.W. (1982). The impact on global food supplies. *Ambio*, 11, 153–157

Openshaw, S., Steadman, P., and Greene, O. (1983). *Doomsday: Britain after Nuclear Attack.* Basil Blackwood, Oxford, England.

Russell, J.S. (1973). Yield trends of different crops in different areas and reflections on the sources of crop yield improvement in the Australian environment. *Journal of Australian Institute of Agricultural Science*, 39, 156–166.

Schlichter, T., Hall, C.A.S., Bolanos, A., and Palmieri, V. (1985). *Energy and Central American agriculture: Analysis for Costa Rica and possibilities for regional indepen-*

dence. Unpublished manuscript.

Scrimshaw, N.S. (1984). Food, nutrition and nuclear war. *New England J. of Medicine*, **311**, 272–276.

Svirezhev, Y.M., Alexandrov, G.A., Arkhipov, P.L., Armand, A.D., Belotelov, N.V., Denisenko, E.A., Fesenko, S.V., Krapivin, V.F., Logofet, D.O., Ovsyannikov, L.L., Pak, S.B., Pasekov, V.P., Pisarenko, N.F., Razzevaikin, V.N., Sarancha, D.A., Semenov, M.A., Shmidt, D.A., Stenchikov, G.L., Tarko, A.M., Vedjushkin, M.A., Vilkova, L.P., and Voinov, A.A. (1985). *Ecological and Demographic Consequences of Nuclear War*. Computer Center of the U.S.S.R. Academy of Sciences, Moscow: 275 pages.

United Nations (1984). *Energy Statistics Yearbook 1983*. United Nations, New York.

Environmental Consequences of Nuclear War Volume II:
Ecological and Agricultural Effects
Edited by M.A. Harwell and T.C. Hutchinson
© 1985 SCOPE. Published by John Wiley & Sons Ltd

CHAPTER 6

Experiences and Extrapolations from Hiroshima and Nagasaki

CHRISTINE C. HARWELL (Editor)

Primary Contributions by: T. Ohkita, Y. Shimazu, T. Urabe,
M. A. Harwell, J. Jacobsen, A. M. Katz, A. Leaf, D. Liverman,
D. Mileti, J. Mitchell, P. Slovic, G. F. White

Additional Contributions: M. Glantz, W. Isard, R. J. Lifton,
M. Lystad, A. Postnov, W. Riebsame, A. Schweiger

This chapter examines the events following the atomic bombings of Hiroshima and Nagasaki in 1945 and extrapolates from these experiences to further understand the possible consequences of detonations on a local area from weapons in the current world nuclear arsenal.

The first section deals with a report of the events that occurred in Hiroshima and Nagasaki just after the 1945 bombings with respect to the physical conditions of the affected areas, the immediate effects on humans, the psychological response of the victims, and the nature of outside assistance. Because there can be no experimental data to validate the effects on cities and their populations of detonations from current weapons, the data from the actual explosions on Hiroshima and Nagasaki provide a point of departure.

The second section examines possible extrapolations from and comparisons with the Hiroshima and Nagasaki experiences. The limitations of drawing upon the Hiroshima and Nagasaki experiences are discussed. A comparison is made of the scale of effects from other major disasters for urban systems, such as damages from the conventional bombings of cities during World War II, the consequences of major earthquakes, the historical effects of the Black Plague and widespread famines, and other extreme natural events. The potential effects of detonating a modern 1 MT warhead on the city of Hiroshima as it exists today are simulated. This is extended to the local effects on a targeted city from a global nuclear war, and attention is directed to problems of estimating the societal effects from such a war.

6.1 LESSONS FROM HIROSHIMA AND NAGASAKI

6.1.1 Introduction

At 08:15, 6 August 1945, an atomic bomb was detonated over Hiroshima, and three days later, on 9 August 1945, at 11:02, another atomic bomb was exploded over Nagasaki. The energy yields of these two bombs were estimated to be 15 ($\pm$3) kT at Hiroshima and 21 ($\pm$2) kT at Nagasaki (Ishikawa and Swain, 1981; U.S.–Japan Joint Workshop, 1985), which are very small compared to the present stage of development of nuclear weapons.

Hiroshima is built on a delta at the mouth of the Ota River, which flows into the Seto Inland Sea from the northern mountains. The east and west are walled off by hills, and the southern delta area faces the Seto Inland Sea. Because the explosion occurred at a height of about 580 m above the center of this fanshaped, flat city, the damage extended throughout the city in all directions. The degree of damage decreased with distance from the hypocenter, but 92% of all structures were damaged to some extent. Virtually the entire city was devastated instantaneously.

Soon after the explosion many fires broke out in the devastated area, merging quickly and spreading in all directions. In Hiroshima, thousands of wooden dwellings and shops were crowded together along narrow streets and were filled with combustible materials. The level terrain was conducive to rapid firespread, and there had been no rain for three weeks, conditions ideal for a firestorm. Winds reached a velocity of 18 m sec^{-1} within two to three hours, with the outbreak of the firestorm. From 11:00 to 15:00, a violent wind blew locally from the center toward the northern part of the city (Uda et al., 1953). The wind gradually decreased and became calm by about 17:00. All combustible materials within a radius of 2 km of the hypocenter were burned by the firestorm.

Nagasaki is built around the Nakashima River basin, the Urakami River basin, and Nagasaki Bay, into which both rivers flow. The city's two basin districts are separated by a hill about 200 m above sea level. The commercial center, the prefectural and municipal offices, and other government offices were concentrated in the Nakashima River district. Along the Urakami River district lies a relatively broad expanse between hills running north and south. There were intermittent rows of factories on the west bank of Nagasaki Bay, and there were also many residences and schools in this district.

The atomic bomb exploded at a height of about 500 m above the center of the Urakami River district. The damages caused by thermal radiation and blast were almost entirely restricted to this area, while most of the Nakashima River district was protected by the hills; however, 36% of all structures in both districts were damaged.

Fires broke out about 90 minutes after the explosion at several locations quite far from the hypocenter. Though the firestorm in Nagasaki was not so large as that in Hiroshima, about two hours after the explosion, when the fire became violent, a southeast wind blew between the hills at a speed of 15 m sec^{-1}. This wind extended the fire toward the north of the valley, where there were fewer residences. About seven hours later, the direction of the wind changed to the east, with a drop in wind speed (Nagasaki City Office, 1977).

The fire-fighting facilities were almost totally destroyed in Hiroshima and Nagasaki. Even where facilities and fire-fighting personnel escaped disaster, blocked roads interfered with fire-fighting activities except along the perimeters of the firestorm areas. Countless water pipes inside damaged buildings were broken, and pumping stations were disabled by the interruption of electric power, causing loss of water pressure and water supply.

In Hiroshima, a mild wind was blowing toward the west at the time of the explosion, and the 'black rain', containing radioactive materials, fell from the north to the west of the hypocenter. Radioactivity was later detected throughout a wide area in the part where rain fell (Yamazaki, 1953; Pace and Smith, 1959; Takeshita, 1975).

In Nagasaki, a wind was blowing toward the east-northeast at the time of the explosion, and rain containing radioactivity was concentrated near the Nishiyama water reservoir 3 km east of the hypocenter. Substantial radioactivity was detected at the Nishiyama district (Shinohara et al., 1953; Pace and Smith, 1959; Takeshita, 1975). It has been said that there were cases of serious biological damage among the persons exposed to black rain or to residual radiation, but there are insufficient objective data available to confirm this.

Many factors influenced the scope of destruction and the number of casualties. Those factors pertaining to the bombs, such as energy, height, and location of the explosion, were highly significant (Glasstone and Dolan, 1977; Ishikawa and Swain, 1981), but the experiences in Hiroshima and Nagasaki reveal the importance of the conditions within the target area as affecting the degree of the catastrophe.

The first factor was the surprise nature of the attack. In neither city was an air-raid alert sounded at the time of the bombings. A large part of the population was in the open or in light wooden dwellings and thus received a minimum amount of protection. The second factor was the protection provided by the terrain. The flat terrain in Hiroshima gave almost no protection, except in the shadow of Hijiyama hill, located about 2 km east of the hypocenter. The rivers within the city, about 100 to 150 m wide, had little or no limiting effect on the firestorm. Because of the hilly terrain in Nagasaki, the area of destruction was largely confined to the Urakami valley district. Moreover, the reported mortality and casualty rates were lower in those parts of the bombed area shielded by the hills, even in districts at about the same distance from the hypocenter (Oughterson and Warren, 1956). The third factor was the immediate paralysis of fire fighting, rescue work, and medical care. There were heavy casualties among physicians and nurses, in the fire-fighting and police personnel, and among local government officials. Many institutions central to the medical, rescue, and fire-fighting systems were completely destroyed. The consequent hampering of rescue work and medical care increased the total mortality in the general population.

6.1.2 Immediate Effects on Humans

According to observations in Hiroshima and Nagasaki, the general course of atomic bomb injury can be divided into four stages (Science Council of Japan, 1951; Glasstone and Dolan, 1977; Ishikawa and Swain, 1981):

1.) initial stage—The greatest number of casualties occurred from immediately after the explosion until the end of the second week; approximately 90% of the fatalities occurred during this stage. The majority of the injured persons receiving medical care for several days after the explosion complained of burn injuries.

2.) intermediate stage—Many moderate injuries caused by radiation were encountered from the beginning of the third week until the end of the eighth week, and most of the remaining 10% of the fatal cases died. The initial and intermediate stages encompassed the acute stage of injury.

3.) late stage—From the beginning of the third month until the end of the fourth, most of those injured survivors showed some improvement, although a few cases died from complications. By the end of the fourth month, most persons suffering from the disasters in both cities had recovered from the acute effects.

4.) delayed effects—After five months, there were various delayed effects: distortions, contractures, and keloids following recovery from burn injuries or mechanical injuries; anemia as a result of bone marrow depression caused by radiation exposure; and disturbances to reproductive functions, such as sterility.

6.1.2.1 Blast

The blast pressures generated by the Hiroshima and Nagasaki bombs at ground zero are estimated to have been 6.4–9.5 psi (44–66 kPa) and 8.5–11.4 psi (59–79 kPa), respectively. The blast wave consisted of two phases: compression and suction. The duration of the compression phase is estimated to have been approximately 0.5–1.0 second. Mechanical injuries resulting from the blasts were direct and indirect, mostly the latter, and were mainly from collapsing buildings, flying debris, or both. There are no reliably established deaths attributable to direct blast effects, that is, resulting from the direct blast pressure on human bodies alone, exclusive of blast-induced contact with other objects. Indirectly, the blasts caused many instantaneous deaths. Middleton (1982) estimated that the LD_{50} for blast alone (i.e., the level at which 50% of those exposed would be directly killed) is about 12 psi, and that some humans could survive blasts of up to 30 psi. The incidence of indirect mechanical injuries among survivors was inversely proportional to the exposure distance from the hypocenter (Table 6.1). Blast injuries occurred mostly among people in structures, less among those outdoors with shielding, and least frequently among those outdoors without shielding— exactly the reverse order from that of burns. Under the condition of enormous blast pressure, buildings and walls offered more risk than protection, especially at close range.

Blast-induced physical injuries of survivors were of all degrees, from minor scratches to severe lacerations and compound fractures. The most common injury was laceration by small glass fragments. Fractures were infre-

TABLE 6.1

TYPES AND SEVERITY OF INJURIES IN RELATION
TO EXPOSURE AT HIROSHIMA[a]

DISTANCE FROM HYPOCENTER (KM)		0	1	2	3	4	5	6
Outdoors (unshielded)	Blast	high	low					
	Burn	high	mod.	low	low			
	Radiation	high	mod.	low	low			
Outdoors (shielded)	Blast	low	low					
	Burn	low	low					
	Radiation	mod.	low	low				
Indoors (wood structure)	Blast	high	high	mod.	mod.	low	low	
	Burn	low	low					
	Radiation	mod.	low	low				
Indoors (concrete structure)	Blast	low	low					
	Burn	low	low					
	Radiation	mod./low						

Casualty Rate (%): high = 50%-100%; moderate = 10%-50%; low = 0-10%.

[a] Data from Science Council of Japan (1951).

quent, but many who did not survive probably had severe fractures. With the extreme scarcity of medical care soon after the bombings and because of lowered white blood cell counts resulting from ionizing radiation, minor lacerations and abrasions, which ordinarily would have promptly healed, often resulted in severe infections.

Rupture of eardrums was considered evidence of direct blast injury among survivors, but its frequency was rather low. For instance, less than 10% of a sample of 200 Nagasaki survivors exposed within 1 km had ruptured eardrums. Several percent of survivors were also reported as temporarily deaf. Other less-defined symptoms may have been blast-related, such as vertigo, buzzing or ringing in the ears, and headache without evidence of trauma. About 15% of the survivors surveyed soon after the bombings complained of these symptoms. Most of them had been within 2.5 km. Transitory unconsciousness immediately after the explosions was frequently described. These symptoms were more likely caused by violent displacement, such as being thrown to the ground, rather than by direct blast. Regarding later effects of mechanical injuries, no data for precise numbers of disabled survivors are available.

6.1.2.2 Thermal Radiation

The intensity of the heat generated by the explosions in Japan is estimated to have been 3000–4000°C at ground level near the hypocenters. Its duration was exceedingly short, approximately 0.5–1.0 second. The heat markedly attenuated with increasing distances from the hypocenters (Table 6.1). There is, however, evidence (e.g., peeling of granite surfaces) that it was more than 575°C at distances of 1.1 and 1.6 km from the hypocenters in Hiroshima and Nagasaki, respectively.

Thermal radiation caused burns directly, or indirectly from fires ignited by the flash from the fireball. Direct burns, often called 'flash burns', were characteristically restricted to one side of the body and were sharply outlined. Indirect burns, or 'flame burns', might involve any part of the body and tended to penetrate much deeper than flash burns. Both types of burns were often combined, but those observed among survivors were predominantly flash burns. When the bombs were dropped, most people wore only short-sleeved, light summer clothes. The effects of radiant heat were enhanced on the bare skin, since clothing was protective to a variable degree, depending on its quality and color and the intensity of the heat. The frequency of burn injuries was exceptionally high. Those in the open without appreciable protection received severe burns within 1.5 km of the hypocenters together with significant doses of ionizing radiation, moderate but still fatal burns within 2.5 km, and mild burns at distances of 3.0–4.0 km. According to a survey conducted in Hiroshima, the frequency of burns was nearly 100%

among unshielded survivors who were alive after 60 days and were exposed at a distance up to 2.5 km; beyond 3 km, it decreased abruptly. Burns were, of course, most frequent in persons outdoors and unshielded, considerably less frequent in those outdoors and shielded, and least frequent among those who were indoors. Persons inside buildings were burned by flash only when the thermal radiation reached them through doors or windows. After the healing of severe burns, overgrowth of scar tissue or keloids was frequently observed, especially among female survivors who were within 2.5 km of the hypocenters. Though it was once suggested that this might have been a consequence of radiation effects, there is no clear evidence to support this. By 1952, there was appreciable regression of protruding scars or keloids in most cases (Ishikawa and Swain, 1981).

6.1.2.3 Ionizing Radiation

Because of the relatively low explosive yields of the atomic bombs, the initial radiation (fast neutrons and gamma rays) produced during a period of about one minute after the explosions played the essential role in radiation-induced health effects. The air dose values of the initial radiation decreased with increasing distances from the hypocenters (Table 6.1). Reassessment of the radiation dosimetry by a joint committee of scientists in Japan and the United States is now in progress, and the final conclusions of this committee are expected in 1986. According to the latest dose estimates, made in 1965 (known as the Tentative 1965 Dose or T65D), air dose values were about 450 rad at 1.0 km and 2.5 rad at 2 km in Hiroshima. In Nagasaki, these values were 925 rad and 18 rad, respectively (Milton and Shohoji, 1968). After extensive surveys of radioactivity over wide areas, including the bombed and fallout areas, conducted by Japanese and American teams, it is generally accepted that residual radiation in the bombed areas mainly resulted from induced radioactivity, and that the contribution of early fallout was not great, except within a few hours after the explosions. Radioactive fallout areas closely approximated the black rain areas, and biological effects of the residual radiation were much less than that of the initial radiation in both cities.

Little is known of the severe radiation injuries that caused instantaneous deaths because these cases were not autopsied in the chaotic conditions immediately after the detonations. For victims who survived for a week or so, the course of those having acute radiation syndrome was predictable by the severity and duration of the early symptoms, dependent on the quantity of radiation doses absorbed. The symptoms and signs of typical radiation injuries resulting from whole-body exposure can be categorized chronologically in the following phases:

1.) the prodromal radiation syndrome, usually consisting of lassitude and gastrointestinal symptoms, such as nausea, vomiting, and anorexia, starting shortly after the exposure and persisting for one or more days;

2.) a period of relative well-being of variable duration inversely proportional to the exposure dose;

3.) a febrile period lasting several weeks, with epilation, oropharyngeal ulcerations, infections, hemorrhagic manifestations, and diarrhea; and

4.) either death or prolonged convalescence with eventual recovery.

In the most severely injured, the febrile phase usually began between the fifth and seventh days, sometimes as early as the third, severe diarrhea being its most prominent manifestation, continuing until death. Many suffered from cerebral symptoms, including convulsions and delirium. The severely exposed usually died within two weeks. In the less severely injured, epilation began about one to two weeks after exposure and initiated the febrile phase, soon followed by pupura and oropharyngeal ulcerations. The less severely but fatally exposed died, as a rule, before the end of the sixth to eighth week after exposure.

The cells of the human body that are very active in proliferation are, in general, most sensitive to radiation exposure. For example, cells of lymphatic tissue, proliferating immature blood cells in the bone marrow, gastrointestinal epithelia, spermatogonia of the testes, and follicle cells of the ovaries are particularly liable to injury from radiation. Among these, depletion of bone marrow cells and denudation of intestinal epithelia by a sufficiently large dose of deeply penetrating ionizing radiation are considered to be the most critical mechanisms for mortality.

The first case of radiation-induced cataract in Hiroshima was discovered in 1948 (Ikui, 1967), and this was followed by many reports of this disease in both Hiroshima and Nagasaki (Hirose and Fujino, 1950). Leukemia among survivors first appeared in 1945 in Nagasaki (Misao et al., 1953) and in 1946 in Hiroshima (Komiya, 1947). Its incidence rose gradually thereafter, reaching its peak between 1950 and 1953, and has maintained high levels since. From 10 to 15 years after the explosion, a general trend in the increase of various cancers, such as thyroid, breast, lung, and multiple myeloma was found among those receiving significant doses of radiation. Microcephaly and other developmental disturbances were encountered among children exposed in utero, particularly within about 17 weeks of gestation (Miller and Blot, 1972). Chromosome aberrations of blood lymphocytes and bone marrow cells have been detected among heavily exposed survivors.

Genetic effects have also been carefully studied. Investigations to date have revealed no adverse genetic effects in the first filial generation born to exposed parents (Kato and Shigematsu, 1985). These results, however, do not necessarily mean that radiation would not cause genetic effects. The genetic effects have thus far proved to be too small to be detected by the methods available during the last four decades (Hamilton, 1985). Although no statistically significant genetic effects have yet been detected in the first filial generation, it is possible that recessive effects will appear in later generations. It is somewhat reassuring that humans do not exhibit a high sensitivity to radiation-induced genetic disorders, but it may be premature to conclude that genetic changes will not occur later from the exposure in Hiroshima and Nagasaki. Investigations need to be continued.

6.1.2.4 Epidemics

Questions have been raised as to whether there were epidemics among the surviving populations of Hiroshima and Nagasaki. The ingredients for development of an epidemic are:

1.) a sufficient number of susceptible individuals in a population to sustain a high incidence of the disease in epidemic proportions;

2.) an infectious agent of sufficient infectivity and virulence to sustain a high prevalence of the disease in the community; and

3.) a means of spreading the infectious agent through the population.

These conditions were fulfilled in the aftermath of the Japanese atomic bombings. The many unburied corpses, the large numbers of injured in unsanitary shelters, the destruction of city water supplies, the failure of the sewage system, the proliferation of flies, and other potential vectors would seem to provide the necessary ingredients. However, the very large proportions of the population which sustained some blast, thermal, or radiation injuries, all of which increase likelihood of secondary infections, make it difficult to distinguish which diarrhea and which sepsis resulted from incidental infection unrelated to the atomic bomb injury and which were directly related to the primary injury. Undoubtedly, the unsanitary conditions that prevailed in both cities in the period immediately following the bombings could have set the stage for epidemics of infectious diseases. However, the extensive injuries would make it almost impossible to separate epidemic infections from those subsequent to the bomb injuries.

Furthermore, bacteriologic facilities were not sufficiently available to isolate infectious organisms to determine whether particular strains were responsible for the many infections that occurred or whether infectious organisms were manifold as expected among the secondary infections contracted by the many injured individuals. In fact, there are only two reports of bacteriological examinations conducted within two months after the bombings. In the first report, blood cultures of 19 survivors who had symptoms of radiation illness, especially with high fever, were carried out in Hiroshima on 30 August and 4 September 1945. Of these, positive results suggesting septicaemia were obtained in five patients. None of these patients survived. Bacteriological examinations of stool from the survivors with mucoid bloody diarrhea, who had symptoms suggesting bacillary dysentery, were performed in August on 200 such cases. Only one case had a positive culture. Results of examinations for typhoid fever on the same survivors were all negative. Stool cultures were also performed on 100 patients with radiation illness. Results were all negative for usual pathogens (U. S. Strategic Bombing Survey, 1946). In the second report, stool cultures were carried out in Nagasaki from 14–22 September 1945, on 37 survivors with diarrhea, or who had past history of severe diarrhea up to that time. Dysentery bacilli were detected in one case (E'njoji and Inoue, 1953). It is presumed that more cases of bacillary dysentery might have been found among victims with mucoid bloody diarrhea, which was generally thought to be one of the symptoms of acute radiation illness, if stool cultures could have been properly performed during the period following the bombings. No such service was available and, accordingly, no conclusion can be drawn about the occurrence of epidemics in either city.

6.1.3 Psychological Responses of Victims

6.1.3.1 Acute Psychological Responses

The psychological state of survivors was the subject of an interview survey conducted in Hiroshima from 1949 to 1952 (Kubo, 1952). An initial, instinctive behavior for protection from various dangers of the devastation of the atomic detonations was for survivors to leave as a mass exodus from the vicinity of destruction. Second, when they recognized the calamity caused by the bombing and observed the disastrous damages never experienced before, they fell into a 'chaotic' state of consciousness in which they could not judge what had happened. Panic occurred, and they took reckless actions which could be considered a reaction to catastrophe. Third, the panic was intensified by further stimuli, including the sudden change of environment because of the disaster and loss of information. With this, they lost the ability to react to external stimuli. They simply followed others and arrived finally at a place which seemed to be safe, where they rested, slept, received nursing care, and at last began to recover their mental function.

Proximally exposed persons, however, were greatly hindered from recognizing the situation because they had developed physical disorders including burns, external wounds, etc., so that their mental conditions cannot be considered apart from their physical condition. However, some of the physical disturbances were later thought to be psychogenic disturbances.

Kubo (1952) reports that recovery of mental function proceeded rapidly soon after the bombing. Proximally exposed survivors developed acute radiation illness in the period one to three weeks after the bombing and again lived in fear of death. It is understood that survivors who did not develop acute radiation illness established a posture of accommodation by confirming the death of family members and the destruction of the community to which they belonged, displaying understanding and judgment of their own situation. Some survivors showed neurasthenic symptoms from 2–3 weeks to 2–3 months after the bombing and some of them developed neuroses (Okumura and Hidaka, 1949).

6.1.3.2 Long-term Psychological Impacts

In a neuropsychiatric study of survivors 10–20 years after the bombing, it was reported that psychosomatic and/or neurotic complaints and symptoms were more frequent in the survivors than in controls (Nishikawa and Tsuiki, 1961). Survivors have what can be considered neurotic conditions; they continue to have mental adherence to the atomic bombings. These complaints have increased with age; a variety of neurotic complaints and symptoms appears in some cases (Konuma et al., 1953). Konuma describes this as the developmental mechanism of a diencephalic syndrome.

As years elapsed after the bombings, survivors remained psychologically precarious for several reasons. First, there was always the threat to their health from delayed radiation effects. Second, there was the fear that their children would be unhealthy or malformed. Third, economic instability threatened if delayed radiation effects decreased their ability to work or care for themselves and also required increased medical expenses. Fourth, death, sickness, and decline or loss of ability to work and manage could further accelerate the disintegration of their families. Fifth, discrimination against them by non-victims added to difficulties in social life, especially the burned victims whose suffering and distress were intensified by the appearance of keloid scars. These multiple effects on health, life, and livelihood imposed a great psychological burden on the victims.

The existence of almost purely psychological phenomena, however, cannot be denied. Such are closely connected with what Lifton (1967) terms the 'taint of death' and 'death guilt', or what Ishida (1973) explains as a 'sense of guilt and shame'. Lifton's 'taint of death' refers to a consciousness deeply imprinted in the minds of the bombing victims 'by three aspects of their ordeal: the suddenness and totality of their death saturation, the permanent taint of death associated with radiation aftereffects, and their continuing group relationship to world fears of nuclear extermination' (Lifton, 1967).

The 'death guilt' he described as stemming from the profoundly inappropriate premature death of many people, which provoked in the survivors the virtually insurmountable feeling that their survival was made possible by others' deaths. Ishida's 'sense of guilt and shame' refers to the victims' self-condemnation with respect to the behavior they inevitably engaged in immediately following the bombings (Ishida, 1973).

6.1.4 Outside Assistance

In addition to examining the purely physical and psychological effects of the bombing, there are other factors which deserve attention, including those which affected the ability of the population to deal with and recover from the bombings. Of particular significance was the availability of assistance to the survivors from both within and without the communities directly affected by the detonations. The nature and extent of this assistance reveal important insights into the ability of communities to cope with such unexpected and unprecedented events.

Prior to August 1945, the city and prefecture of Hiroshima had, under the Wartime Casualties Care Law, established an air defense headquarters, evacuated people, demolished certain buildings to create firebreaks, organized a medical rescue system, and stocked medical supplies. The bombing of Hiroshima on the morning of 6 August left the entire city momentarily immobilized. A 1943 directive by the governor of Hiroshima Prefecture had authorized an 'air defense medical rescue plan', which forbade evacuation of medical doctors and ordered formation of medical rescue squads consisting of one physician, one dentist, one pharmacist, three nurses, and one clerk. Township councils and civil defense teams were to work with these medical squads for the protection and relief of each local district. Of the 298 mobilized doctors in Hiroshima, 270 became atomic bomb victims. Casualty rates among pharmacists and nurses ranged between 80–93%. The well-prepared medical care system for conventional air raids was rendered totally useless. Prefecture and municipal agencies, where the air defense headquarters were located, also suffered heavy damage to personnel and buildings.

By the evening of 6 August, a temporary air defense headquarters was set up by surviving officials of the Hiroshima Prefecture. Requests were sent to the national government and to neighboring prefectures for doctors, and medical and food supplies.

Even though the casualties of military personnel were also great, eleven relief stations were set up soon after the bombing to take care of the injured victims. Relief crews from army and navy bases in and near the city serviced these relief stations. In this immediate post-detonation period, military units played a major role in securing food and drinking water, disposing of corpses, removing debris, and restoring communications and transport services. Japanese military leadership came to an end, however, with the surrender on 15 August 1945.

Right after the detonation, the surviving members of the Hiroshima City Medical, Dental, and Pharmacists Associations were actively engaged in relief efforts, despite the fact that they themselves were suffering from injuries. Doctors from medical associations in adjacent cities and counties and from outside the Hiroshima Prefecture reached the city beginning on 7 August. The number of relief stations in the city reached a peak of 53 on 9 August, gradually decreasing to 11 by 5 October.

Medical teams also came from outside hospitals; it was reported that more than 3000 medical personnel were in Hiroshima by 5 October. A medical survey team was sent on 8 August by the Army Medical School and the Tokyo First Army Hospital. Subsequently, other survey teams came from Tokyo, Kyoto, and Osaka Universities. Apart from the medical relief teams, many persons came from outside the city to assist in coping with the devastation.

At the same time, streams of survivors were flowing out of Hiroshima to the towns and villages of adjacent counties. The total number of people who left Hiroshima at this time is estimated to have been about 150,000 (Hiroshima A-bomb Medical Care History Editorial Committee, 1961). Faced with this sudden influx of refugees, the surrounding towns and villages had an urgent need of increased medical personnel and supplies, but in most of these places it was impossible to meet the demand for help. Thousands of injured persons were accommodated in provisional relief stations such as primary schools and were taken into private homes, without receiving any substantial medical treatment.

In Nagasaki, the defense headquarters had been established in 1944, and the Nagasaki Defense Mobilization Council in 1945. Rescue and relief precautions centered on the city's medical association. There were 22 designated relief stations, and 327 persons were organized to service these stations. Nagasaki Medical University Hospital and Mitsubishi Hospital were also expected to serve as key relief centers (Nagasaki City Office, 1977). But the destructive power of the atomic bomb far exceeded such defense and relief capabilities.

The main buildings and lecture rooms of Nagasaki Medical University were demolished and burned, and almost all teaching staff either died instantly or within a few days. The number of casualties among the administrative staff, nursing staff, and medical and pharmacy students was great. Three other hospitals in the bombed area had similar conditions.

Wounded civilians gathered at places designated prior to the bombing as relief stations. Relief work was begun, despite the lack of medical supplies, in more than 10 such provisional shelters by surviving staff of the medical university and of other hospitals as well as other surviving medical personnel.

Medical relief teams also soon reached the city from naval hospitals, army hospitals, and outside medical associations.

Large numbers of victims left the city soon after the bombing by foot, truck, and train. Hospitals outside the area received more than several thousand surviving patients. Neighboring towns and villages also received streams of injured victims. It was reported that approximately 20% of these patients died within the next two months.

6.2 EXTRAPOLATIONS FROM HIROSHIMA AND NAGASAKI AND OTHER DISASTERS

In addition to examining the factual data about the effects of the bombings of Hiroshima and Nagasaki in order to understand the lessons that can be drawn, it can be instructive to appraise these data to formulate more general conclusions about the effects of large-scale but localized disasters. To put this information into proper perspective, discussions in the following section deal with comparisons of the effects of other disasters which have been visited on communities and populations from sources both natural and anthropogenic.

6.2.1 Comparisons with Other Major Disasters for Urban Systems

When the possible destructiveness for humans of a major nuclear war is estimated, whether for a major exchange or even a single 1 MT detonation, it is difficult to find disasters in recent centuries that are comparable in magnitude and severity. The Hiroshima and Nagasaki explosions were much smaller than any now expected from strategic weapons.

Table 6.2 presents estimates of the human deaths that occurred following a variety of extreme epidemics and natural and technological events for which moderately detailed data are available. Table 6.3 summarizes the estimates of mortalities for the nuclear war scenarios published by the World Health Organization Committee (Bergstrom et al., 1983), Ambio (Ambio Advisory Group, 1982), and the U.S. Office of Technology Assessment (OTA, 1979). From these it is seen that only a few of the recorded historical episodes were of the minimum size contemplated in the nuclear war scenarios considered in this report, and that none approached in absolute terms the expected losses. When the fatalities are taken as proportions of the total population at risk from the threat, only a few of the past episodes are noteworthy.

The largest non-nuclear disasters, in terms of the proportion of affected population that died, were in places devastated by earthquakes, tidal storms, floods, and the plague. In absolute numbers, the two World Wars exacted heavy tolls of lives, rivaling in size the world-wide influenza epidemic of 1919.

In considering the potential effects of current disasters, both nuclear and non-nuclear in origin, several factors should be noted. The concentration of population into big cities is accelerating. The gap between overall capacities of urban and rural areas appears to be increasing in many regions, so that large urban systems become too big to be supported in an emergency by the immediately surrounding areas. Today, in general, levels of food stocks at individual homes are low, and distribution systems are centralized; situations are similar in energy supply and consumption. In these regards, urban systems are becoming even more vulnerable to catastrophes.

The nature of current nuclear weapons makes many advance actions other than evacuation useless. Even if a mass evacuation outside a city could be effectively done, there would be no homes to return to. For example, precautions against fires would be insignificant in the reduction of injuries because the primary fire by the thermal radiation from a detonated nuclear weapon is so intense. Casualties per unit area are great; thus, medical aid is crucial after a nuclear attack. The British Medical Association report (1983) on the medical effects of nuclear war reached the conclusion that such a nuclear attack would cause the medical services in a country to collapse (see also Abrams and von Kaenal, 1981). The possibility of providing individual medical or nursing attention for victims of a nuclear attack could become remote, at some point disappearing completely, with only primitive first aid attention from fellow survivors available.

6.2.1.1 Earthquakes

To predict the impacts of local nuclear attack to cities, the lessons from other types of disasters may be useful. Earthquakes have a special relevance, at least in Japan.

Japan is a seismically active region, and the statistics imply that a major earthquake with M = 8 occurs on the average of once every century. The Tokyo earthquake of September, 1923, with an intensity of M = 7.9, is described briefly here for reference. The disasters accompanying this earthquake were characterized by secondary mass fires which burned an area of 38 km^2, or 44% of the entire city. Total deaths were 68,600, of which 90% were losses associated with the fires. Mass fires broke out in 92 places, and a firestorm was generated with wind speeds reaching 30 m sec^{-1}. The fires were not brought under control until 42 hours after the earthquake. The causes of fire outbreak were: home kitchens (34%), storage of chemicals (31%), and commercial kitchens (28%). The high density of wooden houses was the major factor in exacerbating the damage from the mass fire. Within 30 days of the earthquake, 2,221,000 people, or about half the total inhabitants who lost their houses, were moved to other cities as refugees.

Martial law was instituted and the urban systems were maintained by military troops coming from surrounding areas. Since the support system at

MAJOR DISASTERS IN HISTORY[a]

TABLE 6.2

	EVENT	FATALITIES	POPULATION AFFECTED	AREA AFFECTED	REFERENCE
FLOODS	1887 Huang Ho, Yellow River, China	$1.5 - 7.0 \times 10^6$	1500 villages	$1 \times 10^4 mi^2$	Champ (1982)
	1931 Yangtze, China	3.7×10^6	------	$7 \times 10^4 mi^2$	Champ (1982)
	1938 Honin, Yellow River, China	0.5×10^6	6.0×10^6	------	Champ (1982)
FAMINES	1869-1870 Bengal, India	$3.0 - 10.0 \times 10^6$	30%	-----	Gibney (1978)
	1876-1877 Madras, India	3.5×10^6	20.0×10^6	$4.0 \times 10^4 mi^2$	Gibney (1978)
	1877-1878 North China	$9.5 - 13.0 \times 10^6$	70×10^6	-----	Nash (1977)
	1968-1974 Sahel, Africa	$0.1 - 0.2 \times 10^6$	22.0×10^6	$1.5 \times 10^6 mi^2$	Glantz (1976)
EARTHQUAKES	1556 Honan, Shensi, Shansi, China	0.83×10^6	-----	-----	U.S. Department of Commerce (1979)
	1773 Calcutta, India	0.3×10^6	-----	-----	Nash (1977)
	1976 Hopei, China	$0.2 - 0.99 \times 10^6$	12.8×10^6	$1.0 \times 10^4 mi^2$	Time (9 Aug 1976)
STORMS	1737 Bay of Bengal, India	0.3×10^6	-----	-----	Nash (1977)
	1970 Ganges Delta, East Pakistan	$0.16 - 0.5 \times 10^6$	3.0×10^6	$3.0 \times 10^3 mi^2$	Time (7 Dec 1970)
FIRES	1857 Tokyo, Japan	10.7×10^4	-----	-----	Ishikawa and Swain (1981)
	1923 Tokyo, Japan	6.8×10^4	4.0×10^6	$38 km^2$	this volume
VOLCANOS	1793 Miya-Yama, Java	5.3×10^4	-----	-----	Nash (1977)
	1883 Krakatoa, Java	3.6×10^4	-----	-----	Nash (1977)

[a] Compiled by Axel Schweiger.

	EVENT	FATALITIES	POPULATION AFFECTED	AREA AFFECTED	REFERENCE
AVALANCHES	218 B.C., Alps	1.8×10^4	4.6×10^4	——	Nash (1977)
	1962 Huascaran, Peru	0.4×10^4	9 villages	——	Nash (1977)
INDUSTRIAL	1949 Joh.-Georgenstadt, East Germany	0.3-0.4×10^4	——	——	Nash (1977)
	1984 Bhopal, India	0.14-1.0×10^4	2.0×10^5	——	Der Spiegel (22 Apr 1985)
SHIPS	1865 Sultana USA	0.15×10^4	0.24×10^4	——	Nash (1977)
	1912 Titanic Britain	0.15×10^4	0.22×10^4	——	Nash (1977)
AIR CRASHES	1974 Orly France	346	346	——	Ferrara (1979)
	1977 Teneriffe	582	652	——	Newsweek (11 Apr 1977)
	1980 Riyad Saudi Arabia	301	301	——	New York Times (21 Aug 1980)
	1985 Ireland	329	329	——	The Times (UK) (24 June 1985)
	1985 Tokyo Japan	520	524	——	The Times (UK) (14 Aug 1985)
RAILROAD	1915 Guadalajara, Mexico	600	900	——	Nash (1977)
	1917 Modane, France	543	1200	——	Nash (1977)
EPIDEMICS	1346-1350 plague Europe, Asia	25×10^6	30%	——	McNeill (1976); Garb and Eng (1969)
	1919 influenza worldwide	20×10^6	1.65×10^9	——	Garb and Eng (1969)
WARS	1914-1918 World War I	12×10^6	——	——	Richardson (1960)
	1939-1945 World War II	30-40×10^6	——	——	Richardson (1960)
	1945 Hiroshima	0.12×10^6	3.2×10^6	——	Ishikawa and Swain (1981)

TABLE 6.3

FATALITIES AND CASUALTIES FROM HYPOTHESIZED NUCLEAR ATTACKS[a]

SCENARIO	FATALITIES	INJURIES	POPULATION AFFECTED	AREA AFFECTED	REFERENCE
Hiroshima (1 MT)	$0.4\text{-}0.6\times10^6$	0.2×10^6	1.0×10^6	-----	Urabe (1985)
W.H.O. (10,000 MT)	1.15×10^9	1.1×10^9	4.0×10^9	world	W.H.O. (1983)
AMBIO (5700 MT)	0.75×10^9	0.34×10^9	1.29×10^9	Northern Hemisphere	AMBIO (1982)
limited nuclear war	$8.0\text{-}14.0\times10^6$	$8.0\text{-}14.0\times10^6$	2.2×10^8	U.S.	Katz (1982)
Harwell (5700 MT)	$1.2\text{-}1.3\times10^7$	$3.0\text{-}5.0\times10^6$	2.2×10^8	U.S.	Harwell (1984)

[a] Compiled by Axel Schweiger.

the national level was effective, the recovery was rather rapid; e.g., electric service was reinstituted within 9 days, telephones within 29 days, and transportation by railroad within 3 days. Infectious disease cases were twice those in the normal summer; prices of food and other daily necessities doubled for a month. Total damages cost three times the national government budget of Japan in 1923 (Tokyo City Office, 1925).

On 28 July 1976, the city of Tangshan, China, was virtually destroyed by an earthquake of M = 7.8. At least 250,000 people died, according to city officials. The greatest damage occurred around the railway line that connects Peking, 150 km to the west, with Shenyang, an industrial city to the northeast. All electrical power and communications were disrupted. Notice to the outside came from reconnaissance overflights; outside assistance appeared 12 hours after the initial shock. Within two weeks, 100,000 army troops were transported to Tangshan, along with 30,000 medical personnel and 30,000 construction workers. Injured civilians were evacuated by airlift. Bodies of the dead were buried in mass graves in a deserted open-pit mine.

The city has largely been rebuilt, with new buildings designed to resist a maximum shock of M = 6.3. The population of the city and surrounding countryside has increased since the time of the earthquake from ≈ 1.0 to 1.3 million (Burns, 1985).

Table 6.4 compares damages from the Tokyo earthquake of 1923 with the Tokyo air raid of 1945 and the atomic bombings of Hiroshima and Nagasaki. The extraordinarily high number of deaths per unit area in Hiroshima and Nagasaki implies that the type of destructive force used led to more deaths than injuries in the burned areas, compared to the effects of the other forces on Tokyo, although the Hiroshima and Nagasaki numbers partly include retarded secondary deaths and deaths of non-permanent residents.

TABLE 6.4

COMPARISON OF DESTRUCTION IN JAPAN[a]

	TOKYO EARTHQUAKE 1923	TOKYO AIR RAID 1945	HIROSHIMA 1945	NAGASAKI 1945
Population (x 10^6)	4.0	6.5	0.26	0.17
Burned area (km^2)	38	40	13[b]	6.7[b]
Demolished/burned buildings	0.37×10^6	0.27×10^6	0.05×10^6	0.13×10^6
Fatalities (number) (% of population)	68,000 0.017%	83,600 0.013%	>118,000 45%	>60,000 35%
Fatalities km^{-2}	1,600	2,100	>9,000	>8,900

[a] After Shimazu (1985).

[b] Areas subjected to blast and thermal radiation (primary fire) are included with areas burned by secondary fires.

Disasters by both earthquake and air raids in Tokyo were characterized by large numbers of fatalities from secondary fires. Some conclusions are that requiring the fire- and earthquake-proofing of buildings by revision of building codes is effective in reducing casualties, and that promotion of precautions against firespread is also quite effective. These are the major objectives of the urban disaster reduction program in Japan since World War II. They have been fairly well achieved, and the outbreaks of fires and deaths by burning have been significantly reduced in subsequent earthquakes. For instance, there was no mass fire and only 27 persons were lost by an earthquake of M = 7.4 which struck Sendai city (population 640,000) in 1978.

This is mainly a result of the revision of building codes and the switching off of the sources of fire by civilians. Use of shock-sensitive oil heaters was also helpful. Such actions, however, are not likely to affect substantially the initiation, propagation, and development of urban fires from a nuclear detonation.

Although damage by fire after earthquakes has been reduced significantly in Japan, another type of urban disaster has risen in importance: paralysis of urban systems of electricity, water, gas, food supplies, communications, and transportation. In the Sendai earthquake, for instance, it took more than one month before the water and gas supplies were restored, and the overload of telephone lines caused panic among civilians. Damage of traffic signals also led to large traffic jams, which inhibited evacuation from devastated areas and inhibited influx of outside assistance.

One major problem in counteracting the effects of a disaster is the possibility of an outbreak of mass panic, although in many modern disasters neither panic nor rioting and looting occurred. Urban systems are characterized by a separation of living place and working place, i.e., a significant increase in the daytime center city population density; therefore, outward movement from the city centers would start immediately after the warning.This transient stage is highly vulnerable to the occurrence of damage from disasters such as earthquakes. Detailed simulation of a coupling of warning with the potential behavior of civilians implies that it would take about three times the length of normal commuting time to evacuate a city center (Leaning and Keyes, 1983). This evacuation of a normal daytime population is improbable when the population of the city exceeds 2 million. This means that if a warning were to be issued several hours before a projected earthquake in a city the size of Tokyo, evacuation would likely reach a catastrophic state before the earthquake occurred (Hiramatsu, 1980).

6.2.1.2 Conventional Bombings of World War II

Tokyo was attacked by numerous mass air raids during World War II (see Table 6.4). Among 130 attacks, the largest one occurred on 10 March 1945, from which 40 km^2 were burned; 267,000 houses and 83,600 people were lost within two hours from mass fires caused by conventional weapons totalling only 1.7 kT in energy yield. The fire attack was aimed at the downtown areas with a population density of 5,000 people km^{-2}. The deaths per kT from the bombing on 10 March were about 20 times the average from attacks on other Japanese cities. According to the reports by bomber crews, the height of the ensuing firestorm was greater than 10 km and could be observed 250 km from Tokyo. The wind speed of the firestorm at the surface was estimated at 30 m sec^{-1}. Another major air raid on Tokyo occurred in May 1945, and the urban systems nearly collapsed. The population decreased from 6.5 million before 10 March to 3.5 million after May 1945.

The estimates made of total loss of life in Germany from bombing attacks by the Allied Air Forces during World War II approach 800,000. The greatest losses of life in individual attacks were those where great fires occurred, particularly Dresden and Hamburg. Attacks in July 1943 on Hamburg led to one large fire from which 60,000 persons perished. Reports from Dresden indicate as many as 300,000 deaths there from attacks during the closing days of the war in 1945 (Bond, 1946).

The most prominent causes of death, studied at the time by the German Luftwaffe, were: 1.) death from external injury—burial under rubble and debris and injury from flying fragments; 2.) secondary injuries from explosions—drowning, scalding, chemical burns, poisoning from by-products of exploded bombs; 3.) burns; 4.) tetanus secondary to burns; and 5.) internal injuries.

There was a definite relationship between the type of bomb dropped and the mechanism of death or injury. An incendiary raid was expected to cause more dead than wounded, through the effects of heat and carbon monoxide; in bombings with high explosives, on the other hand, mechanical injuries outnumbered deaths. Season, geographical location, and type of city bombed were important factors in the evaluation of air raid casualties (Bauer, 1945).

During the attack on Hamburg, incendiary bombs started fires which spread particularly in inhabited areas in a very short period of time. The heat increased rapidly and produced a wind of typhoon strength, creating the conditions necessary for a firestorm. It is estimated that within 20 minutes of the initiation of bombing, two of every three buildings were burning within a 11.7 km^2 area; the rising column of heated air created an incoming draft of ground-surface air which reached a speed of 33 km hr^{-1}. In a short time, the temperature reached the ignition point for all combustibles, and the entire area was ablaze. Because of the rapid spread of the fires, people crowded into shelters which were already occupied beyond their capacity. As the temperatures increased in the streets from the spread of the firestorm, many of the occupants of the shelters realized the danger in the situation, yet few tried to escape. Carbon monoxide poisoning became the major cause of death of those who stayed in the shelters (Bond, 1946).

By comparison of proportions of casualties from the single nuclear weapon detonations over Hiroshima and Nagasaki and the conventional bombing attacks on Dresden and Hamburg, the total effectiveness of the bombings could be said to have been the same. The creation of firestorms led to the majority of casualties from fire in all instances. The differences lie not in the effects of the weapons themselves, but in the ease and economy with which these weapons could be delivered. In Hiroshima and Nagasaki, delivery of single weapons from single planes effected the same degree of damage as from all the planes and all the weapons dropped over Hamburg and Dresden.

6.2.1.3 Leningrad

The siege of Leningrad lasted 29 months, beginning in September, 1941. The city was virtually isolated from the mainland. In 1939, Leningrad's population was approximately 3 million; at the beginning of the siege, there were more than 2.5 million inhabitants there (Pavlov, 1967). By the end of 1943, the population had dropped to approximately 600,000. Deaths caused by bombardment totalled about 17,000, and about 800,000 perished because of starvation and cold.

Considerable food stocks were lost because of bombardment and the fires which ensued, in addition to the loss of food imports from surrounding areas because of the siege. Rationing was instituted, but civilians received fewer then their alloted calories as a result of difficulties in obtaining food supplies in large volumes for distribution, in spite of the evacuation of almost one million residents. This major loss of life occurred in spite of the continued existence of a social infrastructure in the city and despite the relatively small physical damage which was incurred.

6.2.1.4 Plague

It has been suggested by some that the bubonic plague which swept from the Crimea through Europe during the 14th century, with the total losses presented in Table 6.2, was most nearly comparable to what might be expected following a nuclear war. The spread of the Black Death (*Pasteurella pestis*), beginning in 1331 and peaking during 1346–1350 (McNeill, 1976), brought tremendous loss of life. McNeill estimated that approximately one-third of the total population of Western Europe died. The estimates for Great Britain range between 20–45%. Some places, such as Milan, were unaffected, while some smaller towns were totally extinguished.

The impacts, however, were not comparable to those expected from nuclear war for at least six reasons:

1.) No buildings, roads, or other physical infrastructures were destroyed, although some suffered from lack of maintenance.

2.) Plants and domestic animals were not directly affected, so that agricultural production was reduced chiefly by lack of labor.

3.) The health of the survivors, especially of those immune to the disease, was not impaired seriously in either the short- or long-range time period, although their state of mind was affected.

4.) Thus, the survivors were left with access to increased stocks of physical equipment and natural resources per capita.

5.) The plague left few places of long-lasting contamination inasmuch as the survivors were immune.

6.) The spread of the infestation occurred over periods of months or years, and while the death rate typically showed pronounced peaks during the epidemic, there usually were periods of slow build-up and decline.

For these reasons, the social impacts of the plague, beyond those of the high mortality and the psychological distress, have little in common with those likely to follow nuclear war.

6.2.1.5 Famines

Throughout history, famines have involved people living impoverished lives who experience an extreme, usually natural, event such as drought, flood, or crop disease. Famine is defined here as severe hunger occurring long enough and over a large enough area to result in deaths sufficiently in excess of normal death rates to cause social disruption. While an extreme event is not in itself a sufficient condition for famine (e.g., the United States weathered the 1930's Dust Bowl years without famine), probably an extreme event is a necessary condition for famine. The event need not be natural; extreme human-caused events are entirely capable of causing famine, as war has throughout history. Human intervention can exacerbate the consequences of an extreme event; for example, food price increases can turn a modest production decline into a famine, and aid that is little, late, or misdirected can allow what would have been merely a bad year to evolve into famine.

The condition required for famine has historically been a particular kind of poverty; i.e., the absence of methods of coping with lean years.People in societies that are vulnerable to famines either have never had, or have been deprived of having practices that provide some form of insurance to rely on in bad years: either stored food or saved wealth with which to buy food.

Famine experiences help put into perspective the problems that might arise following a nuclear war concerning the potential shortages of food and other resources necessary to produce food. Any country on Earth with people living precarious lives without a buffer against lean years might experience famine in the event of a major disaster, such as nuclear war, even though food supplies were adequate. Dominant political events can cause and exacerbate famine; economic events can worsen slight declines in physical outputs of food. Both the climatic effects and the social and economic disarray likely to accompany nuclear war could trigger famine among countries and among people living outside the combatant zone.

In a compilation of famine statistics, Walford (1878) listed 350 famines covering roughly a 250-year period. Europe, and especially the British Isles, dominate the list prior to 1700, though China, Russia, Mexico, and Africa each appear once, and India appears several times. After 1700, 34 of the 58 famines listed occurred in India. Except for the Chinese famine of 1877-78, the remainder occurred in Europe, notably Ireland. Since World War II, famine has been limited almost exclusively to Africa, especially the Sahel region and Ethiopia. The major exception is the Bangladeshi famine of 1974, and some war-related hunger that has occurred in Southeast Asia, most notably Cambodia (McHenry and Bird, 1977; Stief, 1980) and Vietnam (Karnow, 1983).

Lucas (1930) synthesized numerous medieval sources to describe the famine that affected virtually all of Europe in the early part of the 14th century. The famine followed continuous and extraordinary rainfall during the summer and fall of 1315 that ruined nearly all crops in that one harvest year. In Ireland during the mid-1800's, the failure of the potato crops from blight and the bitterly cold winters brought an estimated 2.4 million people to starvation levels (Woodham-Smith, 1962). Between 1860 and 1890, India suffered continual famine years partly because of the changeover to a more national agricultural economy (Bhatia, 1967).

A situation more applicable to the problems of food supply in a post-nuclear war world occurred in Bengal during 1943. Part of the 1942 winter rice crop was destroyed by a typhoon, followed by floods and fungal disease. Rice imports from Burma had been cut off, resulting in about 10% less rice than usual available in Bengal. Despite this seemingly modest decline, an estimated three million people died over the next year. This appears to have resulted from government response to the initiation of starvation, uncontrolled price increases, and maldistribution of the remaining crops (Sen, 1981).

In the 1970's, famine struck Ethiopia and the Sahel region of Africa, primed by an insufficiency of rainfall over a prolonged period. In 1973-74, it is estimated that 200,000 people out of a population of 27 million died of starvation and hunger-related diseases in Ethiopia (Shepherd, 1975). A similar number died in the Sahel between 1968 and 1973 (Sheets and Morris, 1976). The poor distribution system within the country or area and the lack of immediate recognition of the severity of the problem allowed the numbers of deaths to reach such levels, despite the fact that the overall supplies of food in the regions were not drastically reduced nor was there significantly increased demand throughout the time period of drought.

Historical famine situations suggest that even small overall decreases in agricultural production might have very large effects on populations. The major factor in the large numbers of deaths in years with low productivity seems to have been the response of the social system as opposed to solely the absolute levels of food supplies (Glantz, 1976). The failure of distribution systems, inappropriate decisions on exports, and the inability to enforce equalized methods of conservation appear more likely to affect the numbers of deaths than the failure of crops or decreases in yields caused by natural adversities, when agricultural yields fall by a few percent. At higher levels of food reductions, the societal responses may further exacerbate a situation in which food is insufficient in absolute terms.

6.2.1.6 Other Hazards

Prospects for large-scale survival and early recovery from major environmental dislocations are not promising if the modern record of responses to natural disasters is taken as a guide. Although some impressive gains in improved safety and shorter recovery times have been registered in connection with floods, hurricanes, severe storms, landslides, volcanic eruptions, and earthquakes, disaster losses appear to be accelerating throughout much of the world, largely as a result of increasing human vulnerability to natural hazards and the failure to adopt mitigating measures.

The anticipated pervasiveness and severity of nuclear war-induced events exceed any natural disaster yet experienced. Scientific understanding of human responses to extreme natural catastrophes is limited and does not permit confident prediction of behavior in unprecedented situations. Nonetheless, past and present disasters offer some information about potential consequences of a nuclear catastrophe (Clausen and Dombrowsky, 1983; Burton et al., 1978; Drabek and Key, 1983; Dynes, 1975; Fritz, 1968; Mileti et al., 1975; Quarantelli and Dynes, 1973). For example, involuntary local self-reliance is widely assumed to be characteristic of a post-nuclear war world. Small oceanic islands provide opportunities to test the effectiveness of disaster responses in the absence of significant external assistance. Available data suggest that disaster impacts on islands are disproportionately severe and long-lasting and are associated with extremely high potential for further catastrophe. Many similar lessons from natural events are available. They relate to responses to warnings, evacuation operations, the organization of relief, and numerous other aspects of catastrophic episodes. These have been appraised from the standpoint of organizations (Clausen and Dombrowsky, 1983) as well as in terms of the mental health of individuals (Lystad, 1985).

Insofar as a large-scale nuclear war would be a previously unexperienced event, the record of responses to newly emergent hazards is instructive. Lack of knowledge, indecision, and delayed responses have characterized the handling of compound natural and technological hazards at Three Mile Island, Bhopal, Times Beach, Sevesa, Italy, and other locations. Unaccustomed and portentous natural disasters may compel increased public attention, but that does not guarantee that resulting responses will be either prompt or entirely effective.

Recent sub-continental droughts reflect another possible distinguishing feature of a nuclear war, namely, the existence of extreme, spatially extensive, and protracted atmospheric changes. While there is mounting evidence that developed nations can successfully absorb the impacts of significant but smaller-scale climatic fluctuations, experience from the Sahel illustrates both the counterproductive nature of poorly implemented large-scale disaster relief and the stunted capacity of many low-income nations to survive long-lasting natural disasters by using impoverished indigenous coping strategies.

At the global scale, as indicated in the discussion of famine in section 6.2.1.5, areas of marginal human subsistence and particularly those in course of social transition are disproportionately subject to chronic severe disasters. In a post-nuclear war world, the areas of concentration of inhabitants would likely shrink and become more fragmented, and social systems would be stressed, thus magnifying the types of conditions that existing natural disaster relief programs have been least able to ameliorate.

While much can be learned about prospective human responses to a nuclear war by close analysis of natural disaster analogs, the transfer of experience is subject to at least two obvious limitations: 1.) natural disaster impacts occur on considerably smaller geographic scales; and 2.) natural disasters are widely perceived as temporary departures from an assumed normal state.

6.2.2 Extrapolations Beyond Hiroshima and Nagasaki

The remainder of this chapter deals with the possibility of extrapolating information from the Hiroshima and Nagasaki experiences and of using Hiroshima as a case study in order to illustrate potential effects on one city of a nuclear detonation from a modern arsenal. Local effects are viewed in the framework of quantifying the direct effects of a hypothesized 1 MT warhead detonated on Hiroshima and of discussing the local effects on a targeted city of a global nuclear war.

There are many limitations to drawing upon the Hiroshima and Nagasaki experiences during World War II directly to extrapolate potential effects from the use of a modern warhead on a city such as Hiroshima, among which are:

1.) quantitative—Contemporary nuclear warheads are much larger than those used at Hiroshima and Nagasaki. Because of the inherent limitations of extrapolating for effects from a smaller warhead experience, a simulation model for the human impacts of a local attack from a 1 MT warhead was developed.

2.) qualitative—While in the case of a global exchange, the direct effects of each detonation is a local attack from the target perspective, support from outside cannot be expected at either the regional or national level. In addition, urban systems have become much more sophisticated during the past forty years, especially in their dependency on administration and information systems. Vulnerability of urban systems has increased with respect to energy, food supply, transportation, and communication.

6.2.3 Direct Effects of a Modern Warhead: Hiroshima as a Case Example

In 1945, the city of Hiroshima was destroyed by the first use of an atomic bomb. Approximately one-third of the total population of 320,000 was killed, and another one-third was injured (Table 6.5). As people acquired some knowledge about radioactivity, they came to believe that no life would return to Hiroshima for hundreds of years. The city has been successfully reconstructed, however, and its present population is about 900,000, or three times that in 1945. Many survivors still suffer from long-term effects of the atomic detonation. The number of 'health book holders' living in Hiroshima, i.e., civilians known to be injured by exposure to the atomic detonation in 1945, amounted to over 100,000 in 1977, or about 12% of the total population. It is instructive to compare the potential effects of present weapons with those of the 1945 bombing, which caused long-term effects which still persist.

TABLE 6.5

COMPARISON OF CASUALTIES FROM ACTUAL EXPERIENCE
AND SIMULATED 1 MT DETONATION ON HIROSHIMA[a]

	15 KT OBSERVED IN 1945	1 MT SIMULATED Ground Burst (SE wind) (S wind)		Air Burst
Uninjured	118,613	0.5×10^6	0.4×10^6	0.25×10^6
Injured	0.2×10^6 (severe) 48,606 (less severe)	30,524	0.15×10^6	0.15×10^6
Fatalities	118,661	0.4×10^6	0.5×10^6	0.6×10^6
Unknown	3,677			

[a] Simulations conducted by T. Urabe.

6.2.3.1 Background

Hiroshima is located about 800 km west of Tokyo, on a small plain surrounded by mountains and the Seto Inland Sea. The population pattern obtained by the census in 1980 had a density exceeding 20,000 km^{-2} in some areas. The total population of the illustrated area, containing Hiroshima and its adjacent towns, is about 1.1 million. It is noted that almost all of the flat area is covered by housing. Recently, development into the mountain area has occurred. Since all the arable area is now urban, agricultural self-support within the illustrated area after a nuclear war is very unlikely.

The railway runs along the shore, and the super express railway (Shinkansen) runs straight in an east-west direction through the Hiroshima station. Main roads run parallel to the railway, and the industrial zone has been constructed on land reclaimed from the sea. The city center has a high population density even at night, while larger cities like Tokyo show a clear contrast between low night population and high daytime population in the central business district. The daytime population pattern in Hiroshima differs little from the night population, with only a small increase in the central zone of the city and industrial areas.

6.2.3.2 Simulations of a 1 MT Detonation

As discussed in Volume I (Pittock et al., 1985), the effects from a surface burst and from an air burst are different in many ways. If the altitude of detonation is low enough so that the fireball comes into direct contact with the ground surface, then much of the energy associated with the blast wave is directed into the excavation of surface materials. In addition, much of the thermal energy that originates from absorption of the thermal X-rays by the air immediately surrounding the nuclear detonation would be absorbed by the surface itself or by particles entrained in the fireball associated with a surface burst. These factors reduce the area affected by the blast wave and thermal pulse in a surface burst compared to an air burst detonation (Glasstone and Dolan, 1977).

The distances to which particular levels of effects from the blast wave, the thermal pulse, and initial ionizing radiation extend follow relationships specified in Glasstone and Dolan (1977). These distances are a function of the yield of the warhead, the height of burst, and the local conditions at the point of detonation, such as atmospheric transmissivity. The present discussion is concerned with a 1 MT detonation, for which the effects are characterized in Table 6.6.

A simulation model of the effects of a 1 MT detonation from an air or surface burst was developed and analyzed by T. Urabe for the SCOPE-ENUWAR project. In addition to the effects of blast, thermal radiation,

TABLE 6.6

DIRECT EFFECTS OF A 1 MT DETONATION[a]

	Blast effects[b]		Thermal effects[c]		Initial radiation effects[d]	
	5 psi	2 psi	100%	50%	450 rem	200 rem
	(all distances are ground ranges [km] from ground zero)					
Surface[e] burst	4.56	7.57	8.55	10.92	2.7	2.8
Air[f] burst	6.72	12.41	12.62	16.35	2.7	2.8

[a] Tabulated values from Harwell (1984) based on formulae from Glasstone and Dolan (1977).

[b] The 5 psi distance is considered to define the lethal area (Lewis, 1979; Barnaby and Rotblat, 1982; Harwell, 1984); the 2 psi distance is considered to define the injury area (Katz, 1982; Harwell, 1984).

[c] From Harwell (1984) based on data from Glasstone and Dolan (1977); 100% lethality is assumed to occur to those individuals exposed to about 8 to 10 cal cm^{-2}; 50% lethality, 50% injury is assumed to occur to those individuals exposed to between 6 and 8 cal cm^{-2}. Distances are based on a visibility of 20 km.

[d] Ground distances at which the least indicated dose would be absorbed by exposed individuals from the initial burst of fast neutrons and gamma rays; does not include exposure to residual radiation (fallout). From Harwell (1984), based on data in Glasstone and Dolan (1977) and Rotblat (1981).

[e] Detonation at which fireball comes in contact with the ground surface.

[f] Detonation assumed to occur at optimal height, $h = 1100 W^{0.45}$ (Glasstone and Dolan, 1977); for a 1 MT detonation, this height is 3.35 km (Harwell, 1984).

and initial ionizing radiation, the Urabe model included the effects of local fallout from a surface burst, based on fallout patterns from Rotblat (1981) for an ambient wind of 3 m sec^{-1} from the southeast (the conditions on the day of the bombing in Hiroshima in 1945); a separate analysis was done for a wind from the south. Essentially no local fallout would occur after an air burst, so radiation exposure estimates from an air burst in the simulation were limited to that in the initial ionizing radiation.

The combination of effects was translated to human fatalities and injuries following relationships given in OTA (1979) for distance versus human health effects (as percentage killed and injuries from the exposed population). Exposure to thermal radiation was expected to occur for a range of 1%–25% of the total population within a specified distance; the remainder of the population was assumed to be shielded from the thermal rays at the time of the detonation. Account was kept of each individual effect for each location on a grid superimposed on the Hiroshima area map.Combined effects were done as proposed by the British Medical Association (1983), in which a sublethal effect from each of two or more factors was treated as a fatality for the affected individual. By evaluating each grid location for the combined human effects of the stresses at that location and by considering the population within that grid location based on 1980 Hiroshima population data, the total direct effects of a 1 MT detonation on the current population were estimated. This methodology is appropriate for any location and for surface or air bursts of different yields; however, the population distribution grid is specific to Hiroshima and would require adaptation to other cities.

The results from the Hiroshima attack scenarios are presented in Table 6.5. The human fatalities from an air burst are seen to be greater than from a surface burst because of the greater ranges to which the blast and thermal pulse are lethal. In partial compensation for this, the surface burst fatality estimates include deaths from radiation arriving from local fallout; this effect does not occur for the air burst. Further, unlike the situation from the actual 15 kT detonation that occurred over Hiroshima, initial ionizing radiation would not contribute to fatalities, since the distances to which lethal levels of initial ionizing radiation would be absorbed from a 1 MT detonation are well within the distances to which blast and the thermal pulse would be fatal (Table 6.6); the latter effects would result in much earlier deaths than would ensue from lethal doses of initial ionizing radiation, so the individuals lethally exposed would already be dead before radiation symptoms could be evident.

6.2.3.3 Other Concerns

From the results of the simulation model, the direct casualties from a 1 MT explosion are estimated to be about half of the total population. Even if it is assumed that other cities remain in an unharmed state, rescue activities in Hiroshima and areas similar to it would be hampered. Hiroshima is surrounded by mountains, and if the railway, airport, and road systems were destroyed, access to the city from the land and air would be difficult. In addition, the sea which Hiroshima faces is an inland sea, and the passage is usually crowded and could be blocked by a few destroyed ships.

Another significant point about rescue activities in Japan would be the extreme sensitivity of the Japanese people to the presence of radioactivity. After the end of the war, people came to understand that some of the medical effects in Hiroshima and Nagasaki were caused by radioactivity. Sensitivity to the subject of radioactivity was amplified by the Bikini accident, when Japanese fishermen were injured by fallout. Psychological sensitivity to the idea of radioactivity is still a national characteristic.

6.2.4 Additional Effects from Global Stresses

The discussion thus far in this section has focused on the effects on Hiroshima from a single 1 MT detonation in the context of no other nuclear detonations occurring elsewhere at the same time. In the more likely event of a nuclear detonation over Hiroshima during a modern nuclear war, other nuclear detonations would occur over cities and other targets. The qualitatively new effects from multiple detonations discussed throughout this report would be in addition to the direct effects calculated for Hiroshima. These additional effects include the following:

- direct effects from other detonations on the same city: Other detonations would initiate some additive factors, such as doses from local fallout originating from several different sources, but most of the direct effects would interact in nonlinear ways. For instance, a blast wave passing through an area from one detonation could make the area more vulnerable to the effects of blast from a second detonation.

- local fallout: In addition to proximally originated fallout, a large number of cities would experience additional local fallout from surface detonations over other targets upwind of the city.

- lack of outside assistance: Outside assistance was an important factor in the early response at Hiroshima and Nagasaki, as discussed above, particularly in providing food, medical expertise, medical supplies, and social order. It also was key to the long-term recovery of the city. The processes that were seen in the redevelopment of a modern, thriving post-war Hiroshima could not be repeated in the aftermath of a large-scale nuclear war.

- disruption of communications: The effects of an electromagnetic pulse on modern communications and electrical power systems would interfere with transfer of information about what had happened and would hamper efforts for post-nuclear war response.

- psychological effects: The knowledge of the essential disruption of the Earth's civilization would be a totally new experience far beyond that felt at Hiroshima and Nagasaki. For those with prior knowledge of the possibility of nuclear war-induced climatic alterations, the prospects of facing the long-term consequences of nuclear war would likely have a considerable impact on their reactions.

- economic effects: The disruption of the world's economic base and associated international exchange of goods would lead to the loss of food imports. Food availability would be insufficient within a short time, and many of the survivors would starve to death (see Chapter 5 for discussion of loss of food imports). The loss of fossil fuel energy sources and products would reduce potential agricultural productivity. Post-nuclear war life would also be affected by the reduced capabilities of survivors to migrate to areas less affected by direct perturbations; the reduced capability to manufacture essential goods such as pharmaceuticals; the difficulty in acquiring uncontaminated water from deep aquifers; and a host of other similar effects.

- direct effects from climatic disturbances: The people surviving the direct effects of the nuclear detonation might be subject to greatly reduced temperatures and near darkness within a few days of the detonation. Many of those injured and left homeless would die from exposure.

- indirect effects from climatic disturbances: The loss of agricultural productivity that would follow the acute effects of significant nuclear war-induced climatic disturbances occurring during the spring or summer, and chronic effects occurring during the growing season, would result in reduced food for the survivors of a detonation, and many would die of starvation, as discussed in Chapters 4 and 5. Over the long term, reduced levels of precipitation could lead to insufficient water availability for the survivors.

- ecosystem-mediated effects: The longer term responses of ecological systems could include the outbreak of pests that could transmit disease to surviving humans. Other adverse environmental conditions could include increased air and water pollution; pathways for radioactivity to contribute to internal doses to humans; incidents of flooding as climatic extremes abated and snow and ice melted, and increased flooding because of loss of vegetation cover over watersheds; increased levels of ultraviolet radiation, leading perhaps to increased blindness and skin cancers; and other environmental disruptions.

6.2.4.1 Estimating Effects on Social Structure and Processes

To determine the total consequences of nuclear war, it is critical to consider the physical effects within the framework of their implications for the functioning of complex technical–industrial national systems and the world economy. Based on the experiences at Hiroshima and Nagasaki, the likely impacts of individual detonations on humans can be objectively estimated, such as the losses sustained in the medical care system; educational facilities and infrastructure; industrial base; energy supply, production, and distribution systems; and food production, processing, and distribution systems. Additional questions arise about the human management of these systems under stress and the flexibility and improvisational capabilities of highly integrated systems in circumstances where key elements may be destroyed.

One detonation of a modern nuclear warhead would cause horrendous and unprecedented human distress, but experience from other large disasters suggests the dimensions of possible social consequences. Studies by economists, geographers, psychologists, sociologists, and political scientists have examined the ways in which people respond in disaster situations. Those responses include immediate relief, rescue, emergency aid, evacuation, and reconstruction. Such activities take place within societies that maintain their organization, are able to accept evacuees, albeit with distress, and can provide some assistance from within or outside the country.

For a large-scale nuclear war, the immediate and direct environmental effects within the range of each detonation would be of the same nature as described for the single detonations over Hiroshima and Nagasaki. Social responses to a large-scale nuclear war, however, would be different than those expected from a simple increase in the number of areas destroyed. To the extent that neighboring areas and transportation facilities were destroyed, the opportunities for either evacuation or outside aid would be reduced. Conditions would be altered drastically in the event of multiple nuclear explosions. The prospects for aid from nearby areas would be greatly reduced or in many instances eliminated, so that the opportunities for direct relief would be curtailed, as described for the availability of health services in the WHO report (Bergstrom et al., 1983; see also Abrams and von Kaenal, 1981). Capability in fighting fires would be minimal. Rescue and reconstruction activities in areas suspected of contamination by radiation would be impeded. The capacity of local and national governments to continue to provide elementary security, transportation, and food distribution would be undermined.

Destruction of electronic capacities and power transmission systems by EMP would cut off many lines of communication on which intricate public and individual activities depend, particularly following a catastrophe. No modern society has been subjected to this kind of disaster, and there is no precedent for estimating how the ordinary processes of social organization would respond.

If weather disturbances of the type and magnitude suggested in Volume I were introduced, projections of likely social responses become far more difficult. All of the impacts noted above would prevail, but they would be exacerbated by the additional physical and biological impacts outlined in Volume I and preceding chapters of this volume. The reductions in temperature, sunlight, and precipitation, and the accompanying impacts on entire ecosystems and especially on the agricultural productivity of the world would stress the social structure and process in fundamentally unique ways. How the components of social processes might be altered by experience of the physical and biological impacts, and by perception of their possible results, is an area of investigation requiring future attention.

A little is known of how some populations perceive the hazard of nuclear war in comparison with other, more familiar hazards such as airplane accidents or earthquakes (Slovic et al., 1980). Nuclear war is seen by many as being in a different category than the others. The reality of nuclear war, if it ever were to occur, would confront people already disposed to view it as something different and more horrifying than anything they had ever known, with stress unlike that borne initially by the residents of Hiroshima and Nagasaki, who did not learn the nature of the bomb until later. These initial experiences would affect immediate survivors who would have little or no information about the global nature and extent of the nuclear war. There would be extreme uncertainty about the future course of events in the minds of those survivors, who would begin to contend with the prospects for delayed, global consequences.

Ecosystem changes are mediated by perturbations induced by changes in the physical environment, such as climatic alterations, fallout, increased UV-B, air pollutants, and a host of other stresses. These would lead to much more complex alterations in human social and economic systems. These influence and in turn are influenced by human perceptions of the threat of war and, in the event of war, of its effects on natural and social environments.

Earlier discussion outlined ways in which the impacts of nuclear detonations would be different from those induced by the natural and technological disasters with which there has been some experience.Those differences are so important that it seems unwise at this time to venture any but the most general quantitative estimates of the societal consequences of widespread nuclear war. It seems more prudent to indicate the kinds of analyses that might be used in making such estimates with more time and resources, a few of the problems that would be encountered, and some of the directions in which further research might lend accuracy and validity to the results.

6.2.4.2 Estimating Effects on Economic Systems

The effects of a nuclear war on economic systems would occur at several levels. First, there would be the direct destruction of physical structures and effects on the labor force. As significant would be the disruption of surviving industry by the loss of raw materials or critical manufactured goods.

Beginning with the range of large-scale physical and biological perturbations discussed in previous sections of this volume and of Volume 1, a few methods of studying possible impacts on production of goods and services present themselves. Some of these have been appraised in the SCOPE examination of climate impact assessment (Kates et al., 1985), and several might be based upon models of global interrelationships. None commends itself to direct and immediate application, but all suggest directions in which further research might proceed.

One assessment of the possible effects of nuclear detonations on the economy of a region examined the impacts on the State of Massachusetts and the United States from a limited and a large-scale nuclear war (Katz, 1982). Casualties, economic impacts, food supply and distribution, electricity and fuel oil, medical care, and other social impacts were considered. The complications entailed in emergency relocation of populations during a pre-war period were discussed. These latter issues were examined in more depth in Leaning and Keyes (1983). Examination was also made in Katz (1982) of the implications for the global economy and political system of massive destruction in the U.S. and U.S.S.R. No consideration was given to local environmental changes or to climatic alterations.

The early 1970's saw the design and application of a number of global simulation models of resource–environment–economic interactions, including World 3, the World Integrated Model, the Bariloche Model, and the United Nations World Model by Leontiev. These models have been used to investigate global issues, such as the relationship between resources and population, developed–developing world interdependence, and energy forecasts and impacts. These and others have been reviewed and appraised in recent years (Hughes, 1980; Meadows et al., 1982; US Congress, 1982). A key problem with all, whatever their applications, is that they have not been sufficiently tested or validated.

The models have a number of problems for use in assessing the possible economic impacts of climate change, including:

1.) aggregation based on economic criteria but which is inappropriate for considering nuclear war stresses, e.g., the Mesarovic–Pestel model lumps Canada, Australia, Israel, South Africa, and Japan together;

2.) simplicity of the agricultural components of the models, with little differentiation among crop types; inputs such as irrigation, fertilizer, and pesticides are combined into a surrogate capital investment term; and very simple functions relate production to capital and labor;

3.) oversensitivity to sudden changes and extreme variability in climate-related variables like crop yields; and

4.) inability to replicate actual events such as historical climate–food relationships.

Other models that do not have these limitations are dependent on economic variables, such as the price for a commodity, which would be exceedingly sensitive to the perturbations on the agricultural and economic systems following a nuclear war.

One type of model that could be used for a localized post-nuclear war economic assessment is a static input–output model of the world economy such as the Leontiev model. Here the inputs (e.g., labor and crop yields) could be changed to reflect production in the aftermath of a nuclear war and linked linearly to changes in output. avoiding instability problems of the dynamical behavior of systems models. However, input-output models could not be used to examine longer term impacts because the coefficients would not be valid for a global economy in the aftermath of a nuclear war.

In summary, the current global models were constructed to monitor slow trends and interactions, based on an understanding of existing structures and resources. They were not designed to investigate a global catastrophe like nuclear war, and different models need to be developed for that purpose.

6.3 SUMMARY

The survivors of the immediate aftermath of a modern nuclear war would experience some situations for which there are historical precedents, but many other factors would be unique in human history. This summary section recapitulates those factors in the context of what life would be like for persons living in combatant areas and for those who would not directly experience nuclear detonations.

For those who actually experienced a nuclear detonation, but who were far enough removed or somehow protected from the direct lethal effects, the environment they would initially experience would seem much like the early period after the detonations over Hiroshima and Nagasaki.Precedent experiences from Hiroshima and Nagasaki would include the almost instantaneous disruption of the physical system; the initiation and spread of fires; the loss of communications and an understanding of what had happened; the psychological shocks of experiencing the suddenness and overwhelming nature of the devastation surrounding the survivors; mass migration from the scene of destruction; disruption or elimination of fire-fighting capabilities; disruption or elimination of medical systems; extremely large numbers of civilian injured, primarily suffering from the effects of blast and burns; disruption or elimination of social infrastructure, including modes of public order, energy supply, and transportation; and early exposure to radiation, with symptoms appearing within a few days or weeks. In addition, there would soon be some effects for the survivors of a nuclear detonation associated with global phenomena for which there are some precedents among past natural disaster experiences, including lack of food; insufficient supplies of uncontaminated water; and threat of outbreaks of epidemics.

A few of the experiences of those not in combatant areas would have been observed before; particularly instructive would be experiences of wartime sieges, famines, and disease epidemics. But by far most of the post-nuclear war experiences of those not directly affected by detonations, as well as of the survivors of direct detonation, would have no historical precedent. These factors include:

- the scale of devastation, precluding outside assistance and precluding a refugia for exodus of the afflicted population;
- the onset of extreme climatic events on a global scale;
- the insufficiency of food, energy, and other subsistence factors both locally and over large areas of the world;
- the presence of a radioactively contaminated landscape of unknown extent or hazard;
- the impairment or destruction of the economic and social systems on a global scale;
- the psychological challenges to order and stability among survivors in a world undergoing rapid readjustment;
- other global-scale disruptions of the natural environment, including pollution, pest outbreaks, habitat destruction, and loss of species;
- synergistic combinations of the various perturbations; having these extreme perturbations occur simultaneously and on such a scale would likely result in even greater impacts than would be projected from the effects of individual stresses alone.

The ability to predict the responses of humans and societal systems to any of these factors, individually or in combination, is limited by the totally unprecedented nature of these situations. Mere extrapolation from the experiences of the localized atomic bombings of Hiroshima and Nagasaki has consistently led to a gross underestimation of what the consequences of the next nuclear war would be for the global human population.

REFERENCES

Abrams, H., and von Kaenal, W. (1981). Medical problems of survivors of nuclear war. *New Eng. J. Med.*, **305**, 1226–1232.

Ambio Advisory Group. (1982). Reference scenario: How a nuclear war might be fought. *Ambio*, **1**, 94–99.

Barnaby, F., and Rotblat, J. (1982). The effects of nuclear weapons. *Ambio*, **11**, 84–93.

Bauer, F.K. (1945). The nature of air raid casualties. In *U. S. Strategic Bombing Survey. The Effect of Bombing on Health and Medical Care in Germany.* U.S. Government Printing Office, Washington. D. C.

Bergstrom, S., Black, D., Bochkov, N.P., Eklund, S.. Kruisinga, R.J.H.. Leaf, A.,

Obasanjo, O., Shigematsu, I., Tubiana, M., and Whittembury, G. (1983). *Effects of a Nuclear War on Health and Health Services. Report of the International Committee of Experts in Medical Sciences and Public Health.* WHO Pub. A36.12. World Health Organization Publications, Geneva: 176 pages.

Bhatia, B.M. (1967). *Famines in India: A Study of Some Aspects of the Economic History of India 1860–1965.* Asia Publishing House, New York.

Bond, H. (1946). Fire casualties of the German attacks. In Bond, H. (Ed.) *Fire and the Air War.* National Fire Protection Association, Boston: 262 pages.

British Medical Association. (1983). *The Medical Effects of Nuclear War.* John Wiley & Sons, Chichester.

Burns, J.F. (1985). Twenty-three seconds in '76, and a Chinese city still aches. *New York Times,* 13 February 1985.

Burton, T., Kates, R.W., and White, G.F. (1978). *The Environment as Hazard.* Oxford University Press, New York: 240 pages.

Champ, C. (1982). Flood. In Time-Life Series: *Planet Earth.* 37–64. Time-Life, Inc., Chicago.

Clausen, L., and Dumbrowsky, (Eds.) (1983). Einfhrung in die sociologue der katastrophen. *Zivilschutz-Forschung,* **14**, 1–209. (in German).

—. Wir warten alle auf unser Grab. *Der Spiegel,* 22 April 1985. (in German).

Drabek, T., and Key, W.H. (1983). *Conquering Disaster: Family Recovery and Long-Term Consequences.* Irvington, New York: 487 pages.

Dynes, R.R. (1975). The comparative study of disaster: A social organizational approach. *Mass Emergencies,* **1**, 21–31.

E'njoji, M., and Inoue, I. (1953). Bacteriological and serological analysis on diarrheas following A-bomb exposure in Nagasaki. Cited in Shimazu, Y. (Ed.). (1985). *Lessons from Hiroshima and Nagasaki.* Contributions to SCOPE–ENUWAR Workshop. Hiroshima, Japan.

Ferrara, G.M. (1979). *The Disaster File: The 1970's.* Facts on File, New York: 173 pages.

Fritz, C.E. (1968). Disaster. *International Encyclopedia of the Social Sciences,* New York: 202–207.

Garb, S., and Eng, E. (1969). *Disaster Handbook.* Springer-Verlag, New York: 310 pages.

Gibney, E. (Ed.) (1978). *Disaster, when Nature Strikes Back.* Bantam/Britannica Books, New York: 377 pages.

Glantz, M. (1976). Nine fallacies of natural disaster: The case of the Sahel. In Glantz, M. (Ed.) *The Politics of Natural Disaster.* 3–24. Praeger, New York.

Glasstone, S., and Dolan, P.J. (Eds.) (1977). *The Effects of Nuclear Weapons* 3rd. ed. U.S. Government Printing Office, Washington, D. C.: 653 pages.

Hamilton, H.B. (1985). *Genetics and the atomic bombs in Hiroshima and Nagasaki.* CLS Lifelines, National Research Council, 10, 3.

Harwell, M.A. (1984). *Nuclear Winter: The Human and Environmental Consequences of Nuclear War.* Springer-Verlag, New York: 179 pages.

Hiramatsu, H. (1980). Urban earthquake hazards and risk assessment of earthquake prediction. *Jour. Phys. Earth,* **28**, 59–101.

Hirose, K., and Fujino, S. (1950). Cataracts due to atomic bomb exposure. *Acta Societatis Ophthalmologicae Japonicae,* **54**, 449. (in Japanese).

Hiroshima A-bomb Medical Care History Editorial Committee. (1961). *Hiroshima A-bomb Medical Care History.* Hiroshima Medical Association, Hiroshima: 108 pages. (in Japanese).

Hughes, B.B. (1980). *World Modeling.* Lexington Books, Lexington, KY: 227 pages.

Ikui, H. (1967). Ocular lesions caused by the atomic bombings of Nagasaki and Hiroshima: Early disorders. *J. Hiroshima Med. Ass.* (special series), **20**, 160. (in Japanese).

Ishida, T. (Ed.) (1973). *More against Atomic Bombs: Life History of Nagasaki Atomic Bomb Survivors.* Miraisha, Tokyo: 54 pages. (in Japanese).

Ishikawa, I.., and Swain, D. (1981). Hiroshima and Nagasaki: *The Physical, Medical, and Social Effects of the Atomic Bombings.* Basic Books, New York: 706 pages.

Karnow, S. (1983). *Vietnam: A History.* Penguin Books, New York: 752 pages.

Kates, R.W., Ausubel. J.H., and Berberian, M. (Eds.) (1985). *Climate Impact Assessment: Studies of the Interaction of Climate and Society.* John Wiley & Sons, Chichester.

Kato, H., and Shigematsu, I. (1985). Late effects. In Shimazu, Y. (Ed.) *Lessons from Hiroshima and Nagasaki.* 51. Contributions to SCOPE–ENUWAR Workshop. Hiroshima, Japan.

Katz, A.M. (1982). *Life after Nuclear War–The Economic and Social Impacts of Nuclear Attacks on the United States.* Ballinger, Cambridge, MA: 422 pages.

Komiya, E., and Yamamoto, S. (1947). A case of acute leukemia of survivors of the atomic bomb. *Diagnosis and Treatment,* **35**, 8. (in Japanese).

Konuma, M., Furutani, M., and Kubo, S. (1953). Diencephalic syndrome as a delayed A-bomb effect. *Japanese Medical Journal,* **1547**, 4853. (in Japanese).

Kubo, Y. (1952). Study of human behavior immediately after the atomic bombing of Hiroshima: Socio-psychological study pertaining to the atomic bomb and atomic energy. *Japanese J. Psychology,* **22**, 103. (in Japanese).

Leaning, J., and Keyes. L. (Eds.) (1983). *The Counterfeit Ark.* Ballinger, Cambridge, MA: 337 pages.

Lewis, K.N. (1979). The prompt and delayed effects of nuclear war. *Sci. Amer.,* **241**(1), 35–47.

Lifton, R.J. (1967). *Death in Life: Survivors of Hiroshima.* Random House, New York.

Lucas, H.S. (1930). The great European famine of 1315, 1316, and 1317. *Speculum, A Journal of Medieval Studies,* **5**, 343.

Lystad, M. (1985). Human response to mass emergencies. *Emotional First Aid: A Journal of Crisis Intervention,* **2**, 5–18.

McHenry, D.F., and Bird, K. (1977). Food bungle in Bangladesh. *Foreign Policy,* **27**, 72.

McNeill, W.H. (1976). *Plagues and Peoples.* 149. University of Chicago Press, Chicago.

Meadows, D., Richardson, J., and Bruckmann, G. (1982). *Groping in the Dark: The First Decade of Global Modelling.* John Wiley & Sons, Chichester: 311 pages.

Middleton, H. (1982). Epidemiology: The future is sickness and death. *Ambio,* **11**, 100–105.

Mileti, D.S., Drabek, T.E., and Haas, J.E. (1975). *Human Systems in Extreme Environments: A Sociological Perspective.* University of Colorado, Boulder: 165 pages.

Miller, R.W., and Blot, W.J. (1972). Small head size after in utero exposure to atomic radiation. *Lancet,* **ii**, 784.

Milton, R.C., and Shohoji, T. (1968). *Tentative 1965 Radiation Dose (T65D) Estimation for Atomic Bomb Survivors, Hiroshima and Nagasaki.* ABCC TR 1: 68.

Misao, T., Haraguchi, Y., and Hattori, K. (1953). A case of monocytic leukemia developed after the acute symptoms by atomic bomb exposure. In *Collection of the Reports on the Investigation of the Atomic Bomb Casualties,* Vol. II. 1041. Science Council of Japan, Tokyo. (in Japanese).

Nagasaki City Office. (1977). *Record of the Nagasaki A-bomb War Disaster*, Vol. I. 190–262. Nagasaki International Cultural Hall, Nagasaki. (in Japanese).

Nash, J.R. (1977). *Darkest Hours*. Wallaby, New York: 792 pages.

—. (1977). Collision course. *Newsweek*, 11 April 1977.

—. (1980). Riyad crash. *New York Times*, 21 August 1980.

Nishikawa, T., and Tsuiki, S. (1961). Psychiatric investigations of atomic bomb survivors. *Nagasaki Medical Journal*, **36**, 717. (in Japanese).

Okumura, N., and Hidaka, H. (1949). Results of psychoneurological studies on atomic bomb survivors. *Kyushu Neuropsychiatry*, **1**, 50. (in Japanese).

OTA. (1979). *The Effects of Nuclear War*. U.S. Congress, Office of Technology Assessment. Washington, D.C.: 151 pages.

Oughterson, A.W., and Warren, S. (Eds.) (1956). *Medical Effects of the Atomic Bomb in Japan*. 447–458. McGraw-Hill, New York.

Pace, N., and Smith, R.E. (1959). *Measurement of the Residual Radiation Intensity at the Sites of the Hiroshima and Nagasaki Atomic Bombs*. ABCC TR 26:59.

Pavlov, D.B. (1967). *Leningrad in Siege*. USSR Ministry of Defense Publishers, Moscow: 208 pages.

Pittock, A.B., Ackerman, T.A., Crutzen, P., MacCracken, M., Shapiro, C., and Turco, R.P. (1985). *The Environmental Consequences of Nuclear War*. Volume I: Physical. SCOPE 28a. John Wiley & Sons, Chichester.

Quarantelli, E.L., and Dynes, R.R. (1973). *Images of Disaster Behavior: Myths and Consequences*. Disaster Research Center, Columbus, OH.

Richardson, L.F. (1960). Statistics of deadly quarrels. In Wright, Q., and Lienau, C.C. (Eds.). *Statistics of Deadly Quarrels*. 8–40. Quadrangle Press, Chicago.

Rotblat, J. (1981). *Nuclear Radiation in Warfare*. Stockholm International Peace Research Institute. Oelgeschlager, Gunn, and Hain, Cambridge, MA: 149 pages.

Science Council of Japan. (1951). *Summary Report of the Investigation of the Atomic Bomb Casualties*. Science Council of Japan, Tokyo. (in Japanese).

Sen, A. (1981). *Poverty and Famines: An Essay on Entitlement and Deprivation*. Clarendon Press, Oxford.

Sheets, H., and Morris, R. (1976). Disaster in the desert. In Glantz, M.H. (Ed.). *The Politics of Natural Disaster: The Case of the Sahel Drought*. Praeger, New York.

Shepherd, J. (1975). *The Politics of Starvation*. Carnegie Endowment for International Peace, New York.

Shimazu, Y. (Ed.) (1985). *Lessons from Hiroshima and Nagasaki*. Contributions to SCOPE–ENUWAR Workshop, Hiroshima, Japan.

Shinohara, K., Morita, S., Koura, K., Kawai, N., and Yokota, M. (1953). Radiation on the ground in Nagasaki city and vicinity. II: Radiation near the Nishiyama reservoir. In *Collection of the Reports on the Investigation of the Atomic Bomb Casualties*, Vol. I: 45. Science Council of Japan, Tokyo. (in Japanese).

Slovic, P., Fischhoff, B., and Lichtenstein, S. (1980) Facts and fears: Understanding perceived risk. In Schwing, R., and Albors, W. (Eds.) *Societal Risk Management: How Safe Is Safe Enough?* 181–214. Plenum Press, New York.

Stief, W. (1980). Cambodian calamity: The making of a holocaust. *The Progressive*, **44**, 46.

Takeshita, K. (1975). A review of thirty years' study of Hiroshima and Nagasaki atomic bomb survivors. I. Dosimetry, C. Dose estimation from residual and fall-out radioactivity–aerial surveys. *J Radiat Res.*, **16** (supp), 24.

—. (1970). East Pakistan: The politics of a catastrophe. *Time*, 7 December 1970.

—. (1976). China: Shock and terror in the night. *Time*, 9 August 1976.

Tokyo City Office. (1925). *Record of Damage in the 1923 Earthquake*. Tokyo City

Office, Tokyo. (in Japanese).

Uda, M., Sugahara, Y., and Kita, I. (1953). Meteorological conditions related to the atomic bomb explosion in Hiroshima. In *Collection of the Reports on the Investigation of the Atomic Bomb Casualties,* Vol. I: 98. Science Council of Japan, Tokyo. (in Japanese).

Urabe, T. (1985). *Human impacts of low-level detonations: A case study on Hiroshima.* Unpublished manuscript contributed to SCOPE–ENUWAR.

U.S.-Japan Joint Workshop (1985). *Proceedings of the 3rd U.S.–Japan Joint Workshop for Reassessment of Atomic Bomb Radiation Dosimetry in Hiroshima and Nagasaki.*

U.S. Congress. (1982). *Global Models, World Futures and Public Policy: A Critique.* U.S. Government Printing Office, Washington, D.C.: 63 pages.

U.S. Department of Commerce. World Data Center. (1979). *Catalog of Significant Earthquakes: 2000 B.C.–1979.* National Geophysical Data Center, Boulder, CO: 154 pages.

U.S. Strategic Bombing Survey. (1946). The effects of atomic bombs on Hiroshima and Nagasaki. In Bond, H. (Ed.). *Fire and the Air War.* National Fire Protection Association, Boston, MA.: 262 pages.

Walford, C. (1878). *The famines of the world: Past and present.* Journal of the British Statistical Society, 9, 433.

Woodham-Smith, C. (1962). *The Great Hunger: Ireland 1845–1849.* Harper & Row, New York.

World Health Organization (WHO). (1983). *Effects of Nuclear War on Health and Health Services.* WHO, Geneva: 176 pages.

Yamazaki, F. (1953). Residual radiation in west Hiroshima following the atomic bomb explosion. In *Collection of the Reports on the Investigation of the Atomic Bomb Casualties,* Vol I: 25. Science Council of Japan, Tokyo. (in Japanese).

Environmental Consequences of Nuclear War Volume II:
Ecological and Agricultural Effects
Edited by M.A. Harwell and T.C. Hutchinson
© 1985 SCOPE. Published by John Wiley & Sons Ltd

CHAPTER 7

Integration of Effects on Human Populations

MARK A. HARWELL AND CHRISTINE C. HARWELL

Primary Contributions: W. P. Cropper, Jr., S. J. Risch

Additional Contributions: K. Limburg, J. Vandermeer, E. Zubrow

7.1. INTRODUCTION

The two volumes of this SCOPE–ENUWAR report constitute a synthesis of existing information estimating the types of global environmental consequences that could ensue from a large-scale nuclear war. There are many uncertainties and much research remains to be done. The biological responses to projected physical environmental perturbations cannot be detailed with precision because of: 1.) the unprecedented scale of such perturbations; 2.) the lack of an adequate empirical data base drawn from relevant experiments; 3.) the tremendous complexities that characterize biological and human systems and their interactions, especially with respect to their dynamics in response to stress; and 4.) the wide range of potential environmental disturbances being estimated by the physical scientists, associated with a wide range of nuclear war scenarios, and the continuing revision of those estimates over time. The previous chapters in this volume have described and utilized numerous methodologies and a variety of analytical approaches in evaluating the consequences of nuclear war. Clearly, no single analysis or methodology can describe the myriad of environmental responses to nuclear war; nevertheless, the combined analyses presented here portray a picture of the potential effects of a large-scale nuclear war on ecological and agricultural systems; emphasis has been placed in Parts II and III of this volume on the vulnerability of the Earth's human population to disruptions in the global food production and distribution systems. These and the other environmental consequences discussed in Part I are fundamentally important in the context of ultimate human impacts.

The previous discussions of the separate effects of nuclear war on the ecological and agricultural support bases for humans can be integrated, at least in a qualitative manner, into a discussion of potential effects on the world's surviving population. In the following sections, initial consideration is given to the projected effects on human populations from the immediate perturbations of nuclear detonations, drawing on previous analyses, especially the recent World Health Organization study (Bergstrom et al., 1984). The human casualties from the direct effects of nuclear blast, thermal radiation, and ionizing radiation are projected to be in the range of several hundred million humans, distributed primarily in the Northern mid-latitudes (WHO, 1984; Harwell, 1984; Ambio, 1982). Such population losses and the large-scale indirect perturbations such as alterations in global climatic conditions, other physical stresses, and disruptions in human support systems provide the inputs, or initial conditions, for analyses of longer-term, global environmental consequences of nuclear war.

The physical responses to nuclear war extend across a broad range of possibilities. Therefore, it is impossible for the biological analyses to operate with exactitude, even if the stress-response relationships were fully understood. Nevertheless, there is much that can be said concerning the effects on human populations if differing scenarios are systematically addressed and if the bounds of consequences on humans are identified, especially those bounds limited by physical constraints rather than determined by speculative societal and other responses. Two time frames are considered: the first year after a nuclear war, in which climatic and societal disruptions could lead to significant losses of agricultural productivity on a large spatial scale, and subsequent periods, after pre-war food supplies became largely depleted and after the climatic effects, if any, would have settled into a chronic state.

7.2 EFFECTS DURING THE INITIAL YEAR

7.2.1 Direct Effects of Nuclear Detonations

The initial consideration is of the impacts of the nuclear detonations themselves. This is an area largely outside the scope of the present analyses, and reliance is placed primarily on the recent World Health Organization study (Bergstrom et al., 1984), and analyses by Svirezhev et al. (1985), Harwell (1984), and Ambio (1982). Each of those studies considered the immediate effects of a large-scale nuclear war in which 5000 MT or more of total nuclear warhead yield were detonated over military and industrial targets, including urban areas above a certain size (typically 100,000 or 200,000 inhabitants). The specific targeting scenario varies among these and other studies, and, naturally, the immediate effects on human populations are sensitive to the specific scenario. In general, however, the range of direct human impacts is consistent among the studies, with projections on the order of several hundred million human fatalities from direct effects, i.e., from blast, thermal radiation, and fallout. As a severe case analysis, the WHO study included urban targeting on cities throughout the world that led in their calculations to total projected human fatalities of 1.1 billion. Harwell (1984) calculated that about 50%–75% of the population of the United States could succumb to the direct effects of nuclear detonations, including local fallout, and suggested that similar proportions could ensue for Europe and the U.S.S.R. These estimates are in concert with the Ambio study projections (Middleton, 1982) and others (e.g., Haaland et al., 1976; OTA, 1979). In short, the direct effects on *targeted* countries could lead to the loss of a large proportion of their populations and to the concomitant disruption or elimination of the critical social support systems in at least those countries.

Such an effect, however, would be nonhomogeneously distributed over the Earth. Combatant countries are presumed to be primarily in the Northern Hemisphere mid-latitudes, with little or no targeting in the Southern Hemisphere. The direct effects of nuclear detonations are largely quite localized with respect to blast, initial ionizing radiation, thermal radiation, and fires, as discussed in Volume I (Pittock et al., 1985). More regionally distributed would be the effects of local fallout, which would alone be responsible for virtually all of the radiation-induced fatalities from nuclear war; i.e., globally distributed fallout is not projected to reach sufficiently high levels for widespread fatalities from acute radiation exposure (Volume I). Local fallout, then, would tend to result in human fatalities within the boundaries of the targeted country, with the exception that most of Europe could be subjected to substantial doses of local fallout radiation.

The numbers of fatalities occurring during the immediate post-nuclear war period would be affected by the responses of social systems. Medical systems would be called upon on an unprecedented scale, and extreme difficulties in response could be anticipated (Abrams and Von Kaenel, 1981). The extent to which reliance could be placed on outside assistance is uncertain, and depends on geographical and societal factors, among others, which would vary enormously among locations. These considerations are outside the purview of this report, but this is clearly an area of study needing detailed exploration.

In order to identify the extent of such potential uneven distribution of immediate effects across the global landscape, an approximate calculation of the human population within broad latitudinal bands was made by assigning direct fatalities to the major and peripheral combatant countries (using estimates from WHO(1984), Harwell (1984), and Ambio (1982)) and comparing the surviving population level with the present population level (as characterized by the 1982 census data). These data are shown in Figure 7.1. It should again be emphasized that the projections of immediate casualties are rather scenario dependent; this figure illustrates the situation in response to a moderate-sized nuclear war scenario, and lesser or greater direct effects could ensue.

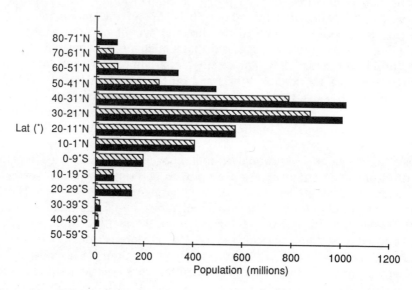

Figure 7.1   Human population distributed across latitudinal bands at current levels (solid bars) and after the direct effects of a large-scale nuclear war (striped bars) (based on calculations derived from Harwell, 1984; Ambio, 1982; and Bergstrom et al., 1983)

7.2.2 Effects on Humans of Reduced Temperatures

The possibility exists for some humans to die directly from exposure to adverse environmental conditions, particularly in tropical regions if extreme temperatures were experienced there; this is because of the general lack of adaptation to cold temperatures by humans and because of the unavailability of basic resources to protect many individuals from adverse conditions among those normally experiencing marginal human existence. However, insofar as warm clothing and fuel resources remained readily available during the period of climatic perturbations, it is not to be expected that a large proportion of the surviving population on Earth would suffer direct fatalities in response to the cold temperatures.

7.2.3 Effects from Loss of Food Imports

Indirect effects would be likely to cause much greater human impacts than exposure to cold temperatures. One area of major potential for human consequences is the effect of societal disruptions. These issues have not been the primary focus of the present study, and many such factors and their human impacts are considered to be highly speculative. Few quantitative or even qualitative evaluations of societal effects have been undertaken, yet the disruptions in economic, social order, infrastructure maintenance, and other systems offer the potential for substantial impacts. For instance, the possibility of extreme competition for limited resources, beginning in the immediate period and potentially extending far into the long term, could be expected to result in considerable impacts. It is beyond the scope of this study to evaluate such issues, but this is clearly is an area requiring concerted attention.

We can, however, separate some physical constraints on human survival that are linked to the possible disruption of societal systems. In particular, the issue of food production and exchange of food resources globally can be at least investigated with respect to the vulnerability of the current world food system.

Subsequent to the direct effects of nuclear detonations would be the effects of availability of food supplies for the surviving populations. Depending on the time of onset of a nuclear war in relation to local crop growing seasons, varying degrees of reliance would have to be placed on stored food and imports. One assumption that was used in the food availability calculations (Chapter 5) is that the export of food from countries that currently export grains would be terminated in the aftermath of a major nuclear war because of: 1.) disruptions in combatant countries, which would likely constitute the major food exporters; 2.) the likely extreme disruptions of the world economic system; and 3.) the disruption of intra- and inter-regional food distribution systems. In contrast to the assumption of termination of food exchanges between countries, it was assumed that within a country there would be an *optimal* distribution of food stores and production (i.e., equal distribution only to those who would be eventual survivors). By choosing such an assumption, which based on historical evidence from famines is clearly unrealistic for the post-nuclear war environment in combatant or non-combatant countries, evaluation can be made of the *minimum* effect that loss of food imports would entail.

To provide some perspective on the vulnerability of the current human population to loss of imports, data on grain production and imports for 135 countries of the world were examined (FAO, 1982c,d). The fraction of the total available food resources (imports plus indigenous production) that gross imports constitute was calculated on a country-by-country basis, as well as regionally and globally. The range of values is from much less than 1% to about 99%, reflecting the great divergence among countries in dependency on other countries for basic food support. A more consistent pattern emerges, however, by looking at continental scales, where the calculations show gross import fractions of 23% in Africa, 11% in Asia, 18% in South America, 20% in Europe, 13% in North America, and 12% for the world in total.

It is not simple to translate such a reduction in the food resource base to population reductions on a global scale, since many factors determine the effects of loss of imports on human support. For example, in many countries, no food imports would be needed if the current agricultural production being fed to domesticated animals were to go strictly into feeding humans directly. In another example, current agricultural production in many countries, especially in tropical regions, involves a large proportion of arable land used for export crops or non-food crops grown on typically the most productive lands, and replacement of these with food crops could reduce or alleviate the need for food importation. Further, major shifts in the consumption patterns among the surviving human population within a country could occur in a post-nuclear war environment, as changes in diet became necessary in response to differential food availability, storage capability, and other factors.

Thus, a reduction in the current level of imports that constitute, for example, the 23% of total grains in Africa might not necessarily translate into a 23% reduction in the human population of Africa, if compensatory mechanisms operated. On the other hand, the past episodes of famine illustrate vulnerability to relatively small reductions in food availability; e.g., the 1943 Bengalese famine, during which there was a loss of only about 10% of rice availability accompanied by disruptions in economic and social systems, was associated with the death of 3 million people (Sen, 1981; see Chapter 6). This example, among many others that have occurred within the historical record, indicates that there is a substantial sensitivity to the loss of small fractions of total food resources and that nonlinear societal responses can lead to disproportionate human population effects. This issue is graphically portrayed in Scrimshaw's (1984) discussion of the societal responses and feedbacks associated with historical famines, which followed perturbations of a much smaller scale than that of a major nuclear war. Further, many historical famines occurred without substantial reductions in the total food resource base.

Even though the effect of loss of imports on a global scale cannot be readily evaluated, examples for some countries can provide a suggestion of the degree of this vulnerability. Australia provides an example of a country that would have essentially no effects from the loss of imports of grains, since the fraction of its total grain imports compared to the total of grain production plus imports is less than 0.05% (and *net* imports are negative for this grain-exporting country). Loss of this level of grain inputs to the food availability system is not likely to have any noticeable effect on the Australian population. By sharp contrast, the case of Japan is a particularly instructive example of a highly sensitive country.

In Figure 7.2, 100% of indigenous production plus imports can be seen potentially to support a population that is about 150% of the current Japanese population. This increase in the support capability by 50% would occur if grains were only fed to humans and if the diet were altered to 1500 calories per person per day of grain consumption (out of a total assumed minimum requirement of 2000 cal person^{-1} day^{-1}; see Chapter 5). The figure indicates, however, that loss of imports, i.e., reliance on 100% of indigenous production alone, under the same assumptions would lead to a maximum

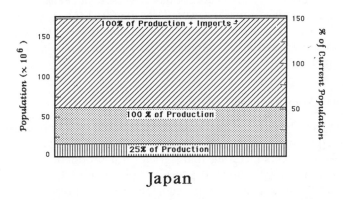

Figure 7.2   Vulnerability of Japan to reductions in food importans and food production

support for only about 50% of the current human population. This dramatically shows the extreme vulnerability in absolute terms in a region heavily dependent on imports, such as Japan, to the loss of imports. This does not consider the potential multiplying effect of societal nonlinearities under conditions of insufficient food resources. If a nuclear war did not directly impact such a region and did not indirectly involve it in exposure to climatic or other physical perturbations, loss of food imports could still lead to the death of a substantial fraction of the affected population. Either the population would have to: 1.) increase its food production markedly (an unlikely situation in the aftermath of a nuclear war, which would probably result in the loss of fossil fuel imports along with the loss of food imports, and an unlikely event in the aftermath of climatic alterations, to which Japan's rice crop is particularly sensitive); 2.) experience massive-scale exodus to other parts of the world by at least half of the Japanese population before food stores were depleted (also highly unlikely in a post-nuclear war world because of loss of transportation capabilities and unavailability of appropriate refugia for such a large number of people); or 3.) be subject to widespread fatalities associated with starvation based on the simple physical limit of insufficient quantities of food. In the latter case, the assumption of an optimal distribution pattern for the remaining food production would not likely reflect the actual situation, and even greater population losses would have to ensue.

Note, however, that the loss of food imports would not necessarily be additive to losses from other effects; thus, in the event of direct nuclear detonations on such areas as Japan, the loss of population from the immediate effects of nuclear detonations would reduce the food consumption requirements for the remaining population, perhaps to the level that loss of imports would have a greatly reduced additional effect. Nevertheless, the situation in Japan is instructive in understanding the potential for very consequential effects from a large-scale nuclear war on countries far removed from nuclear detonations, even in the absence of any physical perturbations on the global environment.

7.2.4 Effects from Reduced Food Production

Climatic alterations following a nuclear war could greatly increase the difficulty of providing adequate food supplies. Chapter 4 provided a number of lines of evidence suggesting that agricultural production is quite sensitive to climatic changes and to the loss of human subsidies. These analyses indicate that if climatic alterations occurred in which there were even brief temperature excursions near or below freezing during the growing season, there would be loss of grain crops of virtually every variety. Additionally, for many crops, most notably rice which is the mainstay of grain consumption for much of the world, brief temperature excursions down to nighttime levels of 10°C or even to 15°C (depending on the timing within the growing season) would result in loss of the crop, even though the rice plants themselves would survive. The analyses of longer periods of reduced *average* temperatures were also seen to limit agricultural crops markedly. For most crops, a 5–7°C reduction in average temperature over a growing season would limit or essentially eliminate crop yield; some crops are sensitive to as little as 1–3°C reductions. Similarly, potential reductions in precipitation were seen to lead directly to crop productivity losses. Light limitations, reduced during the chronic period by only 10%–20% below ambient normals, were estimated potentially to cause nonlinear impacts on crop productivity. The loss of human subsidies was demonstrated potentially to reduce crop productivity significantly, following similar analyses by Svirezhev et al. (1985). Global increases in ultraviolet radiation were identified as possibly resulting in crop productivity reductions, as were local incidences of air pollution, soil contamination and erosion, nutrient depletion, and many other perturbations. In short, many mechanisms have been identified, and at least in part characterized, by which a nuclear war would likely reduce the production of food.

But beyond the effects of each of these factors acting independently are the issues of interactions among perturbations. In some instances, there could be antagonistic effects, i.e., where the imposition of one stress would reduce the sensitivity to another stress. As an example, reduced temperatures can reduce the requirements for available water for the crop plant, partially offsetting the effects from the potential lowering of precipitation inputs. In far more typical situations, however, combinations of effects *increase* the impacts, and synergisms are the rule rather than the exception. These synergisms have not been adequately studied, and in large part we cannot address them quantitatively. Examples of possible synergisms are:

- Crops could have increased vulnerability to disease and pests when subject to such stresses as radiation and air pollution.

- Reduced temperatures could result in the decreased availability of insects that perform essential roles in pollination of crop plants.

- Disruptions of weather and crop information services would coincide with an increased uncertainty about the future climatic conditions to be experienced at a location.

- Societal disruptions could interfere with the optimal distribution of food among survivors.

- Societal disruptions could affect the availability of human labor for agricultural productivity.

- Overexploitation of crops and the environment, such as harvesting consumable plant parts prior to completion of the crop life cycles, could reduce long-term productivity.

- Reduced caloric and nutrient inputs in the diets of human survivors would increase the incidence and susceptibility of people to disease.

- More rapid recovery of opportunistic species of animals could enhance the vectors for disease spread to and among humans.

The list of possible synergisms extends into countless other examples. In total, the potential for such synergisms strongly suggests that the direct reduction in food producing capabilities and the direct human responses to such reductions would be worse, rather than better, than individual stress-response calculations would imply.

These considerations show that the loss of crop production within certain areas is highly likely to occur in the aftermath of a large-scale nuclear war. One key issue that remains to be adequately defined is the spatial extent of areas of lost crop productivity. This cannot be precisely characterized, because nuclear war scenarios and climatological predictions remain uncertain and may never be adequately refined to specify those areas of the Earth that would receive sufficient climatic alterations for lowered productivity. Nevertheless, the deliberations in Volume I suggest very strongly that climatic perturbations would likely be substantial and at least hemispheric—if not global—in scale. It should be clear from the discussions in the present volume that agricultural productivity is much more vulnerable than many people suppose, and that relatively small climatic alterations, or the societal effects after a large-scale nuclear war even in the absence of any climatic alterations, would each be adequate to disrupt agricultural productivity on a large scale.

The atmospheric scientists cannot tell which regions would experience subfreezing or near freezing temperatures after a nuclear war, but rather provide ranges of values that depend on uncertainties associated with the initiating nuclear war scenario as well as with the consequences of a particular scenario. In order to evaluate the potential vulnerability of the Earth to climatic and other perturbations, however, one does not have to be limited to a particular set of climatic projections. Rather, exploration can be made of what the consequences would be in absolute terms if there were *no* agricultural productivity. By making this assessment, no projection is being made that this would occur, with a particular probability; rather, the *vulnerability* of human populations to disruptions in agricultural productivity is being characterized. Such a vulnerability is manifested historically in regional areas (e.g., the sub-Sahel), but nuclear war offers the unique circumstance of imposing on a global scale the types of perturbations to which agricultural productivity is so sensitive.

7.2.5 Duration of Food Stores

If there were no agricultural productivity for the first growing season, the relevant analyses are of the amounts and duration of food stores that would exist at the time of a nuclear war and that were not destroyed directly by nuclear detonations (see Chapter 5). Such calculations provide the upper bound, i.e., the *maximum* population that could avoid starvation based on the *physical* limitations of energy requirements for human survival. That is, it was assumed that: 1.) there were total homogeneity of distribution of food stores within a country (i.e., full and equal access for all who would survive); 2.) those who would *eventually* die from starvation (i.e., the number of people in excess of the one-year food supply capacity) would do so instantaneously at the beginning of the post-nuclear war period, thereby not reducing food resources for the ultimate human survivors; and 3.) changes in dietary patterns would be made to reflect the increased reliance in general on grain calories for minimal human subsistence. Based on these assumptions, calculations can be made of the absolute upper limit of human survival under a situation of no food production for one growing season and no exchange of food across national boundaries. It should be understood that such analyses do not rely on any speculation as to human responses to a limited-food situation on the scale for an individual, a community, or a country. Rather, if one assumes no agricultural production, these calculations are the best physically limited outcome that could happen to food supplies for the human population. Other considerations of food hoarding and maldistribution, societal conflicts over limited resources, less than perfect allocation of food from the very beginning to only those who would eventually survive, vitamin and protein deficiency, increased caloric requirements in response to manual labor for food production, food spoilage and contamination, and other such factors that seem probable to ensue, but that are too speculative to characterize, would each *reduce* the number of humans that could be kept alive through the first year below the estimates provided here.

Detailed analyses constrained by these considerations were presented in Chapter 5 for 15 representative countries, along with summary analyses for 135 countries, which showed tremendous vulnerability in most countries to the loss of one year's food production. Integration across the globe can be made to provide an estimate of total human consequences. As discussed previously, the timing of the nuclear war would have a major influence on these calculations, since the stores of food on hand within a particular country vary over the annual cycle. The worst case would be represented by food stores being limited to only carryover values, i.e., if the perturbations occurred just prior to harvesting of crops when food stores were at a minimum.

Again to provide a bounding example, the effects of loss of food production for one growing season were calculated as if that were to occur when all countries had only carryover food supplies, i.e., the *minimum* stocks of food in storage. This result is presented in Figure 7.3. The extreme vulnerability of the Earth's human population to the loss of one year's food production is graphically indicated. Indeed, population levels would be reduced even below those shown because of non-food related reasons; these values, again, are *physically limited upper bounds*.

The effect of seasonality of a nuclear war on the maximum human support from extant median level food stores is illustrated in Figure 7.4. In this graph, it can be seen that much greater population support would follow the loss of food production occurring when food stocks were at their median level for each country.

Nevertheless, in comparing this figure with Figure 7.1, it becomes clear

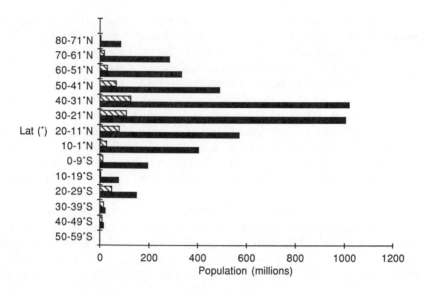

Figure 7.3 Vulnerability of human population to loss of food production if occurring when food stores are at a minimum. Current population (solid bars) and optimal number of survivors after one year (striped bars) (see discussion of assumptions in text) are shown across latitudinal bands

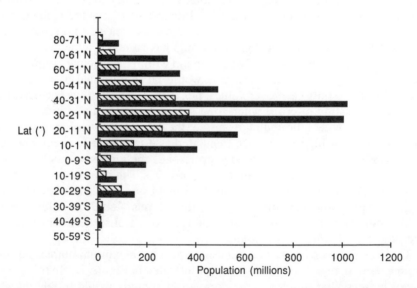

Figure 7.4 Vulnerability of human population to loss of food production if occurring when food stores are at the median level. Current population (solid bars) and optimal number of survivors after one year (striped bars) (see discussion of assumptions in text) are shown across latitudinal bands

that the human population impacts from the loss of one growing season in response to climatic and other effects of nuclear war would at a *minimum* far exceed the estimated direct effects from nuclear detonations on urban and other targets. Alternative targeting scenarios could lead to changes in the fatalities suggested in Figure 7.1, but it would be almost impossible to target nuclear weapons in order to effect direct fatalities of the magnitude and extent of potential indirect human effects shown in Figure 7.4, let alone Figure 7.3. In essence, these figures illustrate *the extreme sensitivity of human life on Earth to disruptions in the agricultural, economic, and societal bases that maintain populations far above the carrying capacity of natural ecosystems*, i.e., the levels possible without any agricultural production.

Whether or not an eventuality such as depicted in Figures 7.3 or 7.4 would actually occur would in part be determined by the spatial extent, severity, and timing of climatic perturbations, issues remaining to be resolved. That climatic perturbations sufficient to cause agricultural losses over some areas would follow a large-scale nuclear war seems quite plausible, as presented in Volume I; projections of such acute effects on a hemispheric or global scale are possible but less certain. *What can be said with assurance, however, is that the Earth's human population has a much greater vulnerability to the indirect effects of nuclear war, especially mediated through impacts on food productivity and food availability, than to the direct effects of nuclear war itself.*

7.3 EFFECTS DURING SUBSEQUENT YEARS

Many of the same issues discussed above would continue to apply in years after the first post-nuclear war year. For instance, agricultural productivity could be expected to remain reduced for long periods because of, among many factors, possible climatic alterations and their continued reverberations, continued economic and societal disruptions, lack of available energy sources, and adverse interactions with ecological systems undergoing their own reverberations. Again, it is difficult to predict quantitatively the net outcome of these and other factors acting over the long term; rather, the bounds of human population levels should be examined as determined by physical constraints associated with specific assumptions. These provide indications of the range of long-term potentialities, from which other analysts can select their own best estimates of the perturbations and derive the associated levels of human impacts.

7.3.1 Chronic Food Production Effects

One major approach to accomplishing this is to look at the situation in the post-nuclear war world at a time after food reserves from pre-war systems became largely depleted. Then the bounding calculations are of how large a human population could be maintained in a steady-state situation as a function of various levels of agricultural productivity. The same approach that was used for the detailed analyses of 15 countries for acute calculations (Chapter 5) was applied to this issue. In these analyses, the assumptions were that: 1.) there were no pre-nuclear war food stores remaining, so human support would be linked solely to extant agricultural productivity; 2.) there were no imports of food or energy resources from other countries; 3.) dietary patterns were altered to 1500 cal person^{-1} day^{-1} grain consumption out of a subsistence diet totaling 2000 cal person^{-1} day^{-1}; 4.) all grains were consumed directly by humans, rather than fed to livestock; and 5.) the maximum number of people were kept alive through perfect distribution of food at the minimally sustaining consumption rates, i.e., provided equally but *only* to those individuals who would continue to survive. These assumptions lead to an upper bound of the *maximum* number of people who could be maintained indefinitely under the physical constraints of food availability. Thus, again the important issues of societal effects, maldistribution of food, synergisms, and the many other issues discussed previously were *not* taken into account, but would tend to *reduce* the numbers of humans who could be maintained below these estimates.

Assessing the global effects of reduced long-term agricultural productivity is difficult because of differing vulnerabilities and differing perturbations that would be experienced among countries. In the assessments of the effects in individual countries, several situations were considered, as represented in Figures 5.3–5.32

1.) the effects from the loss of imports alone—This is represented by the 100% production graphic; for those countries that currently require imports to meet the food needs that would occur under the altered-consumption assumptions (e.g., Japan, Nigeria) (Figures 5.20 and 5.24), the difference between the support provided by 100% indigenous production and full population support reflects the *vulnerability* of that country to loss of imports.

2.) the effects from a limited set of human perturbations, specifically the loss of energy subsidies, energy imports, fertilizer availability, pesticide availability, etc.—This is represented by the range of production reduction levels selected based on examining the current energy dependency of the individual country with respect to agricultural productivity and the assignment of the country to a combatant or non-combatant status (i.e., whether or not it would experience direct effects of detonations).

3.) the additional effects of chronic climatic disturbances, including a few degrees of temperature reductions on average below normal, associated reductions in solar insolation, and reductions in precipitation—In the analyses, the likely range of agricultural productivity reductions associated with these physical perturbations were selected as if they were in addition to the loss of subsidies effects discussed above.

One can now look across the combined range of medium and severe chronic climatic effects, ranging from 1–5°C reductions in temperature and from 10% to 50% reductions in precipitation. The combined effect across the 15 countries was estimated by 1.) converting the fraction of population reduction associated with a particular country under particular assumptions to absolute numbers of people, 2.) summing across countries, and 3.) comparing against the current populations in those countries. The results indicate that under a scenario containing *no* climatic alterations, but with loss of imports and high energy subsidies to agriculture, from 60% to 130% of the current population of the 15 countries could be maintained indefinitely. (The apparent possibility of supporting an increased population level of 30% above the current level reflects the assumptions of altered dietary consumption, especially feeding grain production only to humans.) Thus, these summaries indicate the potential for population decreases of 0% to 40% as a result of the long-term effects of nuclear war in the 15 countries analyzed, not including potential acute or chronic climatic effects and not including the immediate fatalities from nuclear detonations. The sensitivity of these results to the specific countries selected was partially tested by performing the same analyses on a subset of these countries that did not include the U.S., Canada, and the U.S.S.R.; results were essentially unchanged, suggesting that they might be applicable to the whole global population.

One caution, however, is that the possibility of losing up to 40% of the world's population in the absence of any climatic disturbances or any immediate effects would not necessarily be additive to the losses from those effects. In particular, the reduction in the world's population by up to 20% (in the extreme case) from the immediate, direct effects of a large-scale nuclear war would reduce the food demand among the survivors. Similarly, loss of a major fraction of the world's population resulting from widespread acute-period crop failure and subsequent food stores depletion would reduce demand for food in the chronic period. On the other hand, the carryover effects into the chronic period from human losses during the first year could act to enhance the importance of long-term societal and other factors that could affect long-term human support.

Superimposing onto the effects from losses of human subsidies the ranges of effects estimated to ensue from chronic climatic conditions for the 15 countries, the combined effect is that about 30% to 80% of the population could be maintained indefinitely. Again, these calculations for the reduced set of countries (i.e., not including the U.S., Canada, and U.S.S.R.) gave essentially the same range of levels. Extrapolation to the world population would suggest a potential loss of about one to a few billion humans from long-term consequences; this wide range incorporates a wide range of differing potential environmental and societal disturbances. This calculation does *not* count the losses from direct effects or the potential losses from starvation in the first year if food supplies were depleted in response to widespread crop failures; again, these are not necessarily additive to those other effects, because the same individual cannot be killed twice, and because reduced population numbers decrease food demand. *Nevertheless, these numbers do give a sense of the extreme vulnerability of the world's human population to chronic-term effects, even if the first year's effects are not considered.*

7.3.2 Ecosystem Considerations

Chapter 3 briefly discussed the carrying capacities of natural ecological systems. The relationships between ecological productivity or other measures of ecosystem functioning and human carrying capacity are poorly understood and poorly researched. The simple calculations presented previously suggest that only a very small fraction (probably below 1%) of the current human population could be maintained indefinitely in the absence of the agricultural and societal systems that have developed over long periods of cultural evolution. This alone indicates the essential reliance on those human systems for human population support and the concomitant high vulnerability of the Earth's human population to large-scale disruption in those systems.

But it seems likely that in response to disruptions in human systems, there would be an increased reliance on natural ecological systems for human support, e.g., for food, fuel, and shelter. This increased reliance would coincide with the historically unprecedented disruptions to those ecological systems, discussed in Chapters 1–3 of this volume.

It is neither possible nor necessary to quantify how ecological disruptions would translate into a reduced carrying capacity for humans; it is enough to recognize that the *sole* reliance on ecological systems would result in almost total elimination of the current human population, and that the additional disturbance to those ecological systems would further reduce the carrying capacity to well below the 1% level. One adverse, positive feedback that could be important would be the likely overexploitation of the natural ecological systems by humans struggling for survival during the months and years after a nuclear war, retarding the recovery of those ecosystems and reducing the support they could provide humans.

7.3.3 Summary

It is apparent from these considerations of effects on agricultural, societal, and ecological systems that the *total* loss of human agricultural and societal support systems would result in the loss of almost all humans on Earth, essentially equally among combatant and non-combatant countries alike. We do not predict that such a total collapse in global systems would ensue. But it is not clear just how effective a large-scale nuclear war would be in disrupting those global systems. As the nuclear war-induced physical and societal perturbations become better characterized in future studies, and as alternate assumptions are made for stress responses, the information in the present volume can be used to evaluate the alternate impacts on humans.

7.4 FACTORS AFFECTING LONG-TERM AGRICULTURAL REDEVELOPMENT

Under any set of assumptions, there would come a point in time at which the human population would reach a minimum value and, if that level were not zero, would begin a gradual recovery. How quickly that would occur and what the recovery rates would be are not possible to estimate at this time. However, some important factors can be identified that would influence the redevelopment, or retardation of development, of the agricultural and natural ecosystem bases needed for human support. The earlier discussion of the agricultural consequences of the altered climatic variables focused on the period of the first growing season and the few years thereafter. This section identifies some of the factors that could affect the longer-term agricultural system redevelopment after the period of maximum responses to the changes in climate, the altered state of the natural biotic systems, and the human and societal inputs to agricultural productivity.

7.4.1 Physical Factors

While the extremes of global climatic disturbances are unlikely to be persistent, it is nevertheless not possible to rule out agriculturally significant climatic alterations continuing several years into the future. The effects of these types of climatic alterations were examined in the earlier discussion in Chapter 4 on the chronic effects of temperature, light, and precipitation changes on agricultural systems. Immediate survivors of a nuclear war could be faced with the prospects for long-term increases in risks of crop failure or substantial losses of crop production. These risks could result from: 1.) continued alterations in the average climatic conditions; 2.) increased frequency of occurrence of episodic events of adverse weather; and 3.) continued disruptions and insufficiencies in the availability of subsidies for agriculture.

In addition to the loss or diminution of crop productivity, longer-term climatic perturbations could exacerbate the loss of seed supplies, on which future productivity would depend. This would occur in three ways: 1.) The acute phase of the climatic disturbances could directly cause the loss of crops and the seed derived therefrom, if the acute phase occurred prior to the maturation of a crop. 2.) The chronic perturbation phase, if it occurred, would diminish the productivity of many types of crops. There would likely be a concomitant reduction in the proportion of crop production that could be set aside as seed for the next growing season, without conflicting with the immediate food needs of those dependent on that crop; this could be a particularly important factor in the event of widespread famine. 3.) Seeds planted for crops that subsequently failed, such as because of an adverse climatic episode occurring during the chronic phase, would be effectively wasted.

One of the vital inputs into successful agricultural production is the ability to predict what actions are necessary and when they would be most beneficial. These decisions involve the timing of the actions taken during the various phases of cultivation and the nature of the crop types planted in particular areas. Most of these decisions are based on an understanding, derived from experience, of what indicators to use in minimizing the risk of crop failure by choosing appropriate planting dates and seed types. The post-nuclear war situation would not allow the cultivator reasonably to rely on information from the immediate past, since the nature of the future climate would be poorly known. Further, the time lags between observations of climate and crop responses in one year and the decisions to be made in the following year would not necessarily lead to the correct decisions extrapolated from growing season to growing season, nor, for that matter, from one local area to another. Obviously, there would not likely be readily available world-scale weather information from which long-range forecasting could be made, and the value of any weather forecasting, given the nature of the potential information-isolation of regions from one another, would be minimal. Additionally, episodic climatic events of potentially large impact on agricultural productivity in a region would not be easily predictable, even in the absence of communications difficulties. For example, long-term precipitation effects might be felt locally or regionally in response to presently unknown interactions with ocean currents; as another example, local-to regional-scale climatic responses to feedbacks from devegetated areas, particularly in the tropics, could affect the hydrologic cycle.

Another physical factor affecting the longer-term productivity of agricultural systems is the extent of damage to soil productivity. Fires in both natural and cultivated areas, and the failure to protect soils during cultivation, harvesting, and periods of quiescence could result in widespread erosion (see also Svirezhev et al., 1985). This could lead to the loss of nutrients available for future crops and to a lowering of potential crop productivity. The possibility exists for local cycles of desertification which, depending on soil structure and surface winds, might feed dust into the air; such atmospheric inputs are known to affect local weather conditions. Long-term contamination of soils by radiation from local fallout and heavy metal deposition from urban fires could affect crop productivity, could reduce the areas of arable land available for safe cultivation, and could have human health effects which would vary enormously among localities. Finally, other long-term environmental perturbations could constrain restoration of full agricultural productivity; for example, the potential effects of increased UV-B from disruptions in the ozone layer (see Chapter 3).

7.4.2 Biological Factors

Physical factors alone would not determine the long-term response of agricultural systems to the stresses that could result from a nuclear war. A number of biotic inputs to agricultural production influence its degree of success. Throughout the period when agricultural systems would be subjected to some level of climatic abnormalities and in subsequent years, there would likely continue to be problems associated with interactions between agricultural and natural ecological systems. These would relate primarily to exchanges of organisms and seed sources, and to fluctuations in natural systems which could directly or indirectly affect agricultural systems.

For instance, one of the most influential factors could be the incidence of pest outbreaks (Svirezhev et al., 1985). Disruption of the industrial base for pesticide production and disruption of a distribution system which could effectively deploy remaining stores of pesticides would be expected to result in an increase in pest damage to crops, both while growing and during storage. Perturbations of natural ecosystems could influence the spread of insect and other pest species to areas of agricultural production, and continued environmental stresses could act to increase the probability that plant diseases and spoilage of stored crops would increase dramatically over those experienced before the nuclear war. Risk-reducing strategies, such as natural pest predator introduction, might be sought by those who could envision methods of combating these pest outbreaks in the absence of industrially produced chemical applications, but the uncertainties in predicting outbreaks of opportunistic species, especially in severely damaged ecological systems, would severely limit the large-scale efficacy of this approach.

The absence of an energy-intensive agricultural system would require the increased dependence on a labor-intensive and non-mechanized methodology for food production (see discussion on loss of human subsidies, Chapter 4). Draft animals would assume an increased importance in tilling, cultivating, and harvesting. Problems associated with this increased demand would include: 1.) the necessary time to replace those animals that were casualties of the conflict or were themselves food sources in the immediate post-war period; 2.) the maldistribution of the available animals among areas where there became a demand; and 3.) problems associated with the availability of breeding stocks.

Alternate planting strategies might be attempted to reduce the risks associated with agriculture in the absence of a high technological base; these could include experiments with intercropping and companion cropping (Vandermeer, 1981; Gliessman and Altieri, 1982; Horwith, 1985). Problems arise here in the areas of the adequacy of information bases on which decisions would have to be made, the distribution of this information, and the availability of seed sources.

7.4.3 Human and Social Factors

There are a number of factors potentially affecting the development of post-war agriculture that originate primarily from activities related to human and social systems decisions, as opposed to being controlled entirely by physical factors beyond the influence of individuals. In beginning the resumption of agricultural practices, it would be necessary for there to be seed sources available for planting during the first subsequent growing season. Under the pressures of possible widespread destruction of stored food sources, increased and unevenly distributed demand for food supplies for survivors, and lack of knowledge by those unfamiliar with agricultural practices, it would be possible that substantial quantities of seed sources would themselves be consumed directly as food. This, of course, would affect the extent and productivity of any planting done. For those seed sources that did survive the immediate destruction and subsequent hazards, disruption of the seed distribution system would hamper efforts to establish widespread agriculture. Additionally, those seed sources that were obtained might not be the appropriate cultivars for use at a particular location or under local weather and soil conditions. It would seem likely that, in light of possible long-term climatic alterations, there might be an increased emphasis on planting cold- and drought-hardy annuals and perennials that require relatively little processing; an important issue would be the availability of seeds for such crops that would allow such a crop-shifting strategy.

As a corollary to this, there would be an increased number of people who would be directly relying upon and initiating involvement with agricultural practices. A lack of appropriate information and an adequate base of cultural knowledge concerning agricultural practices would exacerbate an already difficult situation; regions in which largely rural populations have only recently concentrated in urban areas might fare better than older industrialized regions. For those unfamiliar with conservative agricultural practices or who attempted to rush production to provide food as quickly as possible, overexploitation of farm land could result after some time period. As the population diminished in an area, the pool of information which could lead to innovative solutions to agricultural problems might diminish (Boserup, 1965, 1983; Simon, 1983).

The widespread destruction of industrial bases could lead to a difficulty in obtaining mechanical parts for those agricultural implements that somehow remained in service through use of available energy sources. There would be some time lag between the lowering or cessation of industrial output of these parts and the initiation of severe shortages, during which time parts would likely be scavenged from local sources.

The ability to migrate to areas with increased probability of producing adequate food would be determined by many societal and physical factors, including the geography of a particular area. Populations tend to concentrate in areas with adequate rainfall for agricultural purposes; uncontaminated sources of readily available drinking water, especially along river banks; available natural resources such as energy sources; and societal resources, such as functioning technological centers and sources of medical care.

It is not unreasonable that there could arise societal conflicts, as nomadic groups came into agricultural areas and attempted to obtain food from those who were producing food in an agrarian strategy (Bronowski, 1973). At best, this interaction, with its potential for serious conflicts, could result in further disruption of agricultural efficiency and a reduction in overall distribution in the local area of production. On a much wider scale, the interactions between combatant and noncombatant areas of the world could involve issues associated with supply and demand, i.e., competition for limited resources. This might be especially evident in Northern and Southern Hemisphere interactions.

As reported in Chapters 4 and 5, widespread starvation would be the prevailing pattern for much of the world if severe climatic and/or societal disturbances resulted in loss of a substantial portion of a year's agricultural productivity. Effects of this lowering of nutritional input could carry over into the longer-term problems of agricultural redevelopment, such as relying on increased human labor by a weakened population. There would be a differential mortality across cultural and economic groups, coupled with the potential for societal conflicts associated with extreme competition for limited food that inevitably would be maldistributed. The demographic repercussions of differential mortality among age classes would play an important role in the long-term redevelopment of agricultural systems.

Psychological, medical, and sociological factors would all influence the redevelopment of post-nuclear war agriculture. These factors would be unpredictable, and they would differ across different locations in response to different climatic conditions, different nuclear war direct damage conditions, and different pre-war societal conditions.

7.5 SUMMARY

While it is not possible to make precise estimates of the total effects of nuclear war on humans or of the duration for which effects would continue to be felt, the previous discussions do provide a basis for readers to come to their own conclusions concerning the total global consequences. It seems possible that several hundred millions of humans could die from the direct effects of nuclear war. The indirect effects could result in the loss of one to several *billions* of humans. How close the latter projection would come to loss of *all* humans is problematical, but the current best estimation is that this result would not follow from the physical and societal perturbations currently projected to occur after a large-scale nuclear war.

One important issue of scale to keep in mind is the difference between estimating that on a global scale the bases for human support would be undermined for a particular fraction of the population (e.g., estimating insufficient food to support more than a certain fraction of the current population), and predicting the survival strategies of small groups of people. Projections of global-scale population losses do not mean that even in those areas in which humans would be expected to die, all would suffer the same fate. No analyses have been attempted here concerning the capability of selected humans on a relatively small scale (e.g., individual, family, community level) to find a successful strategy for survival. That a person or group in a combatant country might find a way to escape the effects of radiation, societal disruptions, climatic alterations, and the host of other potential disruptions, and still continue to survive seems possible, even in devastated areas. *That billions of people could do so in the absence of a sufficient food support base is impossible.* Thus, one needs to distinguish carefully between possible survival strategies on a small scale, and the physical limitations of support for massive numbers of people on a large scale.

In the previous discussion, predictions of specific perturbations or specific human population levels have been carefully avoided. Rather, the basis has been provided for evaluating the physical bounds that would limit human populations under differing assumptions and scenarios. It is quite clear, however, that the potential exists for climatic alterations and societal disruptions to occur on a global scale. Further, the great vulnerability of human population levels to disruptions in food support systems alone indicates that if such global-scale disruptions were to occur, then the impacts on the human populations from these indirect effects of a large-scale nuclear war would exceed in magnitude and in duration the effects from the nuclear detonations themselves.

This conclusion demonstrates that extrapolations of effects from the single nuclear detonations that occurred at the end of World War II cannot begin to characterize the reality of the world after a large-scale nuclear war. A fundamentally different picture of global suffering among peoples of non-combatant and combatant countries alike must become the new standard perception for decision-makers throughout the world if the visions portrayed in this study are to remain just intellectual exercises and not the irreversible future of humanity.

REFERENCES

Abrams. H.L.. and Von Kaenel, W.E. (1981). Medical problems of survivors of nuclear war. Infection and the spread of communicable disease. *New England J. Medicine.* **305**(20). 1226–1232.

Ambio Advisory Group. (1982). Reference scenario: How a nuclear war might be fought. *Ambio,* **1**, 94–99.

Bergstrom. S.. Black. D., Bochkov, N.P., Eklund, S., Kruisinga. R.J.H., Leaf, A., Obasanjo. O.. Shigematsu. I., Tubiana, M., and Whittembury, G. (1983). *Effects of a Nuclear War on Health and Health Services.* Report of the International Committee of Experts in Medical Sciences and Public Health. WHO Pub. A36.12. World Health Organization Publications, Geneva: 176 pages.

Boserup, E. (1965). *The Conditions of Agricultural Growth: The Economics of Agrarian Change under Population Pressure.* Allen and Unwin Ltd., London: 124 pages.

Boserup, E. (1983). The impact of scarcity and planting on development. *J. Interdis. Hist.,* **14**, 383–407.

Bronowski, J. (1973). *The Ascent of Man.* Little, Brown, and Co., Boston, Massachusetts: 448 pages.

FAO (1982c). *FAO Production Yearbook.* Food and Agriculture Organization of the United Nations, Rome, Italy.

FAO (1982d). *FAO Trade Yearbook.* Food and Agriculture Organization of the United Nations, Rome, Italy.

Gliessman, S.J., and Altieri, M. (1982). Polyculture cropping has advantages. *Calif. Agric.,* **36**, 14–16.

Haaland, C.M., Chester, C.V., and Wigner, E.P. (1976). *Survival of the Relocated Population of the U.S. after a Nuclear Attack.* ORNL-5041. U.S. Civil Defense Preparedness Agency, Washington, D.C.

Harwell, M.A. (1984). *Nuclear Winter: The Human and Environmental Consequences of Nuclear War.* Springer-Verlag, New York: 179 pages.

Horwith, B. (1985). A role for intercropping in modern agriculture. *BioScience,* **35**, 286–291.

Middleton, H. (1982). Epidemiology: The future is sickness and death. *Ambio,* **11**, 100–105.

OTA. (1979). *The Effects of Nuclear War.* U.S. Congress, Office of Technology Assessment, Washington, D.C.: 151 pages.

Pittock, A.B.. Ackerman, T.A., Crutzen, P.. MacCracken, M., Shapiro, C., and Turco, R.P. (1985). **The Environmental Consequences of Nuclear War.** Volume I: Physical. SCOPE 28a. John Wiley & Sons, Chichester.

Scrimshaw, N.S. (1984). Food, nutrition, and nuclear war. *New England J. Medicine,* **311**(4), 272–276.

Sen, A. (1981). *Poverty and Famines: An Essay on Entitlement and Deprivation.* Clarendon Press, Oxford.

Simon, J.L. (1983). The effects of population on nutrition and economic well-being. In Rotberg, R.I.. and Rabb, T.K. (Eds.). *Hunger and History.* 215-239. Cambridge University Press, Cambridge.

Svirezhev, Y.M., Alexandrov, G.A., Arkhipov, P.L., Armand, A.D., Belotelov, N.V., Denisenko, E.A., Fesenko, S.V., Krapivin, V.F., Logofet, D.O., Ovsyannikov, L.L., Pak, S.B., Pasekov, V.P., Pisarenko, N.F., Razzevaikin, V.N., Sarancha, D.A., Semenov, M.A., Shmidt, D.A., Stenchikov, G.L., Tarko, A.M., Vedjushkin, M.A., Vilkova, L.P., and Voinov, A.A. (1985). *Ecological and Demographic Consequences of Nuclear War.* Computer Center of the U.S.S.R. Academy of Sciences, Moscow: 275 pages.

Vandermeer, J.H. (1981) The interference production principle: An ecological theory for agriculture. *BioScience,* **31,** 361–364.

World Health Organization (WHO). (1984). *Effects of Nuclear War on Health and Health Services.* WHO, Geneva: 176 pages.

APPENDIX A
List of Participants

Name	Participant Technical Workshop[1]	Contributor to Manuscript	Review Team Participant
T.M. Addiscott (UK)	E		
F. Antoni (Hungary)	S,T		
A.G. Antoshechkin (USSR)	L		
L. Arias (Venezuela)	C		
R.N. Athavale (India)	D		
A.N. Auclair (Canada)	T		
S.A. Barber (USA)	E		
D. Barraclough (UK)	E		
E. Barrios (Venezuela)	C		
F. A. Bazzaz (USA)	C,T		
S. Beagle (USA)	T		
J. Bénard (France)	H,P		
J. Berry (USA)	T		

[1] Workshop abbreviations:
C = Caracas, Venezuela (tropical agriculture and ecosystems)
D = New Delhi, India (planning and issues identification)
E = Essex (temperate agriculture)
H = Hiroshima and Tokyo, Japan (human effects and lessons from Hiroshima and Nagasaki)
L = Leningrad, USSR (planning and issues identification)
M = Melbourne, Australia (Southern Hemisphere agriculture and ecosystems)
P = Paris, France (radiation effects)
S = Stockholm, Sweden (planning and issues identification)
T = Toronto, Canada (Northern temperate ecosystems)

Name	Participant Technical Workshop	Contributor to Manuscript	Review Team Participant
S.K.D. Bergstrom (Sweden)	L,P,S		
T. Bezuneh (Burkina-Faso)	C		
L.C. Bliss (USA)	T	•	•
A. Brace (Australia)	M		
J. Bromley (UK)	E,P		•
E. Brown-Weiss (USA)	D		
G. Budowski (Costa Rica)	C		
A.B. Cairnie (Canada)	P,T		
G.S. Campbell (UK)	E		
M.G.R. Cannell (UK)	T		
T.J. Carleton (Canada)	T		
N. Cherry (New Zealand)	M	•	
E. Chiozza (Argentina)	C		
V.L. Chopra (India)	D		
J.A. Clark (UK)	E	•	
M. Clarke (Australia)	M		
J.R. Coleman (Canada)	T		
C.F. Cooper (USA)	T		
W. P. Cropper, Jr. (USA)	C,E,T	•	
L. Cwynar (Canada)	T		
W. Day (UK)	E		
M.D. Dennett (UK)	E		
J.K. Detling (USA)	E,T	•	
E. Drew (Australia)	M		
B. Dutrillaux (France)	P		

Name	Participant Technical Workshop	Contributor to Manuscript	Review Team Participant
J.H. Edwards (UK)	P		•
R. Feddes (Netherlands)	E		
A. Forester (Canada)	T		
A.C. Freeman (UK)	C,D,E,H L,P,S,T	•	
P. Froggatt (Canada)	T		
Y. Fukushima (Japan)	H		
G. Goldstein (Venezuela)	C		
O. Green (UK)	E		
D. Greenwood (UK)	E		
P.J. Gregory (UK)	E		
J.P. Grime (UK)	T	•	•
H.D. Grover (USA)	E,T	•	•
J. Hanson (USA)		•	
C.C. Harwell (USA)	M	•	
M.A. Harwell (USA)	C,D,E,H,L M,P,S,T	•	
M. Havas (Canada)	T	•	
R. Herrera (Venezuela)	C,T	•	
H. Hughes (New Zealand)	M		
T.C. Hutchinson (Canada)	C,D,E,P,T	•	
V.V. Ivanitchshev (USSR)	L		
R.L. Jefferies (Canada)	T		
P. Jovanovic (Yugoslavia)	P		
A. Keast (Canada)	T	•	
G.J. Kelly (Australia)	M	•	

Name	Participant Technical Workshop	Contributor to Manuscript	Review Team Participant
J.R. Kelly (USA)	T	•	
P.M. Kelly (UK)E,	T	•	
R. Kirchmann (Belgium)	P		
V.F. Krapivin (USSR)	L		
S. Krishnaswamy (India)	D		
A. Kuzin (USSR)	P		•
M.S. Labouriau (Venezuela)	C		
N. Lakshmipathi (India)	D		
A. Leaf (USA)	H	•	•
J. Levitt (USA)	T	•	
K. Limburg (USA)		•	
E.S. Lopes (Brazil)	C	•	
N.K. Lukyanov (USSR)	D,H,L	•	•
H. Lundberg (Sweden)	D,S		
D. Martell (Canada)	T		
J. McKenna (USA)		•	
A. McKenzie (Australia)	M		
S.J. McNaughton (USA)	C,T	•	
E. Medina (Venezuela)	C		
K. Meema (Canada)	C,E,T	•	
R.L. Myers (USA)	C	•	
J.R. Naidu (USA)	D,S		
N. Nicholls (Australia)	M	•	
J. Ohasti (Venezuela)	C		
T. Ohkita (Japan)	H	•	•

Name	Participant Technical Workshop	Contributor to Manuscript	Review Team Participant
S. Pacenka (USA)		•	
J. Palau (Spain)	L,P		
R. Petty (Australia)	M		
D. Pimentel (USA)	E	•	
J. Porter (UK)	E	•	
A. Postnov (USSR)	L	•	
D.J. Potter (Australia)	M		
A. Radkin (Australia)	M		
R.C. Rainey (UK)	E		
P. Ramana (India)	D		
S.J. Risch (USA)	C,E,T	•	•
J.C. Ritchie (Canada)	T		
M.H. Robson (UK)	E		
T. Rosswall (Sweden)	D,S		
J. Rotblat (UK)	H,P		
M.J. Salinger (New Zealand)	M	•	•
E. Sanhueza (Venezuela)	C		
T. Schlichter (Argentina)	C		
A. Seymour (USA)	T	•	
R. Sgrillo (Brazil)	C		
C. Shapiro (USA)	P,T	•	
Y. Shimazu (Japan)	H,P	•	
T. Sinclair (USA)	E	•	
W. Sinclair (USA)	P		
D. Sisler (USA)	E	•	•

Name	Participant Technical Workshop	Contributor to Manuscript	Review Team Participant
E.I. Slepyan (USSR)	L		
N.N. Smirnov (USSR)	L		
V. Smirnyagin (USSR)	L		
R.B. Stewart (Canada)	E,T	•	•
B. Stocks (Canada)	T		
J.C. Su (Taiwan)	D		
A. Summerfield (UK)	L		
Y.M. Svirezhev (USSR)	T	•	•
J. Svoboda (Canada)	T		
A.M. Tarko (USSR)	L		
H.W. Taylor (Canada)	T		
J.M. Teal (USA)	T	•	
P.B. Tinker (UK)	E	•	
A. Travesi (Spain)	P		
Z. Uchijima (Japan)	H	•	
M.H. Unsworth (UK)	E	•	•
T. Urabe (Japan)	H,L	•	
J. Vandermeer (USA)	C	•	
M. Verstraete (USA)		•	
B. Walker (South Africa)	D		
D.W.H. Walton (UK)	T	•	•
R. Warrick (UK)	E		
C. Weeramantry (Australia)	H		
R.W. Wein (Canada)	T		
J. Westgate (Canada)	T		

Name	Participant Technical Workshop	Contributor to Manuscript	Review Team Participant
G.F. White (USA)	D,H	•	
M. Wik (Sweden)	P		
P.G. Williams (Australia)	M		
A.W. Wolfendale (UK)	P		
G.M. Woodwell (USA)	P,S		
R.C. Worrest (USA)	T	•	
G.A. Zavarzin (USSR)	P		
E. Zubrow (USA)	E	•	

APPENDIX B
Recommendations for Further Research

One of the more important outcomes of the process of holding workshops around the world to investigate the environmental consequences of nuclear war has been the recognition of the broad subject areas that have not yet received adequate research treatment. It is instructive to realize that many of the following listed topic areas involve the field of stress ecology; thus, improved understanding of the environmental consequences of nuclear war will progress in concert with advances in stress ecology.

During the synthesis workshop held at the Wivenhoe Conference Center, University of Essex in June, 1985, the review committee for this volume compiled their recommendations for further research. (See Appendix A for a listing of review committee members.) Those recommendations are listed below, supplemented by a more detailed list compiled by M. Harwell, T. Hutchinson, W. Cropper, Jr., and C. Harwell.

Review Committee Preamble:

'We recognized that progress in this field will be strongly dependent on research efforts in stress ecology, but we are confident that these investigations will continue to enjoy strong support.'

REVIEW COMMITTEE RECOMMENDATIONS:

1.) Biological and physical scientists should work cooperatively in developing regional and global models that reflect the climatic consequences of nuclear war, with particular attention to feedback from the biological analysts. This would help to produce the types of information needed for ecological considerations.

2.) There is a need for models of environmental and ecosystem responses extending into the chronic post-nuclear war phase. These should include better estimates of chronic phase parameters of temperature, light, and precipitation. These should also include much more experimental work on the effects of beta-radiation on plants and crops. Microcosm or enclosure experiments would be appropriate.

501

3.) Interactive atmosphere–ocean models need to be improved to allow simulations of post-nuclear war climatic disturbances.

4.) Experiments are needed to give a better understanding of the importance and role of seed and seedling banks in world ecosystems and their vulnerability to climatic perturbations.

5.) Explicit experimentation is needed to investigate synergisms including, for example, the interactive effects on biota of radiation, UV-B, and air pollution.

ADDITIONAL RESEARCH NEEDS (from the Volume II authors):

1.) Synthetic studies addressing the specific conditions at local, regional, and national levels are the next logical step in the process of understanding the effects of global nuclear war.

2.) There is a need for further analysis of food stores, the likelihood of their destruction in a major nuclear war, their location, and other data, on a country-by-country basis.

3.) Experiments need to be conducted using microcosms and enclosed whole ecosystems and agricultural systems to examine systems-level responses to climatic disturbances; particular attention can be given to recovery processes by using this approach.

4.) New model development is needed to determine responses of ecosystems to climatic perturbations. Such models will have general applicability to other important issues in addition nuclear war.

5.) Experimental manipulations of grasslands, such as the response of their root system when subjected to cold temperatures, would provide a good example of the response of perennials to post-nuclear war climatic alterations.

6.) Environmental triggers for pest outbreaks need investigation; this should deal particularly with the relationship of pest outbreaks to unusual climatic events.

7.) There needs to be an enhanced cooperation between physical and biological scientists in identifying the research priorities of the physical scientists. Examples of biologically based suggestions include:

- Climatologists need to do research on short-term variability in climate and the relationships between average climatic conditions and variances in climatic conditions in a post-nuclear war framework.

- Better resolution is needed of the potential levels of air pollution likely to result from a nuclear war.

- Better resolution is needed of the potential levels of precipitation reductions likely to result from a nuclear war.

- The potential for long-term climatic changes needs investigation, particularly involving feedback mechanisms, such as albedo changes, ice pack dynamics, and greenhouse-effect gases.

8.) Existing sophisticated models of local fallout patterns need to be used to evaluate the range of dose levels that would be experienced after a nuclear war, based on a variety of nuclear war scenarios and weather conditions. Similarly, existing dose models need to be used to evaluate the range of internal radiation doses to be expected in the aftermath of a large-scale nuclear war.

9.) There is a critical need for comprehensive and concerted study of the potential societal responses to nuclear war.

10.) Full consideration of the policy implications of the above kinds of research needs to be addressed.

APPENDIX C
Executive Summary of Volume I

Physical and Atmospheric Effects

A.B. Pittock, T.P. Ackerman, P.J. Crutzen,
M.C. MacCracken, C.S. Shapiro, and R.P. Turco

This volume presents the results of an assessment of the climatic and atmospheric effects of a large nuclear war. The chapters in the volume follow a logical sequence of development, starting with discussions of nuclear weapons effects and possible characteristics of a nuclear war. The report continues with a treatment of the consequent fires, smoke emissions, and dust injections and their effects on the physical and chemical processes of the atmosphere. This is followed by a chapter dealing with long-term radiological doses. The concluding chapter contains recommendations for future research and study.

In assessments of this type, a variety of procedural options are available, including, for example, "worst case" analyses, risk analyses, and "most probable" analyses. All of these approaches have relevance for the subject addressed here due to the large uncertainties which surround many aspects of the problem. Some of these uncertainties are inherent in studies of nuclear war and some are simply the result of limited information about natural physical processes. In general, in making assumptions about scenarios, models, and magnitudes of injections, and in estimating their atmospheric effects, an attempt has been made to avoid "minimum" and "worst case" analyses in favor of a "middle ground" that encompasses, with reasonable probability, the atmospheric and climatic consequences of a major nuclear exchange.

The principal results of this assessment, arranged roughly in the same order as the more detailed discussions contained in the body of this volume, are summarized below.

1. DIRECT EFFECTS OF NUCLEAR EXPLOSIONS

The two comparatively small detonations of nuclear weapons in Japan in 1945 and the subsequent higher yield atmospheric nuclear tests preceding the atmospheric test ban treaty of 1963 have provided some information on the direct effects of nuclear explosions. Typical modern weapons carried by today's missiles and aircraft have yields of hundreds of kilotons or more. If detonated, such explosions would have the following effects:

- In each explosion, thermal (heat) radiation and blast waves would result in death and devastation over an area of up to 500 km^2 per megaton, km^2, an area typical of a major city. The extent of these direct effects depends on the yield of the explosion, height of burst, and state of the local environment. The destruction of Hiroshima and Nagasaki by atomic bombs near the end of World War II provides examples of the effects of relatively *small* nuclear explosions.

- Nuclear weapons are extremely efficient incendiary devices. The thermal radiation emitted by the nuclear fireball, in combination with the accidental ignitions caused by the blast, would ignite fires in urban/industrial areas and wildlands of a size unprecedented in history. These fires would generate massive plumes of smoke and toxic chemicals. The newly recognized atmospheric effects of the smoke from a large number of such fires are the major focus of this report.

- For nuclear explosions that contact land surfaces (surface bursts), large amounts (of the order of 100,000 tonne per megaton of yield) of dust, soil, and debris are drawn up with the fireball. The larger dust particles, carrying about half of the bomb's radioactivity, fall back to the surface mostly within the first day, thereby contaminating hundreds of square kilometers near and downwind of the explosion site. This local fallout can exceed the lethal dose level.

- All of the radioactivity from nuclear explosions well above the surface (airbursts) and about half of the radioactivity from surface bursts would be lofted on particles into the upper troposphere or stratosphere by the rising fireballs and contribute to longer term radioactive fallout on a global scale.

- Nuclear explosions high in the atmosphere, or in space, would generate an intense electromagnetic pulse capable of inducing strong electric currents that could damage electronic equipment and communications networks over continent-size regions.

2. STRATEGIES AND SCENARIOS FOR A NUCLEAR WAR

In the forty years since the first nuclear explosion, the five nuclear powers, but primarily the U.S. and the U.S.S.R., have accumulated very large arsenals of nuclear weapons. It is impossible to forecast in detail the evolution of potential military conflicts. Nevertheless, enough of the general principles of strategic planning have been discussed that plausible scenarios for the development and immediate consequences of a large-scale nuclear war can be derived for analysis.

- NATO and Warsaw Pact nuclear arsenals include about 24,000 strategic and theatre nuclear warheads totaling about 12,000 megatons. The arsenals now contain the equivalent explosive power of about one million "Hiroshima-size" bombs.

- A plausible scenario for a global nuclear war could involve on the order of 6000 Mt divided between more than 12,000 warheads. Because of its obvious importance, the potential environmental consequences of an exchange of roughly this size are examined. The smoke-induced atmospheric consequences discussed in this volume are, however, more dependent on the number of nuclear explosions occurring over cities and industrial centers than on any of the other assumptions of the particular exchange.

- Many targets of nuclear warheads, such as missile silos and some military bases, are isolated geographically from population centers. Nevertheless, enough important military and strategic targets are located near or within cities so that collateral damage in urban and industrial centers from a counterforce nuclear strike could be extensive. As a result, even relatively limited nuclear attacks directed at military-related targets could cause large fires and smoke production.

- Current strategic deterrence policies imply that, in an escalating nuclear conflict, many warheads might be used directly against urban and industrial centers. Such targeting would have far-reaching implications because of the potential for fires, smoke production, and climatic change.

3. THE EXTENT OF FIRES AND GENERATION OF SMOKE

During World War II, intense city fires covering areas as large as 10 to 30 square kilometers were ignited by massive incendiary bombing raids, as well as by the relatively small nuclear explosions over Hiroshima and Nagasaki. Because these fires were distributed over many months, the total atmospheric accumulation of smoke generated by these fires was small. Today, in a major nuclear conflict, thousands of very intense fires, each covering up to a few hundred square kilometers, could be ignited simultaneously in urban areas, fossil fuel processing plants and storage depots, wildlands, and other locations. Because there have never been fires as large and as intense as may be expected, no appropriate smoke emission measurements have been made. Estimates of emissions from such fires rely upon extrapolation from data on much smaller fires. This procedure may introduce considerable error in quantifying smoke emissions, especially in making estimates for intense fire situations.

- About 70% of the populations of Europe, North America and the Soviet Union live in urban and suburban areas covering a few hundred thousand square kilometers and containing more than ten thousand million tonne of combustible wood and paper. If about 25–30% of this were to be ignited, in just a few hours or days, tens of millions to more than a hundred million tonne of smoke could be generated. About a quarter to a third of the emitted smoke from the flaming combustion of this material would be amorphous elemental carbon, which is black and efficiently absorbs sunlight.

- Fossil fuels (e.g., oil, gasoline, and kerosene) and fossil fuel-derived products (including plastics, rubber, asphalt, roofing materials, and organochemicals) are heavily concentrated in cities and industrial areas; flaming combustion of a small fraction (~25–30%) of the few thousand million tonne of such materials currently available could generate 50–150 million tonne of very sooty smoke containing a large fraction (50% or greater) of amorphous elemental carbon. The burning of 25–30% of the combustible materials of the developed world could occur with near total burnout of less than one hundred of the largest industrialized urban areas.

- Fires ignited in forests and other wildlands could consume tens to hundreds of thousands of square kilometers of vegetation over days to weeks, depending on the state of the vegetation, and the extent of firespread. These fires could produce tens of millions of tonne of smoke in the summer half of the year, but considerably less in the winter half of the year. Because wildland fire smoke contains only about 10% amorphous elemental carbon, it would be of secondary importance compared to the smoke created by urban and industrial fires, although its effects would not be negligible.

- The several tens of millions of tonne of sub-micron dust particles that could be lofted to stratospheric altitudes by surface bursts could reside in the atmosphere for a year or more. The potential climatic effects of the dust emissions, although substantially less than those of the smoke, also must be considered.

4. THE EVOLUTION AND RADIATIVE EFFECTS OF THE SMOKE

The sooty smoke particles rising in the hot plumes of large fires would consist of a mixture of amorphous elemental carbon, condensed hydrocarbons, debris particles, and other substances. The amount of elemental carbon in particles with effective spherical diameters on the order of 0.1 μm to perhaps 1.0 μm would be of most importance in calculating the potential effect on solar radiation. Such particles can be spread globally by the winds and remain suspended for days to months.

- Large hot fires create converging surface winds and rapidly rising fire plumes which, within minutes, can carry smoke particles, ash and other fire products, windblown debris, and water from combustion and the surrounding air to as high as 10–15 kilometers. The mass of particles deposited aloft would depend on the rate of smoke generation, the intensity of the fire, local weather conditions, and the effectiveness of scavenging processes in the convective column.

- As smoke-laden, heated air from over the fire rises, adiabatic expansion and entrainment would cause cooling and condensation of water vapor that could lead, in some cases, to the formation of a cumulonimbus cloud system. Condensation-induced latent heating of the rising air parcels would help to loft the smoke particles to higher altitudes than expected from the heat of combustion alone.

- Although much of the water vapor drawn up from the boundary layer would condense, precipitation might form for only a fraction of the fire plumes. In the rising fire columns of such fires, soot particles would tend to be collected inefficiently by the water in the cloud. Smoke particles however, are generally composed of a mixture of substances and might, at least partially, be incorporated in water droplets or ice particles by processes not now well understood. Smoke particles that are captured could again be released to the atmosphere as the ice or water particles evaporate in the cloud anvils or in the environment surrounding the convective clouds. Altogether, an unknown fraction of the smoke entering the cloud would be captured in droplets and promptly removed from the atmosphere by precipitation.

- Not all fires would, however, induce strong convective activity. This depends on fuel loading characteristics and meteorological conditions. It is assumed in current studies that 30–50% of the smoke injected into the atmosphere from all fires would be removed by precipitation within the first day, and not be available to affect longer-term large-scale, meteorological processes. This assumption is a major uncertainty in all current assessments. For the fire and smoke assumptions made in this study, the net input of smoke to the atmosphere after early scavenging is estimated to range from 50 to 150 million tonne, containing about 30 million tonne of amorphous elemental carbon.

- Smoke particles generated by urban and fossil fuel fires would be strong absorbers of solar radiation, but would be likely to have comparatively limited effects on terrestrial longwave radiation, except perhaps under some special circumstances. If 30 million tonne of amorphous elemental carbon were produced by urban/industrial fires and spread over Northern Hemisphere mid-latitudes, the insolation at the ground would be reduced by at least 90%. The larger quantities of smoke that are possible in a major nuclear exchange could reduce light levels under dense patches to less than 1% of normal, and, on a daily average, to just several percent of normal, even after the smoke has spread widely.

- Because of the large numbers of particles in the rising smoke plumes and the very dense patches of smoke lasting several days thereafter, coagulation (adhering collisions) would lead to formation of fewer, but somewhat larger, particles. Coagulation of the particles could also occur as a result of coalescence and subsequent evaporation of rain droplets or ice particles. Because optical properties of aerosols are dependent on particle size and morphology, the aggreated aerosols may have different optical properties than the initial smoke particles, but the details, and even the sign, of such changes are poorly understood. The optical properties of fluffy soot aggregates that may be formed in dense oil plumes, however, seem to be relatively insensitive to their size. This is not the case for more consolidated particle agglomerates.

- Little consideration has yet been given to the possible role of meteorological processes on domains between fire plume and continental scales. Mesoscale and synoptic-scale motions might significantly alter, mix, or remove the smoke particles during the first several days. Studies to examine quantitatively the microphysical evolution of smoke particles during this period are needed. While changes in detailed understanding are expected, a significant fraction of the injected smoke particles is likely to remain in the atmosphere and affect the large-scale weather and climate.

5. SMOKE-INDUCED ATMOSPHERIC PERTURBATIONS

In a major nuclear war, continental scale smoke clouds could be generated within a few days over North America, Europe, and much of Asia. Careful analysis and a hierarchy of numerical models (ranging from one-dimensional global-average to three-dimensional global-scale models) have been used to estimate the transport, transformation, and removal of the smoke particles and the effects of the smoke on temperature, precipitation, winds, and other important atmospheric properties. All of the simulations indicate a strong potential for large-scale weather disruptions as a result of the smoke injected by extensive post-nuclear fires. These models, however, still have important simplifications and uncertainties that may affect the fidelity and the details of their predictions. Nonetheless, these uncertainties probably do not affect the general character of the calculated atmospheric response.

- For large smoke injections reaching altitudes of several kilometers or more and occurring from spring through early fall in the Northern Hemisphere, average land surface temperatures beneath dense smoke patches could decrease by 20–40°C below normal in continental areas within a few days, depending on the duration of the dense smoke pall and the particular meteorology. Some of these patches could be carried long distances and create episodic cooling. During this initial period of smoke dispersion, anomalies could be spatially and temporally quite variable while patchy smoke clouds strongly modulate the insolation reaching the surface.

- Smoke particles would be spread throughout much of the Northern Hemisphere within a few weeks, although the smoke layer would still be far from homogeneous. For spring to early fall injections, solar heating of the particles could rapidly warm the smoke layer and lead to a net upward motion of a substantial fraction of the smoke into the upper troposphere and stratosphere. The warming of these elevated layers could stabilize the atmosphere and suppress vertical movement of the air below these layers, thereby extending the lifetime of the particles from days to perhaps several months or more.

- Average summertime land surface temperatures in the Northern Hemisphere mid-latitudes could drop to levels typical of fall or early winter for periods of weeks or more with convective precipitation being essentially eliminated, except possibly at the southern edge of the smoke pall. Cold, near-surface air layers might lead initially to fog and drizzle, especially in coastal regions, lowland areas, and river valleys. In continental interiors, periods of very cold, mid-winter-like temperatures are possible. In winter, light levels would be strongly reduced, but the initial temperature and precipitation perturbations would be much less pronounced and might be essentially indistinguishable in many areas from severe winters currently experienced from time to time. However, such conditions would occur simultaneously over a large fraction of the mid-latitude region of the Northern Hemisphere and freezing cold air outbreaks could penetrate southward into regions that rarely or never experience frost conditions.

- In Northern Hemisphere subtropical latitudes, temperatures in any season could drop well below typical cool season conditions for large smoke injections. Temperatures could be near or below freezing in regions where temperatures are not typically strongly moderated by warming influence from the oceans. The convectively driven monsoon circulation, which is of critical importance to subtropical ecosystems, agriculture, and is the main source of water in these regions, could be essentially eliminated. Smaller scale, coastal precipitation might, however, be initiated.

- Strong solar heating of smoke injected into the Northern Hemisphere between April and September would carry the smoke upwards and equatorward, strongly augmenting the normal high altitude flow to the Southern Hemisphere (where induced downward motions might tend to slightly suppress precipitation). Within one or two weeks, thin, extended smoke layers could appear in the low to mid-latitude regions of the Southern Hemisphere as a precursor to the development of a more uniform veil of smoke with a significant optical depth (although substantially smaller than in the Northern Hemisphere). The smoke could induce modest cooling of land areas not well buffered by air masses warmed over nearby ocean areas. Since mid-latitudes in the Southern Hemisphere would already be experiencing their cool season, temperature reductions would not likely be more than several degrees. In more severe, but less probable, smoke injection scenarios, climatic effects in the Southern Hemisphere could be enhanced significantly, particularly during the following austral spring and summer.

- Much less analysis has been made of the atmospheric perturbations following the several week, acute climatic phase subsequent to a nuclear war involving large smoke injections. Significant uncertainties remain concerning processes governing the longer-term removal of smoke particles by precipitation scavenging, chemical oxidation, and other physical and chemical factors. The ultimate fate of smoke particles in the perturbed atmospheric circulation is also uncertain, both for particles in the sunlit and stabilized upper troposphere and stratosphere and in the winter polar regions, where cooling could result in subsidence that could move particles downward from the stratosphere to altitudes where they could later be scavenged by precipitation.

- Present estimates suggest that smoke lofted to levels (either directly by fire plumes or under the influence of solar heating) which are, or become, stabilized, could remain in the atmosphere for a year or more and induce long-term (months to years) global-scale cooling of several degrees, especially after the oceans have cooled significantly. For such conditions, precipitation could also be reduced significantly. Reduction of the intensity of the summer monsoon over Asia and Africa could be a particular concern. Decreased ocean temperatures, climatic feedback mechanisms (e.g., ice-albedo feedback), and concurrent ecological changes could also prolong the period of meteorological disturbances.

6. ATMOSPHERIC CHEMISTRY IN A POST-NUCLEAR-WAR ENVIRONMENT

Nuclear explosions and the resultant fires could generate large quantities of chemical compounds that might themselves be toxic. In addition, the chemicals could alter the atmospheric composition and radiative fluxes in ways that could affect human health, the biosphere, and the climate.

- Nitrogen oxides (NO_x) created by nuclear explosions of greater than several hundred kilotons would be lofted into the stratosphere. Depending on the total number of high yield weapons exploded, the NO_x would catalyze chemical reactions that, within a few months time, could reduce Northern Hemisphere stratospheric ozone concentrations by 10 to 30% in an atmosphere free of aerosols. Recovery would take several years. However, if the atmosphere were highly perturbed due to smoke heating and by injection of gaseous products from fires, the long-term ozone changes could be enhanced substantially in ways that cannot yet be predicted.

- Ozone reductions of tens of percent could increase surface intensities of biologically-active ultraviolet (UV) radiation by percentages of up to a few times as much. The presence of smoke would initially prevent UV-radiation from reaching the surface by absorbing it. The smoke, however, might also prolong and further augment the long-term ozone reduction as a result of smoke-induced lofting of soot and reactive chemicals, consequent heating of the stratosphere, and the occurrence of additional chemical reactions.

- Large amounts of carbon monoxide, hydrocarbons, nitrogen and sulfur oxides, hydrochloric acid, pyrotoxins, heavy metals, asbestos, and other materials would be injected into the lower atmosphere near the surface by flaming and smoldering combustion of several thousand million tonne of cellulosic and fossil fuel products and wind-blown debris. Before deposition or removal, these substances, some of which are toxic, could be directly and/or indirectly harmful to many forms of life. In addition, numerous toxic chemical compounds could be released directly into the environment by blast and spillage, contaminating both soil and water. This complex and potentially very serious subject has so far received only cursory consideration.

- If the hydrocarbons and nitrogen oxides were injected into an otherwise unperturbed troposphere, they could enhance average background ozone concentrations several-fold. Such ozone increases would not significantly offset the stratospheric ozone decrease, which also would be longer lasting. It is highly questionable, however, whether such large ozone increases could indeed occur in the presence of smoke because ozone generation in the troposphere requires sunlight as well as oxides of nitrogen. It is possible that, in the smoke perturbed atmosphere, the fire-generated oxides of nitrogen could be removed before photochemical ozone production could take place.

- Precipitation scavenging of nitrogen, sulfur, and chlorine compounds dispersed by the fire plumes throughout the troposphere could increase rainfall acidity by about an order of magnitude over large regions for up to several months. This increased acidity could be neutralized to some degree by alkaline dust or other basic (as opposed to acidic) compounds.

- Rapid smoke-induced cooling of the surface under dense smoke clouds could induce the formation of shallow, stable cold layers that might trap chemical emissions from prolonged smoldering fires near the ground. In such layers, concentrations of CO, $HC\ell$, pyrotoxins, and acid fogs could reach dangerous levels. The potential for local and regional effects in areas such as populated lowland areas and river valleys merits close attention.

7. RADIOLOGICAL DOSE

Near the site of an explosion, the health effects of prompt ionizing radiation from strategic nuclear warheads would be overshadowed by the effects of the blast and thermal radiation. However, because nuclear explosions create highly radioactive fission products and the emitted neutrons may also induce radioactivity in initially inert material near the detonation, radiological doses would be delivered to survivors both just downwind (local fallout) and out to hemispheric and global scales (global fallout).

- Local fallout of relatively large radioactive particles lofted by the number of surface explosions in the scenario postulated in this study could lead to lethal external gamma-ray doses (assuming no protective action is taken) during the first few days over about 7 percent of the land areas of the NATO and Warsaw Pact countries. Areas downwind of missile silos and other hardened targets would suffer especially high exposures. Survivors outside of lethal fallout zones could still receive debilitating radiation doses (exposure at half the lethal level can induce severe radiation sickness). In combination with other injuries or stresses, such doses could increase mortality. If large populations could be mobilized to move from highly radioactive zones or take substantial protective measures, the human impact of fallout could be greatly reduced.

- The uncertainty in these calculations of local fallout is large. Doses and areas for single nuclear explosions could vary by factors of 2–4 depending on meteorological conditions and assumptions in the models. A detailed treatment of overlapping fallout plumes from multiple explosions could increase the areas considerably (by a factor of 3 in one sample case). Results are also sensitive to variations in the detonation scenario.

- Global fallout following the gradual deposition of the relatively small radioactive particles created by strategic air and surface bursts could lead to average Northern Hemisphere lifetime external gamma ray doses on the order of 10 to 20 rads. The peak values would lie in the northern mid-latitudes where the average doses for the major nuclear war considered would be about 20 to 60 rads. Such doses, in the absence of other stresses, would be expected to have relatively minor carcinogenic and mutagenic effects (i.e., increase incidence at most a few percent above current levels). Smoke-induced perturbations that tend to stabilize the atmosphere and slow deposition of radioactive particles might reduce these estimated average doses by perhaps 15%.

- Intermediate time scale and long term global fallout would be deposited unevenly, largely because of meteorological effects, leading to "hotspots" of several hundred thousand square kilometers in which average doses could be as high as 100 rads and, consequently, large areas where doses would be substantially less than the average value.

- In the Southern Hemisphere and tropical latitudes, global fallout would produce much smaller, relatively insignificant, radiological doses about one-twentieth those in the Northern Hemisphere, even if cross-equatorial transport were accelerated by the smoke clouds. Additional local fallout would be important only within a few hundred kilometers downwind of any surface burst in the Southern Hemisphere.

- Additional considerations not factored into the above estimates are possible from several sources. Doses from ingestion or inhalation of radioactive particles could be important, especially over the longer term. Beta radiation could have a significant effect on the biota coming into contact with the local fallout. Fission fractions of smaller modern weapons could be twice the assumed value of 0.5; adding these to the scenario mix could cause a 20% increase in areas of lethal fallout. General tactical and theater nuclear weapons, ignored in these calculations, could also cause a 20% increase in lethal local fallout areas in certain geographical regions, particularly in Europe. The injection into the atmosphere of radionuclides created and stored by the civilian nuclear power industry and military reactors, a possibility considered remote by some, could increase estimates of long-term local and global radiological doses to several times those estimated for weapons alone.

8. TASKS FOR THE FUTURE

Extensive research and careful assessment over the past few years have indicated that nuclear war has the potential to modify the physical environment in ways that would dramatically impair biological processes. The perturbations could impact agriculture, the proper functioning of natural ecosystems, the purity of essential air and water resources, and other important elements of the global biosphere. Because current scientific conclusions concerning the response of the atmosphere to the effects of nuclear war include uncertainties, research can and should be undertaken to reduce those uncertainties that are accessible to investigation.

- Laboratory and field experiments are needed to improve estimates of the amount and physical characteristics of the smoke particles that would be produced by large fires, particularly by the combustion of fossil fuels and fossil fuel-derived products present in urban and industrial regions. Experimental conditions should be designed to emulate as much as possible the effects of large-scale fires.

- Laboratory, field, and theoretical studies are needed to determine the potential scavenging rates of smoke particles in the convective plumes of large fires and the scavenging processes that operate on intermediate and global scales as the particles disperse.

- Further theoretical calculations of the seasonal response of the atmosphere to smoke emissions from large fires are needed, particularly of the extent of the perturbation to be expected at early times, when the smoke is freshly injected and patchy. Simulations must be made for later times from months to a year or more, when the atmosphere has been highly perturbed and a substantial fraction of the smoke may have been lofted to high altitudes. Closer attention should be paid to the possible effects in low latitudes and in the Southern Hemisphere, where the climatic effects are likely to be much more important than the direct effects of the nuclear detonations, which are expected to be confined largely to the Northern Hemisphere.

- Laboratory and theoretical studies are needed of the potential chemical alterations of the atmosphere on global and local scales, and of the extent that smoke particles could affect and might be removed by chemical reactions high in the atmosphere.

- Radiological calculations should be undertaken using models that more realistically treat the overlap of fallout plumes, complex meteorological conditions, and that consider both external and internal doses. The question of the possible release of radioactivity from nuclear fuel cycle facilities in a nuclear war should be explored more thoroughly. Patterns of land use and likely targeting strategy should be used in estimating the potential significance of various scenarios.

Index